The Policy Process

The Policy Process

A reader

Second edition

edited by
Michael Hill
University of Newcastle upon Tyne

PEARSON
Prentice
Hall

London • New York • Toronto • Sydney • Tokyo • Singapore
Hong Kong • Cape Town • Madrid • Paris • Amsterdam • Munich • Milan

Pearson Education Limited
Edinburgh Gate
Harlow
Essex CM20 2JE
England

and Associated Companies throughout the world

Visit us on the World Wide Web at:
http://www.pearsoned.co.uk

First published 1993
This second edition published 1997

Typeset in 10/12pt Times by
Hands Fotoset, Ratby, Leicester

Printed and bound in Great Britain by
4edge Ltd, Hockley. www.4edge.co.uk

Library of Congress Cataloging-in-Publication Data

Available from the publisher

British Library Cataloguing-in-Publication Data

A catalogue record for this book is available from
the British Library

ISBN-10: 0-13-616947-3
ISBN-13: 978-0-13-616947-5

---

10 9 8
07 06

Contents

Preface

This is the second edition of a reader first published in 1993. It has been revised at a time when I have also just finished revising the textbook it is designed to accompany: *The Policy Process in the Modern State*. The revision of the reader has been carried out to ensure that it closely shadows the textbook. Part I is readings designed to accompany Chapter 1 of the textbook. Part II is readings relating to Chapters 2–4 of the textbook. Part III and Chapter 5 of the textbook have common concerns. Part IV relates to Chapter 6 of the book, and Part V deals with issues explored in Chapters 7–9.

There are seven new items amongst the readings, whilst five items have been discarded. The introductory sections offer summaries of the issues considered in each part and comments on the readings, together with a new feature – suggestions on further readings.

The idea for the original reader was suggested by Clare Grist. I am grateful to her help at that time and for the more recent help from her colleague Christina Wipf in managing the transition to the new edition.

Acknowledgements

Grateful acknowledgement is made to the following sources for permission to reproduce in this book material previously published elsewhere. Every effort has been made to trace copyright holders, but, if any have been inadvertently overlooked, the publisher will be pleased to make the necessary arrangement at the first opportunity.

The *Australian Journal of Public Administration*, P. Degeling and H. Colebatch for 'Structure and action as constructs in the practice of public administration', *Australian Journal of Public Administration*, **43**, 1984, pp. 320–1.

Blackwell Publishers for extracts from the following: G. McLennan, *Marxism, Pluralism and Beyond*, Polity Press, 1989, pp. 43–56; C. Pollitt, *Managerialism and the Public Services*, Blackwell, 1990; J. G. March and J. P. Olsen, 'Institutional perspectives on political institutions', *Governance*, **9**, 1996, pp. 248–64; P. Hoggett, 'New modes of control in the public service', *Public Administration*, **74**, 1996, pp. 9–32.

Andrew Blowers for 'Master of fate or victim of circumstance – the exercise of corporate power in environmental policy-making', *Policy and Politics*, **11**, 1983, pp. 393–415.

Cambridge University Press and Theda Skocpol for material from P. B. Evans, D. Rueschemeyer and T. Skocpol, *Bringing the State Back In*, 1985, pp. 9–20.

Cambridge University Press and Paul A. Sabatier for P. A. Sabatier, 'Top-down and bottom-up approaches to implementation research: a critical analysis and suggested synthesis', *Journal of Public Policy*, **6**, 1986, pp. 21–8.

Falmer Press Ltd for B. Hudson, 'Michael Lipsky and street level bureaucracy: a neglected perspective', in L. Barton (ed.), *Disability and Dependency*, 1989, pp. 42–55.

The Free Press, a Division of Simon and Schuster, from *The Theory of Social and Economic Organization* by Max Weber, translated by A. M. Henderson and Talcott Parsons. Edited by Talcott Parsons. © 1947, renewed 1975 by Talcott Parsons.

Ian Gordon, Janet Lewis and Ken Young for an extract from 'Perspectives on policy analysis', *Public Administration Bulletin*, **25**, 1977, pp. 26–30.

Robert J. Gregory for 'Political rationality or "incrementalism"? Charles E. Lindblom's enduring contribution to public policy making theory', *Policy and Politics*, **17**, 1989, pp. 139–53.

The President and Fellows of Harvard University for R. Elmore, 'Organizational models of social program implementation', *Public Policy*, **26**, 1978, pp. 185–228.

Harvester Wheatsheaf for the following extracts: M. J. Smith, *Pressure, Power and Policy*, 1993, pp. 56–65; P. Dunleavy, *Democracy, Bureaucracy and Public Choice*, 1991, pp. 174–209.

Bob Hudson for 'Collaboration in social welfare: a framework for analysis', *Policy and Politics*, **15**, 1987, pp. 175–82.

The Institute of Economic Affairs for an extract from G. Tullock, *The Vote Motive*, 1976, pp. 26–40.

W. I. Jenkins for an extract from *Policy Analysis*, Martin Robertson, 1978, pp. 15–25.

Jan-Erik Lane for an extract from 'Implementation, accountability and trust', *European Journal of Political Research*, **15**, 1987, pp. 527–46.

Macmillan Press Ltd for extracts from the following: S. Lukes, *Power: A radical view*, 1974, pp. 25 and 36–45; Dunleavy and O'Leary, *Theories of the State*, 1987, pp. 236–58.

Martin Minogue for 'Theory and practice in public policy and administration', *Policy and Politics*, 11, 1983, pp. 63–85.

Oxford University Press for extracts from the following: © Brian W. Hogwood and Lewis A. Gunn 1985. Reprinted from *Policy Analysis for the Real World* by Brian W. Hogwood and Lewis A. Gunn (1985) by permission of Oxford University Press; © Robert Baldwin 1995. Reprinted from *Rules and Government* by Robert Baldwin (1995) by permission of Oxford University Press.

The Policy Press for G. Smith and D. May, 'The artificial debate between rationalist and incrementalist models of decision making', *Policy and Politics*, **8**, 1980, pp. 147–61.

David O. Porter and Benny Hjern for 'Implementation structures: a new unit of administrative analysis', *Organization Studies*, **2**, 1981, pp. 211–27.

Public Policy and Administration for C. Hood, 'Contemporary public management: a new global paradigm?', *Public Policy and Administration*, **10**, 1995, pp. 104–17.

The Russell Sage Foundation for an extract from M. Lipsky, *Street-level Bureaucracy: Dilemmas of the Individual in Public Service*, 1980.

Part I

The policy process and policy analysis

Introduction

In the first of the extracts in this reader Gordon, Lewis and Young highlight a crucial distinction – between 'analysis for' and 'analysis of' policy. This book of readings is concerned with 'analysis of' policy, and even more specifically with 'analysis of policy determination' rather than 'analysis of policy content'. The extract from Gordon, Lewis and Young shows clearly the relation between this aspect of the study of public policy and other aspects.

Readers will continually find that those who write about the policy process, from almost any perspective, are very concerned to answer ultimate prescriptive questions about how policy *should* be made and implemented. In trying to do this they have been very preoccupied with the extent to which the policy process can be evaluated in terms of how it measures up to what Gordon, Lewis and Young describe in their useful discussion of 'assumptions' as 'the rational model' having a 'status as a normative model and as a "dignified myth" which is often shared by the policy-makers themselves'.

Whilst it is possible to conceive of the study of policy as a detached academic study, and it is at times important to try to achieve detachment, to have a clear view of what is going on, nevertheless the ultimate rationale for our subject is bound to be concern about improving the policy process. That, of course, need not at the same time imply an identification with the goals of those who control the process; we may want to understand it better in order to subvert it in its present form. The complex relationship between policy analysis as a form of 'management science' in which the goals of management are very much at the forefront, and as an academic development out of political science, is explored in the article by Minogue, who makes his overall point pithily in a section headed 'Management versus politics: united they stand, divided they fall'. Within Minogue's analysis lies an important argument about why those who are principally interested in analysis 'for' policy should give some attention to analysis 'of' policy. If they fail to understand policy-making and implementation as a *political* process they will prepare recommendations which are ill adapted to the real world.

A leading textbook on policy analysis (Hogwood and Gunn 1984) claims in its title to offer 'policy analysis for the real world' yet its very adherence to the rational model detracts in places from that goal. Yet to discard entirely the rational model is to collude cynically with those who care neither about good policy nor about good policy processes. We must not forget moreover that the concept of rational model is here

3

particularly applied to solving policy problems in a systematic way. It may also be applied to solving them in a democratic way. But, perhaps most importantly we may want to reserve the use of the concept of rationality to the policies adopted. There is an important conflict of notions of 'rationality' here, explored further in Part III in this book (in the introduction and in the article by Gregory).

The extract from Jenkins' book takes us rather more directly into the issues about studying the policy process in a systematic way. He offers us a conceptual scheme, and comments upon some of the pitfalls about approaching this in too mechanical a way. Later in the book some of the readings may suggest that even Jenkins' careful approach is too systematic to make sense of some aspects of the policy process where clear policies are hard to ascertain and policy output emerges out of grass roots interactions.

All of these introductory readings have been chosen to introduce readers to some of the terminology, to sensitize them to some of the distinctions (which may or may not be made in practice) and to highlight some of the key characteristics of the study of the policy process. For those readers who want to go more deeply into the complexities of the relationships between the various approaches to policy analysis, Wayne Parsons' book*Public Policy*, which is appropriately subtitled 'An Introduction to the Theory and Practice of Policy Analysis', is recommended.

References

Hogwood, B. W. and L. A. Gunn (1984) *Policy Analysis for the Real World*, Oxford: Oxford University Press.
Parsons, W. (1995) *Public Policy*, Aldershot: Edward Elgar.

Perspectives on policy analysis

Ian Gordon, Janet Lewis and Ken Young

A typology of policy analysis

The most obvious distinction in varieties of policy analysis is in terms of explicit purpose and/or client, separating analysis *for* policy from analysis *of* policy. In terms of established lines of research this is probably the most important distinction, and it also reflects a division of disciplinary concerns. Yet within this dichotomy lies a continuum of activities from policy advocacy at one end to the analysis of policy content at the other.

Analysis for policy		Analysis of policy		
Policy advocacy	Information for policy	Policy monitoring and evaluation	Analysis of policy determination	Analysis of policy content

Policy advocacy
We use this term to denote any research that terminates in the direct advocacy of a single policy, or of a group of related policies, identified as serving some end taken as valued by the researchers. The connection of such research with the decision network may be rather less direct. It may be aimed at policy-makers, in which case it assumes a degree of value correspondence (which may or may not be a tenable assumption), or it may serve to challenge existing policies and appeal to rival groups or public opinion at large. In some cases policy advocates argue from their findings toward a particular conclusion, which is offered as a recommendation. In other cases, where a very strong commitment to a particular course of action predates the research, whatever analysis was conducted may have been designed, consciously or unconsciously, to support the case to be argued. Information is gathered and organised in order to sustain a point. This style of policy analysis [. . .] is often carried out by reformist pressure groups, although it is by no means entirely absent from some types of university research.

From I. Gordon, J. Lewis and K. Young, 'Perspectives on policy analysis', *Public Administration Bulletin*, **25**, 1977, pp. 26–30.

Information for policy

In this mode, the researcher's task is to provide policy-makers with information and perhaps advice. It assumes a case for action, in terms of either the introduction of a new policy, or the revision of an existing one. It may be carried out within the research branch of a government department; by outside researchers funded by that department; by independently funded researchers; or by unfunded individuals or associates who have simply chosen to address their scholarly activities to policy issues. The activity itself may be confined to the provision of useful data (e.g. on demographic change) for consideration in policy-making. It may, however, go beyond this to elucidate causal relationships, and thereby to suggest definite policy options. [. . .]

Policy monitoring and evaluation

Policy monitoring and evaluation frequently take the form of *post hoc* analysis of policies and programmes. In an obvious sense, all public agencies perform monitoring and evaluation functions in respect of their own activities, although some may be facile, uncritical or self-legitimising. Evaluation for policy*review* is, on the other hand a more self-conscious business, particularly where the policy or programme in question has an experimental aspect. [. . .]

Monitoring and evaluation can be aimed at providing direct results to policy-makers about the impact and effectiveness of specific policies. But it can do more than this. *Post hoc* review of policy impact may be used for feasibility analysis in future policy design, via the specification of a feasible *set* of actions. In this mode, the object of policy analysis is to inform policy-makers of the limits of possibility. 'Better' policies might then be those which are more closely tailored to the constraints of feasibility imposed by the intractable external world of the policy-makers.

Analysis of policy determination

The emphasis here is upon the inputs and transformational processes operating upon the *construction* of public policy. Attempts to analyse the policy process are inescapably based upon explicit or implicit models of the policy system. In some cases the model is seen as being 'driven' by environmental forces, in others by internal objectives and goals, in yet others by the internal perceptions of the external environment. In contrast with 'advocacy' or 'information' this mode can tend to over-emphasise the constraints upon action to the point where patterns of activity are portrayed as the necessary outcomes of a confluence of forces.

Analysis of policy content

This category of activity includes many studies which have been carried out, within the social administration and social policy field, of the origin, intentions and operation of *specific* policies. Typical of this category are the numerous descriptive accounts which have been given by academics on such policy areas as housing, education, health and social services. While their results may help to inform policy-makers, this is not usually an explicit aim of such studies, for they are conducted for academic advancement rather than public impact. In their more sophisticated variants, content studies engage in 'value analysis' and show social policies as institutionalising social theories.

Assumptions about 'policy' and 'policy-making'

Before discussing the varieties of policy analysis further it is necessary to clarify certain assumptions about the nature of policy and policy-making, since a misunderstanding of these can lead to an unduly narrow view of appropriate research strategies.

Assumptions about the process

The common threads in 'policy' studies can be seen to include some interest in the *content* (as well as the institutions, ideology and procedures) of government activity, some concern for its *outcomes* and an assumption that this activity is in some degree instrumental or *purposive*. The basic orientation is compatible, however, with very different implicit models of the policy process, leading to different strategies for analysis and its application.

To take ideal cases, researchers may on the one hand adopt the assumption that policy-making is essentially a rational process based on the classic steps from problem formulation and evaluation of alternatives through to implementation. Conflicts over goals or perceptions of the situation may be admitted, but these are assumed to result in stable and determinate outcomes which do not interfere with the consistency of the system's operations. Typically the problem is seen as technical, the climate as consensual and the process as controlled. On the other hand, policy-making may be seen as an inescapably *political* activity into which the perceptions and interests of individual actors enter at all stages. In this case implementation becomes a problematic activity rather than something that can be taken for granted, as in the rational process model; policy is seen as a bargained outcome, the environment as conflictful and the process itself is characterised by diversity and constraint.

The power and survival ability of the 'rational system' model is surprising, given that its assumptions have been undermined by empirical studies of the policy process, and that its predictive record is uneven. The main explanation for its continuing existence must lie in its status as a normative model and as a 'dignified' myth which is often shared by the policy-makers themselves. Acceptance of the rational model helps the researcher towards a comfortable life; it enables him or her to appear to engage in direct debate with the policy-makers on the basis that information provided by the researchers will be an aid to better policy-making. If, however, as we believe, policy-making systems approximate more closely to the 'political' model, these prospects can only be superficially attractive.

Assumptions about policy

The concept of 'policy' has a particular status in the 'rational' model as the relatively durable element against which other premises and actions are supposed to be tested for consistency. It is in this sense that we may speak of 'foreign policy' or 'social policy' or 'marketing policy' as if the terms denoted local variants of a universal theme. Yet each of these examples represents very different ways of manipulating, via purposive action, the external environment of particular organisations. Moreover, the term 'policy' is used even within ostensibly similar governmental agencies to describe a range of different activities including (i) defining objectives (ii) setting priorities (iii) describing a plan and (iv) specifying decision rules. These characterisations of 'policy' differ not only in their generality and the level at which it is supposed to occur but also in whether 'policy' is assumed to be entirely prior to action or (as we believe is often the case) at least partly a *post hoc* generalisation or rationalisation. We suggest here that there is a *recursive* relation between policy and action, with 'policy' itself representing an essentially dynamic set of constructions of the situation. In this case, we argue that it is a mistake to conceive of policy analysis as the study of identifiable things called policies which are produced, or crystallise, at a particular stage in the decision process.

Assumptions about 'boundaries'

A feature of the rational model of policy-making is that it conceives the policy system as tightly bounded, and its operations upon the external world as unproblematic. To depart from the assumptions of classical rationality is inevitably to widen the boundaries of the 'relevant' in the analysis of policy-making. 'Policy-makers' are seen as negotiating both within their own organisations and externally, with a host of other organisations and actors whose concurrence may be necessary to policy implementation. The focus shifts from 'decision analysis' to encompass the range of activities from formulation to implementation and impact. Inter-organisational politics and the manipulation of networks (*réseaux*) enter the picture, and it becomes less plausible to speak of locating the 'real' policy-makers. Policy-making, like 'power', appears as a dynamic yet diffused element in the relations between public actors and the world on which they act. This, *the analysis of policy systems*, is perhaps the most neglected aspect of the field.

Assumptions about problem definition

In addition to the assumptions made about the policy-making process, assumptions about problem definition also affect almost all policy analysis. It has been suggested that in every government department there are 'deep structures' of policy – the implicit collection of beliefs about the aims and intentions of the departments and about the relevant actors who influence or benefit from the policy. These constitute what Laski called the 'inarticulate major premises' of the policy-makers. Policy analysts are in the position either of having to accept the 'deep structures' and the consequent assumptions made about problem definition and the range of possible solutions, or of trying to stand outside the organisational consensus and bring new perceptions to old problems. The former role may be more congenial to the policy-makers themselves, but the major potential contribution of the social scientist lies in challenging the deep structures of policy-making. In order that this potential be realised, policy studies must engage in the analysis *of* policy processes, systems and content – a narrowly utilitarian approach to funding policy research will in the long term be self-defeating.

Theory and practice in public policy and administration

Martin Minogue

Introduction

Both the interest and the complexity of the study of public policy lie in its propensity to disrupt disciplinary boundaries, and to call for examination of the social, economic and political environment in which the state operates. The search for a general explanatory theory of public policy necessarily implies a synthesis of social, political and economic theories, for 'what governments do' embraces the whole of economic, social and political life. Public policies do things to economies and societies, so that ultimately any satisfactory explanatory theory of public policy must also explain the inter-relations between the state, politics, economy and society. This is also why people from so many 'disciplines' – economics, politics, sociology, anthropology, geography, planning, management and even applied sciences – share an interest in and make contributions to the study of public policy. But synthesis here becomes a matter of considerable controversy: the scale of interest and intellectual development allows speculation, hypothesis, theorising, argument, much of it brilliant and suggestive; but our state of social knowledge is such that no one theory is capable of proof. Theories themselves may become both heuristic tools and practical ideologies: a good example is provided by Marxist and neo-Marxist political economy. This complexity breeds competition between theories, conflicts over methods, and disagreement over what constitutes the proper mode of analysis.[1]

The interests of policy students are inexhaustible. They may seek to examine:

- a particular public policy system, for example, the policy processes of British or Nigerian or Indian government; or
- a particular area of policy within or across these systems, e.g. foreign policy, health policy, industrial policy, rural development policy.

From M. Minogue, 'Theory and practice in public policy and administration', *Policy and Politics*, **11**, 1983, pp. 63–85.

- a particular decision, e.g. to mount a military attack on another country, to establish free health services for all, to devalue the pound, to increase income tax, to build a motorway, to abolish corporal punishment.

Whatever the particular interest of the student of policy, what cannot be avoided is the need to incorporate the other dimensions. The 'system' cannot be understood without reference to particular areas of policy; areas of policy cannot be understood without reference to specific decisions and actions; specific decisions and actions may be interesting in themselves but have no meaning beyond themselves except to the extent that they contribute to understanding of the policy area within which they are located, and to the general policy system which provides the context for both decision and policy. In brief, the policy analyst, who seeks to provide description of and prescription for specific decisions on particular policies, cannot ignore the overall policy process which is created by the interaction of decisions, policy networks, organisations, actors and events. Nor can he avoid the broader environment within which the public policy process is located; that is, he must pay due regard to the interaction of society and economy, in the effort to understand the political consequences of this interaction. Wildavsky, indeed, identifies 'interaction' as the crucial focus for policy studies, whether at the level of individuals or organisations or within society as a whole. A central concern with interaction will tend to produce an obsession with inter-relationships, which might be dealt with as discrete behavioural patterns, or simplified into systematic models, or elevated into 'grand theory'.

The danger, then, to which policy analysis is notably prone is to downgrade the significance of cause and effect: this frequently shows itself in the ahistorical approach of the bulk of policy studies. It is useful, sometimes, to establish systemic patterns, in which the parts contribute through clearly established relationships to a recognisable whole; but to think that this is enough, or that such analysis can be a reliable guide to present or future practice, is to be very shortsighted about what constitutes an adequate form of explanation. How did the parts come to look as they do? Were they always like that or have they changed? That is, what relationships of cause and effect underlie the relationships of action and interaction? Some analysts who embrace the comfortable rationality of systems theory are, of course, aware of this: but awareness leads them invariably into the position: 'if only we didn't have to start from here, we could much more easily reach our destination'. This can even lead to what Wildavsky terms 'retrodiction', or the prediction of the past. Policy theorists, on the other hand, concerned to avoid such pitfalls and to establish a working set of theoretical propositions, exhibit a rather different fault, though one to which 'comprehensive rationality' adherents are vulnerable: that is, in their concern with policy process and social interaction they are liable to treat particular events and cases with something akin to contempt. In their understandable concern to build up explanatory models at a level which transcends the messy complexity of activities on the ground, they must needs extract some bits of actuality and leave out (suppress?) others. In doing so, they may establish a useful set of regularities, which recur often enough to manipulate into matrices, models, even general theories, but they then, inevitably, falsify any particular piece of actuality;[2] and their 'theory' will quite fail to predict any future piece of actuality, even if it manages to predict a general pattern within which actualities will be likely to occur. This falsification of reality, and so of prediction, is the greatest weakness of theory in the policy sciences. It is scarcely surprising that we therefore find the field full of alternative, competing constructions of reality. Nor is it surprising that the practitioner shuns theory because the gap between theory and practice is more self-evident to the practitioner than it is to the theorist.

This problem lies at the heart of the theoretical catholicity of policy studies, and resides partly in the lack of experience of policy in practice among those who predominate in the theoretical field. The greatest problem for most policy analysts is their inability to cope with politics. I turn, therefore, to a consideration of the place of politics in policy studies, and will proceed by counter-posing political science and management science as competing disciplinary approaches.

Management versus politics: united they stand, divided they fall

The study of politics and the state has a long tradition; the study of administration and management is a much more recent phenomenon. A conventional and dominant tradition in the study of the state has always been the study of constitutions and laws, and the treatment of the state as a neutral instrument of law. In such an approach the principal activity of the state was administration of law and regulation of society within established law. As the scope of the state expanded, so did the scale of its operation and its administrative activities. The academic outgrowth which responded to these developments came to be known as 'public administration'. Public administration is still in use as a terminology, but is now essentially devoid of conceptual meaning. The idea that there is something called public administration which can be defined and recognised as distinctive from other 'disciplines' – like politics, or economics or management science – would be regarded as absurd by any social scientist. [. . .]

We can see at once, if we think about the great variety of disciplines which contribute to the study of activities carried out by 'the public administrator', that the term 'public administration' only has any meaning if it is given an extremely narrow connotation, that is of the administrative rules, procedures and routines which characterise the public service in action. If we shift our gaze beyond this narrow frame, say, to administrative practices, we are at once in a much bigger arena, where there are few certainties and fewer concepts with which to label the phenomena we observe. If we broaden our view to policies, increasing complexity increases our uncertainty: and we must employ some sort of conceptual apparatus if we are to make any sense of it all. 'Public administration' offers no such conceptual framework: it is rather an empty receptacle ready to receive whatever people prefer to put in it.[3] We can then discern a battle of preferences, or competing forms of explanation of what happens in public administration (which naturally become alternative prescriptions as to what *should* happen). Peter Self has said that 'the study of administration could be viewed as a battleground between the contending perspectives of the political scientist and the organisation or management theorists; but the potential contestants are on such different wavelengths that the battle is rarely joined'.[4]

Management science is a house with many rooms: but it is distinguished principally by the claim to offer a superior application of rationality both in making decisions (policy) and in implementing decisions (administration); it would also lay claim to more rigorous methods of investigation, and more effective regard for efficient means of operation. In short, management science holds out to us the promise of better policies which are better administered. We can see how attractive this promise must be to practical men of affairs, particularly so in a period of public concern about the effective use of scarce public resources. The political scientist interested in policy-making is, by contrast, disinclined to give hostages to fortune. His claim rather would be to provide a superior mode of explanation, which would strip away the outer disguises of government and lay bare the structures, processes and relationships of power which constitute the flesh and bones of 'real' government. The argument here would be that there exists a political rationality which may be defined as 'the capacity to make decisions in the future, to mobilise support for substance' which is 'at least as important as generating economic growth so that there will be resources to allocate'.[5] But how are we to choose between these opponents: managerial rationality and political rationality?

In the public sector, it is difficult to draw distinctions between 'management' and 'policymaking'. If we examine the three conventionally defined stages of government activity (decision making, implementation, and evaluation) it can be argued that at each stage the 'policy' perspective provides a more plausible account of events than the 'managerial' perspective. It follows that the policy perspective gives us a more plausible account of the whole governmental system; and that the contribution to public affairs of the managerialist, and of managerial ideologies, is always in the long run likely to be inferior to the contribution of the policy analyst and of policy studies. This is a debate of considerable appositeness at a time when the ideology of management has made strong progress in numerous state bureaucracies, and where 'better management' is all too frequently and simplistically offered as a solution to what is said to be the central problem of bureaucratic inadequacy; whereas the real issue is that of policy failure.

Decision making

It is, of course, arbitrary to reduce complex processes to distinct categories, but orthodox accounts do this as a matter of course, and regard such neat formulations as virtuous. The primary theoretical characteristic of managerialism is the emphasis it places upon rationality. Processes must be orderly. Structures must be logical, and relate clearly to functions. Activity must be systematic: that is, it must flow in a predictable way through the established structures, with predetermined consequences. Decisions must also be rationally ordered, in discernible stages: a stage of formulation, in which clear objectives will be established; a stage of implementation, by which these objectives will be translated into actions; and a stage of evaluation, where practice will be monitored and information fed back systematically into a new cycle, starting with the reformulation of objectives. This type of rationality implies that there can be a perfect system of decision making and that decisions can be perfectly administered.

But managerialism goes beyond the provision of a decision making system; it also tells us that there are rational means for making the choices which the system will translate into action.[6] Numerous devices are offered for our inspection, the principal devices being cost-benefit analysis, systems analysis and programme budgeting. All are rather different, in both theory and practice (and for some governments they are very much in practice), but share at least two characteristics. First, they are all essentially drawn from the work of economists interested in efficiency, here defined as meeting specified objectives at the least possible cost. Secondly, all such techniques rely on hard information, and lots of it, which should be quantifiable.

In *cost-benefit analysis* (CBA) allowances are made for variations in available information by postulating separable categories of decision making:

- decision making under certainty· where a specific action will lead to a predictable specific outcome;
- decision making under risk: where action is broken down into a set of possible specific outcomes, to each of which a quantified level of 'probability' can be attached;
- decision making under uncertainty: where range of possible outcomes may be predicted, but where it is not possible to attach levels of probability to specific outcomes.

In theory, the information and the arithmetic combine to produce the most profitable, or 'best', choice or decision, and therefore the best outcome.

In *systems analysis*, there is less reliance than in the CBA on quantitative methods, more reliance on judgement. Essentially, systems analysis builds models which abstract from 'reality', but represent what are held to be the crucial relationships in reality. Objectives are taken as specified, but as likely to be imprecise and in need of clearer definition. The claim made for systems analysis is that it can clarify objectives, cut the costs of meeting these objectives, and identify bottlenecks which are causing problems: in short, the aim of systems analysis is to eliminate inefficiency, and to create a more effective 'system'.

Programming budgeting cannot be so easily defined as the foregoing devices, except by reference to its application in practice (for example in the USA and in the UK). The general idea is to relate expenditure budgeting to defined goals and outputs, again with the intention of controlling the costs of achieving set objectives.

Most managerialists and many self-described policy analysts would embrace these devices with enthusiasm, stoutly defend their merits, and seek to apply them in the real world of government. But what of the student of public policy who is primarily concerned to locate decision making in the 'real world of government' within an explanatory framework related to political analysis? His reaction will be almost to ridicule such procedures, on the ground that they are so far removed from what a literary critic recently called 'the odd unsymmetry of actual life'.[7] These managerialist approaches incorporate assumptions which in the context of *public* policy processes and *public* organisations are simply not tenable. The assumptions most open to objection relate to *objectives* and *information*.

Objectives

The assumption is either that objectives are given, and the question is only what are the best means to achieve these ends; or that objectives, if not already properly established, can be given clear definition and closely related to specific means; and in both instances, an assumption that public organisations are predominantly concerned with a rational relationship between means and ends.

The policy scientist knows that the 'actual life' of government does not offer much support for these assumptions. First, governmental organisations rarely have clear and precisely defined goals; indeed, such stark definition is deliberately avoided. This is because, characteristically, any specific policy arena is marked by conflict over objectives. The conflict may take a partisan form: i.e. conflict between political ideologies, or between political groups competing for office. Or conflict may take an organisational form: i.e. conflict within public organisations, e.g. ministers vs. officials, higher officials vs. lower officials, departments vs. departments, ministers vs. ministers, and so on; yet again partisan conflicts and organisational conflicts will frequently be inter-related, through interaction between the executive and the legislature, or between the executive and interest groups. In this sort of political-organisational setting, to specify objectives is to pre-empt, or try to pre-empt, someone's interest in an alternative objective. Typically, decisions emerge from a complex process of bargaining[8] and, in a bargaining process, to specify objectives too clearly or too quickly is to invite difficulty. To make clear your objectives is to make a concession to opponents or competitors, and gives them information upon which they can base more effective resistance.

A second assumption to be challenged even where objectives are specified is that these are the real objectives, and that there is unity over objectives. Organisational analysis tells us[9] that organisations are made up of interests, which are engaged in a competition for resources and power (or influence). The competition may be far more significant than the policies upon which competition turns; means are likely to be of much greater concern than ends. Indeed, characteristically, the means – the construction of powerful organisation – often becomes the principal end for those who inhabit the organisation. In relation to British government, you only have to read the Crossman Diaries[10] to see the force of this statement: or note, for example, a quotation from Crossman's famous *éminence grise*, Lady Evelyn Sharpe, who said of the British machinery of government that the distribution of functions did not proceed on the basis of analysis and judgement, but on a basis of guesswork and personalities. In British central government the definition of the whole range of organisational objectives would be (and is) impossible for the outsider, and undesirable (if possible) for the insider. Yet managerial philosophies insist that objectives can be rationally defined and efficiently achieved. In truth, objectives are the products of interaction between key participants, not the prime mover of such interaction.[11]

Information

A further managerial assumption is that necessary and sufficient information is available to the decision maker. There are two comments to be made here. First, in public policymaking, information is frequently inadequate or simply not available, yet these are constraints supplied by time and events; the decision maker cannot wait until he has all the information he needs. Second, information is a resource, to be used and manipulated. It may even be denied to key participants (like one policy adviser to the British Secretary of State for Health and Society Security; he was the Minister's personal representative and informant on a departmental working party on social security benefit, but at the point where crucial decisions had to be made, the officials changed the venue of the meeting at the last minute and 'forgot' to tell the policy adviser).

Moreover, too much information may be an embarrassment. Maynard Keynes once wrote: 'there is nothing a Government hates more than to be well-informed; for it makes the process of arriving at decisions much more complicated and difficult.'[12] This emphasises again the highly political nature of decision making in public life: rational methods may be in principle more desirable than 'the hurried judgements of bargainers' but a political system needs ambiguity if bargains are to be negotiated.

An assumption related to the question of information is that choices between competing objectives can be rationally determined on the basis of accurate formulations of knowledge. But practice has appeared to offer other lessons. For example, in relation to 'big' issues, CBA cannot deal with the problem of choosing between programmes which serve different objectives and constituencies: in what 'rational' way could you choose between the allocation of resources to education as opposed to health, or health as opposed to industrial subsidy? Such choices must, can be and are made: but they are made through political processes in which groups representing different policy areas bargain, and construct trade-offs; or alternatively, where some groups, or one group, succeed in imposing their political power (however based) to the extent of winning a larger share of resources than other groups. Moreover, similar competitive struggles take place not only between policy arenas but within specific policy areas. The outcomes of such struggles are not determined by rational techniques of decision making.

A major problem for rational methods is the reliance upon knowledge which is quantifiable. As Henderson put it in his analysis of Concorde, 'only that which can be counted is permitted to count';[13] and he suggests sardonically that on this score CBA represents 'a greatly superior design of fig-leaf'.[14] It is almost trite to make the point that in the complex social and economic world to which public policies are addressed, and from which in part they spring, a considerable range of factors simply cannot be quantified, except in the most arbitrary manner: how do you put numbers to the quality of a lively sixth form, or the worries of an old, sick person, or the desperation of an unemployed youth? Yet it is factors such as these which generate political enthusiasms and hatreds, and it is just such passions which will, in part at least, influence the political process through which real decisions will emerge. Within such processes, numbers can sometimes be seen to be useful, but only where their projections accord with some strong interest in the decision making arena. As Lord Beveridge once put it: 'Reason and special knowledge have their chance only if there is a channel of access to those who have power.'

Henderson comments that CBA analysts always have excellent statistics of the future, but not of the present or the past. E. S. Quade, the Rand Corporation expert who is said to have 'invented' systems analysis, admitted that 'systems analysis is still largely a form of art'.[15] The major result of the application of programme budgeting in Britain appears at first glance to be public expenditure deficits of breathtaking proportions. We may, I think, conclude this part of the discussion with the view that the claims for rational techniques to make an actual and potential contribution to better public decision making need to be treated with considerable scepticism.

Implementation

Let us turn, then, to an alternative claim for managerialism: that it offers both a method and a philosophy for achieving efficient and effective administration. Here the focus must be on implementation, the crucial business of translating decisions into events: of 'getting things done'. It is, perhaps, the claim to be able to 'get things done' which distinguishes the management system and the management man. It is an appealing philosophy and a seductive promise, and it is this promise (explicit or implicit) which has made management so fashionable in the last decade or so. When governments fail, the problem is frequently identified as 'poor management', and the remedy, of course, is better management: frequently, 'better' management is construed as the practices and attitudes of private sector business management.[16]

The policy scientist can at least agree that getting things done, or implementation, is a crucial aspect of the real world of public policy-making, and one which has been neglected in theoretical literature.[17] He would seek to make a significant distinction, though, between implementation and outcome. Implementation relates to 'specified objectives', the translation into practice of the policies that emerge from the complex process of decision making. Outcome, by contrast, refers to the results of decision-plus-implementation, or what actually happens. My *motif* here would be a quotation from B. J. Loasby: 'It is dangerous to assume either that what has been decided will be achieved, or what happens is what was intended.'[18] This can be explained partly by reference to the problem of objectives: that organisations do not quite know what they are, or cannot agree on them, or pursue conflicting objectives, or even set objectives (either deliberately or unintentionally) which cannot be implemented. But it is also a matter of administration, which means 'good management', and may also mean planning. I do not take the view that administration is in practice redundant, or in theory so dependent a variable as to lack explanatory significance. An extreme view of the first notion was expressed in early Marxist-Leninist ideology, with the belief that planned administration would be rendered unnecessary by the pervasiveness of socialist ideals throughout Soviet society: in *The ABC of Communism* (1920) Bukharin and Preobrazhensky wrote: 'The main direction will be entrusted to various kinds of book-keeping offices or statistical bureaux . . . and since all will understand that this work is necessary and that life goes easier when everything is done according to a pre-arranged plan . . . all will work in accordance with the indications of these statistical bureaux. There will be no need for special Ministers of State, for police and prisons, for laws and decrees – nothing of the sort. Just as in an orchestra all the performers watch the conductor's baton, so here all will consult the statistical reports and will direct their work accordingly.'[19]

But we see that in practice, the Soviet state has notably failed to 'wither away', and indeed represents a strong example of the pervasiveness of state bureaucracy, and arguably of the 'bureaucratisation of politics'. Soviet ideology places the strongest possible emphasis on directive planning of policies, and upon the efficient management of those policies. So do most new states. Similar views have everywhere been gaining ground in the industrialised capitalist states. Management of state policies might be said, then, to be of universal interest, which makes more essential a proper scrutiny of the claims of managerialism.

The policy scientist is likely, in a word, to be sceptical of those claims; sceptical of planning, but not opposed to commonsense attempts to forecast future problems; sceptical of how much effect 'management' can have on the success or failure of public policies, but not opposed to attempts to disposes resources and activities in an orderly way. In particular, he would question two propositions which are implicit and explicit in managerialist literature and practice:

(i) that the expression of efficient management fathers the deed: all managers claim that they are good managers, though many are not; and many public organisations claim that they have introduced 'good management' despite the evidence that they have not (an excellent example of the latter is the British civil service response to the Fulton reforms).[20]

(ii) that a virtue of management is the exclusion of politics: management is 'good' and 'rational'; politics is 'bad' and 'irrational'. Management can deliver desirable results; politics frustrates desirable results. Management represents an instrumental rationality which is functionally necessary; politics represents a dysfunctional irrationality, which is both objectionable and unnecessary; management is 'clean', politics is 'dirty'.

Two questions arise here. First, what is 'good' administration/management; second, is politics necessary? The first point may be dealt with by borrowing the formulation (by Christopher Hood) of a model of perfect administration. Hood proposes the model and then 'relaxes' it to accord with real administration. It takes five pages to propose the perfect model; and 195 pages to give an account of real organisational life which leaves the model in shattered pieces.[21] The model may be summarised as follows:

(a)   An administrative system should be unitary like a large army with a single line of authority: there must be no conflicts of authority, for this would weaken administrative control;

(b) Objectives must be given, uniform, explicit, and known throughout the system;
(c) Clear and authoritative objectives must still be implemented: to achieve this the system must ensure either perfect obedience, or perfect control (to eliminate resistance): the assumption must be that every action of every individual can be recorded and scrutinised;
(d) There must be perfect information and communication, with all tasks unambiguously specified and precisely coordinated;
(e) All these conditions require an adequate time-scale for fulfilment.

Simply to state this model is to highlight the absurdity of the managerialist position: such systems do not, and could not, exist. The 'limits of administration' are clear enough: limited resources, ambiguity of objectives, internal organisational competition. Above all stands the political limit, which might be described thus:

(i) nothing gets done which is unacceptable to dominant or influential political groups, which may be defined to include the 'bureaucratic leadership' group;
(ii) activities which 'get done' externally may generate a hostile and uncooperative response, referred to by Hood as 'recalcitrance'.

There are two insurmountable problems for the analysis which wants to exclude politics. First, the internal world of the organisation cannot be isolated from the world external to the organisation. This is overwhelmingly the case with the public administrative system, which in myriad ways is inter-related with the wider political system; at the centre of affairs the two systems are almost inextricably intertwined. External politics cannot simply be left out.

Secondly, the approach contains the assumption that internal organisation does not involve politics. This assumption could only be sustained by defining politics so narrowly as to render it meaningless. All organisations have politics, in the sense that they contain groups of people, and individuals, who will compete with each other to control and manipulate resources, policies, practices, each other, and the organisation itself. In public organisations, no meaningful distinction between policy and administration is possible; and policies proposed and authorised by formal political institutions and participants are in a wide variety of ways influenced, mediated, even altered by formal administrative institutions and participants at both the higher and the lower levels. (Hood calls this, in the implementation stage, knocking off the corners to get the policy through the front door.)[22]

The problem of making clear definitions of what is involved in good management can be further illustrated by reference to the question of information. Hood's model says that information must be accurate and must be communicated. So does textbook management. There are endless examples to show that the assumption is over-optimistic, mainly because it treats information as neutral. We have already noted that information is a resource which in practice is manipulated by competitors within organisations; and in the case of the state information is an instrument which can be manipulated to maintain domination over policies, to deny influence to external competition for influence over policies and to reduce 'recalcitrance' in the external political environment. Perhaps the most telling examples may be drawn from Soviet and Chinese economic planning, where we might assume the highest possible combination of specified objectives and administrative control. For example, Stalin used to be shown films of tables groaning with fruit, poultry and agricultural produce to illustrate the successful implementation of the rural collectivisation programme; in actuality, the collectives were famine-stricken and impoverished.[23] A different sort of example is provided by World War II fighter pilots, who consistently exaggerated the number of enemy planes they had shot down: they gave to each other, and their superiors (and thence to the wider public), not the truth, but the false information that everyone wanted to hear.[24] We know from studies of real organisations that not only may real information be screened out if it doesn't accord with established beliefs and preferences;[25] but that competent critical people may also be 'screened out' in favour of incompetent uncritical people: we need to look no further than the Nixon Administration in the USA for an example.

Evaluation

A closely related question is that of ignorance, the lack of information or knowledge. This may be an organisational matter too; for as Michel Crozier says, 'People who make the decisions cannot have direct first-hand knowledge of the problems they are called upon to solve. On the other hand, the field officers who know these problems can never have the power necessary to adjust, to experiment, and to innovate.'[26] Even if policymakers had the best of intentions; they would still come up hard against the real limits imposed by ignorance. Public policies are addressed to a world of social and economic interaction of such complexity and scale that our ignorance of it is probably more substantial than our knowledge. In this context, public policies might more usefully be described as social experiments; experiments, moreover, distinguished by guesswork rather than scientific method. It is this facet with explains the need to conceptualise the outcome or impact of public policy. We often do not know what the results and consequences of policies will be until we see them in action.

Clearly it is essential for governments to estimate results, to measure these results, and learn from them. The literature, too, places considerable emphasis upon evaluation: systems analysis calls it feedback, and technically such feedback operates as a self-adjusting mechanism; alternatively, evaluation might generate more data on which to base improved calculations of 'best' future policies. A rather different approach is Lindblom's concept of disjointed incrementalism, which through processes of 'partisan mutual adjustment' ensures that experience is learned from and policy adjusted within the limits imposed by internal organisational politics and external social and political configurations.[27]

Both approaches considerably over-emphasise and contain values of stability and continuity. They make few allowances for conditions of marked economic and social change: conditions which prevail in most countries in the latter part of the twentieth century. Not only is our knowledge of how societies work so limited that policies addressed to societies frequently turn out to be misjudged, or ineffective; but the time scale required for the construction and operation of a major policy is so great that it is highly likely, when operated, to be addressed to a problem which has already changed its nature. In this sense, policy always lags behind events, except to the extent that policies themselves provide part of the social framework within which changes take place. Therefore, the argument is not that policies cannot have effective consequences; but that policies at the very least are always likely to have unintended consequences. If we seek to improve policymaking, we must improve our stock of social knowledge; and as part of this activity, analysis of the results of policies is of profound importance.

Major problems arise here with the nature of political leadership and organisational behaviour. Political leaders will not be anxious to have too critical an examination of their failures; this will be particularly so if, as with many national economic plans in new states, political leaders have never intended implementation (with all its real difficulties and resource-hungry characteristics) but sought only the easy fruits of political rhetoric.[28] For similar reasons, bureaucratic leaders do not frequently show an interest in serious evaluation of policies: this may be because of the fear that the information which results may provide a resource to the enemy/competitor of the organisation. It is, of course, possible that top policymakers well understand the gaps which exist between their policies and the real external world, and so avoid evaluation because they do not wish these frailties to be exposed.

We need to understand yet again that evaluation is not merely a technical matter, nor even a question of good practice: it is, or may be, a highly political issue. We are always, therefore, likely to find that an absence of evaluation contributes further to the uncertainties and unsystematic nature of public policy, and in its analysis, the uncertainty principle must be given great regard. It is worth quoting again that wise man of public affairs, J. M. Keynes: 'The sense in which I am using the term uncertainty is that in which the prospect of European war is uncertain, or the price of copper and the rate of interest twenty years on, or the obsolescence of a new invention . . . About these matters there is no basis on which to form any calculable probability whatever. We simply do not know. . .'.[29]

The limits of managerialism

I propose now to set out some judgements based on these prior arguments, about the limitations of managerialism as an approach to the study, teaching and practice of public policy.

(1) Managerialism constructs a false and naive view of the policy process; in leaving out politics, it puts out the baby with the bathwater. Decisional 'systems' which leave out politics will produce unreal, unworkable or unacceptable decisions.

(2) Efficiency is not enough, if it leaves out problems of choice, and the analysis of choice is inept if it leaves out values. In short, managerialism leaves out morality.

Can we say that a state, like the German Third Reich, which cheaply and with great efficiency achieves a specified objective, that is, the extinction of a significant group of its citizens, is a 'good', a well-managed state? Insofar as managerialism leaves aside consideration of the desirability of objectives it may actually be dangerous. Indeed, Rein suggests that the dilemmas posed by competing objectives are 'desirable, because they pose moral choices and hence permit a debate about moral purposes'.[30]

(3) Managerialism addresses itself too much to the future, too little to the past or the present. The answer to 'bad management now' is 'better management in the future'; in the end, managerialism is an 'if only' conception. It is not rooted in present realities. Far from addressing itself in a practical way to practical men, it is principally in the business of mythmaking.

(4) Managerialism conceals the inner politics of bureaucracies, by bureaucratising political exchanges which are articulated as organisational exchanges.[31] This is a deception convenient both to managers and to managerial analysts. The danger here is that managerialism may lead to enormous policy errors if it succeeds in neutralising political exchanges or reducing political intervention in policy discussion: Henderson's account of the AGR reactor programme gives a good example.[32] British local government also provides an interesting example of the bureaucratisation of politics.[33]

(5) Managerialism can be successfully turned against itself merely by assertion, e.g. by using managerial concepts and language to describe 'reality' but avoiding real analysis by constructing a false reality; examples are provided by:

(i) the practice of economic ministries in new states of reporting the achievement of planned objectives when these objectives have not really been met, or even implemented;

(ii) the assertion that there exists, say, a system of management by objectives, or financial programme management, where these are not in practice effective, nor intended to be, but aim to provide the semblance of a response to calls for 'better management'. One example here is the history of British government's fairly brief flirtation with 'management by objectives', now in effect discarded, and 'programme analysis review', now defunct (a recent internal report suggested that one way to achieve more efficiency would be to reduce the number of efficiency experts!).

Finally, this counterposition of 'managerialism' and 'politics' in public policy analysis depends upon a counterposition of types of rationality. Let Wildavsky sum up the view consistently argued in this section: 'the method called the "rational paradigm" (order objectives, compose alternatives, compare the highest ranking) is mistaken as describing either how decisions are or ought to be made. This paradigm conveys the wrong-headed impression that all one has to do to answer a question is to ask it.'[34] By contrast, political rationality consists of identifying what are the problems to be answered; then, in constructing support for the solutions proposed: here, 'rationality resides in results'.[35]

The limits of policy science

This section might be subtitled: if managerialism fails, can policy science do better? The answer is yes, in that the policy scientist insists on including the political context of public service management in his explanations and analysis, and would incorporate the political dimension into his prescriptions; and yes, in that the policy scientist penetrates real organisational life, seeking to lay bare the political and behavioural processes which generate actual policies, and govern the form, style and pervasiveness of state bureaucracies. But policy science too has serious limitations, and must not, any more than managerialism, state its claim too confidently.

A principal limitation resides in the problem of theory alluded to briefly in the first part of this paper. Policy 'science' has no real claim to be a science; it has no agreed theoretical foundation on which to build models and test hypotheses, but encounters several theoretical possibilities. As always in situations of theoretical fragmentation, policy scientists spend an excessive amount of energy in addressing each other, and in struggling to incorporate a variety of disciplinary approaches. To say this is not to attack the search for a workable and distinctive theory; but to point up the limitations which this continued search produces, at a time when the main contributing disciplines (economics, sociology and politics) are themselves, arguably, in a state of crisis.

One significant effect is to widen the gap which exists between theory and practice. The gap is created in a variety of ways. The most obvious problem is the absence of real political or administrative experience in those who teach and theorise about public policy. This partly explains the 'remoteness' of theory from the real world of policy, but also tends to promote a greater respect for theory than for practice, since academics move in a world where the highest value is placed upon the construction and refinement of theory; even the application of theory may be pursued in an intellectual rather than a practical context. Indeed, some policy studies specialists would quite deliberately avoid any involvement in the real world of policy on the ground that this might impose upon them unwanted intellectual constrictions, as well as quite practical constraints. It is not difficult to understand this tension between academic and practitioner: each threatens to interfere with the activities and preferences of the other. The theorist wishes to distance himself intellectually from the real policy world to avoid the ideological contamination which inevitably comes from actual participation in an area of policy. The practitioner tends to avoid over-exposure to a wide range of ideas, and is rarely anxious to cultivate external critical analysis. C. H. Sisson, himself a former British civil servant, put this rather well: 'the official is a man who has been trained to a practical operation, not to an exposition of theory or a search for truth. There is no need for the administrator to be a man of ideas. His distinguishing quality should rather be a certain freedom from ideas.'[36]

An unfortunate consequence of the gap between the theoretician and the practitioner is that each manifests something uncomfortably close to contempt for the other, a contempt strengthened rather than weakened by being based in a defensive insecurity (the academic insecure about the crisis of theory, the practitioner insecure about the failures of practice). It might be held that decisional and other techniques at least offer to bridge the divide; but the antagonistic feelings of the practitioner are strengthened when he perceives the weaknesses and limited use of such techniques; in any case, the able official will manipulate these techniques and their findings in the political arena, and is able therefore to manipulate the policy analyst. The policy adviser, who is concerned less with techniques than content, and perceives the real policy process more accurately than the 'technician', will be a stronger opponent. But the danger then is the tendency for the policy adviser to think that he is the sole repository of truth, and that his perceived truth must prevail of its own force. Martin Rein makes the point that the policy adviser who seeks to influence practice enters an arena in which several holders of 'truth', as they see it, fight their corners.[37] It is not a question so much of speaking Truth to Power':[38] Power decides what Truth is. To the extent that the policy adviser wishes his version to be chosen, he must enter the power struggle: and once he does so, to the extent that he has to participate in bargains and accommodations, so will the value of his real insights or knowledge be reduced. Rein makes some other interesting suggestions:

(i) that action is significant to the policy analyst because it generates inquiry, not (as the purist would like to think), the other way about;
(ii) knowledge is not always cumulative: decision makers do not always learn from experience even when it is analysed for them, or rather, the factors which condition policymaking may screen out unwanted learning or knowledge (a point recently emphasised in *New Society*: 'not only does social science cost money, but it persists in finding out things the government does not want to know').[39]

On the basis of these arguments, Rein suggests that it is not so much social science which is important for public policymaking, as the social scientist; the values, personality, ambitions and preferences of the individual policy adviser may combine to make a distinctive contribution to real policy. Wildavsky's idea is rather similar: that policy analysis is synonymous with creativity, and with defining problems rather than offering handy solutions: 'in policy analysis the most creative calculations concern finding problems for which solutions might be attempted'.[40]

Rein and Wildavsky are optimistic about the possibility of a genuine role for the external policy analyst, and so for the improvement of public policies. Wildavsky places what can only be described as faith in the possibility of producing better policies and better government through a process by which bright graduates are trained in the 'art and craft', as well as the techniques, of policy analysis. This approach envisages that Graduate Schools of Public Policy will provide a stream of well-trained, knowledgeable policy analysts who will move into governmental agencies and actively participate in policy activities. Yehezkel Dror, ostensibly more attached to 'rationality', shows a similar enthusiasm for the 'preparation of policy sciences professionals'.[41] Other writers, geared to narrower formulations of policy analysis in terms of decision making skills, also take a highly optimistic view of the utility of professional analysts. For example, one recent work of this type promotes the concept of 'performance administration' as an antidote to ineffective policymaking: 'performance administration combines the traditional approaches of public administration with contemporary concepts of systems analysis and comprehensive planning in an attempt to achieve a coordinative process capable of yielding more rational public policies and decisions': this 'must be more than a handful of strategies and techniques . . . it is a set of attitudes . . . a management style.'[42]

But neither the stylish perceptiveness of Wildavsky, the earnest idealism of Dror, nor the careful reasonableness of Steiss and Daneke really gives us much help in relating their varieties of analysis to the sheer messiness of real-world political and organisational life. These political realities are acknowledged, but not dealt with in any convincing way when it comes to prescription. There is no sense of the conflicts and problems which these brave new policy sciences professionals will encounter, no attempt to discuss the limitations by which they will be hamstrung. For example, Dror makes out a case for a code of ethics as part of the 'professionalisation' of the policy scientist, which includes:

(b) When the goals and values of a particular client contradict basic beliefs of the policy scientist, the policy scientist should resign . . .
(c) . . . a policy scientist should not hide an alternative because it contradicts his own personal values and preferences . . .
(e) . . . a policy scientist should refuse to prepare studies, the sole purpose of which is to provide a supporting brief to an alternative already finally decided upon for other reasons . . .
(f) . . . policy scientists should not work for clients who do not provide necessary access to information . . .[43]

Dror clearly believes that such 'policy science professionals' do not exist; but the equally implicit assumption that they should, and can, exist is based on a fundamental lack of understanding of what real life in real public bureaucracies is like. If Dror's graduates were to follow his recommendations, there would soon be none of them left in public service jobs, and this can scarcely be Dror's intention. Dror has left a gap between the ideal and the actual, and gives no guidance on how this gap is to be bridged. There is, in formulations like this, a sort of implied wish that awkward political realities would somehow wither away: but of course they will not, and the failure here is to understand the functional rationality of what might appear otherwise to be irrational political behaviour. Too many policy scientists share the management scientists' tendency to 'leave out the politics', or assume it away. But there will be no adequate theory of public policymaking which does not convincingly account for political phenomena as well as organisational reality. And it is unlikely that an adequate theory can be produced, when it is primarily in the hands of those who do not inhabit the actual world of public political organisations and only get occasional glimpses of that world. These glimpses mean that much theoretical work is shot through with flashes of illumination, but the flashes seem so bright because of the prevailing darkness.

The problem does not rest only with the theorists: they are, at least, trying to make sense of a puzzling, half-hidden world, illuminated less by a flaming torch than a spluttering candle. Practitioners themselves constitute part of the problem. Self-interest pushes them towards concealment rather than open dealing, towards disguises rather than revelations. It becomes an organisational virtue to keep apart policy information and policy analysts, especially if these analysts are outside the organisation; even 'insider' analysts may often find themselves treated with reserve and suspicion. The greatest weakness of the practitioner is the inability to perceive himself, and to understand that all his own actions and activities are just as ideologically framed as the theories of the non-practitioner. The 'pragmatic' bureaucrat is just as beset by values, beliefs and preferences as the 'objective' academic. Both produce work which rests on assumptions, even on world views. Neither can really sustain a claim to objectivity. Just as there is no such thing as value free social science, so there is no such thing as value free administration or value free public policymaking. At least some policy scientists acknowledge the impossibility of detachment: most bureaucrats would not, and the failure of the official to comprehend the ideological nature of his own activities brings a myopic vision which is thoroughly damaging to public policy itself.

The distaste often shown by practitioners for the work of academics is less subtle and more visible. But it is equally damaging to public policy when it involves a deliberate evasion of knowledge; and since knowledge is subject to manipulation by power, the practitioner is invariably well placed to ensure that his version of knowledge prevails. The policy analyst who wishes to influence 'real policy' may follow one of two paths. He may choose to work inside the decision making bureaucracy, using whatever influence he can muster to support his authoritative knowledge. Or he may work through the political process, by way of specific pressure groups or political parties; or in some types of political system, through specific political authority figures, or patronage networks.

What the policy analyst can never assume is that authoritative knowledge will do the trick by itself;[44] though the dissemination of such knowledge may well, in the long run, have important effects upon those who control policy decisions. There is, of course, a view that knowledge will inevitably assert itself in the long run, that it will cause changes in general social values and that these social values must eventually find expression in the public policies which form the framework for social action. But this gradualist view runs into serious opposition, notably from the contrary view that social values reflect economic and social configurations which are deterministic in nature: so that, as Marx said: 'The ruling ideas are everywhere the ideas of the ruling classes', and all knowledge, too, is subject to this formulation, having no political authority except that bestowed by attachment to power.[45]

Whichever underlying view one adopts, political practice seems to indicate that expert knowledge may be necessary to the achievement of desired public policy, but is not sufficient for such achievement. This is probably as it should be: for there is no reason to suppose that the public policies 'desired' by the expert will conform to the policies generally desired by the public, or even that what the expert analyst believes to be the public interest is in actuality in the public interest. We could only rely on a firm connection between the policy analyst and the general public interest if the recent past were more comprehensible and the near future more predictable than they are. If we cannot rely on the state of knowledge of the academic theorist, we can rely even less on the state of knowledge of the professional bureaucrat or politician: as the rate of social and economic change seems constantly to increase, and as political, social and economic systems come more and more to be characterised by 'turbulence', then we might agree with the comment that 'public officials often do not know where they are, let alone where they are going'.[46] In short, social systems are simply not predictable enough to be described as manageable; rational management and control in such circumstances are impossible.

Conclusion

The foregoing analysis might seem to lead to pessimistic conclusions: if the prospects for the efficient management of effective public policies are so constricted and uncertain, is there any point in teaching policy studies, and pursuing policy research and analysis?

The study of public policy is fashionable, of practical importance, and theoretically incoherent: it follows that, though it increasingly attracts students, it is not an easy subject either to teach or to learn: indeed Wildavsky once wrote that policy analysis may be learned but not taught! A subject which holds immense fascination can be turned into a tedious rehearsal of tired concepts, especially where too much emphasis is laid on theory, too little on the investigation of real issues and problems. In the last resort, teachers will follow their own noses, but should be careful to remember that students have noses too, and may not relish the same smells. It is tempting, given the current disarray of the social sciences, to suggest that we should avoid the worship of what usually turn out to be false gods, and seek to develop new ways of tackling the subject, and new ways of involving students in it. Yet the thrust of this paper suggests that the pursuit of the timehonoured method of discrete analysis of issues and problems, on the basis of sound historical groundwork, and informed by a strongly developed consciousness of the primary influence of politics remains the most interesting and illuminating method; for it combines a decent analytical method with the theoretically sound perception that issues of public policy do not lend themselves to neutral, value free, scientific analysis. As Charles Darwin once wrote: 'How odd it is that anyone should not see that all observation must be for or against some view if it is to be of any service.'[47]

Notes

1. Marxist political economy has been strangely neglected in public policy studies: yet the burgeoning interest in the state and its relations with society owes at least as much to this radical strand as it does to the work of more conventionally located policy theorists; for example, Ian Gough, *The Political Economy of the Welfare State* (London: Macmillan, 1979); R. K. Mishra, *Society and Social Policy* (London: Macmillan, 1977); R. Miliband, *The State in Capitalist Society* (London: Weidenfeld & Nicolson, 1970); N. Poulantzas, *State, Power,*

Socialism (London: New Left Books, 1978). For a stimulating discussion of the possibilities for radical theory in the field of public administration, see Patrick Dunleavy, 'Is there a radical approach to Public Administration?', *Public Administration*, Vol. 60, No. 2 (1982), 215–24.

2. This is a crude summary of a detailed and convincing argument in Q. R. D. Skinner, 'The limits of historical explanations', *Philosophy*, Vol. 41, No. 157 (1966) 199–215.

3. The same comment holds good for 'Social Administration': see Michael Hill, *Understanding Social Policy* (Oxford: Blackwell and Martin Robertson, 1980), Chap. I.

4. P. Self, *Administrative Theories and Politics* (London: Allen & Unwin, 1972 edn.), 14–15.

5. A. Wildavsky, *The Art and Craft of Policy Analysis* (London: Macmillan, 1980), 3.

6. The following analysis draws on Wildavsky's articles, 'The political economy of efficiency: cost benefit analysis, systems analysis, and program budgeting', *Public Administration Review*, Vol. 26 (1966), 292–310; and 'Rescuing policy analysis from PPBS', *Public Administration Review*, Vol. 29 (1969), 189–202.

7. Graham Hough, *The London Review of Books*, 1980.

8. Note C. E. Lindblom's concepts of 'disjointed incrementalism' and 'partisan mutual adjustment', elaborated as a critique of the 'comprehensive rationality' approach; see *The Intelligence of Democracy* (New York: Free Press, 1965) and *The Policymaking Process* (New York: Prentice Hall, 1968). Lindblom's incrementalist approach has attracted much criticism, most notably from Y. Dror, *Public Policymaking Re-examined* (Chandler, 1968).

9. The literature is well surveyed in A. Dunsire, *The Execution Process*, Vol. 1 (Oxford: Martin Robertson, 1978), 16–90.

10. R. H. S. Crossman, *The Diaries of a Cabinet Minister* (3 vols, London: Jonathan Cape and Hamish Hamilton, 1975–7).

11. For a discussion of the ways in which problem definition is manipulated and can be linked to policy failure, see Joan K. Stringer and J. J. Richardson, 'Managing the political agenda: problem definition and policymaking in Britain', *Parliamentary Affairs*, Vol. 33 (1980), 23–39.

12. Quoted in Michael Ellman, *Socialist Planning* (Cambridge University Press, 1979).

13. P. D. Henderson, 'Two British errors; their probable size and some possible lessons', *Oxford Economic Papers*, July 1977.

14. *Ibid*.

15. E. S. Quade, quoted in Wildavsky (1966).

16. Notable examples in the British system are provided by the Fulton Committee's Report on the Civil Service (1968); and more recently by the initiatives endorsed by the Thatcher administration: see especially Michael Heseltine, 'Ministers and management in Whitehall', *Management Services in Government* (May 1980), and J. M. Lee, 'The machinery of government under Mrs Thatcher's administration', *Parliamentary Affairs* (Autumn 1980). For a full account of the 'management movement' in British central administration, see John Garrett, *Managing the Civil Service* (London: Heinemann, 1980).

17. A useful survey of this literature is provided by Michael Hill and Susan Barrett in 'Implementation theory and research: a new branch of policy studies, or a new name for old interests?', unpublished paper based on their report to the SSRC Central–Local Government Relations Panel.

18. B. J. Loasby, *Choice, Complexity and Ignorance* (Cambridge University Press, 1976), 89.

19. N. I. Bukharin and E. Preobrazhensky, *The ABC of Communism* (1920, trans. Penguin, 1969).

20. Garrett, *op. cit.*

21. C. Hood, *The Limits of Administration* (John Wiley, 1976).
22. *Ibid.*, 10.
23. Ellman, *op. cit.*, 70.
24. Len Deighton, *Fighter* (Panther, 1979), 186.
25. See J. D. Steinbruner, *The Cybernetic Theory of Decisions* (Princeton, 1974): 'information which is threatening to established belief systems is not processed in a fashion wholly dominated by the reality principle'.
26. M. Crozier, *The Bureaucratic Phenomenon* (Tavistock, 1964), 190.
27. Lindblom, *op. cit.*
28. See C. Leys, 'The analysis of planning' in C. Leys, ed., *Politics and Change in Developing Countries* (Cambridge University Press, 1969); and A. Killick, 'The possibilities of development planning', *Oxford Economic Papers* (July 1976).
29. J. M. Keynes, in 1937, quoted in Ellman, *op. cit.*
30. M. Rein, *Social Science and Public Policy* (London: Penguin, 1976), 259.
31. For an elaboration of this argument, see B. Schaffer, 'Insiders and outsiders: insidedness, incorporation, and bureaucratic politics', *Development and Change*, Vol. II (1980), 187–210.
32. Henderson, *op. cit.*
33. For a detailed account see John Dearlove, *The Reorganisation of British Local Government: Old orthodoxies and a political perspective* (Cambridge University Press, 1979).
34. Wildavsky (1980), 8.
35. *Ibid.*, 10.
36. C. H. Sisson, *The Spirit of British Administration* (London: Faber, 1959), 23.
37. See especially the chapter 'Social science for social policy'; Rein, *op. cit.*, 247–68.
38. Wildavsky (1980), 401–5.
39. *New Society* (28 May 1981), 341.
40. Wildavsky (1980), 3.
41. Y. Dror, *Design for Policy Sciences* (Elsevier, 1971), especially 'Teaching of policy sciences', Chap. 14, 100–16.
42. A. W. Steiss and G. A. Daneke, *Performance Administration* (Lexington, 1980), Chap. 1.
43. Dror (1971), 119.
44. See, for example, the extent to which expert evidence commissioned by governments is disregarded. There are many examples in development planning in the third world; for British examples, see Martin Bulmer, ed., *Social Research and Royal Commissions* (London: Allen & Unwin, 1980).
45. For a surprisingly similar, since non-Marxist, view, see David E. Apter, ed., *Ideology and Discontent* (New York: Free Press, 1964), 18.
46. R. Rose and E. Page, 'Incrementalism or instability?: managing local government financial systems in a turbulent time', paper to SSRC/CSPP Conference, Strathclyde University (June 1981).
47. Quoted in Ralph Ruddock, *Ideologies*, Manchester Monographs 15 (Department of Adult and Higher Education, University of Manchester, 1981).

Policy analysis
Models and approaches

Bill Jenkins

Models and approaches: some attempts to cope

What *is* public policy and why the current concern to focus on it, analyse it and reform it? Pursuit of the first question leads one down the tangled path towards a definition where many have been before and from which few have emerged unscathed. There is, as Lineberry and Masotti point out, little in the way of a consistent conceptualisation of the term 'policy' itself and pages could be, and have been, filled with competing definitions.[1] The problem may be to provide an account that captures the detail and density of the activities embraced by the policy arena. With this in mind, it is worth considering the following definition of public policy:

> A set of interrelated decisions taken by a political actor or group of actors concerning the selection of goals and the means of achieving them within a specified situation where these decisions should, in principle, be within the power of these actors to achieve.[2]

Such a definition should not be seen as all-encompassing. For example, it points to the adoption of a course of action and the means of implementing it, but it does not build implementation into the policy itself. However, the definition has strengths, in that it incorporates the possibility of inaction (the decision not to move), and separates policy from ambition by linking policy decisions to available resources. Further, it stresses the point that policy is more than a single decision. As Anderson has argued, 'policy making typically involves a pattern of action extending *over time* and involving *many decisions*' (author's italics).[3] Public policy, therefore, must be considered to be much more than simply governmental outputs. Moreover, there may be *types of policy* corresponding to distinctive sets of decisions taken within the political system. Thus to focus on outputs alone may result in a partial and incomplete view of the dynamics and totality of public policy.[4] Further, policies have identifiable characteristics, according to which they may occupy different parts of the political spectrum and may need to be dealt with in different ways. For example, policies concerning national defence involve different actors and different structures and are likely to be processed in a different

From W. I. Jenkins, *Policy Analysis* (1978), Oxford: Martin Robertson, Ch. 1.

fashion from those concerning welfare matters. To pursue this line of argument indicates another conceptual issue with which the analyst must deal: the separation of *policy content*, the substance of policy, from *policy process*, the given set of methods, strategies and techniques by which a policy is made. To make such a distinction is not to deny that content and process can be, and often are, interdependent. In fact, some would go as far as proclaiming that content may determine process [. . .]. However, for many process is a central, if not the central, focus, to the extent that they argue that a conceptual understanding of the policy process is fundamental to an analysis of public policy.

Issues enter the political system; information feeds into decision; policies emerge and are implemented. How can such fragmentary events be linked? Is there an inherent and consistent logic connected with the way that policy is made in political systems? To address oneself to this problem is to conceptualise the policy process, and here one of the simplest and most frequently used models is that of the functional set of categories first offered by Harold Lasswell and adopted and developed by others since. An indication of this model is given in Figure 1. Basically, it assumes that policy emerges via a logical path; an issue moves through the political system in a processual way from point of entry, through decision and implementation, until a final choice is made to proceed with or terminate a course of action. Such a scheme, it is argued, is useful in drawing attention to the ordering of policy activities – certain bodies at certain times are more likely to be connected with one stage of the process rather than another. Few who offer this model would consider it as anything but an ideal representation of reality and fewer still would claim that political behaviour ever takes place in such an ordered fashion. Given such reservations, the utility of such an approach, particularly as a vehicle for hypothesis generation, becomes problematic and, in the face of such criticism, some have argued that it may be more productive to consider the policy process in terms of an adapted input–output model of the political system derived from the work of David Easton. Such a perspective is favoured by Sharkansky, Dye and others.[5][. . .] Its major dimensions are indicated in Figure 2, from which it will be clear that the focus of this approach is the dynamics and processes of a political system operating in its environment. Thus its advocates would wish to differentiate between:

(i) *policy demands*: demands for action arising from both inside and outside the political system;
(ii) *policy decisions*: authoritative rather than routine decisions by the political authorities;
(iii) *policy outputs*: what the system does – thus, while goods and services are the most tangible outputs, the concept is not restricted to this;
(iv) *policy outcomes* (or *impacts*): consequences intended or unintended resulting from political action or inaction.

In this way, it becomes possible to define and explore the process of policy while becoming aware of the various interconnections existing within this process. Once

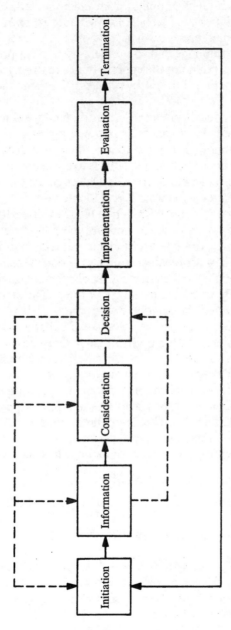

Figure 1 Schematic presentation of process perspective on policy (*Source*: Suggested by G. K. Roberts in a private communication)

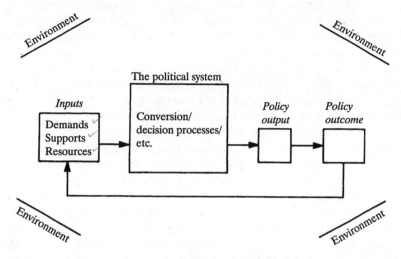

Environment: includes social, economic and political influences
              on inputs, systems variables, policy outputs and
              policy outcomes.

Figure 2 Systems model of the policy process

more, the model may be too neat and too simplistic. Still, granted such caveats, a
systems model indicates possibilities of coping with some of the conceptual problems
of policy analysis already mentioned: the questions of linking variable patterns of
political action with varying political demands [. . .], of explaining outputs, and of
distinguishing outputs from outcomes. [. . .] Thus, via systems approaches, policy
analysis can clearly be seen as an activity involved in disaggregating and understanding
the specific policy-related aspects of the political process.

At this juncture, however, it may be as well to indicate some wider points concerning
the development of policy theory, in particular the preferred directions in which some
observers would like analysis to go. Hence for many, undoubtedly, the ultimate goal is
the 'scientific' study of policy, in which central concepts would be open to scientific
verification and ideas such as 'responsibility' or 'rational policy formation' would be
eliminated. According to this view, what policy analysis should aim for is a conceptual
framework which yields variables capable of systematic and rigorous testing. Such an
approach has much to commend it, although it also introduces problems by down-
grading certain variables, in particular behavioural ones. Rigour of this nature may be
no bad thing. It also has its disadvantages.[6] [. . .]

The move towards a scientific attack on policy has also been accompanied by moves
towards comparative research and a suspicion of, if not a positive disregard for, case
studies. Case studies are considered static, with a tendency to isolate decisions
unreasonably and to confine an investigation too closely to central actors. The

limitations of case studies, it is argued, can be overcome by careful comparative analysis. But comparison over what time period and taking into account what variables? Many case studies may well misuse historical explanation, but the problem with much comparative policy research is that it is blatantly and erroneously ahistorical. Perhaps a major task facing policy studies is to synthesise comparative theory and case study. [. . .] In the long run, indeed, this may offer possibilities; in the short run it would seem too early to jettison case-study material and the concepts that arise from it simply in exchange for quantitative sophistication.[7]

Moves towards scientific hardness, comparative research and a more careful conceptualisation of variables mark recent trends in academic interest in the policy field, many of which can be linked with the increasing popularity of systems models of analysis. Associated with these trends, although often separate from them, is the use of a variety of other conceptual approaches to explore problems such as policy formation and implementation. The majority of such approaches have emerged from within the area of political science although, more recently, others have been drawn in from outside. The political sciences contribution has, in the major part, been met before in, for example, rational and incremental theories of policy making and élite and group models of political behaviour. Again, since full details of these are available elsewhere, they will only be noted in passing here.[8] Broadly, however, their development and use in the policy field indicates a problem of choice, i.e. how does the analyst choose between theoretical approaches to attack the issues of policy? In confronting this problem the first point to remember is [. . .] simply that there is no one best way. The nature of the policy problem is such that a variety of approaches are required to deal with the complexity of the process. As Anderson argues:

> Each [of the models] focuses attention on different aspects of politics and policy making and seems more useful for some purposes or some situations than others. Generally, one should not permit oneself to be bound too rigidly or too dogmatically to a particular model . . . It is my belief that the explanation of political behaviour, rather than the validation of a given theoretical approach, should be the main purpose of political inquiry and analysis.[9]

This quotation is significant. Indeed, we would extend Anderson's argument by stressing that any analysis of policy and the policy process can only be achieved through the linking of a number of differing perspectives. [. . .]

The need for an extended perspective?

The focus on policy here is primarily a systemic one. We would argue that public policy is best understood by considering the operation of a political system in its environment and by examining how such a system maintains itself and changes over time. This is basically, very basically, a starting point.[10] The more detailed perspective we adopt is somewhat broader (see Figure 3). But even this is offered primarily as a guide to thought, since it is grossly oversimplified as it stands, such simplifications being particularly apparent with regard to the model's representation of (a) *the policy environment* and (b) *the political system itself*.

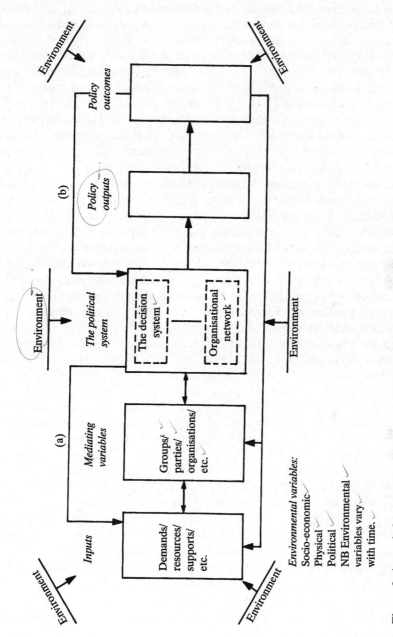

Figure 3 Amended systems model of the policy process

In traditional systems models inputs arise out of the environment, are aggregated in some fashion, and impact on the political system. In all this the environment is defined broadly in socio-economic, physical and political terms. For the general purpose of understanding political life, and for the specific purposes of analysing policy, such a conceptualisation is too crude. The environment is not structureless. It may be made up of individuals, groups and organisations with values and interests, operating alone or together *over time*. Further, the strength of environmental influences may vary with their proximity to the political system, although this is not to argue for a linear relationship between proximity and demand pressures. Interestingly enough, arguments concerning environmental changes and environmental structures have been a feature of organisational sociology for some years, the thesis being that, to account for organisational behaviour, one requires a better conceptualisation of environmental influences.[11] The same point would seem to hold in the study of public policy. In particular, one needs to explore the relationship between demand patterns and what have been termed here 'mediating variables' (see Figure 3). Further, it seems crucial to investigate whether there is any relationship between political action and the presence or absence, over time, of such variables. [. . .] What passes for the 'environment', therefore, requires thought and attention. Indeed, because of the way systems models are usually presented, the all-embracing nature of environmental influences is rarely realised. As usually defined, the environment surrounds the whole process, influencing anything and everything (see Figure 3). While useful as a first approximation, this is too gross a representation of environmental influences. A more detailed focus on environmental variables may be crucial for policy studies.

Much of the comment and criticism in the discussion above could be applied with equal force to the usual conceptualisation of the 'political system'. Too often this has been taken as a black box from which policies emerge or, at best, in which the solution to patterns of political action can be found in the size and variation of political majorities or modes of élite control. In terms of understanding policy such a position is simply not adequate. [. . .] Often the *process of choice* may be as important as the *actual choice* itself. Moreover, decision systems may be constrained by the networks within which they operate. [. . .] The latter question touches on an issue already referred to above: the possible role of administrative systems in the *formation* rather than in the *execution* of public policy, a feature often missed by an analysis that concentrates on political decision-making élites. In brief, the argument here is that policy analysis needs to disaggregate and explore the political system. This point is illustrated by Figure 3, in which a distinction is made between decision systems and organisational networks, and to this should be added another often-ignored factor, the capacity of political systems to influence their environment directly (indicated by (a) in Figure 3). Too often policy is seen simply as the response to pressure, but why is there sometimes no pressure? Why [. . .] may demands fail to emerge? Such problems, again, are the concern of the policy analyst, especially if he purports to explain the non-action as well as the action of political systems.

It is, therefore, doubtful whether the policy process can be captured in any great detail by the simple linear feedback model which political systems theory initially offers. Interactions both across and within systems must be considered, while it may also be important to account for stances and positions adopted by political actors which have no immediate and tangible policy output. A separate point concerns the relationship between decisions and outcomes. The tendency to see the latter relationship as a discrete sequence, initiated by changes in demand or support inputs, is problematic in that it may lead to the neglect of the possibility of a direct relationship between outcome and decision (see (b) in Figure 3). [. . .]

Thus the policy analyst needs to explore in more detail the nature of the political system and the relationship between such variables as decision processes and outcomes. To explain outcomes, however, involves another vital but often downgraded aspect of the whole problem: the need to establish some conceptual grasp of motivation and behaviour. Without such a grasp, responses to policy can be neither understood nor anticipated. To assume individuals or organisational élites behave rationally (perhaps the most elementary behavioural model) is often an oversimplification. An understanding of behaviour and motivation is central to an understanding of policy outcome and impact. More than this, however, such an understanding also appears crucial to an investigation of other aspects of the policy process, in particular the internal operation of the political system itself: for example, why are attempts to rationalise policy or change decision systems so often resisted? [. . .]

To explore the policy world, therefore, demands a more detailed conceptual schema than has previously been offered. To this end, an extended systems model acts as a useful heuristic map; useful in alerting one to areas that need more attention (e.g. the environment, the political system); useful in emphasising links on which theory could be usefully brought to bear (e.g. the extent to which the political system itself controls inputs rather than inputs determine political action). Moreover, to articulate the problem in such a way has value in demonstrating the view, already expressed by Anderson above, that different conceptual models may be required to explore different aspects of the overall process. Figure 3, therefore, presents in the first instance a guide for thought and analysis. As it stands, however, it is open to much of the usual abuse directed at models of this type. Indeed, it cannot be denied that the very act of starting from a systems perspective may pose problems from which it is difficult to escape: the problems of accepting uncritically a goal model of organisations, of adopting the broad assumptions of welfare economics, of slipping towards a pluralistic model of politics. Nevertheless, it must be disputed that one necessarily falls into an ontological trap;[12] rather, in using an extended systems model as an initial focus it becomes possible to explore some of the diverse directions in which policy theory has developed.

Notes

1. On definitional problems, see J. Anderson, *Public Policy Making* (Nelson, 1975), Ch. 1; also R. L. Lineberry and L. Masotti (eds.), *Urban Problems and Public Policy* (Lexington Books, 1975), xi.

2. This definition is adapted from G. K. Roberts, *A Dictionary of Political Analysis* (Longman, 1971), 152–3, and private communications with the same author.

3. Anderson, *op. cit.*, p. 10. For a similar point, see also J. Stewart, 'Public administration and the study of public policy making', *Public Administration Committee Bulletin*, 11 (1971), 42–56.

4. For a perspective on this, see T. Lowi, 'Decision making vs. public policy', *Public Administration Review*, 30 (1970), 314–25, and 'Four systems of policy, politics and choice', *Public Administration Review*, 32 (1972), 298–310. Also note R. Salisbury and J. Heinz, 'A Theory of Policy Analysis', in I. Sharkansky (ed.), *Policy Analysis in Political Science* (Markham, 1970).

5. Lasswell's original process model appears in 'The decision process', in N. Polsby *et al.*, *Politics and Social Life* (Houghton Mifflin, 1963), while for a more contemporary perspective using a similar process schema, see R. Rose, 'Comparing public policy', *European Journal of Political Research*, 1 (1973), 67–94. An Easton-type model is used by a number of writers, who each give it a different emphasis; for example, see T. Dye, *Understanding Public Policy* (Prentice Hall, 1972); I. Sharkansky, *Public Administration: Policy making in government agencies* (Markham, 1970); and, in the context of urban politics, R. Lineberry and I. Sharkansky, *Urban Politics and Public Policy* (Harper & Row, 1971).

6. For a typical argument on the advantages of a scientific and comparative approach to policy-making studies, see R. L. Hofferbert, *The Study of Public Policy* (Bobbs Merrill, 1974), in particular Chs. 1–3.

7. Against case studies, see also Hofferbert, *op. cit.*, but for a differing perspective, note P. Hall *et al.*, *Change, Choice and Conflict in Social Policy* (Heinemann, 1975), in particular Pts. I and II.

8. A full discussion of these and other approaches used in policy studies appears in Dye, *op. cit.*, and Anderson, *op. cit.*

9. Anderson, *op. cit.*, p. 25.

10. The 'black box' models appearing in policy studies are frequently only crude simplifications of the more elaborate systems framework developed by David Easton. For more comprehensive details of the latter, see D. Easton, *A Framework for Political Analysis* (Prentice Hall, 1965), or his earlier *The Political System* (A. Knopf, 1953).

11. For a discussion of organisational environments, see, for example, S. Terberry, 'The evolution of organisational environments', in J. Thomas and W. Bennis (eds.), *The Management of Change and Conflict* (Penguin, 1972); also, R. Osborn and J. Hunt, 'Environment and organisational effectiveness', *Administrative Science Quarterly*, 19 (1974), 231–46. More generally, note the discussion in J. Child, 'Organisational structure, environment and performance', *Sociology*, 6 (1972), 1–22.

12. These points are raised by G. M. Dillon, 'Policy, and dramaturgy: a critique of current conceptions of policy making', *Policy and Politics*, 5, No. 1 (1976), 47–62.

Part II

Theories of the state

Introduction

In order to understand the policy process it is necessary to relate it to the power structure of a society as a whole. Policy is the product of the exercise of political influence, determining what the state does and setting limits to what it does. Any detailed attention to the policy process, including policy implementation, needs to be set in this wider context.

Controversy about power in society was for long centred upon a debate between pluralism, a theory which sees access to influence upon the state as comparatively open to citizens, and theories which emphasize structured power inequalities. Many of the latter derive either from Karl Marx's analysis of power under the domination of capitalism or from theories about the dominance of power elites, propounded by those who accept Marx's views about the concentration of power but reject the view that this can be satisfactorily explained by his analysis of capitalism. The first three extracts in this part deal with aspects of this controversy. Lukes sets out the basic dimensions of the debate, linking it to the conceptual and methodological problems that were encountered by the simpler forms of pluralist theory. Pluralism was in the first place an adaption of nineteenth-century individualist thinking, which had to be modified to recognize that in a complex society citizens relate to the state through intermediary groups. That adaption, sometimes described as 'democratic elitism', had then to face the problem that the relationship between groups and the state is often complex and obscure with the 'elitism' sometimes more evident than the 'democracy'.

Lukes' critique of pluralism is followed in this reader by McLennan's analysis of the way in which political scientists in the pluralist tradition have gradually modified their stance, conceding the importance of structured inequalities. McLennan's discussion of pluralism comes from a book in which he shows how the two traditions of pluralism and Marxism have converged as they have had to confront difficulties with their own models of the power structure.

The corresponding way in which the Marxist approach has been modified is explored in the extract from Dunleavy and O'Leary. The Marxist approach has had to come to terms with the way in which the complexity of economic and social relations in modern societies cannot simply be analysed in terms of a confrontation between two simple elements of capital and labour. Structural analysis has to recognize the importance of a number of different structured conflicts in society, and a wide range of differences within groups postulated, in simplistic Marxist theory, as having opposing interests. In doing this neo-Marxist theory, whilst holding on to the importance of structured interests which may be obscured in the ways discussed in Lukes' second and third dimensions of power, has conceded that actual conflicts in society may have some of the more open characteristics set out in the pluralist model.

Both pluralism and Marxism have long had to contend with a criticism that they disregard the extent to which the state is itself a source of power. They tend to treat it as something neutral to be captured. Early in the twentieth century the main challenge to this view came from the 'elitist' writers like Pareto and Mosca who opposed the Marxist view of the state as 'the executive of the ruling class'. This approach always faced a difficulty in dealing with questions about the original power source of these elites. More recent writing tends to disregard this problem and simply emphasize the extent to which, once complex state institutions were set up, the elevation of individuals or groups to the control of these created a power elite who were then likely to take steps to develop and perpetuate that power. In doing so they would not necessarily remain committed to the interests of the classes or groups which initially enabled them to acquire these positions. Rather they would be likely to develop interests of their own, and start to recruit to their own ranks and influence access to state institutions. Further down the line, as we are in societies which have had massive state institutions for a long period of time, this 'autonomy' has become an important feature of power structures.

Dunleavy and O'Leary discuss the way some Marxist theory has tried to come to terms with this issue. But the other five extracts in this part take this issue further, in a variety of ways.

The extract from Smith's book emphasizes how network analysis may be used to explore the way organized interests outside the state interact with the diverse range of organized interests within the state. Smith makes use of two concepts – policy networks and policy communities – seeing the latter as more cohesive and stable variations of the former. In his book Smith argues (pp. 66–75) that network analysis can be integrated with any of the more general theories of the state. Yet it is in many respects most recognizably a development from pluralism, building upon aspects of 'corporatist' theory which are now seen as offering a less satisfactory way of integrating state theory and pluralist theory.

With the rise of the political influence of the 'new right' a body of theory has been developed which is generally labelled 'public choice' theory. This uses ideas derived from economics to explore political behaviour, emphasizing the notion that there is a political market place in which groups compete for public support. Some writers on theories of the state (e.g. Dunleavy and O'Leary in the book from which the extract here on Marxist theory has been drawn) treat this as offering a separate theory of the state. An alternative view, adopted in the companion text-book to this reader, is to see much of this work as essentially a development of the ideas about competition for support embodied in pluralist theory. However, where public choice theory does go beyond pluralism in a challenging way is in raising questions about the behaviour of state actors as the 'sellers' of public services in situations of monopoly or oligopoly. Hence the extract here from a pamphlet by Tullock in which he analyses, using economic theory about monopoly, what he postulates will be the behaviour of state bureaucrats who can practise 'bureau-maximization' uninhibited by competition.

This theory obviously offers a perspective on the way the state will behave, and has influenced many contemporary developments in public administration (particularly the 'new public management' movement discussed in Part V). However, critics have argued that Tullock and his 'public choice' colleagues offer too simple a model of bureaucratic behaviour (see in particular Self, 1993). Dunleavy in his book *Democracy, Bureaucracy and Public Choice* examines the premises upon which this theory is based but then goes on to argue that if we are to give attention to the motivation structures of bureaucrats we are likely to find that they are more complex than is suggested in Tullock's analysis. He offers us a model which sees bureaucrats as 'bureau-shapers' but not necessarily 'bureau-maximizers'. The extract used here from Dunleavy's book sets out a variety of ways in which bureaus may be expected to be 'shaped', according to their tasks and institutional settings.

The last two extracts in this part offer variants of a body of American work sometimes given the label 'new institutionalism', exploring the way the institutions of government may influence the policy process. The first of these is part of Skocpol's introductory essay in a collection which explores the importance of 'state-centred' theory for the explanation of state behaviour.

The other is a recent article by March and Olsen. These two writers initially provided a lively and provocative statement of the institutionalist position in an article published in 1984. There they argued:

> Political democracy depends not only on economic and social conditions but also on the design of political institutions. The bureaucratic agency, the legislative committee, and the appellate court are arenas for contending social forces, but they are also collections of standard operating procedures and structures that define and defend interests. They are political actors in their own right. (1984, p. 738)

In the course of that article they also set out in a colourful way the most extreme version of the perspective that sees policy making as a haphazard and irrational process when they wrote of a 'garbage-can model' which 'assumes that problems, solutions, decision-makers, and choice opportunities are independent, exogenous streams flowing through a system' (*ibid.*, p. 746). They went on to elaborate their ideas in a book published in 1989. It was difficult to know what to choose from these interesting writers, but in the end it was decided to set out here a more recent statement of their perspective, an article published in 1996.

This large part thus includes an initial selection of three articles concerned with the classic debate about the nature of the democratic state. Readers who want to follow this up will find Schwarzmantel's *The State in Contemporary Society* offers a lively exploration of the relevance of the various theoretical positions today. However, the inclusion of five items which involve, in various respects, ways of relating developments within the state to pressures upon it indicates the way in which analysts have risen to Skocpol's challenge 'to bring the state back in'. To follow up on this theme the books from which the contributions are drawn are certainly relevant. To these should be added an edited volume by Steinmo, Thelen and Longstreth (1992).

References

March, J. G. and Olsen, J. P. (1984) 'The New Institutionalism: organisational factors in political life', *American Political Science Review*, 78, pp. 734–49.

March, J. G. and Olsen, J. P. (1989) *Rediscovering Institutions*, New York: Free Press.

Schwarzmantel, J. (1994) *The State in Contemporary Society*, Hemel Hempstead: Harvester Wheatsheaf.

Self, P. (1993) *Government by the Market?*, Basingstoke: Macmillan.

Steinmo, S., Thelen, K. and Longstreth, F. (eds.)(1992) *Structuring Politics: Historical Institutionalism in Comparative Analysis*, Cambridge: Cambridge University Press.

Three distinctive views of power compared

Steven Lukes

The distinctive features of the three views of power presented are summarised below.

One-dimensional view of power
Focus on (a) behaviour
       (b) decision-making
       (c) (key) issues
       (d) observable (overt) conflict
       (e) (subjective) interests, seen as policy preferences revealed by political participation

Two-dimensional view of power
(Qualified) critique of behavioural focus
Focus on (a) decision-making and non-decision-making
       (b) issues and potential issues
       (c) observable (overt or covert) conflict
       (d) (subjective) interests, seen as policy preferences or grievances

Three-dimensional view of power
Critique of behavioural focus
Focus on (a) decision-making and control over political agenda (not necessarily through decisions)
       (b) issues and potential issues
       (c) observable (overt or covert) and latent conflict
       (d) subjective and real interests [. . .]

The three views compared

I now turn to consider the relative strengths and weaknesses of the three views of power I have outlined.

From S. Lukes, *Power: A radical view* (1974), London: Macmillan, Chapter 7.

The virtues of the decision-making or one-dimensional view are obvious and have often been stressed: by means of it, to cite Merelman, the pluralists 'studied actual behavior, stressed operational definitions, and turned up evidence' (Merelman, 1968, p. 451). However, the trouble is that, by doing this, by studying the making of important decisions within the community, they were simply taking over and reproducing the bias of the system they were studying. By analysing the decisions on urban redevelopment, public education and political nominations, Dahl tells us a good deal about the *diversity* of decision-making power in New Haven. He shows that these issue areas are independent of one another, and that, by and large, different individuals exercise power in different areas and therefore no set of individuals and thus no single elite has decision-making power ranging across different issue areas. He further argues that the decision-making process is responsive to the preferences of citizens because the elected politicians and officials engaged in it anticipate the results of future elections. It would, he writes, 'be unwise to underestimate the extent to which voters may exert *indirect* influence on the decisions of leaders by means of elections' (Dahl, 1961, p. 101): no issue of importance to the former is likely to be ignored for long by the latter. Thus Dahl pictures pluralist politics as both diverse and open: he writes, '[T]he independence, penetrability, and heterogeneity of the various segments of the political stratum all but guarantee that any dissatisfied group will find spokesmen in the political stratum' (p. 93). But the diversity and openness Dahl sees may be highly misleading if power is being exercised within the system to limit decisionmaking to acceptable issues. Individuals and elites may act separately in making acceptable decisions, but they may act in concert – or even fail to act at all – in such a way as to keep unacceptable issues out of politics, thereby preventing the system from becoming any more diverse than it is. 'A polity', it has been suggested, 'that is pluralistic in its decision-making can be unified in its non-decisionmaking' (Crenson, 1971, p. 179). The decision-making method prevents this possibility from being considered. Dahl concludes that the system is penetrable by any dissatisfied group, but he does so only by studying cases of successful penetration, and never examines failed attempts at such penetration. Moreover, the thesis that indirect influence gives the electorate control over leaders can be turned on its head. Indirect influence can equally operate to prevent politicians, officials or others from raising issues or proposals known to be unacceptable to some group or institution in the community. It can serve the interests of an elite, not only that of the electorate. In brief, the one-dimensional view of power cannot reveal the less visible ways in which a pluralist system may be biased in favour of certain groups and against others.

The two-dimensional view goes some way to revealing this – which is a considerable advance in itself – but it confines itself to studying situations where the mobilisation of bias can be attributed to individuals' decisions that have the effect of preventing current observable grievances (overt or covert) from becoming issues within the political process. This, I think, largely accounts for the very thin and inadequate character of Bachrach and Baratz's study of poverty, race and politics in Baltimore (Bachrach and Baratz, 1970). All that study really amounts to is an account of various decisions by the mayor and various business leaders to deflect the inchoate demands of

Baltimore's blacks from becoming politically threatening issues – by such devices as making certain appointments, establishing task forces to defuse the poverty issue, supporting certain kinds of welfare measures, etc. – together with an account of how the blacks gained political access through overt struggle involving riots. The analysis remains superficial precisely because it confines itself to studying individual decisions made to avert potentially threatening demands from becoming politically dangerous. A deeper analysis would also concern itself with all the complex and subtle ways in which the *inactivity* of leaders and the sheer weight of institutions – political, industrial and educational – served for so long to keep the blacks out of Baltimore politics; and indeed for a long period kept them from even trying to get into it.

The three-dimensional view offers the possibility of such an analysis. It offers, in other words, the prospect of a serious sociological and not merely personalised explanation of how political systems prevent demands from becoming political issues or even from being made. Now the classical objection to doing this has often been stated by pluralists: how can one study, let alone explain, what does not happen? Polsby writes:

> ... it has been suggested that non-events make more significant policy than do policy-making events. This is the kind of statement that has a certain plausibility and attractiveness but that presents truly insuperable obstacles to research. We can sound the depths of the abyss very quickly by agreeing that non-events are much more important than events, and inquiring precisely *which* non-events are to be regarded as most significant in the community. Surely not *all* of them. For every event (no matter how defined) that occurs there must be an infinity of alternatives. Then which non-events are to be regarded as significant? One satisfactory answer might be: those outcomes desired by a significant number of actors in the community but not achieved. Insofar as these goals are in some way explicitly pursued by people in the community, the method of study used in New Haven has a reasonable chance of capturing them. A wholly unsatisfactory answer would be: certain non-events stipulated by outside observers without reference to the desires or activities of community residents. The answer is unsatisfactory because it is obviously inappropriate for outsiders to pick among all the possible outcomes that did not take place a set which they regard as important but which community citizens do not. This approach is likely to prejudice the outcomes of research. ... (Polsby, 1963, pp. 96–7)

Similarly, Wolfinger argues that the 'infinite variety of possible nondecisions . . . reveals the idea's adaptability to various ideological perspectives' (Wolfinger, 1971, p. 1078). Moreover, suppose we advance 'a theory of political interests and rational behavior' specifying how people would behave in certain situations if left to themselves, and use it to support the claim that their failure so to behave is due to the exercise of power. In this case, Wolfinger argues, we have no means of deciding between two possibilities: either that there was an exercise of power, or that the theory was wrong (p. 1078).

The first point to be made against these apparently powerful arguments is that they move from a methodological difficulty to a substantive assertion. It does not follow that, just because it is difficult or even impossible to show that power has been exercised in a given situation, we can conclude that it has not. But, more importantly, I do not believe that it is impossible to identify an exercise of power of this type.

What is an exercise of power? What is it to exercise power? On close inspection it turns out that the locution 'exercise of power' and 'exercising power' is problematic in at least two ways.

In the first place, it carries, in everyday usage, a doubly unfortunate connotation: it is sometimes assumed to be both individualistic and intentional, that is, it seems to carry the suggestion that the exercise of power is a matter of individuals consciously acting to affect others. Some appear to feel discomfort in speaking either of groups, institutions or collectivities 'exercising' power, or of individuals or collectivities doing so unconsciously. This is an interesting case of individualistic and intentional assumptions being built into our language – but that in itself provides no reason for adopting such assumptions. In what follows I propose to abandon these assumptions and to speak of the exercise of power whether by individuals or by groups, institutions, etc., and whether consciously or not. A negative justification for this revisionary usage is that there is no other available word that meets the bill (thus 'exerting' power is little different from 'exercising' it); I shall offer a positive justification below.

The second way in which the phrase 'exercising power' is problematic is that it conceals an interesting and important ambiguity. I referred above to Dahl's definition of the exercise of power in terms of A getting B to do something he would not otherwise do. However, this is, as it stands, too simple.

Suppose that A can *normally* affect B. This is to suppose that, against the background of (what is assumed to be) a normally ongoing situation, if A does x, he gets B to do what he would not otherwise do. Here A's action, x, is sufficient to get B to do what he would not otherwise do. Suppose, however, that exactly the same is true of A_1. He can also normally affect B: his action, y, is also sufficient to get B to do what he would not otherwise do, in just the same way. Now, suppose that A and A_1 both act in relation to B simultaneously and B changes his action accordingly. Here, it is clear, B's action or change of course is overdetermined: both A and A_1 have affected B by 'exercising power', but the result is the same as that which would have occurred had either affected him singly. In this case it is a pointless question to ask which of them produced the change of course, that is, which of them made a difference to the result: they both did. They both 'exercised power', in a sense – that is, a power *sufficient* to produce the result – yet one cannot say that *either* of them made a difference to the result. Let us call this sense of 'exercising power' the operative sense.

Contrast this case with the case where A *does* make a difference to the result: that is, against the background of a normally ongoing situation, A, by doing x, actually gets B to do what B would not otherwise do. Here x is an intervening cause which distorts the normal course of events – by contrast with the first, overdetermined case, where there are, *ex hypothesi*, *two* intervening sufficient conditions, so that neither can be said to have 'made a difference', just because of the presence of the other: there the normal course of events is itself distorted by the presence of the other intervening sufficient condition. In this case, by contrast, A's intervention can be said to make a difference to the result. Let us call this sense of 'exercising power' the *effective* sense.

(It is worth adding a further distinction, which turns on *what* difference A makes to the result. A wishes B to do some particular thing, but, in exercising effective power over him, he may succeed in changing B's course in a wide variety of ways. Only in the case where B's change of course corresponds to A's wishes, that is, where A secures B's compliance, can we speak properly of a *successful* exercise of power: here 'affecting' becomes 'control'. It is, incidentally, this case of the successful exercise of power, or the securing of compliance, on which Bachrach and Baratz exclusively concentrate. The successful exercise of power can be seen as a sub-species of the effective exercise of power – though one could maintain that, where the operative exercise of power issues in compliance, this also is an [indeterminate] form of its successful exercise.)

We can now turn to the analysis of what exactly is involved in identifying an exercise of power. An attribution of the exercise of power involves, among other things, the double claim that A acts (or fails to act) in a certain way and that B does what he would not otherwise do (I use the term 'do' here in a very wide sense, to include 'think', 'want', 'feel', etc.). In the case of an effective exercise of power, A gets B to do what he would not otherwise do; in the case of an operative exercise of power, A, together with another or other sufficient conditions, gets B to do what he would not otherwise do. Hence, in general, any attribution of the exercise of power (including, of course, those by Dahl and his colleagues) always implies a relevant counterfactual, to the effect that (but for A, or but for A together with any other sufficient conditions) B would otherwise have done, let us say, b. This is one reason why so many thinkers (mistakenly) insist on actual, observable conflict as essential to power (though there are doubtless other theoretical and, indeed, ideological reasons). For such conflict provides the relevant counterfactual, so to speak, ready-made. If A and B are in conflict with one another, A wanting a and B wanting b, then if A prevails over B, we can assume that B would otherwise have done b. Where there is no observable conflict between A and B, then we must provide other grounds for asserting the relevant counterfactual. That is, we must provide other, indirect, grounds for asserting that if A had not acted (or failed to act) in a certain way – and, in the case of operative power, if other sufficient conditions had not been operative – then B would have thought and acted differently from the way he does actually think and act. In brief, we need to justify our expectation that B would have thought or acted differently; and we also need to specify the means or mechanism by which A has prevented, or else acted (or abstained from acting) in a manner sufficient to prevent, B from doing so.

I can see no reason to suppose that either of these claims cannot in principle be supported – though I do not claim it is easy. Doing so certainly requires one to go much deeper than most analyses of power in contemporary political science and sociology. Fortunately, Matthew Crenson's book, *The Un-Politics of Air Pollution: A study of non-decisionmaking in the cities* (Crenson, 1971), provides a good example of how the task can be approached. The theoretical framework of this book can be seen as lying on the borderline of the two-dimensional and the three-dimensional views of power: I see it as a serious attempt empirically to apply the former, together with certain elements of the latter. For that reason, it marks a real theoretical advance in the empirical study of power relations.

It explicitly attempts to find a way to explain 'things that do not happen', on the assumption that 'the proper object of investigation is not political activity but political inactivity' (pp. vii, 26). Why, he asks, was the issue of air pollution not raised as early or as effectively in some American cities as it was in others? His object, in other words, is to 'discover . . . why many cities and towns in the United States failed to make a political issue of their air pollution problems' (p. vii), thereby illuminating the character of local political systems – particularly with respect to their 'penetrability'. He first shows that differences in the treatment of pollution cannot be attributed solely to differences in the actual pollution level or to social characteristics of the populations in question. He then provides a detailed study of two neighbouring cities in Indiana, both equally polluted and with similar populations, one of which, East Chicago, took action to clean its air in 1949, while the other, Gary, held its breath until 1962. Briefly, his explanation of the difference is that Gary is a one-company town dominated by U.S. Steel, with a strong party organisation, whereas East Chicago had a number of steel companies and no strong party organisation when it passed its air pollution control ordinance.

His case (which he documents with convincing detail) is that U.S. Steel, which had built Gary and was responsible for its prosperity, for a long time effectively prevented the issue from even being raised, through its power reputation operating on anticipated reactions, then for a number of years thwarted attempts to raise the issue, and decisively influenced the content of the anti-pollution ordinance finally enacted. Moreover, it did all this without acting or entering into the political arena. Its 'mere reputation for power, unsupported by acts of power' was 'sufficient to inhibit the emergence of the dirty air issue' (p. 124); and, when it eventually did emerge (largely because of the threat of Federal or State action), 'U.S. Steel . . . influenced the content of the pollution ordinance without taking any action on it, and thus defied the pluralist dictum that political power belongs to political actors' (pp. 69–70). U.S. Steel, Crenson argues, exercised influence 'from points outside the range of observable political behaviour. . . . Though the corporation seldom intervened directly in the deliberations of the town's air pollution policymakers, it was nevertheless able to affect their scope and direction' (p. 107). He writes:

> Gary's anti-pollution activists were long unable to get U.S. Steel to take a clear stand. One of them, looking back on the bleak days of the dirty air debate, cited the evasiveness of the town's largest industrial corporation as a decisive factor in frustrating early efforts to enact a pollution control ordinance. The company executives, he said, would just nod sympathetically 'and agree that air pollution was terrible, and pat you on the head. But they never *did* anything one way or the other. If only there had been a fight, then something might have been accomplished!' What U.S. Steel did not do was probably more important to the career of Gary's air pollution issue than what it did do. (pp. 76–7)

He then moves from these two detailed case studies to a comparative analysis of interview data with political leaders taken from fifty-one cities, aimed at testing the hypotheses arising out of the two case studies. Briefly, his conclusions are that 'the air pollution issue tends not to flourish in cities where industry enjoys a reputation for power' (p. 145) – and that 'where industry remains silent about dirty air, the life chances of the pollution issue are likely to be diminished' (p. 124). Again, a strong and influential party organisation will also inhibit the growth of the pollution issue, since demands for clean air are unlikely to yield the kind of specific benefits that American party machines seek – though where industry has a high power reputation, a strong party will increase the pollution issue's life chances, since it will seek to purchase industrial influence. In general Crenson plausibly argues that pollution control is a good example of a collective good, whose specific costs are concentrated on industry: thus the latter's opposition will be strong, while the support for it will be relatively weak, since its benefits are diffuse and likely to have little appeal to party leaders engaged in influence brokerage. Moreover, and very interestingly, Crenson argues, against the pluralists, that political issues tend to be interconnected; and thus collective issues tend to promote other collective issues, and vice versa. Thus by 'promoting one political agenda item, civic activists may succeed in driving other issues away' (p.170):

> where business and industrial development is a topic of local concern, the dirty air problem tends to be ignored. The prominence of one issue appears to be connected with the subordination of the other, and the existence of this connection calls into question the pluralist view that different political issues tend to rise and subside independently. (p.165)

Crenson's general case is that there are 'politically imposed limitations upon the scope of decision-making', such that 'decision-making activity is channelled and directed by the process of non-decision making' (p. 178). Pluralism, in other words, is 'no guarantee of political openness or popular sovereignty'; and neither the study of decision-making nor the existence of 'visible diversity' will tell us anything about 'those groups and issues which may have been shut out of a town's political life' (p. 181).

I suggested above that the theoretical framework of Crenson's analysis lies on the borderline of the two-dimensional and the three-dimensional views of power. It is, on the face of it, a two-dimensional study of non-decision-making à la Bachrach and Baratz. On the other hand, it begins to advance beyond their position (as presented in their book) in three ways. First, it does not interpret non-decision-making behaviourally, as exhibited only in decisions (hence the stress on inaction – 'What U.S. Steel did not do . . .'); second, it is non-individualistic and considers institutional power, and third, it considers ways in which demands are prevented, through the exercise of such power, from being raised: thus,

> Local political forms and practices may even inhibit citizens' ability to transform some diffuse discontent into an explicit demand. In short, there is something like an inarticulate ideology in political institutions, even in those that appear to be most open-minded, flexible and disjointed – an ideology in the sense that it promotes the selective perception and articulation of social problems and conflicts. . . . (p. 23)

In this way, 'local political institutions and political leaders may . . . exercise considerable control over what people choose to care about and how forcefully they articulate their cares' (p. 27): restrictions on the scope of decision-making may 'stunt the political consciousness of the local public' by confining minority opinions to minorities and denying 'minorities the opportunity to grow to majorities' (pp. 180–1).

Crenson's analysis is impressive because it fulfils the double requirement mentioned above: there is good reason to expect that, other things being equal, people would rather not be poisoned (assuming, in particular, that pollution control does not necessarily mean unemployment) – even where they may not even articulate this preference; and hard evidence is given of the ways in which institutions, specifically U.S. Steel, largely through inaction, prevented the citizens' interest in not being poisoned from being acted on (though other factors, institutional and ideological, would need to enter a fuller explanation). Thus both the relevant counterfactual and the identification of a power mechanism are justified.

References

Bachrach, P., and M. S. Baratz (1970), *Power and Poverty*, New York: Oxford University Press.

Crenson, M. A. (1971), *The Un-Politics of Air Pollution: A study of non-decisionmaking in the cities*, Baltimore: Johns Hopkins University Press.

Dahl, R. A. (1961), *Who Governs?*, New Haven: Yale University Press.

Merelman, R. M. (1968), 'On the neo-elitist critique of community power', *American Political Science Review*, 62, pp. 451–60.

Polsby, N. W. (1963), *Community Power and Political Theory*, New Haven: Yale University Press.

Wolfinger, R. E. (1971), 'Nondecisions and the study of local politics', *American Political Science Review*, 65, pp. 1063–80.

The evolution of pluralist theory

Gregor McLennan

Critical pluralism

The force of at least two of the standard sets of criticisms of conventional pluralism needs to be deflected to some extent. First, there was the issue of the different sorts of interest group brought under the same heading for analytic purposes. The problem with conventional pluralist analysis is not that the need for distinctions was ignored, nor that inequalities between groups were considered insignificant. Bentley finally plumped for a kind of materialism in arriving at a manageable categorization of the basis of group life. His 'underlying' groups were, in effect, principles of potential social stratification and included those based on differences of environmental conditions, race, wealth and trade (Bentley 1967: 462). Writers such as Pendleton Herring and Peter Odegard in the 1930s developed an approach to group analysis which deliberately undercut any all-purpose usage of the notion of interests. Under later pressure from critical voices such as those of Schattschneider and Easton, the pluralist persistence with the notion of interest groups was not so much a naive and uncritical levelling of differences as the retention of a convenient label within which more detailed distinctions and comparisons could be made. Dahl's argument against marxism, for example, was not that class was unimportant, but that when considered as somehow more 'real' than other bases of social differences, the importance of the latter (e.g. language, religion, race) was undermined (Dahl 1971: 106–7). His argument – at least as reviewed in retrospect – was that the undeniable persistence of class division in modern society did not entail that class was always and everywhere the major determinant of politics (Dahl 1982: 62). In this context, Dahl is probably right to dismiss as 'rather absurd' the charge that the conventional pluralists theorized groups as being equally open, equally well resourced, and equally heard at the political level (Dahl 1982: 208–9).

Some pluralists, certainly, were more aware of group inequalities than others. V. O. Key, for example, was an influential 'empirical democratic theorist' whose wry tone

From G. McLennan, *Marxism, Pluralism and Beyond* (1989), Cambridge: Polity Press, Chapter 2.

and clear mind were not conducive to mystification. Key (1964, 1st edn. 1942) looked at a range of pressure groups with a view to their potential for coherence and internal division. He pointed out that while sectional interests cut across the business community, the latter was able to achieve solidarity on political questions due to their special powers of class unity in the face of challenges to their control of wealth (Key 1964: 73f.). Business, however, is a minority interest, so in a democracy the problem for businessmen (which they generally overcome) is to generate the kind of public opinion that acquiesces to their high status in the economic order (1964: 91). For Key, an element of 'economic determinism' here is quite palatable – provided it does not obliterate other, non-economic sources of interest-conflict (1964: 103).

A second objection to pluralism – that it ignores the organized power of the state – also stands in need of modification. It is true that group theory does play down 'the state' as a concept and focuses instead on the representative and responsive political system. But this is not merely a 'bias' of pluralism since the tradition in the US from the early part of this century has been unimpressed by idealist concepts of the general will and common good which the state was held to 'represent'. The turn to group interests was a more empiricist and behavioural approach, but it was also a substantive sociological impulse which can be defended as such. Additionally, it does not follow from pluralists' relative neglect of the state that they were wholly unaware of interest-group activity *within* the level of the political system. On the contrary, Latham for one pointed out the perpetual 'group struggle' within officialdom itself (1952: 35). And Dahl's whole concern was to establish the political as well as the social prerequisites for polyarchy, since societal pluralism could not of itself guarantee that a range of interests would be taken up by parties and leaders. The frequency in pluralist writings of terms such as 'leaders' as marking a contrast between the groups represented and the political representatives in a polyarchy indicates the pluralist awareness of self-interest on the parts of officials and politicians. Dahl's major empirical study of the interest group influence on local decision-making, *Who Governs?* (1961), comes out with quite 'anti-pluralist' conclusions, if pluralism is taken in any pure sense. The city government of New Haven is clearly perceived and portrayed by Dahl as an independent agent and the various interest groups identified do not appear to have great impact on the outcome of the political process (1961: 5–6).

The condensation of pluralist thinking on the state into a convenient metaphor suggesting responsive representation can therefore be misleading. Truman, for example, described the 'weathervane' picture, in which government as a single entity is moved this way and that by the balance of forces amongst social interests, as 'much too simple' (Truman 1951: 106). Latham not only saw officials as constituting interest groups, he accepted that in some sense the state had to act independently as the 'custodian of the consensus' (1952: 14). Clearly, this conception, like Dahl's continual assertion of the imperfections of modern democracy, entails a powerful semi-autonomous governmental interest. The bargaining amongst the various powers, interests and organizations in pluralist theory is not, after all, an even-handed process. Some groups in society are in a stronger position to bargain than others, and those in the political system itself are often in a position to brush off the pressures created by social constituencies.

The main critical charges against pluralism are therefore relative ones. It is true that in comparison with other types of political theory 'the state' is *relatively* neglected. It is true that in *some* expressions of pluralism, democratic consensus is assumed to operate and the impression is given that all serious interests can be both balanced out and partially satisfied. *Occasionally* pluralists tend to take suggestive images and parallels for real: the state as broker or umpire, for example, or the social system as tending to equilibrium. Overall, though, it is the contradictoriness of pluralist discourse which is striking, and this does involve a culpable theoretical forgetfulness. For example, in spite of his acute analysis of class interests amongst the most powerful group in society, Key is able to generalize – in a characteristic pluralistic phrase – that power remains widely dispersed and that groups interact in a 'complex and kaleidoscopic manner' (1964: 8). In parallel, and in spite of the recognition of the autonomy of political elites, the pluralists do frequently return to the constraints on leadership imposed by a variety of social interests and indeed the norms of the democratic culture.

This lack of a stable set of conceptual hierarchies is one reason why pluralism is seldom expounded as a specific theory. It also explains why attempts definitively to pin down conventional pluralism tend to run into trouble. For example, two recent commentators have argued that pluralism presents an 'image of society as an aggregate of interacting individuals socialized into cultural values and engaging in diverse communications and exchanges, especially in markets' (Alford and Friedland 1985: 17). This interpretation rightly highlights the role pluralism allots to the civic culture in providing the subjective bonding in an atomistic and competitive market society. Yet the characteristic element which marks pluralism off from straightforward liberal individualism – the sociology and psychology of *group* formation – is glaringly absent from the sketch.

Another critical reviewer assimilates pluralism into the tradition of the theory of political elites (Graham 1986: 125ff.). The logic of this move is that pluralism's 'realistic' side is emphasized at the expense of its 'normative' elements. Thus, the pluralists' emphasis on competing groups, parties and organizations, plus their 'realism' about the necessary limitations of popular rule in a modern society, produce a somewhat cynical rationale for the long-favoured 'iron law of oligarchies'. This interpretation is also plausible, but it does tend to underestimate the normative aspect of pluralist theory. Although minority groups do compete for power under the banner of self-interest, pluralists believe (perhaps mistakenly) that a wide range of groups are able to exercise a democratic voice. From below, pluralist society emits a strong (and ever-changing) flow of citizen concerns. From above, the condition of democratic stability is that groups ensconced in the political system must show themselves to be sensitive to societal demands and to the expectations of the democratic culture generally.

This unstable amalgam of hard-headed realism about the imperfect democracy and a certain idealism about the virtues of pluralist market society came unstuck in the later 1960s. The notion that deep social polarity was a thing of the past and that an end to ideological politics was in the offing simply evaporated as serious strife re-entered the fabric of modern democracies. The complacency of the pluralist suggestion that minority voices can be heard without resort to conflict was rudely shattered by the racial and social violence which erupted in a spread of major US cities. The rediscovery of millions of free Americans living in poverty bluntly dented the feeling that democracy and affluence went hand in hand. The onset of economic recession spoiled the technocratic vision of smooth growth. The systematic questioning of the social order by students – the very sons and daughters of middle America – revealed that a concerned voice for internal change and for the rest of the world would not, it seemed, be listened to in the normal process of institutional democratic politics.

The impact of the political and cultural alternatives on respectable America was closely connected to the fact that, and the way in which, the strongest country in the world was conducting a war on one of the poorest peasant societies: Vietnam. Not the cosy picture of articulate pressure groups securing a response from a friendly local senator, but harrowing images of the bombing and napalming of peasant communities, became part of the underbelly and substance of domestic western politics in the late 1960s. Nothing could more dramatically reveal, radical critics felt, the coercion which lay behind consensus, the brutalization behind homilies on freedom, and the imperial interests which sustained an advanced economy upon which, according to pluralism, democratic norms depended. In response to the emergent radicalism behind that disillusionment, middle America turned to the more openly disciplinary politics of the Nixon era. But the promise of trust and openness could no longer be maintained without question, and the Watergate bugging scandal of 1973–4 seemed the apotheosis of the transformation of democratic promise to a polyarchy which was imperfect indeed.

The impact of these events on pluralist thinking was profound. Some political theorists were moved by these and parallel European developments to separate further the question of democratic *stability* from that of societal pluralism. By the mid 1970s a strong anti-pluralist current was prominent in international political science: the 'crisis' of the democracies was asserted to lie in the expression of *too many* turbulent group voices, *too much* responsiveness on the part of increasingly 'overloaded' government (cf. Crozier *et al.* 1975). For several of the key conventional pluralists, notably Dahl and Lindblom, a more apt response was to move in a self-critical direction. In their important 1976 Preface to *Politics, Economics and Welfare*, these authors argue that polyarchy has taken an adverse turn, due to the growth of an 'imperial presidency', the entrenched accumulations of private wealth in the face of public squalor, and a singular failure to combat social inequality. The remedy, if one is to be found, must involve a far greater degree of active popular participation.

One aspect of the development from conventional to critical pluralism is the questioning of the somewhat functionalist and 'technicist' account of social evolution it embodied. Pluralism did not, as is sometimes alleged, lack a sense of history, or even of historical *conflict* (cf. Beer 1969), but it did assume that economic growth was a steady, necessary foundation for democracy, and that such a process is relatively independent of the social conflict surrounding it. In the later phase of pluralism, an element of this equation of growth, pluralism and democracy remains (e.g. Dahl 1971: 78), but there is a newly perceived sense of ecological and democratic danger in any neutral and limitless conception of economic advance. The realization that global resources are finite and that the choice of sources is itself a matter for careful moral consideration is one part of the questioning of growth. Another is the sense that the waste and pollution spawned by the very industry which sustained modern society now threatens to engulf and poison it. Yet another is the awareness of chronic 'under-development' in some lands as a *consequence*, and not just a contingent accompani-ment, of advanced development in others. This seriously undermines the idea that the west's 'lead' in technology is ultimately the hope for the rest of the world. These issues are mentioned only in passing in the new introduction to *Politics, Economics and Welfare* (1976, xxii) but they are seen as involving a qualitatively new set of problems for classical pluralism. Above all, as Dahl and Lindblom recognize, political issues of this sort are essentially *collective* in nature: of necessity they posit the need for action towards a common good. The theoretical currency of competing interest-group bargaining is not well equipped to provide a positive appreciation of such increasingly important items on the socio-political agenda.

Another – by now obvious – source of pluralist revision is an enhanced awareness of distinctions amongst groups. There is a greater sense than before that the configur-ation of interests requires an emphasis on profound social *division* rather than overlapping commonalities. Cleavage and conflict are now as much at the centre of analysis as consensus and freely undertaken negotiations (Dahl 1980: 20). The very notion of social 'interests' appears to have been sharpened too. In the earlier texts, the political importance of those interests which could take the form of *organized* pressure groups already went against the idea of spontaneously achieved democratic balance. In the last work of his 'conventional' phase, Dahl indeed had moved away from any temptation to convene totally different entities under the label 'interest group'. Organized political lobbies constituted one group-type; but the sociologically rich notion of 'subcultures' (Dahl 1971: 203) indicates a rather different order of analytic concern. An interest in the distinction between local, societal and international dimensions of interest-formation is evident too. True, Dahl for one continues to keep a line open to small group psychology when he asserts that local solidarities might simply be *recalcitrant* in the face of the rather abstract identities produced by structural reflection. But it is taken for granted that the complexion of local campaigns and attachments is likely to stem from the way in which general societal patterns and interests are locally embodied (Dahl 1982: 62f.).

The privileged role of business interests, as we have seen, was recognized to an extent in conventional pluralism. In the critical variety business is uniquely charged with having an effective *veto* on the entire political system (Dahl and Lindblom 1976: xxxvi–xxxvii). As well as acknowledging the personal influence of entrepreneurs in decision-making circles, a more general structural imperative is sketched whereby the political system is driven by its concern for business interests.

It becomes a major task of government to design and maintain an inducement system for businessmen, to be solicitous of business interests, and to grant them, for its value as an incentive, intimacy of participation in government itself. In all these respects the relation between government and business is unlike the relation between government and any other interest group in society. (Dahl and Lindblom 1976: xxxvii)

A conventional pluralist thought was that in a polyarchy business privilege could be neutralized. Lindblom, however, has now broken with that proposition, disturbing the hitherto implicit link between democracy and free market society.

The mere possibility that business and property dominate polyarchy opens up the paradoxical possibility that polyarchy is tied to the market system not because it is democratic, but because it is not. (Lindblom 1977: 168–9)

In other words, Lindblom is asking whether democracy-as-we-know-it (polyarchy) works in favour of a capitalist system precisely by giving the *appearance* (but not the reality) of equal pluralist participation in decision-making. This suggestion bears surprising resemblance to Lenin's well-known phrase that (bourgeois) democracy provides capitalism with its 'best possible shell' by conceding to the working class a degree of political freedom while continuing to enslave them economically. In a similarly quasi-marxist vein, Lindblom reasons that labour cannot possibly have a tendentially equal influence in the polity since the state has no need to offer workers inducements in the same way as it has to placate employers. On the contrary, workers will continue to contribute to the system without inducements 'because they have no choice but to do so' (Lindblom 1977: 176).

One of the real-world features which has caused the pluralists to become less sanguine about their earlier propositions is the continued centralization of the economy in private hands, in spite of considerable state intervention in the free market. That process overturns the impression that economic development represents a public good and a vital public domain. The interests of the giant corporations, pluralists now think, are governed principally by the imperatives of global expansion and profit. Rather than, as before, trying to theorize the role of business *within* polyarchy, the very accountability of private assets to public criteria of utility is seen as a threat to democracy. Critical pluralists are persuaded that in effect a systematic *rivalry* between business and polyarchy has developed, a contest between 'the voters' and 'the rich capitalists' (Duverger 1974: 5).

In order to appraise this problem adequately, pluralists have had to reverse exactly the terms of their analytical discourse. Not only is the previous idea of parity between interest groups now strictly 'unthinkable' (Lindblom 1977: 193), the very concept of pluralist politics as a market-place wherein groups bargain for advantage must be rejected. The pluralists perhaps did not embrace this free-enterprise terminology as openly as Joseph Schumpeter (1943) or the 'economics of politics' theorists who regarded political choice as a species of consumer preference (Tomlinson 1981). And in an effort to emphasize the purely political character of pluralist theory, Truman (1951: 48) and Dahl and Lindblom (1953: 516–17) tried to theorize a 'third way' between the 'grand alternatives' of individual enterprise and state centralism, capitalism and socialism. Even so, the earlier pluralist work is pervaded by images drawn from 'bourgeois' economics.

Lately, Dahl in particular has jettisoned this terminology and its dominant paradigm. In an important switch of priorities, he is now concerned to examine economic organization itself in *democratic* terms, rather than the other way around, and he has come up with some radical equations. If the assumption of democracy is that binding collective decisions ought to be made only by those persons subject to them, then why does the principle not apply to a central arena of decision-making, namely economic enterprises (Dahl 1985: 57)? Currently, limited ownership and control of enterprises secures political inequality through its adverse effect on equal access, resources and life-chances. This is partly because capitalist enterprises are themselves fundamentally undemocratic in structure and decision-making. The democratization of capitalist firms is therefore a major prerequisite if a genuine pluralist democracy is to emerge. Here, much greater recognition is given by pluralists to the substantive conditions of formal democracy and participation. For full political liberty to be secured, the argument goes, workers must become 'citizens of the enterprise' (Dahl 1985: 92). And, in turn, for that to happen, there must be a substantial equalization of ownership and control.

On political grounds, corporate capitalism is inimical to democracy ('I do not see how private ownership of corporate enterprise can be a fundamental moral right') (1985: 74). The implication that it is capitalist economic organization which supports the pluralism which in turn sustains democracy has, with these arguments, dramatically been turned around. Without economic democracy and a radical spread of effective collective control, the new view suggests, pluralist democracy will remain superficial at best.

Dahl lays down some fairly stringent conditions for democracy, and his list in *A Preface to Economic Democracy* looks considerably more substantive in character than the somewhat formal analogue in *A Preface to Democractic Theory* almost twenty years before. In addition to equal votes, Dahl specifies effective participation, enlightened understanding, inclusive membership of the polity, and final control of the political agenda by the *demos* (Dahl 1985: 59–60). These considerations are far from constituting a technical checklist; yet they reflect a renewed concern for the norms of classical democracy, however 'unrealistic' these might appear in our complex civilization.

Some of the specified items clearly derive from reflections on the state of the civic culture. If societal pluralism cannot of itself produce effective polyarchy, never mind democracy, then the criteria of citizen participation and subjective commitment to political norms are ever more important. We noted that some doubt was expressed in conventional pluralism about how freely formed any democratic consensus could be. But there seemed a degree of genuine optimism that the people were at least content with the workings of the political system and that the level of participation was acceptable. Such optimism – or perhaps it is sheer contradictoriness – now strikes the critical pluralists as problematic. They perceive a decisively causal relationship between the very restricted terms of the political consensus and general 'indoctrinated complacency' (Dahl and Lindblom 1976: xxxix). This is secured, it is asserted, through the uniquely powerful mass media and education system. The narrowness of the basis of political agreement reflects and sustains, according to Dahl, an 'irrational and deformed public consciousness' (Dahl 1980: 29). Consciousness is deformed, the argument now goes, because the very legitimacy of the system itself is never placed before intelligent democratic judgement. Thus the grand or primary issues about the social system itself are removed from the political agenda, and indoctrination in the myth of balance encourages passivity and homogeneity in the public mind. The tones of a conspiracy theory in these sentiments involve no extraneous imposition of vulgar marxism on these democratic pluralist reflections. Lindblom especially sees the agencies of ideology as actively promoting business interests, and in general regards the 'core' beliefs of the polyarchies as 'the product of a rigged, lopsided competition of ideas' where the appearance of open belief-formation is secured mainly by the closed, circular operation of propaganda (Lindblom 1977: 202–12). [. . .]

Let me summarize the current political contours of pluralist theory by reference to Steven Lukes's influential analysis of models of power (Lukes 1974).

[The account of Lukes has been omitted as a section from Lukes's own work forms the previous chapter.]

The elaboration of this model represented an attempt to show the poverty of conventional pluralist theory. What is interesting for our purposes is that 'critical pluralism' as I have outlined its development now conforms to a large degree with the three-dimensional view. Lukes rightly noted Dahl's concern, in *Who Governs?*, to show how *indirect* were the influences on political decisions, thus in a way breaching the confines of the one-dimensional view. Phase two pluralism goes much further, revealing the strength of structural as well as personal influence by businessmen and corporations. It has sketched in greater detail the logic of non-participation in polyarchies and that of 'agenda-setting', thus enriching its understanding of popular democracy in the process. And it has openly asserted that inequalities of resources and responses, which themselves render the grand edifice of open government a façade, are systematically sustained by a *rhetoric* of consensus which is generated through the socialization process and the ideological institutions. Pluralist theory has always had two faces, one of which looked somewhat cynically towards the reality of elite rule in formally democratic nations. The other face was turned optimistically to the future in the hope that imperfect democracy could be steadily enhanced. On waking up from their American dream, the pluralists have attractively revised their previous, limited conception of democracy.

References

Alford, R. R., and R. Friedland (1985), *Powers of Theory*, Cambridge: Cambridge University Press.

Beer, S. H. (1969), *Modern British Politics*, London: Faber and Faber.

Bentley, A. F. (1967), *The Process of Government*, Cambridge, MA: Belknap Press.

Crozier, M. J., *et al.* (1975), *The Crisis of Democracy*, London: The Trilateral Commission.

Dahl, R. A. (1961), *Who Governs?*, New Haven: Yale University Press.

Dahl, R. A. (1971), *Polyarchy*, New Haven: Yale University Press.

Dahl, R. A. (1980), 'Pluralism revisited', in Erlich and Wooton (eds.).

Dahl, R. A. (1982), *Dilemmas of Pluralist Democracy*, New Haven: Yale University Press.

Dahl, R. A. (1985), *A Preface to Economic Democracy*, Cambridge: Polity Press.

Dahl, R. A., and C. E. Lindblom (1953), *Politics, Economics and Welfare*, 2nd edn., 1976. Chicago: University of Chicago Press.

Duverger, M. (1974), *Modern Democracies: Economic power versus political power*, Illinois: Dryden Press.

Graham, K. (1986), *The Battle of Democracy*, Brighton: Wheatsheaf Books.

Key, V. O. (1964), *Politics, Parties and Pressure Groups*, 5th edn., New York: Crowell.

Latham, E. (1952), *The Group Bases of Politics*, Ithaca: Cornell University Press.

Lindblom, C. E. (1977), *Politics and Markets*, New York: Basic Books.

Lukes, S. (1974), *Power: A radical view*, London: Macmillan.

Schumpeter, J. (1943), *Capitalism, Socialism and Democracy*, London: Unwin.

Tomlinson, J. (1981), 'The "economics of politics" and public expenditure: a critique', *Economy and Society*, 10.

Truman, D. (1951), *The Governmental Process*, New York: Alfred Knopf.

The evolution of Marxist approaches to state organization

Patrick Dunleavy and Brendan O'Leary

State organization

Relatively detailed Marxist accounts of how state institutions operate have emerged only in the post-war period, and are associated chiefly with the growth of Western neo-Marxisms – new forms of expressing Marx and Engels' ideas, distinguished chiefly by their willingness to engage 'bourgeois' social science directly in debate. While orthodox Marxist-Leninism of the Comintern period offered no serious accounts of liberal democratic practices and institutions, neo-Marxists have tried to come to terms with phenomena which classical Marxists did not anticipate, especially the advent of some form of mixed economy and the growth of an extended welfare state in every advanced capitalist society. Previous Marxist descriptions of the democratic state as a nakedly repressive apparatus attuned only to the behests of capitalists sat unsatisfactorily with the apparent emergence of government planning and 'caring capitalism', at least in the period from the early 1950s to the late 1970s. The emergence of new-right governments in the 1980s has called in question the previous welfare consensus, and apparently signalled a drive towards the 'recommodification' of areas of social life previously handled by public policy decision. But no attempt to dismantle radically the fabric of state regulation or public service provision has yet been pushed through in any liberal democracy, so that the public policy configuration now remains quite distinct from that prevailing before 1945.

If the problems requiring analysis are thus quite novel, the Marxist toolkit available for constructing a response has remained heavily influenced by the three approaches to the state articulated in Marx and Engels' own work, namely, the instrumental, arbiter and functionalist models. [...] We cover neo-Marxists' modern instrumentalist, arbiter and functionalist models in turn, summarizing the differences from Marx and Engels' classical accounts, and describing how each approach analyses the workings of

From P. Dunleavy and B. O'Leary, *Theories of the State* (1987), Basingstoke: Macmillan, Chapter 5.

state institutions and policy-making. We conclude our accounts of each approach by looking at some of its distinctive variants to demonstrate the range of options in the neo-Marxist literature.

Modern instrumentalist models

We noted above that Marx and Engels most commonly relied on an instrumentalist account of the liberal state as a machine directly controlled from outside by capitalists and hence bound to act in furthering their interests. They refined their account to acknowledge the possibility of indirect control of the state by capitalists, taking account of the persistence of aristocratic and monarchical governments in late nineteenth-century Europe. Modern instrumen-talism has adapted this strategy to explain how it is that the election of social democratic parties into government, or the advent of other coalitions orientated in part to working-class voters (such as Franklin Roosevelt's 'new deal' administration in the USA), has not qualified the fundamentally capitalist character of the liberal democratic state. Modern instrumentalists elaborate Kautsky's proposition that the capitalist class rules but does not itself govern, contenting itself with ruling successive governments, a claim which is commonly elaborated through a point-by-point critique of pluralism. [. . .]

The next stage of the modern instrumentalist argument has close affinities with elite theory, arguing that capitalists, state bureaucrats and political leaders are unified into a single cohesive group by their common social origin, similar lifestyles and values, and by the existence of numerous networks and forums where co-ordinated strategies for public policy are hammered out. While direct participation in government by personnel from big business has characteristically declined in modern liberal democracies (except in the USA), the state apparatus remains staffed overwhelmingly by strata of society who can be relied on to adopt pro-capitalist stances on economic and industrial issues – for example, members of professions, lawyers, accountants and farmers. Where leftist governments do gain power, international financial markets and the loss of business confidence automatically create unfavourable climates for radical social reforms, normally shaping the 'economic facts of life' to constrain any fundamental alteration of capitalism long before the ultimate weapons available to domestic business (such as investment strikes) have to be brought into play.

The consequences of capitalist domination can be traced in the consistent orien-tation of much state intervention to supporting domestic capital against foreign competition, underpinning advanced technology, and imposing restrictive state controls on industrial relations. Most mixed economy interventions involve the state in subsidizing or taking over the organization of necessary economic activities un-profitable for capital; and most welfare policies can be understood as attempts to socialize labour costs falling on businesses, which become financed out of general taxation instead of showing up directly in employers' wage bills and production costs. The absolutely preponderant orientation of the state in capitalist society is towards 'the containment of pressure' from below (Miliband, 1982, pp. 54–93).

Instrumentalists have never paid great attention to the detailed institutional organization of the liberal democratic state. Most instrumentalists agree with Marx that parliamentary processes are meaningless charades, significant only as a means of maintaining the key ideological illusion that there is effective popular control of state policy-making. Legislatures are ineffectual, and real power is concentrated in the executive branch of government. For example, in the web of agencies which surround the US presidency and make key foreign and defence policy decisions, Domhoff (1970, 1978) claims to detect clear evidence of capitalist control over both popular and elite opinion-making agencies, which set the agenda for policy-making. The American executive branch of the state is overwhelmingly staffed by the upper class; Congress serves at most as a place in which dissident members of the upper class can air grievances. Debate and apparent pluralism in the institutions of representative government mask internal and technical disagreements amongst the ruling class about how to manage the discontent of subordinate classes. Instrumentalists regard administrative elites as simply functionaries who make policy according to the rational interests of the capitalist class. Bureaucracies exist primarily to respond to the problems and contradictions of a capitalist economy: there is no necessary reason for their existence independent of their class-biased role. This simple view also extends to the legal system. Instrumentalists agree with radical elite theorists that the class origins of the judiciary are reflected in the use of judicial discretion in a consistently biased fashion against labour unions and radical social movements. Judges consistently use the law of contract against trade unions (labour monopolists) as opposed to capitalist monopolists.

In instrumentalist writings the state is seen in the last resort as a unified organization. Federal decentralization of domestic policy responsibilities to regional governments, local government organizations and/or the separation of powers are alike dismissed as window dressing. Any apparent fragmentation is a ruling-class stratagem designed to divide exploited classes which develop revolutionary or reformist consciousness. Should apparent fragmentation get out of hand, control over policy will be overtly centralized, or a new but equally fraudulent decentralization of state organizations will be devised. Reorganizations which alter the legal powers and managerial patterns of local governments are interpreted as the implementation of the national capitalists' will. Local or regional governments originally served as the executive committees for managing the common affairs of the local or regional bourgeoisie. In the modern period capital is instead organized at a national or transnational scale so that the previous (capitalist) rationale for sub-national government has withered away, except for a few spatially constrained sectors of capital, such as development interests or companies engaged in extracting mineral resources. Current local state functions are a microcosm of the repressive and class-biased strategies which apply at central state level (Cockburn, 1977). If this situation threatens to change, as when radical left parties gain control of local authorities, then sub-national government is simply bypassed, or its powers are drastically reduced. Conflicts between central and local governments are the only serious ones which can arise within the liberal democratic state, and are invariably resolved in favour of the centre, where the executive committee of the national bourgeoisie is located. In the absence of such conflicts the local or regional state acts as the instrument of local or regional capitalists, except when their interests are too parochial. [. . .]

The arbiter model

Marx and Engels' arbiter model of the state suggested that if class forces in society were for a time evenly balanced, then the state bureaucracy and a strong political-military leader could intervene to impose stabilizing policies which were not controllable by capital, although they would be bound to maintain capitalist predominance in economic life. The modern arbiter model suggests that this distinct policy stance by state agencies and political leaders could be a much more common and long-lasting phenomenon than Marx or Engels ever acknowledged. Poulantzas (1978) suggests that the state in liberal democracies acts as a condensation of class struggle, mirroring in a distorted and class-biased way the balance of class forces in the broader society. Elections, strikes, riots, pressure group lobbying, and decisions by law courts continuously serve to adjust state policies to keep them in touch with movements and realignments of multiple class fractions and strata. Within modern capitalist societies the monopoly corporations constitute the dominant class fraction. If their influence over public policy is to be maintained, it is essential that the state ensures a broader degree of support for state policy from other fractions of capital, from intermediate class categones (such as the petit bourgeoisie and non-manual groups), and from significant sections of the working class. Flexible and adaptive public policy configurations co-opt popular struggles and disorganize working-class militancy.

Maintaining this configuration requires that the state apparatus should operate with a considerable degree of autonomy from the dominant class fraction, and that the leaders who assemble and co-ordinate the ruling 'power bloc' should appear on the political stage as independent actors. But this autonomy for stage agencies is *relative*, since in the last instance the requirements of capitalism as an economic system will always prevail over any contradictory state policies, even supposing that these should reach the point of being explicitly formulated. Nonetheless, because the relatively autonomous state in advanced capitalism acts in a way which gauges and responds to the balance of class forces, there is the possibility of a partial socialization of capitalism as an economic system – i.e. the introduction of elements of a socialist mode of production, an argument which purely repressive or instrumental models of the state emphatically deny.

The arbiter model has been developed to analyse major institutional changes in post-war liberal democracies by Poulantzas' concept of *authoritarian statism*. This model particularly set out to explain the consolidation of the Gaullist regime in France after the Fifth French Republic was established with a strong president in 1958, a change which inaugurated an unbroken dominance of French national politics by right-wing parties for over two decades. Poulantzas identified the rise of authoritarian statism as the principal trend in contemporary liberal democratic politics, and defined it as 'intensified state control over every sphere of socio-economic life combined with a radical decline of the institutions of political democracy, and with draconian and multiform curtailment of so-called "formal" liberties' (Poulantzas, 1978, pp. 203–4).

Five features are important. First, the decline of parliaments and the strengthening of executive power corresponds to the decline of liberal bourgeois politics and presages the possible demise of liberal democracy altogether. Second, the whole separation of powers doctrine – which prescribes no institutional connections between the executive, the legislature and the judiciary – has begun to dissolve, and liberal democratic states systematically violate their own laws. Third, political parties have declined as serious inputs into policy-making, either because a single party grouping has emerged as dominant over all alternatives (as in Japan or Gaullist France), or because where two party groupings alternate in power, executive authority is always monopolized by a centrist bloc which spans both possible parties of government (as in Britain or West Germany). Fourth, the 'legitimating process is shifting towards plebiscitary and purely manipulatory circuits (the media) dominated by the administration and the executive' (Poulantzas, 1978, p. 229). The fifth feature is the development of so-called 'parallel networks', which cross-cut the formal or official organization of the state, and cause a concentration of powers to accumulate at the very top of the executive. Political leaders and presidents increasingly seem to run government in a directly personalized, discretionary way. At the same time quasi-governmental agencies have multiplied beyond the reach of any effective control by representative politics. Authoritarian statism carries the 'seeds or certain scattered elements of fascism' and Poulantzas asserts in conclusion that 'All contemporary power is functional to authoritarian statism' (1978, p. 239).

The arbiter approach dismisses instrumentalist arguments that the state apparatus operates to support capitalism because the social backgrounds, values and networks of contacts for senior bureaucrats and political leaders tie them into a directly pro-business orientation. In Poulantzas' view the co-ordination of the capitalist state is achieved by the political executive and higher administrative civil service, irrespective of the type of personnel who staff these posts. The institutional separation of the state from the capitalist class is not simply a charade. The constitutional and organizational arrangements filter the interests of state personnel towards the long-run interests of the capitalists. The mechanisms of legal and political accountability were initially developed to serve the interests of particular capitalists in removing the corrupt exploitation of state offices. In the modern period the institutional separation preserves harmony amongst different types of capital and makes the state appear open to the interests of all citizens, including the working class. The state must appear class-neutral, the better to preserve the long-run interests of the capitalist class.

Civil servants in an advanced industrial state are meritocratically selected (Therborn, 1978) even though their tasks are to plan in the long-run interests of capitalism. State officials are dependent upon capitalist economic development and growth if they are going to be able to pursue their interests and sustain themselves in office, so they are constrained to act in the interests of capital, although not necessarily in its optimal interests (Offe, 1984). Planning cannot be socially rational, as it would be under socialism, where planning for need would replace production for profit. But planning can be made rational *for a particular class* or for the 'power bloc' created to sustain monopoly capital's predominance. A range of policy technologies, including Keynesian demand management, incomes policies, regional policies, indicative planning and welfare management, can be used by state officials. These interventions will be implemented despite short-term business protests if state managers deem them class-rational. In the long run administrators try to make capitalism a positive-sum game from which all classes can gain. Such strategies prevent the breakdown of capitalism into class conflicts. They can only succeed by imposing long-run discipline upon capitalists. Conspiracies or strong personal relations between business and state elites, such as corruption, nepotism or clientelism, are syndromes of under-development for arbiter theorists. Such lapses from the liberal democratic ethos are the legacy of feudalism, not intrinsic features of bourgeois democracy.

Arbiter theorists have a comparatively complex outlook on law, which is regarded as a partly autonomous sphere of social action, not controllable by capitalists. Legal procedures bind judges against straightforward manipulation, and subordinate classes can take advantage of these legal procedures despite the obstacles placed in their way. Jury systems, and the segmentation of the legal system into spheres which are in no obvious sense class-based, are given due significance in this view (Thompson, 1975). The successful struggle of labour movements in various liberal democracies to transform the practice of contract and labour law is not ignored, as in instrumentalist models. However, arbiter theorists have no faith in the long-run neutrality of the courts. Concessions which judges make to workers at one moment in the class struggle may be removed at another. The relative autonomy of law has to be constantly maintained by successful working-class mobilization into politics and the labour movement.

Arbiter theorists also recognize that liberal democratic states vary greatly in their internal organization between federal and unitary forms. Local governments also possess very different degrees of policy-making and financial autonomy; and a historically given separation of powers may still significantly affect the cohesion of the state. Since the state as a whole is relatively autonomous from the short-run interests of capitalists, each state sub-organization is also relatively autonomous from the relevant short-run interests of the capitalists, and other class interests must be accommodated in some degree. The changing institutional structure of the state is a historical artefact of class struggle which follows a simple pattern. The successes of subordinate classes in capturing state organizations are met by reorganizations which benefit the long-run interests of capital, as in Britain, where local government units have been completely modernized and increased in size to make them less vulnerable to electoral capture by the labour movement (Dearlove, 1979). American federalism was also explained by Charles Beard (1935) as a device which promoted national integration in the long-run interests of the merchant class. The fragmentation of the state apparatus also conveniently diverts the class struggle to multiple fronts. A thoroughly centralized state is avoided by an intelligent bourgeoisie because it is not in their long-run interest to build a state machine which could quickly be converted to serve socialist purposes. Decentralization fragments the scope of radical change and raises the thresholds required for it to be achieved, a maxim which constitutional and administrative designers take seriously in many liberal democracies. That decentralized state structures serve to reduce the scope of welfare state expansion and socialist incumbency is one of the few findings in the comparative public policy literature on which there is near unanimity (Castles, 1985, p. 120). Constitutions embodying decentralization bind the bourgeoisie against the short-run pursuit of their material interests, reflecting an abstentionist strategic rationality.

There are no developed variants of the arbiter model. Indeed, as we shall see below, many of its key protagonists (such as Poulantzas and Therborn) also switch back and forth between the arbiter model and functionalist arguments. However, there is an interesting and well-developed literature which is worth considering in its own right, namely the application of the arbiter model to explain the existence of *authoritarian regimes under capitalism*. Marxists have traditionally agreed that liberal democracy is the 'normal' form of political system for an advanced industrial state. Marx explained the regime of Napoleon III as an arbiter state temporarily gaining autonomy from the balance of class forces, a situation which he insisted could occur only when the transition from capitalism to socialism was already in train. Orthodox Marxists in the inter-war period accordingly hailed the widespread growth of fascist exceptional regimes as a sign that the death agonies of European capitalism were imminent. But the strength and resilience of those fascist societies, none of which fell because of internal collapse, and their replacement after 1945 by liberal democratic capitalism seemed to refute such interpretations. Equally the long-lived persistence of authoritarian regimes in post-war capitalist societies (as in Spain, Portugal, Greece, Brazil and Argentina) reawakened Marxist writers' interest in explaining 'exceptional' regimes. Trotsky (1971) suggested that fascist governments emerge not where class forces are 'balanced', but rather when the bourgeoisie has already lost its battle with the working class; only in these circumstances will capitalists concede a very high level of autonomy to a fascist political party or social movement which they cannot control. In trying to explain post-war authoritarian regimes Poulantzas radically extended the arbiter model to suggest that an autonomous state is the generalized form of political system for advanced capitalism, and that 'exceptional' and liberal democratic govern-ments are both equally possible and common alternatives by which a necessary degree and appropriate form of state autonomy can be achieved.

Modern functionalist approaches

The functionalist model in Marx and Engels' work stressed the shaping of state organization and policy-making by the fundamental imperatives of maintaining capitalist development. Changes in the economic base of society determine shifts in the political and legal superstructure. Modern functionalist approaches continue to emphasize that state intervention is best explained by an impersonal logic of the development of advanced capitalism. Like the views of their predecessors in classical Marxist thought, modern functionalist views do not regard it as useful or necessary to demonstrate the precise mechanisms by which state policy responds to structural imperatives; instead they focus on macro-social issues and trends. Some important Marxist functional approaches have been defined as attempts to respond to grand sociological theories formulated in the USA and Western Europe. Conservative writers have developed complex theoretical systems to explain the maintenance of social stability and legitimacy [. . .]. Neo-Marxist functionalist schemas try to match their conceptual sophistication, and to adapt the concepts of system theory to demonstrate the necessary class biases and contradictions of state interventions. Although economic imperatives remain dominant in these schemas, all modern functionalist accounts acknowledge the existence of separate political–ideological structures or cultural processes with their own distinctive logic of development. For example, Althusser argues that revolutionary situations can only occur when the economic system is in crisis at the same time as the political and ideological structures are in crisis. Habermas argues that crises have been displaced from the economic realm into the state apparatus itself or into the cultural system.

There are few if any developed functionalist accounts of state institutions, although Therborn's (1978) analysis of the decline of parliaments is a mixture of functional and arbiter model arguments. He argues that the traditional forms of representative government, which effectively excluded the popular masses or isolated and controlled them through local notables, is 'no longer an adequate instrument'. In most liberal democracies it has gradually been supplemented by a new plebiscitary politics, based on the cult of charismatic leaders built up through the mass media. Plebiscitary politics enhances, indeed exalts, executive preponderance in policy-making and implementation, at the expense of legislatures. This change is functional for the stability of monopoly capitalism because the pseudo-democracy of direct voting by a mass electorate for leaders or policies increases the legitimacy of the political system, allows the mass of citizens to be co-opted into compliance, and poses no real risk of losing control over key state decisions to the masses. Similarly O'Connor (1973, p. 78) argues that the American executive branch remains independent of particular class interests, and serves the interests of monopoly capital as a whole. These interests are sifted, ranked and transmitted by the state administration to the president and his key aides, who initiate appropriate political action on them.

The characteristics of politicians or civil servants on which instrumentalist accounts focus barely matter in a functionalist analysis. State personnel simply fill given roles; their behaviour is largely predetermined by structural forces in line with the functional imperatives of the capitalist mode of production. Their policy-making styles vary according to what is optimal for the function concerned. Similarly the state's organization at any time is assumed to be *optimally* organized for the needs of capital at that time. Specify capitalism's need at any time and the structure of state organization is explained – except of course in periods of acute crisis. A strictly functionalist Marxist must accordingly believe that problems of state co-ordination cannot exist, except in a revolutionary crisis. In normal circumstances the capitalist state can successfully conceal its class character. The state's function is to co-ordinate and manage the economic crises generated by the mode of production through political and ideological interventions. Threatening co-ordination difficulties can arise if and only if the system's managers cannot resolve the displacement of crises because of serious dysfunctions in the economy or some sort of collapse in the cultural–ideological system.

But since Marxists believe that capitalism as a social system is doomed, it follows that capitalism cannot be rationally planned for ever. Ruling-class strategies and responses to functional imperatives from an internally contradictory mode of production are permanently unstable. Even in the functionalist version of Marxism the state's performance is contingent on class struggle (although the two explanatory mechanisms, classes in struggle and functional imperatives, are never combined convincingly). Functionalist Marxists continue to insist that rational comprehensive planning is only possible under socialism, despite a complete lack of evidence for this judgement in the operation of planning in the Soviet Union or its allied states (Nove, 1983). Many Western Marxists still deny that the experience of Eastern bloc countries has any direct relevance for the future planned performance of Western economies following their transformation into socialism. However, there is some evidence of a recent reappraisal of this entrenched attitude.

Yet there have been some areas where functionalist accounts have been elaborated to try to explain the persistence of both stability and internal tensions within the state apparatus. A quite developed model of the reasons for fragmentation of government into different tiers and sectors is provided by *the dual state thesis*, which presents a Marxist alternative to liberal corporatist theory [. . .].

The thesis has three main stages (O'Connor, 1973; Wolfe, 1977; Cawson and Saunders, 1983). First, three functions of the state in the capitalist mode of production are deduced from the functional requirements of the mode of production. They are the preservation of order, the promotion of capital accumulation and the manufacture of legitimation. Second, forms of state expenditure corresponding to each of these functions are identified. Order is maintained through 'social expenses' policy; accumulation is fostered directly by 'social investment' expenditures to reduce production costs; and social cohesion is boosted by 'social consumption' spending, which boosts workers' living standards (and hence only indirectly contributes to increased profitability). State organizations can be classified according to which function is furthered by their budgets. Thus police organizations which preserve order fall in the social expenses category, nuclear power plants supposedly providing cheap electricity constitute social investment, and welfare agencies which promote legitimation fall in the social consumption category. Third, the direction of state organizations is structured so that accumulation functions are ranked higher than legitimation functions. An appropriate ranking is achieved by creating two sets of institutions. The central government or politically uncontrolled quasi-governmental agencies monopolize social investment functions of critical significance for capital. Here decision-making is characteristically corporatist, future-orientated, and concerned to integrate external interests in achieving state policy goals. The central government also monopolizes social expenses functions of key significance for social stability, but these are administered in a rigidly bureaucratic way, without any attempt to co-opt external interests. At the same time local government structures, and perhaps some politically visible sections of the national state apparatus, are entrusted with responsibility for social consumption spending. Policy-making in this area is deliberately pluralist, mopping up political energies, providing a reassuring appearance of controversy and popular influence, and sustaining a needs-orientated ideology which seems to indicate the social neutrality of state policy. In practice local governments or elected regional governments are rigidly controlled by the centre to prevent them adopting policies hostile to capital interests, and their decisions are extensively determined by prior central state commitments of resources. Nonetheless, conflicts in central–local relations reveal the structural tensions between the accumulation and legitimation imperatives acting upon the capitalist state.

Critics of the dual state thesis argue that in practice public expenditures can be classified according to their function only through a *post hoc* evaluation of their consequences or by knowing which organizations implemented the programmes (which would make the whole schema tautologous). Thus only after the event can one evaluate whether expenditure on public health services contributed to capital accumulation, legitimation, and/or social order (Dunleavy, 1984). Nor is the comparative evidence of the allocation of functions between state organizations in liberal democracies very favourable for the theory (Sharpe, 1984). In some countries major social consumption functions are controlled by the central government and social investment functions by local governments.

A second major area of functionalist thinking is in *accounts of the legal system* which are based on Marx's base–superstructure metaphor (Cohen, 1978). The legal system existing at any time is explained as functional for the development of the productive forces at that time, or (in another version) for the relations of production at that time. As Cohen presents the functionalist model, law changes in accordance with changes in the power relations between classes, a feature particularly true of the law of the labour contract. There may be time lags and a degree of sub-optimality in the correspondence between relations of production and legal relations, but otherwise law is functional for the economic base. Critics of the functionalist base–superstructure distinction argue that law is in fact part of the property relations governing production, so it is not possible to separate the two (Lukes, 1983). Nonetheless, the base–superstructure model is the dominant Marxist approach to law. Renner (1949) argued with some plausible empirical evidence that legal norms which appear to persist for lengthy historical periods, spanning different modes of production, in fact change their substantive functions in response to developments in economic structures. However, Renner's arguments did not imply that law is a passive reflection of its class-divided environment. Judges and the legal system play an active role in the maintenance and alteration of social relations. Pashukanis (1979) stressed the formal resemblance between law and capitalist rationality. Law mirrors the abstract individuality and formal equality of contracting parties in the capitalist market. Law will consequently disappear under socialism, where substantive collective goals (embodied in the plan) will replace formal legal equality, which would be dysfunctional to socialism. However, in some functionalist versions of Marxism, the legal system does have the capacity to be class-neutral, because it does not recognize classes, only abstract individuals (Poulantzas, 1973). Nonetheless, this judicial fiction functions in a class-biased way, maintaining the capitalist mode of production through the 'juridical illusion' that social conflicts can be settled or refereed outside the class struggle.

There has been a considerable fashion for functionalist accounts among Western Marxists, since an apparently more elegant intellectual apparatus than those of orthodox instrumentalists can be constructed. Three distinctive variants of the functionalist approach have been noteworthy: structuralist Marxism, the capital logic school, and German neo-Marxism.

Structuralist Marxism originated in France in the 1960s, especially in the work of the communist philosopher Louis Althusser, although other key writers have included Poulantzas (who sometimes uses the arbiter model and sometimes a functional approach). In structuralist accounts the state is seen as essentially a factor of cohesion in society, which functions to organize the dominant class and to disorganize the subordinate classes through the use of either repressive or ideological apparatuses (Althusser, 1969). Repressive state apparatuses (RSAs) are new labels for armies and police forces. Ideological state apparatuses (ISAs) include a very wide range of institutions which are said to perform the 'state' function of ensuring social stability. Althusser's list includes religious, educational, trade union and mass media organizations, and the family. But remarkably no mention is made of welfare agencies, public enterprises or planning bodies, all of which are major additions in the extended welfare state. RSAs and ISAs continually create the 'conditions of existence' of the capitalist mode of production, producing docile, disciplined and fragmented 'individuals' whose viewpoints and behaviour are suitable for capitalist life. It is to capture this function that Althusser defined the state to include almost all non-economic organizations, except the revolutionary party of the working class, in the process definitionally obliterating the difference between input politics and state organization, or between the state and society (Polan, 1984, pp. 34–5).

Althusser denies that there is anything specific to explain about liberal democracy except its illusory existence. His ISA concept implies that the populations of the capitalist state are living under a dictatorship, a bourgeois dictatorship. What they think is private is in fact public. Liberal democracy, private life, civil rights and interest groups are all simply ideological constructs designed to pacify and mislead. [. . .] Althusser insists that political and ideological structures exist with their own rhythm and laws of development quite distinct from those in the economic sphere. One might have expected an examination of the non-economic bases of liberal democracy or of bureaucracy in understanding the distinction between 'class power' and 'state power', or 'the specificity of the political' (Laclau, 1977). However, structuralist Marxists fail to carry through their qualification of economic determinism. Social classes, political parties, ideologies and state organizations still seem to be 'explained' by the logic of the mode of production. Some critics also argue that any qualification of economic determinism threatens the distinctiveness of Marxism. For example, neo-Marxist analyses of bureaucracy and the division of labour have converged on the accounts given by elite theorists (Parkin, 1979); and post-Althusserian and post-Gramscian Marxism is indistinguishable from pluralism except in its vocabulary (Laclau and Mouffe, 1985).

A further problem for structuralist Marxists is the relation between class struggle and functionalist state theory. They later came to argue that class struggle goes on in state institutions (Althusser, 1976; Poulantzas, 1978). But such class struggle cannot originate in the political and ideological levels of the mode of production, because in their scheme the functions of these levels are to stabilize the mode of production. On the other hand, if the class struggle going on inside the state originates at the economic sphere, then surely there is no separation of the economic and the political–ideological levels at all?

The capital logic school of neo-Marxist theories (sometimes also called the 'state derivation' approach) set out to deduce the functional necessity of the state from analysis of the capitalist mode of production (Altvater, 1973; Holloway and Picciotto, 1978). For example, legal and monetary systems necessary for the production and exchange of commodities and the circulation of capital are 'deduced' from the functional needs of capitalism. The state as a whole functions as 'an ideal collective capitalist' (Altvater, 1973), a political institution which corresponds to the common needs of capital. Whereas public choice theorists explain state activities, such as the production of public goods, as a result of intentional rationality [. . .], the capital logic school deduces the functional necessity of the state from analysis of the imputed needs of capital. They similarly deduce the need for the contemporary state to intervene extensively to regulate the crisis-prone capitalist economy in four ways – providing the general, material conditions of production; establishing general, legal relations; regulating and suppressing conflicts between capital and wage-labour; and protecting national capital in the world market (Altvater, 1978, p. 42). However, there are limits to the functional capacities of the state – it cannot transcend the contradictions of capitalism.

German neo-Marxism is influenced by the Frankfurt School of critical theory and by systems thinking (Jay, 1973). A leading author in the genre, Claus Offe, defines the capitalist state as an institutionalized form of political power which 'seeks to implement and guarantee the *collective* interests of all members of a class society dominated by capital' (Offe, 1984, p. 120). This conception mixes an organizational and functional definition of the state. It presupposes that the functionally optimal capitalist state is in some senses class-neutral. Offe believes that the institutional operations of the state are guided by three conditions. First, the state is excluded from organizing production according to its own 'political' criteria. This 'exclusion principle' means that investment decisions in any liberal democracy lie with capitalists, outside direct state control. Second, state policy is constrained because government depends for taxation revenue upon maintaining successful capital accumulation. State officials must be interested, for the sake of their own power, in guaranteeing and safeguarding healthy capital accumulation, an argument which anticipates the neo-pluralist position of Charles Lindblom [. . .]. Third, the capitalist state is built upon this combination of exclusion from direct production and dependence on capital accumulation, but an ideal form of state also requires democratic legitimation. The state's function, *par excellence*, is to manage potential crises which may occur in the economy, in its own fiscal resources, or in the legitimacy of existing social arrangements.

Marxist critics argue that functionalist accounts of the state are vacuous because they consist of citing the consequences of particular actions as their causes (Elster, 1986 [. . .]). Because a particular action achieves a given result, the action is seen as made necessary in order to achieve that result, and a loose typology of the 'needs' of capital is constructed to demonstrate the functionality of any particular outcome. Thus we 'know' that the creation of an extended welfare state was functional for capital in the three decades after 1945 because that was what occurred. Equally we know that cutbacks and retrenchment of welfare services have become functional for capital since the mid-1970s because that too has occurred. In short, whatever the state does is functional for the capitalist class in the long run, so the theory is immunized against any conflicting evidence. Instrumentalists also claim that Poulantzas' conception of the state as the factor of cohesion in the social formation is equally unhelpful. To say that the reproduction of the capitalist mode of production requires a number of conditions to be met is not an explanation of how they are met, of what happens if they are not met, of whether they can be met in 'functionally equivalent ways', or of *why* these needs are met.

The relative autonomy of the state

All neo-Marxist word-processors have been programmed with the phrase 'the *relative autonomy* of the capitalist state', so it may be useful in rounding off this section to recap very briefly on how the three approaches actually use this concept. In fact there are two different meanings hidden away in this phrase: the state can be relatively autonomous of the capitalist class, which is appropriate for an organizational model of the state (Figure 1). Alternatively the state may be relatively autonomous of the capitalist mode of production, which is appropriate for a functionalist approach.

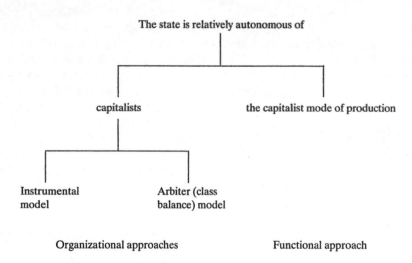

Figure 1 Marxist conceptions of the 'relative autonomy' of the state

References

Althusser, L. (1969) *For Marx* (Harmondsworth: Penguin), translated B. Brewster.

Althusser, L. (1976) *Essays in Self-Criticism* (London: New Left Books).

Altvater, E. (1973) 'Notes on some problems of state interventionism', *Kapitatstate*, 1 and 2.

Altvater, E. (1978) 'Some problems of state interventionism', in J. Holloway and S. Picciotto (eds.), *State and Capital* (London: Arnold).

Beard, C. (1935) *An Economic Interpretation of the Constitution of the United States* (New York: Macmillan).

Castles, F. G. (1985) *The Working Class and Welfare: Rejections on the political development of the welfare state in Australia and New Zealand, 1890–1980* (Wellington: Allen & Unwin).

Cawson, A. and Saunders, P. (1983) 'Corporatism, competitive politics and class struggle', in R. King (ed.), *Capital and Politics* (London: Routledge & Kegan Paul).

Cockburn, C. (1977) *The Local State* (London: Pluto Press).

Cohen, G. A. (1978) *Karl Marx's Theory of History: A defence* (Oxford: Oxford University Press).

Dearlove, J. (1979) *The Reorganization of British Local Government* (Cambridge: Cambridge University Press).

Domhoff, W. (1970) *The Higher Circles* (New York: Random House).

Domhoff, W. (1978) *The Powers that Be* (New York: Random House).

Dunleavy, P. (1984) 'The limits to local government', in M. Boddy and C. Fudge (eds.), *Local Socialism? Labour councils and new left alternatives* (London: Macmillan).

Elster, J. (1986) 'Further thoughts on Marxism, functionalism and game theory', in J. Roemer (ed.), *Analytical Marxism* (Cambridge: Cambridge University Press).

Holloway, J. and Picciotto, S. (eds.) (1978) *State and Capital: A German debate* (London: Edward Arnold).

Jay, M. (1973) *The Dialectical Imagination* (London: Heinemann).

Laclau, E. (1977) *Politics and Ideology in Marxist Thought* (London: New Left Books).

Laclau, E. and Mouffe, C. (1985) *Hegemony and Socialist Strategy* (London: Verso).

Lukes, S. (1983) 'Can the base be distinguished from the superstructure?', in D. Miller and L. Siedentop (eds.), *The Nature of Political Theory* (Oxford: Oxford University Press).

Miliband, R. (1982) *Capitalist Democracy in Britain* (Oxford: Oxford University Press).

Nove, A. (1983) *The Economics of Feasible Socialism* (London: Allen & Unwin).

O'Connor, J. (1973) *The Fiscal Crisis of the State* (New York: St Martin's Press).

Offe, C. (1984) *The Contradictions of the Welfare State* (London: Hutchinson University Library).

Parkin, F. (1979) *Marxism and Class Theory: A bourgeois critique* (Oxford: Oxford University Press).

Pashukanis, E. B. (1979) *Selected Writings on Marxism and Law* (London and New York: Academic Press).

Polan, A. (1984) *Lenin and the End of Politics* (London: Methuen).

Poulantzas, N. (1973) *Political Power and Social Classes* (London: New Left Books).

Poulantzas, N. (1978) *State, Power, Socialism* (London: New Left Books).

Renner, K. (1949) *The Institutions of Private Law and Their Social Functions* (London: Routledge & Kegan Paul).

Sharpe, L. J. (1984) 'Functional allocation in the welfare state', *Local Government Studies*, January–February, pp. 27–45.

Therborn, G. (1978) *What Does the Ruling Class Do When It Rules?* (London: New Left Books).

Thompson, E. P. (1975) *Whigs and Hunters* (Harmondsworth: Penguin).

Trotsky, L. (1971) *The Struggle Against Fascism in Germany* (New York: Pathfinder).

Wolfe, A. (1977) *The Limits of Legitimacy* (New York: Free Press).

| Policy networks

M. J. Smith

It was suggested [. . .] that state autonomy has to be examined within the context of state/group relationships. This chapter will examine the nature of the potential relationships, analyse the types of policy networks that exist, and examine their impact on policy outcomes.

Within modern government, policy-making 'tends to fragment and specialise as a result of two fundamental trends, the expansion in the scope of governmental responsibility, and the increasing complexity of public affairs' (Campbell *et al.* 1989: 86). This leads some analysts of public policy to suggest that policy-making is becoming increasingly pluralistic as the policy process fragments and an increasing number of groups are admitted into the policy arena (Heclo 1978). However Campbell *et al.* (1989) maintain that this fragmentation is leading to policy being made within increasingly specialised arenas with a limited number of participants. The reality seems to be that in different policy arenas a range of group/government relationships exist.

Policy networks are a means of categorising the relationships that exist between groups and the government. Policy networks occur when there is an exchange of information between groups and government (or between different groups or parts of the government) and this exchange of information leads to the recognition that a group has an interest in a certain policy area. The exchange of information can be minimal – a group's name being placed on a consultation list, a group sending in a submission on a green paper – or it can be very intense with groups having institutionalised access to government and being involved in the detailed development of policy and, consequently, constantly exchanging a very high level of detailed information. According to Laumann and Knoke (1987: 13), 'The greater the variety of information and the more diverse the sources that a consequential actor can tap, the better situated the actor is to anticipate, and to respond to, policy events that can affect its interests.'

The state can be divided into a distinct number of policy domains. 'A policy domain is . . . a set of actors with major concerns, whose preferences and actions on policy events must be taken into account by other domain participants' (Laumann and Knoke 1987: 10). The number of participants, the degree of their integration into government and the degree of influence they have depend on the nature of the policy network

From M. J. Smith, *Pressure, Power and Policy* (1993), Hemel Hempstead: Harvester Wheat-sheaf, pp. 56–65.

within the particular domain. Potential policy networks can be arranged along a continuum from an issue network to a policy community (Hogwood 1986). This section will review the different types of networks and the impact that they have on state autonomy and policy outcomes. It will begin by examining the concept of policy networks.

Policy networks, and their importance for understanding group/government relations, derive from the notion of subgovernment in the United States (Ripley and Franklin 1980) and the work of Jordan and Richardson in Britain on policy communities (Richardson and Jordan 1979, 1985; Jordan and Richardson 1987) (see Jordan 1990 and Rhodes 1990 for a full discussion of these developments). In both cases, the development of these concepts was a recognition that there were problems with the pluralist view of the world. In particular policy areas, policy-making is not open but is made within subgovernments which are 'clusters of individuals that make most of the routine decisions in a given substantive area of policy' (Ripley and Franklin 1980: 8). Most decisions on non-controversial issues are made within small groups which include the key congressional subcommittees, government agencies and interest groups.

Richardson and Jordan (1979) likewise suggest that policy-making is segmented and that policy is made between a myriad of interconnecting and interpenetrating organisations. 'It is the relationship involved in committees, the *policy community* of departments and groups . . . that perhaps better accounts for policy outcomes than do examinations of party stances, of manifestos or of parliamentary influence' (Richardson and Jordan 1979: 74). Accordingly, the distinction between the governed and governors becomes blurred and the dominant style in policy-making is co-operation and consensus (Jordan and Richardson 1982).

The notion of policy communities and subgovernments as used by Richardson and Jordan tends to describe relationships between groups and government rather than explain how these affect policy outcomes. Moreover, they make little attempt to distinguish between types of communities and so the term policy community is used very liberally as a means of describing all types of group/government relations. No real distinction is made between the integrity and intensity of different relationships. In addition, they to some extent undermine their own notion of a closed and regularised relationship by seeing most policy communities as being relatively open. They stress that departments in Britain are always willing to consult a whole range of groups; that there is a tendency for policy communities to break down into issue networks and that often policy communities have numerous linkages and overlapping membership (Jordan 1981; Jordan and Richardson 1987: 145). This approach to policy communities is used as a description of a range of relationships and is very much within a pluralist framework by continuing to emphasise access and fragmentation.

Recently there have been attempts to make the concept of policy networks more theoretically informed. Rhodes in his work on local government and sub-central government has significantly extended the use and usefulness of the notion of policy networks (Rhodes 1986, 1988). Rhodes, from Benson (1982), sees a policy network as a 'complex of organisations connected to each other by resource dependencies and distinguished from other complexes by breaks in the structure of resource dependencies'. Rhodes (1988: 77–8) suggests that networks vary across five key dimensions:

1. Constellation of interests – the interests of those involved in a network vary according to service/function/territory or client group.
2. Membership – who are the members, are they public or private groups?
3. Vertical independence – to what extent is a policy network dependent or independent on the actors above or below it?
4. Horizontal independence – what are the interconnections between networks?
5. The distribution of resources – what resources do participants have to exchange?

Using these criteria, Rhodes identifies six types of communities: policy communities and issue networks, which will be discussed below; professionalised networks where a professional group is dominant; intergovernmental networks where the local government is represented at national level; territorial communities which include the major territorial interests of Scotland, Wales and Northern Ireland; and producer networks where economic groups play a key role. Rhodes then uses the concept to analyse a number of policy areas. He mainly restricts his use of these concepts to policy areas which involve aspects of the welfare state and hence he is largely dealing with interaction between different government actors. Rhodes admits that 'the utility of policy networks for analysing relationships between producer groups is yet to be demonstrated' (Rhodes 1988: 371). [. . .] The remainder of this chapter will extend Rhodes's notion of policy networks to interest group intermediation.

Policy networks and pressure groups

Policy networks demonstrate that relationships between groups and government are segmented, and that relationships vary from policy sector to policy sector. In addition, as Rhodes has demonstrated from his study of local government (Rhodes 1981; Marsh and Rhodes 1992), relationships between groups and government cannot be seen as zero-sum. It is not a case of pressure groups outside the system lobbying government in order to achieve specific goals. Rather, the relationship is one of dependency: 'Any organisation is dependent on another organisation for resources.' This of course applies more readily to intergovernmental relationships than in group/government relationships where each side can survive without the other. However, in particular situations when the government wishes to achieve specific policy goals, and groups wish to influence policy, groups and government are mutually dependent.

In order to achieve goals, resources have to be exchanged (Rhodes 1981). If the government does want to achieve a particular policy goal with the minimum of conflict, it needs the assistance of groups in the development and implementation of policy. Government can exchange access to the policy process for cooperation and thus establish a policy network.

Moreover, the dominant coalition retains discretion, determines the rules of the game and regulates 'the process of exchange'. The government/government agencies remain, as we have seen, dominant. It has resources which are much greater than those of other groups and is therefore able to determine what resources should be exchanged and how. It is ultimately the government which calls the shots. 'The relationship is asymmetric'; it is government which creates the network, controls access to the network and the rules of the game (Rhodes 1988: 82). Finally, the impact of the network on policy depends on the 'relative power potential of interacting organisations', i.e. the resources that they have and the way they are exchanged. So for Laumann and Knoke (1987: 13), 'an organization's power and influence in a system is a function of its position or location in the overall resource exchange networks generated out of dyadic resource exchanges'.

Because power is the result of dependency based on an exchange of resources, governments and groups have an incentive to build networks. Despite Rhodes's insistence that the government creates and controls access to the community, the type of network that develops is not always determined by the government. The government has an interest in developing closed policy communities. Nevertheless, the type of network that develops often depends on the groups involved, the interests of various actors within government, the nature of the policy and the institutional arrangements that are available. Consequently, a whole range of networks which integrate groups and governments to varying degrees develop.

Marsh and Rhodes (1992: 251) have outlined a number of dimensions which determine a network's position on the policy community–issue network continuum (see Table 1). First, a network depends on the number of participants. In a policy community the number of participants will be limited. It will usually involve one government agency or section within that agency. Occasionally a policy community will involve more than one department, for example the trade policy community in the United States [. . .] or the food policy community in Britain. However, if this policy community is to remain closed, one of the government actors must accept the lead of the other. In Britain, both the Department of Health and the Ministry of Agriculture were involved in the food policy community but Health was prepared to accept the leadership of Agriculture (Smith 1991; Mills 1992). The departmental role in a policy community is usually played by a department but on many occasions individual politicians will become involved. The community will also include one or two interest groups. These interest groups will be perceived as representative of a particular interest and have a near monopoly of membership. If there is more than one pressure group, those involved will not be competing but represent different interests within the policy arena. Food producers, farmers and doctors were involved in the food policy community but a single organisation represented each group.

Certain policy communities involve '"experts", inside government, in universities or other institutions, who research and think about policy' (Campbell *et al.* 1989: 86). Often this is the case in very technical areas such as nuclear power where the role of scientist and technician is central to the development of policy (Saward 1992). In the US, the particular role and resources of Congress mean that there is also a legislative role. This does not mean that Congress has a major input into policy. Congressional

Table 1 The characteristics of policy networks

Dimension	Policy community	Issue network
Membership		
Number of participants	Very limited, some conscious exclusion	Large
Type of interest	Economic/professional	Wide range of groups
Integration		
Frequency of interaction	Frequent, high quality	Contacts fluctuate
Continuity	Membership, values, outcomes persistent	Fluctuating access
Consensus	All participants share basic values	A degree of agreement but conflict present
Resources		
Distribution of resources within network	All participants have resources. Relationship is one of exchange	Some participants have resources, but limited
Distribution of resources within participating organisations	Hierarchical leaders can deliver members	Varied and variable distribution and capacity to regulate members
Power	There is a balance among members. One group may be dominant but power is positive-sum	Unequal power. Power zero-sum

Source: Marsh and Rhodes (1992).

input is likely to come through the committee system. In addition, 'a concerted effort is made to insure that the membership of the subcommittee is supportive of the goals of the subgovernment' (McCool 1990: 282).

Therefore access to a policy community is highly restricted. As Laffin (1986: 6–7) points out:

> Those within the community generally operate quite stringent entry criteria, these vary among issue areas but include such criteria as possession of expert knowledge; occupancy of a senior position in a relevant organisation; what civil servants call 'soundness', meaning that the person can be trusted to observe the norms of the community; and a reputation for getting things done.

There are a set of 'rules of the game' which actors have to abide by in order to gain entry to the policy community. The 'rules of the game' govern how participants have to behave if they are to gain access to the network: they will act constitutionally; they will accept the final decision of government; they can be trusted; the demands that they make are reasonable (Rhodes 1986). If a group wants to have access to a policy community it must forgo conducting high profile campaigns and become an insider developing policies in private (Jordan and Richardson 1987; Grant 1989).

Consequently, it is easy for a policy community to exclude radical groups. In order to attract attention they have to take overt action like demonstrations but in doing so they are breaking the rules of the game and so are excluded (Saunders 1975: 38).

Policy communities also have an institutional basis that provides a further means of exclusion. Within most policy communities there are particular institutions which are central to the policy process and membership of these institutions ensures access to the policy community. Often this will involve an advisory committee, an *ad hoc* committee created to deal with a particular problem or a particular section within a department which provides the focus for group/government interaction.

However, even exclusion is not simple. Within policy communities there are usually degrees of exclusion. Laumann and Knoke (1987: 229) suggest that the

> global network structure contains a few central positions occupied by actors that maintain close ties with many others . . . and a larger number of peripheral positions occupied by actors with lower visibility, fewer ties and generally tenuous involvement in the system.

A policy community tends to have a core and periphery (Laumann and Knoke 1987) or, in other words, a primary and secondary community. The primary core contains the key actors who set the rules of the game, determine membership and the main policy direction of the community. They are continuously involved in the policy process on a day-to-day level. In the secondary community are the groups which also abide by the rules of the game but do not have enough resources to exert a continuous influence on policy. Therefore, the secondary community tends to involve groups which are important on particular issues and which have occasional access to the policy process. [. . .] There is also a third layer of groups which are completely excluded and have no access at all to the policy community.

Whilst membership in a policy community is limited, in an issue network it is extremely large. There are likely to be several government departments, agencies or subcommittees. The range of interest groups could be in the hundreds, and constantly changing, with groups continuously entering and leaving the policy arena. Heclo believes that in many areas of policy-making in the US there are 'a large number of participants with quite variable degrees of mutual commitment' and so 'it is all but impossible to identify clearly who the dominant actors are' (Heclo 1978: 102). An issue network contains a large number of actors with relatively limited resources. There are several government agencies and access to the network is fairly open, which enables groups to move easily in and out of the policy arena.

This leads directly to the second dimension of a policy network: continuity. The limited number of actors in a policy community means that the participants tend to be stable over a long period of time. The groups involved do not change frequently. In an issue network, as we have just seen, the membership is constantly changing as groups move in and out of the arena. The third dimension is frequency of interaction. In a policy community, the government agency and the key interests will be constantly involved in the policy process and so interaction is daily and of high quality. In an issue network interaction is erratic. The degree and importance of interaction will constantly change and who has contact with whom will also vary.

The fourth dimension is the degree of consensus. If a network is to develop into a policy community there has to be a high degree of consensus on policy aims and the rules of the game. 'Where there are no such shared attitudes, no policy community exists' (Jordan 1990: 327). In fact a policy community often has more than a consensus; it actually has an ideology which determines the community's 'world-view'. Ideology is a way of making sense of the world by defining and ordering it (Therborn 1980: 15 and 18). Ideology defines not only what policy options are available but what problems exist. In other words, it defines the agenda of issues with which the policy community has to deal. Therefore members of a policy community agree on both the range of existing problems and the potential solutions to these problems. Laffin maintains that a policy community has a 'cognitive order', which is agreement on what passes as accepted knowledge in the community and a 'normative order' which is agreement on the values that underpin the community (Laffin 1986: 12).

The ideology thus privileges certain ideas within the policy process. In doing so it ensures that the interests of the dominant actors within the policy community are served and it acts as a further means of exclusion. By maintaining agreement on accepted problems, groups which try to raise new problems or suggest alternative solutions are automatically excluded. The policy community can suggest that new problems either do not exist or are the responsibility of a different network. Alternative solutions are defined as extreme or demonstrating a lack of knowledge about a problem and as such are again excluded. Therefore, within a policy community, power is exercised through Lukes' third dimension. By determining what problems and solutions are acceptable, it ensures that other alternatives are not even conceived of within the community (and sometimes outside the community). An attempt to conceive of them would destroy the consensus and thus the community.

In a policy community there is a consensus or ideology' which limits 'the range of arguments that are permissible, legitimate and likely to be accepted as valid forms of controversy' (Laumann and Knoke 1987: 315). As a consequence, issues within a policy community are often depoliticised. They are seen as technical issues to be resolved by insiders because no conflict is perceived over the potential policy options. Therefore, there is no need to include other groups in the discussion of an issue. If the ideology is fully effective groups outside the community will not even claim the need to be involved in the policy community. The consensus on policy will be accepted by all. Hence groups which possibly could have opposed the policy community will remain potential groups (see Gaventa 1980).

In an issue network, it is unlikely that there will be a consensus – the sheer number of groups means that consensus is practically unachievable. Policy is likely to be highly political because so many groups with various different problems and solutions exist within the policy domain. There is often conflict between the various government agencies and departments. There may be conflict over who is responsible for a policy or an issue, who should be involved and what action should be taken. This conflict between government agencies is often a key reason why an issue network develops. The conflict between agencies makes the problem political and subject to debate. Agencies attempt to attract pressure groups into the arena in order to strengthen their position against other agencies and to increase their legitimacy. Consequently, the arena becomes increasingly political and further groups are drawn into the arena. This makes the possibility of consensus even more remote.

The fifth dimension which determines the nature of a policy network is the nature of the relationship. In a policy community it is likely that the relationship will be an exchange relationship. In other words, the groups involved will have resources that they can exchange. Groups with this level of resources have information, legitimacy, implementation resources, which can be exchanged for a position in the policy process, and some control over policy. In an issue network, although some actors have resources, they are likely to be limited. Most of the interest groups are likely to have little information to exchange and little control over the implementation of policy. Consequently, they are forced into overt lobbying activities. Likewise, government agencies, which do not have a monopoly of the policy area, cannot guarantee that an interest group has a role in the policy process.

Sixth, it follows from the nature of the relationship that resources also affect the nature of interaction. If groups have resources to exchange the interaction is likely to involve bargaining and negotiation over the direction of policy. If the government agencies want some of the pressure groups' resources, they have to offer some input into policy, and if the group is to stay within the policy community it is likely to want policy that favours its interests. In an issue network the relationship will be based on consultation at best. This consultation might involve a simple exchange of information and is unlikely to have much effect on policy outcomes (Jordan and Richardson 1987).

Seventh, in a policy community power is a positive-sum. In other words a policy community does not involve one group sacrificing power to another. It could involve each group in a mutual expansion of power as each increases its influence over policy. In an issue network power is unequal and there are likely to be losers and winners. As the losers have few resources they can do little if their interests are sacrificed in the development of policy.

The final dimension is the structure of participating organisations. The type of network that develops depends to some extent on the nature of the pressure groups involved. If a policy community is to develop, the leadership of a pressure group has to ensure that once agreement is reached, the membership will accept the policy. If the leadership cannot, there will be disagreement within the group and the policy consensus will collapse. In an issue network control over group membership is not an important factor.

In a policy community there are a limited number of groups which are stable over time and agree on the parameters of policy. They have resources to exchange which results in a process of policy-making that is based on negotiation and presumes that once an agreement is reached a pressure group can ensure that the membership will abide by the decision. A policy community involves the conscious and unconscious exclusion of particular groups. Groups are excluded through conscious decisions not to involve a particular group. They are also excluded through ideologies, rules of the game and the structure of policy-making. Policy communities involve particular informal and formal institutions. Informal institutions could be *ad hoc* committees, regular meetings between officials and interest group leaders, or informal day-to-day contact. Formal institutions include advisory committees, and other such committees, established to ensure the representation of particular interests in government. These institutions enable officials to determine who will be the insiders and the outsiders.

Issue networks generally lack formal institutionalised contacts between groups and government. There is little agreement on the nature of policy problems or how they should be resolved. There is little exchange of resources, and almost no exclusion, and as a result groups are constantly moving in and out of the policy arena. Issue networks can occur in areas of great political importance where it is difficult to establish a consensus [. . .] or where the issue is seen, in Lindblom's (1977) term, as a 'secondary' issue and so not one where a government agency feels the need to develop a monopoly and exclude certain groups (for example abortion issues). Issue networks also develop in new policy areas where no groups have established dominance or where there are no established institutions to enable exclusion. It is important to note that issue networks are not completely open. They are relationships that are distinguished from the general pressure group universe. In order to be an issue network, groups have to be recognised as having some interest in the area and minimal resources to exchange (Marsh and Rhodes 1992).

It must be emphasised that these terms are ideal types at either end of a continuum. It is seldom, if ever, the case that a network will exist which conforms to the eight dimensions outlined above. Often relationships will vary across each of these dimensions and so the number of networks is practically infinite. Nevertheless, these are dimensions that have important empirical relevance and as such help us to understand the types of relationships that exist between groups and government. The clearest example of a policy community which has many of the features outlined above is in British Agricultural Policy. [. . .] Rhodes provides a useful example of an issue network in British inner city policy. Rhodes (1988) demonstrates the difficulty of establishing an inner city policy due to the number of actors involved. The network involved several Ministries, the Treasury, the Departments of Employment, Education, Industry and Social Security, and the Home Office. It also included several agencies within the Department of Employment, and a number of subnational government bodies such as different tiers of local government, area health authorities and a range of interest groups. The failure to achieve agreement between these bodies resulted in 'the continuing failure of innercity policy' (Rhodes 1988: 359). The most fundamental failure of the network was the inability to define the problems it faced.

It is also important to point out that policy networks can develop at different levels of government and can involve vertical integration. For example, a policy community concerned with the issue of agricultural prices and agricultural policy in general can exist at the departmental level whilst within the Ministry of Agriculture a policy community concerned with land drainage and sea defences exists at the level of a specific section of the department (see Cunningham 1992). Rhodes demonstrates how policy networks can link subnational bodies to national bodies. In addition, policy networks can also include an international element. With Britain's integration into the EC, a large number of policy areas now involve EC institutions and groups in the network. Likewise, trade policy is made in an international context with GATT being a key institution within the policy network. It is also possible for networks to exist with little or no key government actors. Grant*et al.* (1988) demonstrate that in the chemical sector, the central role in the network is performed by the key chemical companies.

Hence a policy network can exist at varying levels of government (national or local); in different policy areas (agricultural, industrial or health); or in a subsector of policy (land drainage, chemical policy, community care) or even around particular issues.

References

Benson, J. K. (1982) 'A Framework for Policy Analysis' in D. Rogers *et al.*, *Interorganizational Coordination*, Ames: Iowa State University Press.

Campbell, J. C., Baskin, M. A., Baumgartner, F. R. and Halpern, N. P. (1989) 'Afterword on Policy Communities: A Framework for Comparative Research', *Governance*, 2, pp. 86–94.

Cunningham, C. (1992) 'Sea Defences: A Professionalised Network?' in D. Marsh and R. A. W. Rhodes (eds.) *Policy Networks in British Government*, Oxford: Oxford University Press.

Gaventa, J. (1980) *Power and Powerlessness*, Oxford: Clarendon Press.

Grant, W. P. (1989) *Pressure Groups, Politics and Democracy in Britain*, London: Philip Allan.

Grant, W. P., Paterson, W. and Whitson, C. (1988) *Government and the Chemical Industry*, Oxford: Clarendon.

Heclo, H. (1978) 'Issue Networks and the Executive Establishment' in A. King (ed.) *The New American Political System*, Washington DC: American Enterprise Institute.

Hogwood, B. W. (1986) 'If Consultation is Everything then Maybe it is Nothing', *Strathclyde Papers in Government and Politics*, 44.

Jordan, A. G. (1981) 'Iron Triangles, Woolly Corporatism and Elastic Nets: Images of the Policy Process', *The Journal of the Policy Process*, 1, pp. 95–123.

Jordan, A. G. (1990) 'Sub-governments, Policy Communities and Networks: Refilling the Old Bottles', *Journal of Theoretical Politics*, 2, pp. 319–38.

Jordan, A. G. and Richardson, J. J. (1982) 'The British Policy Style or the Logic of Negotiation?' in J. J. Richardson (ed.) *Policy Styles in Western Europe*, London: George Allen and Unwin.

Jordan, A. G. and Richardson, J. J. (1987) *Government and Pressure Groups in Britain*, Oxford: Clarendon.

Laffin, M. (1986) *Professionalism and Policy: The Role of the Professions in the Centre–Local Government Relations*, Aldershot: Gower.

Laumann, E. O. and Knoke, D. (1987) *The Organisational State*, Madison, WI: The University of Wisconsin Press.

Lindblom, C. E. (1977) *Politics and Markets*, New York: Basic Books.

McCool, D. (1990) 'Subgovernments as Determinants of Political Viability', *Political Science Quarterly*, 105, pp. 269–93.

Marsh, D. and Rhodes, R. A. W. (1992) 'Policy Communities and Issue Networks: Beyond Typology' in D. Marsh and R. A. W. Rhodes (eds.) *Policy Networks in British Government*, Oxford: Oxford University Press.

Mills, M. (1992) 'Networks and Policy on Diet and Heart Disease' in D. Marsh and R. A. W. Rhodes (eds.) *Policy Networks in British Government*, Oxford: Oxford University Press.

Rhodes, R. A. W. (1981) Control and Power in Centre–Local Government Relations, Farnborough: Gower/SSRC.

Rhodes, R. A. W. (1986) *The National World of Local Government*, London: Allen and Unwin.

Rhodes, R. A. W. (1988) *Beyond Westminster and Whitehall*, London: Unwin Hyman.

Rhodes, R. A. W. (1990) 'Policy Networks: A British Perspective', *Journal of Theoretical Politics*, 2, pp. 293–317.

Richardson, J. J. and Jordan, A. G. (1979) *Governing Under Pressure*, Oxford: Martin Robertson.

Richardson, J. J. and Jordan, A. G. (1985) *Governing Under Pressure* (2nd edn), Oxford: Martin Robertson.

Ripley, R. and Franklin, G. (1980) *Congress, the Bureaucracy and Public Policy*, Illinois: Dorsey Press.

Saunders, P. (1975) 'They Make the Rules', *Policy and Politics*, 4, pp. 31–58.

Saward, M. (1992) 'The Civil Nuclear Network in Britain' in D. Marsh and R. A. W. Rhodes (eds.) *Policy Networks in British Government*, Oxford: Oxford University Press.

Smith, M. J. (1991) 'From Policy Community to Issue Network: Salmonella in Eggs and the New Politics of Food', *Public Administration*, 69, pp. 235–55.

Therborn, G. (1980) *The Power of Ideology and the Ideology of Power*, London: Verso.

The economic theory of bureaucracy

Gordon Tullock

Bureaucracy

Bureaucrats are like other men. This proposition sounds very simple and straight-forward, but the consequences are a radical departure from orthodox economic theory.

If bureaucrats are ordinary men, they will make most of (not all) their decisions in terms of what benefits them, not society as a whole. Like other men, they may occasionally sacrifice their own well-being for the wider good, but we should expect this to be exceptional behaviour.

Most of the existing literature on the machinery of government assumes that, when an activity is delegated to a bureaucrat, he will either carry out the rules and regulations or will make decisions in the public interest regardless of whether it benefits him or not. We do not make this assumption about businessmen. We do not make it about consumers in the market. I see no reason why we should make it about bureaucrats.

Bureaucrats and businessmen

A businessman, in an environment that is reasonably competitive and without severe externalities, will normally make a decision which is more or less in accord with the well-being of society, but not because he is consciously *aiming* at the public good. His general aim is simply to make as much money as he can, and he makes the most by doing what is in the social interest. The bureaucrat will also do what is in the social interest if the constraints to which he is subject are such that his own personal interest is identical to the social interest.

The theory of bureaucracy should be based upon the assumption that bureaucrats are as self-seeking as businessmen, and it should concern itself with the design of constraints which will make the bureaucrats' self-interest identical with the interests of society. We should not expect the identity to be perfect – we do not have perfection in the market – but we should expect at least a high correlation. Unfortunately it is harder to arrange such a high correlation in a bureaucratic context than in the market [. . .].

From G. Tullock, *The Vote Motive* (1976), London: Institute of Economic Affairs.

To return to the main theme of this paper, since we have no perfect solution we must choose among imperfect instrumentalities. What, then, are the imperfections of the bureaucratic process?

Bureaucrats and elected representatives
In most modern countries, an immense number of decisions are taken by bureaucrats. They are supposedly in accord with the decisions of the elected representatives in democracies (or of the dictator in despotisms); but often the influence of these representatives is in practice modest. Indeed there seems now to be developing a mystique under which the bureaucrats are not even supposed to be under the control of elected officials. [. . .] The view that many decisions should be separated from political control by being put solely under the control of bureaucrats (sometimes in that oldest branch of the bureaucracy, the judiciary) is wide-spread.

Motives of bureaucrats
What does happen in a bureaucracy? What are the motivations of bureaucrats? Like everyone else, bureaucrats presumably try to improve their own utility. Their utility, again like everyone else's, is partly based upon their immediate ability to consume goods and partly on their appreciation of good things happening to other people. In other words, they are partly selfish and partly public-interested.

In most business activities, the approximation that the businessman is trying to maximise his money income turns out to work rather well, although seldom perfectly. In the bureaucracy, we would like a somewhat similar approximation. If we look over aims in which a bureaucrat might be interested, we can begin by listing those which are of primary concern to him: his salary, his conditions of work – office furniture, etc. (strictly apportioned according to rank in most bureaucracies), his power over other people, his public respect and reputation. In addition to these self-regarding values, let us assume he is also interested in the public good and consciously wants to accomplish something in his job. We can easily think of circumstances in which the two would be in clear conflict. Mr James Smith, for example, is due for promotion to department head, a job which will lead in due course to his becoming Sir James; but Mr Charles Brown is the best man for the job. It is, on the whole, doubtful whether Mr Smith will bring that truth firmly to the attention of his superiors.

On the other hand, we will easily find circumstances where Mr Smith would, for purely *selfish* reasons, be motivated to serve the interest of society. If we assume in this example that he is much abler than Mr Brown, his *selfish* motives would point in the correct direction.

(One of the advantages of the simple profit-maximising assumption in business is that it permits us to assume a single 'maximand' and make calculations. If we consider the businessman as maximising his utility . . . we no longer have as easy a problem. His utility is, to him, a simple 'function' which he can maximise; but, to us as outsiders, what is observed is a number of different elements, such as his income, respect in his profession, the beauty of his secretary, other aspects of his office, etc. We would have to work out a complex function of all those variables and them attempt to maximise it;

and this complex function would have to be identical to the one he uses in utility maximising. In general, economists have abandoned this problem, and assume a simple, single goal: the profit. The loss in accuracy is fortunately slight.)

What does the bureaucrat try to maximise?

Is there a similar maximand we can use for bureaucracies? The answer is, unfortunately, 'No', if we want to be completely general. Bureaucrats tend to maximise different collections of activity. But it is true that if we confine ourselves to the type of bureaucracy found in most Western countries, there is a 'not bad' approximation: *size*.

As a general rule, a bureaucrat will find that his possibilities for promotion increase, his power, influence, and public respect improve, and even the physical conditions of his office improve, if the bureaucracy in which he works expands. This proposition is fairly general. Almost any bureaucrat gains at least something if the *whole* bureaucracy expands. He gains more, however, if *his* Ministry expands, and more yet if the subdivision in which he is employed expands.

I have confined this proposition to *most* bureaucracies in *modern Western democracies*. It is not necessarily true of all these bureaucracies, or of bureaucracies in other political systems. The real issue here is whether the reward structure in the bureaucracy is such that people gain when their burden expands. This is not necessarily true everywhere. Further, there is one important limitation on profit-maximisation which also applies to size-maximisation for bureaucrats: in general, people do not like hard work!

A bureaucrat ordered to do research on, say, improving the bid process for North Sea oil is presumably not totally uninterested in discovering a better method of letting the bids; but he is apt to give more consideration to the opportunity this project gives him to expand the size of his office, and hence improve his probability of promotion, prestige, etc. However, it is by no means certain that he will work hard to achieve either of these goals. Indeed, in the pathological case, he will devote the bulk of this time to essentially leisure activities (some of which, like reading history or solving crosswords, may be located in his office), and time he devotes to work will be solely devoted to an effort to expand his office with no concern at all for its ostensible object. In the more normal non-pathological case, although he may not engage in what we would normally refer to as hard work, he will devote a good deal of attention both to improving the bid process and to using the project to expand his office.

Assume the bureaucrats are simply attempting to maximise the size of their bureaucracies and leave aside, for the time being, their desire to consume leisure (technically described as 'shirking' in the management literature). Economists have gone a long way with their simple, one-argument 'utility function' for businessmen (profit-maximisation); if we cannot get as far with our one-argument utility function for bureaucrats (size-maximisation), at least we should make some progress.

Improving the bureaucracy

One way of improving the size of a bureaucracy is to do a good enough job so that people want more of the activity it is producing. [. . .]

To examine the matter a little more formally, assume that a government activity, say police protection, is produced at constant cost, represented by the horizontal line on Figure 1. The demand for it (DD) should slant downward as in Figure 1, and can be thought of as a demand of the citizenry, or of the higher level of government, i.e. the legislature or, perhaps, of the cabinet.

The usual way of organising and supplying the police is to create a series of regional monopolies, all the police in, say, Liverpool being organised under one control. It has its own decision-making process and its own ends (although much writing on administration implicitly assumes otherwise).

If it were somehow possible to buy police services competitively, individuals buying it and competing companies supplying it, the optimum amount would be obtained at point O, the cost would be the rectangle below and to the left of point O, and the consumer surplus generated for the citizenry shown by the triangle DCO.

If we assume the citizenry continue to buy police services independently (we are assuming this is technologically feasible), but they are supplied by a profit-maximising monopoly, it would provide M units of police service at a price of M', and make a profit equivalent to the rectangle above the cost line and to the left of line M. There would still be some consumer surplus, but clearly the consumers would be in a much worse situation than with competitive suppliers.

Let us now more realistically assume that the individuals are not purchasing the police services as individuals but through a governmental agency which has a demand for police services derived from the demand of the individual citizens. The supplier is also a monopoly: there is only one police force in Liverpool; and let us assume that the police attempt to maximise the size of their bureaucracy. What is the likely outcome?

Single buyer v. single seller

First, we have a monopsony (single buyer) against monopoly (single seller), and this is always a difficult situation for economists to analyse. What would happen if one or the other of the two had everything his own way? If the legislature is in complete control of the situation and has a perfect idea of the cost structure facing the police, they could offer the rectangle left of and below O to the police in return for the police producing O amount of police protection, and we would have the same solution as in free competition.

If the police have everything on their side, which means they are able to conceal their own cost from the legislature, they can misrepresent the cost of providing various amounts of police services, and the legislature will not be able to discover their true 'production function'. We then get a most extraordinary situation. The police will provide B police services and charge the amount of the rectangle under the cost line and to the left of B. This means that for the marginal police services they are charging more than they receive and there is a net social waste shown by the shaded triangle. They are able to get away with this, however, because the size of the shaded triangle is the same as DCO. As a perfectly discriminating monopolist always will, they have squeezed out the entire consumer surplus, but have spent it on providing additional police services.

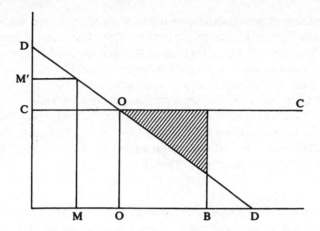

Figure 1 Supply and demand for police services

How do we reach this conclusion? The police department is not assumed to be profit-maximising (it is not possible for the policemen simply to pocket any profit they make), but they are benefited in various ways by the expansion in the size of the force. Since we assume that they are exploiting the demand curve to the maximum, they are also maximising their size by this socially wasteful expansion.

This situation is the ultimate result which could be expected if the bureaucracy worked hard at expanding its budget and was able to exploit the full monopoly gains in all-or-nothing bargaining from the legislature. The taxpayer would be indifferent to having the existing police force or no police force at all, which, of course, also makes possible much lower taxes. It seems doubtful whether any existing bureaucracy has reached this position. Many bureaucracies, from the standpoint of the citizen-taxpayers as a whole, may be beyond this point; but that is because they are satisfying the demands of some persistent and voluble minority. In these circumstances, a true demand curve would be that of the minority and, once again, I doubt whether many real-world bureaucracies have succeeded in exploiting their monopoly positions to the full.

There are a number of reasons why bureaucracies would not be able to reach this goal with any degree of regularity. First, and obviously, the legislature or purchaser of the services from the bureaucracy characteristically has at least some information about the production function of the bureaucracy and is not subject to what we might call 'complete' exploitation. Secondly, since the members of the bureaucracy among other things want leisure, they are unlikely to put in the concentration and hard work required to exploit the legislature to the theoretical maximum.

Ironically, the desire for leisure – what we normally call laziness – has a net benefit for society. Suppose the individuals in the bureaucracy work hard enough to get only 80 per cent of what they could if they devoted full force to achieving it. The cost level line in the diagram would be adjusted upward to indicate that you have to hire more policemen to get a given amount of protection. This clearly would be a disadvantage for the taxpayer-citizen. On the other hand, the bureaucracy in negotiating with the legislature would not get all of the welfare triangle; it would leave 20 per cent of it to the citizen. The citizen would therefore derive some benefit from the service, although if the policemen were energetic and hard-working in both 'policing' and exploiting the legislature, the consumer surplus would be entirely consumed in producing 'efficiently' police services not worth their cost. The citizen-taxpayer is better off with lazy servants than with diligent ones here, but this results simply because the diligent ones will use their diligence to extract surplus value from him.

Odds with the bureaucracy

Does the bureaucracy in practice extort its entire theoretically possible gain from the legislature? This is the classic monopoly-against-monopsony problem, and economists normally say it is insoluble. But there are good reasons for believing the odds will be heavily on the side of the bureaucracy. It will have a good idea of the legislative demand for its services, which is essentially derived from the voters' demand. The bureaucracy has access to the newspapers, television, etc., and therefore has a good idea of the popular demand. In the circumstances, the legislature is not able to keep its demand curve a secret.

These factors are exaggerated by two special characteristics of governmental demand. First, most government demands are organised by special interest pressure groups, like the farmers, who normally are intimately connected with the bureaucracy which will carry out the policy, the Ministry of Agriculture, which, in turn, is therefore very well informed about the political pressures that can be brought to bear upon Parliament and the government. Secondly, a good part of the demand for bureaucratic services comes not from the people who will *receive* them but from those who will be paid to *supply* them. The bureaucrat who works for the Minister of Agriculture, or the policeman who works for the chief constable, is also a voter. In voting, he (and his family) have two demands for their bureaucracy's service. First, they, like other citizens, gain whatever benefits it generates; but, secondly, they gain privately from the payments made to them.

They are part of the demand for their own services, and a particularly important part. They combine very good information about their bureau with strong motivation. And, indeed, they seem to represent a larger percentage of the voting population than of the total population, because they are more likely to vote. Rough estimates in the United States indicate that about one out of five Americans derives his support from a government job in the family, but about one out of four voters does so.

If the bureaucracy has a good idea of the demand for the service, the government has difficulty determining the cost of providing it. In general, the only source of such information is the bureaucracy, which is apt not only to say that economies are impossible but also, if economies are imposed, to act so as to maximise their cost instead of attempting to do the best job it can in the new circumstances.

Bureaucrats resist 'cuts' by superior knowledge

Three examples readily come to mind. The first occurred when I was serving on the council of the American Political Science Association. We were in one of the budget crises which afflict learned societies from time to time. The APSA maintains in Washington, DC, a large office, engaged in not too well defined activities. It was suggested that one of the ways we could escape from our budget problem was to reduce expenses in this office. The permanent secretary of the society, who had been responsible for building up the office after he was appointed, immediately said that 'Yes, that could be done'; it would be possible for him to lay off two or three of the employees in the subscription service branch, i.e. those who took care of seeing to it that everyone got their *American Political Review, P.S.*, and other documents circulated to members. The result clearly would be that members were inconvenienced. He did not suggest that any of the 'policy officials' might be dispensed with, although it was never clear what the bulk of them were doing.

My second example involves the Federal Customs Service. Its budget was reduced. The civil servant in charge laid off every Customs Inspector in the United States but not one person in any other part of the Customs Service. This was too extreme, and he was transferred in a burst of unfavourable publicity; but he was not fired.

The third case, more recent, concerns newspaper reports that the Immigration Service is deliberately investing its resources in office staff rather than in Inspectors to make it necessary for Congress to increase its budget.

This kind of behaviour is common with bureaucracies; and, in general, congressmen have found it difficult to prevent. Professor William Niskanen, whose book *Bureaucracy and Representative Government*[1] rigorously develops the size-maximising principle, spent most of his life before writing it as an economist in the Department of Defense, attempting to improve its efficiency. Immediately after writing the book, he moved to a higher-level agency, the Office of Management and Budget, the general control agency of the United States government, and found that there, too, it was impossible for him to outmanoeuvre the bureaucrats because they simply knew more about their departments than he did.

Solutions: more information? – reducing bureau monopoly?

What can be done? First, an attempt to develop expertise at the upper layer is required to which the whole development of cost-benefit analysis is directed. More information would help, but it is not obviously going to lead to much improvement. What is needed is some way of lowering the bargaining potential of the monopoly bureaus.

In the market place we do not try to discover the cost structure of companies from whom we buy products or service. All we do is compare the prices and services offered by organisations and choose the one that suits us best. The existence of a monopoly, of course, makes it hard for us to do this, and we tend to feel disadvantaged. Is there some way in which we could provide for Parliament or Congress the same ability to select the lowest price rather than putting upon it the burden of determining the operating efficiency of the bureaucracy? The answer, fortunately, is that such possibilities often exist, and as far as we can tell they improve efficiency.

First, although most government services are produced under monopoly conditions, some are produced with varying degrees of competition. It is very hard to get measures of efficiency, but something can be done. Examining the data,[2] we find that the least efficient bureaus are those which have perfect monopolies.

Second, where, although the individual bureau has a monopoly in one area, several bureaus operate in different areas, the legislature can at least compare cost curves. The police forces, which in both the United States and Britain are organised as a series of local monopolies (except for privately supplied police services) rather than as a national service, are an example. There are, of course, many others, such as refuse-collection, fire-fighting, education, sewerage, etc.

Third, still more efficient are government bureaus which provide a service that is also supplied by private companies. Waste removal in the United States, for example, is sometimes a government activity and sometimes carried out by private companies charging a contract fee. So far as we can tell, the government bureaus, although not as efficient as the private companies (as measured by price and service), are nevertheless markedly more efficient than government bureaus which do not face private competition.

Government bureaus, even in this final negative situation, are almost never as efficient as private companies in a competitive industry.

The question of the efficiency of private industry in monopolistic situations, of course, is not at issue here, since no one (so far as I know) regards this as a particularly desirable organisation of the economy. The reason is simple (Figure 1). If one company protected by a high tariff has a monopoly in motor-car production in its home market, the demand curve is for motor-cars in total. If there are two companies, the motorist who is thinking whether or not to buy a car also has the alternative of buying it from the other company. Similarly with a bureaucracy: the more the competition, the more it is forced to produce close to the optimum output and productive efficiency one would anticipate in a competitive industry.

Introducing competition into the bureaucracy

(a) COMPETITION WITHIN BUREAUS

Can we introduce competition into bureaucracy? First, we could simply stop enacting cartel legislation. Most 'efficiency' studies of government have attempted to root out competition (called 'duplication'). In the United States' automobile market, not only is General Motors 'duplicated' by Ford, Chrysler and American Motors, but a lot of odd foreigners like British Leyland, Fiat, Volkswagen, and Toyota are also 'duplicating activity'. Wouldn't we be much more efficient if we abolished 'duplication'?

The absurdity of this proposition would not in any way be reduced if we substituted a government service for production of motor-cars. In the United States, highways are characteristically constructed by a large number of private companies. Their repair and maintenance, however, is normally done by monopolistic government enterprises. In some areas – Blacksburg, Virginia, where I live, is an example – a good deal of the maintenance is let out on bids to competing private companies. We pay lower repair prices than we would if a monopolistic agency was doing all the repairing. Furthermore, the competing companies ready and willing to replace bureaucracies in other cities and counties also make the road repair bureaucracies there careful about prices.

Thus one way of increasing the competitiveness of government services is simply to contract them out. Many services are contracted out in various places in the world. The entire line of public utilities – telephone, telegraph, radio and television transmission, water supply, sewage removal, electricity, and gas – are sometimes provided privately and sometimes publicly. Usually the private companies are given some kind of government monopoly, which sharply reduces their efficiency; but sometimes one or more of the utilities are generated by competing private companies. It is not obvious that this arrangement is ideal, but it would certainly be worth careful investigation. The mere act of looking into this possibility would probably lead to very sharp improvements in efficiency in the corresponding government agencies.

There are also many other government activities which can be performed by private agencies on contract. Fire protection is, in general, a government activity, but for some obscure reason a private fire protection industry has developed in the state of Arizona. The private fire protection companies enter into contracts with the smaller cities to provide them with fire protection, and also offer their services to private individuals. Comparative studies[3] seem to indicate that the private companies provide fire protection for about *half* the cost of public fire departments serving similar communities. Further, the private companies – tiny though they are – have been the cutting edge of scientific progress in the fire protection industry. They have invented an entirely new technology which, granted the extraordinarily small funds they have for research, is a remarkable achievement. This technology is beginning to spread through the United States government fire departments, but only very slowly, since there are few fire commissioners who really want to cut their budgets in half.

(b) COMPETITION BETWEEN BUREAUS

A second way to impose competition on bureaucracies is to retain bureaucratic control but permit competition within it. The area served by a bureaucracy might simply be divided into smaller areas with separate budgets. It would help efficiency if Parliament made a habit of changing the geographic scope of the small bureaucracies handling, say, police protection. If, for example, the Commander in charge of division I seems to have done better one year than the Commander in charge of neighbouring division II, 15 per cent of II might be added to I, the Commander of I promoted, and the Commander of II reduced. In the following year, at the very least a good deal of thought on methods of improving efficiency by both might be expected. Perhaps the 15 per cent could be shifted back at the end of the next year.

Notes

1. Aldine-Atherton, New York, 1971; the argument is summarised in *Bureaucracy: Servant or master?*, Hobart Paperback No. 5, IEA, 1973.

2. Thomas E. Borcherding (ed.), *Budgets and Bureaucrats: The origins of government growth*, Duke University Press, Durham, NC, 1976.
3. A popular account of this phenomenon is William C. Wooldridge, *Uncle Sam, the Monopoly Man*, Arlington House, New Rochelle, NY, 1970, pp. 124–7. For a more scholarly account, Roger Ahlbrandt, 'Efficiency in the provision of fire services', *Public Choice*, 16, Fall 1973, pp. 1–15.

The bureau-shaping model

Patrick Dunleavy

Rational bureaucrats have few incentives to pursue budget-maximizing strategies, as this chapter seeks to show by building on the core public choice assumptions. I assume that bureaucrats maximize self-regarding and hard-edged utilities in making official decisions. A bureau's overall policy is set by some combination of individual decisions made by its officials, and by interactions with a sponsor body. Within broad limits, officials' influence on bureau policy is always extensively rank-structured, with those near the top being most influential. Sponsors depend extensively on bureaus for information about their costs, benefits and outputs, although they also receive some general information from citizens.

There are four reasons why rational bureaucrats should not budget-maximize. First, collective action problems exist within bureaucracies and have an important influence upon overall bureau behaviour. Second, the extent to which bureaucrats' utilities are associated with budget increases varies greatly across different components of overall budgets, and across distinct types of agencies. Third, even if some rational officials still budget-maximize, they will do so only up to an internal optimum level, Fourth, senior officials are much more likely to pursue work-related rather than pecuniary utilities – in which case, collective strategies of reshaping their bureaus into different agency types can best advance senior officials' interests. Whether senior bureaucrats pursue bureau-shaping or budget-maximizing strategies varies systematically with agency type.

Collective action problems inside bureaucracies

Bureaus are rank-structured environments. But it is very rare for any sizeable government agency to be completely dominated by one individual or even a small leadership group with cohesive interests: 'The monolithic bureau is a myth' (Downs

From P. Dunleavy, *Democracy, Bureaucracy and Public Choice* (1991), Hemel Hempstead: Harvester Wheatsheaf, pp. 174–209.

97

1967: 133). To realize collective benefits for bureau members will require concerted action by a number of officials which may be quite large, especially in hostile or turbulent environmental conditions. Most US federal departments are congeries of between five and ten major bureaus, administrations or offices, running programmes which operate in quite distinct ways and policy fields. Each bureau or administration has an extensive sub-structure of senior officials, and there is a smallish departmental core of central administrators built around the Office of the Secretary and the Inspector General, who pull overall policy together. In this system, and given the large size of most US federal departments, a large number of officials are involved in constructing bureau or departmental budgets. Even in the much smaller and highly integrated departments characteristic of British central government there may be up to eighty policy-level staff. In neither country can budget-maximization be a private good pursued by a single hegemonic official. But if budget-maximizing requires a collective effort, how do officials choose between individual or collective strategies for boosting their welfare, and between increasing sectional or overall bureau budgets? And do bureaucrats encounter collective action problems in maximizing budgets?

Budget-maximizing as a collective strategy

Any given bureaucrat has a range of both individual and collective strategies open for boosting her welfare. She can most directly and strongly improve her personal position using an individual strategy – for here a successful effort generates a pay-off which does not need to be shared with others. By contrast, with any collective strategy there is a more indirect and complex link between a successful outcome and a welfare boost for the individual. When multiple officials shape a bureau's policy, then budget-maximization is a collective rather than an individual way of increasing bureaucrats' welfare:

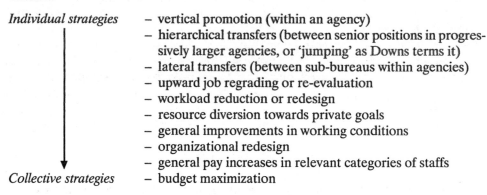

Individual strategies
- vertical promotion (within an agency)
- hierarchical transfers (between senior positions in progressively larger agencies, or 'jumping' as Downs terms it)
- lateral transfers (between sub-bureaus within agencies)
- upward job regrading or re-evaluation
- workload reduction or redesign
- resource diversion towards private goals
- general improvements in working conditions
- organizational redesign
- general pay increases in relevant categories of staffs

Collective strategies
- budget maximization

An overall budget increase for the agency has particularly indeterminate implications for any official, however senior. Consequently, rational bureaucrats put their efforts primarily into individual utility-maximizing strategies. They only pursue collective goods strategies if other options are foreclosed or are already fully exploited.

Studies in occupational sociology show that blue-collar workers are more attracted to collective forms of pay bargaining than white-collar staffs, because people in manual grades have little prospect of significantly improving their situation by individual strategies of promotion, career advancement, or renegotiating individual contracts with employers (Crouch 1982: 67–74). Similarly, we might expect that within a government agency the opportunities for individual welfare maximization will be fewest in the bottom ranks of bureaucrats: here collective strategies for improving officials' welfare may be resorted to more readily. But senior officials have much greater scope for exploiting individual strategies, so they are less likely to resort to collective strategies.

A closely related issue arises over the assumption in the existing public choice literature that budget-maximization focuses solely on boosting an agency's entire expenditure, its global budget. With multiple officials influencing policy, surely rational officials will primarily seek budget increments for their section or division inside the agency? Sectional budget increases could offer individual benefits to the one or two policy-level staff in each division. So surely a more realistic focus on budget increments tagged to specific sections can rescue Niskanen's assumption of a single hegemonic official?

But in practice dropping a whole-bureau focus on the global budget is difficult, and cannot rescue budget-maximizing models from their difficulties. Trying to model bureaucratic behaviour *vis-à-vis* sectional budgets requires very complex models which are even more difficult to operationalize than those focusing on global budgets. I noted above that US federal departments are congeries of bureaus, but this is not the end of the story. Even within bureaus or administrations there are sub-offices running distinct programmes. The degree of sectionalization of bureaus and the ways in which senior staffs aggregate sectional budget bids also vary widely across agencies. A developed apparatus for measuring both these properties in a standardized fashion would be needed if a disaggregated model were to be developed. It is highly improbable that officials in general would see their interests as advanced by all (tagged) budget increases inside their bureau or department, as budget-maximizing models assume. Instead, rational bureaucrats will only favour sectional budget increases with positive implications for them. They are likely to be indifferent towards, or to oppose, budget increments going to other sections of their own organization. Officials in stagnant or slow-growing sections of an agency could easily face severe welfare losses because of budget increases in more dynamic sections. Not only would they experience 'relative deprivation', but the balance of influence and prestige within the agency would shift towards the growth areas at their expense.

Consequently, an account of how officials behave with sectional rather than global budget increases would need to be constructed in terms of the emergence of minimum winning coalitions for certain types of budgetary expansion rather than others. Because such an approach would be very complex and require great methodological sophistication before it could be applied empirically, the analysis here follows the existing public choice literature's focus on global budgets. None the less I recognize explicitly that this is a drastic simplifying assumption, which should ideally be superseded at a later stage by a more complex account.

Collective action and maximizing budgets

Because bureaucracies are significantly rank-structured organizations, the existing public choice literature assumes that collective action problems have no bearing upon agency policies. Yet once we recognize multiple policy-level officials, then a rational official must meet the following condition before deciding to pursue the shared goals of global budget-maximization:

$$(B_j * P_j) - C_j > A_j$$

In words, B_j the official's net utility derived from a marginal budget increment (i.e. the individual benefits she receives after allowing for any costs associated with budgetary growths); discounted by P_j, the probability that the individual official's advocacy will be decisive in securing the budget increase; minus C_j, the costs of personally advocating the budget increment; must be greater than A_j, the rate of return on individual efforts to improve her welfare, or available on alternative collective strategies.

In the theory-of-the-firm debate a number of authors pointed out early on that even if a collective goal such as profit-maximization could be plausibly ascribed to a large firm, managers' behaviour could rationally diverge from it (Loasby 1968):

> Any individual manager is one amongst many and as such he might rightly assume that his activities will only make a small contribution to the achievement of the collective goal. It would be rational for him to assume that the others are contributing to the goal, thereby allowing him to serve his own goals and to become a 'free-rider' in the group. (Jackson 1982: 55)

Only one or two public choice authors recognize collective action problems inside bureaus, and most assume that officials' work conditions are calculated to produce co-operative behaviour:

> Hierarchy and organization are especially effective at concentrating the interactions between specific individuals. A bureaucracy is structured so that people specialize, and so that people working on related tasks are grouped together. This organizational practice increases the frequency of interactions, making it easier for workers to develop stable cooperative relationships. Moreover, when an issue requires coordination between different branches of the organization, the hierarchical structure allows the issue to be referred to policy makers at higher levels who frequently deal with each other on just such issues. By binding people together in a long-term, multilevel game, organizations increase the number and importance of future interactions, and thereby promote the experience of cooperation among groups too large to interact individually. (Axelrod 1984: 130–1)

... [A] bureaucracy is a strongly defined exogenous group, with a clear group identity of which all bureau members are aware. By retaining a whole-bureau focus on global rather than sectional budgets, difficulties arising from potentially conflicting identities are excluded. So in respect of budgets at least, bureaucrats automatically perceive their collective interest, although they may not rank it highly compared with individual strategies for maximizing their welfare.

However, the rank-structured nature of bureaucracy also changes the basic collective action problem in an interesting and important way which is likely to more than offset these influences fostering co-operation. Each of the terms in the equation above – undiscounted benefits, probability of influence, advocacy costs and returns on alternative strategies – will vary systematically across 'top'-, 'middle'- and 'bottom'-ranked officials, as shown in Figure 1.

The utility pay-offs from generalized budgetary increments are likely to vary, roughly inversely with rank. People who are already senior officials gain least, since their position is already well established. The same features of public service systems which foster co-operative behaviour (such as civil service tenure systems) also heavily insulate existing permanent staff from being affected by budget fluctuations. Really large benefits from budget increments will be concentrated on marginal staff – those with no job security, people acting as consultants, spin-off staffs or those on part-time contracts. Certainly these groups have most to lose from budget reductions, and they are a significant (if largely unstudied) component. In the United States, where federal government employment has been subject to strict manpower limits set by Congress, minimum estimates suggest that an extra 5 to 25 per cent of staff are 'contracted in', that is, employed by federal agencies directly without ever showing up in official personnel returns (Bennett and Johnson 1980: 36–41). The wide range of variation here also reflects a hazy boundary with the much larger phenomenon of agencies' contracting out tasks to firms.

The probability that an individual's advocacy of a budget increment is decisive obviously increases dramatically with rank. Top-down, hierarchic forms of organization clearly imply that part-time, hived-off and bottom-rank officials have negligible individual impact upon their agency's policy, while the influence of middle ranks is not much more. Within policy-making ranks, however, the probability of influence rises sharply with seniority, reaching a threshold of maximum influence which is environmentally determined. In a super-favourable environment the combined probability of top officials in securing increases may approximate 1. But, contrary to Niskanen's account, such a situation is very exceptional (Goodin 1982). In a hostile or turbulent environment, the agency's overall probability of success declines rapidly, and even the most influential official can have only a fraction of that chance to be decisive in getting a budget increment approved by the sponsor.

With the distribution of influence shown here, environmental conditions have a major impact upon how top bureaucrats discount their utility pay-offs from budget increments. Formal models of the interactions between bureaucracies and legislatures demonstrate exactly this relationship, suggesting that increases in the legislature's oversight activities can dramatically curb the ability of budget-maximizing bureaucrats to secure increments (Bendor and Moe 1985: 772). But external changes hardly affect the attitudes of lower staffs, whose probable influence is small, even in a favourable environment. Top bureaucrats are also likely to be much better informed about shifting environmental conditions than lower-ranking officials, so that their reactions will adapt more quickly and accurately to external developments. By contrast, bottom-rank bureaucrats often have anachronistic attitudes, remaining conservative in environments suitable for organizational growth, or carrying over established growth orientations into an era of cutbacks.

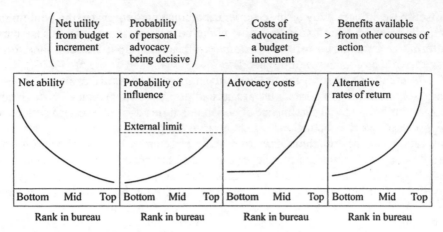

$$\left(\begin{array}{ccc} \text{Net utility} & & \text{Probability} \\ \text{from budget} & \times & \text{of personal} \\ \text{increment} & & \text{advocacy} \\ & & \text{being decisive} \end{array}\right) \quad - \quad \begin{array}{c} \text{Costs of} \\ \text{advocating} \\ \text{a budget} \\ \text{increment} \end{array} \quad > \quad \begin{array}{c} \text{Benefits available} \\ \text{from other courses of} \\ \text{action} \end{array}$$

Figure 1 The distribution of net utilities, influence probabilities, advocacy costs and alternative rates of return within a hypothetical bureau

The costs of advocating a budget increment are also significantly rank-structured. Because bottom-rank personnel have little chance to influence bureau policy, their pursuit of collective gains from budget increments may be confined to supporting a labour movement case for more spending. Beyond the middle ranks of the organization, greater opportunities for actively promoting budgetary expansion (over and above normal or technical incremental adjustments for inflation, etc.) mean that advocacy costs rise steeply with rank. For top officials a budgetary increase typically involves preparing special papers, attending difficult meetings, cultivating external allies and contacts, responding to sponsor criticisms or investigations and justifying the bureau's case in public. Empirical studies of budget-making show that most budget scrutiny, negotiations and controversy concentrates on marginal changes to a largely unanalysed 'base budget' (Jackson 1982: ch 5). So the advocacy costs of seeking increases on the base budget are substantial in senior ranks.

Alternative rates of return on individual welfare-boosting efforts will be much higher for senior officials (with multiple opportunities to better their positions) than for rank-and-file workers (for whom other options are foreclosed or ineffective). I also argue below that alternative collective strategies focusing on work-related utilities are more important to senior officials (see the final section of this chapter). On both counts, top bureaucrats require higher individual benefits before it is worthwhile to commit effort to budget-maximizing, while lower-ranked officials have fewer viable alternatives.

With utilities, influence probabilities, advocacy costs and alternatives patterned as in Figure 1, then bureaucrats will experience severe collective action problems in maximizing budgets, even though annual budgeting is a frequently reiterated game. Even if budget-maximization could benefit bureau members as a whole, officials will none the less free-ride on advocating increases, for different reasons. Bottom-rank bureaucrats gain most from budget increases, but they also know that they can make virtually no difference to the outcome individually. Hence even though their advocacy costs are small, and they have fewer welfare-boosting options to pursue, low-ranking officials with secure jobs are unlikely to find it worth their while to press for increased spending. By contrast, officials at the top of the bureau can significantly affect outcomes, but stand to gain least from budgetary expansion, confront high advocacy costs in exercising their influence and have more opportunity to boost their welfare in alternative ways. They are particularly unlikely to incur high advocacy costs in a hostile or turbulent environment where the agency's overall chance of success is low or unpredictable.

Of course, much will depend on the cardinal values assigned to the variables in the equation above. By itself this analysis cannot demonstrate that bureaucrats *necessarily* confront collective action problems in maximizing budgets. But fleshing out the equation with some intuitively realistic values and examples suggests that collective action problems will be the norm rather than the exception.

Key concepts for analysing budgets and agencies

To claim that bureaucrats maximize budgets is unilluminating until we can know precisely *which* elements of agency expenditure rational officials seek to boost. Although this chapter deals with whole-agency budgetary changes rather than sectional budgets, important distinctions are still feasible within this focus. And differentiating types of (whole-agency) budgets highlights the existence of very different kinds of agency, many of which do not conform with the line bureaucracy paradigm in existing public choice accounts.

Types of budget
An agency's *core budget* (CB) consists of those expenditures which are spent directly on its own operations (rather than going outside the agency in transfers, contracts or grants to other public sector bodies). The CB includes items such as salaries and personnel costs, equipment and material costs consumed directly in the agency's basic functions (such as office equipment or computers), and accommodation expenditures (such as rent for premises and recurrent capital spending on buildings). The concept is very similar to the definition of 'running costs' used in the UK central government (Thain and Wright 1989), except that the CB also includes some capital spending on the agency's own operations.

The *bureau budget* (BB) includes all the core budget items above, plus any monies which the agency pays out to the private sector, for example by awarding contracts to private firms, or by making transfer payments to individuals or firms, or by directly paying interest on capital debts. In Western countries, most spending on construction and major equipment purchasing is included in the bureau budget, since these tasks are carried out under contract by private firms. The BB covers all expenditures which are directly controlled by the bureau's own decisions. So long as the funding stays inside the public sector (e.g. up to the point where contracts are let or transfers disbursed), policy implementation rests solely with the bureau's own staff. No separate or subordinate public sector organizations are involved in handling any part of the BB.

An agency's *programme budget* (PB) includes its bureau budget, plus any monies which the agency passes on to other public sector bodies for them to spend. Thus the PB encompasses any expenditure for which the agency must account to the sponsor (and the courts), and over which it exercises some direct supervision – even if large parts of this total are passed on to other public sector agencies for final implementation. Inter-organizational transfers of this last kind can only be included in the agency's programme budget total if it exercises some degree of hierarchical control over the ways in which the funding is spent.

Finally, the *super-programme budget* (SPB) consists of the agency's programme budget plus any spending by other bureaus from their own resources, over which the agency none the less either exercises some policy responsibilities, or which it can limit or expand in planning terms, or for which it can wholly or partially claim political credit (and hence also incur political blame). This concept may well have no application in countries with a federal constitution, but is useful in analysing centralized unitary states such as the United Kingdom.

These types of budget interrelate like Chinese boxes (Figure 2). The core budget is at the centre, enclosed by the larger bureau budget, which is in turn enclosed by the larger programme budget. Each level has a different theoretical significance. The core budget is the agency's own activity spending; the bureau budget is the public spending over which it retains complete authority and control (before it reaches private sector firms or individuals); the programme budget is the agency's total throughput of funding from the sponsor, including money channelled elsewhere in the public sector. For many agencies, the PB is the end of the story.

However, the super-programme budget concept is necessary because in some countries top-tier agencies which make inter-governmental transfers to regional or local governments thereby acquire the ability to control large chunks of these lower-tier agencies' spending. Sometimes the existence of grant funding is used to justify legislation giving top-tier agencies extensive policy control or supervisory powers, which are especially strong in European countries like the United Kingdom, the Netherlands and Eire. Alternatively, with linked or matching grants, each unit of central government entitlement has to be paired with some locally sourced funding. These and other devices (such as formula-based grants) often mean that cuts or increases in top-tier agencies' grants have multiplier effects on lower-tier governments' finances and behaviour.

Types of agency
The relative sizes of core, bureau and programme budget levels fluctuate systematically across agencies, creating an important basis for distinguishing theoretically based agency types. In deciding what is to count as an 'agency', it is normally necessary to decompose officially unified organizations into components consisting of the different agency types set out below, which are themselves functionally defined.

Delivery agencies are the classic line bureaucracies of Weberian theory and economic

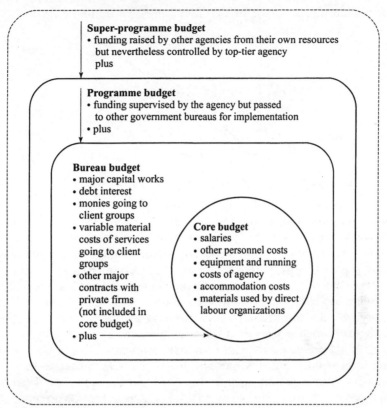

Figure 2 Components of core, bureau, programme and super-programme budgets

analyses. They directly produce outputs or deliver services to citizens or enterprises, using their own personnel to carry out most policy implementation. Employees no doubt often work in complex networks of sub-bureaus. But there is a clear line of authority or responsibility from top bureau officials to those at the grass roots. Delivery agency functions are usually labour-intensive. Consequently they tend to have large budgets in relation to their functions. And their core budgets absorb a high proportion of their bureau and programme budgets, mostly on staffing costs. Delivery agencies tend not to have significant relationships with subordinate public sector bodies, so that there is no super-programme budget increment over and above the programme budget. Picturing the stylized inter-relationships between types of budgets as in Figure 3, both the core budget and the bureau budget rise steadily with programme budget increases, with the CB absorbing the great preponderance of the PB. A good example of a delivery agency in the US federal government is the health services wing of the Department of Veterans' Affairs, which employs 200,000 staff, and spends 91 per cent of its $10 billion budget (in 1988) on its own operations. A smaller-scale example is the National Parks Service (in the Department of the Interior) which employs 16,500 staff, and spends 83 per cent of its $1 billion budget on running costs.

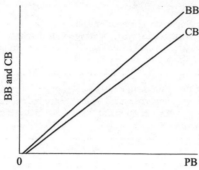

Figure 3 How budgets change in delivery and regulatory agencies

Regulatory agencies have the same CB/BB and BB/PB curves as delivery agencies, but much smaller budgets. Regulatory agencies' key tasks are to limit or control the behaviour of individuals, enterprises or other bodies, using licensing systems, reporting controls, performance standards or some similar system. All these devices externalize many of the costs onto the people being regulated, so regulatory agencies appear relatively cheap to run in tax-funding or public expenditure terms. Because regulatory agencies are primarily paper-moving and inspecting organizations, their core budgets absorb a high proportion of their bureau and programme budgets. However, if subsidies are used as secondary elements to back up regulations, the bureau budget may differ somewhat from the CB. Because they externalize compliance costs, regulatory agencies employ far fewer staff than delivery agencies, and their programme budgets are much smaller. Again, there is no super-programme budget increment. A good US example is the Food Safety and Inspection Service (in the Department of Agriculture) which employs just over 9,000 staff, and spends 87 per cent of its $390 million budget (in 1988) on administrative costs.

Transfer agencies handle payments of some form of subsidy or entitlement by government to private individuals or firms. They are above all money-moving organizations. Since subsidy payments are easily systematized within centrally administered administrations, all national governments are likely to have at least one transfer agency with a large staff. None the less the administration costs of transfer payments are small in relation to the subsidies paid out, so that the core budget should absorb a very low proportion of the bureau budget. Transfer agencies do not usually pass on much money to other public sector bodies, unless a decentralized implementing tier is required for a particular benefit. (If such intermediating bodies are used very extensively to carry out direct service implementation, then the top-tier bureau will be reclassified in my schema as a control agency – see below.) So the bureau budget usually absorbs almost all of a transfer agency's programme budget. The inter-relationship of the core, bureau and programme budgets to be expected on theoretical grounds is shown in Figure 4. Here, unlike delivery or regulatory agencies, the core budget does not keep on expanding with the programme budget. Once a basic administrative apparatus is in place, sizeable BB and PB increases may have no impact

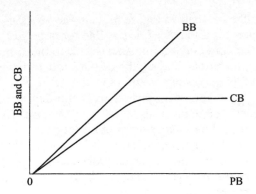

Figure 4 How budgets change in transfer and contract agencies

on running costs. For example, an agency paying out public pensions could simply inscribe larger values on the cheques it mails to the elderly, without its core budget changing at all. The benefits wing of the US Department of Veterans' Affairs is a good example, employing nearly 19,000 staff, with administrative costs of $840 million, which none the less amount to only 4 per cent of its programme budget of nearly $20 billion (in 1988).

Contracts agencies are concerned with developing service specifications or capital projects for tendering, and then letting contracts to private sector firms (or to commercially run public sector organizations, such as public corporations). Contracts agencies' staff work on research and development into projects, drawing up equipment or service specifications, liaising with companies, contract management and compliance, etc. The actual implementation of the projects or services, the ordering of plant and materials, the employment of most of the staff needed and the production of physical outputs are all carried out by contractors. Consequently, contracts agencies' core budgets typically absorb only a modest share of their bureau budget (following the pattern of Figure 4), although considerably more than would be the case for transfer agencies. A typical CB/PB ratio is 20–30 per cent. Bureau budgets, of course, absorb almost all of contracts agencies' programme budgets, and there is again no super-programme budget increment. The US space agency NASA is a good example. Its 22,000 staff carry out research and development and prepare contracts for space projects, at a cost of $2.2 billion, just over a fifth of the agency's $10 billion programme budget, the remainder going in contracts to private firms.

Control agencies are the last of the basic agency types. Their primary task is to channel funding to other public sector bureaus in the form of grants or inter-governmental transfers, and to supervise how these other state organizations spend the money and implement policy. Again, the administrative costs involved comprise only a small fraction of the sums transferred, but this time the bureau budget is also only a minor part of the programme budget. Because they often supervise sub-national governments or bureaus, control agencies' super-programme budgets can show large-scale increases over programme budget levels. The interrelationship of control agency budgets is shown schematically in Figure 5. As in the previous diagram, once a basic organizational apparatus is in place it is possible for large PB increases to take place without affecting the core budget. But since grants to other public sector bodies are also excluded from the bureau budget, the BB line, too, remains flat. Finally, a super-programme budget line growing faster than the 45 degree angle is sketched in, indicating that in some countries the provision of central funding confers leverage over subordinate agencies' spending from all sources. A good American example of a control agency (but with no super-programme budget) is the Federal Highways Administration (in the Department of Transport), which employs just 3,400 staff, at a cost of $194 million, but pays out grants and subsidies for national highways totalling $13 billion, chiefly to the state governments. The FHA's core budget absorbs just 1.5 per cent of its programme budget.

In addition to these basic types, some additional categories need to be included to achieve comprehensive coverage. *Taxing agencies* raise government finances. They closely resemble regulatory agencies in externalizing administrative costs onto individuals, enterprises or other bureaus, and in being labour-intensive, paper-moving organizations. Their administration costs tend to be small in relation to the yield of taxes gathered. However, taxing agencies are much larger in staffing and core budget terms for a number of reasons. In Western Europe, governments have used fewer and more general taxes, such as simplified income taxes or value-added tax, concentrating personnel into one or two major taxing organizations (Rose and Karran 1988; Rose 1981: 94–127). In all liberal democracies subsidy systems have been extensively integrated into the tax collection apparatus, with tax expenditures seen as a politically acceptable substitute for public spending in areas such as home ownership, occupational pensions, company cars or private health insurance. So taxing agencies have gained a stake in many different policy areas. In the US federal government the Internal Revenue Service employs 113,000 staff and has a programme budget of $9.5 billion (in 1988), of which some $5 billion is in the core budget (virtually all the rest is repayment of over-collected taxes).

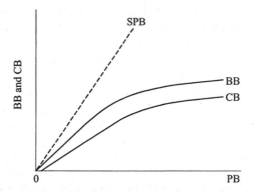

Figure 5 How budgets change in control agencies

Trading agencies were defined for the UK central government analysis as full governmental bodies (that is, excluding public corporations with their own inter-mediating board from the scope of the central state). In other contexts a broader definition might be more appropriate. These agencies operate directly in economic markets in a fully or quasi-commercial mode, and when they deliver service to other public sector bodies they do so on a full recharging basis. Trading agencies normally do a single job, without other policy responsibilities. Good US examples are the various Power Marketing Administrations (in the Department of Energy) which distribute electricity generated from government-built hydro-electric schemes to utilities and other customers in the south-west United States.

Servicing agencies are very similar in function, providing services or facilities to other government bodies, sometimes on a recharged basis but with no private sector customers, or else on a non-priced basis where their outputs are seen as collective benefits for a set of agencies or a whole tier of government. The General Services Agency which manages land acquisitions and property for the US federal government is an example.

[A section on 'Agency types: empirical evidence' has been omitted here.]

The conditions for budget-maximizing

Whether officials want to maximize their budgets can vary in three main ways: depending on their rank and the type of budget; on the type of agency involved; and on variations over time. The last part of the section sums up the arguments about variations by showing how bureaucrats' optimal programme budget levels are deter-mined.

Variations with type of budget

The personal utilities of bureau members are unlikely to be equally involved in the expansion of different elements of the overall budget. Table 1 shows a rough-and-ready list of the reasons why public choice writers have seen budget-maximization as improving bureaucrats' welfare. The first section of this chapter strongly suggested that the salience of different utility considerations will vary considerably for top, middle and low-rank bureaucrats.

The most basic individual utility gains from budget increases, and those which are most important for bottom- and middle-ranking officials, are all associated with the core budget. By contrast, the more diffuse utility gains from budgetary expansion, and those which are most important for top-ranking officials, are primarily linked to the bureau budget. In this group of pay-offs only facilitating non-conflictual management of the bureau can be regarded as associated primarily with the core budget. And only an agency's patronage power is positively and directly associated with the expansion of the programme budget. An enlarged programme budget allows top managers to build up slack resources, which can be deployed to cope with sudden crises or calls for action. But since most of the programme budget may have to be passed on to other agencies,

Table 1 Welfare gains for bureaucrats from budget-maximization

Type of welfare gain	Associated budget	Salience for ranks		
		Bottom	Middle	Top
Improving job security	CB	++	+	0
Expanding career prospects	CB	+	++	0
Increased demand for skills and labour	CB	+	++	0
Triggering upward regrading	CB	0	++	+
Reducing conflict in bureau management	CB	0	+	++
Boosting bureau prestige	BB	0	+	++
Improved relations with clients or contractors	BB	0	+	++
'Slack' creation to cope in crises	BB/PB	0	+	++
Increased patronage powers	PB	0	0	++

Notes: ++ = high salience;   + = medium salience;
              0 = low salience;   CB = core budget;
              BB = bureau budget; PB = programme budget.

top officials gain maximum flexibility from retaining any slack in the bureau budget under their own direct control.

Turning to the costs of advocating budgetary expansion (note that these are not the drawbacks of budgetary growth itself, but of advocating it), an important asymmetry becomes apparent. While the benefits of budgetary expansion are associated mainly with the core budget or the bureau budget, the costs of advocacy (in terms of time spent, effort and resources required, increased scrutiny by the sponsor and the public, and level of external criticism received) are all likely to be closely associated with the programme budget. It is on programme budget performance that sponsor bodies and citizens in general base their judgements about the overall funding levels appropriate in particular policy areas. Within a given level of environmental hostility, a rise in that part of an agency's programme budget flowing outside the agency tends to squeeze its chances of achieving core budget increases. Similarly, both core and bureau budget increases will be more difficult if funds flow to expanding subordinate public sector bureaus.

Variations with type of agency
To the extent that rational bureaucrats are primarily concerned to maximize their core budget and perhaps their bureau budget, this incentive will be strongest in organizations where there is a close relationship between core, bureau and programme budgets. Delivery agencies are the largest budget organizations which fit this pattern, and here the welfare of both senior and lower-ranking officials seems to be the most closely tied to programme budget increases. The same pattern of CB/BB/PB ratios holds for regulatory agencies; but they are much smaller bodies and officials may make utility gains by externalizing costs as well as pushing up budgets. Taxing agencies are large and spend most of their money on their own operations. Budget-maximizing pressures may also be present here, especially where revenue yields are high *vis-à-vis*

administrative costs – although environmental hostility (and hence scrutiny by critics in the legislature) is also high in most Western countries. Trading and service agencies also have core, bureau and programme budgets which are similar. However, market opportunities and competitive pressures (from other suppliers, or from other goods) normally inhibit trading agencies' expansion, together with requirements to break even or make a given financial return. Servicing agencies are fairly small and their growth is constrained because demand for their services depends on other agencies.

In some kinds of contracts and transfer agencies, self-interested senior officials may also have a strong incentive to maximize their bureau budgets. These agencies' core budgets account for only a fraction of the programme budget, so that lower-level staffs have little reason to seek PB expansion. However, senior managers may be able to derive large welfare gains from pushing up the bureau budget (here almost identical with the PB), so long as certain conditions are met. These include:

- the scale of single decisions about contracts or transfers must be large;
- final decisions about the allocation of funding must be one-off and discretionary in character, and made at top levels – rather than routinized, rule-bound, or formula-based, and made at grass roots level;
- the recipients of contracts or transfers must be a relatively few, large organizations – such as big corporations or meso-corporatist interest groupings or lobbies;
- these recipients must be able to organize a flowback of benefits in return for officials' exercising patronage on their behalf.

For example, officials in procurement agencies like the Pentagon or NASA have strong reasons to maximize their bureau budgets, since defence and other contracts often confer considerable patronage potential. There are many opportunities for corporations involved in tendering to organize substantial reciprocal benefits for official contacts who are helpful: benefits such as side deals which help win promotion, or yield lucrative opportunities for what the French call *pantouflage*; career moves into the corporate sector for the still vigorous managers; or post-retirement directorships for older individuals. Where transfer agencies are dealing with very well-organized corporate 'clients', such as the powerful farmers' organizations and food-manufacturing interests in most liberal democracies, the same sort of incentives apply for top officials. In these circumstances, it could be rational for bureaucrats to push up bureau budgets, even though the extra monies involved mainly flow outside the agency in question.

However, for all control agencies, and for the remaining contracts and transfer agencies dealing with multiple, fragmented 'clients' (for example, small firms in a highly competitive industry, or recipients of state welfare benefits), no such incentives apply. These agencies' core budgets are only a small fraction of the programme budget, and no significant flowback of benefits will follow for senior officials if the bureau or programme budgets are inflated. For example, the Department of Education in the US federal government and the Department of Education and Science in Britain both spend less than 2 per cent of the total budget they control on their own activities. Hence it is highly unlikely in public choice terms that self-interested officials would constantly seek programme budget increases. No rational actor in policy-level ranks would seem to have much reason to push for increases in funding (still less Niskanen's oversupply levels of funding), when the monies concerned are almost all passed on to low-status or disorganized private sector recipients, or are channelled to other public sector agencies. To take another example, why should policy-level staff at a welfare agency want to push up payments to the unemployed or to old-age pensioners? Rational managers in top-tier agencies have even less reason to care about whether the super-programme budget spent by lower-tier agencies in their policy area increases or declines. To worry about such totals, central officials would have to make a fetish out of a particular budgetary aggregate, or be mission-committed, or be afflicted by some form of altruism – all motivations which need to be excluded from any useful public choice model. Indeed, for officials in these types of agency, programme or bureau budget increases may be a liability. Since costs attach to the programme budget, but benefits to the core or bureau budgets, overall funding boosts can substantially raise environmental hostility while carrying no significant utility gains for top managers. Control agencies in particular may become even more dependent upon subordinate agencies' performance if programme budgets grow.

Variations over time
So far I have assumed that the relationship between core, bureau and programme budgets is fairly constant, after an initial phase of bureau-consolidating growth. But for any substantial agency there may be a limit beyond which it cannot expand without becoming too unwieldy or unmanageable. Common constraints include:

- the funnelling of management into political-administrative bottlenecks, especially representative institutions with finite capabilities and size;
- the spreading of top management and political attention over too wide an area, and too thinly;
- the accumulation of inertia in very large departments.

For example, in British central government problems of limited ministerial time, finite spans of control and giganticism have repeatedly led to the splitting of departments and the failure of experiments such as 'super-ministries' in the post-war period (Pollitt 1983; Kellner and Crowther-Hunt 1980: 174–238).

A large agency coming up against such constraints and pushing for further growth can trigger a period in which it loses some of its existing functions to other (rival) agencies. At the central government level, such rivals could be other departments which acquire slices of territory, or they could be quasi-government agencies set up to hive-off less salient functions. Either threat could produce a zig-zag growth curve for the core and bureau budgets graphed against the programme budget (Figure 6). With this sort of curve, rational budget-maximizing officials in senior positions should not advocate programme budget increases when the bureau's growth has brought it within the danger area – shaded in Figure 6. To do so could produce a quantum reduction in

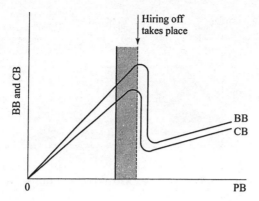

Figure 6 Zig-zag bureau budget curves

the core and bureau budgets to which their utilities are most linked. Zig-zag core and bureau budget curves are most likely to occur in delivery agencies, plus those contracts, transfer and taxing agencies with large staffs.

The relationship between core, bureau and programme budgets also raises some interesting issues when contracts or control agencies enter a period of *declining budgets*. Dwindling programme budgets can be associated with a period of rising core and bureau budgets as the control agency re-centralizes powers or functions from subordinate agencies, or as the contract agency brings back in-house functions it has previously sent to outside professionals (Figure 7). After a while, the re-centralization phase might be followed by cutbacks striking home within the central department itself. But there may well be extensive periods when officials in contract or control agencies welcome cutbacks in the programme budget as a means of increasing or stabilizing their bureau budgets, to which their utilities are linked. For example, Dunleavy (1981) demonstrates that in the mid-1960s, at the height of a public housing boom managed by British local authorities, council architects actually designed only half of the dwellings involved, private architects 30 per cent and construction corporation architects 20 per cent. By 1973, when the level of public housing starts was half its previous size, the local authority architects' share had increased to 75 per cent. What this meant for one large city, Birmingham, was that in the mid-1960s its architects designed virtually no housing at all – their role was limited solely to contract drafting and supervision, plus minor landscape architecture. Ten years later the council architects had regained full design control of most of their housing output. This kind of effect will exist wherever public agency staffing does not expand fully to accommodate workloads in 'boom' periods, so that the character of agencies' work tasks stretches to absorb the variation – even in delivery agencies which use consultants or contractors. Staff utilities at all levels in the agency may rise quite sharply in periods of limited budgetary reductions when workloads are reinternalized.

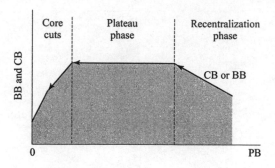

Figure 7 How recentralization cutbacks can expand core or bureau budgets

Bureaucrats' optimal budget levels

Thus there are multiple reasons why self-interested officials vary greatly in the extent to which they push up expenditures, so that Niskanen's (1971) picture of bureaucrats as open-ended budget-maximizers is highly unlikely to be accurate. Summing up the previous discussion, there are two ways of picturing how senior officials make budget decisions. The first is a diagram of the influences upon an individual bureaucrat analogous to those already given for potential interest group members and for voters (Figure 8). An obvious difference from earlier diagrams is the importance of rank inside bureaucracies. Rank conditions the undiscounted benefits that officials receive from programme budget increments, their individual influence assessments and their costs of advocating budgetary growth. In addition the type of agency determines what stake senior officials have in programme budget increases, and to a lesser degree the advocacy costs which they confront. Both these influences have the effect of endogenizing senior bureaucrats' preferences, so that the context in which they are operating conditions what it is they want. Lastly, no private benefits from budget-maximization are shown – officials must pursue individual strategies to reap private benefits, not an inherently collective effort to push up programme budgets.

A second key method of representing bureaucrats' decisions is a demand-and-supply model of the conditions in which bureaucrats seek further budget increments. The demand curve for advocacy of budget increases shows how officials' discounted marginal utilities (DMU) change with programme budget increments; and the supply curve shows how advocacy costs change as the PB goes up. The point where these curves intersect indicates bureaucrats' optimal level of programme budget, which is internally determined (Figure 9).

Discounted marginal utility curves are influenced mainly by: first, the probability of influence – top bureaucrats' curves are quite far away from the origin while bottom bureaucrats' curves are much closer in and shallower; and second, the relationship between core, bureau and programme budgets – top bureaucrats in delivery, contract and regulatory agencies have fairly elastic slopes, but those in control and transfer agencies have steeply declining curves.

Marginal advocacy cost curves are influenced mainly by: first, the size of the existing

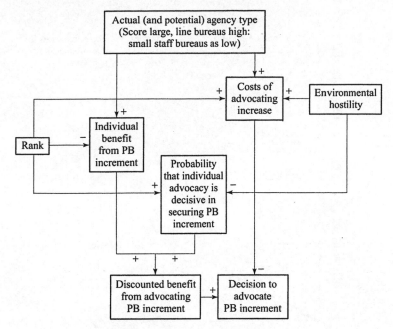

Figure 8 Influences on whether bureaucrats budget-maximize

PB, set against the sorts of functions which the agency is carrying out, since with constant functions successive budgetary increments become progressively more costly to obtain; second, external hostility to an agency getting a PB increment – at the point where an agency is unlikely to get a further increase however hard it pushes, the cost curve becomes vertical (for top bureaucrats especially); third, changes in external hostility – if it increases or decreases then the cost curve shifts up to the right or down to the left respectively; fourth, alternative rates of return – since marginal advocacy costs are net costs, they take account of other welfare-boosting options, which are extensive for top bureaucrats; and fifth, rank – cost curves are higher and rise more steeply the further up the rank hierarchy officials are located.

In these graphs bureaucrats advocate expansion in the agency's activities if its current programme budget is to the left of their equilibrium PB position. But if the bureau's current position is to the right of the equilibrium, officials do nothing, switching attention instead to other individual or collective strategies for improving their welfare. Note that the alternative to budget maximization is inaction, not advocacy of budgetary reductions.

Because of the varying shapes of the discounted marginal utility and marginal cost curves, changes in the external environment have different impacts upon bureaucratic behaviour. For senior bureaucrats in delivery, contract or regulatory agencies a shift of cost curves to the left triggers large decreases in the equilibrium level of PB, since increased external hostility produces sharp adjustments of the cost curve back along a

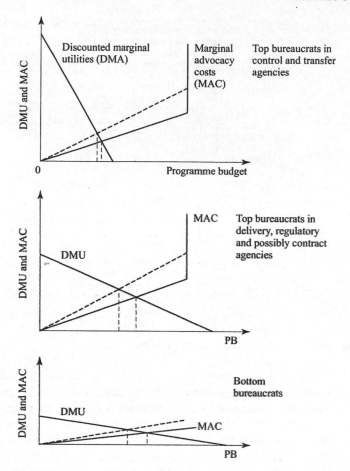

Figure 9 The choice problem for bureaucrats in deciding whether to advocate budgetary increases

utility curve that slopes fairly gently. But in control or transfer agencies at the same rank a large-scale adjustment in the marginal advocacy cost curve may not affect bureaucratic behaviour much because their DMU curve is already so inelastic. For bottom bureaucrats the same external shifts which manifest themselves as marked changes in the top bureaucrats' cost curves will produce only small increases in the shallow slope of cost curves. But since their discounted utility curves typically are also shallow, even a small shift may produce a sharp fall in their equilibrium PB level.

Bureaucrats' motivations and bureau-shaping strategies

The bureaucratic empire-builder is not an off-beat theoretical construct, but also an important everyday image of government officials, especially in the United States (Lineberry 1989: ch. 15; Kaufman 1981). To define an alternative model of what bureaucrats want therefore entails uncovering a more plausible set of official objectives, one which can explain observed behaviour with more precision or over a wider range of situations than the budget-maximization hypothesis. This section develops such an account, the bureau-shaping model. I explore bureaucrats' motivations; the collective strategies which facilitate bureau-shaping; and how differently situated officials choose between bureau-shaping or budget-maximizing strategies.

Motives for bureau-shaping

Welfare-maximizing officials in policy-making ranks are primarily concerned to improve their welfare by providing themselves with congenial work and a valued work environment for three main reasons. First, there is a general presumption in the existing public choice literature, most organization theory and in the first section of this chapter, that senior managers put less stress than lower-ranking bureau members on the pecuniary or near-pecuniary components of their utility function (such as income, job security, or perks). Instead, higher-ranked bureaucrats place more emphasis upon non-pecuniary utilities: such as status, prestige, patronage and influence, and most especially the interest and importance of their work tasks (Halperin 1974; Kingdon 1984).

Second, public service employment systems are designed to place severe limits on officials' ability to increase their pecuniary utilities by either individual or collective action, whether budget-maximization strategies or the discretionary ability to divert resources to personal welfare-boosting. Salaries are constrained within restrictive and standardized upper salary ceilings. In Sweden, West Germany and the United Kingdom the ratio between top civil service salaries and the wages of bottom-rank government employees consistently declined from 1950 to 1980, when the three countries' figures were 6.0, 4.3 and 5.5 respectively (Peters 1989: 41–4). Hence there is no public sector counterpart to the very large and individualized 'prizes' paid out as salaries to key executives in private corporations. Similarly, blanket limits on staff numbers, centralized audit systems, and lifetime career paths to senior positions, are all common features of public service employment systems which tend to reduce officials' ability to pursue their individual interests in pecuniary terms. In addition, public sector perks are strictly controlled, with very few company cars or fringe benefits, strict rules against officials having additional employment or business activities, standardized provision of accommodation and equipment, and scarce support of secretarial staff rationed out by across-the-board formulae. In most public administration systems personnel, accommodation, finance and information technology are centrally administered to minimize the creation of slack by individual managers. Only recently have such patterns begun to be eroded by 'cost centre' budgeting imported from the private sector.

Compared with their counterparts in private companies, senior government officials are likely to find that budget-maximization is a remarkably frustrating activity in terms of direct near-pecuniary utility pay-offs. The distinctive traits of public service systems are designed to displace senior officials' energies and efforts into work and policy-related aspects of their careers rather than into feathering personal nests. Senior officials' pay and conditions are normally maintained at levels sufficient to preserve their pre-existing position in the occupational class structure. But they are also calculated to sift out from promotion people anxious to maximize pecuniary utilities. Thus a realistic individual-level model of why people enter career paths leading to senior positions in public agencies, or of why people temporarily transfer into such positions from the private sector in the United States, is likely to emphasize non-pecuniary utilities related to the intrinsic characteristics of the work involved.

Third, work-related utilities seem to be a major continuing influence on the ways in which officials behave within the public sector. Without positing an other-regarding or ideological commitment by officials to their bureau or its mission, a good deal of evidence suggests that self-interested officials have strong preferences about the kind of work they want to do, and the kind of agency they want to work in. Table 2 gives a list of the most common pro and anti values cited in the administrative sociology literature, and which can plausibly be ascribed to self-regarding bureaucrats pursuing their own welfare.

Clearly, there is always a pecuniary parameter in bureaucrats' concerns – a level of income and of near-money benefits which they will seek to achieve as a condition of the pursuit of other utilities. But this is likely to be a constraint which is surmounted relatively easily and thereafter is not very influential positively or negatively in structuring individual behaviour, especially when officials are making policy decisions. Officials are certainly not likely to be trying to maximize pecuniary elements of their utilities. There will be sharp differences in the perceived welfare of officials who share

Table 2 Positive and negative values ascribable to bureaucrats

Positively valued	Negatively valued
Staff functions	*Line functions*
• individually innovative work	• routine work
• longer time horizons	• short-time horizons
• broad scope of concerns	• narrow scope of concerns
• developmental rhythm	• repetitive rhythm
• high level of managerial discretion	• low level of managerial discretion
• low level of public visibility	• high level of grass roots/public visibility
Collegial atmosphere	*Corporate atmosphere*
• small-sized work unit	• large-sized work units
• restricted hierarchy and predominance of elite personnel	• extended hierarchy and predominance of non-elite personnel
• co-operative work patterns	• work patterns characterized by coercion and resistance
• congenial personal relations	• conflictual personal relations
Central location	*Peripheral location*
• proximate to the political power centres	• remote from political contacts
• metropolitan (capital city location)	• provincial location
• conferring high-status social contacts	• remote from high-status contacts

comparable salaries but are located in different agencies and positions. Rational officials want to work in small, elite, collegial bureaus close to political power centres. They do not want to head up heavily staffed, large budget but routine, conflictual and low-status agencies.

Collective strategies for bureau-shaping

If officials have the values posited in Table 2, they can most effectively pursue these objectives at an individual level, searching for career or promotion paths which lead them to an appropriate rank in a suitable sort of agency – just as I argued in the first section that officials pursuing pecuniary utilities can best do so using individual means, rather than relying on collective budget increments.

None the less, once individual opportunities are exhausted or show diminishing returns, or in addition to them, are there collective strategies (akin to budget-maximization) by which bureaucrats can foster their work-related utilities? And can these strategies be continuously developed – as with budget-maximization because of the annual budgetary cycle? I argue that rational bureaucrats oriented primarily to work-related utilities pursue a *bureau-shaping strategy* designed to bring their bureau into a progressively closer approximation to 'staff' (rather than 'line') functions, a collegial atmosphere and a central location. Essentially, these pro-values imply that national-level delivery agencies in particular become transformed over time into control, transfer or contracts agencies. Policy-level officials maximize this objective within a continuous bureau budget constraint, but one which varies systematically with the character and size of the agency. At each stage of the process, senior officials seek to achieve a satisfactory level of budget, but this level in turn is set by their previous success in restructuring the bureau's tasks and organization. As a reshaped bureau takes on more of the small, central, elite character – becomes more of a control, transfer or contracts agency – then the budget constraint is eased. Senior officials' utilities become progressively unlinked from dependence on a high absolute level of programme or bureau budget.

There are five key means of pursuing bureau-shaping strategies.

1. *Major internal reorganizations.* Changes in structure can regularly increase the degree to which an agency conforms with the elite policy-making ideal. Expansion is concentrated at the policy-making level, while existing routine functions are shunted into well-defined enclaves which need to be involved as little as possible with senior management. Often geographical separation is a key means of achieving this result, especially where it saves costs or fits with regional policy objectives. Other current functions inconsistent with the bureau's ideal image may be 'hived-in' to separately designated departmental agencies or accountable management units.

2. *Transformation of internal work practices.* Policy-level officials want to increase the interest of their work tasks, lengthen the time horizons used in decision-making and extend their discretionary ability to control policy. A shift towards more sophisticated management and policy analysis systems insulates the agency from criticism by rival bureaus, external partners or the sponsor body. It also tends to change

the balance of bureau personnel towards more high-level, skilled or professional staffs, improving existing bureau members' status and work content, as well as their career advancement prospects.

If personnel ceilings are being enforced then the automation or computerization of clerical tasks can free manpower quotas to be redeployed at policy-making levels (for instance, by hiring in more policy analysts). In many public service systems restrictive personnel limits are placed on whole groups of agencies by political fiat. Congress has long imposed rigid manpower ceilings on the US federal government departments. In Britain the incoming Conservative government froze civil service manpower in 1979, and then programmed manpower targets reduced by 15 per cent over five years (Fry 1986: 102; Dunsire and Hood 1989: 17–19). Where such constraints apply, a pre-condition for regrading changes may be the contracting out, reduction, computerization or automation of routine work tasks so that the staffing allocations involved can be redeployed in ways which confer more fruitful pay-offs for senior officials. Bureau policy staffs also tend to promote more accountable management for routine enclave areas or lower-level staffs, but emphasize collegial decision-making, 'team production' methods and hence diffused responsibility amongst policy-rank officials.

3. *Redefinition of relationships with external 'partners'.* Where agencies deal extensively with external organizations – such as subordinate public agencies, contractors, regulatees or client interest group – these relationships can be readjusted so as to cut down on routine workloads while maximizing the agency's policy control. Policy-level officials promote hands-off, autopilot controls for run-of-the-mill matters but increased discretionary involvement in policy-relevant issues – often implying a shift towards a more corporatist style of relationship (Cawson 1982; 1985). The bureau also tries to minimize its dependence upon external organizations, as the inter-organizational literature argues (Hanf and Scharpf 1978). A high-density managerial or control workload can be a liability for a bureau if external or subordinate organizations refuse to co-operate. Replacing such arrangements with a more robust and insulating control apparatus is usually a priority. Bureaus also seek to extend the scope of their patronage of external bodies, but only where this can be achieved in line with their preferred image.

4. *Competition with other bureaus.* Bureaus always defend the scope of responsibilities involved in their existing programme budget, although they may be only weakly committed to defending given programme budget levels. Agencies are by no means simple-minded imperialists. They compete with rival bureaus at the same tier of government for programme tasks and policy areas which fit in with their ideal bureau form (especially those tasks with a high proportion of policy-level staff, which command useful resources and confer prestige or influence, and which tend to increase the average level of managerial discretion within the bureau). But bureaus may want to export troublesome and costly low-grade tasks to rivals, especially where doing so carries no major implications for a reduced programme budget.

5. *Load-shedding, hiving-off and contracting out.* By far the most radical possibilities for top-tier agencies to reshape their functions arise from their ability to export responsibility for functions inconsistent with senior officials' agency-type ideal. Especially in

unitary states, central government departments may simply be able to legislate the transfer of functions to sub-central governments, as the UK Department of Health and Social Security did in 1985, transferring a complex and troublesome system of implementing housing benefits administration to local governments. Alternatively, routine or non-core bureau functions can be hived-off to closely supervised quasi-government agencies (QGAs). Both load-shedding to subordinate governments and hiving-off to QGAs preserve bureaus' programme budget levels, but reduce core and bureau budgets. Finally, ancillary functions especially can be contracted out to private firms or made subject to competitive tendering, producing radical reductions in the personnel absorbed on routine functions. Core budgets fall, but the contracted services remain within the agency's bureau budget.

Individual officials in policy ranks can contribute to bureau-shaping strategies just as easily and frequently as they can push up budgets. Like budget-maximization, the pursuit of a bureau-shaping strategy requires collective action, especially by top- (and perhaps also, middle-) ranking officials. But bureau-shaping has a much more important and visible connection with these officials' welfare than does generalized budgetary expansion *per se*. Maximizing a bureau's conformity to an ideal, high-status organizational pattern, within a budget constraint contingent on the existing bureau configuration, provides a powerful explanation of a wide range of observed administrative behaviour. Bureau-shaping activity appears to be every bit as commonplace and as frequently pointed out by scholars of administrative behaviour as are tendencies to budget-maximization.

Choosing between bureau-shaping and budget-maximization
The graphs of discounted marginal utilities and advocacy costs developed above can be used to diagram the rival ways in which budget-maximizing and bureau-shaping strategies expand bureaucrats' welfare. Niskanen's model suggests that oversupplying bureaucrats are always trying to push outwards against a restrictive external constraint imposed by the legislature or other sponsor body (Figure 10a). Hence the DMU curve often intersects the MAC curve in its vertical section at point A, because of the requirement that the bureau be at least neutral in its impact on social welfare. However, officials realize that if the vertical section of the MAC curve could be pushed further outwards, a new equilibrium at point B would be feasible.

Figure 10a implies that no long-term budgetary expansion can take place, unless officials are in a position to change the shape of the MAC curve. In fact, new right accounts stress that bureaucrats invest in reorganization because it shifts the DMU curve upwards, as in Figure 10b where DMU_2 and DMU_3 are the curves after successive reorganizations. Even if the MAC curve stays at MAC_1, reorganization can improve officials' welfare, as in the shift from J to R. However, reorganizations also normally enable officials to expand the legislature's tolerance of budget increases, so shifting the vertical section of the MAC curve outwards as shown to MAC_2 and later MAC_3. Agencies will promise that reorganization or work automation will increase efficiency, improve service quality, modernize service standards, or allow them to undertake new tasks with resources freed up by reorganization. Thus the equilibrium

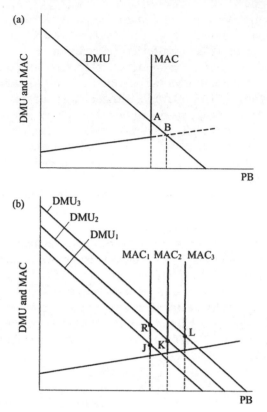

Figure 10 The new right's view of the impacts of reorganization in a line bureau

programme budget levels will continuously expand over time, from J to K and L. On this account, the level of PB which bureaucrats seek can only stabilize when further expansion of the DMU and MAC curves is ruled out by a taxpayers' revolt, constitutional amendment, or accession to power of a new right government (Mitchell 1983).

By contrast, the bureau-shaping model argues that normally equilibrium programme budget levels lie on the sloping section of the MAC curve, because senior officials respond to changes in environmental favourability or hostility in much more sensitive and diffident ways than budget-maximizing accounts assume, and these responses affect the shape and placing of the whole MAC curve, not just its vertical section. In many circumstances, the existing PB level could already be larger than senior officials' optimum, and the agency quiescent. Over the longer term, the bureau-shaping model argues that major internal reorganizations are very unlikely to simply inflate the DMU curve along its existing shape. Far more commonly, the DMU curve changes shape, swinging in a clockwise direction so as to maximize the benefits which senior bureaucrats derive from lower levels of the programme budget, while reducing their dependence on high levels of PB in order to maintain their welfare (Figure 11).

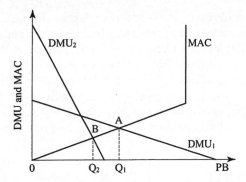

Figure 11 The bureau-shaping model's view of the impacts of reorganization in a line bureau

Numerous strategies discussed above allow top bureaucrats directly to improve their own welfare: for example, by shedding troublesome direct managerial responsibilities and gaining increased staff and time resources for intellectually more attractive tasks such as planning and guidance. All these kinds of change will produce shifts like that from DMU_1, to DMU_2 shown here. So long as the marginal cost curve cuts these utility curves in their lower reaches as shown, then the equilibrium budget level declines from Q_1 to Q_2. Only if the marginal cost curve cuts the DMU curves in their upper reaches (i.e. if the external constraints on budgetary expansion are anyway exceptionally restrictive) will the equilibrium programme budget position move outwards if the DMU curves rotate. As in the earlier example, if the DMU and marginal advocacy cost curves intersect in the vertical section of the advocacy costs curve the equilibrium PB position is static.

A particularly interesting example of rotating DMU curves occurs where a delivery agency has been progressively transformed into a control agency, transfer agency or contracts agency. This change shifts the DMU radically clockwise, at the same time changing its shape from an elastic to an inelastic curve. Other things being equal, the optimum programme budget level for top bureaucrats in the new small agency is lower than that advocated while they still had direct line responsibilities. It should be clear that a prerequisite for an internal reorganization of this kind is that the area under the DMU curve but above the advocacy costs curve should be greater with a control/transfer/contract agency configuration than under delivery agency arrangements – as in the curves diagrammed here.

Conclusion

Public choice models of bureaucracy which predict open-ended budget-maximization are badly flawed internally. Bureaucrats typically do not embark on collective action modes of improving their welfare unless they have exhausted individual welfare-boosting strategies. If they do choose to try to increase budgets, rational officials usually confront familiar collective action problems. In particular, although lower-ranking bureaucrats have most to gain from budgetary expansion, they will know that the attainment of increments is almost completely insensitive to their individual advocacy, so that even though their advocacy costs are small, campaigning for budgetary expansion is unlikely to advance their individual utility. Higher-ranking officials are aware that the attainment of budgetary growth will be much more sensitive to their personal contribution, but typically they have much less to gain from increments and confront substantial advocacy costs in seeking to push through increases in the agency's base budget.

Budget-maximization is anyway an ambiguous concept, since utility pay-offs are primarily associated with growth in the agency's core or bureau budgets, while advocacy costs are associated with the programme budget. In addition, there are major differences between agency types in the extent to which officials associate their welfare with the growth of the programme budget. In delivery agencies (the classic line bureaucracies dwelt on in public choice models) the connection is close and positive. But in control agencies it is remote and variable. Top bureaucrats' decisions about budget-maximizing can be modelled in terms of discounted marginal utilities and marginal advocacy costs, whose interaction identifies an optimal budget position which is an equilibrium point.

The characteristics of public service employment systems make it likely that the welfare of higher-ranking bureaucrats is closely bound up with the intrinsic characteristics of their work, rather than near-pecuniary utilities. Rational bureaucrats therefore concentrate on developing bureau-shaping strategies designed to bring their agency into line with an ideal configuration conferring high status and agreeable work tasks, within a budgetary constraint contingent on the existing and potential shape of the agency's activities. Changes in the ways in which agencies are organized may shift this equilibrium point outwards over time – if the change involves simply reorganizing the way in which an agency carries out a fixed role. Alternatively, organizational changes can cause the equilibrium PB point to become smaller – if the change involves reshaping an established delivery agency by hiving-off line functions so that it becomes a central control, transfer or contracts agency.

References

Axelrod, R. (1984) *The Evolution of Co-operation*, New York: Basic Books.

Bendor, J. and Moe, T. (1985) 'An adaptive model of bureaucratic politics', *American Political Science Review* 79, 3, pp. 755–74.

Bennett, J. T. and Johnson, M. H. (1980) *The Political Economy of Federal Government Growth, 1959–1978*, College Station, TX: A&M University Press.

Cawson, A. (1982) *Corporatism and Social Policy*, London: Heinemann.

Cawson, A. (ed.) (1985) *Organized Interests and the State: Studies in meso-corporatism*, London: Sage.

Crouch, C. (1982) *Trade Unions: The logic of collective action*, London: Fontana.

Downs, A. (1967) *Inside Bureaucracy*, Boston: Little, Brown.

Dunleavy, P. (1981) *The Politics of Mass Housing in Britain, 1945–75: Corporate power and professional influence in the welfare state*, Oxford: Clarendon Press.

Dunsire, A. and Hood, C. with Huby, M. (1989) *Cutback Management in Public Bureaucracies: Popular theories and observed outcomes in Whitehall*, Cambridge: Cambridge University Press.

Fry, G. (1986) 'Inside Whitehall', in H, Drucker, P. Dunleavy, A. Gamble and G. Peele, *Developments in British Politics 2*, London: Macmillan, pp. 88–106.

Goodin, R. E. (1982) 'Rational politicians in Washington and Whitehall', *Public Administration* 62, 1, pp. 23–41.

Halperin, M. (1974) *Bureaucratic Politics and Foreign Policy*, Washington, DC: Brookings Institution.

Hanf, K. and Scharpf, F. (eds) (1978) *International Policy-making*, London and Beverly Hills: Sage.

Jackson, P. M. (1982) *The Political Economy of Bureaucracy*, Deddington, Oxford: Philip Allan.

Kaufman, H. (1981) 'Fear of bureaucracy: a raging pandemic', *Public Administration Review* 41, 1, pp. 1–9.

Kellner, P. and Crowther-Hunt, Lord (1980) *The Civil Servants: An inquiry into Britain's ruling class*, London: Macmillan.

Kingdon, J. (1984) *Agendas, Alternatives and Public Policies*, Boston: Little, Brown.

Lineberry, R. (1989) *Government in America: People, politics and policy*, Glenview, IL: Scott, Foresman.

Loasby, B. J. (1968) 'The decision-maker in the organization', *Journal of Management Studies* 5, 3, pp. 352–64.

Mitchell, W. C. (1983) 'Fiscal behaviour of the modern fiscal state: public choice perspectives and contributions', in L. Wade (ed.) (1983) pp. 69–122.

Niskanen, W. A. (1971) *Bureaucracy and Representative Government*, Chicago: Aldine-Atherton.

Peters, B. G. (1989) 'The European bureaucrat: the applicability of "Bureaucracy and Representative Government" to non-American settings'. Paper to a conference on 'The Budget-Maximizing Bureaucrat', University of Montreal, Montreal, Quebec, 13–15 April.

Pollitt, C. (1983) *Manipulating the Machine*, London: Allen and Unwin.

Rose, R. (1981) *Understanding Big Government: The programme appoach*, London and Beverly Hills: Sage.

Rose, R. and Karran, T. (1988) *Taxation by Political Inertia: Financing the growth of government*, London: Allen and Unwin.

Thain, C. and Wright, M. (1989) 'Running costs: a new agenda for controlling public spending?' Paper to the UK Political Studies Association Annual Conference, University of Warwick, 4 April.

Wade, L. (ed.) (1983) *Political Economy: Recent views*, Boston: Kluwer-Nijhoff.

Bringing the state back in

Theda Skocpol

The autonomy and capacity of states

States conceived as organizations claiming control over territories and people may formulate and pursue goals that are not simply reflective of the demands or interests of social groups, classes, or society. This is what is usually meant by 'state autonomy'. Unless such independent goal formulation occurs, there is little need to talk about states as important actors. Pursuing matters further, one may then explore the 'capacities' of states to implement official goals, especially over the actual or potential opposition of powerful social groups or in the face of recalcitrant socioeconomic circumstances. What are the determinants of state autonomy and state capacities? Let us sample the arguments of a range of recent studies that address these questions.

States as actors
Several lines of reasoning have been used, singly or in combination, to account for why and how states formulate and pursue their own goals. The linkage of states into transnational structures and into international flows of communication may encourage leading state officials to pursue transformative strategies even in the face of indifference or resistance from politically weighty social forces. Similarly, the basic need of states to maintain control and order may spur state-initiated reforms (as well as simple repression). As for who, exactly, is more likely to act in such circumstances, it seems that organizationally coherent collectivities of state officials, especially collectivities of career officials relatively insulated from ties to currently dominant socioeconomic interests, are likely to launch distinctive new state strategies in times of crisis. Likewise, collectivities of officials may elaborate already established public policies in distinctive ways, acting relatively continuously over long stretches of time.

The extranational orientations of states, the challenges they may face in maintaining domestic order, and the organizational resources that collectivities of state officials may be able to draw on and deploy – all of these features of the state as viewed from a Weberian–Hintzean perspective can help to explain autonomous state action.

From T. Skocpol, 'Bringing the state back in: current research', in P. B. Evans, D. Reuschemeyer and T. Skocpol (eds.), *Bringing the State Back In* (1985), Cambridge: Cambridge University Press, Chapter 1.

In an especially clear-cut way, combinations of these factors figure in Alfred Stepan's and Ellen Kay Trimberger's explanations of what may be considered extreme instances of autonomous state action – historical situations in which strategic elites use military force to take control of an entire national state and then employ bureaucratic means to enforce reformist or revolutionary changes from above.

Stepan's book *The State and Society: Peru in comparative perspective* investigates attempts by state elites in Latin America to install 'inclusionary' or 'exclusionary' corporatist regimes.[1] A key element in Stepan's explanation of such episodes is the formation of a strategically located cadre of officials enjoying great organizational strength inside and through existing state organizations and also enjoying a unified sense of ideological purpose about the possibility and desirability of using state intervention to ensure political order and promote national economic development. For Brazil's 'exclusionary' corporatist coup in 1964 and for Peru's 'inclusionary' corporatist coup in 1968, Stepan stresses the prior socialization of what he calls 'new military professionals.' These were career military officers who, together, passed through training' schools that taught techniques and ideas of national economic planning and counterinsurgency, along with more traditional military skills. Subsequently, such new military professionals installed corporatist regimes in response to perceived crises of political order and of national economic development. The military professionals used state power to stave off or deflect threats to national order from nondominant classes and groups. They also used state power to implement socioeconomic reforms or plans for further national industrialization, something they saw as a basic requisite for improved international standing in the modern world.

Ellen Kay Trimberger's *Revolution from Above* focuses on a set of historical cases – Japan's Meiji restoration, Turkey's Ataturk revolution, Egypt's Nasser revolution, and Peru's 1968 coup – in which 'dynamically autonomous' bureaucrats, including military officials, seized and reorganized state power. Then they used the state to destroy an existing dominant class, a landed upper class or aristocracy, and to reorient national economic development.[2] Like Stepan, Trimberger stresses the formation through prior career interests and socialization of a coherent official elite with a statist and nationalist ideological orientation. She also agrees with Stepan's emphasis on the elite's concern to contain any possible uppheavals from below. Yet, perhaps because she is in fact explaining a more thoroughly transformative version of autonomous state action to reshape society, Trimberger places more stress than Stepan on the role of foreign threats to national autonomy as a precipitant of 'revolution from above.' And she highlights a structural variable that Stepan ignored: the relationship of the state elite to dominant economic classes. As Trimberger puts it, 'A bureaucratic state apparatus, or a segment of it, can be said to be relatively autonomous when those who hold high civil and/or military posts satisfy two conditions: (1) they are not recruited from the dominant landed, commercial, or industrial classes; and (2) they do not form close personal and economic ties with those classes after their elevation to high office.'[3] Trimberger also examines the state elite's relationship to dominant economic classes in order to predict the extensiveness of socioeconomic changes a state may attempt in response to 'a crisis situation – when the existing social, political, and economic order is threatened by external forces and by upheaval from below.'[4] State-initiated authoritarian *reforms* may occur when bureaucratic elites retain ties to existing dominant classes, as, for example, in Prussia in 1806–1814, Russia in the 1860s, and Brazil after 1964. But the more sweeping structural changes that Trimberger labels 'revolution from above,' including the actual dispossession of a dominant class, occur in crisis situations only when bureaucratic state elites are free of ties or alliances with dominant classes.[5] As should be apparent, Trimberger has given the neo-Marxist notion of the relative autonomy of the state new analytical power as a tool for predicting the possible sociopolitical consequences of *various* societal and historical configurations of state and class power.

State autonomy in constitutional polities

Stepan and Trimberger deal in somewhat different, though overlapping, terms with extraordinary instances of state autonomy – instances in which nonconstitutionally ruling officials attempt to use the state as a whole to direct and restructure society and politics. Meanwhile, other scholars have teased out more circumscribed instances of state autonomy in the histories of public policy making in liberal democratic, constitutional polities, such as Britain, Sweden, and the United States.[6] In different forms, the same basic analytical factors – the international orientations of states, their domestic order-keeping functions, and the organizational possibilities for official collectivities to formulate and pursue their own policies – also enter into these analyses.

Hugh Heclo's *Modern Social Politics in Britain and Sweden* provides an intricate comparative-historical account of the long-term development of unemployment insurance and policies of old-age assistance in these two nations.[7] Without being explicitly presented as such, Heclo's book is about autonomous state contributions to social policy making. But the autonomous state actions Heclo highlights are not all acts of coercion or domination; they are, instead, the intellectual activities of civil administrators engaged in diagnosing societal problems and framing policy alternatives to deal with them. As Heclo puts it:

> Governments not only 'power' (or whatever the verb form of that approach might be); they also puzzle. Policy-making is a form of collective puzzlement on society's behalf; it entails both deciding and knowing. The process of making pension, unemployment, and superannuation policies has extended beyond deciding what 'wants' to accommodate, to include problems of knowing who might want something, what is wanted, what should be wanted, and how to turn even the most sweet-tempered general agreement into concrete collective action. This process is political, not because all policy is a by-product of power and conflict but because some men have undertaken to act in the name of others.[8]

According to Heclo's comparative history, civil service administrators in both Britain and Sweden have consistently made more important contributions to social policy development than political parties or interest groups. Socioeconomic conditions, especially crises, have stimulated only sporadic demands from parties and interest groups, argues Heclo. It has been civil servants, drawing on 'administrative resources of information, analysis, and expertise' who have framed the terms of new policy elaborations as 'corrective[s] less to social conditions as such and more to the perceived failings of previous policy' in terms of 'the government bureaucracy's own conception of what it has been doing.'[9] Heclo's evidence also reveals that the auto-nomous bureaucratic shaping of social policy has been greater in Sweden than in Britain, for Sweden's premodern centralized bureaucratic state was, from the start of industrialization and before the full liberalization and democratization of national politics, in a position to take the initiative in diagnosing social problems and proposing universalistic solutions for administering to them.

Heclo says much less than he might about the influences shaping the timing and content of distinctive state initiatives. He does, however, present evidence of the sensitivity of civil administrators to the requisites of maintaining order in the face of dislocations caused by industrial unemployment. He also points to the constant awareness by administrators of foreign precedents and models of social policy. Above all, Heclo demonstrates that collectivities of administrative officials can have pervasive direct and indirect effects on the content and development of major government policies. His work suggests how to locate and analyze autonomous state contributions to policy making, even within constitutional polities nominally directed by legislatures and electoral parties.

Along these lines, it is worth looking briefly at two works that argue for autonomous state contributions to public policy making even in the United States, a polity in which virtually all scholars agree that there is less structural basis for such autonomy than in any other modern liberal capitalist regime. The United States did not inherit a central-ized bureaucratic state from preindustrial and predemocratic times. Moreover, the dispersion of authority through the federal system, the division of sovereignty among branches of the national government, and the close symbiosis between segments of the federal administration and Congressional committees all help to ensure that state power in the twentieth-century United States is fragmented, dispersed, and every-where permeated by organized societal interests. The national government, moreover, lacks such possible underpinnings of strong state power as a prestigious and status-conscious career civil service with predictable access to key executive posts; authori-tative planning agencies; direct executive control over a national central bank; and public ownership of strategic parts of the economy. Given such characteristics of the US government, the concept of state autonomy has not often been used by scholars to explain American policy developments.

Nevertheless, Stephen Krasner in his *Defending the National Interest* does use the concept to explain twentieth-century continuities in the formulation of U.S. foreign policy about issues of international investments in the production and marketing of raw materials.[10] A clever heuristic tactic lies behind Krasner's selection of this 'issue area' for systematic historical investigation: It is an issue area located at the intersection of properly geopolitical state interests and the economic interests of (often) powerful private corporations. Thus, Krasner can ask whether the short-term push and pull of business interests shapes the definition of the U.S. 'national interest' with respect to raw materials production abroad or whether an autonomous state interest is consistently at work. He finds the latter pattern and attributes it to actors in a special location within the otherwise weak, fragmented, and societally permeated U.S. government:

> For U.S. foreign policy the central state actors are the President and the Secretary of State and the most important institutions are the White House and the State Department. What distinguishes these roles and agencies is their high degree of insulation from specific societal pressures and a set of formal and informal obligations that charge them with furthering the nation's general interests.[11]

Unfortunately, Krasner does not expand on the concept of 'insulated' parts of the state. In particular, he does not tell us whether various organizational features of state agencies make for greater or lesser insulation. Instead, Krasner primarily emphasizes the degree to which different parts of the federal executive are subject to Congressional influences.[12] And he cannot fully dispel the suspicion that the Presidency and the State Department may simply be subject to class-based rather than interest-based business influences.[13] Nevertheless, he does show that public policies on raw materials have been most likely to diverge from powerful corporate demands precisely when distinctively geopolitical issues of foreign military intervention and broad ideological conceptions of U.S. world hegemony have been involved. Thus, Krasner's study suggests that distinctive state-like contributions to U.S. policy making occur exactly in those instances and arenas where a Weberian–Hintzean perspective would insist that they should occur, no matter how unpropitious the overall governmental potential for autonomous state action. As J. P. Nettl once put it, 'Whatever the state may or may not be internally, ... there have ... been few challenges to its sovereignty *and* its autonomy in "foreign affairs."'[14]

My own work with Kenneth Finegold on the origins of New Deal agricultural policies also suggests that autonomous state contributions to domestic policy making can occur within a 'weak state.' Such autonomous state contributions happen in specific policy areas at given historical moments, even if they are not generally discernible across all policy areas and even if they unintentionally help to create political forces that subsequently severely circumscribe further autonomous state action.[15] Finegold and I argue that, by the period after World War I, the U.S. Department of Agriculture was 'an island of state strength in an ocean of weakness.'[16] We attribute the formulation of New Deal agricultural interventions – policies that responded to a long-standing 'agrarian crisis' but *not* simply in ways directly demanded by powerful farm interest groups – to the unique resources of administrative capacity, prior public planning, and practical governmental experience available to federal agricultural experts at the dawn of the New Deal. Our argument resembles Hugh Heclo's findings about innovative civil officials in Britain and Sweden. Essentially, we found a *part* of the early-twentieth-century U.S. national government that allowed official expertise to function in a restricted policy area in ways that were similar to the ways it functioned in Sweden, or in Britain between 1900 and 1920.

In addition, however, we trace the political fate of the New Deal's administrative interventions in agriculture. We show that, in the overall context of the U.S. state structure, this initially autonomous state intervention inadvertently strengthened a particular lobbying group, the American Farm Bureau Federation, and gave it the final increments of electoral and administrative leverage that it needed to 'capture' preponderant influence over post-1936 federal agricultural policies. Subsequent state planning efforts, especially those that implied redistribution of economic, racial, or social-class power, were then circumscribed and destroyed by the established commercial farming interests championed by the Farm Bureau.

In short, 'state autonomy' is not a fixed structural feature of any governmental system. It can come and go. This is true not only because crises may precipitate the formulation of official strategies and policies by elites or administrators who otherwise might not mobilize their own potentials for autonomous action. It is also true because the very *structural potentials* for autonomous state actions change over time, as the organizations of coercion and administration undergo transformations, both internally and in their relations to societal groups and to representative parts of government. Thus, although cross-national research can indicate in general terms whether a governmental system has 'stronger' or 'weaker' tendencies toward autonomous state action, the full potential of this concept can be realized only in truly historical studies that are sensitive to structural variations and conjunctural changes within given polities.

Are state actions 'rational'?
An additional set of comments must be made about the rationality of autonomous state actions. Often such actions are considered more capable of addressing 'the capitalist class interest' or 'society's general interests' or 'the national interest' than are governmental decisions strongly influenced by the push and pull of demands from interest groups, voting blocs, or particular business enterprises.[17] In such perspectives, state officials are judged to be especially capable of formulating holistic and long-term strategies transcending partial, short-sighted demands from profit-seeking capitalists or narrowly self-interested social groups. But scholars skeptical about the notion of state autonomy often respond that state officials' own self-legitimating arguments, their claims to know and represent 'general' or 'national' interests, should not be taken at face value. State officials have no privileged claims to adequate knowledge of societal problems or solutions for them, argue the skeptics. Besides, their legitimating symbols may merely mask policies formulated to help particular interests or class fractions.

Surely such doubts about the superior rationality of state actions deserve respectful attention; yet we need not entirely dismiss the possibility that partially or fully autonomous state actions *may* be able to address problems and even find 'solutions' beyond the reach of societal actors and those parts of government closely constrained by them. Partly, the realization of such possibilities will depend on the availability and (even more problematically) the appropriate use of sound ideas about what the state can and should do to address societal problems. Partly, it will depend on the fit (or lack thereof) between the scope of an autonomous state organization's authority and the scale and depth of action appropriate for addressing a given kind of problem. Planning for coordinated systems of national transportation, for example, is unlikely to be achieved by state agencies with authority only over particular regions or kinds of transportation, no matter how knowledgeable and capable of autonomous official action those agencies may be. In sum, autonomous official initiatives can be stupid or misdirected, and autonomous initiatives may be fragmented and partial and work at cross-purposes to one another. Notwithstanding all of these possibilities, however, state actions may sometimes be coherent and appropriate.

Still, no matter how appropriate (for dealing with a given kind of crisis or problem) autonomous state activity might be, it can never really be 'disinterested' in any meaningful sense. This is true not only because all state actions necessarily benefit some social interests and disadvantage others (even without the social beneficiaries' having worked for or caused the state actions). More to the point, autonomous state actions will regularly take forms that attempt to reinforce the authority, political longevity, and social control of the state organizations whose incumbents generated the relevant policies or policy ideas. We can hypothesize that one (hidden or overt) feature of all autonomous state actions will be the reinforcement of the prerogatives of collectivities of state officials. Whether rational policies result may depend on how 'rational' is defined and might even be largely accidental. The point is that policies different from those demanded by societal actors will be produced. The most basic research task for those interested in state autonomy surely is to explore why, when, and how such distinctive policies are fashioned by states. Then it will be possible to wonder about their rationality for dealing with the problems they address – and we will be able to explore this issue without making starry-eyed assumptions about the omniscience or disinterestedness of states.

Can states achieve their goals?

Some comparative-historical scholars not only have investigated the underpinnings of autonomous state actions, but have also tackled the still more challenging task of explaining the various *capacities* of states to implement their policies. Of course, the explanation of state capacities is closely connected to the explanation of autonomous goal formation by states, because state officials are most likely to try to do things that seem feasible with the means at hand. Nevertheless, not infrequently, states do pursue goals (whether their own or those pressed on them by powerful social groups) that are beyond their reach. Moreover, the implementation of state policies often leads to unintended as well as intended consequences, both when states attempt tasks they cannot complete and when the means they use produce unforeseen structural changes and sociopolitical reactions. Thus, the capacities of states to implement strategies and policies deserve close analysis in their own right. [. . .]

A few basic things can be said about the general underpinnings of state capacities. Obviously, sheer sovereign integrity and the stable administrative–military control of a given territory are preconditions for any state's ability to implement policies.[18] Beyond this, loyal and skilled officials and plentiful financial resources are basic to state effectiveness in attaining all sorts of goals. It is not surprising that histories of state building zero in on exactly these universal sinews of state power.[19] Certain of these resources come to be rooted in institutional relationships that are slow to change and relatively impervious to short-term manipulations. For example, do state offices attract and retain career-oriented incumbents with a wide array of skills and keen motivation? The answer may well depend on historically evolved relationships among elite educational institutions, state organizations, and private enterprises that compete with the state for educated personnel. The best situation for the state may be a regular flow of elite university graduates, including many with sophisticated technical training, into official careers that are of such high status as to keep the most ambitious and successful from moving on to nonstate positions. But if this situation has not been historically established by the start of the industrial era, it is difficult to undo alternative patterns less favorable to the state.[20]

Factors determining a state's financial resources may be somewhat more manipulable over time, though not always. The amounts and forms of revenues and credit available to a state grow out of structurally conditioned, yet historically shifting political balances and bargains among states and between a state and social classes. Basic sets of facts to sort out in any study of state capacities involve the sources and amounts of state revenues and the degree of flexibility possible in their collection and deployment. Domestic institutional arrangements and international situations set difficult to change limits within which state elites must maneuver to extract taxes and obtain credit: Does a state depend on export taxes (for example, from a scarce national resource or from products vulnerable to sudden world market fluctuations)?[21] Does a nonhegemonic state's geopolitical position allow it to reap the state-building benefits of military aid, or must it rely on international bankers or aid agencies that insist on favoring nonpublic investments and restrict the domestic political options of the borrower state?[22] What established authority does a state have to collect taxes, to borrow, or to invest in potentially profitable public enterprises? And how much 'room' is there in the existing constitutional–political system to change patterns of revenue collection unfavorable to the state?

Finally, what authority and organizational means does a state have to deploy whatever financial resources it does enjoy? Are particular kinds of revenues rigidly 'earmarked' for special uses that cannot easily be altered by official decision makers?[23] Can the state channel (and manipulate) flows of credit to particular enterprises and industrial sectors, or do established constitutional–political practices favor only aggregate categorical expenditures? All of these *sorts* of questions must be asked in any study of state capacities. The answers to them, taken together, provide the best general insight into the direct and indirect leverage a state is likely to have for realizing any goal it may pursue. A state's means of raising and deploying financial resources tell us more than could any other single factor about its existing (and immediately potential) capacities to create or strengthen state organizations, to employ personnel, to coopt political support, to subsidize economic enterprises, and to fund social programs.[24]

State capacities to pursue specific kinds of policies

Basic questions about a state's territorial integrity, financial means, and staffing may be the place to start in any investigation of its capacities to realize goals; yet the most fruitful studies of state capacities tend to focus on particular policy areas. As Stephen Krasner puts it:

> There is no reason to assume *a priori* that the pattern of strengths and weaknesses will be the same for all policies. One state may be unable to alter the structure of its medical system but be able to construct an efficient transportation network, while another can deal relatively easily with getting its citizens around but cannot get their illnesses cured.[25]

Those who study a comprehensive state-propelled strategy for change, such as a 'revolution from above' or a major episode of bureaucratically sponsored reforms, may need to assess the overall capacity of a state to realize transformative goals across multiple spheres. Moreover, as Krasner points out, it may be useful to establish that 'despite variations among issue areas within countries, there are modal differences in the power of the state among [for example] the advanced market-economy countries.'[26] Nevertheless, such overall assessments are perhaps best built up from sectorally specific investigations, for one of the most important facts about the power of a state may be its *unevenness* across policy areas. And the most telling result, even of a far-reaching revolution or reform from above, may be the *disparate* transformations produced across sociopolitical sectors.

Thus, in a provocative article, 'Constitutionalism, class, and the limits of choice in the U.S. foreign policy,' Ira Katznelson and Kenneth Prewitt show how U.S. policies toward Latin America have been partly conditioned by the uneven capacities of the American national government: strongly able to intervene abroad, yet lacking the domestic planning capacities necessary 'to direct the internal distribution of costs entailed by a less imperialist foreign policy.'[27] [. . .]

Many studies of the capacities of states to realize particular kinds of goals use the concept of 'policy instrument' to refer to the relevant means that a state may have at its disposal.[28] Cross-national comparisons are necessary to determine the nature and range of institutional mechanisms that state officials may conceivably be able to bring to bear on a given set of issues. For example, Susan and Norman Fainstein compare the urban policies of northwest European nations with those of the United States. Accordingly, they are able to conclude that the U.S. national state lacks certain instruments for dealing with urban crises that are available to European states, instruments such as central planning agencies, state-controlled pools of investment capital, and directly administered national welfare programs.[29]

Analogously, Peter Katzenstein brings together a set of related studies of how six advanced industrial-capitalist countries manage the international trade, investment, and monetary involvements of their economies.[30] Katzenstein is able to draw fairly clear distinctions between the strategies open to states such as the Japanese and the French, which have policy instruments that enable them to apply policies at the level of particular industrial sectors, and other states, such as the British and U.S., which must rely on aggregate macroeconomic manipulations of fiscal and monetary parameters. Once again, as in the Fainstein study, it is the juxtaposition of different nations' approaches to a given policy area that allows relevant policy instruments to be highlighted. Neither study, however, treats such 'instruments' as deliberate short-term creations of state managers. Both studies move out toward macroscopic explorations of the broad institutional patterns of divergent national histories that explain why countries now have, or do not have, policy instruments for dealing with particular problems or crises.

States in relation to socioeconomic settings
Fully specified studies of state capacities not only entail examinations of the resources and instruments that states may have for dealing with particular problems; they also necessarily look at more than states as such. They examine states *in relation* to particular kinds of socioeconomic and political environments populated by actors with given interests and resources. One obvious use of a relational perspective is to investigate the power of states over domestic or transnational nonstate actors and structures, especially economically dominant ones. What capacities do states have to change the behavior or oppose the demands of such actors or to transform recalcitrant structures? Answers lie not only in features of states themselves, but also in the balances of states' resources and situational advantages compared with those of nonstate actors. This sort of relational approach is used by Stephen Krasner in his exploration of the efforts of U.S. policy makers to implement foreign raw materials policy in interactions with large corporations, whose preferences and established practices have frequently run counter to the state's definition of the national interest.[31] [. . .]

In Peter Katzenstein's *Between Power and Plenty*, [. . .] (as indicated earlier) the object of explanation is ultimately not state *power over* nonstate actors, but nations' strategies for managing 'interdependence' within the world capitalist economy. One notion centrally invoked in the Katzenstein collection is that of a 'policy network' embodying a patterned relationship between state and society. In Katzenstein's words:

> The actors in society and state influencing the definition of foreign economic policy objectives consist of the major interest groups and political action groups. The former represent the relations of production (including industry, finance, commerce, labor, and agriculture); the latter derive from the structure of political authority (primarily the state bureaucracy and political parties). The governing coalitions . . . in each of the advanced industrial states find their institutional expression in distinct policy networks which link the public and the private sector in the implementation of foreign policy.[32]

Katzenstein argues that the definition and implementation of foreign economic policies grow out of the nexus of state and society. Both state goals and the interests of powerful classes may influence national policy orientations. And the implementation of policies is shaped not only by the policy instruments available to the state, but also by the organized support it receives from key societal groups.

Thus, policy objectives such as industrial reorganization might be effectively implemented because a central state administration controls credit and can intervene in industrial sectors. Yet it may be of equal importance that industries are organized into disciplined associations willing to cooperate with state officials. A complete analysis, in short, requires examination of the organization and interests of the state, specification of the organization and interests of socioeconomic groups, and inquiries into the complementary as well as conflicting relationships of state and societal actors. [. . .]

Bringing the state back in to a central place in analyses of policy making and social change does require a break with some of the most encompassing social-determinist assumptions of pluralism, structure–functionalist developmentalism, and the various neo-Marxisms. But it does not mean that old theoretical emphases should simply be turned on their heads: Studies of states alone are not to be substituted for concerns with classes or groups; nor are purely state-determinist arguments to be fashioned in the place of society-centered explanations. The need to analyze states in relation to socioeconomic and sociocultural contexts is convincingly demonstrated in the best current research on state capacities.

Notes

1. Alfred Stepan, *The State and Society: Peru in comparative perspective*, Chaps. 3 and 4. See also Alfred Stepan, 'The new professionalism of internal warfare and military role expansion,' in *Authoritarian Brazil*, ed. A. Stepan (New Haven, Conn.: Yale University Press, 1973), pp. 47–65.
2. Ellen Kay Trimberger, *Revolution from Above*.
3. *Ibid.*, p. 4.
4. *Ibid.*, p. 5.
5. Thus, in commenting on Stepan's work, Trimberger argues that he could have explained the repressive and 'exclusionary' nature of the Brazilian coup (in contrast to Peru's 'inclusionary' reforms, which included mass political mobilization and expropriation of hacienda landlords) by focusing on the Brazilian military's ties to Brazilian and multinational capitalists. In fact, Stepan does report ('The new professionalism,' p. 54) that Brazilian military professionals received their training alongside elite civilians, including industrialists, bankers, and commercial elites, who also attended the Superior War College of Brazil in the period before 1964.
6. For France, there is an especially rich literature on state autonomy, its consequences and its limits. I am deliberately leaving it aside here, because France is such an obvious case for the application of ideas about state autonomy. See, however, Stephen Cohen, *Modern Capitalist Planning: The French experience* (Berkeley: University of California Press, 1976); and Richard F. Kuisel, *Capitalism and the State in Modern France: Renovation and economic management in the twentieth century* (Cambridge and New York: Cambridge University Press, 1981).
7. Hugh Heclo, *Modern Social Politics in Britain and Sweden*.
8. *Ibid.*, p. 305.
9. *Ibid.*, pp. 305–6, 303.
10. Stephen Krasner, *Defending the National Interest*.
11. *Ibid.*, p. 11.
12. See also Krasner, 'United States commercial and monetary policy,' pp. 51–87.
13. Thus, Krasner has the most difficulty in distinguishing his argument for 'state autonomy' from the structural Marxist perspective according to which the state acts for the class interests of capital as a whole. His solution, to stress 'nonrational' ideological objectives of

state policy as evidence against the class-interest argument, does not strike me as being very convincing. Could an imperialist ideology not be evidence of class consciousness as well as of state purpose? One might stress, instead, the perceived geopolitical 'interests' at work in U.S. interventions abroad. 'Free-world' justifications for such interventions are not obviously irrational, given certain understandings of U.S. geopolitical interests.

14. J. P. Nettl, 'The state as a conceptual variable,' *World Politics* 20 (1968): 563–4.

15. Kenneth Finegold and Theda Skocpol, 'Capitalists, farmers, and workers in the New Deal – the ironies of government intervention' (paper presented at the annual meeting of the American Political Science Association, Washington, D.C., August 31, 1980). Part of this paper was subsequently published as Theda Skocpol and Kenneth Finegold, 'State capacity and economic intervention in the early New Deal,' *Political Science Quarterly* 97 (1982): 255–78.

16. Skocpol and Finegold, 'State capacity,' p. 271.

17. In contrasting ways, both Krasner's *Defending the National Interest* and Poulantzas's *Political Power and Social Classes* exemplify this point.

18. Or perhaps one should say that any state or state-building movement preoccupied with sheer administrative–military control will, at best, only be able (as well as likely) to implement policies connected to that overriding goal. This principle is a good guide to understanding many of the social changes that accompany state-building struggles during revolutionary interregnums.

19. See Tilly, ed., *Formation of National States*; Michael Mann, 'State and society, 1130–1815: an analysis of English state finances,' *Political Power and Social Theory* (Greenwich, Conn.: JAI Press, 1980), vol. 1, pp. 165–208; and Stephen Skowronek, *Building a New American State: The expansion of national administrative capacities* (Cambridge and New York: Cambridge University Press, 1982).

20. See Bernard Silberman's important comparative-historical work on alternative modes of state bureaucratization in relation to processes of professionalization: 'State bureaucratization: a comparative analysis' (Department of Political Science, the University of Chicago, 1982).

21. Windfall revenues from international oil sales, for example, can render states *both* more autonomous from societal controls and, because social roots and political pacts are weak, more vulnerable in moments of crisis. I argue along these lines in 'Rentier state and Shi'a Islam in the Iranian Revolution,' *Theory and Society* 11 (1982): 265–83. The Joint Committee on the Near and Middle East of the American Council of Learned Societies and the Social Science Research Council currently has a project entitled 'Social Change in Arab Oil-Producing Societies' that is investigating the impact of oil revenues on state–society relationships.

22. See Robert E. Wood, 'Foreign aid and the capitalist state in under-developed countries,' *Politics and Society* 10 (1) (1980): 1–34. Wood's essay primarily documents and discusses the anti-state-building effects of most foreign aid, but it also notes that 'the "overdeveloped" military institutions fostered by aid can provide a springboard for statist experimentation unintended by aid donors' (p. 34). Taiwan and South Korea would both seem to be good examples of this.

23. See John A. Dunn, Jr., 'The importance of being earmarked: transport policy and highway finance in Great Britain and the United States,' *Comparative Studies in Society and History* 20(1) (1978): 29–53.

24. For 'classic' statements on the social analysis of state finances, see especially Lorenz von Stein, 'On taxation,' and Rudolf Goldscheid, 'A sociological approach to problems of public

finance,' both in *Classics in the Theory of Public Finance*, ed. Richard A. Musgrave and Alan T. Peacock (New York: Macmillan, 1958), pp. 202–13 and 28–36, respectively.

25. Krasner, *Defending the National Interest*, p. 58.
26. *Ibid.*
27. Ira Katznelson and Kenneth Prewitt, 'Constitutionalism, class, and the limits of choice in U.S. foreign policy,' in *Capitalism and the State in U.S.–Latin American Relations*, ed. Richard Fagen (Stanford, Calif.: Stanford University Press, 1979), p. 38.
28. This concept is discussed by Peter Katzenstein in *Between Power and Plenty*, pp. 16, 297–8.
29. Susan S. and Norman I. Fainstein, 'National policy and urban development,' *Social Problems* 26 (1978): 125–46; see especially pp. 140–1.
30. Katzenstein, ed., *Between Power and Plenty*.
31. Krasner, *Defending the National Interest*, especially Parts 2 and 3.
32. Katzenstein, ed., *Between Power and Plenty*, p. 19.

Institutional perspectives on political institutions

James G. March and Johan P. Olsen

Abstract: This article examines some basic assumptions about the nature of political institutions, the ways in which practices and rules that comprise institutions are established, sustained, and transformed, and the ways in which those practices and rules are converted into political behavior through the mediation of interpretation and capability. We discuss an institutional approach to political life that emphasizes the endogenous nature and social construction of political institutions, identities, accounts, and capabilities.

Political science as a field is defined less by a set of theoretical concepts than by an empirical focus on concrete political institutions and processes. Legislatures, bureaucracies, legal systems, political parties, mass media, and all the other institutions of contemporary politics are objects of study. Although political scientists occasionally examine other institutions, such as business firms, churches, or armies, and use various forms of political analysis to interpret them, the discipline persistently retreats from attempts to generate distinctive theoretical tools and returns to concerns about identifiable political institutions.[1]

Historically, theoretical political science has been more an interweaving of metaphors than a theoretically coherent discipline or even an arena for competition among alternative metaphors. It has combined the traditions of Aristotle and Tocqueville with those of Hobbes and Bentham and grafted onto those roots various elements of the wisdom of Freud, Marx, Durkheim, Adam Smith, and Darwin. In recent years, this pragmatic approach to ideas has been expressed most conspicuously in efforts to reconcile an exchange conception of politics drawn particularly from ideas of social contracts, the utilitarians, and modern microeconomics with an institutional conception that builds on jurisprudence, sociological and psychological conceptions of identity, and modern organization theory.

This chapter is in that tradition of political science. We examine some basic assumptions about the nature of political institutions, the ways in which the practices and rules that comprise institutions are established, sustained, and transformed, and the ways in

From James G. March and Johan P. Olsen, 'Institutional perspectives on political institutions', *Governance*, **9** (3), 1996, pp. 248–64.

which those practices and rules are converted into political behavior through the mediation of interpretation and capability. Without denying the elements of exchange in politics and the many ways in which politics aggregates exogenous individual preferences and responds to exogenous distributions of resources and capabilities, we discuss an institutional approach to political life – one that emphasizes the endogenous nature and social construction of political institutions, identities, accounts, and capabilities.

Telling stories about politics

The stories of politics are stories attached to real political events in real political institutions. Why did the Weimar Republic fail? How do we account for the historical divergence of the political institutions of Canada and the United States? What explains post-communist political developments in Hungary? The stories about such events and institutions constructed within political science are organized around a few themes of how political institutions work. Politics is organized by (and helps to organize) these stories of history.

There are two conventional stories of democratic politics. The first story sees politics as a market for trades in which individual and group interests are pursued by rational actors. It emphasizes the negotiation of coalitions and 'voluntary' exchanges. The second story is an institutional one. It characterizes politics in a more integrative fashion, emphasizing the creation of identities and institutions as well as their structuring effects on political life.

Politics as arranging exchanges

Politics can be seen as aggregating individual preferences into collective actions by some procedures of bargaining, negotiation, coalition formation, and exchange (Riker 1962; Coleman 1966; Downs 1967; March 1970; Niskanen 1971). In such a view, individual actors have prior desires (preferences, interests) which they use to determine the attractiveness of expected consequences. Collective action depends on the negotiation of bargains and side-payments among potential trading partners. Exchange stories of politics and governance have roots in the doctrines of social contract theory which arose in the seventeenth century. The political community is seen as atomistic. Society is constituted of individuals for the fulfilment of individual ends. Individuals have rights but no obligations or bonds, except those created through consent and contracts based on calculated advantage (Taylor 1985: 187–229).

The ability of any particular actor to realize his or her desires in such a system of exchange depends on what the desires are, what exchangeable resources that actor possesses, and what political rights he or she has. Wants that are consistent with the wants of others are more easily satisfied than wants that compete with others. The greater the exchangeable resources (initial endowments) and the more rights to political voice, the stronger the trading position. One version of the exchange story emphasizes the pareto-optimal qualities of exchange and gains from trade – the achievement of outcomes that make at least some people better off and no one worse off than before the exchanges. A second version of the exchange story emphasizes the coercive qualities of exchange when initial endowments are unequal, the way in which 'voluntary exchange' results in one group of actors imposing its will on other groups (Moe 1990; Sened 1991; Olsen 1992).

Politics as creating and sustaining institutions
An alternative story emphasizes the role of institutions. The exchange vision of human nature as static and universal and unaffected by politics is replaced by a view of the political actor as flexible, varied, malleable, culture-dependent and socially constructed. Intentional, calculative action is embedded in rules and institutions that are constituted, sustained, and interpreted in a political system. The core notion is that life is organized by sets of shared meanings and practices that come to be taken as given for a long time. Political actors act and organize themselves in accordance with rules and practices which are socially constructed, publicly known, anticipated and accepted. Actions of individuals and collectivities occur within these shared meanings and practices, which can be called institutions and identities (Meyer and Rowan 1977; March and Olsen 1984; 1989; North 1990).

In the institutional story, people act, think, feel and organize themselves on the basis of exemplary or authoritative (and sometimes competing or conflicting) rules derived from socially constructed identities, belongings and roles. Institutions organize hopes, dreams, and fears as well as purposeful actions. Institutionalized rules proscribe or prescribe emotions and expression of emotions (Flam 1990a; 1990b). Sentiments of love, loyalty, devotion, respect, friendship, as well as hate, anger, fear, envy, and guilt are made appropriate to particular identities in particular situations.

Institutions constitute and legitimize political actors and provide them with consistent behavioral rules, conceptions of reality, standards of assessment, affective ties, and endowments, and thereby with a capacity for purposeful action (Douglas 1986; Thompson *et al.* 1990; March and Olsen 1995). Along the way, political institutions create rules regulating the possession and use of political rights and resources. Even the conception of an autonomous agent with a particularistic way of feeling, acting, and expression is an acquired identity, a socialized understanding of self and others (Taylor 1985: 205).

Action is taken on the basis of a logic of appropriateness associated with roles, routines, rights, obligations, standard operating procedures and practices. The perspective is more behavioral than moral but it echoes an Aristotelian judgment: 'As man is the best of all animals when he has reached his full development, so he is the worst of all when divorced from law and morals' (Aristotle 1980: 29).

Institutional perspectives

The word 'institutional' has come to mean rather different things to different authors.[2] The institutional alternatives to voluntary exchange stories about politics with which we are concerned here are infused with two basic themes:

1. a theme that pictures political action as driven less by anticipation of its uncertain consequences and preferences for them than by a logic of appropriateness reflected in a structure of rules and conceptions of identities;
2. a theme that pictures political change as matching institutions, behaviors, and contexts in ways that take time and have multiple, path-dependent equilibria, thus as being susceptible to timely interventions to affect the meander of history and to deliberate efforts to improve institutional adaptiveness.

Institutional conceptions of political action

Institutional theories supplement exchange theories of political action in two primary ways: first, they emphasize the role of institutions in defining the terms of rational exchange. Rational action depends on subjective perceptions of alternatives, their consequences, and their evaluations. Pictures of reality and feelings about it are constructed within social and political institutions (Cyert and March 1992; March and Simon 1993). Second, without denying the reality of calculations and anticipations of consequences, institutional conceptions see such calculations and anticipations as occurring within a broader framework of rules, roles, and identities (North 1981; 1990; Shepsle and Weingast 1987; Shepsle 1989; 1990). Indeed, at the limit, self-interested calculation can be seen as simply one of many systems of rules that may be socially legitimized under certain circumstances (Taylor 1985; Nauta 1992).

INSTITUTIONAL BASES OF RATIONAL EXCHANGE

In exchange theories, political action (decision-making, resource allocation) is a result of bargains negotiated among individual actors pursuing individual interests. The theories presume that individuals pursue their interests by considering alternative bargains in terms of their anticipated consequences for individual preferences and choosing those combinations of bargains that serve their preferences best. Political actors are imagined to be endowed with preferences or interests that are consistent, stable, and exogenous to the political system. They act on the basis of incomplete and possibly biased information. In short, exchange theories of politics are special cases of rational actor theories of human behavior.

Institutional theories focus on the behavioral and social bases of information and preferences in a theory of rational choice. They picture preferences as inconsistent, changing, and at least partly endogenous, formed within political institutions. Interests and cleavages are seen as created by institutional arrangements and maintained by institutional processes of socialization and co-optation (Selznick 1949; Lipset and Rokkan 1967; Eisenstadt and Rokkan 1973; Wildavsky 1987; Sunstein 1990; Greber and Jackson 1993). Institutional theories similarly emphasize the ways in which institutions shape the definition of alternatives and influence the perception and construction of the reality within which action takes place. Institutional capabilities and structures affect the flow of information, the kinds of search undertaken, and the interpretations made of the results (Cyert and March 1963; March and Olsen 1989; 1995; Olsen and Peters 1996).

Awareness of the limits of rationality and of the embedding of rationality in an institutional context has led to a considerable restructuring of theories of rational exchange, including political theories based on an exchange perspective. This restructuring has come to picture rational exchange as framed by and dependent on political norms, identities, and institutions. In so far as political actors act by making choices, they act within definitions of alternatives, consequences, preferences (interests), and strategic options that are strongly affected by the institutional context in which the actors find themselves. Exploring the ways in which institutions affect the definition of alternatives, consequences, and preferences, the cleavages that produce conflict, and the enforcement of bargains have become major activities within modern choice theory (Laitin 1985).

RULES AND IDENTITIES

Institutional conceptions of action, however, differ from rational models in a more fundamental way. Most people in politics and political institutions follow rules most of the time if they can (Searing 1991). The uncertainties they face are less uncertainties about consequences and preferences than they are uncertainties about the demands of identity. Actions are expressions of what is exemplary, natural, or acceptable behavior according to the (internalized) purposes, codes of rights and duties, practices, methods, and techniques of the constituent group and of the self. As a result, the institutional axiomatics for political action begin not with subjective consequences and preferences but with rules, identities, and roles (Friedrich 1950; Tussman 1960).

Political institutions matter. Institutionalized identities create individuals: citizens, officials, engineers, doctors, spouses (Dworkin 1986). Rule-following can be viewed as contractual – an implicit agreement to act appropriately in return for being treated appropriately. Such a contractual view has led game theorists and some legal theorists to interpret norms and institutions as meta-game agreements (Shepsie 1990; Gibbons 1992), but the term 'contract' is potentially misleading. The terms are often unclear enough to be better called a 'pact' (Selznick 1992) than a 'contract,' and socialization into rules and their appropriateness is ordinarily not a case of willful entering into an explicit contract.

Within an institutional framework, 'choice,' if it can be called that, is based more on a logic of appropriateness than on the logic of consequence that underlies conceptions of rational action. Institutionalized rules, duties, rights, and roles define acts as appropriate (normal, natural, right, good) or inappropriate (uncharacteristic, unnatural, wrong, bad). The impact of rules of appropriateness and standard operating procedures in routine situations is well known (March and Simon 1958; Cyert and March 1963). But the logic of appropriateness is by no means limited to repetitive, routine worlds. It is also characteristic of human action in ill-defined, novel situations (Dynes 1970; Quarantelli and Dynes 1977). Civil unrest, demands for comprehensive redistribution of political power and welfare, as well as political revolutions and major reforms often follow from identity-driven conceptions of appropriateness more than conscious calculations of costs and benefits (Lefort 1988; Elster 1989b). Appropriateness has overtones of morality, but it is in this context primarily a cognitive, or perhaps teleological, concept. Rules of action are derived from reasoning about the nature of the self. People act from understandings of the nature of things, from self-conceptions and conceptions of society, and from images of proper behavior. Identities define the nature of things and are implemented by a cognitive process of interpretation (March and Olsen 1989; 1994).

Neither the definition of an identity nor its achievement is necessarily trivial. Fulfilling an identity through following appropriate rules involves matching a changing (and often ambiguous) set of contingent rules to a changing (and often ambiguous) set of situations. As a result, institutional approaches to behavior make a distinction between a rule and its behavioral realization in a particular instance (Apter 1991; Thelen and Steinmo 1992: 15). Identities and rules assure neither consistency nor simplicity (Biddle 1986; Berscheid 1994). The elements of openness in their interpretation mean that while institutions structure politics, they ordinarily do not determine political behavior precisely. The processes through which rules are translated into actual behavior through constructive interpretation and available resources have to be specified.

As they try to understand history and self, and as they try to improve the often confusing, uncertain, and ambiguous world they live in, individuals and collectivities interpret what rules and identities exist, which ones are relevant, and what different rules and identities demand in specific situations or spheres of behavior. Individuals may have a difficult time resolving conflicts among contending imperatives of appropriateness, among alternative concepts of the self. They may not know what to do. They may also know what to do but not have the capabilities to do it. They are limited by the complexities of the demands upon them and by the distribution and regulation of resources, competencies and organizing capacities – that is by the capability for acting appropriately.

Processes of constructive interpretation, criticism and justification of rules and identities are processes familiar to the intellectual traditions of the law (Dworkin 1986; Sunstein 1990; Teubner 1993). Such processes are highly relevant for the ambiguities of identities, rules and factual situations. They give specific content in specific situations both to such heroic identities as patriot or statesman and to such everyday identities as those of an accountant, police officer, or citizen (Kaufman 1960; Maanen 1973; Spradeley and Mann 1975).

IDENTITIES, INTERESTS, AND THE COMMON GOOD

Some of the more celebrated differences between exchange theories of politics and institutional theories concern the concept of the 'common good,' the idea that individuals might, under some circumstances, act not in the name of individual or group interest but in the name of the good of the community. Exchange traditions downplay the significance or meaning of virtue in the values of the citizenry and doubt the relevance of social investment in citizenship. The assumption is that interests cannot (and should not) be eliminated or influenced. The object is to provide a neutral arena for voluntary exchange among them. If leaders wish to control the outcomes of this self-seeking behavior, they do so by designing incentives that induce self-interested individuals to act in desired ways as much as possible (Hart and Holmström

1987; Levinthal 1988). Political norms are seen as negotiated constraints on fundamental processes of self-serving rationality rather than constitutive (Coleman 1986; Shepsle 1990). From this perspective, a community of virtuous citizens is *Gemeinschaftschwermerei* – a romantic dream (Yack 1985). The fantasy in some democratic thought that modern society can be held together by, and that conflicts can be resolved through, reference to either a moral consensus or a shared conception of the common good is deemed to be wrong as a description and pernicious as an objective.[3]

In virtually all institutional theories of politics, on the other hand, humans (through their institutions) are seen as able to share a common life and identity, and to have concern for others. Either what is good for one individual is the same as what is good for other members of the community, or actions are supposed to be governed by what is best for the community as a whole. Although the idea of a common good is plagued by the difficulty of defining what is meant by the term and by the opportunities for exploitation of individual gullibility that lie in an uncritical embrace of hopes for community values, many institutional theorists criticize presumptions of individual self-interested behavior that are standard in the rational tradition (Mansbridge 1990; Mulhall and Swift 1992; Chapman and Galston 1992).

Indeed, the civic basis of identities is often intrinsic to the concept of a person, citizen, or public official. Giving priority to private interests and preferences is not merely a corruption of the political process but also a corruption of the soul and a fall from grace. Social identities are the building blocks of the self. Anyone incapable of achieving an identity based on constitutive attachments – if such a person could be imagined – should not be described as a free and rational agent, but as a being without character or moral depth, a non-person (Sandel 1982; 1984).

This folding of communication values into institutional theories of politics is almost universal in modern discussions of political democracy, and it leads to a tendency to confuse two related but distinct notions. The first notion is the idea that political democracy requires a sense of community. Exactly what constitutes a sense of community varies a bit from one communitarian author to another, but a common element is the idea that individuals might (and should) have empathy for the feelings and desires of others and under some circumstances might (and should) subordinate their own individual or group interests to the collective good of the community (Sabine 1952; Olsen 1990).

The second notion is the idea that democracy is built upon visions of civic identity and a framework of rule-based action – what we have called a logic of appropriateness. Embedded in this notion are ideas about the obligations of citizenship and office, the commitment to fulfill an identity without regard to its consequences for personal or group preferences or interests. The self becomes central to personhood, and civic identity becomes central to the self (Turner 1990).

The two notions share some common presumptions, but they have quite different perspectives about the fundamental basis for democratic action. The communitarian ideal of shared preferences, including a preference for the common good, presumes that individual action is based on individual values and preferences. The model is one of individual, consequential, preference-based action. Strategies for achieving democracy emphasize constructing acceptable preferences.

On the other hand, the civic identity ideal presumes, that action is rule-based, that it involves matching the obligations of an identity to a situation. Pursuit of the common good is not so much a personal value as a constitutive part of democratic political identities and the construction of a meaningful person. The community is created by its rules, not by its intentions. Strategies for achieving democracy emphasize molding rules and identities and socializing individuals into them (Elster and Slagstad 1988; Elster 1989a).

The distinctions are worth maintaining. When they are confounded, there is a tendency to see the problems of modern polities as lying primarily in the value premises of individual preference-based action rather than in a structure of political rules, institutions, and identities. In fact, many of the greatest dangers to the democratic polity come not from particularistic individual self-seeking but from deep, group-based identities that are inconsistent with democracy, for example, strong feelings of religious, class, and national identities. And efforts to build a personal set of communitarian values enhancing concern for the common good will be of little use – even if successful – if anti-democratic action stems primarily not from preferences and their associated values but from commitments to identities that are inconsistent with democratic institutions.

Institutional conceptions of political change

Exchange theories of political exchange are largely theories of the adjustment of political bargains to exogenous changes in interests, rights, and resources. When values change, political coalitions change. For example, when attitudes with respect to the role of women in society shift, so also do political parties. When resources are redistributed, political coalitions change. For example, when the age composition of society shifts in the direction of older citizens, so also do political programs. The presumption is that political bargains adjust quickly and in a necessary way to exogenous changes.

In contrast to political accounts drawn from an exchange tradition, which are organized primarily around stories of how resources and interests shape the outcomes of politics, students of political institutions are generally less confident of the efficiency of history in matching political outcomes to exogenous pressures. They see the match between an environment of interests and resources on the one hand and political institutions on the other as less automatic, less continuous, and less precise. They see a world of historical possibilities that includes multiple stable equilibria. They see the pressures of survival as sporadic rather than constant, crude rather than precise. They see institutions and identities as having lives and deaths of their own, sometimes enduring in the face of apparent inconsistency with their environments, sometimes collapsing without obvious external cause (Krasner 1988; March and Olsen 1989).

THE NATURE OF HISTORY

Although their many different manifestations allow numerous variations on theories of history, institutional and exchange conceptions of politics tend to be divided by a grand debate in historical interpretation. On one side in that debate is the idea that politics follows a course dictated uniquely by exogenous factors. From such a perspective, history is efficient in the sense that it matches political institutions and outcomes to environments uniquely and relatively quickly. This side of the debate is typical of exchange theories and theories of rational choice.

Some version of an efficient history assumption also underlies traditional comparative statics as applied to political institutions. Why do political institutions differ from one country to another? It is because the social and economic environments of the countries differ. How does one explain specific differences in institutions? It is by pointing to specific differences in their environments. As long as history is efficient in the sense of deriving institutions to a unique equilibrium quickly, variations in institutional structures can be predicted without identifying the underlying processes of change (Furubotn and Richter 1984).

On the other side of the debate is the idea typical of institutional theories that history follows a less determinate, more endogenous course. They generally presume that the conditions under which political development is driven quickly to a unique outcome in which the match between a political system and the political environment has some properties of unique survival advantage seem relatively restricted (Kitcher 1985; Baum and Singh 1994). There is no guarantee that the development of identities and institutions will instantaneously or uniquely reflect functional imperatives or demands for change. Political institutions and identities develop in a world of multiple viable possibilities. Moreover, the paths they follow seem determined in part by internal dynamics only loosely connected to changes in their environments.

Even in an exogenous environment, there are lags in matching an environment, multiple equilibria, path dependencies, and interconnected networks of diffusion. In addition, environments are rarely exogenous. Environments adapt to institutions at the same time as institutions adapt to environments. Institutions and their linkages coevolve. They are inter-twined in ecologies of competition, cooperation, and other forms of interaction. And institutions are nested, so that some adapting institutions (e.g. bureaus) are integral parts of other adapting institutions (e.g. ministries).

The complications tend to convert history into a meander (March 1994b). There are irreversible branches, involving experimentation, political alliances, communication contacts, and fortuitous opportunities. The direction taken at any particular branch sometimes seems almost chance-like, yet it is likely to be decisive in its effect on subsequent history (Brady 1988; Lipset 1990). Institutional histories require an understanding of both the origins of an institution and the paths by which it has developed (Berman 1983).

The path of development is produced by a comprehensible process, but because of its indeterminate meander the realized course of institutional development is difficult to predict very far in advance. Wars, conquests, and occupation are significant in changing the political maps of the world (Tilly 1975; 1993; Giddens 1985). 'Timely interventions' at historical junctions may make a difference. This ability to create change, however, does not guarantee either that any arbitrary change can be made at any time or that changes will turn out to be consistent with prior intentions (March 1981). Institutions may be established to serve the interests of a specific group, but the long run results may be quite deleterious to the same interests (Rothstein 1992).

In general, neither competitive pressure nor current conditions uniquely determines institutional options or outcomes (Herzog 1989; North 1990). Institutional development depends not only on satisfying current environmental and political conditions but also on an institution's origin and history (Berman 1983). Political technologies and practices are stabilized by positive local feedback leading to the endurance of institutions, competency traps, and misplaced specialization (Levitt and March 1988). The adaptation of identities and institutions to an external environment is shaped and constrained by internal dynamics by which identities and institutions modify themselves endogenously.

AUTONOMOUS INSTITUTIONAL DEVELOPMENT

Politics is not simply a matter of negotiating coalitions of interests within given constraints of rights, rules, preferences, and resources. Politics extends to shaping those constraints, to constructing accounts of politics, history, and self that are not only bases for instrumental action but also central concerns of life.

AUTONOMOUS IDENTITIES

Identities are responsive to external forces. Religious movements, great social and economic transformations, war, conquest, and migration all leave their marks (Tilly 1975; Flora 1983). But political identities, such as those of the citizen or the public official, also evolve endogenously within a political process that includes conflict, public discourse, civic education, and socialization. Politics develops values and identities. In the context of political life, citizens struggle to understand 'who they are, where they come from historically, what they stand for, and what is to be done about the perils and possibilities that lie ahead of them as a people' (Wolin 1989: 14).

In the course of that struggle, individuals come to define identities such as that of the democratic citizen and public official and to mold those identities to a specific set of historical and political experiences and conditions. Clearly, there are limits. It has been argued that there are eradicable and irreconcilable differences among cultures, making some immigrants 'unassimilable.' For instance, the processes that used to turn foreigners into Frenchmen are faltering (Brubaker 1992; Hoffmann 1991: 66). Nevertheless, the self is not so much a premise of politics as it is one of its primary creations (Sandel 1982; 1984).

AUTONOMOUS INSTITUTIONS

The story of institutional change is a story of many failed experiments. At every level of adaptation – at the level of interpretations, rules, institutional forms, and specific institutions – changes usually lead to increased vulnerability. Nevertheless, in the struggle to survive, institutions transform themselves. Changes may be discontinuous, contested, and problematic (Skowronek 1982; Orren and Skowronek 1994). They may represent 'punctuated equilibrium' (Krasner 1988) and 'critical junctions' (Collier and Collier 1991), and be linked to 'performance crises' (March and Olsen 1989) which stimulate departures from established routines and practices. Many important institutional changes have been associated with the rare cataclysms and metamorphoses at breaking points in history where considerable resources are mobilized and one definition of appropriateness replaces another (Krasner 1988; March and Olsen 1989).

However, change also occurs through mundane processes of interpretation, reasoning, education, imitation and adaptation. Institutions create elements of temporary and imperfect order and historical continuity. They give rules communicable meaning so they can be diffused and passed on to new generations. Indeed, institutions are usually associated with routinization and repetition, persistence and predictability, rather than with political change and flexibility, agency, creativity and discretion. Surviving institutions seem to stabilize their norms, rules, and meanings so that procedures and forms adopted at birth have surprising durability (Stinchcombe 1965; Hannan and Freeman 1989).

The processes of securing stability, however, introduce two important sources of change. First, the same institutional stability that provides advantage (and may even be essential to survival in the short run) can easily become a source of vulnerability. Institutional competence and reliability become a barrier to change, thus a likely precursor of long run obsolescence (Levinthal and March 1994). Second, communicable meaning is subject to reinterpretation. Institutions change as individuals learn the culture (or fail to), forget (parts of) it, revolt against it, modify it or reinterpret it (McNeil and Thompson 1971; Lægreid and Olsen 1978; 1984). The resulting drifts in meaning lead to changes that explore alternative political paths and create the divergences of politics.

THE PURSUIT OF INTELLIGENCE

The logic of consequence and the logic of appropriateness are equally logics of thoughtfulness, and the cognitive demands for each are substantial. In the case of a logic of consequence, there are requirements for knowledge about the future and for consistency and clarity in preferences. In the case of a logic of appropriateness, there are requirements for knowledge about the situation and for consistency and clarity in identities. Under appropriate circumstances action based on either logic can lead to achieving outcomes that are judged to be attractive or contribute (over some time horizon) to survival advantage. However, neither rational exchange nor rule-following (and the learning and selection of rules that lies behind it) is assured of being intelligent (March 1994a). The intelligence of each depends on the ways in which their imperatives are interpreted and on the extent to which capabilities for meeting them exist.

Implications for a research agenda

Institutional perspectives on political institutions and politics provide a set of ideas for thinking about research that is different from ideas drawn from an exchange perspective. Emphasis on modeling the bargaining of exchanges among self-interested individuals within constraints of prior preferences, resources, and rights is replaced by a broader conception that includes attention to the constraints, indeed places them at the center of attention.

Such a framework invites research on the ways in which a political order of rights, rules, and institutions is constructed and maintained through active education and socialization of citizens and officials; on the ways individual and collective capabilities for action evolve endogenously through the allocation of resources and capabilities; on the ways conceptions of identity are developed and shared; on the construction of meaning, including an understanding of history and self, through political and social experience; and on histories in which institutions, behaviors, and contexts are matched in ways that take time and have multiple, path-dependent equilibria.

Within such a conception, research might focus particularly on four grand factors in political development:

First, politics depends on the *identities* of citizens and communities in the political environment. Preferences, expectations, beliefs, identities, and interests are not exogenous to political history. They are created and changed within that history. Political actors act on the basis of identities that are themselves shaped by political institutions and processes. When they act in ways that support a democratic system, they do so because they have come to see such action as part of their own identities.

Second, politics depends on the distribution of *capabilities* for appropriate political action among citizens, groups, and institutions. Acting appropriately to fulfill an identity requires not only the will to do so but also the ability. Those capabilities are not just imposed on a political system or the individuals in it but are distributed and developed within the system as well. It is possible to study the ways individuals and institutions garner the rights, authorities, resources, competencies, and organizing capacities necessary to do what is expected of them and the processes by which they achieve or fail to achieve the fruits of those capabilities.

Third, politics depends on *accounts* of political events and responsibility for them, interpretations of political history. Accounts form the basis for defining situations within which identities are relevant. Meanings and histories are socially constructed. Political myths are developed and transmitted. Accountability is established. It is possible to study the processes by which a current situation is defined or history is understood and by which political events and possibilities are interpreted, as well as the possibilities for transmission, retention, and retrieval of the lessons of history.

Fourth, politics depends on the ways in which a political system *adapts* to changing demands and changing environments. Such adaptiveness involves a balance between exploring new possibilities and exploiting existing capabilities, a balance that is easily upset by dynamics leading to excessive experimentation or excessive stability. Studies of the ways in which political systems reinterpret the meaning of stable identities and institutions and the circumstances and manner in which they are transformed are essential to a comprehension of political continuity and change.

Notes

1. An earlier version of this chapter was presented at the International Political Science Association World Congress, Berlin, August 1994. It draws extensively from March and Olsen 1994, 1995. The research has been supported by the Spencer Foundation, the Stanford Graduate School of Business, the Norwegian Research Centre in Organization and Management, the Center for Advanced Study in the Behavioral Sciences at Stanford, and the ARENA-program (Advanced Research on the Europeanization of the Nation-State) financed by the Norwegian Research Council.
2. Compare for instance, the various uses of 'institution' in political science (Shepsle and Weingast 1987; Lepsius 1988; March and Olsen 1989; Shepsle 1989; Moe 1990; Apter 1991; Grafstein 1992; Steinmo, Thelen, and Longstreth 1992; Weaver and Rockman 1993; Orren and Skowronek 1994) as well as sociology (Meyer and Rowan 1977; Scott 1987; Thomas *et al.* 1987; Hechter *et al.* 1990; Powell and DiMaggio 1991), anthropology (Douglas 1986), economics (Furubotn and Richter 1984; 1993; North 1990; Eggertsson 1990), and law (Broderick 1970; MacCormick and Weinberger 1986; Smith 1988).
3. Both Habermas and Rawls suggest that we have to avoid models which overburden citizens ethically by assuming a political community united by a comprehensive substantive doctrine. At the same time, both seem to suggest that citizens may share some aims and ends which do not make up a comprehensive doctrine, as well as basic rules for regulating their political co-existence in the face of persistent disagreements and different ways of life (Habermas 1992; 1994; Rawls 1993).

References

Apter, D. A. (1991) 'Institutionalism reconsidered', *International Social Science Journal* 8: 463–81.

Aristotle (1980) *Politics*, Harmondsworth: Penguin.

Baum, J. and J. Singh (eds.) (1994) *The Evolutionary Dynamics of Organizations*, New York: Oxford University Press.

Berman, H. J. (1983) *Law and Revolution. The Formation of the Western Legal Tradition*, Cambridge, MA: Harvard University Press.

Berscheid, E. (1994) 'Interpersonal Relationships', *Annual Review of Psychology* 45: 79–129.

Biddle, B. J. (1986) 'Recent developments in role theory', *Annual Review of Sociology* 12: 67–92.

Brady, D. W. (1988) *Critical Elections and Congressional Policy Making*, Stanford, CA: Stanford University Press.

Broderick, A. (1970) *The French Institutionalists*, Cambridge, MA: Harvard University Press.

Brubaker, R. (1992) *Citizenship and Nationhood in France and Germany*, Cambridge, MA: Harvard University Press.

Chapman, J. W. and W. A. Galston (eds.) (1992) *Virtue*, Nomos XXXIV, New York: New York University Press.

Coleman, J. S. (1966) 'The possibility of a social welfare function', *American Economic Review* 56: 1105–22.

Coleman, J. S. (1986) *Individual Interests and Collective Action*, Cambridge: Cambridge University Press.

Collier, R. B. and D. Collier (1991) *Shaping the Political Arena: Critical Junctures, the Labor Movement, and Regime Dynamics in Latin America*, Princeton, NJ: Princeton University Press.

Cyert, R. M. and J. G. March (1963) *A Behavioral Theory of the Firm*, Englewood Cliffs, NJ: Prentice-Hall (2nd edn 1992: Blackwell).

Douglas, M. (1986) *How Institutions Think*, Syracuse: Syracuse University Press.

Downs, A. (1967) *Inside Bureaucracy*, Boston: Little, Brown.

Dworkin, R. (1986) *Law's Empire*, Cambridge, MA: Belknap, Harvard University Press.

Dynes, R. R. (1970) *Organized Behavior in Disaster*, Lexington, MA: Heath Lexington Books.

Eggertsson, T. (1990) *Economic Behavior and Institutions*, Cambridge: Cambridge University Press.

Eisenstadt, S. and S. Rokkan (eds.) (1973) *Building States and Nations* I, II, Beverly Hills: Sage.

Elster, J. (1989a) *The Cement of Society*, Cambridge: Cambridge University Press.

Elster, J. (1989b) 'Demokratiets verdigrunnlag og verdikonflikter', in *Vitenskap og politikk*, ed. J. Elster. Oslo: Universitetsforlaget.

Elster, J. and R. Slagstad (eds.) (1988) *Constitutionalism and Democracy*, Oslo: Norwegian University Press.

Flam, H. (1990a) 'Emotional man and the problem of collective action', *International Sociology* 5: 39–56.

Flam, H. (1990b) 'Emotional Man II: Corporate Actors as Emotion-motivated Emotion Managers', *International Sociology* 5: 225–34.

Flora, P. (1983) *State, Economy, and Society in Western Europe 1815–1975*, Frankfurt: Campus Press.

Friedrich, C. J. (1950) *Constitutional Government and Democracy* (rev. ed.), Boston, MA: Ginn and Company.

Furubotn, E. G. and R. Richter (eds.) (1984) 'The new institutional economics. A symposium', Special Issue: *Zeitschrift für die gesamte Staatswissenschaft* 140 (1).

Furubotn, E. G. and R. Richter (eds.) (1993) 'The new institutional economics. Recent progress; expanding frontiers', Special Issue, *Zeitschrift für die gesamte Staatswissenschaft* 149 (1).

Gibbons, R. (1992) *Game Theory for Applied Economists*, Princeton, NJ: Princeton University Press.

Giddens, A. (1985) *The Nation-State and Violence*, Berkeley: University of California Press.

Grafstein, R. (1992) *Institutional Realism*, New Haven, CT: Yale University Press.

Greber, E. R. and J. E. Jackson (1993) 'Endogenous Preferences and the Study of Institutions', *American Political Science Review* 87: 639–56.

Habermas, J. (1992) *Faktizität und Geltung: Beiträge zur Diskurstheorie des rechts und des demokratischen Rechtsstaats*, Frankfurt am Main: Suhrkamp.

Habermas, J. (1994) 'Three Normative Models of Democracy' (manuscript).

Hannan, M. T and J. Freeman (1989) *Organizational Ecology*, Cambridge, MA: Harvard University Press.

Hart, O. and B. Holmström (1987) 'The Theory of Contracts', in T. Bewley (ed.) *Advances in Economic Theory*, Cambridge: Cambridge University Press.

Hechter, M., K.-D. Opp, and R. Wippler (1990) *Social Institutions. Their Emergence, Maintenance and Effects*, New York: deGruyter.

Herzog, Don (1989) *Happy Slaves. A Critique of Consent Theory*, Chicago: University of Chicago Press.

Hoffmann, S. (1991) 'Thoughts on the French Nation Today', *Dædalus* 122: 63–79.

Kaufman, H. (1960) *The Forest Ranger*, Baltimore, MD: Johns Hopkins University Press.

Kitcher, P. (1985) *Vaulting Ambition*. Cambridge, MA: MIT Press.

Krasner, S. D. (1988) 'Sovereignty: An institutional perspective', *Comparative Political Studies* 21: 66–94.

Laitin, D. D. (1985) 'Hegemony and Religious Conflict: British Imperial Control and Political Cleavages in Yorubaland', in *Bringing the State Back In*, eds. P. B. Evans, D. Rueschemeyer and T. Skocpol, Cambridge: Cambridge University Press.

Lefort, C. (1988) *Democracy and Political Theory*, Cambridge: Polity Press.

Lepsius, M. R. (1988) *Interessen, Ideen und Institutionen*, Opladen: Westdeutscher Verlag.

Levinthal, D. A. (1988) 'A Survey of Agency Models of Organizations', *Journal of Economic Behavior and Organization* 9: 153–85.

Levinthal, D. A. and J. G. March (1994) 'The Myopia of Learning', *Strategic Management Journal* 14: 95–112.

Levitt B. and J. G. March (1988) 'Organizational Learning', *Annual Review of Sociology* 14: 319–40.

Lipset, S. M. (1990) *Continental Divide*, New York: Routledge.

Lipset, S. M. and S. Rokkan (1967) 'Cleavage Structures, Party Systems and Voter Alignments: An Introduction', in *Party Systems and Voter Alignments*, eds. S. M. Lipset and S. Rokkan, New York: Free Press.

Lægreid, P. and J. P. Olsen (1978) *Byråkrati og beslutninger*, Bergen: Universitetsforlaget.

Lægreid, P. and J. P. Olsen (1984) 'Top Civil Servants in Norway: Key Players – on Different Teams', in *Bureaucrats & Policy Making*, ed. E. N. Suleiman. New York: Holmes & Meier.

Maanen, J. van (1973) 'Observations on the Making of Policemen', *Human Organization* 32: 407–18.

MacCormick, N. and O. Weinberger (1986) *An Institutional Theory of Law*, Dordrecht: D. Reidel.

Mansbridge, J. J. (ed.) (1990) *Beyond Self-Interest*, Chicago: University of Chicago Press.

McNeil, K. and J. D. Thompson (1971) 'The Regeneration of Social Organizations', *American Sociological Review* 36: 624–37.

March, J. G. (1970) 'Politics and the City', in *Urban Processes as Viewed by the Social Sciences*, eds. K. Arrow; J. S. Coleman, A. Downs, and J. G. March. Washington, DC: The Urban Institute Press.

March, J. G. (1981) 'Footnotes to Organizational Change', *Administrative Science Quarterly* 26: 563–77.

March, J. G. (1991) 'Exploration and Exploitation in Organizational Learning', *Organizational Science* 2: 71–87.

March, J. G. (1994a) *A Primer on Decision-Making*, New York: Free Press.

March, J. G. (1994b) 'The evolution of evolution', in *Evolutionary Dynamics of Organizations*, eds. J. Baum and J. Singh, New York: Oxford University Press.

March, J. G. and J. P. Olsen (1984) 'The New Institutionalism: Organizational Factors in Political Life', *American Political Science Review* 78: 734–49.

March, J. G. and J. P. Olsen (1989) *Rediscovering Institutions*, New York: Free Press.

March, J. G. and J. P. Olsen (1994) 'Institutional Perspectives on Governance', in *Systemrationalitat und Partialinteresse*, eds. H. U. Derlien, U. Gerhardt and F. W. Scharpf, Baden-Baden: Nomos.

March, J. G. and J. P. Olsen (1995) *Democratic Governance*, New York: Free Press.

March, J. G. and H. A. Simon (1958)*Organizations*, New York: Wiley (2nd edn 1993: Blackwell).

Meyer, J. W. and B. Rowan (1977) 'Institutionalized Organizations: Formal Structure as Myth and Ceremony',*American Journal of Sociology* 83: 340–63.

Moe, T. M. (1990) 'Political Institutions: The Neglected Side of the Story', *Journal of Law, Economics, and Organizations* 6: 213–66.

Mulhall, S. and A. Swift (1992) *Liberals and Communitarians*, Oxford: Blackwell.

Nauta, L. (1992) 'Changing Conceptions of Citizenship', *Praxis International* 12: 20–34.

Niskanen, W. A. (1971) *Bureaucracy and Representative Government*, Chicago: Rand McNally.

North, D. C. (1981) *Structure and Change in Economic History*, New York: Norton.

North, D. C. (1990) *Institutions, Institutional Change and Economic Performance*, Cambridge: Cambridge University Press.

Olsen, J. P. (1990) *Demokrati på svenska*, Stockholm: Carlssons.

Olsen, J. P. (1992) 'Analyzing Institutional Dynamics', *Staatswissenschaften und Staatspraxis* 2: 247–71.

Olsen, J. P. and B. G. Peters (eds.) (1996) *Lessons from Experience. Experiential Learning in Administrative Reforms in Eight Democracies*, Oslo: Scandinavian University Press.

Orren, K. and S. Skowronek (1994) 'Beyond the Iconography of Order: Notes for a "New Institutionalism"', in *The Dynamics of American Politics*, eds. L. C. Dodd and C. Jillson, Boulder: Westview Press.

Powell, W. W. and P. J. DiMaggio (eds.) (1991) *The New Institutionalism in Organizational Analysis*, Chicago: The University of Chicago Press.

Quarantelli, E. L. and R. R. Dynes (1977) 'Responses to Social Crisis and Disaster', *Annual Review of Sociology* 3: 23–49.

Rawls, J. (1993) *Political Liberalism*, New York: Columbia University Press.

Riker, W. H. (1962) *The Theory of Political Coalitions*, New Haven, CT: Yale University Press.

Rothstein, B. (1992) 'Labor-Market Institutions and Working Class Strength', in *Structuring Politics. Historical Institutionalism in Comparative Analysis*, eds. S. Steinmo, K. Thelen and F. Longstreeth, Cambridge: Cambridge University Press.

Sabine, G. H. (1952) 'The Two Democratic Traditions', *The Philosophical Review* 5: 493–511.

Sandel, M. J. (1982) *Liberalism and the Limits of Justice*, Cambridge: Cambridge University Press.

Sandel, M. J. (1984) 'The Procedural Republic and the Unencumbered Self', *Political Threory* 12: 81–96.

Scott, W. R. (1987) 'The Adolescence of Institutional Theory',*Administrative Science Quarterly* 32: 493–511.

Searing, D. D. (1991) 'Roles, Rules and Rationality in the New Institutionalism', *American Political Science Review* 85: 1239–60.

Selznick, P. (1949) *TVA and the Grass Roots*, Berkeley: University of California Press.

Selznick, P. (1992) *The Moral Commonwealth*, Berkeley: University of California Press.

Sened, I. (1991) 'Contemporary Theory of Institutions in Perspective', *Journal of Theoretical Politics* 3: 379–402.

Shepsle, K. A. (1989) 'Studying Institutions. Some Lessons from the Rational Choice Approach',*Journal of Theoretical Politics* 1: 131–47.

Shepsle, K. A. (1990) *Perspectives on Positive Economy*, Cambridge: Cambridge University Press.

Shepsle, K. A. and B. Weingast (1987) 'The Institutional Foundations of Committee Power', *American Political Science Review* 81: 85–104.

Skowronek, S. (1982) *Building a New American State*, Cambridge: Cambridge University Press.

Smith, R. M. (1988) 'Political Jurisprudence, the "New Institutionalism" and the Future of Public Law', *American Political Science Review* 82: 89–108.

Spradley, J. P. and B. J. Mann (1975) *The Cocktail Waitress*, New York: Wiley.

Steinmo, S., K. Thelen and F. Longstreth (eds.) (1992) *Structuring Politics. Historical Institutionalism in Comparative Analysis*, Cambridge: Cambridge University Press.

Stinchcombe, A. L. (1965) 'Social Structure and Organizations', in *Handbook of Organizations*, ed. J. G. March, Chicago: Rand McNally.

Sunstein, C. (1990) *After the Rights Revolution*, Cambridge, MA: Harvard University Press.

Taylor, Charles (1985) *Philosophy and the Human Sciences*, Cambridge: Cambridge University Press.

Teubner, G. (1993) *Law as an Autopoietic System*, Oxford: Blackwell.

Thelen, K. and S. Steinmo (1992) 'Historical Institutionalism in Comparative Politics', in *Structuring Politics. Historical Institutionalism in Comparative Analysis*, eds. S. Steinmo, K. Thelen and F. Longstreth, Cambridge: Cambridge University Press.

Thomas, G. M. *et al.* (1987) *Institutional Structure. Constituting State, Society, and the Individual*, Beverly Hills, CA: Sage.

Thompson, M., R. Ellis and A. Wildavsky (1990) *Cultural Theory*, Boulder: Westview Press.

Tilly, C. (ed.) (1975) *The Formation of National States in Western Europe*, Princeton, NJ: Princeton University Press.

Tilly, C. (1993) rev. edn, *Coercion, Capital, and European States*, Oxford: Blackwell.

Turner, B. S. (1990) 'Outline of a Theory of Citizenship', *Sociology* 24: 189–217.

Tussman, J. (1960) *Obligation and the Body Politic*, London: Oxford University Press.

Weaver, R. K. and B. A. Rockman (eds.) (1993) *Do Institutions Matter?*, Washington, DC: Brookings.

Wildavsky, A. (1987) 'Choosing Preferences by Constructing Institutions: A Cultural Theory of Preference Formation', *American Political Science Review* 81: 3–22.

Wolin, S. S. (1989) *The Presence of the Past. Essays on the State and the Constitution*, Baltimore: Johns Hopkins University Press.

Yack, B. (1985) 'Concept of Political Community in Aristotle's Philosophy', *Review of Politics* 47: 92–112.

Part III

The policy process

Introduction

The first two articles in this section deal with an important debate about the policy process, efforts to specify how policy *should* be made. This may seem to take us off in an inappropriate direction in a Reader on how policy *is* made. But the intimate connections between these two concerns have already been emphasized in Part I, and in this case we will find critics confronting the arguments for an ideal with what is suggested as a more realistic account of the policy process.

Two comparatively recent contributions to a debate which has a rather longer history have been chosen. The debate goes back to an argument advanced from a very clearly prescriptive viewpoint by Herbert Simon in his *Administrative Behavior*. He set out to recommend a rational approach to the making of policy decisions whilst nevertheless taking into account organizational and political realities. Simon recommended an approach involving careful examination of options to arrive at a decision which would 'satisfice' in terms of policy goals even if it was not the ideal or optimal decision.

This approach was challenged by Braybrooke and Lindblom on two grounds, both rooted in the pluralist analysis of politics. One was that in many circumstances the pressures upon decision-makers are such that this kind of 'rationality' is unattainable, and many decisions are 'incremental' involving small adjustments to what has been done before. This process is one of 'partisan mutual adjustment' in the light of pluralist competition to influence decisions. The other objection derived specifically from the pluralist ideal that the best kind of democratic process involves this sort of incremental adjustment. Hence to attempt rational decision-making would mean engaging in the kind of social engineering in which political elites endeavoured to disregard the popular pressures upon them. Subsequently many writers tried to find the middle ground between these two positions. Of particular interest here was the evolution of the thinking of one of the main protagonists, Lindblom, who, as McLennan showed in his piece in Part II, increasingly came to recognize that pluralism was often biased. Hence, he can be seen as taking an increasingly state-centred view in which some approach to 'rational' decision-making by administrators may be important to counteract the impact of powerful interests (see Lindblom and Woodhouse 1993).

The article by Smith and May seeks to help us find our way through this debate, by showing how prescriptive and descriptive positions are mixed together within it. In their view the rationalism position is particularly clearly prescriptive whilst the

159

incrementalist position provides a good description of what is likely to occur in the real world. However, that straightforward distinction, which is generally helpful to us in sorting our way through this debate, is challenged a little in the second article. Here Gregory celebrates Lindblom's important contribution to policy-making theory, emphasizing a *prescriptive* point that 'good' decision-making is likely to be that which is best adjusted to the political realities which require it to be incremental.

Gregory's thoughtful analysis of this subject highlights a point mentioned in the introduction to Part I. It is a peculiarity of our use of language in the study of the policy process that the word rationality has been appropriated to describe a process as opposed to an outcome. It is, moreover, a process more concerned with relating means to ends than with ensuring that there is a mandate for those ends. This turns on its head a body of philosophical work which was concerned with the extent to which totalitarian regimes (see, in particular the work of Popper 1966) tried to practise wholesale social engineering without reference to the views, needs or interests of their subjects. This was seen as deeply irrational in terms of its outcomes, however carefully it related means to ends. It brings us back to the issues about the 'autonomous state', in which the people engaged in 'rational' planning may be Orwellian 'big brothers'. The point is also applicable to some of the 'new right' thinkers who seek to use the policy process to effect massive ideologically driven reversals of past policy.

This is not necessarily to argue that the pluralist optimism of the original Braybrooke and Lindblom work was right all along. Devastating events have occurred as a result of a chain of incremental decisions; look, for example, at the way the United States gradually moved into engagement in war in Vietnam. Moreover, a simple pluralist faith in popular mandates here may not be sufficient, some appalling human acts have been justified in terms of their popular support (here, of course, the analysis offered by Lukes in Part II indicates some of the difficulties with this notion). It is therefore not so easy to take a simplistic stance on the decision-making debate when it is set out in abstract terms. Our answers may depend upon the issues and will certainly depend upon more detailed analysis of who controls the policy outputs of the state and how they control it.

The third piece in this part is rather different. The discussions of the policy process in this part and the last one have been essentially theoretical; the article by Blowers applies theory to a case study. In the analysis of policy processes contrasting theoretical approaches may be used together, either by pulling out pieces from each or by comparing and contrasting explanations to see how they illuminate the policy process in different ways. Policy analysis is not an exact science. It involves trying to understand and explain events in situations in which we never have complete information about what happened and why it happened, and our interpretations are influenced by our frames of reference and our ideologies.

Blowers contrasts two perspectives – the pluralist and the political economy perspective. The second perspective is the one which derives from Marxist theory and emphasizes structured economic determinants of action. Blowers subsequently examined this story at much greater length, and with even more elaborate use of the theories, in his book *Something in the Air: Corporate Power and the Environment*. In this article he ends by stressing the way in which two explanations may stand side by side, illuminating the story in different ways. In his book he goes further to suggest ways in which the theories may be differentially used to illuminate different parts and different phases in the long saga of pollution control policy in the brickfields he studied.

Ideally, a reader of this kind should include a range of case studies but space prevents this. Readers looking for others will find them in M. J. Smith's book *Pressure, Power and Policy* from which an excerpt was included in Part II, in the book on the institutional approach edited by Steinmo, Thelen and Longstreth also recommended in Part II, and in Marsh and Rhodes' *Implementing Thatcherite Policies*, which is as much about policy-making as about implementation.

References

Blowers, A. (1984) *Something in the Air: Corporate Power and the Environment*, London: Harper and Row.

Lindblom, C. E. and Woodhouse, E. J. (1993) *The Policy Making Process*, Englewood Cliffs, NJ: Prentice Hall.

Marsh, D. and Rhodes, R. A. W. (1992) *Implementing Thatcherite Policies*, Buckingham: Open University Press.

Popper, K. R. (1966) *The Open Society and its Enemies* (5th edn), London: Routledge and Kegan Paul.

Simon, H. A. (1957) *Administrative Behavior* (2nd edn), New York: Macmillan.

The artificial debate between rationalist and incrementalist models of decision making

Gilbert Smith and David May

Introduction

As students of the formation and implementation of government policies have become dissatisfied with a predominantly descriptive and generally atheoretical approach to their subject, so more express attention to the abstract concepts and ideas which guide data collection and analysis in policy studies has become indispensable. The notion of 'decision making' is indisputably central to studying the process through which policies are both designed and effected and this paper is about the components of that idea. Such analysis may be thought redundant for 'decision' is a common enough term. But, as the already extended discussions of 'key concepts' such as poverty,[1] need,[2] justice,[3] implementation[4] or control[5] have shown, commonsense notions in everyday usage tend initially to be rather blunt instruments when pressed into service as tools for research. And as any good craftsman knows, there are few things more dangerous than using blunt tools.

In the literature on public administration[6] a debate about the relative merits of rationalistic as opposed to incrementalist models of decision making has featured for some years now and although the terms of this debate are rather well known it has had comparatively little impact upon empirical research in the area of either policy or administrative studies. However, an awareness of the limits to rational decision making in institutions has exerted a significant influence upon the direction of the more sociologically oriented work in the field of organisational analysis.[7] It is the purpose of this note to suggest that, when work from these several fields is considered together, it is apparent that (1) the components of 'decision making' in social policy are by no means obvious, (2) the rationalism versus incrementalism debate is in certain respects an artificial dispute and (3) this has implications for the design and conduct of empirical research on decision making which aspires to be policy relevant.

From G. Smith and D. May, 'The artificial debate between rationalist and incrementalist models of decision making', *Policy and Politics*, **8**, 1980, pp. 147–61.

Two models of decision making

An essentially rationalistic approach to decision making has predominated in the study of organisations. This approach advances a definition of decision making which is described by Scott as consisting of a process with the following components:

1. A search process to discover goals.
2. The formulation of objectives after search.
3. The selection of alternatives (strategies) to accomplish objectives.
4. The evaluation of outcomes.[8]

These are the elements which are viewed as common to the making of all kinds of decisions – and rightly so. That is, good decisions are those which conform to this pattern. As Etzioni observes:

> Rationalistic models are widely held conceptions about how decisions are and ought to be made. An actor becomes aware of a problem, posits a goal, carefully weighs alternative means, and chooses among them according to his estimate of their respective merit, with reference to the state of affairs he prefers.[9]

It is important to note that the approach purports to offer a framework which is at one and the same time explanatory and normative.

The rationalistic approach, however, has been widely criticised. First, it is regarded as being too narrow. It neglects the range of political variables which limits the extent of choice available in the light of the power of relevant vested interests. Most decision makers in policy contexts do not work in an environment devoid of constraints. They are simply not free to consider all possible options and often they are compelled to shortlist, if not actually recommend, options that they would not even pretend to justify as the most appropriate in terms of a simple means–ends schema. This is the well-known process of pressure group politics. And students of the policy process are showing considerable interest in the pluralist and related theories which have been a regular part of the political science parentage of public administration.[10]

Secondly, the rationalistic approach is seen as utopian. Most policy decisions have numerous unanticipated consequences which are neither as inconsequential nor disposed of nearly as readily as the model tends to imply. The model represents, perhaps, the planner's dream but in the real world, it is argued, ends are not that clear, decisions are not that neat and evaluation is not that systematic. Indeed it has been argued[11] that ambiguity is actually a rather central feature of most policy and should be acknowledged and studied as such. Since,

> the executive's . . . task of translating ambiguous political directives into operational agency policy . . . is one which requires a far more sensitive value theory than any now available in the context of administrative scholarship,[12]

McCleery sees the rational model as appropriate only to those limited kinds of bureaucracy where the executive is given very precise guidance. But in practice policy institutions of this kind may well be the exception rather than the rule.

Thirdly, the rationalistic approach is accused of being value biased in that rationality is itself a quality prized in varying degrees. There is by no means consensus on the fact that rationality represents some universal good nor even upon the definition of rationality.[13] Particularly in an organisational context the model is accused of favouring management and senior professions to the detriment of low-ranking staff, clients and patients, whose perspectives are in practice neglected. There is a tendency to equate rationality with the smooth running of the organisation. Although clearly we need to know a great deal about the way in which claimants and clients, patients and the general public approach service agencies, there is some evidence, in studies of welfare services for example,[14] that the importance attached to the smooth running of different aspects of a service may in significant respects differ between groups associated with the agency.

Fourthly, rationalistic models are seen as too rigid in drawing sharp distinctions between ends and means, values and decisions, and facts and values. What counts as 'fact' is notoriously subject to the interests and values of the parties involved.

> Traditional conduct, like other forms of unreflected social process, does not differentiate between means and ends, nor between the criteria for truth and good conduct. What is good and what works must be true.[15]

As Lindblom,[16] in his much quoted article, points out, means and ends are often chosen simultaneously within the administrative process. The frequent absence of any clear means–ends relationship is often particularly apparent when several of the stages of implementing policy are examined together and overall. (Policy research is habitually handicapped by the fact that individual research projects can so seldom examine all stages in the process. Not infrequently it is what happens *between* major stages that is most interesting.) Cassidy and Turner,[17] for example, have used the idea of 'up stream causality' in studying systems of criminal justice to suggest, for instance, that rates of apprehension and charging may be a function of the proportion of those charged found guilty in the courts, rather than vice versa. Thus means often precede ends, become ends or even cause ends. Ends become means as one decision merges into the next. Values may rationalise rather than determine decisions and certainly actors are often unable to rank their values independently of specific choices. The ambiguity of means, ends and their relationship is substantially greater than rational models allow.

A final criticism of rationalistic models is that they are impractical. Even with the aid of computer technology a review and evaluation of all *possible* answers to a problem in order to select the optimal solution is seldom plausible and the cost of the search may well exceed the savings achieved by the solution eventually discovered. This is one of the dilemmas faced by policy makers in deciding whether or not it is worth commissioning research. The Seebohm Committee, for example, set up to examine the reorganisation of the personal social services in Britain, is only one of a number of government committees and commissions that have felt that the delay in producing their report which would be occasioned by awaiting the results of a programme of research would not be justified.[18] It is easy for supposedly rationally minded social scientists to criticise policy makers for neglecting systematic research. It is less easy actually to demonstrate its utility when weighed against the costs.[19] Even if the savings of a novel policy option do exceed the search costs there is no way of knowing about that before the search begins. Inevitably, it is argued, at least some choices must be made without reference to the relationship between means and ends.

In reaction to these criticisms Lindblom has set out the alternative approach termed, provocatively, 'muddling through', or 'disjointed incrementalism'.[20] This model posits the decision maker as starting not with some ideal goal but with the policies currently in force. Decision making entails considering only incremental change, or changes at the margins. Only a rather restricted number of policy alternatives is reviewed and only a limited number of consequences is envisaged and evaluated for any given alternative. In empirical support of this view Jansson and Taylor,[21] while commenting upon the virtual absence of studies which assess the effectiveness of planning procedures in social agencies, rank only one third of the sample of agencies which they studied, as undertaking extensive search activity for new policies. In contrast to the conventional view which sees means adjusted to ends, incrementalism promotes the opposite, allowing for a continuous and reciprocal relationship between means and ends. It is argued that in this way the problems of decision makers are rendered more manageable, for what counts as 'the problem' is constantly subject to redefinition in the light of available means to solve it. Thus the very subject of the decision may be transformed and reinterpreted through the analysis. Evaluation is thus seen not as a separate activity but as taking place in series with decision making. Braybrooke and Lindblom conclude:

> Since policy analysis is incremental, exploratory, serial, and marked by adjustment of ends to means, it is to be expected that stable long-term aspirations will not appear as dominant critical values in the eyes of the analyst. The characteristics of the strategy support and encourage the analyst to identify situations or ills from which to move *away* rather than goals *towards* which to move (original italics).[22]

Like the rationalistic model, the incrementalist approach has also been subjected to important criticisms. It is accused of being conservative in that it copes with only remedial and short-term change and reinforces inertia. Dror[23] suggests that it is a valid approach only if the results of present policies are generally satisfactory, if the nature of the problem is relatively stable and if means for dealing with that problem are continuously available. Generally, however, he regards 'its [incrementalism's] main impact as an ideological reinforcement of the pro-inertia and anti-innovation forces prevalent in all human organisations, administrative and policy making'.[24] Certainly there *are* major barriers to policy innovation. Booth,[25] for example, has described those factors in the machinery of local government in Britain which have inhibited the introduction of alternatives to residential care in the personal social services, in spite of a strong 'rational' case against the extensive supply of residential provision. Dror concludes:

> The 'rational-comprehensive' model has at least the advantage of stimulating administrators to get a little outside their regular routine, while Lindblom's model justifies a policy of 'no effort'.

Taken together, the limited validity of the 'muddling through' thesis and its inertia-reinforcing implications constitute a very serious weakness.[26]

The incrementalist approach is also accused of being unjust since 'good' decisions are assessed not by their ranking on some objective evaluative criterion but simply by their acceptability in a particular situation. The approach is therefore thought to favour the interests of the most powerful and systemically to under-represent the interests of the underprivileged and politically unorganised. Incrementalism, too, is felt to be more narrow and more limited than the model it seeks to replace. Incremental decisions take place within the context of more fundamental decisions and the approach has little to say about how decisions of this more fundamental kind are made. While it may afford a strategy for researching some of the more detailed workings of the decision making process it is incomplete as a framework for 'macro' analysis.

Finally it is argued that although much has been made of the practicality of the incrementalist approach in fact it is extremely costly. Although the costs of rational decision making are high the costs of failing to explore radical alternatives to existing policies may be even higher. Admittedly the optimal solution is not to be preferred if the costs of discovering it are greater than the savings incurred. But the incrementalist approach is accused of offering no way of informing participants that a sub-optimal solution which has emerged is so costly comparatively as to represent an outcome that decision makers would find unacceptable if the costs were apparent. This is the situation that techniques such as cost benefit analysis[27] and planning strategies such as corporate management seek to avoid, although the few case studies available show substantial disparity between practical experience and the ideal accounts.[28] Nevertheless, Hyderbrand concludes,

> the question remains whether gradual incremental change is only a form of adaptation which leaves basically intact what *ought* to be changed (original italics).[29]

Two 'third' approaches

Now this debate has generated important criticisms of both rationalist and incrementalist approaches and the study of decision making can hardly proceed without taking them into account. Certainly neither model has survived unscathed as the basis for research in social policy, and both Etzioni[30] and Dror[31] have attempted to avoid the weaknesses of rationalist and incrementalist models by combining the strongest features of the two. Each offers a 'third' alternative. Etzioni describes the 'mixed-scanning approach' and Dror outlines what he calls the 'normative-optimum model for policy making'. But both have limitations.

Mixed scanning entails a decision making process in two phases. Initially a broad sweep is made of policy options and these are assessed against stated values in general terms. Then, within this framework, decision making proceeds incrementally in matters of detail. Etzioni claims that:

each of the two elements in mixed-scanning helps to reduce the effects of the particular shortcomings of the other; incrementalism reduces the unrealistic aspects of rationalism by limiting the details required in fundamental decisions, and contextuating rationalism helps to overcome the conservative slant of incrementalism by exploring longer-run alternatives.[32]

But in fact it is not clear that the unrealistic and conservative shortcomings would actually be avoided. They might merely be confined or moved to different sectors of the decision making process. There is no guarantee that within these confines they might not even be accentuated. We would need to examine mixed scanning in practice before we could judge. Other issues are sidestepped. For example, Etzioni retains the presumption that decision makers can summarise and rank their values, at least ordinally. As we have mentioned, it has been argued with conviction that values are ordered only in contexts of specific choice.

However, the central weakness of mixed scanning lies in the importance attached to a distinction between two different kinds of decision.

> It is essential to differentiate fundamental decisions from incremental ones. Fundamental decisions are made by exploring the main alternatives the actor sees in view of his conception of his goals, but – unlike what rationalism would indicate – details and specifications are omitted so that an overview is feasible. Incremental decisions are made but within the contexts set by fundamental decisions (and fundamental reviews).[33]

But just as the distinction between means and ends is flexible, as we have seen, so fundamental decisions in one context are incremental in another and vice versa. It is at least possible that decision makers would define decisions in different ways, either quoting or ignoring detail and either exploring or neglecting alternatives, as suited their purposes in particular situations. Without further empirical data the doubt remains that mixed scanning is just as utopian as rational planning and just as lethargic as 'muddling through'. The important point is that rationalism and incrementalism embody diametrically opposed principles which are not reconciled by mixed scanning's sampling of either side.

Dror also seeks a model to 'increase rationality-content' in decision making while acknowledging that, 'Extrarational processes play a significant role in optimal policy making on complex issues'.[34] Essentially his alternative consists of a recapitulation of some of the aspects of rational planning but with heavy caveats of the form, '*some* clarification of values' or '*preliminary* estimation of pay-offs' or 'explicit arrangements to stimulate creativity'. Lindblom has criticised Dror for offering no more than a series of discrete statements which do not connect and cannot be said to constitute a 'model' for decision making.[35] However, the weakest feature of Dror's statement is the role assigned to 'intuition' and 'experience'. These are disconcertingly vague variables and hardly more than residual categories for non-rational sources of information. The whole model borders on the tautologous as an extended restatement of the opening commitment to both rational and non-rational elements. Again the important point is that the central features of the dispute between rationalist and incremental models of decision making remain largely unmarred by this attempt to offer this 'third' alternative.

An artificial debate

These, then, are the terms of the argument. But in this note we are not proposing to come down in favour of one side or the other, nor indeed in favour of the attempts that have been made to construct a 'third' model of decision making as a compromise between the two. For in spite of prolonged dissension between rationalist and incrementalist models of decision making, both they and the several versions of a rapprochement have in common epistemological features the significance of which outweigh any specific points of variance. What we are proposing to do is to suggest that in certain respects the debate is somewhat artificial, firstly because it is not at all clear that the protagonists are actually arguing about the same thing and, secondly, because there is an important issue – of what it takes to act in accord with a set of rules about decision making behaviour – which is largely ignored on both sides. As policy research seeks clarification of the notion of 'decision making' it seems important initially to question some ground rules of the debate as it stands.

First, it is a mark of all the models that we have discussed that they should serve both explanatory and normative purposes. Bittner has commented on the general concept of rational organisation that, 'Even though one finds only *"is"* and *"is not"* in the substantive determination, there attaches the sense of *"ought"* to the entire scheme' (original italics).[36] In this debate that inclination is widespread and quite explicit. We have already mentioned Etzioni's observation that rationalistic models are widely held conceptions about how decisions *are* and *ought to be* made. It is also an important aspect of Lindblom's thesis that incrementalism both describes decision makers' behaviour and formalises an account of how they should behave. Furthermore Etzioni claims of the mixed scanning tactic that:

> Mixed-scanning provides both a realistic description of the strategy used by actors in a large variety of fields and the strategy for effective actors to follow[37]

and adds that the approach should be, 'at once *more realistic and more effective* than its components' (italics added).[38] And Dror, too, retains this commitment to a concurrently descriptive and prescriptive enterprise:

> What is needed is a model which fits reality while being directed towards its improvement, and which can in fact be applied to policy making while motivating a maximum effort to arrive at better policies.[39]

It is perhaps an indication of how deeply ingrained is this dual commitment within the disciplines of administrative and policy studies that such a statement does not immediately stand out as odd, confused and confusing as a basis for empirical research.

However, it *is* anomalous to presume *a priori* that 'is' and 'ought' in modes of decision making correlate. Certainly the authors who adopt this position do not explain at all clearly how a model is supposed to serve simultaneously as an accurate description of how decisions are made and as a description of how they might be made differently by way of improvement. Can these decision making models serve both functions? The debate which this note has been reviewing suggests not. Indeed the frequency with which current practices are criticised and changes advocated indicates precisely the opposite; namely that quite different frameworks may be required for explanatory and normative discussion. We are not of course arguing that explanatory social research can have no prescriptive policy implications. (A legitimate concern with improving both substantive policy and the way in which it is made and implemented is the *raison d'être* of much research in this field.) But to press either rationalist or incrementalist models into service for both functions at the same time is to risk what Bittner has termed 'ambiguities that defy clarification'.[40] Certainly as the debate is currently structured concepts in use for analysis and practice are utterly confused and it is hard to see how lucidity can be distilled.

One way forward may lie in the suggestion that the protagonists in the 'rationalism versus incrementalism' debate are really arguing about different kinds of things and that the term 'decision making' is thus in danger of being applied insensitively to a variety of phenomena and to confusing effect. It may be helpful to make some distinctions.

It will be apparent from discussion earlier in this note that few commentators generally doubt rationalistic models to be rather accurate pictures of widely held images about ideal decision making procedures. Criticism centres on the fact that rationalistic models are empirically inaccurate, or unrealistic. *That is not the way things are.* On the other hand there is a degree of sympathy for the view that the incrementalist approach has much validity as an empirical model of how policies are made (or, as McCleery puts it, 'more often, not made').[41] Criticism here centres on the claims of this approach to be useful normatively. *That is not the way things should be.*

Now viewed in this light it can be seen that the debate between rationalistic and incrementalist models is artificial in the sense that it is based on what Etzioni[42] elsewhere has pointed to as the confusion of comparing real with ideal states of affairs and expecting them to be the same. The two models are about different social phenomena and as such should seek to perform different functions. We should not expect them to agree. It certainly comes as no surprise to students of organisational behaviour to learn that the ideal accounts offered by organisational members of their practices are only a partial basis for explanation. As Bittner notes:

> It has been one of the most abiding points of interest of modern organisational research to study how well the programmatically intended formal structures of organisations describe what is going on within them, and what unintended, unprogrammed and thus informal structures tend to accompany them.[43]

And with a degree of consistency which is unusual in the social sciences, study after study has concluded that we require more than one account to describe the several facets of organisational life. The problem is not to reconcile the differences between contrasting rational and incremental models, nor to construct some third alternative which combines the strongest features of each. The problem is to relate the two in the sense of spelling out the relationship between the social realities with which each is concerned.

If this point is a valid one it has implications for policy related research. It means that more sophisticated accounts than those currently available are required of the impact of policy makers' ideologies, about the nature of decision making, upon the conduct and outcomes of the various stages of the policy process. In that sense what is called for is a data-based metatheory, delineating more precisely the role and functions of existing decision making models within the machinery of policy and administration. Methodologically that may be difficult for it must probably rest upon participant and other forms of observational data as well as upon interviews and records which so often reflect primarily ideological variables. But it is hard even to begin those tasks while 'is' and 'ought' remain so totally confused.

A second general feature of the debate is that both incrementalist and rationalist models, again together with the proponents of a 'third' view, largely ignore the issue of *what it takes*[44] to constitute conformity to the rules of either rationalist or incrementalist principles. That is, insufficient attention has been paid to organisational members' own coding practice. For activity which may be classified by the organisational analyst in one set of terms may be described by the decision makers themselves, either prospectively or restrospectively, in another. What then is the relative status of the member's and analyst's coding manual? For instance, much apparent confusion of means and ends and objectiveless behaviour, from an incrementalist stance, may well be held by members as quite in accord with rational conduct. In the welfare services, for example, social workers are often accused by their critics of 'muddling through' yet persist in rational accounts of their own professional practices and decisions.

The point is that there is much flexibility in the way in which decision making can be described and it would be naive to suppose that members do not employ this flexibility in their own interests. For models of decision making are as much 'active elements of the concrete phenomenon of organisation' as a 'disinterested statement about it'.[45] As Turner[46] has argued, we must at least consider the possibility that social scientists have been 'set up' for their view of organisational life and thus been systematically misled about its character by presuming that the relationship of correspondence between an organisational concept and the practical activities that constitute that concept *in situ* is unambiguous. It is not. Since concepts and rules in organisations are used both prospectively and retrospectively to assign meaning to courses of action, what a scheme of ideas practically entails is a matter for empirical research. We may even find that it does not substantially affect the outcome of events whichever approach decision makers themselves claim to be following. They are likely to choose whatever is situationally most convenient and then justify their mode of choice in whatever terms appear most likely to prove acceptable.

One example of this can be seen in the field of British central government funding of applied social research. The Rothschild Report[47] recommended changes in the way in which decisions about financing projects were to be made. Although this may have altered the relationship between central government and some of the research councils, many established commissioning practices in departments' external research programmes and in relations between departments and government research units undoubtedly continued unchanged, but under the revised terminology of the 'customer–contractor principle'. Bittner has made the general point thus:

Extending to the rule the respect of compliance, while finding in the rule the means of doing whatever need be done, is the gambit that characterises organisational acumen.[48]

Again if the point is a valid one it has implications for research. For it casts doubt upon the utility of expending any more intellectual energy in developing *a priori* 'models' of decision making. The way forward lies in producing more, and more carefully researched, data based answers to the following questions. What do relevant professionals, administrators, policy makers and laymen actually mean by 'decision making'? What activities do they include within these rubrics? What tactics do they employ? When? Where? How? And to what effects?

A concluding observation within Bittner's programmatic statement summarises the wider enterprise of which this kind of research would form a part:

> The problem that requires investigation is how various evaluations can be used as credits, and what sorts of credits have the consequence of assimilating some partial performance closer to the larger enterprise. The investigation of this problem would reveal the negotiable relationship between policy and politics.[49]

It is central to research in the field of policy and administration to understand not only how individual policy decisions are operationalised but also how decision makers at all stages of the policy process operationalise the notion of 'decision making' itself.

Conclusion

Empirical research in policy studies rightly involves the uncomfortable process of moving continually from theory to data and back again. While research in this area has sometimes been criticised for its atheoretical features, it is also important that concepts and models hastily adopted from allied fields should not be allowed to distort the phenomena under review. The concept of 'decision' is undoubtedly central to the processes of both making and implementing policy but in this note we have been suggesting that its components are by no means obvious, that this in itself constitutes a topic for enquiry and that the debate between rationalist and incrementalist models of decision making, as it is currently structured, provides an inadequate basis for policy research.

We have discussed incrementalist and rationalist models as well as attempts to provide a 'third' alternative. We have concluded that the debate is an artificial one for two reasons. Firstly, the relationship between 'is' and 'ought' is confused and there are good grounds for suggesting that whereas incrementalist models may perform an explanatory function, rationalist models are largely confined to a prescriptive role. Secondly the debate does not consider seriously the issue of what it takes to act in accord with any set of decision making rules and thus neglects the way in which policy makers and administrators may use 'decision making' as a gloss for a range of practices.

Throughout we have suggested that if these arguments are valid they have implications for policy research. They imply a commitment to an adequate explanatory account of decision making practices in the policy process as a precursor to prescriptions about how decisions ought to be made. They imply too the need for empirical studies of what decision makers mean by 'decision making' and how that varies in the varied contexts in which policy arises and gains practical effect.

Notes

1. P. Townsend (ed.), *The Concept of Poverty* (London: Heinemann, 1970).
2. A. Forder, *Concepts of Social Administration* (London: Routledge & Kegan Paul, 1974).
3. B. Davies, *Social Needs and Resources in Local Services* (London: Michael Joseph, 1968).
4. A. Dunsire, *The Execution Process. Volume 1, Implementation in a Bureaucracy, Volume 2, Control in a Bureaucracy* (London: Martin Robertson, 1978).
5. *Ibid.*
6. C. E. Lindblom, 'The science of "muddling through",' *Public Administration*, Vol. 19 (1959), 79–99. Y. Dror, '"Muddling through" – "science" or inertia?', *Public Administration Review*, Vol. 24 (1964), 153–7. A contribution to 'Government decision making', a symposium with contributions from Y. Dror, C. E. Lindblom, R. W. Jones, Mickey McCleery and Wolf Hyderbrand, *Public Administration Review*, Vol. 24 (1964), 153–65.
7. G. Salaman and K. Thompson (eds.), *People and Organisations* (London: Longman for the Open University Press, 1973).
8. W. G. Scott, 'Decision concepts', in F. G. Castles *et al.* (eds.), *Decisions, Organisations and Society* (Harmondsworth: Penguin Books, 1971), 19.
9. A. Etzioni, 'Mixed-scanning: a "third" approach to decision-making', *Public Administration Review*, Vol. 27 (1967), 385. Etzioni is quoted with particular relevance to this note in K. N. Wright, 'An exchange strategy for the interface of community-based corrections into the service system', *Human Relations*, Vol. 30 (1977), 879–97.
10. See, for example, P. Hall *et al.*, *Change, Choice and Conflict in Social Policy* (London: Heinemann, 1975).
11. See, for example, D. May, 'Rhetoric and reality: the consequences of unacknowledged ambiguity in the children's panel system', *The British Journal of Criminology*, Vol. 17 (1977), 209–27; G. Smith, 'The place of "professional ideology" in the analysis of "social policy": some theoretical conclusions from a pilot study of the children's panels', *The Sociological Review*, Vol. 25 (1977), 843–65; D. M. Hill, 'Political ambiguity and policy: the case of welfare', *Social and Economic Administration*, Vol. 12 (1978), 89–119.
12. M. McCleery, 'On remarks taken out of context', *Public Administration Review*, Vol. 24 (1964), 161.
13. B. R. Wilson (ed.), *Rationality* (Oxford: Blackwell, 1970).
14. J. Mayer and N. Timms, *The Client Speaks* (London: Routledge & Kegan Paul, 1970); E. Sainsbury, *Social Work with Families* (London: Routledge & Kegan Paul, 1975); S. Rees, *Social Work Face to Face* (London: Edward Arnold, 1978).
15. R. Hyderbrand, 'Administration of social change', *Public Administration Review*, Vol. 24 (1964), 164.
16. *Op. cit.*
17. R. G. Cassidy and R. E. Turner, 'Criminal justice system behaviour', *Behavioural Science*, Vol. 23 (1978), 99–108.
18. *Report of the Committee on Local Authority and Allied Personal Social Services* (The Seebohm Report), Cmnd. 3703 (London: HMSO, 1968), para. 115.

19. See A. B. Cherns, R. Sinclair and W. I. Jenkins, *Social Science and Government: Policies and problems* (London: Tavistock, 1972).
20. *Op. cit.* See also D. Braybrooke and C. E. Lindblom, *A Strategy of Decision* (New York: Free Press, 1963).
21. D. S. Jansson and S. H. Taylor, 'Search activity in social agencies: institutional factors that influence policy analysis', *Social Service Review*, Vol. 52 (1978), 189–201.
22. *Op. cit.*, 102.
23. *Op. cit.*
24. *Ibid.*, 155.
25. T. Booth, 'Finding alternatives to residential care – the problem of innovation in the personal social services', *Local Government Studies*, Vol. 9 (1978), 3–14.
26. *Op. cit.*, 155.
27. See, for example, A. Williams and R. Anderson, *Efficiency in the Social Services* (Oxford: Blackwell; London: Martin Robertson, 1975).
28. See, for example, A. P. Kakabadse, 'Corporate management in local government: a case study', *Journal of Management Studies*, Vol. 14 (1977), 341–51.
29. *Op. cit.*, 164.
30. *Op. cit.*
31. *Op. cit.*
32. *Op. cit.*, 390.
33. *Ibid.*
34. *Op. cit.*, 155.
35. C. E. Lindblom, 'Contexts for change and strategy: a reply', *Public Administration Review*, Vol. 24 (1964), 157–8.
36. E. Bittner, 'The concept of organisation', *Social Research*, Vol. 32 (1965), 250.
37. *Op. cit.*, 388.
38. *Op. cit.*, 390.
39. *Op. cit.*, 156.
40. *Op. cit.*
41. *Op. cit.*
42. A. Etzioni, 'Two approaches to organisation analysis: a critique and a suggestion', *Administrative Science Quarterly*, Vol. 5 (1960), 257–78.
43. *Op. cit.*, 237.
44. See especially on this point D. H. Zimmerman, 'The practicalities of rule use', in J. D. Douglas (ed.), *Understanding Everyday Life* (London: Routledge & Kegan Paul, 1971), Chapter 9.
45. E. Bittner, *op. cit.*
46. S. Turner, 'Complex organisations as savage tribes', *Journal for the Theory of Social Behaviour*, Vol. 7 (1977), 99–125.
47. *A Framework for Government Research and Development* (The Rothschild Report), Cmnd. 4148 (London: HMSO).
48. *Op. cit.*, 251.
49. *Ibid.*, 254.

Political rationality or incrementalism?

Robert Gregory

Introduction

The name of C. E. Lindblom is synonymous with the concept of incrementalism in the academic literature on public policy making. From the early 1950s he developed an incisive critique of theoretical approaches which depicted public policy making as an exercise in means/ends rationality based on the analysis of comprehensive information. According to Lindblom, such rational-comprehensive, or synoptic, models grossly misrepresented the real practices of policy making, to which he applied his concepts of successive limited comparisons (Lindblom, 1959) and disjointed incrementalism (Braybrooke and Lindblom, 1963).

He has since developed and refined his thoughts on the role of formal analysis in policy making (Lindblom and Cohen, 1979; Lindblom, 1980); he has abandoned his earlier pluralist assumptions about the distribution of group power in liberal democracies (Lindblom, 1977, 1980); and he has also acknowledged an earlier failure to distinguish clearly enough between incremental *analysis* and incremental *politics*, and among differing types of the former (Lindblom, 1979). He has, however, remained committed to the argument that the synoptic model of policy making is an unrealistic and even morally dubious 'ideal'.

The main criticism levelled against Lindblom is that disjointed incrementalism cannot cope adequately with technical complexity and rapid change in modern society. Yehezkel Dror, Amatai Etzioni and more recently Robert Goodin have argued for the development of what they see as more integrated and comprehensive (less marginal) and better informed (more analytical) policy strategies (Dror, 1964, 1968, 1971; Etzioni, 1967; Goodin, 1982).

The collection of ideas commonly associated with the term 'incrementalism' constitute the Lindblomian paradigm of public policy making, which embodies a particular meaning of rationality. This meaning is substantially different from the two other concepts of rationality that are central to the theoretical debate on public policy

From R. Gregory, 'Political rationality or "incrementalism"? Charles E. Lindblom's enduring contribution to public policy making theory', *Policy and Politics*, **17**, 1989, pp. 139–53.

making, namely, *technical* (or formal) rationality, which is about the selection of appropriate means for achieving given ends, and *economic* rationality, which is about determining the most efficient use of resources among competing purposes (for example, Hartwig, 1978). The two latter concepts either together or separately inform the synoptic – or, as it will sometimes be called here, rationalist – model.

This review does not attempt any philosophical examination of these various concepts of rationality. Instead it concentrates on the notion of objective-setting, in which the essential differences between the Lindblomian and synoptic paradigms are located.

Incrementalism: multiple meanings

The term 'incrementalism' has become a popular shorthand symbol for one or more of several ideas progressively propounded by Lindblom, mainly since his major collaborative work with Robert Dahl (Dahl and Lindblom, 1953), and which taken collectively constitute the Lindblomian paradigm. These are:

1. That in public policy making the level of theoretical understanding of the relationships among relevant variables is low (Lindblom, 1959; Braybrooke and Lindblom, 1963).
2. That policy makers typically confine themselves to consideration of those variables, values and possible consequences that are of immediate concern to themselves and which differ only marginally from the status quo, thus greatly simplifying their analysis of possible options (Lindblom, 1959).
3. That in the face of such limited informational and theoretical input policy movements are based on trial and error interventions of an intendedly marginal kind, so that unanticipated consequences may be coped with more easily (Lindblom, 1959; Braybrooke and Lindblom, 1963).
4. That policy and/or political change occurs only marginally, that is, what will be the case tomorrow will not differ radically from what exists today. This is what Lindblom refers to as incrementalism 'as a political pattern' – its 'core meaning' (Lindblom, 1979, p. 517).
5. That policy making is a process of political and social interaction – negotiation, bargaining, etc. – among groups promoting and protecting differing and competing interests and values. This is Lindblom's (1965) 'partisan mutual adjustment', a political process that contrasts with a system in which policy is driven by centralised, information-based decision-making (either system being capable of producing incremental policy change, which thus is conceptually different from partisan mutual adjustment).
6. That political and policy change is not a function of any coherent set of transcendently guiding goals (Braybrooke and Lindblom, 1963; Lindblom and Cohen, 1979).

These meanings can be aggregated into two groups, which focus attention on two different aspects of public policy making. The first group embraces meanings 1, 2 and 3, and concerns the role of formal analysis in policy making. The second group, encompassing the fourth, fifth and sixth meanings, relates to the socio/political context of public policy making. Thus, Lindblom's central concept of 'disjointed incrementalism' is essentially an amalgam of meanings contained in the first group, in that it attempts to convey how decision-makers simplify their analytical tasks. His 'simple incremental analysis' (the second meaning stated above) is one of several elements in disjointed incremental analysis, while 'disjointed incrementalism' is in turn one of several possible forms of 'strategic analysis', that is, 'analysis limited to any calculated or thoughtfully chosen set of stratagems to simplify complex policy problems' (Lindblom, 1979, p. 518). The 'disjointed' nature of what Lindblom refers to as 'this complex method of analysis' (Lindblom, 1979, p. 517) is a function of the socio/political context in which it operates: many wills mingle in the making of policy, and consequently analysis is always both partial and partisan. This does not refer simply to any biased generation or misrepresentation of evidence, although this is frequently to be expected, but rather to the inevitability of multiple and divergent viewpoints, based on necessarily selective and incomplete information, that characterises political discourse (Lindblom and Cohen, 1979; Lindblom, 1980).

Incrementalism as analysis

Simply stated, the debate between the so-called rationalists and the incrementalists has been about how to 'improve' public policy processes and outcomes. Just what constitutes 'improvement' in public policy making is a matter of preference, and may be measured against an almost infinite range of criteria. Politicians, bureaucratic advisers, policy analysts, public employees working at the counter, and the clients, beneficiaries or victims of policy are all likely to focus on different issues. For theorists who advocate the development of more 'rational' policy, improvement has to do with the degree to which formal analysis overcomes the 'irrationalities' and limitations of political interaction. Problems of policy making are problems of intellect, in that there is seen to be not enough of it about. According to Dror (1971, p. 28), for example:

> The inadequacy of present normal sciences for the purposes of policy making improvement is the result of their basic paradigms. Therefore, in order to produce the scientific inputs necessary for policy making improvement, a scientific revolution is essential.

And Goodin (1982, pp. 37–8) concludes, *inter alia*, that:

> any responsible policy must be based on some theoretical understanding of the system into which it intervenes . . . based on our theoretical understanding of the particular system concerned, it is sometimes appropriate to think big and sometimes appropriate to think small. Clearly, the most dangerous course, however, is to deny the need for theory and refuse to think at all.

On this issue Lindblom and his critics often seem to be talking past one another, arguing perceived differences when in fact they share common ground. To Lindblom, 'achieving impossible feats of synopsis is a bootless, unproductive ideal' (Lindblom, 1979, p. 518). He sees strategic analysis as a more productive ideal because it is practicable. But writers like Dror and Goodin are hardly unaware of the shortcomings of 'pure' rationality, while strategic analysis hardly seems different from Simon's (1947) 'bounded rationality', which is predicated upon a recognition of those short-comings (Paris and Reynolds, 1983, pp. 124–36). To this extent the debate between Lindblom and his critics has been of very limited significance.

Their major differences over the role of analysis in policy making become apparent on a closer examination of the three meanings contained in the first group, above. Common to these is the core issue concerning the level of *theoretical understanding* in policy making. The first meaning addresses this point directly, while numbers 2 and 3 are derived as a secondary consequence of it. The issue of theoretical understanding in policy making is one to which Goodin (1982) has paid particular attention. The three forms of incrementalism that he identifies (Goodin, 1982, Ch. 2) approximate respec-tively the elements identified above. The first type is a small-step, trial and error, totally pragmatic process of decision-making independent of any theoretical understanding; the second is incrementalism that adapts by testing theoretical hypotheses through small changes in a limited range of variables; and the third, a 'minor theme', is where theoretically informed interventions are tested by small changes which do not foreclose future options – 'the smaller the change the more likely it is to be reversible' (Goodin, 1982, p. 36). Goodin argues that incrementalism shuns 'analytical problem-solving' because 'social theories are too infirm to form the basis for policy making' (Goodin, 1982, p. 19).

If Goodin had set out to show that policy makers are, in fact, guided by theoretical assumptions, even if these are only inchoate and unsoundly based, his thesis would have been a valid elucidation of a point not clearly defined by Braybrooke and Lindblom. In other words, even purely pragmatic decision-makers, such as those depicted in Goodin's first case, are guided in their choices of action by *implicit* beliefs about possible or likely outcomes. To call these beliefs or assumptions 'theories' may be stretching a point, but only if we confine the concept of theory to formal and explicit hypotheses about cause and effect. Thus, Lindblom's (1959) decision-maker, who shapes an economic policy not on the basis of complete causal knowledge about the relationships among a range of economic variables, but in light of his or her understanding of the various trade-offs among a range of significant values that are embodied in a number of differing alternative courses of action, is guided by beliefs about the probable consequences of the choice that is made. In effect, these are inchoate 'hypotheses'. Cases where a decision-maker has absolutely *no* speculative idea about causal relationships – irrespective of how ill-founded these ideas might prove to be in practice – are probably so rare as to be insignificant.

Goodin, however, is primarily concerned with formal theory in policy making. His proposition is that incrementalists either fail to use formal theory at all; or, if they do, they do not use enough, or they use it too cautiously. Here he is much less persuasive in his criticism. This is mainly because, if Goodin is to be believed, these incrementalists – of all three varieties – somehow have an aversion to theoretical understanding of the problems and issues they address. While not saying it explicitly, he invites the reader to conclude that this reluctance to engage theory stems from the decision-maker's stupidity, or laziness, or both. But Goodin's impatience with incrementalists reflects his own inadequate appreciation of the *political* context and nature of their work: if only politicians and their advisers ignored the political character of their work then policies would, from the point of view of those who devise them, be much more 'successful'. His example of the management of the British economy in the post-war years is an interesting one. According to Goodin, the failure of successive governments to halt the 'precipitous decline' of the British economy can be attributed to flaws in the first type of incrementalism. Governments had no shortage of theories about how to deal with the economy but, 'faced with profound disagreement among economic advisers and heavy pressure for quick results, (they) approached the decision problem in a highly incremental manner', trying a number of policies but abandoning each as it failed to produce quick results. Goodin refers to two economists who offer good reasons for believing that any of the strategies would have worked, given time, 'but governments, operating in an extremely atheoretical way, had no clear idea how long to ask insistent citizens and Zurich gnomes to wait for results' (Goodin, 1982, p. 23).

Even if Goodin's assumption about the longer-term efficacy of the chosen strategies is correct, the problem that British governments faced was surely a political one. Knowing what Goodin believes they should have known, their problem was how to convince 'insistent citizens' impatient for results in the short term. In situations of that sort the choices confronting governments are inevitably as much about maintaining electoral support as about determining the theoretical validity of alternative policies. To suggest that this ought not to be so, as Goodin implicitly does, is to depict the political context of governmental policy making as some sort of pathological impediment to 'rational' choice. That does not advance understanding very far.

Politics is not for 'curing'. It never goes away, even when governments profess or appear to be sticking to policies that have the blessing of theoretical 'experts'. The Thatcher government would seem to be more to Goodin's liking (although he does not say) since it has become known for the Prime Minister's resoluteness in sticking to macroeconomic policies that are based on Friedmanite theory intended to create conditions for sustainable, non-inflationary growth of output and employment. The Lange (Labour) government in New Zealand provides another pertinent example. In its first term of office it received widespread acclamation for its abandonment of the pragmatic and politically opportunistic policy stances of its predecessors in the post-war years, and for its commitment to the 'new laissez-faire' which is based on economic liberalism, and a belief in the primacy of inflation as the most important economic problem, to be addressed by the pursuit of firm monetary policy (Boston, 1987; Easton, 1987). After three years of massive reforms to the structure of the New Zealand economy the government was returned to office at the 1987 general election with the biggest Parliamentary majority in the country's history.

Does all this indicate that the sort of incrementalist policy making deplored by

Goodin is now on the wane, that at least in the area of macroeconomic management Britain and New Zealand are seeing a new breed of analytical problem-solvers, instructed by formal theory, and impatient with practical political considerations? No. It can be argued, for example, that the Thatcher government has responded more pragmatically than many would allow to the theoretical shortcomings underpinning its policies (Boston, 1987, p. 141). Apart from that, however, while it may appear that these governments, especially the Lange one, have to a greater extent than their predecessors placed their faith in the longer-term efficacy of theoretically informed choices, they have been able to do this only by solving simultaneously their political problem – persuading their 'insistent citizens' that (a) a longer-term perspective is necessary, and (b) it will ultimately deliver.

It cannot be conceded that there is a stronger commitment to theory *per se*. Rather, what has changed has been the theoretical paradigm that policy makers have employed in informing their economic strategies. Prior to the Thatcher and Lange governments the dominant paradigm had been a neo-Keynesian one based on counter-cyclical demand management strategies. This has been replaced by the radically different paradigm of Friedmanite 'neo-conservative' market liberalism. Moreover, especially so in New Zealand, but also in Britain, radical programmes of public sector reform have been driven not by traditional public administration theory, but by the 'public choice' or 'economics of bureaucracy' theoretical framework (see, for example, Gregory, 1987; Hood, 1987; Roberts, 1987). Arguably, contrary to Goodin's belief that British (and, by extension, New Zealand) governments have been too impatient with theoretical prognostications, and have preferred to respond in a pragmatic manner to changing economic and political circumstance, it may be that the neo-Keynesian theoretical framework within which they operated gave rise to their expedient counter-cyclical macroeconomic management. Similarly, because of their radical challenge to the older order of things the reforms introduced under the 'new laissez-faire' theoretical paradigm demand a firm and continuing political commitment (or at least the appearance of it) if they are to produce the outcomes their authors promise.

Goodin claims that the incrementalists' avoidance of theoretical understanding is based on their assumption of quick and complete results which leaves them blind to policy responses that flow from 'threshold' or 'sleeper' effects, and too inclined to precipitate undesirable policy change. 'What we really need in order to anticipate threshold or sleeper effects is a fairly full set of theoretically integrated empirical generalisations' (Goodin, 1982, p. 26). But, particularly in social policy, such generalisations are extraordinarily difficult to generate, are usually inconclusive and politically contentious when they are, and offer an unconvincing 'excuse' for not proceeding on the basis of well-intentioned judgement that acknowledges the need to act until (often unforeseeable) consequences dictate a policy review. Ironically, Goodin's example of what he considers to be a non-incremental policy based on a 'comparatively full theoretical understanding' confirms the centrality of political power and opportunity that his analysis otherwise ignores. Continuing Congressional support for NASA's plan to put a man on the moon was obviously crucial to its ultimate success. But that support was based on a widely shared belief in the scientists' capacity to deliver the goods – which is quite different from 'theoretical understanding of the processes involved in a space launch' (Goodin, 1982, p. 27) – and on the perceived virtues of the plan itself. (Had they the resources most governments would find it much easier to employ theoretical understanding to fly to the moon than to determine an acceptably fair and efficient distribution of public goods and services.)

A similar response is invited by Goodin's critique of his second type of incrementalism. This is where analysts acknowledge their reliance upon theory about how a system works, but use incremental procedures for perfecting the theory (Goodin, 1982, p. 28). He offers here an orthodox statement about the difficulties faced by analysts in ensuring the internal and external validity – contamination and replicability – of social experiments that are intended to inform public policy making (see, for example, Roos, 1975; J. Q. Wilson, 1974). But it is not at all clear as to what Goodin is criticising in this approach, and no alternative possibility is offered. Instead, he rests content with a statement that could well have been lifted from a practitioner's manual on 'muddling through':

> policy makers have no alternative but to plan as best they can with such information and theory as are available to them at the time. This category of cases is of tremendous importance, since the policy environment is typically highly volatile. (Goodin, 1982, p. 33)

What is at issue is a deeper understanding than that offered by Goodin of the relationships – no matter how direct or diffuse – between theory and practice, belief and action, research and application, in public policy making. For example, popular belief in the efficacy of neo-Keynesian demand management strategies was a vital factor in ensuring the success of those policies in the decades following the Great Depression. Goodin has little, if anything, to say about the subtleties of such interactions, which is surprising in light of the fact that Lindblom, the major target of his criticisms, had already offered an exploratory examination of them in his co-authored work with D. K. Cohen (Lindblom and Cohen, 1979). There, the authors argued a point that is fundamentally challenging to Goodin's analysis: that what they call 'professional social inquiry' (which includes the development and testing of theories) is seldom conclusive in its findings and even less often, if ever, 'independently authoritative' in its application (1979, pp. 41–3).

This shortcoming is evident, too, in Goodin's third concept of incrementalism, which has at its centre a belief in 'the virtues of thinking small' (Caiden and Wildavsky, 1974, p. 309), lest non-incremental decisions produce irreversible effects. Goodin rightly points out that there is no necessary relationship between the irreversibility of a policy intervention and its size: large-scale interventions may be just as reversible as small ones, while the converse may also be true. Moreover, according to Goodin, there is nothing intrinsically wrong with irreversibility in any case: 'it is enormously desirable to eradicate evils once and for all' (Goodin, 1982, p. 37).

But Goodin ignores a more compelling truth, namely, that in so many areas of governmental policy, but especially in the vast area of social policy, it is often politically difficult to agree either on what the problems to be 'eradicated' are, or on how they ought to be addressed. As Banfield (1980, p. 18) has observed:

Social problems are at bottom political; they arise from differences of opinion and interest and, except in trivial circumstances, are difficulties to be coped with (ignored, got around, put up with, exorcised by the arts of rhetoric etc.) rather than puzzles to be solved. In coping with difficulties, formal analysis may sometimes be helpful, but it is not always so. (See, too, Blumer, 1971; Rittel and Webber, 1973.)

Such problems do not readily lend themselves to 'solutions' that are – in Lindblom and Cohen's terminology – either scientifically *conclusive* or politically, socially or morally *authoritative*. The 'Final Solution' devised by the Third Reich is a dramatic illustration. Goodin suggests that incremental policy changes are, under his third type, a function of the analyst's desire to avoid the irreversibility that is believed to result from inadequate theoretical understanding. But is it not that policy makers tend to proceed cautiously under circumstances of high political salience, incomplete and ambiguous information, and where 'reversibility' is assessed in terms of political and social cost rather than technical/experimental validity?

Albeit indirectly, however, Goodin's critique does draw attention to a major weakness in the Lindblomian paradigm; for while there is no necessary relationship between reversibility and the size of policy change, neither is there any such relationship between the latter and the degree of political benefit or cost. This will be discussed in the following section, which focuses on those incrementalist ideas contained in group 2, relating to the socio/political character of public policy making.

Incrementalism as politics

The incremental paradigm explains what it sees as the typically marginal and gradualist character of policy change in terms of processes of social and political interaction, whereby different groups and interests seek to protect and pursue their disparate purposes largely without reference to any set of overarching, common, goals. According to Lindblom (1979, p. 522), while this process of incremental *politics* is closely related to disjointed incremental *analysis* it is not to be confused with it. Nor, he points out, should the process of partisan mutual adjustment be confused with incremental politics *per se*:

> One can imagine a nation practising political incrementalism without partisan mutual adjustment, or with only a minimum of it. One can also imagine partisan mutual adjustment for non-incremental policy making. (1979, p. 523)

Notwithstanding these caveats, a reading of all Lindblom's work on incrementalism leaves the strong impression that he has over-stressed the extent to which policy change is and must be marginal. He denies that political incrementalism is, in principle, slow moving:

> A fast-moving sequence of small changes can more speedily accomplish a drastic alteration of the *status quo* than can an only infrequent major policy change. . . . One might reply of course that drastic steps in policy need be no more infrequent than incremental steps. We can be reasonably sure, however, that in almost all circumstances that suggestion is false. *Incremental*

steps can be made quickly because they are only incremental. They do not rock the boat, do not stir up the great antagonisms and paralyzing schisms as do proposals for more drastic change. (Lindblom, 1979, p. 520. Emphasis added)

This may or may not be so. Apart from the fact that what constitutes incremental or radical change is a matter of subjective judgement, a seemingly radical policy change may not be considered undesirable by those affected by it, and may even be warmly welcomed. What is primarily at issue here is not, as Lindblom suggests in regard to the American political system 'a structure of veto powers [in the Constitution, in legislative procedures, and in property rights] that makes even incremental moves difficult and insufficiently frequent' (1979, p. 520). It is the exercise of political power generally – coalition building, and the fostering, maintenance and decline of support, for example (Spread, 1985) – that determines the nature, scope and focus of policy innovation and change.

Lindblom's view that policy change in the United States and Western Europe has been 'insufficiently frequent' simply expresses his own political judgement about the need for change. This in itself represents a departure from his earlier writings, in which – as many of his critics have claimed – he regarded political incrementalism as not only inevitable but desirable, seeing political democracy as being 'often greatly endangered' by non-incremental change (Braybrooke and Lindblom, 1963, p. 73). But his argument that it is necessarily incremental not only serves to mask the subjectivity of the judgement on which that observation is based, but also obscures the much more compelling point that, whether or not policy change is incremental or radical, it is always politically driven, that is, it is always a function of extant power alignments.

This insistence on the marginality of change turned the so-called incrementalist versus rationalist debate into a blind alley. Much of the literature critical of the Lindblomian paradigm espoused the need to produce policy responses that were less incremental, more far-reaching, in scope. But in following Lindblom's lead that it is political obstacles that inhibit change the critics wrongly concluded that larger-scale policy changes could be induced by enhancing the role of formal analysis and rational techniques of calculation. This in turn drew Lindblom into pointing out the intellectual and political unrealities of synoptic analysis, while reasserting the inevitability of disjointed incremental analysis and of marginal political change. In assuming that a more synoptic style of analysis in policy making could achieve what politics could not, Lindblom's critics threw out the baby of political decision-making with what they regarded as the bathwater of gradualist change. The upshot has been an obfuscation and inter-mixing of the ideas contained in each of the two groups of incrementalist meanings. But while Lindblom has greatly over-stressed the extent to which policy change is or must be incremental, and has been rather ethnocentric in his conclusions on this point, unlike his critics he has understood very clearly that the political baby is an extremely resilient one, which, as will be shown below, has a peculiar rationality of its own.

The confusion can be removed simply by asserting that *there is no necessary relationship between the extent of any policy development or change and the degree to which professional social inquiry has informed it* (Lindblom and Cohen, 1979). The two central themes in the debate are logically, and empirically, separate: depending on whether one judges change to be marginal or radical, one can say that just as an incremental change might be guided by a more synoptic analysis with a heavy reliance on theoretical understanding, and just as a radical change might be so guided, the converse is also possible in each case. [. . .]

The reification of incrementalism

The Lindblomian paradigm illuminates the *processes* of public policy making, whereas the rationalist perspective concentrates on the *results* produced by those processes. In coining the phrase 'the science of muddling through' Lindblom sought to represent what he saw as the generic rationality of a process which, judged by the expectations of microeconomic logic, could not be relied upon to produce 'rational' results. But in insisting that disjointed incrementalism is, in fact, a method or system and 'not a failure of method for which administrators ought to apologise' (1959, p. 87), Lindblom has reified the activities and behaviour he has so ably described. In the debate spawned by Lindblom's seminal article both he and his critics tended to promote and sustain a text book illusion that incrementalist or synoptic strategies were available for adoption or rejection by persons whose business was policy making. The exchange took on the appearance of a religious crusade, in which policy makers were invited to choose either salvation or damnation. Zealous reformers preached against seduction by the easy virtues of political and analytical expediency – Goodin, for example, has decried the 'perverse and pervasive doctrine of incrementalism' (1982, p. 19) – while Lindblom sought to show that the road to a policy making hell was paved with the best of rationalist intentions.

   A legacy of all this has been a common propensity to speak, often pejoratively, of a large group of people – the 'incrementalists' (a term we here place in inverted commas) – whose business is policy making, and who are said to behave in the variety of ways depicted in one or both of the two groups of meanings (above), or to talk as if 'incrementalism' were a 'thing in itself'. The literature is replete with examples, but a few will illustrate. Goodin talks of an 'incrementalist in the role of a central banker (who) might learn to raise taxes slightly every time the inflation rate creeps upward without ever bothering to try to discover what was causing the inflation' (1982, p. 20). Cates (1979, p. 528) states that 'incrementalism is an adversary process; competing values and groups reach agreement through compromise', and (echoing Lindblom) that 'incrementalism is best suited to a stable environment where fine-tuning is all that is needed'. Paris and Reynolds (1983, p. 134) argue that 'incrementalist procedures cannot be expected to provide distributive fairness'. Frohock (1979, p. 52) explains that 'an incrementalist decision-maker expects other actors, in other sections of institutions, to correct the mistakes he may make as he operates even within his limitations, and even this remedial function of incrementalist systems depends upon the limited scope of decisions taken by everyone'. Jackson (1982, p. 148) gives standard reasons in answering his own question, 'Why do decision makers use incrementalism as a decision rule?'. And finally, Lindblom himself calls incremental politics a 'suitable instrument for more effectively grappling with our policy problems', and as being 'a way of "smuggling" changes into the political system' (Lindblom, 1979, pp. 520–1).

All such usage is a form of reification: it imputes an objective, concrete 'reality' to forms of human behaviour that are properly explicable in terms of individual motivation within certain socially created contexts (Fay, 1975). Or it simply creates confusion where clarity is needed (see Smith and May, 1980, on this point). Is Goodin's banker just that – a banker, who acts in a particular way under particular circumstances, or is he or she a banker who has decided to be an 'incrementalist' (perhaps having done a university course in policy making theory)? Incrementalism is not an 'adversary process' as Cates argues (confusing, incidentally, Lindblom's concept of incremental politics with the idea of partisan mutual adjustment). It is not a process of any sort, although the term does – as noted above – focus attention on political processes. What Cates might more accurately have said is that *politics* is an adversary process which sometimes/often produces incremental change (which is to say very little). Nor is incrementalism (meaning disjointed incremental analysis) 'best suited' to anything. It just *is*. By its very nature the analysis of policy issues is inevitably partial, partisan and multi-faceted, whether or not the socio/political environment is stable or unstable. If she means that incremental *politics* is best-suited to a stable environment she is merely offering a tautology: little political change is best suited to conditions of little political change. Distributive fairness, which is the focus of Paris' and Reynolds' concern, is denied not by anyone adopting 'incrementalist procedures', but by the political capacity of some interests to prevail over others. Frohock's decision-maker is unlikely to expect other policy actors to 'correct his mistakes'; rather, he or she is much more likely to act according to the aphorism, 'where you stand depends on where you sit' (Miles, 1978), that is, to play the role of policy advocate that that person is institutionally expected (paid?) to play, alongside others playing different roles and advocating different interests. Nor are there 'incrementalist systems' which have 'remedial functions' that are 'dependent upon the limited scopes of decisions taken by everyone'. Instead it is more sensible to say that in politics the pursuit of narrowly defined personal or group interests may produce policy changes which are considered by some, or all, to be an improvement on what went before. In Jackson's case it can be said that decision-makers do not 'use' incrementalism as a 'decision rule'; they do what they can with limited resources of various kinds – information, time, energy, intelligence, and so on. (The argument that disjointed incrementalism is a decision rule that can be collectively, rather than individually, applied is even more fallacious.) Finally, the 'instrument' of incremental politics, to which Lindblom refers, is nothing of the sort: rather, we should speak of a political process, which sometimes (he, of course, would say more often than not) produces small-scale change – by 'smuggling' perhaps, but also by openly declaring the goods and paying political duties on them.

It is particularly significant that in many such instances 'incrementalism' has been used in place of a perfectly good word long since available to describe the same activity: politics.

'Incrementalism' discarded: Lindblom's political rationality

In Lindblom's classical work, *Politics and Markets*, he develops his two models of the role of intellect in the social organisation of world politico-economic systems. While these models are based on the original ones set out in his earlier work, including 'The science of muddling through', in the whole of *Politics and Markets* there are but three brief references to 'incresmentalism' as such. In his co-authored work with Cohen (1979) the term is referred to only once, in a footnotes, as is also the case in the second edition of *The Policy-making Process* (1980). True, in each of these works Lindblom's concerns are much broader than his earlier focus on the shortcomings of rational-comprehensive policy making. Yet it is almost as if by the late 1970s he had concluded that the term was unnecessary, or that it had been the source of too much confusion. (His 1979 article, 'Still muddling, not yet through', was intended to clarify once and for all some of the differing meanings of the term.)

Whether or not that was Lindblom's own belief, his central contribution to public policy theory could better be understood if at the very least the term 'incrementalism' were used with greater discrimination, or preferably if it were dropped from usage altogether. In none of its separate meanings does it adequately capture the central point that is at the heart of virtually all Lindblom's work, but which becomes particu-larly explicit in his later writings, namely, that *public policy making has to be understood essentially as a political process, rather than an analytical, problem-solving, one.* [. . .]

The strength of Lindblom's work lies in the way in which, both directly and indirectly, it illuminates the nature of a rationality of collective, i.e. political, action, the crucial feature of which is its very *collectivity*. In the Lindblomian paradigm of public policy making, no one individual or group has a monopoly on truth, information or analysis. And the power to determine the ends and means of public policy is widely, though of course not equally, shared. These factors, therefore, rather than any technical limitations on the role of human intellect (as important as these might be), render futile any aspiration to the synoptic 'ideal'. While Lindblom himself may not have put it quite so bluntly, his work shows how advocates of synoptic policy making – whether they know it or not – are really presenting politically sanitised and morally dubious prescriptions for an increasingly elitist distribution of power in society. These prescriptions are disguised by a scientistic vocabulary which speaks of X-efficiency, externalities and general equilibrium, of society's inability to 'solve' (or at least develop 'optimal' policies for) its 'social problems', as if 'correct' answers are detectable by those whose proper business is to govern by virtue of their superior knowledge and intellect.

Lindblom's writing (1977, 1980) on the role of intellect in social organisation clearly illustrates that such a prospect has to be understood in terms of political power rather than scientific integrity. One may accept or reject his thesis on the 'privileged position of business' in western democracies (see Mayer, 1982; Vogel, 1987), and one might agree with Gilliatt (1987) that the Lindblomian view of politics as the search for order ignores an alternative perspective which sees it as being by nature a 'quarrelsome activity concerned with promoting conflict and disrupting order'. Nevertheless,

Lindblom is surely correct in recognising that policy making is an essentially non-scientific activity (the art of the possible, no less), and that those who engage in it are not necessarily dunderheads obdurately set against theoretical insight and commitment, but are political actors who in their own 'final analysis' must measure success against a capacity to translate hopes into legitimate reality. The collective nature of political action ensures that what *is* done will depend greatly on what *can* be done, politically and socially, technically and economically, morally and culturally. [. . .]

It may also be that in many places politics has something of a bad name. It carries with it connotations of self-seeking politicians and political parties who continually subvert the collective public interest through the relentless pursuit of partisan and personal advantage. The advent of a particular government, therefore, which appears to be committed to pursuing the common good through strategies purporting to be unsullied by calculations of partisan advantage (except in so far as their 'correctness' is taken to be a measure of their political virtue) is popularly seen as a welcome relief from prevalent political cynicism. The strategies of the Thatcher government in Britain and the Lange government in New Zealand, as noted above, bring them into this category. In both countries the government's over-riding commitment to the primary objective of disinflation seems to give the lie to Lindblom's arguments that there is no one best way, and that values are determined during – not before – consideration of alternative policy options. It appears to belie the message of his initial example in 'The science of muddling through', that economic management is all about negotiating trades-offs among *marginally* differing values; and it suggests that tightly disciplined cabinets in Westminster parliamentary systems can have a unitary identity and monopoly of decision-making power far more readily than is possible in a system of 'separated institutions sharing powers' (Neustadt, 1960, p. 33). Some would say that Lindblom's representation of political decision-making might have been an appropriate description of governmental economic management at the time he presented it, that is in the 1950s and 60s, before the 'stagflation' of the 1970s disrupted the complacent application of neo-Keynesian economic policies.

The evidence for any such conclusions is illusory. As Lindblom (1980) has observed, public policy making in liberal democracies is driven by the often contradictory demands that it be subject to popular control, mindful of individual liberties, and productive of problem solutions. So while changes in economic policies may be far more sweeping in scope than the Lindblomian paradigm would suggest were possible, sooner or later conflicting demands and pressures begin to make themselves felt, and governments can ignore them only at the risk of placing other, democratic, values in jeopardy. The linear, singular strategy may even achieve its main objective – inflation, for example, might be reduced to a promised 5% per annum. The question then is, what next? The objectives of retaining it at such a level has to be weighed against other, maybe more politically pressing, demands: perhaps that the exchange rate be devalued, unemployment reduced, social welfare programmes increased, and the fiscal deficit reduced. A seemingly virtuous determination to pursue objectives when sustained in the face of growing dissent becomes transformed into an arrogant authoritarianism. This is often because governments hoist themselves on the petard of their own specified objectives: a willingness to revise those objectives in the face of changing circumstances can be represented by political opponents as evidence of muddled thinking, inconsistency or lack of commitment.

Implicit in Lindblom's observations on the elusive nature of policy objectives – '(they) have no ultimate validity other than that they are agreed upon' (1959, p. 84) – is the question of whether or not the overwhelming preoccupation with talk of objective-setting and achievement in public policy making is an especially useful way of conceptualising what the process is really about. The one thinker who has made this point an explicit part of his considerable, and much underrated, contribution to public policy theory is Sir Geoffrey Vickers (for example, 1965, 1968, 1972, 1983; and Open Systems Group, 1984), who includes the idea of 'endurance through time' as one of five elements that he considers to be 'repugnant to "scientific" study' (1972, p. 265). Vickers' work shows how policy making is about the complex and continuous process of adjusting the 'value system' to the 'reality system', and vice versa, and how when viewed in this light it becomes much more relevant to talk not of goals and objectives that are achieved, once and for all, but of norms and standards that are maintained or modified over time (policy 'problems' being resolved rather than solved). For example, in the case mentioned in the preceding paragraph, the 'objective' of reducing inflation to 5% per annum should be seen instead as a means of ensuring – at least for the time being – that certain valued relationships are sustained over and above others that are valued less (say a lower trade deficit and a reduced cost of living, as against rising unemployment and lower rates of productive investment). In this, the task of governance is not to reduce inflation to a target figure, thus 'solving the problem' once and for all, but to shape and alter the standards by which policy success or failure is judged over time. (Borrowing Churchill's famous phrase, to avoid those states of affairs up with which the public will not put.)

It is ironical that these enduring insights into the nature of public policy making should have been proffered by a man whose primary intellectual training lies in economics, the discipline which has provided the theoretical foundations of the prescriptive models of policy analysis against which his own critique has been directed. But as a *political* economist Lindblom has always resisted the temptation to regard politics, in any of its multitude of forms, as a pathological obstruction to the achievement of more rational policy outcomes. As he himself has said, 'to understand policy making one must understand all of political life and activity' (1980, p. 5). He sees very clearly that while better formal analysis is always to be welcomed in policy making – 'like a person in a desert who prizes the shade of any single tree he finds' (Lindblom, 1977, p. 259) – governments proceed in ways characterised by the incrementalist features contained in group 2 (above) because they are obliged to act in a socio/political arena rather than a scientific one. The essence of policy making, an iterative rather than a sequential process in which 'public policy is being formed as it is being executed, and . . . executed as it is being formed' (Friedrich, 1940, p. 6), is the search for legitimate collective action rather than the testing of scientific theories. And while not all politics is policy making, nor all policy making necessarily politics, the differences between the values of political action and scientific inquiry – that is, the differences between *advocacy* on the one hand, and *analysis* on the other – underpin the whole policy analysis enterprise, and ultimately those engaged in it must decide for themselves the extent to which they wish to sacrifice political relevance to scientific integrity or vice versa (Bulmer, 1988; Coleman, 1972; Meltsner, 1976; Price, 1965; Rein and White, 1977; Wilson, 1981).

To suggest, as Lindblom does, that in the face of such uncertainty, ambiguity, inadequate theory and information, unintended consequences, social and technical complexity, political complicatedness, and organisational self-centredness, governments in any modern society in effect do not really know what they are doing is to invite disbelief, impatience, and not a little opprobrium. After all, who ever heard of a politician publicly admitting that he or she is not really in the business of providing 'rational' solutions? In an age when people are culturally conditioned to assume the validity of rationalistic norms there are not many votes in that. Moreover, Lindblom's political perspicacity seems to have left him with virtually nothing to say about the criteria of 'good' policy other than that it is collectively agreed upon; and it is but a short step (though one that he himself has not taken) to argue that, after the 'final analysis' has been completed, political might must be right. Yet this lacuna in his writing does not mean that, in particular, economically rational models of policy making can offer any conclusive answers (Paris and Reynolds, 1983). Nor does it compromise Lindblom's recognition that in order to understand the core of public policy making we need to pay close attention to the nature and exercise of political power.

Conclusion

Charles E. Lindblom's enduring message is that public policy making needs to be seen as an essentially political process, driven by a distinctive form of collective rationality. To understand this is to cut through the confusion created by the over-use of the term 'incrementalism', with which his name is so often closely linked. It is virtually impossible to read Lindblom without sensing his own intuitive understanding that political life is larger than technical and economic logic. While this may have led him to overstate the extent to which policy change is marginal in scope, it has also enabled him to see that formal techniques of analysis and theory-building – no matter how desirable – are inevitably mediated by processes of political interaction, and are no substitute for them.

At a time when virtually all western governments are under pressure to demonstrate the rational ordering of their objectives in the interests of enhanced efficiency, when so much public policy innovation is guided by public choice economic theory purporting to offer 'solutions' to all manner of policy problems, and when graduate schools of public policy feel a need to shape their curricula to reflect those same developments, students of public policy could do far worse than grasp what Lindblom made explicit, and left implicit, in 'The science of muddling through'. It would be a pity if they were misled into thinking that as the 'father of incrementalism', he has offered insights of only transient importance.

References

Banfield, E. C. (1980) 'Policy science as metaphysical madness', in Goldwin, R. A. (ed.), *Bureaucrats, Policy Analysts, Statesmen: Who leads?*, Washington, DC: American Enterprise Institute.

Blumer, H. (1971) 'Social problems as collective behaviour', *Social Problems*, 18, 3, pp. 298–306.

Boston, J. (1987) 'Thatcherism and Rogernomics: changing the rules of the game – comparisons and contrasts', *Political Science*, 39, 2, pp. 129–52.

Braybrooke, D. and Lindblom, C. E. (1963) *A Strategy of Decision: Policy evaluation as a social process*, New York: Free Press.

Bulmer, M. (1988) 'Social science expertise and executive-bureaucratic politics in Britain', *Governance*, 1, 1, pp. 26–49.

Caiden, G. and Wildavsky, A. (1974) *Planning and Budgeting in Poor Countries*, New York: Wiley.

Cates, C. (1979) 'Beyond muddling: creativity', *Public Administration Review*, 39, 6, pp. 527–32.

Coleman, J. S. (1972) *Policy Research in the Social Sciences*, Morristown, NJ: General Learning Press.

Dahl, R. A. and Lindblom, C. E. (1953) *Politics, Economics, and Welfare*, New York: Harper & Brothers.

Dror, Y. (1964) 'Muddling through – "science" or inertia?', *Public Administration Review*, 24, 3, pp. 153–7.

Dror, Y. (1968) *Public Policy Making Re-examined*, San Francisco: Chandler.

Dror, Y. (1971) *Design for Policy Sciences*, New York: American Elsevier.

Easton, B. (1987) 'Labour's economic strategy', in Boston, J. and Holland, M. (eds.), *The Fourth Labour Government: Radical Politics in New Zealand*, Auckland: Oxford University Press.

Etzioni, A. (1967) 'Mixed scanning: a "third" approach to decision-making', *Public Administration Review*, 27, 5, pp. 385–92.

Fay, B. (1975) *Social Theory and Political Practice*, London: Allen & Unwin.

Friedrich, C. J. (1940) 'Public policy and the nature of administrative responsibility', *Public Policy*, 1, pp. 3–24.

Frohock, F. M. (1979) *Public Policy: Scope and logic*, Englewood Cliffs, NJ: Prentice Hall.

Gilliatt, S. E. (1987) 'Being political: a quarrelsome view', *International Political Science Review*, pp. 367–84.

Goodin, R. E. (1982) *Political Theory and Public Policy*. Chicago: Chicago University Press.

Gregory, R. J. (1987) 'The reorganisation of the public sector: the quest for efficiency', in Boston, J. and Holland, M. (eds.), *The Fourth Labour Government: Radical politics in New Zealand*, Auckland: Oxford University Press.

Hartwig, R. (1978) 'Rationality and the problems of administrative theory', *Public Administration*, 56, 2, pp. 159–79.

Hood, C. (1987) 'British administrative trends and the public choice revolution', in Lane, J.-E. (ed.), *Bureaucracy and Public Choice*, London: Sage.

Jackson, P. M. (1982) *The Political Economy of Bureaucracy*, Oxford: Philip Allan.

Lindblom, C. E. (1959) 'The science of muddling through', *Public Administration Review*, 19, 2, pp. 79–88.

Lindblom, C. E. (1965) *The Intelligence of Democracy: Decision making through mutual adjustment*, New York: Free Press.

Lindblom, C. E. (1977) *Politics and Markets: The world's political-economic systems*, New York: Basic Books.

Lindblom, C. E. (1979) 'Still muddling, not yet through', *Public Administration Review*, 39, 6, pp. 517–26.

Lindblom, C. E. (1980) *The Policy-making Process*, 2nd edn, Englewood Cliffs, NJ: Prentice Hall.

Lindblom, C. E. and Cohen, D. K. (1979) *Usable Knowledge: Social science and social problem solving*, New Haven, CT: Yale University Press.

Mayer, T. (1982) 'Markets and democracy: a critique of Charles E. Lindblom', *New Political Science*, 3 1/2, pp. 71–92.

Meltsner, A. J. (1976) *Policy Analysts in the Bureaucracy*, Berkeley: University of California Press.

Miles, R. E. Jr (1978) 'The origin and meaning of Miles' Law', *Public Administration Review*, 38, 5, pp. 399–403.

Neustadt, R. E. (1960) *Presidential Power: The politics of leadership*, New York: Wiley.

Open Systems Group (eds.) (1984) *The Vickers Papers*, London: Harper & Row.

Paris, D. C. and Reynolds, J. F. (1983) *The Logic of Policy Inquiry*, New York: Longman.

Price, D. K. (1965) *The Scientific Estate*, Cambridge, MA: Harvard University Press.

Rein, M. and White, S. H. (1977) 'Policy research: belief and doubt', *Policy Analysis*, 3, Spring, pp. 239–71.

Rittel, H. W. and Webber, M. M. (1973) 'Dilemmas in a general theory of planning', *Policy Sciences*, 4, 2, pp. 155–69.

Roberts, J. L. (1987) *Politicians, Public Servants and Public Enterprise: Restructuring the New Zealand Government Executive*, Wellington: Victoria University Press for the Institute of Policy Studies.

Roos, N. P. (1975) 'Contrasting social experimentation with retrospective evaluation: a health care perspective', *Public Policy*, 23, Spring, pp. 241–57.

Simon, H. A. (1947) *Administrative Behavior*, Glencoe, IL.: Free Press.

Smith, G. and May, D. (1980) 'The artificial debate between rationalist and incrementalist models of decision making', *Policy and Politics*, 8, 2, pp. 147–61.

Spread, P. (1985) 'Lindblom, Wildavsky and the role of support', *Political Studies*, 33, 2, pp. 274–95.

Vickers, Sir Geoffrey (1965) *The Art of Judgement: A study of policy making*, London: Chapman & Hall.

Vickers, Sir Geoffrey (1968) *Value Systems and Social Process*, London: Tavistock Publications.

Vickers, Sir Geoffrey (1972) 'Commonly ignored elements in policy making', *Policy Sciences*, 3, 2, pp. 265–6.

Vickers, Sir Geoffrey (1983) *Human Systems are Different*, London: Harper & Row.

Vogel, D. (1987) 'The new political science of corporate power', *The Public Interest*, 87, Spring, pp. 63–79.

Wilson, J. Q. (1974) 'Social experimentation and "public policy analysis', *Public Policy*, 22, Winter, pp. 15–37.

Wilson, J. Q. (1981) '"Policy intellectuals" and public policy', *The Public Interest*, 64, Summer, pp. 31–46.

Master of fate or victim of circumstance?

The exercise of corporate power in environmental policy-making

Andrew Blowers

Introduction

The debate about corporate power has tended to polarise around two theoretical perspectives. One, the *pluralist* view, argues that business is an interest group competing with other interests for access to decision makers in a relatively open political framework. In this view, business pursues its economic objectives but also reacts to social pressures for control over its activities exerted by the interests of consumers, labour and the environment. Strategies of cooperation, concession and compromise are arbitrated through a responsive, representative and democratic policy which engages in consultation with the interests involved, promoting policies which seek to balance economic, social and technological factors. The other view, the *political economy* perspective, defines business as a dominant force engaged in the control of large sectors of economic and political life. Business is 'not simply another interest group: its role [is] actually more akin to that of a ruling class or dominant elite' (Vogel, 1981, pp. 1–2). Business power is all pervasive, controlling the nation's technology, pattern of work organisation, location of industry, market structure, resource allocation and income distribution. Business is able to penetrate all levels of political decision making and, by strategies of manipulation, information control and sanctions,

From A. Blowers, 'Master of fate or victim of circumstance – the exercise of corporate power in environmental policy-making', *Policy and Politics*, **11**, 1983, pp. 393–415.

is able to define the political agenda and resist controls or financial penalties that threaten its continued prosperity.

The debate about corporate power has suffered in that it has been conducted at a largely abstract level and where specific evidence is used it is often transposed into grand generalisations which may be inapplicable across different societies. Temporal and spatial factors have often been neglected. Viewed over time it is possible to conceive different periods during which business was on the defensive, followed by periods when it was able to exert power more aggressively. 'Instead of endlessly debating the power of business in the abstract or focusing on the outcomes of particular policy disputes, political scientists need to pay more attention to the processes by which the power of business as a whole varies over time' (Vogel, *op. cit.*, p. 3). Similarly, the power of business varies according to place. Some countries, or regions within countries, provide a more propitious environment for business expansion than do others. Disadvantages (climate, wage and union structure, resource availability, infrastructure) can be partly overcome by various forms of concession (subsidies, incentives, state spending on services for industry etc.). The question that needs to be answered is how business responds to these temporal and spatial differences. On the one hand it may seek to accommodate to the pressures exerted upon it or, alternatively, it may exploit its power by seeking to undermine constraints or extract concessions which favour its interests.

One way in to understanding the exercise of corporate power is to focus on an aspect of business interaction with government. The environmental problems created by business activity – air and water pollution, dereliction and resource depletion – impose costs on the community which have provoked government intervention in the form of controls, regulations and standards. In support of the pluralist case it can be argued that this intervention reflects the power of environmental groups able to restrain industry by exploiting the available legal and political opportunities. Against this it can be argued that the success of government intervention is more apparent than real. Businessmen may accept certain restrictions but only to the point where business efficiency will be impaired. 'Hence they often predict dire consequences when a new regulation is imposed on them, yet thereafter quickly find ways to prosper under it' (Lindblom, 1977, p. 179). Technological and economic changes have had a far more profound impact on environmental improvement than has been achieved through regulation. For example, changes in fuel type, in housing design and in population density were already reducing the incidence of pollution from smoke and sulphur dioxide when the Clean Air Act was introduced in Britain in 1956 (Waller, 1982). It is possible to conclude that, 'even when policy making and state intervention have appeared to play a part this merely acts to reinforce the economic interests of the polluter and the polluted' (Sandbach, 1982, p. 3). In many cases industry simply claims that pollution control is neither technically nor economically feasible and so little progress is made.

In trying to establish whether or not business has been able to sustain its objectives in the face of environmental pressures we need to define what exactly constitutes the exercise of power. There are various definitions, each stressing a particular outcome of the exercise of power. One definition sees power in terms of dominance in decision making. 'The power of a group or class is a function of its ability to define the political agenda, to win political victories, and to benefit disproportionately from policy outcomes' (Vogel, *op. cit.*, p. 4). The strategies deployed by industry in the environmental field are similar to those outlined by Kimber and Richardson (1974). They include the use of advance intelligence and information, privileged access to officials and decision makers, and raising public consciousness by rational argument on the merits of the case. The control by industry of information sources about the technological and economic implications of control and its superior resources for employing expertise and influencing decisions are critical weapons in defending its cause. But it may be felt these resources have been matched by environmentalist groups using their access and deploying countervailing command of information and expertise, often sufficient to neutralise the power of business.

Another definition of power focuses on its impact. 'By "power" I mean the ability to make decisions having effects upon a substantial portion of the community, or a considerable impact upon a smaller public' (Reagan, 1963, p. 74). Industry may impose costs of pollution and dereliction on a wide public, which stimulates antagonism and organised opposition. But it also confers jobs on a smaller section of that same public and is able to build powerful coalitions of workers and capital to defy environmental groups. And it can also exploit territorial divisions by threatening to remove its activities (and their economic benefits) to more welcoming locations. This threat of investment withdrawal, if it can be carried out, remains the most powerful weapon of business. It suggests a third definition of power, 'the ability of a class or group to realise its own specific objectives' (Sandbach, 1980, p. 135). The objectives of industry are to maintain its productive capacity at least cost in order to achieve maximum profitability. The extent to which it succeeds will determine whether business is dominant, or merely an interest group having to accommodate its objectives in the face of opposing interests.

Environmental issues provide a good test bed for examining the exercise of corporate power. In particular they enable us to confront the alternative versions proffered by pluralists and exponents of political economy. These alternatives can be posed in the form of two propositions,

– *corporate power can be defined as an interest in conflict with other interests (such as environmental interests) each with different objectives. The outcome of this conflict is uncertain and depends on changes in circumstances which favour certain interests against others.*

– *corporate power may be conceived as a class interest able to achieve its objectives in the face of opposition from other interests (such as environmental groups) by adopting strategies that best exploit the circumstances. The outcome in this case is predictable, only the means for achieving it are uncertain.*

By examining a particular case I shall show how both positions can contribute to our understanding of the exercise of corporate power. This example covers a period during which circumstances changed (sometimes dramatically) and in which alternative locations played a part in influencing decisions.

There are, of course, problems in offering generalisations from individual cases but the lack of empirical evidence on this question needs to be remedied. 'Case studies leave to their readers the task of determining how findings add to previous knowledge ... A hypothesis (which sets forth conditions and consequences) even though incorrect is easier to relate to new experience than are collections of unexceptionable but unorganised anecdotes' (Polsby, 1980, pp. 122–3). With this in mind I offer this case study to demonstrate that both the above propositions may prove valid – it is merely a question of how the evidence is interpreted.

London Brick Company

The London Brick Company, by a process of mergers and takeovers conducted over several decades, had achieved by 1974 a monopoly of fletton brickmaking (Hillier, 1981; Cox, 1979). The fletton process is based on the thick Oxford Clay deposits of Buckinghamshire, Bedfordshire and Cambridgeshire. The clay produces bricks of consistent quality and contains a high organic content which enables the bricks virtually to fire themselves. Fletton bricks are, therefore, cheap to produce and can bear transport costs, giving London Brick access to a national market taking about 40% of the total brick output. Demand for bricks is linked to the fortunes of the construction industry. Booms in production (such as in 1973 when London Brick produced over 3,000 million bricks) are followed by slumps and, in the current recession, the company's output is less than half its 1973 figure. London Brick's dominant position in the market and in the Oxford Clay area provides it with support from national interests concerned with construction and from local interests concerned with employment and the local economy. But the fletton brick industry gives rise to major environmental problems. One is the dereliction caused by the excavation of clay; the other is air pollution which results from the emission of sulphur oxides, fluorides and organic substances known as mercaptans which give rise to the offensive smell characteristic of the brickfields. Over time, as dereliction has increased and public sensitivity to environmental issues has developed, these problems have provoked opposition calling for restoration of the clay pits and control of air pollution.

The conflict between economic and environmental interests came to a head in 1979 when the company applied for planning permission to rebuild its major brickworks in the Marston Vale in Bedfordshire. It proposed to build two new 'superworks', one at Stewartby in the centre of the Vale and the other to the south of Ridgmont near the M1. Each works would be built in two phases, each phase having a capacity of 5 million bricks per week, totalling 10 million per week for the works. Effluent gases would be emitted through tall chimneys, one for each phase (two for each works) 400 feet above ground level. Thus four new chimneys would replace the 98 smaller chimneys at existing works and were accepted by the Alkali Inspector as the best practicable means of pollution control. In the Inspector's view the pollutants would be dispersed and diluted and rendered harmless through the tall stacks. He shared the industry's view that pollution abatement was neither technically nor economically feasible but that provision for a third flue should be made during construction of the works in the event of appropriate technology being discovered. These proposals were met with resistance from environmentalists, farmers, local residents and some politicians. Although they accepted the principle of new works for the future prosperity of the industry and the local economy they maintained that permission should be withheld unless pollution control measures were installed.

The environmentalists seized the opportunities afforded them by the dispersal of powers over pollution control. Formally, the control of emissions is a matter for either district councils or the Alkali Inspectorate. The districts (Environmental Health Departments), operating under the Clean Air Acts (1956, 1968), are responsible for the control of smoke emissions from domestic and commercial premises and from furnaces. The districts also have controls (under the Public Health Act, 1936) over industries which cause a nuisance or which are designated as 'offensive trades'. There remain many industrial processes 'which are not subject to any prospective or antici-patory controls' (Wood, 1982, p. 3). But major processes which, because of the quantity of emissions or technical problems of control, cannot be dealt with locally are registered under the Alkali Acts. They are subject to the control of district Alkali Inspectors with prospective powers over new works and retrospective powers over existing works, who apply the concept of 'best practicable means' for abatement. 'The Chief Inspector . . . lays down the broad national policies and, provided they keep within their broad guidelines, inspectors in the field have plenty of flexibility to take into account local circumstances and make suitable decisions' (Hill, p. 13). Inspectors thus work in a negotiating role with industry in reaching decisions (Vogel, 1980). Although the agency is well versed in technical criteria it also considers economic aspects and its lack of formal competence in this area must, according to Bennett, 'cast doubt on the soundness of its decisions' (1979, p. 95).

The close relationship between the Inspectorate and industry excludes environ-mentalist pressures. This has led environmentalists to encourage the use of planning powers to exert greater control over polluters. Planning authorities can influence the source and impact of emissions through their control over location and land use. They may also use discretionary powers in the form of planning conditions, agreements and policies. The possible duplication of powers between authorities has led the Department of the Environment (1981) to remind local planning authorities that 'planning conditions should not be used to regulate pollution where appropriate specific powers can be used'. Nevertheless, the tendency to employ such powers has led to increasing conflict between the environmentalists, applying pressure through planning conditions and policies, and industry, resisting any controls which go beyond those required by the Alkali Inspector. Both sides may be prepared to negotiate and achieve compromise through planning agreements though, as in the following case, this may be insufficient to prevent conflict.

The conflict did not suddenly erupt but had a long period of gestation. It is possible to trace four stages in the development of the conflict. The first, a long period during which environmental issues flared up from time to time, did not produce any significant change in the company's policies towards dereliction or air pollution. This can be described as the *non decisionmaking* phase. The issue became active once the permissions had been applied for in 1979 and, at first, there was a phase of *negotiation* between the opposing groups. Later, when negotiation failed to realise a victory for either side, the conflict deepened into a phase of *confrontation*. Finally, there was the phase of *resolution* when the conflict was settled and the issue, once more, subsided in terms of public debate. In the following account I shall focus on the changes in political and economic circumstances during the course of the conflict and the strategies employed by the company in meeting these changes. What we have to consider is whether changes in the company's strategy were deliberate, based on careful calculation of outcomes, or simply reactions to changing but unforeseen events, pragmatic adjustments rather than preconceived plans.

The phase of non decisionmaking

Throughout the post-war period there has been public concern about the visible problems of dereliction and a less palpable, but more profound, anxiety about the risks to human health, animals and crops from air pollution. From time to time this has erupted in public debate, for example at a public inquiry into a proposal to build a new brickworks at Woburn Sands (Bucks.) in 1966 (Porteous *et al.*, 1977), at a conference on the brickfields at Bedford in 1967 (Beds. County Council, 1967), and during the public consultation on the structure and minerals plans for Bedfordshire during 1976–8 (Beds. County Council, 1976a and b, 1978a and b). Despite all the argument nothing was achieved; in essence it was a period of non decisionmaking in which the company carried on its activities without serious challenge.

Just after the war the various brick companies operating in the Marston Vale were granted a series of planning permissions by the Minister at a time when the national need for bricks was an overriding concern. These permissions covered vast areas, providing the industry with sufficient clay resources to last until well into the next century. The conditions attached to the permissions were very liberal [. . .] and there was no reference to air pollution save in one permission, where the Minister 'observes that your Research Department are working to eliminate to the greatest degree the possibility of damage to the countryside from injurious fumes' (Letter to London Brick Co. Ltd., 26th May 1949). Given such relative freedom to despoil and pollute, the brick companies had no need to take any positive action except some cosmetic tree planting to assist good public relations, or to find material to fill the pits at a profit.

During the 1950s and 60s cases of fluorosis (a debilitating bone disease in cattle attributed to the ingestion of fluorides) were reported in the brickfields. Research had revealed a higher incidence of this disease in Bedfordshire than in other areas, with the clear implication that the problem was caused by the brickworks (Burns and Allcroft, 1964). London Brick tackled this problem in three ways – by buying up land for its own farming; by out of court settlements with farmers negotiated with the National Farmers' Union; and by a clause in which its tenants waived all claims for damage caused by the company's activities. In these ways farming interests were kept relatively quiet until the late 1970s, when they played a major part in the opposition to the company's redevelopment plans.

Armed with its liberal planning permissions the company had little need to stir itself to action to defend its interests. It was able to argue that restoration was only possible if massive amounts of fill could be imported at an economic cost. It could point to contracts negotiated [. . .] to import domestic waste into the brickfields to restore one of the worked out pits. And it could claim, with the support of the Alkali Inspector, that there were no processes of pollution control that were either economic or technically feasible.

However, by the late 1970s the national need for bricks was no longer overriding; new methods of construction had gained ground and construction was at a low level. Research evidence on the hazards of pollution to human health, though statistically inadequate and inconclusive (e.g. Brothwood Report, 1960) had contributed to a growing public concern about the company's activities which reflected a more general shift in values in favour of environmental concerns. The company's failure to provide adequate landscaping or to ensure restoration fuelled public antagonism. Opposition which had, hitherto, been sporadic and ephemeral began to establish a firm base as local action groups made common cause with conservationist and farming interests. They but waited an opportunity. That opportunity came with the company's redevelopment plans. London Brick found itself embattled with powerful and well-organised environmental interests able to exploit political circumstances. In this atmosphere London Brick's long established, largely low profile strategy would no longer serve as an adequate defence.

The phase of negotiation

It was clear that, initially, the company was unaware of the public hostility that could be orchestrated into strong opposition. The Managing Director reflected the mood of the company, observing, 'We thought the plans would be snatched from our hands and we'd be told to get on with it as soon as possible'. This complacent attitude had been encouraged by the lack of resistance to similar plans in neighbouring Cambridgeshire where two new superworks had already been opened. The company were simultaneously applying for permissions for a further new works in Cambridgeshire, and had plans for one in Buckinghamshire as well as the two new Bedfordshire works. Its stated priorities were to build first at Ridgmont, then at Stewartby in a long term programme of complete redevelopment of the fletton industry which would reduce the labour force, thereby increasing productivity and enabling the company at least to maintain its share of a market which was in secular decline. Whether or not it was foreseen at the time, this blanket series of applications would enable the company later to switch its investment priorities, giving it the flexibility needed to outmanoeuvre opposition.

The company made its early approaches through the Bedfordshire planning officials and the Chairman of the Environmental Services Committee (the planning committee). During the period before an application is made companies enjoy confidential and privileged access to authorities and the opportunity to discuss their plans in confidence. This has been called the 'pre-parliamentary' phase by Knoepfel *et al.*, during which companies 'seek to define the problem in such a way that problem solving strategies are considered and ultimately selected which give the emitters a maximum degree of freedom of action and legal security while, at the same time, causing them only minimal costs' (1980, p. 45).

The planning officials had long been concerned with the problem of dereliction but had been frustrated by the permissive conditions which gave them little power to impose restoration on the company. The company recognised that concessions would need to be offered to secure the support of the planning officials and, through them, the elected members. London Brick proposed a package of environmental improvements in return for the permissions. It was agreed the package should be negotiated in the form of a Section 52 Planning Agreement legally binding on the company. Section 52 Agreements are regarded by some commentators as evidence of corporatism in town planning, 'a drift away from the taken-for-granted values and assumptions which underlie pluralist democracy, and towards the values and assumptions inherent in the philosophy of corporatism' (Reade, 1982, pp. 10–11). Such agreements are conducted in secret and bargains are struck in which 'developers and planners are likely to develop shared perspectives as to which things are in "the public interest" and which are not' (p. 13). Agreements are justified as a means of securing planning gains in return for planning permissions and this was certainly how the Bedfordshire agreement was portrayed. 'These environmental advantages amount to a very attractive package indeed and it is difficult to envisage any other circumstances in which such far reaching improvements could be achieved' (Report to Environmental Services Committee, 27th March 1980, p. 50).

The planning officials were also concerned about the siting of the new Ridgmont works. Instead of the existing site on a prominent ridge visible for miles around they preferred a site beneath ground level in an exhausted part of a clay pit. This idea provoked a local action group representing a village downwind of the site to claim that the planners were attempting 'to force a new brickworks and its obnoxious side effects onto an hitherto unaffected residential area' (Cranfield Action Committee, 5th June 1979). The short campaign they mounted was totally successful and the company withdrew the scheme in favour of the site adjacent to the existing works.

Once the application had been submitted in August 1979 the 'parliamentary' phase began. During this phase the outcome 'will depend on the balance of power among the interested actors involved . . . and the strategies they use in pursuing their objectives' (Knoepfel et al., op. cit., p. 14). It soon became evident that pollution rather than dereliction was the key political issue. Opponents claimed that the dangers from pollution had been underestimated and that the company had failed to pursue abatement measures or monitoring of emissions with sufficient vigour. Tall chimneys, they asserted, would only disperse the problem more widely. A cause for concern became a call for control. The pollution issue offered opponents the best prospect of a powerful coalition embracing local action groups and the farming community, already aware of the pollution hazards. Hence fluorides became the main focus of attention, though London Brick continued to stress smell as the main problem. The dangers of fluoride were less obvious but more sinister than smell or sulphur dioxide and, for that reason, became a more compelling issue.

London Brick responded to this new challenge with a predictable defence. They relied on the Alkali Inspector's view, reiterated in successive reports, that levels of fluoride were 'satisfactorily low'; that tall chimneys would virtually eliminate the problem; that pollution control equipment was neither technically nor economically feasible; and that the third flue would be installed to treat gases if it was found to be necessary and if appropriate technology could be proven. They sought to minimise the problem. 'The effluent also contains a minute amount of fluoride, the concentration measured at ground level being about one-hundredth of the threshold limit for possible effects on human health' (London Brick Company; 1978, p. 17). [. . .]

Having selected fluoride as their target the opposition began to mobilise political support. The general background of public disquiet was orchestrated by a group of powerful interests which emerged to spearhead the attack on the company. This group was called Public Review of Brickmaking and the Environment (PROBE) and was chaired by the Marquis of Tavistock, with his seat at Woburn Abbey and extensive land holdings in the county. Its membership included leading county councillors, MPs, local businessmen, medical and engineering experts and a local farmer who claimed his cattle were suffering from fluorosis. Using contacts with the local and national media, with farming interests and with government ministers, PROBE increased the political salience of the pollution issue.

The County Council had commissioned a report from consultants to investigate the effects of pollution, methods of control and monitoring, and to advise the Council on what action should be taken on the permissions. The report concluded, 'The case for fluoride removal, with respect to grazing animals, is unproven at the present time' (Cremer and Warner, 1979, p. A24). Although methods of fluoride removal were possible there was no technique for removing all pollutants. The problems of raw materials, waste disposal and production costs made the known processes unattractive. The report defined odour rather than fluoride as the main problem, recommending that planning permission should be deferred or rejected until alternative kilning techniques had been developed to remove the smell. The report appeared to confirm the company's claims, though on the subject of odour removal it was not aware 'of any practicable or proven technology which will permit the realisation of this objective' (London Brick Company, 1980, p. 1). Still the company was prepared to negotiate. It offered one further concession – a part permission for the first stage of one of the new works using conventional technology and the deferral of the second stage while a research programme was undertaken to demonstrate the feasibility of pollution control measures. This concession did not satisfy the opponents and marked the end of the phase of negotiation.

The phase of confrontation
The limits of negotiation were formally embodied in the Section 52 Agreement. This provided for comprehensive schemes of buffer zones around villages; demolition of old works; landscaping and tree planting; and revocation of the old permissions with

much tighter conditions. It also embraced the concept of a part planning permission and participation by the County Council in a research programme on pollution control. This represented an attempt to secure greater control over areas in which formal planning powers were relatively weak. Environmentalists regarded the Agreement as no more than the company should be expected to offer. They were sceptical about the possibility of enforcement and recognised that the restoration of the pits depended on the unlikely prospect of vast amounts of waste material becoming available. On the pollution issue, too, environmentalists questioned whether concessions had been made. All the company had agreed to do was carry out a research programme prior to the second stage of the works being built. If no techniques were found to be feasible or economic the company could go ahead using conventional technology. The company's plans had in no way been hindered by this agreement. Conversely, London Brick regarded these concessions as the limit to which it could go – any further and its investment programme would be impeded, involving high costs and unacceptable delays. The use of a Planning Agreement to introduce a pollution research programme might be viewed, on the one hand, as an unwarranted intrusion of planning into an area under the jurisdiction of another agency, or an assertion of the local public interest in an area where it might otherwise have been unrepresented.

At this point, with an intransigent opposition matched by an unyielding company, the room for compromise had disappeared and the two sides were in confrontation. The company had exhausted its advantages of privileged access to officials and its negotiations had failed to secure an easy passage for its application. The issue now entered the political arena. On one side were supporters of London Brick, led by the Chairman of the Environmental Services Committee, who were anxious to cooperate with the company and felt a good bargain could be struck which balanced environmental needs against the jobs and wealth resulting from the investment. Opposing them were those who felt that more could be extracted from the company which was portrayed by the Leader of the Council as 'the unacceptable face of capitalism'. Politically, the 71 Conservatives, the dominant group on the Council, were split, representing two strands in the party – a conservationist wing with strong rural interests and a wing favouring private enterprise as embodied in London Brick. The small opposition groups (Labour, 9 members, and Liberal, 2 members) [. . .] opposed the company. It had been agreed that the planning permissions were so significant that they should be decided by the full Council of 83 members.

Delays had already caused the company to review its investment plans. It now wished to develop at Stewartby rather than at Ridgmont to take advantage of the need to open up clay reserves nearby. In March, 1980, the Environmental Services Committee, by a large majority, recommended the Council to grant a part permission for redevelopment at Stewartby. London Brick was confident of success but, at the April meeting of the County Council, another obstacle was encountered. A report on the pollution problem commissioned by the Department of the Environment (1980) was not ready and so a decision was deferred until the following July.

This delay was used by PROBE to undertake an extensive press campaign and lobbying among the uncommitted members of the Council. A pamphlet supporting new brickworks, 'But not at any price!', was issued and members of the Council were provided with free champagne and persuasion in the Portrait Gallery at Woburn Abbey. At the Council meeting in July London Brick's opponents, skilfully led by the Leader of the Council, by a majority of 38 to 28 with 17 absent or abstaining, applied a new condition to the permission for the first phase of the Stewartby works. This required that the brick kilns should be 'so designed as to be capable of removing the pollutants (sulphur dioxide and' fluoride) and odours given off in the firing process' (County Council, 3rd July 1980, Minute 80/73). The Council also deferred a decision on the application for the Ridgmont Works, a decision which was to prove of far greater significance later.

The company had, up to this point, relied on its access to officials to persuade local politicians. Its objectives had been thwarted and so it responded by a more direct approach. Its first move was to reinterpret the condition. The Council, it was argued, having approved the new works would need to apply conditions that were 'both reasonable and not repugnant to the permission'. On legal advice the condition was interpreted to mean, 'the kilns shall be so designed as to be capable of removing the pollutants and odours to the gas treatment plant if and when an appropriate plant can be constructed'. This was followed by a direct appeal by the Chairman of London Brick at a meeting with council members. For the first time a hint was given that the company would, if necessary, withdraw its investment if it did not gain satisfaction from the County Council [. . .].

Despite the sympathy of the Environmental Services Committee the County Council was not persuaded by these new pressures. It was clear that the Council had meant that pollution control should be applied before the works were commissioned and not at some future date, if and when such measures became available. The appearance of the company Chairman at a meeting with members was criticised as an unfortunate precedent. The Council in December 1980 confirmed its original decision by 43 votes to 33. This proved to be the apogee of the opponents' cause. Events now moved swiftly in favour of the company.

The phase of resolution
Unable to gain a permission through negotiation or through political confrontation, the company precipitated a change in the political environment by announcing that it was no longer pursuing its development plans for Stewartby. In February 1981 a permission for a new superworks at Whittlesey was granted by Cambridgeshire County Council without a pollution condition and this became the company's first investment priority, implying it would be up to a decade before it revived its plans for Stewartby or Ridgmont. The initial strategy of applying for several works in different counties appeared to have paid off in that the Achilles' Heel had been found in Cambridgeshire.

Meanwhile, the recession had deepened, weakening the company's outlook but, paradoxically, strengthening its hand with Bedfordshire County Council. During a recession the brick industry combines a reduction in production capacity through short-time working with an increase in stockholding. There comes a point when these measures are unable to reduce the supply of bricks sufficiently and the closure of complete works becomes necessary. The choice of which works to close is economically determined. [. . .] By the beginning of 1981 London Brick was on short-time working and stocks amounted to five months' supply, and there was no hint of improvement in the market. The company decided to close a major works and selected Ridgmont, the second largest works in Bedfordshire, to close in May 1981 with the loss of 1,100 jobs. It justified the decision on the grounds that Ridgmont was an old works producing bricks of variable quality with a high wastage, and that it was of the right size (14% of total output) to achieve the necessary reduction in production capacity. Whether fortuitous or by design the closure of Ridgmont was of major political significance.

Bedfordshire was faced with the twin prospect of no investment in new works and the closure of one of its large old works. Employment, not pollution, was now the major issue. The environmentalist case was fatally weakened and a powerful alliance of material interests – capital and labour – took the initiative. The trade unions exerted telling pressure on councillors, particularly the Labour Group, whose votes had been decisive in opposing the company's plans. With a County Council election due the following May the brickworks issue promised to be an important, and in some seats a crucial, issue.

London Brick, once again, changed their investment strategy. If an acceptable permission could be obtained in Bedfordshire it would receive priority over Cambridgeshire. Further delays had weakened the case for Stewartby and the closure of Ridgmont opened up the opportunity to develop there. Fortuitously the County Council had deferred a decision on the Ridgmont works but the company had not withdrawn its application. The way was therefore still open for the Council to permit a new works at Ridgmont. In the changed economic circumstances the Environmental Services Committee in March 1981, urged on by the councillor for the Ridgmont area and without reference to the County Council, granted permission for the Ridgmont works without any pollution condition on the first phase. It incorporated the Section 52 Agreement for a research programme to investigate pollution control measures that might be applied to later phases of the development.

In economic terms the prospect of lost investment and jobs had motivated labour interests to apply pressure. Politically, a looming election had concentrated the minds of councillors. Procedurally, the undetermined application for Ridgmont and the decision not to refer the matter once again to the Council had presented the company's supporters with the means of achieving victory. But it was a pyrrhic victory since the prospect of investment had receded and the company announced the closure of further works, including one of two remaining in Bedfordshire. A more apposite conclusion would be that everybody had lost – workers had lost jobs, environmentalists had lost the chance of enforcing pollution control measures, the company had lost its investment opportunity, and the community had lost the wealth generated by brickmaking.

Master of fate or victim of circumstance?

We can now return to the propositions reflecting alternative interpretations of corporate power to examine which better stands the test of the evidence from the London Brick case study. On the one hand, the political economy view suggests a close correspondence between economic power and political achievement. The company, in this view, possessed reserves of power so that it could manipulate circumstances in its favour. Its ultimate success was inevitable though the means for achieving it varied. Alternatively, the pluralist view perceives power allocated among competing interests. In this view the company was buffeted by circumstances, shifting from one strategy to another as it faced obstacles strewn in its path by opponents. Throughout the debate the outcome was unclear and depended on the relative power available to different participants. These views may now be compared by providing alternative versions of the conflict.

The political economy interpretation
For a long period London Brick appeared to be inactive – action was unnecessary since the company could not be challenged. The lack of sufficient opposition to influence the company's policies may be explained as a recognition of the company's power and the weakness of its opponents. It was a case of anticipated reactions, a belief that nothing could be achieved by action. In Moodie's words, 'the absence of pressure may therefore be of little significance – it could, conceivably, mean either that the potential pressure is so great that it need not be applied, or that the aggrieved group has no leverage' (1970, p. 65). The planning permissions provided the company with the freedom to avoid action. Certainly the planning officials felt there was no means by which they could force the company to achieve restoration of the clay pits. The company, by undertaking minimal tree planting, by refuting the research evidence on the hazards of pollution and by denying the possibility of pollution control, was able to defeat attempts to exercise some control over its activities. Its largely passive strategy can be seen as a mobilisation of bias sufficient to prevent opponents from realising their common interest in seeking environmental improvements.

The period of non decisionmaking was not unlike that described by Crenson (1971) in Gary (Indiana). [See the extract from Lukes in Part II of the reader.]

There is some evidence of suppression of the air pollution issue by London Brick. When opposition did become manifest in the 1960s over the issue of cattle fluorosis the company acted decisively, buying up land, settling out of court with farmers and employing a tough tenancy clause. Thus by a combination of inaction, and, when necessary, suppression, London Brick avoided interference in its activities for three decades.

When public opposition crystallised around the redevelopment plans the company met it by adjusting its strategy. London Brick recognised that it was most likely to secure its objectives by working closely with the planning officials. Planners, it seemed, would be happy to trade some improvement in the landscape for planning permissions without air pollution controls. The company possessed a shrewd insight into the attitudes of officials.

Yet ordinarily as new problems arise – for example, public demands for restriction on air pollution – businessmen know that government officials will understand their wishes – in this case their unwillingness or incapacity to bear without help the costs of stopping industrial discharges through the air. Businessmen will find the government official ready to acknowledge their special competence and interest, eager to welcome them into negotiation, anxious about the possible adverse effects of costly antipollution measures on prices and production. (Lindblom, *op. cit.*, p.184.)

The company's investment strategy had an inevitable logic. By applying simultaneously for new works in three counties it would be possible to sift out the weakest point. Once this was established the company could divide and rule, achieving permissions at all locations on the terms offered by the most permissive authority, in this case Cambridgeshire. Similarly the company applied for two sites at Ridgmont when only one was required. It could accept the one which attracted the least opposition. The planners, left to choose the site, would face the opprobrium while the company would appear to be responding to public pressure. Again, the apparently perverse switch of investment priorities from Ridgmont to Stewartby and back to Ridgmont can be seen as a calculated manoeuvre to exploit changing circumstances. Delays at Ridgmont left Stewartby as an acceptable proposition. But when the Council impeded its plans London Brick was able to revert to its Ridgmont application, which it had not withdrawn and which the Council had not determined. This shows a subtle appreciation of available opportunities.

Once the pollution issue had emerged the company appeared willing to offer concessions. It was prepared to accept a part permission and to undertake research into pollution before the second stage was commissioned. In reality it had conceded nothing since its investment programme would not be interrupted and it had always accepted the possibility of pollution control if appropriate technology could be proved. Failing a technical break-through the permission enabled it to build the second stage without abatement measures. The company refused to accept fluoride as a problem, arguing that the offensive smells should be tackled first. Thus the initiative on pollution research and control remained firmly with the company.

When the company's concessions failed to convince the Council it shifted to a more ebullient strategy. It first hinted that it would withdraw its investment, usually sufficient to cause the capitulation of opposition. Businessmen 'need only point to the costs of doing business, the state of the economy, the dependence of the economy's stability and growth on their profits or sales prospects – and simply predict, not threaten, that adverse consequences will follow on a refusal of their demands' (Lindblom, *op. cit.*, p. 185). In this case the hint was not quite sufficient and was transformed into a threat with the announcement of a change in investment priorities to Cambridgeshire. Although the deepening recession made the closure of plant inevitable the selection of Ridgmont, it could be argued, happened to exert the maximum amount of pressure on the County Council. Furthermore, the alliance with the unions was another means of extracting an acceptable permission. In sum, when the possibilities of peaceful cooperation with the Council had failed to produce the goods, all the company had to do was to deploy the reserves of power which it commanded to secure a desirable outcome.

In terms of the definitions of power stated earlier it is possible to argue that London Brick had ultimately managed, in Vogel's terms, to set the political agenda and had won a political victory. There was little doubt either that it had the ability to make decisions which would have a major impact on the community in terms of pollution and jobs (Reagan, 1963). It had ample resources, possessed insight into the political process, and could play a waiting game. The acid test of its strategy was a success in realising its objectives (Sandbach, 1982) and here, too, it had gained a planning permission, different in some details, but in principle what it had originally asked for. This political economy interpretation has a neat symmetry and a plausible logic. But it can also be argued that the company failed to benefit from the conflict and that it failed above all to secure the investment, though economic circumstances were responsible for that. The flaws in this interpretation become apparent when the same evidence is examined from a pluralist viewpoint.

The pluralist interpretation

Pluralists would agree that for a long time after the original permissions had been granted action by the company was unnecessary. But they would dispute the explanation for this. Polsby, a leading pluralist, argues, 'If a issue is not raised in a community, there are at least two possible reasons why it is not: either it is being suppressed or there is a genuine consensus that it is not an issue' (*op. cit.*, p. 216). Pluralists would point to the national consensus in favour of brickmaking and the lack of any tangible disquiet about the environmental issue at local level. It is quite conceivable that during this early phase, until the dereliction issue became obvious and anxieties about cattle fluorosis were aroused, the issue was disregarded and public opinion was quiescent. This lack of interest or abstention on the part of the public should occasion no surprise. 'How does abstention differ from apathy, laziness, pessimism, or lack of interest in politics? These are all widespread; indeed they are the common condition. Most people prefer spending their time, money, and skill for purposes other than shaping public policy' (Wolfinger, 1972, p. 1071).

Once opposition was aroused the company was forced to respond and to lean heavily on the support of government bodies, notably the Alkali Inspector. Opponents challenged the company's failure to act in the spirit of the planning permissions and viewed the close relationship between the company and the Alkali Inspector with suspicion. As Bennett observes, 'the Inspectorate chooses to pursue a policy of close cooperation with industry and only rarely resorts to formal enforcement procedures' (1979, p. 95). When the fluorosis issue developed London Brick reacted pragmatically to buy off the opposition. Over the long non decisionmaking phase the company's varied and unpremeditated responses helped to create a climate of suspicion and hostility that would eventually transform the balance of power between London Brick and its opponents.

It appears that the intensity of opposition which greeted the company's redevelopment plans in 1979 took it by surprise, resulting in a change of strategy. Pluralists would see its reaction as defensive with the company uncertain which course to follow. At first, London Brick sensed that its privileged access to the planning officials would enable it to secure the planning permissions. The company seemed to discount the fact that the advice of officials might be rejected by the politicians. Thus, when the sympathy and reassurance it received from officials was not matched by a welcome from the politicians the company was, once again, caught unawares and faced a powerful opposition it had not anticipated.

Pluralists would see little that was sinister in the company applying for several sites in different counties at the same time. The company had adopted a long term investment programme and had presumably not expected permissions to be any more difficult to gain at one site than another. Its priorities were determined by financial criteria. Bedfordshire appeared to be the company's first priority, a point that was later confirmed by the company's Chairman.

> I really cannot commit my Board at this stage to where it starts. The last thing I would like to suggest to you is that our position would be in any way influenced by the fact that we have now permissions both in Buckinghamshire and of course in Cambridgeshire. We will have to decide in terms of the total modernisation programme where we should start ... If it is any help for you and I am talking informally ... I personally would like to see a start in Bedfordshire, but that does not commit the decision taken by the Board. (Report to Environmental Services Committee, 9th December 1980, p. 20.)

As to the decision to apply for alternative sites at Ridgmont, this can be explained in terms of accepting the planners' advice that options should be presented for debate. When public opposition to one site developed the company reacted by agreeing to locate the works at the other site. The shift to Stewartby was again a reaction to events. The delays encountered at Ridgmont meant it was necessary to build first at Stewartby to take advantage of the new clay workings there.

As the conflict deepened the company found itself giving ground. It offered a series of concessions, the Section 52 Agreement and, later, the agreement to accept only a part permission for the first phase of the new Stewartby works. The reports of both the consultants and the Department of the Environment confirmed that smell was the major problem and so it was natural for the company to focus on this rather than the problem of fluoride.

London Brick continued to negotiate through the officials and with the Chairman of the Committee, still failing to perceive the danger to its interests of the well-organised opposition that was lobbying members of the County Council. Its lack of perception and failure to exert any pressure in a changing political environment contributed to its defeat in July 1980. At last recognising its vulnerability, the company was forced to alter its strategy yet again. It still hoped to persuade the Council by its rather feeble attempt to reinterpret the pollution condition and, then, by throwing the weight of the company Chairman into the debate. But the support it gained with the Environmental Services Committee, though crucial to later events, failed to change the Council's mind at its December meeting. This defeat appeared to leave the company with little option but to cuts its losses in Bedfordshire and take its investment to Cambridgeshire. The subsequent closure of Ridgmont was a matter of commercial necessity – it was the optimum size plant needed to reduce production in a falling market. The company insisted the decision had nothing to do with the fate of its planning permissions in Bedfordshire.

London Brick had little idea of the transformation that this decision would bring about. Two quite unforeseen developments came to the beleaguered company's aid. One was the spontaneous intervention of the unions, who, facing the loss of jobs, provided the company with support and weakened the political opposition facing an election. The alliance of labour with capital is characteristic in environmental conflicts. 'On some political and economic issues it tends to identify with industry' (Engler, 1961 p. 492). The other development was pure serendipity – the recognition by a councillor that the Council's failure to determine the Ridgmont permission left the way open to the Environmental Services Committee to grant a permission without the pollution condition and without reference to the Council. Borne along by events, the company accepted the windfall and switched its priorities once again to Ridgmont since, by now, delays at Stewartby had precluded the building of new works in time to take advantage of the new clay workings.

In this version the company appears not as the masterful exploiter of events but as the creature of circumstance. It had not appreciated the force of opposition its plans would engender and was pitched into a battle of opposing interests whose outcome remained, until the end, uncertain. Its investment strategy became the prisoner of events. It was not clear where it would invest first either in terms of which county or even in terms of which specific sites within Bedfordshire. In the end London Brick not only failed to impose its will on the local authority but lost its whole investment strategy, as the delays caused by the conflict ruined its hopes of making a start on its redevelopment plan. In terms of the definitions of power identified earlier the company had not defined the political agenda nor won any political victories which enabled it to benefit. It could be argued, too, that it had failed to realise its specific objectives. It is undeniable that it took decisions which had a considerable impact on the community. The decision to close Ridgmont, though caused by economic circumstances, had a major impact. But it is equally the case that its opponents were able to take decisions which, potentially at least, could affect the company's investment plans and thus its impact on the environment.

Conclusions

The London Brick case illustrates the importance of temporal and spatial factors in corporate decision making. Over a long period the company was able to exercise power by inaction and by taking the requisite steps to thwart opposition. When it found itself in confrontation with environmental interests it sought to negotiate, and when that failed, it retaliated. More generally it is possible to perceive an oscillation in the balance of power as the successes of environmental groups are met by a resurgence of business power. It seems that when business is at its weakest in economic terms it can defend itself against environmental pressures best. When jobs and profits are on the line the business case meets with more sympathy from governments. Large multi-plant companies can also make choices between alternative investment opportunities. In this case London Brick, though tied to its Oxford Clay resource base, was able to select which plants to close and where to redevelop. To pluralists such changes in strategy underline the differences in the balance of power between corporate and environmental interests that exist at different times and in different places. The political economy perspective sees it differently, as evidence of the flexible but overwhelming opportunities for the exercise of power available to business.

This case study has, perhaps, oversimplified two alternative interpretations. It has, however, suggested that both are plausible though both are also flawed. The political economy version contends that business possesses such reserves of power that the eventual outcome is never in doubt. This requires, at some points, a willing suspension of disbelief. For example, did the company fully recognise the opportunities which lay open to it after its defeat by the Council? Perhaps it did not need to since it might have won anyway. The pluralist argument relies, typically, on taking things at their face value. It regards the company as no more than an interest group with roughly equal chances of success in a battle with other interests. It suggests, perhaps, that the company was more naive and innocent than was really the case. But the pluralist stress on the uncertainty of the outcome and the importance of changing circumstances is, at least, as compelling as the notion of the company as an omnipotent giant able to impose its will. We are left, perhaps, to conclude that both perspectives contribute to our understanding of the exercise of corporate power. As Dunleavy argues, 'it does not seem utopian to detect signs of empirically supported common ground, underlying the fundamental theoretical disputes which separate the two halves of the debate' (1981, p. 16).

References

Bedfordshire County Council (1967) *Bedfordshire Brickfield*, October.

Bedfordshire County Council (1976a) *County Structure Plan, Public Participation*, Phase 1, Report, June.

Bedfordshire County Council (1976b) *County Structure Plan, Public Participation*, Phase 2, Report, December.

Bedfordshire County Council (1978a) *Minerals, Appraisals and Issues*, March.

Bedfordshire County Council (1978b) *Minerals, Appraisals and Issues, Public Consultation*, March to July.

Bennett, G. (1979) 'Pollution control in England and Wales: a review', *Environmental Policy and Law*, 5, pp. 93–9, 190–3.

Brothwood Report (1960) *Report on Atmospheric Pollution in the Brickworks Valley*, Bedfordshire County Council, Health Department, October.

Burns, K. N. and Allcroft, R. (1964) 'Fluorosis in cattle. 1. Occurrence and effects in industrial areas of England and Wales 1954–7', Animal Disease Surveys Report No. 2. Pt. 1 Ministry of Agriculture, Fisheries and Food, HMSO.

Cox, A. (1979) *Brickmaking: A history and gazetteer*, Survey of Bedfordshire, Bedfordshire County Council, Royal Commission on Historial Monuments (England), November.

Cremer and Warner (1979) *The Environmental Assessment of the Existing and Proposed Brickworks in the Marston Vale Bedforashire*, Main Report, prepared for Bedfordshire County Council by Cremer and Warner, Consulting Engineers and Scientists, October.

Crenson, M. A. (1971) *The Un-Politics of Air Pollution: A study of non-decisionmaking in the Cities*, Baltimore, The Johns Hopkins Press.

Department of the Environment (1980) *Air Pollution in the Bedfordshire Brickfields*, Report, Directorate of Noise, Clean Air and Waste.

Dunleavy, P. (1981) 'Alternative theories of liberal democratic politics: the pluralist–marxist debate in the 1980s', paper prepared for Social Sciences Foundation Course, The Open University.

Engler, R. (1961) *The Politics of Oil: Private power and democratic directions*, University of Chicago Press.

Hill, M. 'Air pollution control in Britain' (unpublished paper).

Hillier, R. (1981) *Clay that Burns: A history of the fletton brick industry*, London Brick Company.

Kimber, R. and Richardson, J. J. (1974) *Campaigning for the Environment*, London, Routledge & Kegan Paul.

Knoepfel, P., Weidner, H., Hans, K. and Watts, N. (1980) *The Environmental Quality Game: A proposal for an analytical model*, International Institute for Environment and Society, Berlin.

Lindblom, C. E. (1977) *Politics and Markets*, New York, Basic Books.

London Brick Company (1978) *Report and Accounts*.

London Brick Company (1980) *Brickworks Redevelopment Plan*, London Brick Company Assessment and Implications of the Cremer and Warner Report.

Moodie, G. C. (1970) *Opinions, Publics and Pressure Groups*, London, George Allen & Unwin.

Polsby, N. W. (1980) *Community Power and Political Theory*, 2nd edition, New Haven, Yale University Press.

Porteous, A., Attenborough, K. and Pollitt, C. (1977) *Pollution: The professionals and the public*, The Open University Press.

Reade, E. J. (1982) 'Section 52 and corporatism in planning', *Journal of Planning and Environment Law*, January, pp. 8–16.

Reagan, M. D. (1963) *The Managed Economy*, New York, Oxford University Press.

Sandbach, F. (1980) *Environment, Ideology and Policy*, Oxford, Basil Blackwell.

Sandbach, F. (1982) 'Pollution control: in whose interest?', paper given to Conference on Environmental Pollution and Planning, Southampton.

Vogel, D. (1980) 'Coercion versus consultation: a comparison of environmental protection policy in the United States and Great Britain', paper for the British Politics Group, American Political Science Annual Convention, Denver, Colorado.

Vogel, D. (1981) 'How business responds to opposition: corporate political strategies during the 1980s' (draft paper).

Waller, R. E. (1982) 'Air pollution and health', paper given to Conference on Environmental Pollution and Planning, Southampton.

Wolfinger, R. E. (1972), 'Nondecisions and the study of local politics', *American Political Science Review*, vol. 65, pp. 1063–80.

Wood, C. (1982) 'Local planning authority controls over pollution', paper given to Conference on Environmental Pollution and Planning, Southampton.

Part IV

Implementation

Introduction

To understand the policy process as a whole it is necessary to give attention to policy implementation. Thinking about implementation has evolved from a starting point in which the translation of policy into action was seen as being, under normal circumstances, an unproblematical process so long as bureaucracies were clearly subservient to their political masters. This early perspective was dominated by a view of bureaucracy as, by and large, conforming to the Weberian model, with politics as a goal-setting process, along the lines of Simon's notion of rational decision-making, and by a view of the feasibility of separating administration from politics as set out in a classic essay by Woodrow Wilson (Wilson 1887), a political scientist who became President of the United States. This view did not fail to identify that administration was a creative process, elaborating policy to conform to circumstances and needs. What it did tend to disregard was the extent to which this activity would tend to transform policy, often fundamentally. Recognition of this has given implementation studies a crucial importance in the study of the policy process. Yet it is important not to see them as somehow separate from studies of the policy-making process. Rather, implementation must be seen as part of policy-making.

The first wave of implementation studies, of which one by Pressman and Wildavsky (1973) was the most influential, drew attention to this phenomenon, presenting it largely in terms of the subversion of the goals of the original policy-makers. This involved a focus upon the ways in which organizational and inter-organizational phenomena would tend to transform policy. The reading from Hogwood and Gunn belongs very much in this tradition. It looks at the factors which will tend to undermine 'perfect administration' and provides a series of prescriptions to policy-makers to assist them in preventing this occurrence. Implementation is interpreted in top-down terms, accepting the validity of the goals of policy-makers and their capacity to make them explicit. Hogwood and Gunn offer an excellent model or yardstick against which actual implementation processes can be measured. The second wave of implementation studies, however, raises questions about how the 'implementation deficit', likely to be found, should be interpreted.

These later studies raised three different kinds of problems about the top-down approach. First, they questioned whether top level 'policy-makers' really want to, or are able to, set clear policy goals. Second, they suggested that where goals are set they come through in such potentially contradictory ways, particularly as new policies are typically layered on top of earlier ones, that, on methodological grounds, implementation is better studied by looking at the efforts of those at the bottom to make sense of these new inputs from the top. Third, and most fundamentally, some writers challenged the normative view, embedded in the top-down approach, that goal setting inputs *should* come from the top. This last view offered a challenge to the classical 'statist' view of democracy, suggesting that in many circumstances it is best that policy is 'negotiated' at the bottom, between those who are expected to carry it out and those who are affected by it.

All three of these criticisms have been advanced in the work of Hjern. The article by Hjern and Porter reproduced here does not outline them explicitly but rather sets out to show how policy processes occur in complex structures. They advance the view that there is a need for bottom-up analysis of administrative activities in terms of 'implementation structures'.

Readers will also find this sort of view discussed in the reading from Elmore, where the first of his models (the 'systems management model') conforms to the top-down approach whilst the other three diverge in various ways. Elmore's article explores various analytic models of the organization of implementation derived from theory, using an approach he describes as derived from the work of Graham Allison (1971), rather like that used in the earlier extract from Blowers, in which various approaches to analysing the same issue are compared and contrasted for their explanatory power. In this case, however, the normative issues about *control* continuously lurk in the background, with the problems of securing control intensifying as one moves through from the first to the fourth of Elmore's models.

The next extract in this section is an article by Sabatier which explores the strengths and weaknesses of the top-down and bottom-up approaches, and aims to reach some kind of synthesis. Sabatier is particularly concerned with the methodological arguments. He is clearly not prepared to address the normative argument advanced by some of the bottom-uppers, feeling uncomfortable with a view which denies legitimacy to top level policy-makers. Accordingly he is not happy with the extent to which writers from the bottom-up perspective present the distinction between policy formulation and implementation as blurred, seeing it as precluding 'policy evaluation' (which is of course one of their main reasons for drawing attention to the issue).

Sabatier's discomfort highlights a fundamental normative concern, which many will want to resolve either by urging that policy-makers should adopt explicit goals (as in the Hogwood and Gunn approach) or by interposing ideal goals which they, the analysts, believe should be present. The problem with the former is that policy-makers may be adept at suggesting, for political reasons, that they have specific goals even when they know they have not provided the means to attain them (this is an aspect of 'symbolic' policy-making, see Edelman 1971). An example of the latter is an assumption that a specific social policy is concerned to advance equality. The problem with this is that it readily leads into the trap of attributing the specified goal to some of the actors, particularly those with policy-making responsibilities. Whilst both of these procedures may offer valid perspectives for evaluation purposes they may lead, in implementation studies, to assumptions that it is the implementers as opposed to the policy-makers who have subverted the postulated goal.

The final extract comes from an article by Lane in which he tries to get away from the dichotomy offered by the top-down/bottom-up argument. It is worth noting that Lane, like Hjern, is a Scandinavian. It is arguable that in the Scandinavian countries the analysis of implementation has lacked the rather charged form it assumes in the United States – because of conflicts between the federal government and the states – and in Britain – because of the very conflictual relationship between central and local government since 1979. Rather, the policy systems in Sweden, Norway and Denmark have been characterized by high consensus and an acceptance of a negotiated relationship between central 'steering' and local autonomy.

Whilst the readings in this section have been selected to highlight some issues about the study of implementation, in practice the next and final section of the book also explores aspects of implementation and its importance for the policy-process.

Those who want to read more about implementation theory might go back to Pressman and Wildavsky's classic, cited above, for the top-down approach or to a collection edited by Barrett and Fudge (1981) for the bottom-up approach. It may also be appropriate to look at other pieces by Hjern; these are cited by Sabatier.

References

Allison, G. T. (1971) *Essence of Decision*, Boston: Little, Brown.

Barrett, S. and Fudge, C. (eds) (1981) *Policy and Action*, London: Methuen.

Edelman, M. (1971) *Politics as Symbolic Action*, Chicago: Markham.

Pressman, J. and Wildavsky, A. (1973)*Implementation*, Berkeley: University of California Press.

Wilson, W. (1987) 'The Study of Administration', *Political Science Quarterly*, 56(2), pp. 481–506.

Why 'perfect implementation' is unattainable

Brian Hogwood and Lewis Gunn

Why 'perfect implementation' is unattainable

[. . .] In an article entitled 'Why is implementation so difficult?', Gunn (1978) drew upon Hood's analysis (1976) and those of Pressman and Wildavsky (1973), Etzioni (1976), Kaufman (1971), Bardach (1977), Van Meter and Van Horn (1975), and King (1975 and 1976) to provide for civil servants a short guide to some of the reasons why, according to these pioneering writers, any state of 'perfect implementation' was likely to be virtually unattainable in practice. Like Hood again, Gunn emphasized that 'perfection' in this context was an analytical concept or 'idea' and not, in the colloquial sense of the term, an 'ideal' to be achieved. In other words, no prescriptive model was offered and, indeed, several of the logical preconditions of perfect implementation – such as 'perfect obedience' or 'perfect control' – were identified as being morally and politically quite unacceptable as well as unattainable in a pluralist democracy.

What, then, are these preconditions which would have to be satisfied if perfect implementation were to be achieved and why are they unlikely to be achieved in practice?

The circumstances external to the implementing agency do not impose crippling constraints
Some obstacles to implementation are outside the control of administrators because they are external to the policy and the implementing agency. Such obstacles may be physical, as when an agricultural programme is set back by drought or disease. Or they may be political, in that either the policy or the measures needed to achieve it are unacceptable to interests (such as party activists, trade unions, or, in some societies, the military) which have the power to veto them. These constraints are obvious and there is little that administrators can do to overcome them except in their capacity as advisers, by ensuring that such possibilities are borne in mind during the policy-making stage.

From B. W. Hogwood and L. A. Gunn, *Policy Analysis for the Real World* (1984), Oxford: Oxford University Press.

That adequate time and sufficient resources are made available to the programme
This condition partly overlaps the first, in that it often comes within the category of external constraints. However, policies which are physically or politically feasible may still fail to achieve stated intentions. A common reason is that too much is expected too soon, especially when attitudes or behaviour are involved (as, for example, in attempts to alter discriminatory attitudes towards the physically or mentally disabled). Another reason is that politicians sometimes will the policy 'end' but not the 'means', so that expenditure restrictions may starve a statutory programme of adequate resources. This happened in the case of the 1974 Control of Pollution Act, since it coincided with cutbacks in the public sector which denied local authorities sufficient funds to appoint the additional staff needed to implement the Act. A more unusual problem arises when special funds are made available, as in the Urban Programme, but have to be spent within an unrealistically short time, faster than the programme can effectively absorb them. It is important to realize that money is not a resource in itself but only a 'ticket' with which to purchase real resources, and there may be delays in this conversion process. The fear of having to return the 'unspent portion' of funding at the end of the financial year often leads public agencies into a flurry of expenditure, sometimes on relatively trivial items. Attempts to persuade finance officers to allow the carry-over of unspent funds to the next financial year are usually in vain, so that administrators are again quite limited in what they can do to overcome these constraints upon effective implementation. They can only advise politicians about the lead times which may be involved before a programme produces results, plan the annual cash flow to avoid any unspent portion, and seek to anticipate any blockages in converting cash into real resources.

That the required combination of resources is actually available
The third condition follows on naturally from the second, namely that there must not only be constraints in terms of overall resources but also that, at each stage in the implementation process, the appropriate combination of resources must actually be available. In practice, there is often a 'bottleneck' which occurs when, say, a combination of money, manpower, land, equipment, and building material has to come together to construct an emergency landing-strip for the RAF, but one or more of these is delayed and as a result the project as a whole is set back by several months. As noted in [the section above], a temporary shortage of cash may be less serious in such circumstances than a blockage in the supply of some 'real' resource. The flow of additional funding for a programme can be swiftly increased, given political assent, by a turn of the fiscal 'tap', but there can be no guarantee that money can be converted into land, materials, or manpower within the time-scale of the programme. Thus a shortage in, say, the stock of seasoned timber can hold up a building programme for months. Or a dearth of skilled carpenters may seriously constrain a housing rehabilitation programme. In other words, particularly severe disruptions threaten when scarce resources are in the nature of a relatively fixed *stock* rather than a *flow*. The length of a delay in making good a deficiency in the supply of trained manpower, for example, will be determined by the minimum length of the training period involved.

The main responsibility for such crises in implementation properly lies with administrative staff, including programme designers and managers, since they now have available to them a battery of techniques (often with attendant technology) such as network planning and control, manpower forecasting, and inventory control, which should help them to anticipate potential bottlenecks and take appropriate action in terms of generating or redistributing resources within the programme.

That the policy to be implemented is based upon a valid theory of cause and effect
Policies are sometimes ineffective not because they are badly implemented, but because they are bad policies. That is, the policy may be based upon an inadequate understanding of a problem to be solved, its causes and cure; or of an opportunity, its nature, and what is needed to exploit it. Pressman and Wildavsky (1973) describe any policy as a 'hypothesis containing initial conditions and predicted consequences. That is, the typical reasoning of the policy-maker is along the lines of 'if x is done at time t(1) then Y will result at time t(2)'. Thus every policy incorporates a theory of cause and effect (normally unstated in practice) and, if the policy fails, it may be the underlying theory that is at fault rather than the execution of the policy.

Pressman and Wildavsky developed their argument from a detailed case-study of the failure of a programme in the late 1960s aimed at creating employment for members of minority groups in the Californian city of Oakland. The programme provided funds for public works and for making building and other loans available to private firms, in hopes that (a) resulting business opportunities would be taken up by investors and (b) result in the creation of new jobs which would (c) be filled by Blacks and Mexicans. Despite much initial goodwill the programme achieved very little. Few loans were taken up by firms and some proposals for public works came to nothing. Even when funds were spent as intended, the net increase in employment of members of minority groups was disappointingly small. One of Pressman and Wildavsky's conclusions was that the programme was based upon an inadequate theory of work-creation: this seeming failure of implementation was, at least in part, a failure of policy-making. A similar point is made by Bardach (1977, 251–2): 'If this theory is fundamentally incorrect, the policy will fail no matter how well it is implemented. Indeed, it is not exactly clear what "good" implementation of a basically misconceived policy would mean'.

Here, then, is one seeming problem of implementation which can only be tackled by better analysis at the issue definition and options analysis stages of the policy-making process. The difficulties of such analysis should not be underestimated, given the limits of our ability to understand and 'solve' complex social and economic problems, especially since, as Bardach (1977) reminds us, government tends to get landed with the most difficult problems with which no one else has been able to cope. However, we can attempt to improve issue definition [. . .]; we can try to test the 'hypotheses' underlying various policy options; we may be able to learn something from foreign experience (although there is little evidence that we in Britain have learned anything from the policy failures described by Pressman and Wildavsky and other American writers); and finally, we must remember that the 'moment of choice' is not the end of the policy-making process and be prepared constantly to test underlying theory against problems of practice observed at later stages in the process.

That the relationship between cause and effect is direct and that there are few, if any, intervening links

Even from the very broad outline of the Oakland programme, it will be seen that the theory underlying the policy was more complex than a simple 'if X, then Y' and extended the causal chain to 'if X, then Y, and if Y, then Z'. Pressman and Wildavsky argue that policies which depend upon a long sequence of cause and effect relationships have a particular tendency to break down, since 'the longer the chain of causality, the more numerous the reciprocal relationships among the links and the more complex implementation becomes'. In other words, the more links in the chain, the greater the risk that some of them will prove to be poorly conceived or badly executed. In the case of the Oakland programme a cruder but also more direct approach to work-creation might have had greater success. However, given the complexity of some recent British programmes – not least our own attempts to improve the employment prospects of minority groups or to regenerate our declining inner cities – we should not be too critical about American practice.

That dependency relationships are minimal

This condition of 'perfect implementation' requires that there is a single implementing agency which need not depend on other agencies for success, or if other agencies must be involved, that the dependency relationships are minimal in number and importance. Where, as is often the case in practice, implementation requires not only a complex series of events and linkages (see [above]) but also agreement at each event among a large number of participants, then the probability of a successful or even a predictable outcome must be further reduced. Pressman and Wildavsky argue that 'Adding the number of necessary clearances involved in decision points throughout the history of the program will give an idea of the task involved in securing implementation.' (A *decision point* will be reached each time an act of agreement has to be registered for the programme to continue, and *clearance* is the name given to each instance in which a separate participant is required to give his consent.) By a process of simple arithmetical calculation, Pressman and Wildavsky show that, even if there is a high chance of obtaining a clearance from a single participant at a given decision point, when all the probabilities are multiplied together the overall chances of success are extremely slender.

Such calculations are a little misleading since, as Bowen (1982) points out, the chances of success are considerably improved if there are repeated attempts at securing agreement at tricky decision points, concentration of resources on difficult clearances, parallel attempts to achieve similar results by different routes, and the beginning of a 'bandwagon' effect (see also Bardach, 1977, 242–3). Further, Pressman and Wildavsky's calculation was based on an 'all-or-nothing' concept of a favourable outcome at each decision point, whereas the chances of partial success might well be higher. That being said, it still seems likely that the greater the number of clearances required among other bodies involved in implementation, the lower will be the chances of full implementation.

It is not only in a federal system such as the USA that programmes can become overextended in terms of both causal chains and numbers of participating agencies. Anthony King (1976) argues that the capacity of British government to deal with its problems is diminishing because 'the number of dependency relationships in which government is involved has increased substantially'. Thus it is nowadays relatively rare for implementation of a public programme to involve only a government department on the one hand and a group of affected citizens on the other. Instead there is likely to be an intervening network of local authorities, boards and commissions, voluntary associations, and organized groups. An example of multi-stage, multi-agency implementation is the Glasgow Eastern Area Renewal (GEAR) project, involving as it does the Scottish Office, Scottish Development Agency, Scottish Special Housing Association, Manpower Services Commission, Strathclyde Regional Council, City of Glasgow District Council, and several other public bodies – as well as community groups, the inhabitants themselves, and the private businesses and investors who, it is hoped, will be attracted to the regenerated area. The question of whether GEAR is a partial success story or a 'mutually non-effective group of organisations' (Booth, Pitt, and Money, 1982) is the subject of some debate in Scotland. At several points, impatience with the problems of working with so large a group of organizations has led to suggestions that an Urban Development Corporation (similar to those introduced to England) might provide a more effective basis for regenerating Glasgow's declining East End.

That there is understanding of, and agreement on, objectives
The requirement here is that there should be complete understanding of, and agreement on, the objectives to be achieved, and that these conditions should persist throughout the implementation process. (We should perhaps repeat that this 'requirement' is only in terms of the ideal-type model of 'perfect implementation': no prescriptive – far less descriptive – model is offered at this point.)

[. . .] The theory of planning is replete with references to objectives which, we are told by managerialist writers, should be clearly defined, specific, and preferably quantified, understood, and agreed throughout the organization, mutually compatible and supportive, and provide a blueprint against which actual programmes can be monitored. However, [. . .] most research studies suggest that, in real life, the objectives of organizations or programmes are often difficult to identify or couched in vague and evasive terms. Even 'official' objectives, where they exist, may not be compatible with one another, and the possibility of conflict or confusion is increased when professional or other groups proliferate their own 'unofficial' goals within a programme. Official objectives are often poorly understood, perhaps because communications downwards and outwards from headquarters are inadequate. Even if objectives have initially been understood and agreed, it does not follow that this state of affairs will persist throughout the lifetime of the programme, since goals are susceptible to succession, multiplication, expansion, and displacement. Any of these tendencies will complicate the implementation process and even – in the eyes of top management – 'subvert' it. Again we see that apparent 'implementation failures' may stem from features of other stages in the policy process.

That tasks are fully specified in correct sequence

Here the condition is that in moving towards agreed objectives it is possible to specify, in complete detail and perfect sequence, the tasks to be performed by each participant. The difficulties of achieving this condition of perfect implementation are obvious. Also it is surely desirable as well as inevitable that there should be some room for discretion and improvisation in even the most carefully planned programme. But techniques such as network planning and control [. . .] can at least provide a framework within which projects can be planned and implementation controlled, by identifying the tasks to be accomplished, the relationships between these tasks and the logical sequence in which they should be performed. There remain, of course, the managerial problems of actually ensuring that tasks are performed correctly and on time and of taking appropriate remedial action if they are not.

That there is perfect communication and co-ordination

The precondition here is that there would have to be perfect communication among and co-ordination of the various elements or agencies involved in the programme. Hood (1976) argues that for perfect implementation to be achieved it would be necessary to have a completely unitary administrative system – 'like a huge army with a single line of authority' – with no compartmentalism or conflict within. He is not, of course, advocating such a system. Even to state this condition of perfect co-ordination is to know that, leaving aside questions of desirability, its attainment would be all but impossible within and among real-life organizations which are characterized by departmentalism, professionalism, and the activities of many groups with their own values, goals, and interests to protect.

Communication has an important contribution to make to co-ordination and to implementation generally. However, perfect communication is as unattainable a condition as most of the others we have examined. While management information systems (MIS) can assist in matching information flow to needs, they cannot ensure that the resulting data, advice, and instructions are understood as intended by the senders, or indeed, understood at all. Co-ordination is not, of course, simply a matter of communicating information or of setting up suitable administrative structures, but involves the exercise of power, and this leads to the final condition for perfect implementation.

That those in authority can demand and obtain perfect compliance

Hood's phrase is 'perfect obedience' and he expands it to mean 'no resistance to commands at any point in the administrative system'. If there were any potential for resistance it would be identified (in Hood's model of 'perfect administration') by the system's 'perfect information' and forestalled by its 'perfect control'. In other words, the final and perhaps least attainable condition of perfect implementation is that those 'in authority' are also those 'in power' and that they are able to secure total and immediate compliance from others (both internal and external to the agency) whose consent and co-operation are required for the success of the programme. In practice, within an agency there may be compartmentalism, between agencies there may be conflicts of interest and status disputes, and those with the formal authority to demand co-operation may lack the power to back up these demands or the will to exercise it. Every administrative practitioner knows how difficult it would be to achieve the condition of perfect compliance. Most of us would add that we would not want to live or work in such a system.

When implementation involves, as it sometimes does, innovation and the management of change – with major departures from previous policies and practices – there will be particularly high probability of suspicion, recalcitrance, or outright resistance from affected individuals, groups, and interests, especially if insufficient time has been allowed for explanation and consultation or if any previous experience of change has been unfortunate. We cannot (and should not) hope ever to be free from such resistance, but we can learn a good deal about its nature and about the responses open to administrators from the study of individual, group, organizational, and political behaviour. Thus the psychologist, sociologist, and political scientist have at least as much to contribute to our understanding of implementation as have the programme designer, network planner, and information systems analyst. [. . .]

A 'top-down' perspective?

The language, concepts, and approach employed to this point would be regarded by some more recent writers on implementation – or, in their language, 'the policy–action relationship' – as biased and limiting. Barrett and Fudge (1981) argue that much of the literature to which we have so far made reference demonstrates a 'managerial' perspective, reflecting a 'policy-centred' or 'top-down' view in which implementers are seen as 'agents' of those who claim to make policy. They argue that:

> rather than treating implementation as the transmission of policy into a series of consequential actions, the policy–action relationship needs to be regarded as a process of interaction and negotiation, taking place over time, between those seeking to put policy into effect and those upon whom action depends.

From our previous comments on the interdependence of policy-making and implementation, on the scope for officials to initiate and influence policy, and on the limits to centrally imposed objectives, co-ordination, and demands for compliance, it will be obvious that we can agree with much of the above statement as a *description* of what happens in real life. We also agree – indeed, is there anyone who does not? – on the importance of understanding the contribution to 'the complexity of the policy process' of 'environmental, political, and organizational' factors. Thus, in seeking to criticize some at least of the so-called 'top-down' writers, Barrett and Fudge are creating a straw man and sometimes appear to confuse ideal-type models of perfect implementation with a normative or prescriptive model.

Barrett and Fudge themselves often seem to drift between descriptive and prescriptive styles of argument. Hierarchy and the 'chain of command' are clearly out of favour and the term 'top-down' is used virtually as an epithet throughout. They appear not only to argue against but actively to dislike any suggestions that 'politics and administration' might be viewed as separate, though such an argument has the curious effect of not only politicizing administration, but also, more worryingly, of de-politicizing politics. There is, of course, an important area of overlap between politics and administration but there are also more substantial areas of relatively independent functioning which are worth preserving, both analytically and in practice.

If pressed, we must plead guilty to a measure of sympathy with the top-down view, if only on the grounds that 'those seeking to put policy into effect' are usually elected while 'those upon whom action depends' are not, at least in the case of civil servants and the staff of health services, nationalized industries, etc. In the case of local authorities, of course, we have competing democratic legitimacies, since local councils, too, are elected, and we need not elaborate upon the controversy which has been created in the early 1980s by central government's unusually assertive attitude towards, and attempts to exercise dominance over, local authorities. Even in the case of central–local relations, however, we find it difficult to see why the view from the top is necessarily less valid than that from other levels. Of course, anyone can think of favourite examples of national policies so misconceived that they deserved to be stifled at birth and we have already indicated our view that 'implementation failures' can often be traced to inadequate policies. Choose different examples, however, and the 'bottom-up' view looks less attractive. If a Home Secretary is committed to better relations between policemen and black youths, should we view with equanimity the persistence of 'street level' police attitudes and actions which are openly racist? If the central health departments were to take a stronger line on the need for preventive medicine, would it not be a matter of legitimate concern if many clinicians and health authorities continued to direct resources towards 'heroic' medicine which, in terms of lives saved (and the quality of some of those lives), often seem less than good value? If Parliament decided to move from left-hand to right-hand drive on our roads, would we be happy to leave to 'negotiation' between road-users, local authorities, and the central government such questions as when, how, and whether the change-over should take effect?

We do not disagree with Barrett and Fudge when they argue that on many occasions 'lower level actors take decisions which effectively limit hierarchical influence, pre-empt top decision-making, or alter "policies"', but we find it difficult to agree with their ready acceptance of, let alone their seeming acquiescence in, all these aspects of the 'policy/action continuum'. Implementation must involve a process of interaction between organizations, the members of which may have different values, perspectives, and priorities from one another and from those advocating the policy. Much of this interaction can and should take place before policy formulation (e.g. in the form of consultation of local authority associations by central government departments), although there is no guarantee that such prior consultation will produce prior consent. While attempts will subsequently be made by unconvinced local authorities and others 'upon whom action depends' to modify and redirect the policy's thrust, there are surely limits – if only legal and constitutional limits – to how far such post-legislative guerrilla skirmishing should be taken. Finally, we would argue that the prescriptive aspects of policy analysis are concerned precisely with rescuing 'policy' from mere 'action'.

References

Bardach, E. (1977), *The Implementation Game*, Cambridge, MA, MIT Press.

Barrett, S. and C. Fudge (eds.) (1981), *Policy and Action*, London, Methuen.

Booth, S. A. S., D. C. Pitt and W. J. Money (1982), 'Organisational redundancy? A critical appraisal of the GEAR project', *Public Administration*, 60, pp. 56–72.

Bowen, E. R. (1982), 'The Pressman–Wildavsky paradox', *Journal of Public Policy*, 2, 1–22.

Etzioni, A. (1976), *Social Problems*, Englewood Cliffs, NJ, Prentice Hall.

Gunn, L. (1978), 'Why is implementation so difficult?', *Management Services in Government*.

Hood, C. C. (1976), *The Limits of Administration*, London, Wiley.

Kaufman, H. (1971), *The Limits of Organizational Change*, Alabama, University of Alabama Press.

King, A. (1975), 'Overload: problems of governing in the 1970s', *Political Studies*, 23, pp. 284–96.

King, A. (1976), 'The problem of overload', in *Why is Britain becoming Harder to Govern?*, London, BBC Publications.

Pressman, J. I. and A. Wildavsky (1973), *Implementation*, Berkeley, University of California Press.

Van Meter, D. and C. E. Van Horn (1975), 'The policy implementation process, a conceptual framework', *Administration and Society*, 6 (4).

Implementation structures

A new unit of administrative analysis

Benny Hjern and David O. Porter

Introduction

The scope of the public sector in Western democracies has dramatically expanded since the late 1940s as it has tried to keep pace with ever more pervasive externalities, the increasing uncertainties facing industry, and demands by citizens for more social services. Revenues and expenditures have risen, but so has a perception of an 'implementation deficit'. Under the auspices of, first, political science and public administration, and, subsequently, policy studies, a vast literature has focussed on this 'problem'. It would seem public programmes are never adequately implemented. From the perspective of most of these analyses, the modern state has promised programmes which it cannot deliver.

In this article we look at the findings in implementation and interorganizational studies in a somewhat different light. We suggest that perceptions of deficits in programme implementation are distorted and exaggerated by analytic frameworks which use organizations or individuals as the basic unit of analysis. A universal finding in studies of programme implementation is that clusters of public and private actors are involved. To cope with this condition, a theory is needed which bridges the gap between the atomistic theories in economics and comprehensive planning and management theories in public administration. We suggest an administrative theory with 'implementation structures' as the core units of analysis to fill this gap.

The article begins with a critique of administrative and economic theories when applied to programme implementation. It proceeds with an analysis of the administrative imperatives of programmes, and ties these imperatives to the identification of a potential pool of organizations from which localized implementation structures are formed. We then distinguish between organizations and implementation structures,

From B. Hjern and D. O. Porter, 'Implementation structures: a new unit of administrative analysis', *Organization Studies*, **2**, 1981, pp. 211–27.

and follow with an analysis of how complexity is reduced in implementation structures without recourse to hierarchy. Implementation structures and organizations are then contrasted as units for analysing the administration of programmes. The final sections present a phenomenological analysis of the formation of implementation structures, a summary of the observed characteristics of implementation structures, and some of the theoretical and normative implications of using these structures as units for analysis.

Hierarchy and markets

Many themes in the theory of administration were rationalized in the last decades of the 19th century by Max Weber and Woodrow Wilson (see Ostrom 1973: 22–33, for an analysis of these rationalizations). Based on these earlier theories, public administration theorists and practitioners have tried to design comprehensive, functionally uniform, and hierarchical organizations. There should be strong executives who are democratically responsible, and a neutrally competent civil service selected on merit principles (Kaufman 1956). A Lonely Organization Syndrome – 'bring all related functions in "X" (i.e. education, housing, or manpower) together under one roof' – is still the most powerful idea in public administration.

Political economists, seeing the futility of guiding many public sector programmes through bureaucracies, have offered an alternative to the Lonely Organization Syndrome (Ostrom 1973: 74ff.). They have observed that, as in markets, many public services are being provided by numerous and often overlapping governments. Rather than urge consolidation of these governments into ever more comprehensive jurisdictions, the political economists encourage the proliferation of even more of them. Competition among governments, combined with improved techniques for citizens to express their individual preferences, will increase the economic efficiency of government (Bish 1974; Niskanan 1971; Tullock 1970).

Both the Lonely Organization Syndrome and the political economy approach are anachronisms. The social structures on which they were based have changed radically. Once, public organizations prospered in sparsely populated environments. Private firms were, however, more numerous and competitive. With the maturing of industrial society, political democracy, and the social welfare state, the density and interconnectedness of public and private organizations increased. Since World War II in Scandinavia, for instance, the number of organizations has increased at a faster pace than the population (Berrefjord 1978; Elvander 1973). The result has been the emergence of an 'organizational society' in which many important services are provided through multi-organizational programmes. There are interconnected clusters of firms, governments, and associations which come together within the framework of these programmes – implementation structures.

In this setting, programmes are neither implemented by the invisible hand of markets nor with the heavy hand of large government bureaucracies. Programmes are implemented through multiorganizational clusters, some of which are part of markets and others of government bureaucracies. Actors in implementation structures may concurrently have to operate in markets and hierarchies. In policy analysis, few analytical frameworks can.

Observations on implementation

One of the most pervasive findings in studies of programme implementation is that many actors are involved in what outwardly appears to be a confounding set of relationships (Altenstetter and Bjorkman 1978; Friend *et al.* 1974; Lovell 1978; Metcalfe 1978; Pressman and Wildavsky 1973; Scharpf 1977; Welsh 1977 to cite only a few of these studies).

In the implementation of manpower training programmes in Sweden and Germany, we found a bewildering array of organizations and actors. Among the trainees there were the unemployed, those threatened with unemployment, youth, the aged, women, the handicapped, and the hardcore unemployed. Participating in planning, financing, and offering courses were specialized training centres, municipality schools, county or state training directors, union officials, firms, social welfare agencies, county planning departments, vocational training specialists, placement officers, teachers, chambers of commerce, craft-guilds, and a score of local, regional, and national agencies.

It seemed improbable that anything could be produced in such a muddle. But we observed large numbers of students in classes. There were graduations, and the graduates often went on to better jobs than they had previously held. Employers found workers with adequate skills.

But there were problems. Certain types of students systematically dropped out of courses, or never enrolled. Many students were 'trained for unemployment' in occupations which were already overcrowded or where the skills were obsolete. Employers complained about the quality or content of the training. Courses which local actors unanimously agreed were needed were not approved, or were approved only after long delays. New plants opened to find no appropriately trained workers to operate their production lines, even though the firm had announced their plans long in advance and may even have received public financial support to locate in the area.

How can these processes be analysed? Public administration theories, grounded in the Lonely Organization Syndrome, were not sufficient if used alone. No single, comprehensive organization can command all the needed resources. Conventional market analyses were also insufficient. There was a similarity of markets in the actions of many firms, agencies, and other actors. But there were significant 'market failures' too. All actors pursuing their individual interests did not produce a programme which satisfied what participating actors thought were the collective interests. A new formulation was needed which bridged the gap between the atomistic theories in economics and the comprehensive planning and management theories in conventional public administration. What is needed is a strategy for analysing purposive action within a framework where *parts of many public and private organizations* cooperate in the implementation of a programme. We suggest not only the use of *implementation structures* as a new unit of analysis, but also that this unit is the core of a strategy for administering multiorganizational programmes.

Programme and administrative imperatives

As a first step in using implementation structures as units of analysis, we analysed the 'administrative imperatives' behind the legislation authorizing a programme. A brief examination of the programme of labour market training demonstrates the inherent multiorganizational composition of the implementation structures within its imperative. To meet the objective of 'training the unemployed for employment' in a training programme, cooperation among national, regional, and local actors is required. At the national level it is necessary to create an overall framework of regulations and resources. Regional and local actors are involved in providing actual services. Training programmes rely on a 'local presence' (Porter 1980) to provide the essentially local and personal services of training and work creation. The implementation of training programmes at regional and local levels includes the planning of courses to be offered in specific localities; assembling the teachers, equipment, and facilities to teach the courses; and recruiting, teaching, and placing participants. To offer training which will lead to employment, planners must know the employers and occupations within a region. They are dependent on employers, unions, and other public authorities for information. Training facilities have relations with other educational institutions in the region to obtain properly prepared teachers; with employers in the design of up-to-date courses; with other public authorities for facilities and resources. In recruiting students, training institutions and labour exchanges have relations with each other, and with a variety of social service and private organizations. Placement of graduates involves interactions with employers.

Starting from an analysis of the administrative imperative of a programme it is possible to define reasonably accurately the *pool of organizations* within the task environment of a programme. The programme is implemented by members from such pools.

Pools of organizations

With a little imagination it is easy to name the main corporate actors in the pool of organizations which will *potentially* be involved in implementing a manpower training programme. The pool for a manpower training programme includes national, regional, and local labour market agencies, training centres, public and private employers, unions, general county and municipal governments, planning departments, and a variety of social agencies. The regional composition and local presence of organizations with a potential interest in manpower training varies considerably, even in a 'homogeneous' country such as Sweden.

More important, the pools of organizations are not administrative entities. They are the raw materials out of which the operating implementation structures are formed, almost irrespective of mandates from the central levels for one or another agency to implement the programme. Even so, organization pools provide essential information on the background and rules of implementation within a particular locality. However, before examining the processes through which implementation structures are formed out of a pool of organizations, it is necessary to distinguish between organizations and implementation structures as analytic units and administrative entities.

Organization rationales and programme rationales

In providing social services as diverse as housing, education, health, and manpower programmes in countries as varied as the FRG, Sweden, and the United States, we have found two general orientations towards administration and implementation – an organization rationale and a programme rationale (Porter 1980). These rationales are associated with two different administrative entities, which scholars have tried to analyse as if they were a single unit. Organization rationales are embedded within organizations. As purposive entities, organizations are comprised of *parts* of several programmes. Goal structures in organizations have long resisted being reduced to a consistent and clear set of objectives (Perrow 1978), in part because different clusters of goals are associated with each group of activities or programmes.

A *subset* of the members of the organization, usually those associated with general administrative activities, follow an organization rationale. They adapt the goals of the programmes within the organization to fit a 'holistic' strategy which conforms with their perception of the niche the organization fills within its environment. Programmes, in this context, are treated as instruments for insuring the overall survival of an organization.

A Swedish labour exchange, for instance, administers programmes in placement, training, and job creation. As an entity, the exchange is sensitive to pressures from the firms, unions, and local governments in its particular locality. It defines a niche for its activities within this context, continuously moulding the parts of the placement, training, and job creation programmes it participates in to an organizationally sensible rationale which meets the expectations of these surrounding organizations and communities. High performance in any one programme area is subordinated to high performance of the organization as a whole.

But almost no programme is fully implemented by a single organization. Programmes are implemented by a cluster of *parts* of public and private organizations, i.e. implementation structures. An implementation structure is comprised of *subsets* of members within organizations which view a programme as their primary (or an instrumentally important) interest. For these actors, an implementation structure is as much an administrative structure through which purposive actions are taken as the organizations in which they are employed.

The major differences in how actions are taken in organizations and implementation structures are that in the latter:

- there is less formal structure and fewer authoritative relations;
- the social structures which exist are more dynamic and shifting. The cluster of actors does not represent a legally defined entity with its own building and corporate charter; and
- decisions to participate in a programme are 'fuzzy', based on consent and negotiation.

Implementation structures are more likely to be *self-selected* than *designed* through authoritative relationships. They are formed by the initiative of individuals in relation to a programme. These individuals do not necessarily belong to the organization formally charged with programme implementation. Further, much information about implementation structures can only be obtained by identifying their individual members. Put another way, 'the nature of self-organization consists of a self-referential process. . . . A self-organizing system, that is to say, is first and foremost, a problem-posing system, not merely a problem-solving system' (Sahal 1979: 140).

Actors following organization and programme rationales, respectively, interact in similar patterns to those described by scholars of matrix organizations (Davis and Lawrence 1978; Galbraith 1971). These matrix elements are highlighted in Figure 1. Organizations (O_1, O_2, O_3 in Figure 1) participate in *parts* of several programmes (P_1, P_2, and P_3). Persons from within a single organization attempt to adjust these parts of programmes to meet overall organizational objectives. The vertical oval enclosing the parts of the three programmes implemented by O_1 is the area within which an organization rationale is practised. Persons identifying with a programme (P_1) pursue a programme rationale within the horizontal oval, trying to adjust the contributions of the parts of a number of organizations to meet the needs of the programme. Persons occupying positions at any of the nine points of intersection shown in the figure have to serve 'masters' both in programmes and in organizations. Failure to identify implementation structures as administrative entities distinct from organizations has led to

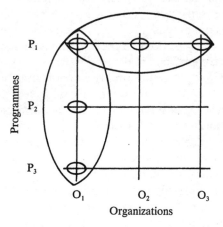

Figure 1 Matrix relationships between organization rationales and programme rationales

severe difficulties in administering the implementation of programmes. When a new programme is enacted, it is assigned to a single organization, and everyone walks away secure in the belief that somehow it will be implemented. If there is a failure, the programme is assigned to another organization, or the department head is fired, or both. Since programmes are implemented by an implementation structure, and not a single organization, such reactions may be inappropriate and dysfunctional.

Complexity and hierarchy

Scholars and bureaucrats complain about what they perceive to be a complexity of relationships within implementation structures, and the seeming intractability of this complexity. In this section, it is suggested that this perception of complexity is rooted primarily in the concepts used to analyse programme implementation, and is unwarranted by the actual situation. Programme implementation is complex, to be sure, but mechanisms operate within these programmes to reduce complexity. If implementation structures are used as the unit for administrative analysis, more effective use of these mechanisms can be made.

One of the acknowledged strengths of hierarchy in organization theory is that it helps to make possible the accomplishment of complex tasks (Simon 1947; Weber 1922: 223ff.). A task is subdivided into a number of small pieces and assigned to different units in an organization. The process of dividing up the tasks and recombining the subsequent work is authoritatively coordinated through a hierarchy. The overall goals or objectives (but not necessarily how the tasks are to be performed [Stinchcombe 1959–60]) are determined by persons at the top of the hierarchy. This mind-set is deeply embedded in what we have characterized as the Lonely Organization Syndrome.

For someone guided by this mind-set, the processes of implementing programmes are a nightmare. To administer a programme leads to splitting headaches and feelings of powerlessness. No one is in charge. There are few formal mechanisms for dividing up tasks. Enforcing decisions is rendered ineffectual because the workers in the field are employed by other organizations. There is so much happening that it is an impossible task to try to comprehend it all.

Complexity is reduced in implementation structures in an entirely different way than is rationalized by this variant of organization theory. In a critique of hierarchically based theories, Ostrom (1973) observed that the implementation of programmes by government often resembles a market. Complexity in markets (i.e. decisions about quantity and quality of production by firms, and decisions about consumers' needs) is reduced by many individual consumers and firms making decisions, via a calculus based on individual self-interest (Knight 1933).

Programme implementation structures are similar to and different from markets in several important ways. They are similar in that there is a need for independent, discretionary action in order to cope with the complexity inherent in so many interdependent actions. As with markets it is difficult within implementation structures to devise a set of rules that authoritatively direct the behaviour of the clusters of relatively autonomous public and private actors. Discretion and independent actions (sometimes encouraged on normative grounds in democracies) are required to cope with the diverse situations.

But, unlike markets, implementation structures are administrative entities. They are organized around specific programmes. In markets, goods and services are moulded by households into a package which satisfies their diverse demands, rather than the objectives of a public programme. The public choice approach has overlooked this crucial difference between programme implementation structures and markets, and therefore has had difficulties suggesting how to guide public industries (Bish and Ostrom 1973).

The existence of commitments separates a rationalization of structures from others using a strictly competitive and individualistic theory of exchange. To the extent that an individual takes notice of a commitment, i.e. does what he *ought* to, rather than what he *wants* to, microeconomic approaches lose much of their applicability. A distinction between commitment and preference is meaningless in a purely individualistic calculus (cf. Hirsch 1976: 14; Sen 1977: 329). Microeconomic theory postulates competitive (i.e. uncommitted) action within a *given* institutional arrangement (i.e. a market or even a hierarchy). To rationalize the behaviour of members of an implementation structure, this postulate must be reversed, i.e. implementation entails commitment to programme objectives by actors who are relatively uncommitted regarding institutional arrangements.

In summary, implementation structures are *allocative and administrative* entities. They fall between market and bureaucratic rationalizations. Goods are allocated through clusters of autonomous and semiautonomous actors – as in a market but unlike a bureaucracy. Objectives are set, plans are formulated, resources made available at the right place and time, services are provided, performance evaluated – as in a bureaucracy but unlike a market.

The processes through which implementation structures are formed may be a guide to assessing how they reduce complexity. Actors self-select or are committed to participate as there are tasks to be accomplished. Thus, complexity may be reduced without recourse to hierarchy. A rationalization of implementation structures, therefore, cannot rely upon the rationalizations and methodologies offered under the Lonely Organization Syndrome or markets. But implementation structures are administrative entities, and to improve their performance they should be treated as administrative entities in a conventional way. Can strategies be developed to improve the planning, budgeting, performance, and evaluation of implementation structures (cf. Fayol 1916; Gulick 1937; Hanf, Hjern, and Porter 1978)?

Alternative units of analysis

We have found it impossible to rationalize observations on the processes of programme implementation and administration using single organizations as the unit for analysis. Such an approach would have forced us to ignore the *cognitions* of practitioners and descriptive researchers. In some organizationally grounded research the perceptions and relations of people in one section of an organization, for instance, are aggregated and compared with the perceptions and relations of people in another section. The boundaries of the sections, as legally defined, are accepted *a priori* as the proper basis for aggregation and comparison, even though the people in each section are more influenced by relationships across section, programme, or organization boundaries. *A priori* decisions on the appropriate principle for aggregation destroy much of the meaning of the data collected. Decisions on the proper unit for aggregation should be solved empirically, not *a priori* (cf. Bachrach 1977).

Lately, through the concept of domain consensus, the same mistake has been made in research on interorganizational fields (see, for example, Benson 1975: 235–8). A 'focal organization' is picked *a priori* as the unit for analysis. The focal organization *and* its domain become a unit. All interactions are treated as if they contribute to an organization rationale because the unit of analysis – the focal organization – was chosen *a priori*, not empirically. We argue that this methodological decision may lead to lumping several different administrative entities together, and treating them as one. Much of the meaning of the data is thus destroyed.

Formation and dynamics of implementation structures

We argued above that implementation structures are formed from within pools of organizations and that they are formed through processes of consensual self-selection. In contrast to other theories that deal with the forming of groups of collective action we postulate that several motives are concurrently at play when implementation structures develop.

Attempts in interorganizational theory to determine *the* motive for participation in multiorganizational networks are instructive but give no conclusive evidence on why such collectivities as implementation structures are formed. (A broader treatise on participation is found in Dachler and Wilpert 1978.) Two interrelated motivational assumptions have been developed in the interorganizational literature. One uses an exchange perspective. Relations are formed when members of two or more organizations perceive mutual benefits from interacting (cf. Bish 1978; Levine and White 1961; Tuite 1972; White 1974). Another orientation – the power dependency approach – maintains that the motive for interaction is asymmetrically defined. Relationships are formed when the motivated party is powerful enough to force or induce the other to interact (cf. Aldrich 1972, 1976; Kochan 1975; Yuchtman and Seashore 1967).

The formation of implementation structures cannot be fully described with only one of these approaches. Both exchange and power dependency motives are often found in the formation of the same implementation structure. (This is in line with other pieces of empirical research, see Schmidt and Kochan 1977.) Further, the existence of asymmetrically defined, or power dependent, motives prohibits the application of

Olson's (1965) classic formulation of collective action in rationalizing the formation of implementation structures. More than a pursuit of individual self-interest is involved (see also Stigler 1975; Chamberlin 1978).

To review, within the same implementation structure there are many different motives for participation. Arbitrarily selecting one motive for participation will not solve the problem of defining and assessing implementation structures. Neither organization theory, with its emphasis on finding a single goal (Simon 1947: 42–3), nor economics, with its focus on individual self-interest maximization (Downs 1967; Niskanen 1971; Tullock 1965), nor interorganization theory, with its emphasis on exchange or power dependency, has been successful in defining and assessing organizations or interorganization fields using an analysis based on a single motive. Why follow the same path in defining and assessing implementation structures? The question of motives for participation should be open to empirical assessment. A phenomenological approach to defining implementation structures is a device to analyse motives for participation without being forced into accepting untenable assumptions. Motives for participation are not the primary concern in a phenomenological approach, rather we are interested in the *use* made of the resources brought together within implementation structures. There is not necessarily a connection between the motives for entering an implementation structure and the use made of resources in an existing one (cf. Simon 1964: 18–19 on this topic).

Another reason for a phenomenological approach is that the cognition and behaviour of individual members or organizations are important for understanding how resources are mobilized and used in implementation structures. As other researchers, we found 'entrepreneurs' operating within implementation structures. It has even been argued that without the reticulist or network management skills of individuals, the implementation of many programmes would grind to a halt (Friend *et al.* 1974; Lovell 1978; O'Toole 1979; Seidman 1970: 170). In rationalizations of 'organization behaviour', such individual skills are largely unaccounted for. The cognitions and behaviours of individuals are compartmentalized and filtered through 'objective' group measures.

This argument for our phenomenological approach is not based on an assumption about the unique situation of individuals. Individual cognitions and behaviour, to a degree, are structured and controlled by groups and cliques within organizations, professions, or programmes. The participants in implementation structures follow a rationale which is sanctioned, but not determined, by the organizations of which they are members as well as by their more general environments. Indeed, in order to make sense of sometimes conflicting and uncertain situations of decision making, we have to assume that the participants draw upon the moral and social conventions and institutions surrounding them. We take issue with some systems analysts who stress the complexity which environments impart on the system or organization. [. . .]

A third, and more practical, reason for using a phenomenological approach is that it provides a cheap and easily understood *methodology* for identifying implementation structures for purposes of administrative analysis. In our research on the local implementation of labour market programmes we focused on mapping implementation structures as they are understood by participants. Administrators in labour market programmes often intuitively seek to identify the implementation structure within which they are, or could be, operating. We have found open-ended interviews the best technique for obtaining this information from participants.

Our interviews were structured to assess interactions in four different aspects of a programme – planning, mobilization of resources, effectuation, and evaluation. (A similar set of administrative processes is identified by Gowler and Legge 1978: 202–4.) This technique yields four 'subimplementation structures', with partly different and partly overlapping members within each substructure. The starting point for defining implementation structures was the pool of organizations in a local labour market, but the participants were not confined to the local setting. We have observed interactions among local, regional, and national actors in implementing a programme at local levels (see Hanf *et al.* 1978 for a report on these specific implementation structures).

The implementation structure approach: a summary

An acronym, PIPIS, summarizes what may become a process for administering programmes. An analysis of the objectives of a *programme* suggests an administrative *imperative*. This imperative points to a potential *pool* of organizations, from which an *implementation structure* is formed.

Implementation structures are not organizations. They are comprised of parts of many organizations; organizations are comprised of parts of many programmes. As analytic constructs, implementation structures are conceptualized to identify the units of purposive action which implement programmes. They are 'phenomenological administrative units', partly defined by their participating members.

We found a number of elements which implementation structures seem to have in common. The actors and organizations in implementation structures have a *variety of goals and motives*. There may be a general interest in education, manpower training, or housing, but each actor and organization is participating in the programme partly for its own reasons. The intensity of interest in the programme varies substantially from one actor to another.

There is a *programme rationale* within which purposive action takes place. Programme-oriented actors view the resources of the various organizations in their implementation structures as a field within which they practise the familiar 'budgetary strategies'. Monetary and non-monetary resources are mobilized. Calculations are made to determine which actors within the structure offer a better potential for providing resources, and which resources could best be moulded to the priorities of the programme.

Authority relationships often focus on professional status, coordinative competence, potential or real power, and resource control. Traditional hierarchical authority tends to be of limited influence. Heads of one organization interact nonauthoritatively with midlevel managers or service providers in another.

There is a great deal of *local discretion*. Regional and national organizations may attempt to influence this discretion, particularly in such programmes as selective labour market policies, but control strategies are of very limited efficiency.

There is no single implementation structure for a national programme; rather there is a *collection of localized implementation structures*, each comprised of a distinctive array of public and private actors.

Within implementation structures, *subgroups of actors and organizations perform specialized roles*. There are substructures *for policy making, planning and intelligence, resource provision, intermediary and coordinating roles, services provision, and evaluation*. Coordination of roles within and among substructures varies considerably from one implementation structure to another.

Finally, implementation structures *differ in their relative cohesiveness*. The state of interrelatedness within particular implementation structures varies both geographically and over time. Some structures are highly *developed and regular*, others are *undeveloped and ad hoc*. The more developed and regular structures can be accurately described as *networks* of relationships in which participants have rather settled expectations about each other's actions. They relate in patterns not unlike the interactions within a cohesive organization. In the more undeveloped and *ad hoc* structures, expectations among the actors are not settled. Patterns of mutually beneficial interaction are poorly understood or have not been negotiated.

Implications and future research

The implications of accepting implementation structures as units for analysis are numerous. When implementation structures are accepted as distinct administrative entities, new lines for research open up in the more positive disciplines of sociology, political science, and psychology. Behaviours and institutions must be described, categorized, and analysed. Phenomena which have been described as anomalous or deviant when analysed within the context of organizations become explicable within implementation structures.

In more normative areas of inquiry, such as administration, democratic theory, accounting, information systems, evaluation, and law, new orientations will be needed to rationalize activities within implementation structures.

The old debate surrounding politics and administration takes on new dimensions when viewed from the analytical perspective of implementation structures. Democracy and pluralism go together, as do pluralism and discretion. Democracy has always been considered a cornerstone in the discipline of public administration, but pluralism and discretion have been troublesome. Perhaps a 'post-Weberian administration' will centre on a strategy for guiding multiorganizational programmes where negotiation, consent, and persuasion replace the biases towards control, command, and aggregate measures enforced through a unified chain of command (cf. Landau and Stout 1979). The basic administrative framework will need to resemble the responsibility centre and matrix administrative formats more than the hierarchical formats now dominant in public administration (Porter 1980).

Further, there have been few theories for intranational and cross-national comparisons of local administration. Subnational administration has been neglected or treated in a series of case studies. The implementation structure approach permits comparisons of the general features of programme administration at the subnational levels. Given the importance of evaluating the provision of social services (which rely on a local presence), such a comparative theory is much needed.

Democratic theory will also need adjustments beyond its applications to public administration. Concepts of political responsibility must be recast to take into account that many key actors in implementation derive their positions and legitimacy from nongovernmental sources. Notions of elective responsibility and corporatism do not have the breadth to cover these phenomena in programme implementation structures.

The areas of accounting, information systems, and evaluation will need to be expanded to consider financial and nonfinancial data from more of the actors within the clusters which comprise implementation structures. With the exception of some limited experience in PPBS (Schick 1980), these fields have used organizations as their units of analysis and considered the multiorganizational characteristics of programme implementation in an unsystematic fashion.

Many legal institutions and procedures also need to be reconsidered. In the absence of clear institutional lines of authority, the formulation and enforcement of legal obligations in the implementation of programmes is more problematic than in a situation where organizations are assumed to be responsible. Investigations will need to examine experiences in setting legal norms within implementation structures (e.g. Ostrom 1962) and attempt to extend principles and practices from these experiences to programme implementation generally.

References

Aldrich, H. (1972) 'An organization–environment perspective on cooperation and conflict in the manpower training system' in *Conflict and Power in Complex Organizations*, A. Negandhi (ed.), Kent, Ohio: CARI, Kent State University.

Aldrich, H. (1976) 'Resource dependence and interorganizational reactions: local employment service offices and social service sector organizations', *Administration and Society* 7: 419–54.

Altenstetter, C., and J. W. Bjorkman (1978) *Federal–State Health Policies and Impacts: The politics of implementation*, Washington, DC: University Press of America.

Bachrach, S. (1977) 'From morphology to political cognitions: toward a status group model of intra-organizational analysis', Cornell University Working Paper.

Benson, K. J. (1975) 'The interorganizational network as a political economy', *Administrative Science Quarterly* 20: 229–49.

Berrefjord, O. (1978) 'Fra embetsmannsstat til embetsmannsstat?' in *Forhandling-sokonomi og Blandningsadministrajon*, G. Hernes (ed.), Oslo: Universitetsforlaget.

Bish, R. L. (1974) *The Public Economy of Metropolitan Areas*, Chicago: Rand McNally/ Markham.

Bish, R. L. (1978) 'Intergovernmental relations in the United States: some concepts and implications from a public choice perspective' in *Interorganizational Policy Making: Limits to coordination and central control*, K. Hanf and F. W. Scharpf (eds.), London and Beverly Hills: Sage.

Bish, R. L., and V. Ostrom (1973) *Understanding Urban Government: Metropolitan reform reconsidered*, Washington, DC: American Enterprise Institute for Public Policy Research.

Chamberlin, J. R. (1978) 'The logic of collective action: some experimental results', *Behavioral Science* 23: 441–5.

Dachler, H. P., and N. Wilpert (1978) 'Conceptual dimensions and boundaries of participation in organizations: a critical evaluation', *Administrative Science Quarterly* 23: 1–39.

Davis, S. M., and P. R. Lawrence (1978) 'Problems of matrix organizations', *Harvard Business Review* May–June: 131–42.

Downs, A. (1967) *Inside Bureaucracy*, Boston: Little, Brown.

Elvander, N. (1973) *Naringslivets 900 Organisationer*, Malmo: Naringliv och Samhalle.

Fayol, H. (1916) *General and Industrial Administration*, London: Pitman. Reprinted 1949.

Friend, J. K., J. M. Power, and C. J. L. Yewlett (1974) *Public Planning: The inter-corporate dimension*, London: Tavistock.

Galbraith, J. R. (1971) 'Matrix organization design', *Business Horizons*, February: 29–40.

Gowler, D., and K. Legge (1978) 'The evaluation of planned organizational change: the necessary art of the possible', *Journal of Enterprise Management* 1: 201–13.

Gulick, L. (1937) 'Notes on the theory of organization' in *Papers on the Science of Administration*, L. Gulick and L. Urwick (eds.), New York: Institute of Public Administration, Columbia University.

Hanf, K., B. Hjern, and D. O. Porter (1978) 'Local networks of manpower training in the Federal Republic of Germany and Sweden' in *Interorganizational Policy Making: Limits to coordination and central control*, K. Hanf and F. W. Scharpf (eds.), Beverly Hills and London: Sage.

Hirsch, E. (1976) *Social Limits to Growth*, Cambridge, MA: Harvard University Press.

Kaufman. H. (1956) 'Emerging conflicts in the doctrines of public administration', *American Political Science Review* 50: 1057–73.

Knight, F. H. (1933) *The Economic Organization*, New York: Harper Torchbook, Harper and Row. Reprinted 1965.

Kochan, T. A. (1975) 'Determinants of the power of boundary units in an interorganizational bargaining relation', *Administrative Science Quarterly* 20: 434–52.

Landau, M., and R. Stout, Jr. (1979) 'To manage is not to control: or the folly of type II errors', *Public Administration Review* 39: 148–56.

Levine, S., and P. White (1961) 'Exchange as a conceptual framework for the study of interorganizational relationships', *Administrative Science Quarterly* 5: 583–601.

Lovell, C. (1978) 'Self-linking networks in local administration'. Paper presented at the Annual Meeting of the American Society of Public Administration, Phoenix, Arizona, April.

Metcalfe, H. L. (1978) 'Policy making in turbulent environments' in *Interorganizational Policy Making: Limits to coordination and central control*, K. Hanf and F. W. Scharpf (eds.), Beverly Hills and London: Sage.

Niskanan, W. A., Jr. (1971) *Bureaucracy and Representative Government*, Chicago: Aldine-Atherton.

Olson, M. (1965) *The Logic of Collective Action*, Cambridge, MA: Harvard University Press.

Ostrom, V. (1962) 'The water economy and its organization', *Natural Resources Journal* 2: 55–75.

Ostrom, V. (1973) *The Intellectual Crisis in American Public Administration*, Alabama: The University of Alabama Press.

O'Toole, L. (1979) 'Inter-organizational cooperation and labor market training: some cases'.

IIM/7–8 in the Publication Series of the International Institute of Management, Berlin: Science Center.

Perrow, C. (1978) 'Demystifying organization' in *The Management of Human Services*, R. C. Sarri and Y. Hasenfeld (eds.), New York: Columbia University Press.

Porter, D. O. (1980) 'Accounting for discretion and local environments in social experimentation and programme administration: some proposed alternative conceptualizations' in *Do Housing Allowances Work?*, K. L. Bradbury and A. Downs (eds.), Washington, DC: Brookings Institute.

Pressman, J. L., and A. Wildavsky (1973) *Implementation*, Berkeley, CA: University of California Press.

Sahal, D. (1979) 'A unified theory of self-organization', *Journal of Cybernetics* 9: 127–42.

Scharpf, F. W. (1977) 'Public organization and the waning of the welfare state: a research perspective', *European Journal of Political Research* 5: 339–62.

Schick, A. (1980) 'Budgeting as an administrative process' in *Perspectives on Budgeting*, A. Schick (ed.), Washington, DC: *American Society for Public Administration*.

Schmidt, S. M., and T. A. Kochan (1977) 'Interorganizational relationships: patterns and motivations', *Administrative Science Quarterly* 22: 220–34.

Seidman, H. (1970) *Politics, Position and Power*, New York: Oxford University Press.

Sen, A. K. (1977) 'Rational fools: a critique of the behavioral foundation of economic theory', *Philosophy and Public Affairs* 6: 317–44.

Simon, H. (1947) *Administrative Behavior: A study of decision-making processes in administrative organizations*, New York: The Free Press. Reprinted 1965.

Simon, H. A. (1964) 'On the concept of organizational goals', *Proceedings of the American Philosophic Society* 106: 18–19, 467–82.

Starling, J. D. (1975) 'System constructs in simplifying complexity' in *Organized Social Complexity*, T. R. LaPorte (ed.), Princeton, NJ: Princeton University Press.

Stigler, G. J. (1975) 'Free riders and collective action: an appendix to theories of economic regulation', *Bell Journal of Economics and Management Science* 5: 359–69.

Stinchcombe, A. L. (1959–60) 'Bureaucratic and craft administration of production: a comparative study', *Administrative Science Quarterly* 4: 168–87.

Tuite, M. F. (1972) 'Toward a theory of joint decision-making' in *Interorganizational Decision-making*, M. F. Tuite, R. Chrisholm and M. Radnor (eds), Chicago: Aldine.

Tullock, G. (1965) *The Politics of Bureaucracy*, New York: Public Affairs Press.

Tullock, G. (1970) *Private Wants, Public Means*, New York: Basic Books.

Weber, M. (1922) *Economy and Society*, New York: The Bedminster Press. Reprinted 1968.

Welsh, W. A. (1977) 'Interregional variations in public goods and services: some methodological issues and a preliminary analysis' in *Yearbook of East-European Economics* 7, 171–212. Munich and Vienna: Gunter Olzop Verlag.

White, P. E. (1974) 'Intra and interorganizational studies', *Administration and Society* 6: 105–52.

Yuchtman, E., and S. E. Seashore (1967) 'A system resource approach to organizational effectiveness', *American Sociological Review* 32: 871–93.

Organizational models of social program implementation

Richard E. Elmore

Concern about the implementation of social programs stems from the recognition that policies cannot be understood in isolation from the means of their execution. A large collection of carefully documented case studies – in education, manpower, housing, and economic development – points consistently to the same basic pattern: grand pretensions, faulty execution, puny results.[1] A reasonably broad consensus has developed among analysts of social policy that the inability of government to deliver on its promises derives only in part from the fact that policies are poorly conceived. In some instances, policies are based on poor and incomplete understandings of the problems they are supposed to address. But in the largest number of cases it is impossible to say whether policies fail because they are based on bad ideas or because they are good ideas poorly executed.[2] Increasingly, policy analysts have begun to focus on the process by which policies are translated into administrative action. Since virtually all public policies are implemented by large public organizations, knowledge of organizations has become a critical component of policy analysis. We cannot say with much certainty what a policy is, or why it is not implemented, without knowing a great deal about how organizations function. [. . .] The translation of an idea into action involves certain crucial simplifications. Organizations are simplifiers; they work on problems by breaking them into discrete, manageable tasks and allocating responsibility for those tasks to specialized units. Only by understanding how organizations work can we understand how policies are shaped in the process of implementation.

The utility of organizational models

If knowledge of organizations is central to the analysis of implementation, then how do we go about putting that knowledge into a form useful for analysis? The single most

From R. Elmore, 'Organizational models of social program implementation', *Public Policy*, **26**, 1978, pp. 185–228.

important feature of organizational theory is its conceptual anarchy. When we look to the literature on organizations for guidance in the analysis of an important practical problem, such as implementation, we find a collection of conflicting and contradictory theories. This diversity of theories is a sure sign that knowledge in the field is 'soft'. This is not to say that it should be, or ever will be, 'hard', but only that it is extremely difficult to use knowledge of this sort as the basis for analysis. Richard Nelson captured this difficulty nicely in his discussion of the intellectual underpinnings of policy analysis. 'The problem of making sensible organizational changes', he argues, 'is beyond the present capacity of the various organizational analysis traditions'. He adds,

> [We] presently lack [a] . . . normative intellectual structure capable of guiding us effectively regarding organizational choice or modification. . . . [We] lack even a language that will enable us to list, and talk about, the organizational alternatives in a helpful manner.[3]

So on this point we're stuck. Having established that analysis of the implementation problem requires knowledge of organizations, we find that there is no single, coherent body of organizational theory that will serve as the basis for analysis. There are two ways of coping with this impasse. One is to make an heroic attempt to synthesize all organizational theory into a tidy set of analytical precepts useful in the analysis of implementation. The other is to acquiesce in the present diversity of thought about organizations and try to distill from that diversity a finite number of distinguishable models that can be used to analyze the implementation problem. I've chosen the latter strategy, largely because I believe the former to be impossible. This approach does not speak to Nelson's plea for an 'effective normative intellectual structure', since it doesn't result in a single set of prescriptions about how implementation should be organized, but it does speak to his plea for a language that supports the discussion of organizational alternatives.

Those familiar with Graham Allison's study of the Cuban missile crisis[4] will recognize that I have cribbed the idea of alternative organizational models directly from him. His was the initial insight, and his is the credit for demonstrating its analytical utility. Readers of Allison will notice, however, that I depart considerably from his treatment. In most instances the differences are attributable to the nature of the subject matter; defense strategy, not surprisingly, raises a set of problems considerably different from the implementation of social programs. Suffice it to say that Allison is not responsible for the use that others make of his ideas.

Viewing the implementation process through a number of different organizational models allows us to be specific about the organizational assumptions we make when we offer prescriptions for improving implementation. Different models, we will see, lead to quite different perceptions and conclusions. 'What we see and judge to be important', Allison argues, '. . . depends not only on the evidence but also on the "conceptual lenses" through which we look at the evidence'.[5] Neither policy analysts nor administrators have been particularly careful about specifying the organizational assumptions that shape their recommendations and actions. Analysts, by and large, have found organizational problems either uninteresting or insufficiently precise. Administrators have a direct stake in organizational problems, but can seldom indulge in the luxury of an extended analysis of organizational alternatives. The consequence of this failure to address organizational issues has been an embarrassingly large gap between the analyst's recommendations and the solutions implemented by administrators.[6] Forcing analysts and administrators to think systematically about organizational alternatives might ultimately drive policy-making in the direction of feasible, or implementable, policies.

Some models are basically normative – they're based on strongly held opinions about how organizations ought to operate. Some models are descriptive – they attempt to capture the essential objective attributes of organizations. In some instances it's difficult to distinguish normative from descriptive elements. But in all instances the model is a simplification of reality, not a surrogate for it.[7] No single model adequately captures the full complexity of the implementation process.

I will develop four organizational models representing the major schools of thought that can be brought to bear on the implementation problem. The *systems management model* captures the organizational assumptions of the mainstream, rationalist tradition of policy analysis. Its point of departure is the assumption of value-maximizing behavior. The *bureaucratic process model* represents the sociological view of organizations, updated to include recent research by students of 'street-level bureaucracy' that bears directly on the analysis of social program implementation. Its point of departure is the assumption that the essential feature of organizations is the interaction between routine and discretion. The *organizational development model* represents a relatively recent combination of sociological and psychological theory that focuses on the conflict between the needs of individuals and the demands of organizational life. Finally, the *conflict and bargaining model* addresses the problem of how people with divergent interests coalesce around a common task. It starts from the assumption that conflict, arising out of the pursuit of relative advantage in a bargaining relationship, is the dominant feature of organizational life.

The most important aspect of these models, however, is not that they represent certain established traditions of academic inquiry. As we shall see, their major appeal is that each contains a commonsense explanation for implementation failures. And each explanation emphasizes different features of the implementation process.

The format of the discussion will be the same for each model. I will first present a list of four propositions that capture the essential features of each model. The first proposition states the central principle of the model; the second states the model's view of the distribution of power in organizations; the third states the model's view of organizational decision-making; and the fourth gives a thumbnail sketch of the implementation process from the perspective of the model. I will then discuss how these assumptions affect the analyst's perception of the implementation process. In Allison's words, I will develop 'a dominant inference pattern' that serves to explain why certain features of the implementation process are more important than others and to predict the consequences of certain administrative actions for the success or failure of implementation efforts. Finally, I will draw some examples from the current case literature on social program implementation that demonstrate the strengths and weaknesses of each model.

Some readers will no doubt chafe at the idea that highly complex bodies of thought about organizations can be reduced to a few simple propositions. My defense is that this is an exercise in the application of theory, not an exercise in theory building. The premium is on capturing the insights that each model brings to the problem, not on making the theory more elegant or defensible. I have tried mightily to avoid creating straw men. Each model is offered as a legitimate analytical perspective.

Model I: Implementation as systems management

Propositions:

1. Organizations should operate as rational value maximizers. The essential attribute of rationality is goal-directed behavior; organizations are effective to the extent that they maximize performance on their central goals and objectives. Each task that an organization performs must contribute to at least one of a set of well-defined objectives that accurately reflect the organization's purpose.
2. Organizations should be structured on the principle of hierarchical control. Responsibility for policy-making and overall system performance rests with top management, which in turn allocates specific tasks and performance objectives to subordinate units and monitors their performance.
3. For every task an organization performs there is some optimal allocation of responsibilities among subunits that maximizes the organization's overall performance on its objectives. Decision-making in organizations consists of finding this optimum and maintaining it by continually adjusting the internal allocation of responsibilities to changes in the environment.
4. Implementation consists of defining a detailed set of objectives that accurately reflect the intent of a given policy, assigning responsibilities and standards of performance to subunits consistent with these objectives, monitoring system performance, and making internal adjustments that enhance the attainment of the organization's goals. The process is dynamic, not static; the environment continually imposes new demands that require internal adjustments. But implementation is always goal-directed and value-maximizing.

A frequent explanation for failures of implementation is 'bad management'. We generally mean by this that policies are poorly defined, responsibilities are not clearly assigned, expected outcomes are not specified, and people are not held accountable for their performance. Good management, of course, is the opposite of all these things, and therein lies the crux of the systems management model. The model starts from the normative assumption that effective management proceeds from goal-directed, value-maximizing behavior. Organizations are thought of as problem-solving 'systems' – functionally integrated collections of parts that are capable of concerted action around a common purpose.[8]

Integration presupposes the existence of a controlling and coordinating authority. In the systems management model, this authority is called the 'management subsystem' – 'the source of binding pronouncements and the locus of the decisionmaking process'.[9]

It provides 'a means of insuring role performance, replacing lost members, coordinating the several subsystems of the organization, responding to external changes and making decisions about how all these things should be accomplished'.[10] Hierarchical control is the single most important element insuring that organizations behave as systems.

The translation of policy into action consists of a deliberate, stepwise process in which goals are elaborated into specific tasks. Robert Anthony's discussion of planning and management control gives a succinct statement of the transition from policy to operations:

> Strategic planning is the process of deciding on objectives, on resources used to obtain these objectives, and on the policies that are to govern acquisition, use and disposition of these resources. . . . Management control is the process by which managers assure that resources are obtained and used effectively and efficiently in the accomplishment of the organization's objectives . . . [and] operational control is the process of assuring that specific tasks are carried out effectively and efficiently.[11]

These functions are distributed in descending order from the highest to lowest levels of the organization. Taken together, they describe a general set of decision rules for the optimal allocation of resources, tasks, and performance criteria among subunits of an organization.

For all its emphasis on hierarchical control, one would expect that the systems management model would make little or no allowance for the exercise of lower-level discretion by subordinates carrying out policy directives. In fact, this is not quite the case. The problem of subordinate discretion figures prominently in the literature of systems management. Understandably, the issue arose in a very visible way during the initial attempts to apply systems analysis to national defense planning. Defense planners found almost immediately that the ability of the management subsystem to control the performance of subunits was limited by the enormous complexity of the total system. Hence, a great deal hinged on discovering the correct mix of hierarchical control and subordinate discretion. Hitch and McKean call this process 'sub-optimization', which they define as an 'attempt to find optimal (or near optimal) solutions, but to sub-problems rather than to a whole problem of the organization in whose welfare or utility we are interested'.[12] In organizational terms, suboptimization consists of holding subunits responsible for a certain level of output but giving subunit managers the discretion to decide on the means of achieving that level. In business parlance, these subunits are called 'profit centers', in the public sector they have been called 'responsibility centers'. Suboptimization provides a means of exercising hierarchical control by focusing on the output of subunits rather than on their technically complex internal operations.

In practice, suboptimization raises some very complex problems – selecting appropriate criteria of subunit performance, accounting for the unintended consequences, or spillovers, of one unit's performance on another's, and choosing the appropriate aggregation of functions for each subunit.[13] But the notion of suboptimization gives the systems management model a degree of flexibility that is not often appreciated by its critics. It is *not* necessary to assume that all organizational decisions are centralized in order to assume that organizations are functionally integrated. If the outputs of delegated decisions are consistent with the overall goals of the organization, then there is room for a certain degree of latitude in the selection of means for achieving those outputs.

A great deal of behavior in organizations can be explained by examining devices of control and compliance. Some are easy to identify, some blend into the subtle social fabric of organizations. One common device is what Herbert Kaufman calls the 'preformed decision'. He argues that 'organizations might disintegrate if each field officer made entirely independent decisions', so organizations develop ways of making decisions for their field officers 'in advance of specific situations requiring choice':

> ... [Events] and conditions in the field are anticipated as fully as possible, and courses of action [for each set of events and conditions] are described. The field officer then need determine only into what category a particular instance falls; once this determination is made, he then simply follows a series of steps applicable to that category. Within each category, therefore, the decisions are 'preformed'.[14]

Much of the work of high-level administrators in the implementation process consists of anticipating recurrent problems at lower levels of the system and attempting to program the behavior of subordinates to respond to these problems in standardized ways.

But not all devices of control are so obvious. In a casual aside, Robert Anthony remarks that 'the system [of management controls] should be so constructed that actions that operating managers take in their perceived self-interest are also in the best interests of the whole organization'.[15] An important ingredient of control, then, is to be found in the way people are socialized to organizations. Social psychologists Katz and Kahn observe that all organizations have 'maintenance subsystems' for recruitment, indoctrination, socialization, reward, and sanction that 'function to maintain the fabric of interdependent behavior necessary for task accomplishment'.[16] [. . .] Organizations often require people to put the requirements of their formal roles above their personal preferences. The effect is to enhance the predictability and control of subordinate behavior in much the same way as preformed decisions and suboptimization. The difference is that instead of shaping decisions, it is the decision-*makers* who are shaped.

The major appeal of the systems management model is that it can be readily translated into a set of normative prescriptions that policy analysts can use to say how the implementation process ought to work. From the model's perspective, effective implementation requires four main ingredients: (1) clearly specified tasks and objectives that accurately reflect the intent of policy: (2) a management plan that allocates task and performance standards to subunits; (3) an objective means of measuring subunit performance; and (4) a system of management controls and social sanctions sufficient to hold subordinates accountable for their performance. Failures of implementation are, by definition, lapses of planning, specification, and control. The analysis of implementation consists of finding, or anticipating, these breakdowns and suggesting how they ought to be remedied.

Analysis is made a good deal easier in this model by virtue of the fact that organizations are assumed to operate as units; a single conception of policy governs all levels of an organization. Success or failure of the organization is judged by observing the discrepancy between the policy declaration and subordinate behavior. The analyst focuses on the 'clarity, precision, comprehensiveness, and reasonableness of the preliminary policy', on 'the technical capacity to implement', and on 'the extent to which the actual outputs of the organization have changed in the expected direction after the introduction of the innovation'.[17] But in order for this conception of analysis to make any sense in organizational terms, one must first assume that policy-makers, administrators, and analysts have a common understanding of policy and have sufficient control of the implementation process to hold subordinates accountable to that understanding.

A great deal would seem to depend, then, on whether organizations can actually be structured on the assumptions of the systems management model. The empirical evidence is suggestive, but hardly conclusive. Herbert Kaufman, who has made a career of studying administrative compliance and control, concludes his classic study of the U.S. Forest Service with the observation that 'overall performance comes remarkably close to the goals set by the leadership'.[18] This was accomplished using a set of management controls and social sanctions that closely approximate the systems management model. The net result is that 'the Rangers want to do the very things that the Forest Service wants them to do, and are able to do them, because these are the decisions and actions that become second nature to them as a result of years of obedience'.[19] [. . .]

The distinctive feature of [this case] is strong management control in the presence of wide geographical dispersion, which suggests that large organizations can approximate the ideal of value-maximizing units. But [. . .] in the existing literature [on implementation] there are no examples that come close to approximating the ideal. One explanation for this is that the literature records only failures. Another is that social programs are characterized by chronically bad management. If we could find successful examples of implementation, one could argue, they would manifest all the essential attributes of the systems management model. This is an empirical question that requires more evidence than we presently have.

But there are at least two other explanations for the lack of systems management examples in the implementation literature, and both point to weaknesses in the model. The first is that the model completely disregards a basic element common to all cases of social program implementation: federalism. Regardless of how well organized an agency might be, its ability to implement programs successfully depends, to some degree, on its ability to influence agencies at other levels of government. [. . .] Where more than one agency is involved in the implementation process, the lines of authority are [. . .] blurred. It is not uncommon for implementors of social policy to be responsible to more than one political jurisdiction – to the federal government for a general declaration of policy and certain specific guidelines, and to a state or local unit for myriad administrative details. These jurisdictional boundaries are a permanent fixture of the American federal system; they exist not to enhance the efficiency of implementation but to protect the political prerogatives of state and local government. [. . .] The systems management model [. . .] fails to account for the weakness of management control across jurisdictional boundaries.

The second possible explanation for the lack of systems management examples in the literature on social program implementation is perhaps that the model is not intended to describe reality. Recall that all propositions on which the model is based are normative; they describe how organizations *ought* to function, not necessarily how they actually do. The distinction is not as disingenuous as it sounds. We frequently rely on normative models to help us evaluate performance, diagnose failure, and propose remedies, even though we understand perfectly well that they have very little descriptive validity. We do so because they provide useful ways of organizing and simplifying complex problems. In this sense, the test of a model is not whether it accurately represents reality, but whether it has some utility as a problem-solving device. The major utility of the systems management model is that it directs our attention toward the mechanisms that policy-makers and high-level administrators have for structuring and controlling the behavior of subordinates.

It is dangerous, however, to focus on the normative utility of the model to the exclusion of its descriptive validity. To say that the model simplifies in useful ways is not the same thing as saying that the implementation process should be structured around the model. This is a mistake that policy analysts are particularly prone to make, and it involves a peculiar and obvious circularity. If the fit between model and reality is poor, the argument goes, then the model should be used to restructure reality. Only then, the analyst concludes triumphantly, can it be determined whether the model 'works' or not. A special form of this argument claims that social programs fail because policies are poorly specified and management control is weak. To the extent that we remedy these problems we can predict a higher ratio of successes to failures. The problem with this argument is that the definition of success is internal to the model, and it may or may not be shared by people who are actually part of the process. The systems management model will almost certainly 'work' if everyone behaves according to its dictates. If we could make value maximizers of all organizations, then we could no doubt prove that all organizations are value maximizers. But the point is that participants in the implementation process don't necessarily share the norms of the model. And it is this fact that leads us to search for alternative models.

Model II: Implementation as bureaucratic process

Propositions:

1. The two central attributes of organizations are discretion and routine; all important behavior in organizations can be explained by the irreducible discretion exercised by individual workers in their day-to-day decisions and the operating routines that they develop to maintain and enhance their position in the organization.

2. The dominance of discretion and routine means that power in organizations tends to be fragmented and dispersed among small units exercising relatively strong control over specific tasks within their sphere of authority. The amount of control that any one organizational unit can exert over another – laterally or hierarchically – is hedged by the fact that, as organizations become increasingly complex, units become more highly specialized and exercise greater control over their internal operations.
3. Decision-making consists of controlling discretion and changing routine. All proposals for change are judged by organizational units in terms of the degree to which they depart from established patterns; hence, organizational decisions tend to be incremental.
4. Implementation consists of identifying where discretion is concentrated and which of an organization's repertoire of routines need changing, devising alternative routines that represent the intent of policy, and inducing organizational units to replace old routines with new ones.

We reach instinctively for bureaucratic explanations of implementation failures. 'There was a major change in policy', we say, 'but the bureaucracy kept right on doing what it did before'. Or alternatively, 'When the bureaucracy got through with it, the policy didn't look anything like what we intended'. Bureaucracy was not always a pejorative term; for Max Weber, it was a form of organization that substituted impersonal, efficient, and routinized authority for that based on personal privilege or divine inspiration. Lately, though, bureaucracy has become an all-purpose explanation for everything that is wrong with government. We use terms like 'the bureaucracy problem'[20] and 'the bureaucratic phenomenon'[21] to describe behavior of public officials that is 'inefficient, unresponsive, unfair, ponderous, or confusing'.[22]

When we look behind these characterizations, the problems of implementing policies in bureaucratic settings can be traced to two basic elements: discretion and routine. As bureaucracies become larger and more complex, they concentrate specialized tasks in subunits. With specialization comes an irreducible discretion in day-to-day decision-making; the ability of any single authority to control all decisions becomes attenuated to the point where it ceases to be real in any practical sense. In the words of Graham Allison, factored problem-solving begets fractionated power.[23] With the growth of discretion also comes the growth of routine. Individuals and subunits manage the space created by discretion so as to maintain and enhance their position in the organization. They create operating routines in part to simplify their work but also to demonstrate their specialized skill in controlling and managing their assigned tasks. Individuals and subunits resist attempts to alter their discretion or to change their operating routines – in other words, they resist hierarchical management – because these things are a concrete expression of their special competence, knowledge, and status in the organization. The central focus of the bureaucracy problem, according to J. Q. Wilson, is 'getting the front-line worker – the teacher, nurse, diplomat, police officer, or welfare worker – to do the right thing'.[24] The job of administration is, purely and simply, 'controlling discretion.'[25]

The standard techniques of hierarchical management – budget and planning cycles, clearance procedures, reporting requirements, and evaluation systems – are the means by which high-level administrators attempt to structure the behavior of subordinates.

To the front-line worker, though, these techniques are often incidental to the 'real' work of the organization. The front-line worker's major concern is learning to cope with the immediate pressures of the job, and this requires inventing and learning a relatively complex set of work routines that go with one's specialized responsibility. This split between high-level administrators and front-line workers accounts for the quizzical, sometimes skeptical, look one often gets from teachers, social workers, and other front-line workers when they're asked about the implementation of policy. 'Policy?' they reply, 'We're so busy getting the work done we haven't much time to think about policy'.

The bureaucratic process model, then, traces the effect of lower-level discretion and routinized behavior on the execution of policy. The central analytical problem is to discover where discretion resides and how existing routines can be shaped to the purposes of policy. The major difference between systems management and bureaucratic process models is that the former assumes that the tools of management control can be used to program subordinate behavior, while the latter posits the existence of discretion and operating routines as means by which subordinates resist control. The systems management model assumes that the totality of an organization's resources can be directed at a single, coherent set of purposes – that organizations can be programmed to respond to changes in policy. The bureaucratic process model assumes that the dominant characteristic of organizations is resistance to change – not simply inertia (the tendency to move in one direction until deflected by some outside force), but as Donald Schon observes, 'dynamic conservatism' (the tendency to fight to remain the same).[26] In the systems management model one assumes that, given the right set of management controls, subunits of an organization will do what they are told; in the bureaucratic process model, one assumes that they will continue to do what they have been doing until some way is found to make them do otherwise.

In the implementation of social programs, new policies must typically travel from one large public bureaucracy to another, and then through several successive layers of the implementing agency before they reach the point of impact on the client. Whether or not the policy has its intended effect on the client depends in large part on whether the force of existing routine at each level of the process operates with or against the policy.

It is frequently at the final stage of this process – the point of delivery from agency to client – that the forces of discretion and routine are most difficult to overcome. This problem is the central concern of students of 'street-level bureaucracy'. The growth of large public service agencies has created a distinguishable class of bureaucrat – one who shoulders virtually all responsibility for direct contact with clients, who exercises a relatively large degree of discretion over detailed decisions of client treatment, and who therefore has considerable potential impact on clients.[27] From the client's perspective, the street-level bureaucrat *is* the government. Clients seldom, if ever, interact with higher-level administrators; in fact, most public service bureaucracies are deliberately designed to prevent this. Because of the frequency and immediacy of the contact between street-level bureaucrats and their clients, it is usually impossible for higher-level administrators to monitor or control all aspects of their job performance.

Consequently, a significant distance opens up between the street-level bureaucrat and his superiors. This distance breeds autonomy and discretion at lower levels of the organization. The distinctive quality of street-level bureaucracy is that 'discretion increases as one moves down the hierarchy'.[28]

But this concentration of discretion at lower levels has a paradoxical quality. For while street-level bureaucrats occupy the most critical position in the delivery process, their working conditions are seldom conducive to the adequate performance of their jobs. More often than not, they find themselves in situations where they lack the organizational and personal resources to perform their jobs adequately, where they are exposed regularly to physical or psychological threat, and where there are conflicting and ambiguous expectations about how they ought to perform their work.[29] Social service delivery jobs are among the most stressful in our society. Street-level bureaucrats are expected to treat clients as individuals, but the high demand for their services forces them to invent routines for mass processing. High-level administrators and policy-makers are preoccupied with the way policy is expressed in legislation, regulations, and guidelines. But the major concern for the street-level implementor is how to control the stress and complexity of day-to-day work. Out of this concern grows a whole set of informal routines that students of street-level bureaucracy call 'coping mechanisms'.

Learning to cope with the stresses of service delivery means learning to rely on simple, standardized sources of information to clients – case histories, employment records, permanent school records, test scores, eligibility forms, and the like. It means developing a facility for classifying and labeling people simply and quickly – 'an alcoholic parent', 'a broken family', 'a history of drug abuse', 'violence-prone and resistant to authority', 'can't hold a job', and so on. It means developing one's 'faculties of suspicion' in order to spot people who pose a threat either to oneself or to the system one is administering. And it means using the formal procedures of the organization to strike an impersonal distance between oneself, as an individual, and the client.[30] All these mechanisms have the effect of reducing and controlling the stress and uncertainty of daily work, and for this reason they figure prominently in the implementation of social policy. On the other hand, they are not typically included in the policy-maker's or the high-level administrator's definition of 'policy'. More often than not, they're either ignored or regarded as external to the implementation process.

Concentrating on formal declarations of policy at the expense of informal coping routines means that 'even the most imaginative manipulations of goals, structure, staff recruitment, training and supervision may . . . represent only superficial changes . . . rather than the fundamental reforms hoped for'.[31] From the perspective of the bureaucratic process model, major shifts in policy have little or no effect until they reach the final transaction between service giver and client. The elaborate superstructure of regulations, guidelines, and management controls that accompany most social programs tend to have weak and unpredictable effects on the delivery of social services because street-level bureaucrats and their clients develop strong patterns of interaction that are relatively immune to change. Implementation failures, from this point of view, are the result of a failure on the part of policy-makers to understand the actual conditions under which social services are delivered.

Empirical evidence demonstrating the effect of organizational routines on the implementation of social policy, while not extensive, is certainly compelling. Probably the first serious attempt to document the street-level effect of a major shift in policy was Miriam Johnson's study of how national manpower policy influenced the operation of local employment service offices in California.[32] The employment service is in some respects the archetypal social service delivery system. Initiated and largely funded by the federal government, it is totally administered by the states under broad guidelines from the federal level. The essential transactions of the employment service, however, occur at the street level, where employers and prospective employees are matched. Prior to the mid-sixties, the state employment services operated largely as labor exchanges; their purpose was simply to match the best person with the available job. During the mid-sixties, new federal manpower policies emphasized the services' responsibility to undertake remedial programs designed to get the poor and unskilled into the labor market. Then, in the early seventies, growing skepticism about the services' ability to help the disadvantaged resulted in a shift back to the original conception of the labor exchange. Johnson gives a client's-eye view of what it was like to deal with the employment service in each of these periods.

In the first phase – the labor exchange – the client's transaction with the employment service was dominated by the impersonal reception line and counter that separated client from bureaucrat. 'There was no way for an applicant to bypass the line', she says, because only by waiting in line could the applicant get the required forms.

> The reception line led to the counter, which stood as a rampart, a boundary that defined the combat areas. It protected and defended the public agency from assault and harassment, from the public it served, from 'they'– the enemy.[33]

When the California State Employment Service began to respond to the federal mandate to provide services for the disadvantaged, it did so by initiating small, experimental projects rather than attempting wholesale reform of the agency. The employment service workers who participated in these projects were given a great deal of latitude in designing them, and the first things they eliminated were the reception line and the counter. For Johnson, these actions were evidence that workers were just as oppressed by the routines of the old system as clients.[34] The counter was replaced by more informal, less structured interactions that often took the form of group counseling sessions. But these experimental projects 'had no significant effect on the designers of new manpower programs and delivery systems'.[35] The remainder of the employment service seemed largely unaffected by the experimental projects.

With the return to the labor exchange idea in the early seventies, employment service officers looked pretty much the same as they always had, but there was one interesting and seemingly minor difference in operating routines at the local level:

> There was still a counter . . . and there was still a receptionist. . . . [But] on the public side of the counter was something of value, . . . access to the jobs themselves. A Job Information

Center was required in all ... local offices by 1970. ... The area was open to the public and it was not necessary to be registered for work in order to use the ... Center. [It] was a self-screening operation in which the office supplied the referral information at the request of the applicant.[36]

It is ironic, after all the bombast and rhetoric of social action in the mid-sixties, that the net effect on the employment service should be something as simple as moving job information from one side of the counter to the other. But the example illustrates both the enormous resilience and the great importance of lower-level discretion and operating routines. Experimental projects had very little effect on the day-to-day operations of local offices, and the one change that did occur might easily have been overlooked by an analyst less sensitive to street-level operations.

Another important example of street-level response to high-level policy is the Weatherly and Lipsky analysis of the Massachusetts Comprehensive Special Education Law.[37] The law is a carefully conceived effort to put an end to arbitrary and discriminatory treatment of handicapped children by the public school system. Each local school district is required to provide an individualized evaluation of a child's needs by a team that includes teachers, specialists, and parents. The evaluation is to result in a plan for each child, outlining the services the school system will offer. If the school system cannot provide the services required, it must pay to have them provided elsewhere. To the extent possible, handicapped children must be included in regular classrooms. And the traditional labels that had stigmatized children with special problems were to be eliminated.

During the first year of its implementation (1974–75), state and local administrators began to discover that the law imposed burdens 'well beyond the capacity of any school system'.[38] Implicit in the implemented program was a cruel dilemma. On the one hand the law required individualized treatment but on the other it created such an enormous administrative burden at the local level that educators were forced to develop routines for mass processing.[39] Local educators developed simple decision rules for differentiating more and less difficult cases: the loudest, most disruptive children were referred for evaluation first; children with easily identified, routine problems were processed perfunctorily, while those with more complex problems or 'disruptive' parents were treated more circumspectly; teachers and administrators collaborated to reduce referrals when the burden became too heavy.[40] The evaluation conferences, which brought together teachers, specialists, and parents, tended to be characterized by largely negative assessments of children, the use of technical jargon, and preoccupation with the assignment of blame – all of which enhanced the position of professionals over parents and made the assessment procedure move more smoothly.[41] The traditional labels for children's problems were eliminated, but new, more euphemistic lables were invented.[42] In other words, routinization at the local level largely undermined the broad purposes of the law.

The basic problem, Weatherly and Lipsky point out, was not that local school personnel were determined to subvert the law. On the contrary, they made great personal sacrifices to make it work. The real problem was that the law reflected absolutely no understanding of how street-level bureaucrats respond to changes in policy and the increased workloads they entail. Faced with a broad legislative mandate and a large, complex new responsibility, local implementors invented operating routines that helped simplify their work but ran counter to the intent of the legislation.

The major advantage of the bureaucratic process model is that it forces us to contend with the mundane patterns of bureaucratic life and to think about how new policies affect the daily routines of people who deliver social services. Policy-makers, analysts, and administrators have a tendency to focus on variables that emphasize control and predictability, often overlooking the factors that undermine control and create anomalies in the implementation process. Bureaucratic routines operate against the grain of many policy changes because they are contrived as buffers against change and uncertainty; they continue to exist precisely because they have an immediate utility to the people who use them in reducing the stress and complexity of work. Failing to account for the force of routine in the implementation of policy leads to serious misperceptions.

Walter Williams argues that most implementation problems grow out of a division of labor between what he calls the 'policy and operations spheres'.[43] In the policy sphere, people tend to focus on global issues and general shifts in the distribution of power among governmental units. Consequently, when the responsibility for implementation shifts to the operations sphere there is little in the way of useful guidance for implementors. The limited case literature on the role of bureaucratic routines bears out this observation. The unresponsiveness of large public bureaucracies to new policy initiatives is more often than not attributable to a failure to connect the 'big ideas' of policy-makers with the mundane coping mechanisms of implementors.

Unlike the systems management model, the bureaucratic process model does not give any clear-cut prescriptions for improving the implementation process. About the only normative advice offered by students of street-level bureaucracy is the rather weak suggestion that 'bureaucratic coping behaviors cannot be eliminated, but they can be monitored and directed' by rewarding 'those that most closely conform to preferred public objectives [and] discouraging objectionable practices'.[44] What this prescription overlooks is that coping routines derive their appeal and resilience from the fact that they are rooted in the immediate demands of work; they are, then, almost generically immune to hierarchical control. It's difficult, within the context of the bureaucratic process model, to think of ways to change street-level behavior in a predictable fashion. But, as we shall see in the following section, it's not at all difficult to solve this problem when we adopt the perspective of another model.

The utility of the bureaucratic process model shouldn't hang entirely on its limited normative power, though, since its major advantages are descriptive: it captures a very common pattern of implementation failure, in which hierarchical controls generated by top management to alter the behavior of subordinates, or by one government agency to structure the behavior of another, simply fail to affect the important street-level transactions that determine the success of a policy.

Model III: Implementation as organizational development

Propositions:

1. Organizations should function to satisfy the basic psychological and social needs of individuals – for autonomy and control over their own work, for participation in decisions affecting them, and for commitment to the purposes of the organization.
2. Organizations should be structured to maximize individual control, participation, and commitment at all levels. Hierarchically structured bureaucracies maximize these things for people in upper levels of the organization at the expense of those in lower levels. Hence, the best organizational structure is one that minimizes hierarchical control and distributes responsibility for decisions among all levels of the organization.
3. Effective decision-making in organizations depends on the creation of effective work groups. The quality of interpersonal relations in organizations largely determines the quality of decisions. Effective work groups are characterized by mutual agreement on goals, open communication among individuals, mutual trust and support among group members, full utilization of members' skills and effective management of conflict. Decision-making consists primarily of building consensus and strong interpersonal relations among group members.
4. The implementation process is necessarily one of consensus-building and accommodation between policy-makers and implementors. The central problem of implementation is not whether implementors conform to prescribed policy but whether the implementation process results in consensus in goals, individual autonomy, and commitment to policy on the part of those who must carry it out.

Another frequent explanation of implementation failures is that those who implement programs are seldom included in decisions that determine the content of those programs. The closer one gets to the point of delivery in social programs, the more frequently one hears the complaint that policy-makers and high-level administrators don't listen to service deliverers. What grates most on the sensibilities of teachers, social workers, employment counselors, and the like is the tacit assumption in most policy directives that they are incapable of making independent judgments and decisions – that their behavior must be programmed by someone else. It's difficult for persons who see themselves as competent, self-sufficient adults to be highly committed to policies that place them in the role of passive executors of someone else's will.

The prevailing theories of organizational behavior represented by the systems management and bureaucratic process models encourage and perpetuate this pathology. Hierarchy, specialization, routine, and control all reinforce the belief that those at the bottom of the organization are less competent decision-makers than those at the top. High-level administrators can be trusted to exercise discretion while those at the bottom must be closely supervised and controlled. Policy is made at the top and implemented at the bottom; implementors must set aside their own views and submit to the superior authority and competence of policy-makers and high-level administrators.

Not surprisingly, this view has become increasingly difficult to defend as the work force has become more professionalized and better educated. It's now relatively clear that there are basic conflicts between the individual's need for autonomy, participation, and commitment and the organization's requirement of structure, control, and subordination. Concern for this conflict has led some to posit a 'democratic alternative' to established theories of organization.[45] The label we will attach to this alternative is 'organizational development'. A number of schools of thought coexist within this tradition, but we will concentrate primarily on the work of Chris Argyris, who has spent an unusually large amount of effort specifying the assumptions on which his view is based.

Argyris begins with the observation that what we define as acceptable adult behavior outside organizations directly contradicts what's acceptable inside. On the outside, adults are defined as people who are self-motivating, responsible for their own actions, and honest about emotions and values. Inside organizations, adults are expected to exhibit dependency and passivity toward their superiors, they resort to indirection and avoid taking responsibility as individuals, and they are forced to submerge emotions and values.[46] Resolving this tension requires a fundamentally different kind of organization and a different theory of organizational behavior. Rational or bureaucratic theories of organization stress abstract, systemic properties – structure, technology, out-puts – at the expense of the social and psychological needs of individuals.[47] The reasonable alternative is a theory that begins from the needs of individuals rather than the abstract properties of organizations. Such a theory leads 'not only to a more humane and democratic system but to a more efficient one'.[48]

The essential transactions of organizational life occur in face-to-face contacts among individuals engaged in a common task, that is, in work groups. Organizational effectiveness and efficiency depend more than anything else on the quality of interpersonal relations in work groups. Effective work groups are characterized by agreement on goals, open communication, mutual trust and support, full utilization of member skills, and effective management of conflict.[49] The cultivation of these attributes requires a special kind of skill, which Argyris calls 'interpersonal competence' to distinguish it from the purely technical competence that comes from the routine performance of a task. Individuals are interpersonally competent when they are able to give and receive feedback in a way that creates minimal defensiveness, to give honest expression to their own feelings, values and attitudes, and to remain open to new ideas.[50] The trappings of bureaucracy and rational decision-making –routines, management controls, objectified accountability – undermine interpersonal competence and group effectiveness, encouraging dependence and passivity while penalizing openness and risk-taking. Hence, 'the very values that are assumed to help make [an organization] effective may actually . . . decrease its effectiveness'.[51]

Nowhere in the literature on organizational development is there a simple composite of the well-structured organization. It's fair to infer from the theory, though, that an effective organization would have at least the following features: most responsibility for decisions would devolve to lower levels of the organization; the focus of organizational activity would be the work group, formed of people engaged in a common task; and information – statements of purpose, evaluative judgments, and expressions of needed changes – would be readily exchanged without negative social consequences at all levels of the organization. All these features originate from the simple assumption that people are more likely to perform at their highest capacity when they are given maximum control over their own work, maximum participation in decisions affecting them, and hence maximum incentives for commitment to the goals of the group.

The organizational development model gives quite a different picture of the implementation process than either the systems management or bureaucratic process models. In the systems management model, implementation consists of the skillful use of management controls to hold subunits accountable for well-defined standards of performance. In the bureaucratic process model, implementation consists of changing the formal and informal work routines of an organization to conform with a declaration of intent. In both instances, *policy is made at the top and implemented at the bottom*. But in the organizational development model the distinction is much less clear. If major responsibility is actually devolved to work groups at lower levels of the organization, it makes very little sense to think of policy as flowing from top to bottom. More about this in a moment.

Implementation failures are not the result of poor management control or the persistence of bureaucratic routines, but arise out of a lack of consensus and commitment among implementors. The features of the implementation process that matter most are those that affect individual motivation and interpersonal cooperation, not those that enhance hierarchical control. Success of an implementation effort can be gauged by looking at the extent to which implementors are involved in the formulation of a program, the extent to which they are encouraged to exercise independent judgment in determining their own behavior, and the extent to which they are encouraged to establish strong work groups for mutual support and problem-solving.

Empirical evidence on the underlying assumptions of the organizational development model is relatively scarce, but the most important piece of evidence in the area of social program implementation comes from a large-scale study done completely outside the organizational development tradition. In 1972, the federal government contracted with the Rand Corporation to conduct a nationwide study of four federally funded education programs, each of which was designed to encourage innovation in the public schools.[52] The programs were administered by different units within the U.S. Office of Education and they used a variety of administrative strategies. Nearly 300 local projects were surveyed, so the potential for variation within and among programs was great. Yet the Rand analysts concluded that overall the 'programs had approximately equal effects on project outcomes, despite their different management strategies'.[53] They also concluded that 'differences between programs explained only a small amount of the variation in implementation outcomes'.[54] In short, the federal government's management of the programs seemed to have virtually no effect on the success or failure of implementation.

Pursuing this issue further, the Rand group analyzed 29 descriptive case studies of local project implementation, attempting to identify what distinguished successful from unsuccessful attempts at change. The characteristics that emerged from this analysis were (1) the existence of a strong local training component; (2) the use of local expertise and technical assistance in project implementation; (3) frequent and regular staff meetings; (4) local development of project materials; (5) the use of voluntary, highly motivated participants; and the like.[55] What is significant about all these factors is that federal administrators have virtually no control over them. Project success depended primarily on the existence and mobilization of local resources. 'Our observations suggest', the analysts concluded, 'that it is extremely unrealistic to expect a school district to do something wise with its federal money if it is not already committed to something wise when the funds are first received'.[56]

Milbrey McLaughlin, a principal author of the study, looked in detail at a number of projects that were intended to change classroom organization. Discussing the importance of local materials development, she observes that it was 'sometimes undertaken because the staff felt they couldn't locate appropriate commercial materials', but she concludes that 'the real contribution lay . . . in providing the staff with a sense of involvement and an opportunity to learn by doing'. She continues,

> Working together to develop materials . . . gave the staff a sense of 'ownership' in the project. It also broke down the traditional isolation of the teacher and provided a sense of professionalism and cooperation not usually available in the school setting. But even more important, development of materials provided an opportunity for users to think through the concepts which underlay the project in practical, operational terms. . . . Although such 'reinvention of the wheel' may not appear efficient in the short run, it appears to be a critical part of the individual learning and development necessary to significant change.[57]

Here, in the concrete language of project-level implementation, are the essential elements of the organizational development model: emphasis on individual motivation and commitment (sense of involvement, ownership in the project), the centrality of strong face-to-face work groups (breaking down the traditional isolation of teachers, enhancing professionalism and cooperation), and the explicit criticism of conventional notions of organizational efficiency (the usefulness of reinventing the wheel).

The picture of implementation that emerges from these findings is one in which the ability of policy-makers and high-level administrators to manipulate the behavior of implementors using the standard devices of hierarchical control is severely limited. The critical variables are those arising out of individual commitment and motivation. The Rand analysts described the implementation process as 'intrinsically' one of 'mutual adaptation'; the policy or innovation is shaped by implementors and, likewise, the behavior of implementors is shaped by the policy or innovation.[58] The only way an innovation can become established in an organization, the Rand analysts argue, is for implementors to learn it, shape it, and claim it for their own.

But the full significance of the Rand findings is not adequately expressed by the plausible idea of mutual adaptation. Every defensible view of implementation contains some gesture toward adaptive behavior – in the systems management model, adaptation is a necessary consequence of feedback on the performance of subunits; in the bureaucratic process model, organizational routines evolve slowly over time in response to changing demands. So it's not the notion of adaptive behavior that distinguishes the organizational development model from other perspectives.

The real significance of the organizational development model, and the import of the Rand evidence, is that it effectively turns the entire implementation process on its head. It reverses what we instinctively regard as the 'normal' flow of policy, from top to bottom. The message of the model is, quite bluntly, that the capacity to implement originates at the bottom of organizations, not at the top. In each of the two previous models the central problem was how policy-makers and high-level administrators could shape the behavior of implementors using the standard devices of hierarchical control. What the organizational development model suggests is that these devices explain almost none of the variation in implementation outcomes. The factors that do affect the behavior of implementors lie outside the domain of direct management control – individual motivation and commitment, and the interaction and mutual support of people in work groups. Hence, the closer one gets to the determinants of effective implementation, the further one gets from the factors that policy-makers and administrators can manipulate. The result is that, in terms of the effective structure of organizations, *the process of initiating and implementing new policy actually begins at the bottom and ends at the top*. Unless organizations already have those properties that predispose them to change, they are not likely to respond to new policy. But if they have those properties, they are capable of initiating change themselves, without the control of policy-makers and administrators. The role of those at the top of the system, then, is necessarily residual; they can provide resources that implementors need to do their work, but they cannot exert direct control over the factors that determine the success or failure of that work.

If one accepts this view, the important business of implementation consists not of developing progressively more sophisticated techniques for managing subordinates' behavior but of enhancing the self-starting capacity of the smallest unit. The organizational capacity to accept innovations necessarily precedes the innovations themselves, so one can't expect individuals to respond to new policies unless they are predisposed to do so. But once this predisposition exists, it is no longer practical to think of imposing changes from above. The only conception of implementation that makes sense under these conditions is one that emphasizes consensus building and accommodation between policy-makers and implementors. Mutual adaptation exists not because it is a pleasing or democratic thing to do, but because it is the only way to insure that implementors have a direct personal stake in the performance of their jobs. This is what the advocates of organizational development mean when they say that more democratic organizations are also more efficient ones.

The organizational development model focuses on those aspects of an organization's internal structure that enhance or inhibit the commitment of implementors. The chief determinants of success are the sort of microvariables identified by the Rand analysts: materials development by implementors, strong interpersonal and professional ties among implementors, non-manipulative support by high-level administrators, and explicit reliance on incentives that elicit individual commitment from implementors rather than those designed to enforce external conformity. To the extent that the implementation process actually becomes these things, it is neither accurate nor useful to think in terms of a single declaration of policy that is translated into subordinate behavior. Policy does not exist in any concrete sense until implementors have shaped it and claimed it for their own; the result is a consensus reflecting the initial intent of policy-makers and the independent judgment of implementors.

The organizational development model also forces us to recognize the narrow limits of one organization's capacity to change the behavior of another. When an agency at one level of government attempts to implement policy through an agency at another level, the implicit assumption is that the former controls factors that are important in determining the performance of the latter. The organizational development model suggests that those factors that have the greatest influence on the success or failure of implementation are precisely the ones over which external agencies have the least control. The maximum that one level of government can do to affect the implementation process is to provide general support that enhances the internal capacity of organizations at another level to respond to the necessity for change, independent of the requirements of specific policies. So, to the extent that the implementation process actually took the shape of the model, the federal government, for example, would invest most of its resources not in enforcing compliance with existing policies, but in assisting state and local agencies to develop an independent capacity to elicit innovative behavior from implementors.

The most powerful criticism of the organizational development model comes, surprisingly, from its strongest supporters. The bias of the model toward consensus, cooperation, and strong interpersonal ties leads us to ignore or downplay the role of conflict in organizations. The model, one of its advocates argues, 'seems most appropriate under conditions of trust, truth, love, and collaboration. But what about conditions of war, conflict, dissent, and violence?' 'The fundamental deficiency in models of change associated with organization development', he concludes, is that they 'systematically avoid the problem of power, or the *politics* of change'.[59] The same criticism may be levelled, to one degree or another, against each of the three models discussed thus far, because none directly confronts the issue of what happens in organizations when control, routine, and consensus fail. A wide range of implementation problems can be understood only as problems of conflict and bargaining.

Model IV: Implementation as conflict and bargaining

Propositions:

1. Organizations are arenas of conflict in which individuals and subunits with specific interests

compete for relative advantage in the exercise of power and the allocation of scarce resources.

2. The distribution of power in organizations is never stable. It depends exclusively on the temporary ability of one individual or unit to mobilize sufficient resources to manipulate the behavior of others. Formal position in the hierarchy of an organization is only one of a multitude of factors that determine the distribution of power. Other factors include specialized knowledge, control of material resources, and the ability to mobilize external political support. Hence, the exercise of power in organizations is only weakly related to their formal structure.

3. Decision-making in organizations consists of bargaining within and among organizational units. Bargained decisions are the result of convergence among actors with different preferences and resources. Bargaining does not require that parties agree on a common set of goals, nor does it even require that all parties concur in the outcome of the bargaining process. It only requires that they agree to adjust their behavior mutually in the interest of preserving the bargaining relationship as a means of allocating resources.

4. Implementation consists of a complex series of bargained decisions reflecting the preferences and resources of participants. Success or failure of implementation cannot be judged by comparing a result against a single declaration of intent, because no single set of purposes can provide an internally consistent statement of the interests of all parties to the bargaining process. Success can only be defined relative to the goals of one party to the bargaining process or in terms of the preservation of the bargaining process itself.

Social programs fail, it is frequently argued, because no single unit of government is sufficiently powerful to force others to conform to a single conception of policy. With each agency pursuing its own interest, implementation does not progress from a single declaration of intent to a result, but is instead characterized by constant conflict over purposes and results and by the pursuit of relative advantage through the use of bargaining. This diversity of purpose leads some participants to characterize programs as 'failures' and some to characterize them as 'successes', based solely on their position in the bargaining process. Conflict and bargaining occur both within and among implementing agencies. Single organizations can be thought of as semi-permanent bargaining coalitions, and the process of moving a declaration of policy across levels of government can be understood as bargaining among separate organizations.

Bargaining can be explicit or tacit. We tend to associate the notion of bargaining only with direct confrontations between well-defined adversaries – labor negotiations, arms limitation talks, and peace negotiations, for example. But many forms of bargaining, especially those in implementation, occur without direct communication and with an imperfect understanding by each party of the others' motives and resources.[60] Seen in this light, implementation becomes essentially a series of strategic moves by a number of individual units of government, each seeking to shape the behavior of others to its own ends.

The key to understanding bargaining behavior is recognizing that conflict implies dependency. Even the strongest adversaries must take account of their opponents' moves when they formulate a bargaining strategy. 'The ability of one participant to gain his ends', Schelling observes, 'is dependent to an important degree on the choices or decisions that the other participant will make'. Furthermore, 'there is a powerful common interest in reaching an outcome that is not enormously destructive of values to both sides'.[61] In implementation, as in all important bargaining problems, parties with strongly divergent interests are locked together by the simple fact that they must preserve the bargaining arena in order to gain something of value. Failure to bargain means exclusion from the process by which resources are allocated. But the mutual advantage that accrues to participants in bargaining has little or nothing to do with their ability to agree explicitly on the goals they're pursuing, or their means for pursuing them. Mutual advantage results only from the fact that by agreeing to bargain they have preserved their access to something of value to each of them.

[. . .] The common element in all forms of bargaining behavior, [Lindblom] argues, is that 'people can coordinate with each other without someone's coordinating them, without a dominant purpose, and without rules that fully prescribe their relations to each other'.[62] This point is essential for understanding the usefulness of the conflict and bargaining model in the analysis of social program implementation. The model permits us to make conceptual sense of the implementation process without assuming the existence of hierarchical control, without asserting that everyone's behavior is governed by a predictable set of bureaucratic routines, and without assuming that concerted action can proceed only from consensus and commitment to a common set of purposes. In short, the model provides a distinct alternative to the limiting assumptions of the previous three. Implementation can, and indeed does, proceed in the absence of a mechanism of coordination external to the actors themselves, such as hierarchical control, routine, or group consensus.

Bargained decisions proceed by convergence, adjustment, and closure among individuals pursuing essentially independent ends. Allison makes this point when he says that 'the decisions and actions of governments are . . . political resultants . . . in the sense that what happens is not chosen as a solution to a problem but rather results from compromise, conflict, and confusion of officials with diverse interests and unequal influence'.[63] The term 'resultant', appropriated from physics, emphasizes the idea that decisions are the product of two or more converging forces. The mechanism of convergence depends on what Schelling calls 'interdependence of expectations'. Parties to the bargaining process must predicate their actions not only on predictions of how others will respond but also on the understanding that others are doing likewise. So bargaining depends as much on shared expectations as it does on concrete actions.

> The outcome is determined by the expectations that each player forms of how the other will play, where each of them knows that their expectations are substantially reciprocal. The players must jointly discover and mutually acquiesce in an outcome or a mode of play that makes the outcome determinate. They must together find 'rules of the game' or together suffer the consequences.[64]

In concrete terms, this means that much of the behavior we observe in the implementation process is designed to shape the expectations of other actors. An agency might, for example, put a great deal of effort into developing an elaborate collection of rules and regulations or an elegant system of management controls, knowing full well that it doesn't have the resources to make them binding on other actors. But the *expectation* that the rules *might* be enforced is sufficient to influence the behavior of other actors. The important fact is not whether the rules are enforced or not, but the effect of their existence on the outcome of the bargaining process.

The outcomes of bargaining are seldom 'optimal' in any objective sense. More often than not, they are simply convenient temporary points of closure. Asking 'what it is that can bring. . . expectations into convergence and bring . . . negotiations to a close', Schelling answers that 'it is the intrinsic magnetism of particular outcomes, especially those that enjoy prominence, uniqueness, simplicity, precedent, or some rationale that makes them qualitatively differentiable' from other alternatives.[65] In other words, the result of bargaining is often not the best nor even the second or third best alternative for any party; all parties can, and frequently do, leave the bargaining process dissatisfied with the result. As long as an opportunity to resume bargaining remains, there is seldom a single determinant result; all resolutions are temporary. So one should not expect the mechanisms of bargaining to lead teleologically from a single purpose to a result.

One is tempted to say that the conflict and bargaining model is not a model of organizational behavior at all, but a model of what happens when organizations fail. This argument is plausible. We tend to associate the term organization with a certain threshold of commonality that allows individuals to cooperate around a common set of goals. If this minimum condition isn't met, it seems reasonable to conclude that there is an absence of organization. Some time ago, though, the theory of organizations took a turn away from this assumption. Cyert and March, dissatisfied with the conventional wisdom of normative economic theory and the sociology of organizations, elaborated an alternative theory, beginning from the premise that organizations are essentially bargaining coalitions.[66] The process of organizational decision-making, they argue, involves continuous conflict among subunits over relatively specific purposes that define each subunit's interest in the organization. The overall goals of an organization, they argue, are calculatedly vague and essentially useless as guides to decision-making. Hence, organizations are not defined by agreement on overall purposes, but only by the process of conflict, bargaining, and coalition building among subunits. The absence of agreement on overall goals, then, is not a sign of organizational failure, but simply a clue directing our attention to the existence of conflict and bargaining as permanent fixtures of organizational life.

The real structure of organizations, then, is to be found in their bargaining processes, rather than in their formal hierarchy or operating routines. Notions of top and bottom have very little meaning. Formal position is a source of power, but only one of many, and it does not necessarily carry with it the ability to manipulate the behavior of subordinates. Many other sources of power – mastery of specialized knowledge, discretionary control over resources, a strong external constituency, and so on – can be used to enhance the bargaining position of subordinates relative to superiors, and vice versa. No simple rules can be set forth for determining the distribution of power in organizations. Stability, if it exists at all, is the short-term product of bargaining on specific decisions.

This view leads to a conception of implementation considerably different from any of the other models. One understands the process by focusing on conflict among actors, the resources they bring to the bargaining process, and the mechanisms by which they adjust to each other's moves. Most important, the distinguishing feature of the conflict and bargaining model is that *it doesn't rest on any assumptions about commonality of purpose*. In each of the previous models, it was possible to say that successful implementation was in some sense dependent on a common conception of policy shared by all participants in the process. In the systems management model, agreement was the product of management control; in the bureaucratic process model, it resulted from incorporation of a new policy into an organization's operating routines; and in the organizational development model, it resulted from consensus among policy-makers and implementors. But in the conflict and bargaining model, the outcomes of implementation are temporary bargained solutions – resultants – that reflect no overall agreement on purposes.

Success or failure of implementation is therefore largely a relative notion, determined by one's position in the process. Actors who are capable of asserting their purposes over others, however temporarily, will argue that the process is 'successful'. Those with a disadvantage in the bargaining process will argue that the process is 'unsuccessful'. It is entirely possible for the process to proceed even when all actors regard it as unsuccessful, because the costs of refusing to bargain may exceed the costs of remaining in a disadvantageous bargaining relationship. Under these circumstances, the only objective measure of success or failure is the preservation of the bargaining process itself. So long as all parties agree to bargain and mutual benefit is to be gained from bargaining, preservation of the bargaining arena constitutes success. Regardless of the level of conflict in social programs, all actors have an interest in maintaining the programs as long as they deliver benefits that are not otherwise accessible.

The empirical evidence on conflict and bargaining in social program implementation is abundant. The implementation of federal educational programs provides some of the best examples, because the process occurs in a system where power is radically dispersed across all levels of government. The Elementary and Secondary Education Act of 1965 was intended not simply to increase federal expenditures on education but also to change the operation of state and local educational agencies. Title I of the Act was intended to focus attention and resources on educationally disadvantaged children at the local level; Title V was designed to enhance the administrative capability of state educational agencies. In both cases, the pattern of interaction among agencies at different levels of government suggests conflict and bargaining rather than simple progression from a purpose to a result. In its first five years, Title I went from a period of 'good working relationships' and 'friendly assistance' between the federal government and local agencies, through a stage of aggressive federal enforcement of program guidelines, and eventually back to a relatively passive federal role. Jerome Murphy demonstrates that the critical element in these shifts was a change in the nature of the bargaining arena in Title I. In the late sixties, civil rights organizations conducted a large-scale study of local abuses of Title I, confirming a widely held suspicion that funds were not being focused on disadvantaged children, and then mounted an aggressive political campaign to force the U.S. Office of Education to take a stronger posture in enforcing program guidelines. After a flurry of enforcement activity that generated a great deal of political counterpressure from state and local agencies, federal administrators backed away from aggressive enforcement.[67] In other words, federal policy – legislation, regulations, and guidelines – served only as a point of departure for bargaining among implementing agencies. Local implementors designed their actions around expectations about the willingness of federal administrators to enforce the policy. When federal administrators were forced to take a different posture, local administrators responded in part with compliance and in part with counterpressure. The policy actually implemented lies somewhere between the literal requirements of the law and regulations and the interests of local implementors. Another flurry of federal enforcement would alter the situation again.

In the implementation of Title V, the federal government dispensed relatively unrestricted funds to state educational agencies for use in strengthening their administrative capacities. Murphy found that, in the aggregate, Title V did not significantly change the activities or functions of state agencies. The dominant pattern was that 'funds were distributed to satisfy the interests of important elements in the organization' and were 'expended mainly to meet pressing problems through the simple expansion of existing modes of operation'.[68] In other words, the infusion of federal funds simply touched off intraorganizational bargaining in which subunits claimed their share of the bounty and proceeded to use it for their own immediate purposes. In the few cases where significant changes in state agencies did occur, they came 'only after strong pressure from outside the organization'.[69] As in the case of Title I, it took a shift in the bargaining arena to force a change in the behavior of implementors.

The extremely diffuse and fluid nature of organizational relationships in the field of education has led Karl Weick to characterize educational organizations as 'loosely coupled systems'.[70] Although conflict and bargaining do not figure prominently in Weick's model, the characteristics of loosely coupled systems that he identifies lead to the same conclusions as the conflict and bargaining model. The lack of structure and determinacy, the absence of teleologically linked events, the dispersion of resources and responsibilities, and the relative absence of binding regulation all add up to the kind of system in which concerned action is possible only through tacit or explicit bargaining among relatively independent actors.

The same pattern exists in a number of other studies of social program implementation. Pressman's analysis of the impact of federal programs on the city of Oakland concludes that action is possible in urban settings only when 'effective bargaining arenas' exist to enforce 'citizens'. . . demands on government and government's willingness to respond'.[71] In the Pressman and Wildavsky study of the Economic Development Administration's job creation project in Oakland, a similar pattern was repeated. Federal administrators underestimated the complexity of local bargaining relationships and overestimated their ability to force a result consistent with their objectives.[72] Derthick's study of the Department of Housing and Urban Development's New Towns program concludes with the observation that federal programs succeed when 'an adjustment between the federal program and local interests is worked out . . . with the net result . . . that programs are neither 'federal' nor 'local' but a blend of the two'.[73] Cuomo's account of the attempt to locate a low-income public housing project in a middle-class neighborhood of Forest Hills, Queens, demonstrates how bargaining between local residents, city, state, and federal administrators converged on an outcome that satisfied no one but temporarily resolved the conflict.[74] The important characteristic of all these cases is that the participants in the bargaining process stood to gain more from bargaining than from not bargaining. A failure to bargain means a loss of access to goods that can be gained only by participation. Even the strongest of adversaries are locked together by the dependency of conflict.

The major contribution of the conflict and bargaining model to our understanding of social program implementation is the insight that parties to the implementation process needn't agree on anything except the necessity to bargain. The bargaining process, whether it occurs among individuals within organizations or among organizations at different levels of government, proceeds by convergence, adjustment, and closure rather than by hierarchical control or consensus. This feature of the model explains why it is such a powerful descriptive device; it allows us to interpret events without attributing an overall purpose to them. But this feature is also the model's greatest weakness: it does not allow us to posit an objective definition of success or failure, since all normative judgments are simply assertions of relative advantage in the bargaining process. The rationalist critique of the conflict and bargaining model is that it elevates confusion and mindless drift to the level of principle, that it provides an easy excuse for acquiescing in results that satisfy no one, and that it provides no basis for improving the implementation process. These criticisms are difficult to counter, except by observing that a failure to understand the intricacies of bargaining is sometimes more costly than a failure to agree on an objective measure of success.

Conclusion

In closing, two obvious but obligatory remarks are in order. The first is that models are necessarily constructs or ideal types. Nothing is immutable about the distinctions I have drawn here, nor do I make any pretense of having captured all that is important in the implementation process. What is useful about the models, I've argued, is that they draw on established traditions of organizational inquiry and they accord with certain commonsense explanations of why social programs fail. The second observation is that the evidence on social program implementation is skimpy; the cases I've used are intended only to suggest that modest empirical support can be found for the assumptions underlying each of the models. This is not to suggest that any of the evidence is very solid or that there is any reason to believe that the evidence favors one model or another. It does suggest a great need for descriptive studies of social program implementation.

The more interesting question is, of what use is the notion of alternative models to the analysis of implementation? Granting that certain models highlight certain features of the process while concealing others, what use could one make of this fact? I would like to suggest, briefly, two possibilities; but before I do, one possible use of alternative models about which I am very skeptical comes immediately to mind. This is the view that the models should be treated as rival hypotheses and that the gradual accumulation of empirical evidence will eventually prove some single model of the process superior to all others. This is unlikely to happen for two reasons. First, models contain not only descriptive information but normative information; in spite of empirical evidence that a process operates in a certain way, people can nevertheless persist in the belief that it *ought* to operate in another way. Second, people have the capacity to shape their behavior in response to models; a neat predictive model of an essentially political process, like implementation, invites people to behave in unpredictable ways to achieve their own ends. Given the diversity of opinion reflected in the four models presented here, it seems highly unlikely that the accumulation of evidence will lead to agreement. It will probably just reinforce the disagreement that currently exists. But, as I indicated above, two ideas about the use of alternative models are more promising.

The first is that applying different models to the same set of events allows us to distinguish certain features of the implementation process from others. In fact, every implementing agency probably has a set of management controls, a firmly entrenched collection of operating routines, some process for eliciting the involvement of implementors, and a set of internal and external bargaining relationships. The important question is not whether these elements exist or not, but how they affect the implementation process. One way of disentangling the effects of these factors is to analyze the same body of evidence from the perspective of several different models. This is the approach taken by Allison in his analysis of the Cuban missile crisis.

The second idea proceeds from the notion that certain kinds of problems are more amenable to solution when using one perspective than when using another. It is conceivable that in certain times and settings, the use of management controls is clearly appropriate, while in other circumstances only bargaining is appropriate. In some instances, wholesale delegation of discretion is the obvious course of action to follow, while in others firm control of discretion is necessary. The point is that models can help analysts and decision-makers distinguish among different kinds of problems. Using management controls in a system in which power is extremely diffuse, for example, is like using a crescent wrench to turn a Phillips screw. The problem is to understand when certain tools of analysis and strategies of action are likely to pay off and when not.

Neither of these approaches requires complete agreement on the nature of the models or on the existence of a single model that captures all essential features of the process. They require only a willingness to treat certain parts of a complex process as analytically separable, plus a high tolerance for ambiguity.

Notes

1. A number of these studies are collected in Walter Williams and Richard E. Elmore (eds.), *Social Program Implementation* (New York: Academic Press, 1976). Another collection, which focuses on the role of regulation in the implementation process, is a special number of *Policy Sciences* 7 (Winter 1976), edited by Francine Rabinovitz, Jeffrey Pressman, and Martin Rein. Two major reviews of the literature on implementation are, Donald Van Meter and Carl Van Horn, 'The policy implementation process: a conceptual framework', in *Administration and Society* 6 (1974): 445–88; and Erwin Hargrove, *The Missing Link: The study of implementation of social policy* (Washington, DC: Urban Institute, 1975).

2. Walter Williams, 'Implementation problems in federally-funded programs', in Williams and Elmore (eds.), *Social Program Implementation*, pp. 15–40.

3. Richard Nelson, 'Intellectualizing about the moon–ghetto metaphor: a study of the current malaise of rational analysis of social problems', *Policy Sciences* 5 (1974): 398. This article has been expanded into a book, *The Moon and the Ghetto* (New York: Norton, 1977), that includes a number of case studies demonstrating what Nelson means by analysis of organizational alternatives. His framework differs considerably from the one developed here.

4. Graham Allison, *Essence of Decision: Explaining the Cuban missile crisis* (Boston: Little, Brown, 1971).

5. *Ibid.*, p. 2.

6. *Ibid.*, p. 267. See also Arnold Meltsner, 'Political feasibility and policy analysis', *Public Administration Review* (November/December 1972): 859–67.

7. This distinction is developed at length in Ralph Strauch, 'A critical look at quantitative methodology', *Policy Analysis* 2 (1976): 121–44.

8. This account of the systems management model is drawn from the following sources: Daniel Katz and Robert Kahn, *The Social Psychology of Organizations* (New York: Wiley, 1966); William Baumol, *Economic Theories and Operations Analysis*, 3rd edn. (Englewood Cliffs, NJ: Prentice Hall, 1972); Robert Anthony, *Planning and Control Systems: A framework of analysis* (Boston: Harvard Graduate School of Business Administration, 1965); C. West Churchman, *The Systems Approach* (New York: Delta, 1968); and Charles Hitch and Roland McKean, *The Economics of Defense in a Nuclear Age* (Cambridge, MA: Harvard University Press, 1963).

9. Katz and Kahn, *The Social Psychology of Organizations*, p. 79.

10. *Ibid.*, p. 203. Cf. Churchman, The Systems Approach, p. 44.

11. Anthony, *Planning and Control Systems*, pp. 16–18.

12. Hitch and McKean, *The Economics of Defense in a Nuclear Age*, pp. 128–9, 396–402. Their choice of the term 'sub-optimization' is perhaps unfortunate because to most of us it communicates the meaning 'less than optimal', which is quite the opposite of the meaning they wish to convey. It is clear from their discussion that they intend the term to mean 'optimizing at lower levels'. Some writers, however, insist on using the term to mean less than optimal. See, e.g., Anthony, *Planning and Control Systems*, p. 35. Two other sources in which the term is used consistently with the meaning of Hitch and McKean are, Baumol, *Economic Theories and Operations Analysis*, p. 395n, and Richard Zeckhauser and Elmer Schaefer, 'Public policy and normative economic theory', in Raymond Bauer and Kenneth Gergen (eds.), *The Study of Policy Formation* (New York: Free Press, 1968), pp. 73–6. A more recent treatment of suboptimization in policy analysis may be found in E. S. Quade, *Analysis for Public Decisions* (New York: Elsevier, 1975), pp. 95–8.

13. Hitch and McKean, *The Economics of Defense in a Nuclear Age*, p. 129.
14. Herbert Kaufman, *The Forest Ranger: A study of administrative behavior* (Baltimore: Johns Hopkins University Press, 1969), p. 91.
15. Anthony, *Planning and Control Systems*, p. 45.
16. Katz and Kahn, *The Social Psychology of Organizations*, p. 40.
17. Williams, 'Implementation analysis and assessment', in Williams and Elmore (eds.), *Social Program Implementation*, pp. 281–2.
18. Kaufman, *The Forest Ranger*, p. 203.
19. *Ibid.*, p. 228.
20. James Q. Wilson, 'The bureaucracy problem', *The Public Interest* 6 (Winter 1967): 3–9.
21. Michel Crozier, *The Bureaucratic Phenomenon* (Chicago: University of Chicago Press, 1964).
22. James Q. Wilson, *Varieties of Police Behavior* (New York: Atheneum, 1973), p. 1.
23. Allison, *Essence of Decision*, p. 80.
24. Wilson, *Varieties of Police Behavior*, pp. 2–3.
25. *Ibid.*, p. 9; see also pp. 64ff.
26. Donald Schon, *Beyond the Stable State* (New York: Random House, 1971), p. 32.
27. Michael Lipsky, 'Toward a theory of street-level bureaucracy', in Willis Hawley and Michael Lipsky (eds.), *Theoretical Perspectives on Urban Politics* (Englewood Cliffs, NJ: Prentice Hall, 1976), p. 197.
28. Wilson, *Varieties of Police Behavior*, p. 7.
29. Lipsky, 'Toward a theory of street-level bureaucracy', pp. 197–8.
30. *Ibid.*, pp. 201ff.
31. Richard Weatherly, 'Toward a theory of client control in street-level bureaucracy', unpublished paper, School of Social Work, University of Washington, 1976, p. 5.
32. Miriam Johnson, *Counter Point: The changing employment service* (Salt Lake City: Olympus, 1973).
33. *Ibid.*, p. 21.
34. *Ibid.*, pp. 63–4.
35. *Ibid.*, pp. 85–6.
36. *Ibid.*, p. 109.
37. Richard Weatherly and Michael Lipsky, 'Street-level bureaucrats and institutional innovation: implementing special-education reform', *Harvard Educational Review* 47 (May 1977): 171–97.
38. *Ibid.*, p. 180.
39. *Ibid.*, p. 182.
40. *Ibid.*, pp. 186–7.
41. *Ibid.*, pp. 189–90.
42. *Ibid.*, pp. 192–3.
43. Williams, 'Implementation problems in federally funded programs', pp. 20–3.
44. Weatherly and Lipsky, 'Street-level bureaucrats and institutional innovation', p. 196.
45. See, e.g., Katz and Kahn, *The Social Psychology of Organizations*, pp. 211ff.
46. Chris Argyris, *Personality and Organization: The conflict between system and individual* (New York: Harper, 1957), pp. 53ff.
47. Chris Argyris, *The Applicability of Organizational Sociology* (London: Cambridge University Press, 1972), *passim*.
48. Warren Bennis, *Organization Development: Its nature, origins, and prospects* (Reading, MA: Addison-Wesley, 1969), p. 28.

49. *Ibid.*, p. 2 [quoting Douglas McGregor, *The Professional Manager* (New York: McGraw Hill, 1967)].

50. Chris Argyris, *Interpersonal Competence and Organizational Effectiveness* (Homewood, IL: Irwin, 1962), p. 42.

51. Chris Argyris, *Integrating the Individual and the Organization* (New York: Wiley, 1964), p. 138.

52. The results are reported in a five-volume study, *Federal Programs Supporting Educational Change* (Santa Monica, CA: Rand Corporation, 1975). The principal authors are Paul Berman, Milbrey McLaughlin, Dale Mann, Peter Greenwood, and John Pincus. A number of other researchers, including this author, worked on parts of the study.

53. Paul Berman and Milbrey McLaughlin, *Federal Programs Supporting Educational Change, Vol. IV: The Findings in Review* (Santa Monica, CA: Rand Corporation, 1975), p. 22.

54. *Ibid.*, see also pp. 45–7.

55. Berman and McLaughlin, *Federal Programs Supporting Change, Vol. III: The Process of Change*, p. 39.

56. *Ibid.*, p. 26.

57. Milbrey McLaughlin, 'Implementation as mutual adaptation: change in classroom organization', in Williams and Elmore (eds.), *Social Program Implementation*, pp. 172–3.

58. Berman and McLaughlin, *Federal Programs Supporting Educational Change, Vol. III: The Process of Change*, pp. 3, 31.

59. Bennis, *Organization Development*, p. 77: emphasis in original.

60. An elegant account of tacit bargaining and coordination is given in Thomas Schelling, *The Strategy of Conflict* (London and New York: Oxford University Press, 1963), pp. 53ff.

61. *Ibid.*, pp. 5–6.

62. Charles Lindblom, *The Intelligence of Democracy: Decision making through mutual adjustment* (New York: Free Press, 1965), p. 3.

63. Allison, *Essence of Decision*, p. 162.

64. Schelling, *The Strategy of Conflict*, pp. 106–7.

65. *Ibid.*, p. 70: Lindblom, *The Intelligence of Democracy*, pp. 205–25.

66. Richard Cyert and James March, *A Behavioral Theory of the Firm* (Englewood Cliffs, NJ: Prentice Hall, 1963), p. 27.

67. Jerome Murphy, 'The education bureaucracies implement novel policy: the politics of Title I of ESEA, 1965–72', in Alan Sindler (ed.), *Policy and Politics in America* (Boston: Little, Brown, 1973), pp. 160–98. See also Milbrey McLaughlin, 'Implementation of ESEA Title I: a problem of compliance', *Teachers College Record* 77 (1976): 397–415.

68. Jerome Murphy, 'Title V of ESEA: the impact of discretionary funds on state education bureaucracies', in Williams and Elmore (eds.), *Social Program Implementation*, pp. 89 and 91. A more extended treatment of this case is found in Murphy's *State Education Agencies and Discretionary Funds* (Lexington, MA: Lexington Books, 1974).

69. *Ibid.*, p. 94.

70. Karl Weick, 'Educational organizations as loosely coupled systems', *Administrative Science Quarterly* 21 (1976): 1–18.

71. Jeffrey Pressman, *Federal Programs and City Politics: The dynamics of the aid process in Oakland* (Berkeley, CA: University of California Press, 1975), pp. 14 and 143–4.

72. Jeffrey Pressman and Aaron Wildavsky, *Implementation* (Berkeley, CA: University of California Press, 1973), *passim*.

73. Martha Derthick, *New Towns in Town: Why a federal program failed* (Washington, DC: Urban Institute, 1972), pp. 97–8. Portions of this study are reprinted in Williams and Elmore, *Social Program Implementation*, pp. 219–39.
74. Mario Cuomo, *Forest Hills Diary: The crisis of low-income housing* (New York: Random House, 1974), *passim*.

Top-down and bottom-up approaches to implementation research

Paul A. Sabatier

The last fifteen years have witnessed an enormous amount of research on policy implementation. While the early work was primarily American – motivated in part by perceived failures in Great Society programs – much of the most interesting recent work has been done in Western Europe. For general reviews, see Yin (1980), Barrett and Fudge (1981), Alexander (1982), and Sabatier and Mazmanian (1983a).

Most of the early American studies were analyses of a single case and came to very pessimistic conclusions about the ability of governments to effectively implement their programs (Derthick, 1972; Pressman and Wildavsky, 1973; Murphy, 1973; Bardach, 1974). The second generation of studies were more analytical and comparative in perspective (Goggin, 1986). They sought to explain variation in implementation success across programs and governmental units by reference to specific variables and conceptual frameworks (Van Meter and Van Horn, 1975; Sabatier and Mazmanian, 1979, 1980). But they maintained the same 'top-down' perspective as earlier writers, i.e. they started with a policy decision (usually a statute) and examined the extent to which its legally-mandated objectives were achieved over time and why.

In the late 1970s and early 1980s, however, a quite different approach emerged in response to the perceived weaknesses of the 'top-down' perspective. Rather than start with a policy decision, these 'bottom-uppers' started with an analysis of the multitude of actors who interact at the operational (local) level on a particular problem or issue. In the process, the familiar policy stages of formulation, implementation, and reformulation tended to disappear. Instead, the focus has been on the strategies pursued by various actors in pursuit of their objectives. Such studies have shown that local actors often deflect centrally-mandated programs toward their own ends (Lipsky, 1971; Berman and McLaughlin, 1976; Hanf and Scharpf, 1978; Ingram, 1977; Elmore, 1979; Browning *et al.*, 1981; Barrett and Fudge, 1981; Hjern and Hull, 1982; Hanf, 1982).

From P. A. Sabatier, 'Top-down and bottom-up approaches to implementation research: a critical analysis and suggested synthesis', *Journal of Public Policy*, **6**, 1986, pp. 21–48.

This paper will first examine the 'top-down' and 'bottom-up' approaches in greater detail, including an analysis of the strengths and weaknesses of each. It will then suggest a synthetic framework which integrates most of the strengths of the respective approaches and applies it to a longer time frame than in most implementation studies.

Top-down approaches: a not entirely disinterested evaluation

In analyzing the two approaches, we shall focus on a representative scholar for each: Daniel Mazmanian and Paul Sabatier for the top-downers, Benny Hjern *et al.* for the bottom-uppers. While this neglects the views of other scholars, it ensures that the work of a leading proponent of each 'school' will be subjected to detailed analysis.

Presentation
The essential features of a top-down approach are that it starts with a policy decision by governmental (often central government) officials and then asks:

1. To what extent were the actions of implementing officials and target groups consistent with (the objectives and procedures outlined in) that policy decision?
2. To what extent were the objectives attained over time, i.e. to what extent were the impacts consistent with the objectives?
3. What were the principal factors affecting policy outputs and impacts, both those relevant to the official policy as well as other politically significant ones?
4. How was the policy reformulated over time on the basis of experience?

The work of Sabatier and Mazmanian serves as a useful example of the top-down approach because it has been around for several years; it has been subjected to extensive empirical testing; and it is viewed by at least a few completely disinterested observers (Alterman, 1983; Goggin, 1984) as a leading proponent of this point of view.

The Sabatier and Mazmanian framework (1979, 1980) took as its point of departure the first generation of implementation research with its very pessimistic conclusions (Pressman and Wildavsky, 1973; Murphy, 1973; Bardach, 1974; Jones, 1975; Berman and McLaughlin, 1976; Elmore, 1978). Sabatier and Mazmanian first identified a variety of legal, political, and 'tractability' variables affecting the different stages of the implementation process (see Figure 1).

They then sought to synthesize this large number of variables into a shorter list of six sufficient and generally necessary conditions for the effective implementation of legal objectives:

1. Clear and consistent objectives.
   Taken from Van Meter and Van Horn (1975), clear legal objectives were viewed as providing both a standard of evaluation and an important legal resource to implementing officials.

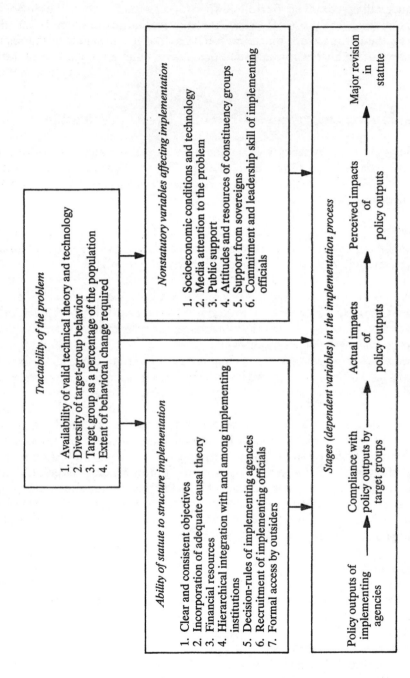

Figure 1 Skeletal flow diagram of the variables involved in the implementation process
(*Source:* Sabatier and Mazmanian, 1980: 542)

2. Adequate causal theory.

Borrowing the fundamental insight of Pressman and Wildavsky (1973) that policy interventions incorporate an implicit theory about how to effectuate social change, Sabatier and Mazmanian pointed to the adequacy of the jurisdiction and policy levers given implementing officials as a means of ascertaining those causal assumptions.

3. Implementation process legally structured to enhance compliance by implementing officials and target groups.

Borrowing again from Pressman and Wildavsky (1973), the authors pointed to a variety of legal mechanisms including the number of veto points involved in program delivery, the sanctions and incentives available to overcome resistance, and the assignment of programs to implementing agencies which would be supportive and give it high priority.

4. Committed and skillful implementing officials.

Recognizing the unavoidable discretion given implementing officials, their commitment to policy objectives and skill in utilizing available resources were viewed as critical (Lipsky, 1971; Lazin, 1973; Levin, 1980). While this could partially be determined by the initial statute, much of it was a product of post-statutory political forces.

5. Support of interest groups and sovereigns.

This simply recognized the need to maintain political support throughout the long implementation process from interest groups and from legislative and executive sovereigns (Downs, 1967; Murphy, 1973; Bardach, 1974; Sabatier, 1975).

6. Changes in socioeconomic conditions which do not substantially undermine political support or causal theory.

This variable simply recognized that changes in socioeconomic conditions, e.g. the Arab oil boycott or the Vietnam War, could have dramatic repercussions on the political support or causal theory of a program (Hofferbert, 1974; Aaron, 1978).

In short, the first three conditions can be dealt with by the initial policy decision (e.g. a statute), whereas the latter three are largely the product of subsequent political and economic pressure during the implementation process.

Although Sabatier and Mazmanian took seriously the arguments of Lipsky (1971), Berman (1978; 1980), and Elmore (1978) concerning the substantial limitations of programmed/hierarchical control, they did not accept the pessimists' conclusion concerning the inevitability of 'adaptive' implementation in which policy-makers are forced largely to acquiesce to the preferences of street-level bureaucrats and target groups. Instead, they sought to identify a number of legal and political mechanisms for affecting the preferences and/or constraining the behavior of street-level bureaucrats and target groups both in the initial policy decision and then subsequently over time. For example, policy-makers normally have some ability to select one set of implementing officials over another; to affect the number of clearance points; to provide appropriate incentives and sanctions; to affect the balance of constituency support; etc. And, as Pressman and Wildavsky (1973) clearly showed, policy-makers can strongly affect the implementation process by basing a program on a valid causal theory rather than a dubious one. In short, while Sabatier and Mazmanian rejected hierarchical *control* – in the sense of tightly constrained behavior – as impossible, they argued that the behavior of street-level bureaucrats and target groups could be kept within acceptable bounds over time if the six conditions were met (Sabatier and Mazmanian, 1979: 489–92, 503–4).

Over the next five years, Sabatier and Mazmanian sought to have the framework tested – by themselves and others – in a variety of policy areas and political systems. The results, summarized in Table 1, indicate that the framework has been applied over twenty times. These cases have involved ten policy areas, including strong representation from land use control, education, and environmental protection. While a majority of cases have been American, many of these have focused on state or local policy initiatives rather than on the implementation of federal policy. In addition, there have been eight cases, primarily in higher education, involving six European countries.

It is now time to assess the results of this research program. This will be done, first, from the standpoint of one of the authors and then from the perspective of their 'bottom-up' critics.

Table 1 Empirical applications of the Sabatier and Mazmanian framework

I. Original research by Sabatier and/or Mazmanian
    1. California Coastal Conservation Act, 1972–80 (Sabatier and Mazmanian, 1983b)
    2. San Francisco Bay Conservation and Development Act, 1965–72 (Sabatier and Klosterman, 1981)
    3. French Coastal Decrees of 1976 and 1979 (Sabatier, 1984)

II. Secondary analysis of others' research by Sabatier and/or Mazmanian
    1. British Open University, 1969–79 (Cerych and Sabatier, 1986)
    2. French Instituts Universitaires de Technologie, 1967–79 (Cerych and Sabatier, 1986)
    3. Norwegian Regional Colleges, 1970–9 (Cerych and Sabatier, 1986)
    4. University of Tromsø (Norway), 1969–79 (Cerych and Sabatier, 1986)
    5. German Gesamthochschulen, 1970–9 (Cerych and Sabatier, 1986)
    6. Swedish 25/5 Scheme (Cerych and Sabatier, 1986)
    7. Polish Preferential University Admissions (Cerych and Sabatier, 1986)
    8. 1970 U.S. Clean Air Act, 1970–9 (Mazmanian and Sabatier, 1983)
    9. U.S. School Desegregation, South and North, 1955–75 (Mazmanian and Sabatier, 1983)
    10. 1965 U.S. Elementary and Secondary Education Act, Title I, 1966–7 (Mazmanian and Sabatier, 1983)
    11. 1970 New Towns Act (U.S.), 1970–8 (Mazmanian and Sabatier, 1983)

III. Utilization by other scholars
    1. Model cities, revenue sharing, and CDBG in SF Bay Area (Browning *et al.*, 1981)
    2. Variety of federal anti-discrimination programs (Bullock, 1981)
    3. Evolution of U.S. welfare policy since 1935 (Goodwin and Moen, 1981)
    4. 1965 ESEA, Title I, 1960–79 (Kirst and Jung, 1982)
    5. Groundwater management in several New York counties (S. Jones, 1984)
    6. U.S. hazardous waste policy (Bowman and Lester, 1986; Lester, 1986; Davis, 1985)
    7. U.S. coastal zone management (Lowry, 1985)

A critical self-appraisal

One ought, of course, to be skeptical of self-evaluations. Authors are often tempted to select cases which fit their theories. In this instance, however, only seven of the twenty-four cases were selected by Mazmanian and Sabatier, thus affording some protection against biased case selection. That still leaves the potential for biased data selection or interpretation of results, but the reader can decide for himself after examining the case evidence.

These caveats notwithstanding, experience has demonstrated some real strengths in the Sabatier/Mazmanian framework.

First the importance it attaches to legal structuring of the implementation process – one of its major innovations – has been confirmed in numerous studies. This is particularly gratifying since one of the most frequent criticisms of the framework has been that the emphasis on structuring is unrealistic, i.e. that the cognitive limitations of policy-makers and the need for compromise at the formulation stage preclude careful structuring (Majone and Wildavsky, 1978; Barrett and Fudge, 1981). The evidence suggests that, while fairly coherent structuring is difficult, it occurs more frequently than critics realize and, when present, proves to be very important.

For example, the framework emphasized the importance of selecting implementing institutions supportive of the new program and suggested creating new agencies as a specific strategy. This turned out to be possible in six of the twenty-odd cases studied [. . .] and in many other cases formulators expressly selected sympathetic existing institutions. When this was not possible, e.g. compensatory education in the U.S., it proved to be a serious impediment to effective implementation.

Likewise, two of the major contributions borrowed from Pressman and Wildavsky (1973) – veto points and causal theory – were confirmed in many studies. In the case of the coastal commissions, for example, the agencies' greater success in protecting scenic views than in providing public access to the beach can largely be explained by reference to the number of veto points: In particular, the coastal commissions had all the legal authority necessary to protect scenic views, while actually providing public access required the cooperation of at least a half-dozen other agencies (Sabatier and Mazmanian, 1983b). The superior ability of U.S. air pollution authorities to regulate automotive emissions than to reduce vehicle miles traveled can be attributed to a greater understanding of, and control over, the factors involved (Mazmanian and Sabatier, 1983b: Chap. 4). The much greater success of the British Open University than the French IUTs in reaching projected enrollments can be partially attributed to the better theory utilized by policy formulators in the former case (Cerych and Sabatier, 1986). While Bowen (1982) rightly cautions that the analysis of veto points is more complicated than envisaged by Pressman and Wildavsky, their contributions remain of the first order.

Perhaps the best evidence of the potential importance of legal structuring is that the two most successful cases studied to date – the California coastal commissions (at least in the short run) and the British Open University – were also the best designed institutions. That is, they structured the process to provide reasonably consistent objectives, a good causal theory, relatively few veto points, sympathetic implementing officials, access of supporters to most decisions, and adequate financial resources.

Second, the six conditions of effective implementation have proven to be a useful checklist of critical factors in understanding variations in program performance and in understanding the strategies of program proponents over time. While the relative importance of specific factors has varied across cases – with implementing agency support being probably the most consistently critical one – all except clear and consistent objectives have been important in many cases. There is also some evidence that interest group support may be more critical in the U.S. than in many European countries – presumably reflecting the greater autonomy of administrative agencies in countries like Great Britain, France, and the German Federal Republic.

Third, the relatively manageable list of variables and the focus in the framework on the formulation–implementation–reformulation cycle encouraged many of our case authors to look at a longer time-frame than was true of earlier implementation studies (i.e. ten years instead of four). This, in turn, led to a discovery of the importance of learning by program proponents over time as they became aware of deficiencies in the original program and sought improved legal and political strategies for dealing with them. The best example is the American compensatory education case, where serious deficiencies revealed by early evaluation studies enabled program proponents to greatly strengthen the legal structure and constituency support over time (Kirst and Jung, 1982; Mazmanian and Sabatier, 1983). For other examples of learning over time, one can cite the supporters of the French IUTs who greatly improved their understanding of the factors affecting student choices over time (Cerych and Sabatier, 1986).

Fourth, our focus on legally-mandated objectives – particularly when combined with the ten-year time span for assessing program effectiveness – helped produce a less pessimistic evaluation of governmental performance than was true of the first generation of implementation studies. On the one hand, the focus on legally-mandated objectives encouraged scholars to carefully distinguish the objectives contained in legal documents from both the political rhetoric surrounding policy formulation and the tendency of critics to evaluate a program on the basis of what they mistakenly perceived to be its objectives – the criticism of the 'failure' of the Open University to meet the needs of working class students being a case in point. In addition, the longer time-frame used in many of these studies meant that several which were initially regarded as failures – U.S. compensatory education and the French IUTs – were regarded in a more favorable light after proponents had had the benefit of a decade of learning and experimentation (Kirst and Jung, 1982; Mazmanian and Sabatier, 1983; Cerych and Sabatier, 1986).

On the other hand, several years' experience with testing the Sabatier/Mazmanian framework has also revealed some significant flaws – quite apart from the more serious methodological criticisms of the 'bottom-uppers.'

First, the emphasis they placed on 'clear and consistent policy objectives' was a mistake. Experience has confirmed the critics' charge that very few programs meet this criterion, either initially or after a decade (Majone and Wildavsky, 1978; MacIntyre, 1985). Instead, the vast majority incorporate a multitude of partially-conflicting objectives. This does not, however, preclude the possibility of assessing program effectiveness. Instead, it simply means that effectiveness needs to be reconceptualized into the 'acceptability space' demarcated by the intersection of the ranges of acceptable values on each of the multiple evaluative dimensions involved. This can be illustrated by the case of the Norwegian regional colleges: They were supposed to serve students from the local region and to foster regionally-relevant research at the same time that they were also mandated to be part of a national educational system in which the transfer of student credits among institutions and the evaluation of faculty research by peers in other institutions had to be protected. While the institutions after a decade were receiving 'excellent' ratings on very few of these dimensions, the evidence suggests they were satisfactory on all of them (Cerych and Sabatier, 1986).

On a related point, most implementation scholars have followed Van Meter and Van Horn (1975) in assuming that, *ceteris paribus*, the probability of effective implementation of a reform is inversely related to the extent of envisaged departure from the status quo ante. In their study of European higher education reforms, however, Cerych and Sabatier (1986) provide evidence that the relationship is not linear but rather curvilinear. They suggest that very incremental reforms – e.g. the Swedish 25/5 Scheme for adult admission to universities – simply do not arouse enough commitment to get much done, while those such as the German *Gesamthochschulen* which envisage a comprehensive reform of the entire system arouse too much resistance to get off the ground. Instead, those reforms – e.g., the British Open University – which are ambitious enough to arouse intense commitment from proponents but rather limited in their effects on the entire (e.g. higher education) system stand the best chance of success.

Second, while Sabatier and Mazmanian encouraged a longer time-frame and provided several examples of policy-oriented learning over time, their framework did not provide a good conceptual vehicle for looking at policy change over periods of a decade or more (Goodwin and Moen, 1981; Browning *et al.*, 1981; Goggin, 1984; Lowry, 1985). This is primarily because, as we shall see below, it focused too much on the perspective of program *proponents*, thereby neglecting the strategies (and learning) by other actors which would provide the cornerstone for a more dynamic model.

The assessment thus far has been from the point of view of the authors or other sympathizers of a top-down perspective. It is now time to examine the more fundamental methodological criticisms raised by 'bottom-uppers,' most notably, Benny Hjern.

The bottom-up critique

The fundamental flaw in top-down models, according to Hjern and Hull (1982), Hanf (1982), Barrett and Fudge (1981), Elmore (1979), and other bottom-uppers, is that they start from the perspective of (central) decision-makers and thus tend to neglect other actors. Their methodology leads top-downers to assume that the framers of the policy decision (e.g. statute) are the key actors and that others are basically impediments. This, in turn, leads them to neglect strategic initiatives coming from the private sector, from street-level bureaucrats or local implementing officials, and from other policy subsystems. While Sabatier and Mazmanian are not entirely guilty of this – in particular, their focus on causal theory and hierarchical integration encourages the analyst to examine the perspectives of other actors – this is certainly a potential Achilles' heel of their model.

A second, and related, criticism of top-down models is that they are difficult to use in situations where there is no dominant policy (statute) or agency, but rather a multitude of governmental directives and actors, none of them preeminent. As this is often the case, particularly in social service delivery, this is a very telling criticism. While Sabatier and Mazmanian can recognize such situations – through the concepts of (inadequate) causal theory and (poor) hierarchical integration – they have very little ability to predict the outcome of such complex situations except to say that the policy they are interested in will probably not be effectively implemented.

A third criticism of top-down models is that they are likely to ignore, or at least underestimate, the strategies used by street-level bureaucrats and target groups to get around (central) policy and/or to divert it to their own purposes (Weatherly and Lipsky, 1977; Elmore, 1978; Berman, 1978). A related point is that such models are likely to neglect many of the counterproductive effects of the policies chosen for analysis. While a really skillful top-downer can attempt to deal with such deficiencies, there is little doubt that these, too, are important criticisms.

Finally, there are a whole series of arguments that the distinction between policy formulation and policy implementation is misleading and/or useless (Nakamura and Smallwood, 1980; Barrett and Fudge, 1981; Hjern and Hull, 1982; Hjern, 1982). These include the following: The distinction ignores the fact that some organizations are involved in both stages and/or that local implementing officials and target groups often simply ignore central legislators and administrators and deal directly with each other; since it is difficult to isolate policy decisions, it is preferable to talk about action and reaction (Barrett and Fudge, 1981); and because policies change as they get implemented, it is better to talk about policy evolution (Majone and Wildavsky, 1978).

This criticism strikes me as much less persuasive than the previous three. On the other hand, there are certainly cases, such as the Swedish 25/5 Scheme (Cerych and Sabatier, 1986), where there is no discernible policy 'decision' but rather a series of very incremental steps over time. But in the vast majority of the cases using the Sabatier and Mazmanian framework, it was not only possible but also highly desirable to retain the distinction between formulation and implementation. In fact, of the twenty-four cases, the 25/5 Scheme was the only one in which anyone even remotely skilled in legal analysis would find it difficult to discern an initial major policy decision. As for the arguments that some organizations are involved in both formulation and implementation, so what? The same organizations also try to influence local and central government; does this suggest that distinction between levels of government ought also to be rejected as useless? Finally, while local officials and target groups may sometimes ignore the legal authority of central officials, if such officials were really as insignificant as Hjern *et al.* suggest then why do the very same local officials and interest groups spend thousands of hours and millions of dollars every year trying to influence them?

Furthermore, obliterating the distinction between formulation and implementation will have two very significant costs (Sabatier and Mazmanian, 1983a). First, it makes it very difficult to distinguish the relative influence of elected officials and civil servants – thus precluding an analysis of democratic accountability and bureaucratic discretion, hardly trivial topics. Second, the view of the policy process as a seamless web of flows without decision points (Majone and Wildavsky, 1978; Barrett and Fudge, 1981) precludes policy evaluation (because there is no policy to evaluate) and the analysis of policy change (as there is never a defined policy at t_0 which changes into another defined policy at t_1).

In sum, while the first three criticisms are reasonably persuasive, the fourth is not. The bottom-uppers have thus been able to advance some rather telling arguments against the top-down approach. Have they also been able to accomplish the more difficult task of developing a more viable alternative?

Bottom-up approaches: the promised land?

In discussing the bottom-up perspective, the focus will be on the work of Benny Hjern and his colleagues – David Porter, Ken Hanf, and Chris Hull – who, while at the Science Center in Berlin during the period from roughly 1975 to 1983, developed a coherent methodology for conducting implementation analysis. It is this willingness to propose an intersubjectively reliable alternative to top-down approaches which distinguishes Hjern *et al.* from many bottom-up critics (e.g. Barrett and Fudge, 1981) and is one of the principal reasons their work has been chosen for analysis.

Presentation
Hjern *et al.* began with an acute awareness of the methodological weaknesses of the top-down approach, a commitment to the development of an intersubjectively reliable methodology, and a concern with policy areas – e.g. manpower training – involving a multitude of public and private organizations.

In contrast to the top-down approach – which starts from a policy decision and focuses on the extent to which its objectives are attained over time and why – the bottom-up approach of Hjern *et al.* starts by identifying the network of actors involved in service delivery in one or more local areas and asks them about their goals, strategies, activities, and contacts. It then uses the contacts as a vehicle for developing a network technique to identify the local, regional, and national actors involved in the planning, financing, and execution of the relevant governmental and non-governmental programs. This provides a mechanism for moving from street-level bureaucrats (the 'bottom') up to the 'top' policy-makers in both the public and private sectors (Hjern *et al.*, 1978; Hjern and Porter, 1981; Hjern and Hull, 1985). Table 2 compares some of the central features of top-down and bottom-up approaches.

The study of Swedish manpower training programs, for example, by Hjern *et al.* (1978) started with the interaction of unions, governmental employment agencies, local governments, and industrial firms in several areas, and then moved from there via

Table 2 Comparison between top-down and bottom-up approaches

	Top-down (Sabatier and Mazmanian)	Bottom-up (Hjern *et al.*)
Initial focus	(Central) government decision, e.g., new pollution control law.	Local implementation structure (network) involved in a policy area, e.g., pollution control.
Identification of major actors in the process	From top down and from government out to private sector (although importance attached to causal theory also calls for accurate understanding of target group's incentive structure).	From bottom (government and private) up.
Evaluative criteria	Focus on extent of attainment of formal objectives (carefully analyzed). May look at other politically significant criteria and unintended consequences, but these are optional.	Much less clear. Basically anything the analyst chooses which is somehow relevant to the policy issue or problem. Certainly does not require any careful analysis of official government decision(s).
Overall focus	How does one steer system to achieve (top) policy-maker's intended policy results?	Strategic interaction among multiple actors in a policy network.

a networking technique to identify the people actually involved in planning, financing, and executing the relevant programs. They concluded that program success was far more dependent upon the skills of specific individuals in 'local implementation structures' than upon the efforts of central government officials.

In addition to their study of manpower training programs in Sweden and the German Federal Republic, Hjern *et al.* have sought to apply this technique to a variety of programs designed to foster the economic viability of small firms in the Federal Republic and several other countries (Hjern and Hull, 1985). They have also encouraged the application of their approach to Swedish energy policy (Wittrock *et al.*, 1982), English manpower training (Davies and Mason, 1982), Dutch pollution control (Hanf, 1982), and Swiss economic development (Ackermann and Steinmann, 1982). It should be noted, however, that – with the exception of Hanf – these latter papers are more united by a bottom-up perspective than by any serious effort to employ the networking methodology first outlined by Hjern and Porter (1981).

Evaluation

The approach developed by Hjern *et al.* has several notable strengths.

First, they have developed an explicit and replicable methodology for identifying a policy network ('implementation structure'). In the small firms study, for example, they started with a random sample of firms in an area, and then interviewed key officials in each firm to ascertain their critical problems, the strategies developed to deal with each, and the persons contacted to execute each of those strategies. They then used those contacts via a networking technique to identify the 'implementation structure' (Hull and Hjern, 1982). In the case of financial problems, for example, the structure would include local (and perhaps regional) banks, officials in agencies with financial assistance programs, and, in the most successful case, an official in a local redevelopment agency who had extensive contacts he could direct firms to. It is this intersubjectively reliable methodology which separates Hjern *et al.* from the vast majority of bottom-up (and even top-down) researchers.

Second, because Hjern *et al.* do not begin with a governmental program but rather with actors' perceived problems and the strategies developed for dealing with them, they are able to assess the relative importance of a variety of governmental programs *vis-à-vis* private organizations and market forces in solving those problems. In contrast, a top-down approach is likely to overestimate the importance of the governmental program which is its focus. For example, Hanf (1982) bottom-up analysis of pollution control in the Netherlands concluded that energy policies and the market price of alternative fuels had more effect on firms' pollution control programs than did governmental pollution control programs – a conclusion which would have been difficult for a top-downer to reach.

Third, because Hjern *et al.* do not start with a focus on the attainment of formal policy objectives, they are free to see all sorts of (unintended) consequences of governmental and private programs.

Fourth, this approach is able to deal with a policy/problem area involving a multitude of public (and private) programs, none of them preeminent. In contrast, such cases present substantial difficulties for top-down approaches.

Finally, because of their focus on the strategies pursued by a wide range of actors, bottom-uppers are better able to deal with strategic interaction over time than are top-downers – who tend to focus on the strategies of program proponents, while neglecting those of other actors.

For all these strengths, however, the Hjern *et al.* approach also has its limitations.

First, just as top-downers are in danger of overemphasizing the importance of the Center *vis-à-vis* the Periphery, bottom-uppers are likely to overemphasize the ability of the Periphery to frustrate the Center.

More specifically, the focus on actors' goals and strategies – the vast majority of whom are at the Periphery – may underestimate the Center's *indirect* influence over those goals and strategies through its ability to affect the institutional structure in which individuals operate (Kiser and Ostrom, 1982). For example, if Hjern *et al.* had studied the California coastal commissions, they would have taken as given that the vast majority of coastal officials were very sympathetic to environmental protection – without ever realizing that the distribution of officials' preferences was a consequence of the prior efforts of the framers of the coastal law to structure the situation in such a way – via the distribution of appointments between state and local governments – as to maximize the probability of that outcome. Likewise, Hjern *et al.* would simply take as granted that Actor A had certain resources without inquiring into the reasons s/he had them. In short, one of the most basic shortcomings of the Hjern *et al.* approach is that it takes the present distribution of preferences and resources as given, without ever inquiring into the efforts of other actors to structure the rules of the game.

Second, in a related point, Hjern *et al.* take the present participants in an implementation structure as given without examining the prior effort of various individuals to affect participation rates. For example, their networking methodology would simply have revealed that environmental groups were frequent litigants in American air pollution cases – thus neglecting the extensive efforts of drafters of the 1970 Clean Air Act to provide such groups with legal 'standing' (formal rights of intervention) to participate in such litigation.

This brings us to a third, and more fundamental, limitation with the Hjern *et al.* approach: Its failure to start from an explicit theory of the factors affecting its subject of interest. Because it relies very heavily on the perceptions and activities of participants, it is their prisoner – and therefore is unlikely to analyze the factors *indirectly* affecting their behavior or even the factors directly affecting such behavior which the participants do not recognize. Hjern *et al.* suffer from all of the limitations – as well as the advantages – of 'grounded theory' (Glaser and Strauss, 1967). Their networking methodology is a useful starting point for identifying many of the actors involved in a policy area, but it needs to be related via an explicit theory to social, economic, and legal factors which structure the perceptions, resources, and participation of those actors.

Scharpf (1978) and Thrasher (1983) have attempted to use exchange theory toward this end, but that hasn't been followed by Hjern *et al.* Likewise, Barrett and Fudge (1981) and Barrett and Hill (1984) have toyed with a number of approaches – mostly related to bargaining – but thus far haven't come close to an explicit conceptual framework. Until they do, the implicit assumptions which are guiding their data collection will remain difficult to discern.

Finally, it is worth observing that top-downers and bottom-uppers have been motivated by somewhat different concerns and thus have developed different approaches. Top-downers have been preoccupied with (a) the effectiveness of specific governmental programs and (b) the ability of elected officials to guide and constrain the behavior of civil servants and target groups. Addressing such concerns requires a careful analysis of the formally-approved objectives of elected officials, an examination of relevant performance indicators, and an analysis of the factors affecting such performance. Bottom-uppers, on the other hand, are far less preoccupied with the extent to which a formally enacted policy *decision* is carried out and much more concerned with accurately mapping the strategies of actors concerned with a policy *problem*. They are not primarily concerned with the implementation (carrying out) of a policy *per se* but rather with understanding actor interaction in a specific policy sector.

Where do we go from here?

Having identified the strengths and weaknesses of the two approaches, there are at least two strategies which can be pursued. The first is to indicate the conditions under which each is the more appropriate approach. The second is to develop one or more syntheses of the competing approaches.

Comparative advantage

The top-down approach is useful, first, in cases where there is a dominant public program in the policy area under consideration or where the analyst is solely interested in the effectiveness of *a* program. In cases like the California coastal commissions or the Open University – where a single public agency clearly dominated the field – the top-down approach is appropriate. On the other hand, in policy areas such as manpower training and employment development – which necessarily involve a multitude of public and private actors – the bottom-up approach is more appropriate. One might in fact be tempted to demarcate entire policy areas – e.g. highways, social security, income taxation – where there is a dominant public agency, but this should only be done with caution as unions and other private actors may turn out to be more important than anticipated.

On a more general note, the top-down approach is more useful in making a preliminary assessment of which approach to use: To the extent that the scores on the six conditions of effective implementation are relatively high and the investigator is primarily interested in the *mean* policy outputs and outcomes, then the top-down approach is appropriate. On the other hand, in cases where the scores on the six conditions are relatively low and one is interested in inter-local variation, then the bottom-up approach should be employed. When scores on the six conditions are moderate or mixed, the appropriate methodology depends on whether one is primarily interested in mean responses or in assessing inter-local variation. The top-down is more appropriate for the former because it focuses on the extent to which the overall system is structured/constrained. The bottom-up focuses on local implementation structures, and thus is better for assessing the dynamics of local variation. One could, of course, aggregate across numerous bottom-up studies to obtain a mean response, but this would normally be prohibitively expensive.

The top-down approach is more useful for making these preliminary assessments because of its greater theoretical development. The identification of specific variables and causal relationships makes predictions possible. On the other hand, the bottom-up approach of Hjern *et al.* (or Barrett and Fudge) has not yet developed much of a substantive theory and thus is poorly equipped to make predictions.

In summary, the top-down approach appears to have a comparative advantage in situations in which (1) there is a dominant piece of legislation structuring the situation or (2) research funds are very limited, one is primarily interested in mean responses, and the situation is structured at least moderately well. In contrast, the bottom-up approach is more appropriate in situations where (1) there is no dominant piece of legislation but rather large numbers of actors without power dependency, or (2) one is primarily interested in the dynamics of different local situations.

Syntheses

A preferred alternative to these either-or choice situations is to synthesize the best features of the two approaches. To date, there have been at least three such efforts.

The most ambitious has been the study of the implementation of programs designed to reduce sulfur dioxide emissions in several European countries directed by Peter Knoepfel and Helmut Weidner. The conceptual framework for the study was explicitly designed to be a synthesis (Knoepfel and Weidner, 1982). [. . .]

A second approach, developed by Richard Elmore (1985), attempts to combine his previous work on 'backward mapping' – one of the bottom-up classics – with what he terms 'forward mapping', essentially a top-down perspective. He argues that policy-makers need to consider both the policy instruments and other resources at their disposal (forward mapping) *and* the incentive structure of ultimate target groups (backward mapping) because program success is contingent on meshing the two. Elmore's paper is primarily concerned with aiding policy practitioners by indicating the need to use multiple perspectives in designing and implementing policies. At that very practical level, it is excellent. It does not purport, however, to provide a model of the policy process which can be used by social scientists to explain outcomes in a wide variety of settings.

The third approach, to be outlined below, explicitly attempts to develop such a general model of the policy process which combines the best features of the bottom-up and top-down approaches, while also applying them to a longer time-frame than is the case in most implementation research.

An advocacy coalition framework of policy change

One of the major contributions of Mazmanian and Sabatier (1983) was their conten-tion that the relatively short time span (4–5 years) used in most implementation studies not only led to premature judgments concerning program failure but also missed some very important features of the policy process, namely the extent of policy-oriented learning.

For example, early studies of Federal compensatory education programs (Title I of ESEA) concluded that the program was bringing about very little change because of ambiguous objectives, dubious causal theories, resistance of implementing officials, and the inability of proponents to organize at the local level (Murphy, 1973). But later studies incorporating a 10–15-year time span portrayed a fair amount of improvement on the part of both school officials and students' educational achievement (Kirst and Jung, 1982; Mazmanian and Sabatier, 1983: Chap. 6). Over time, objectives were clarified; research resulted in more adequate causal theories; and supportive constitu-encies were fostered at both the state and local levels. This suggested a process of policy learning by program proponents, as they discovered deficiencies in the existing program and then developed a series of strategies to deal with them.

While this approach did a good job of illustrating learning by proponents, its top-down assumptions made it difficult to focus equally on learning by opponents. This deficiency can be addressed, however, by incorporating bottom-uppers' techniques for ascertaining the strategies – and, by extension, the learning from experience – of a wider variety of actors concerned with a program. This points to a synthesis which combines top-down and bottom-up approaches in the analysis of policy change over periods of a decade or more.

Elements of the synthesis

The elements of such a conceptual framework are at hand. Consistent with the bottom-uppers, one needs to start from a policy *problem* or subsystem – rather than a law or other policy *decision* – and then examine the strategies employed by relevant actors in both the public and private sectors at various levels of government as they attempt to deal with the issue consistent with their objectives. The networking technique developed by Hjern *et al.* can be one of the methods for determining the actors in a subsystem, although it needs to be combined with other approaches indicating the actors who are indirectly (or even potentially) involved.

Likewise, the concerns of top-down theorists with the manner in which legal and socioeconomic factors structure behavioral options need to be incorporated into the synthesis, as do their concerns with the validity of the causal assumptions behind specific programs and strategies. This leads to a focus on (1) the effects of socio-economic (and other) changes external to the policy network/subsystem on actors' resources and strategies; (2) the attempts by various actors to manipulate the legal attributes of governmental programs in order to achieve their objectives over time; and (3) actors' efforts to improve their understanding of the magnitude of and factors affecting the problem – as well as the impacts of various policy instruments – as they learn from experience.

Attention thus shifts from policy implementation to policy change over periods of 10–20 years. The longer time span creates, however, a need to aggregate actors into a manageable number of groups if the researcher is to avoid severe information overload. After examining several options, the most useful principle of aggregation seems to be by belief system. This produces a focus on 'advocacy coalitions,' i.e. actors from various public and private organizations who share a set of beliefs and who seek to realize their common goals over time.

In short, the synthesis adopts the bottom-uppers' unit of analysis – a whole variety of public and private actors involved with a policy problem – as well as their concerns with understanding the perspectives and strategies of all major categories of actors (not simply program proponents). It then combines this starting point with top-downers' concerns with the manner in which socioeconomic conditions and legal instruments constrain behavior. It applies this synthesized perspective to the analysis of policy change over periods of a decade or more. This time-frame is required to deal with the role of policy-oriented learning – a topic identified as critical in several top-down studies, although by no means inherent to that approach. Finally, the synthesis adopts the intellectual style (or methodological perspective) of many top-downers in its willingness to utilize fairly abstract theoretical constructs and to operate from an admittedly simplified portrait of reality. It is primarily concerned with theory construction rather than with providing guidelines for practitioners or detailed portraits of particular situations.

Overview of the framework

The advocacy coalition framework starts from the premise that the most useful aggregate unit of analysis for understanding policy change in modern industrial societies is not any specific governmental organization but rather a policy subsystem, i.e. those actors from a variety of public and private organizations who are actively concerned with a policy problem or issue such as higher education or air pollution control (Heclo, 1978; Jordan and Richardson, 1983; Milward and Wamsley, 1984; Rose, 1984; Sharpe, 1985).

Figure 2 presents a general overview of the framework. On the left side are two sets of exogenous variables – the one fairly stable, the other dynamic – which affect the constraints and resources of subsystem actors. Air pollution policy, for example, is strongly affected by the nature of air quality as a collective good, by the geographical contours of air basins, and by political boundaries which are usually quite stable over time. But there are also more dynamic factors, including changes in socioeconomic conditions and in system-wide governing coalitions, which provide some of the principal sources of policy change. These are all features drawn from top-down models which 'structure' policy-making.

Within the subsystem, the framework draws heavily upon the bottom-up approach. It assumes, however, that actors can be aggregated into a number of advocacy coalitions – each composed of politicians, agency officials, interest group leaders, and intellectuals who share a set of normative and causal beliefs on core policy issues. At any particular point in time, each coalition adopts a strategy(s) envisaging one or more changes in governmental institutions perceived to further its policy objectives. Conflicting strategies from different coalitions are mediated by a third group of actors, here termed 'policy brokers,' whose principal concern is to find some reasonable compromise which will reduce intense conflict. The end result is legislation or governmental decrees establishing or modifying one or more governmental action programs at the collective choice level (Kiser and Ostrom, 1982; Page, 1985). These in turn produce policy outputs at the operational level (e.g. agency permit decisions). These outputs at the operational level, mediated by a number of other factors (most notably, the validity of the causal theory underlying the program), result in a variety of impacts on targeted problem parameters (e.g. ambient air quality), as well as side effects.

At this point the framework requires additional elements not normally central to implementation studies. Some aspects of public policy clearly change far more frequently than others. In order to get a conceptual handle on this, the framework distinguishes the *core* from the *secondary* aspects of a belief system or a governmental action program. Recall the coalitions are seeking to get their beliefs translated into governmental programs, so the two concepts can be analyzed in similar categories. The extent to which a specific program incorporates the beliefs of any single coalition is, however, an empirical question and will reflect the relative power of that coalition within the subsystem.

Table 3 represents a preliminary attempt to identify the principal topics addressed in the Deep Core, the Near Core, and the Secondary Aspects of a belief system. (Only the latter two are relevant to governmental action programs.) It suggests that coalitions

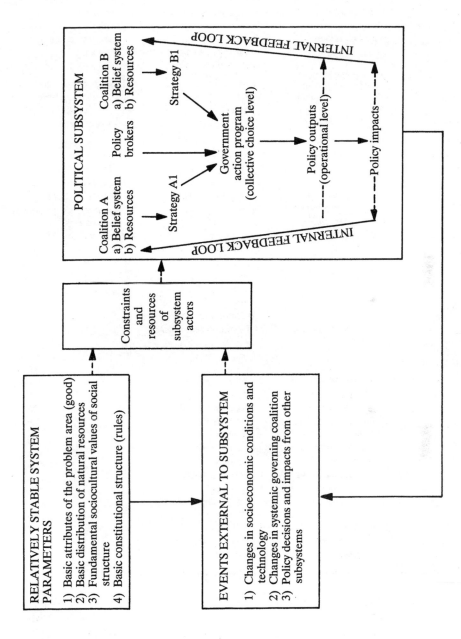

Figure 2 General overview of conceptual framework of policy change

Table 3 Structure of belief systems of policy elites[a]

	Deep (normative) Core	Near (policy) Core	Secondary Aspects
Defining characteristics	Fundamental normative and ontological axioms.	Fundamental policy positions concerning the basic strategies for achieving normative axioms of deep core.	Instrumental decisions and information searches necessary to implement core policy positions.
Susceptibility to change	Very difficult; akin to a religious conversion.	Difficult, but can occur if experience reveals serious anomalies.	Moderately easy; this is the topic of most administrative and even legislative policy-making.
Illustrative components	1) The nature of man 　　i) Inherently evil vs. socially redeemable 　　ii) Part of nature vs. dominion over nature 　　iii) Narrow egoists vs. contractarians 2) Relative priority of health, love, beauty, etc. 3) Basic criteria of distributive justice: Whose welfare counts? Relative weights of self, primary groups, all people, future generations, non-human beings, etc. 4) Ability of society to solve problems 　　i) Zero-sum competition vs. potential for mutual accommodation 　　ii) Technological optimism vs. pessimism	1) Proper scope of governmental (vs. market) activity 2) Proper distribution of authority among various units (e.g. levels) of government 3) Identification of social groups whose welfare is most threatened/critical 4) Orientation on basic policy conflicts e.g. environmental protection vs. economic development 5) Basic choices concerning policy instruments, e.g. coercion vs. inducements vs. persuasion 6) Desirability of participation by various segments of society 7) Perception of relative seriousness of this problem area	1) Most decisions concerning administrative rules, budgetary allocations, disposition of cases, statutory interpretation, and even statutory revision 2) Information concerning program performance, the seriousness of the problems, etc.

[a] The Near Core and Secondary Aspects also apply to governmental action programs.

will be very reluctant to alter their beliefs concerning core issues such as the proper scope of governmental vs. market activity; their orientation on basic policy conflicts; the relative distribution of authority among different levels of government; or their identification of social groups whose welfare is most critical. For example, federal air pollution policy in the U.S. – which essentially reflects the beliefs of the environmental coalition – accords government a very important role in this policy area; places greater priority on public health than on economic development; gives the federal government an unusually preeminent role over states and localities; and places a high priority on protecting the welfare of susceptible health populations, e.g. people suffering from emphysema. These are topics on which neither the environmental coalition nor federal law have changed very much since 1970 (Mazmanian and Sabatier, 1983: Chap. 4).

On the other hand, there has been a great deal of change in the secondary attributes of federal air pollution programs which are instrumental to achieving the core aspects. These include such topics as the appropriate deadlines for meeting particular emission standards; the relative importance of various sources of pollutants affecting air quality; the most valid methods for measuring ambient air quality; the proper enforcement budget of implementing agencies; the perceived feasibility of particular pollution control technologies; and the precise effects of pollution concentrations on specific populations. While these have all been the subject of vigorous debate, they represent rather marginal, instrumental choices within the context of core beliefs.

The framework argues that the core aspects of a governmental action program – and the relative strength of competing advocacy coalitions within a policy subsystem – will typically remain rather stable over periods of a decade or more. Major alterations in the policy core will normally be the product of changes external to the subsystem – particularly large-scale socioeconomic perturbations or changes in the systemwide governing coalition. An example of the latter would be the change in Britain from Parliaments dominated by moderate socialists and conservatives to a system dominated by Mrs Thatcher's wing of the Conservative Party with a *fundamentally* different conception of the proper scope of governmental activity.

While changes in the policy core are usually the result of external perturbations, changes in the secondary aspects of a governmental action program are often the result of policy-oriented learning by various coalitions or policy brokers. Following Heclo (1974: 306), policy-oriented learning refers to relatively enduring alterations of thought or behavioral intentions which result from experience and which are concerned with the attainment or revision of policy objectives. Policy-oriented learning involves the internal feedback loops depicted in Figure 2, as well as increased knowledge of the state of problem parameters and the factors affecting them. For example, a decade of experience and research in U.S. air pollution programs has indicated that efforts to reduce vehicle miles traveled by commuters through the use of, e.g., parking surcharges have only very modest effects on air quality, impose very substantial costs on commuters, and therefore are no longer a feasible policy option (Mazmanian and Sabatier, 1983). Since the vast majority of policy debates involve secondary aspects of a governmental action program – in part because actors realize the futility of challenging core assumptions – such learning can play an important role in policy change. In fact, a principal concern of the framework is to analyze the institutional conditions conducive to such learning and the cases in which cumulative learning may lead to changes in the policy core.

A more extensive exposition of the framework can be found in Sabatier (1986). This overview should, however, indicate how it synthesizes important elements from both top-down and bottom-up perspectives within the implementation literature. But the framework also borrows from a number of other literatures, including those on long term policy change (Heclo, 1974; Derthick, 1979; Browning *et al.*, 1985; Hogwood and Peters, 1983), coalition stability (Dodd, 1976; Hinckley, 1981), elite belief systems (Putnam, 1976), and the utilization of policy research (Weiss, 1977).

References

Aaron, Henry (1978). *Politics and the Professors*. Washington, D.C.: Brookings Institution.

Ackermann, Charbel and Steinmann, Walter (1982). 'Privatized policy making,' *European Journal of Policy Research* 10 (June): 173–85.

Alexander, Robert (1982). 'Implementation: does a literature add up to a theory?' *Journal of the American Planning Association* (Winter): 132–55.

Alterman, Rachelle (1983). 'Implementation analysis: the contours of an emerging debate,' *Journal of Planning Education and Research* 3 (Summer): 63–5.

Bardach, Eugene (1974). *The Implementation Game*. Cambridge, MA: MIT Press.

Barrett, Susan and Fudge, Colin, eds. (1981). *Policy and Action*. London: Methuen.

Barrett, Susan, Fudge, Colin and Hill, Michael (1984). 'Policy, bargaining and structure in implementation theory,' *Policy and Politics* 12: 219–40.

Berman, Paul (1978). 'The study of macro- and micro-implementation,' *Public Policy* 26: 157–84.

Berman, Paul (1980). 'Thinking about programmed and adaptive implementation,' in *Why Policies Succeed or Fail*, ed. by Helen Ingram and Dean Mann. Beverly Hills: Sage.

Berman, Paul and McLaughlin, Milbrey (1976). 'Implementation of ESEA Title I,' *Teacher College Record* 77 (Feb.).

Bowen, Elinor (1982). 'The Pressman-Wildavsky paradox,' *Journal of Public Policy* 2 (February): 1–22.

Bowman, Ann and Lester, James (1986). 'Subnational policy implementation: testing the Sabatier–Mazmanian model,' *Administration and Society*, forthcoming.

Browning, Rufus, Marshall, Dale, and Tabb, David (1981). 'Implementation and political change: sources of local variation in federal social programs,' in *Effective Policy Implementation*, ed. by D. Mazmanian and P. Sabatier. Lexington, MA: D.C. Heath.

Browning, Rufus, Marshall, Dale, and Tabb, David (1985). *Protest Is Not Enough*. Berkeley: University of California Press.

Cerych, Ladislav and Sabatier, Paul (1986). *Great Expectations and Mixed Performance: The implementation of European higher education reforms*. Stoke-on-Trent, United Kingdom: Trentham Books.

Davies, Tom and Mason, Charles (1982). 'Gazing up from the bottoms: problems of minimal response in the implementation of manpower policy,' *European Journal of Political Research* 10 (June): 143–58.

Davis, Charles (1985). 'Perceptions of hazardous waste policy issues among public and private sector administrators,' *Western Political Quarterly* 38 (Sept.): 447–63.

Derthick, Martha (1972). *New Towns In-Town*. Washington: Urban Institute.

Derthick, Martha (1979). *Policymaking for Social Security*. Washington: Brookings.

Dodd, Lawrence (1976). *Coalitions in Parliamentary Governments*. Princeton: Princeton University Press.

Downs, Anthony (1967). *Inside Bureaucracy*. Boston: Little, Brown.

Elmore, Richard (1978). 'Organizational model of social program implementation,' *Public Policy* 26 (Spring): 185–228.

Elmore, Richard (1979). 'Backward mapping,' *Political Science Quarterly* 94 (Winter): 601–16.

Elmore, Richard (1985). 'Foward and backward mapping,' in *Policy Implementation in Federal and Unitary Systems*, ed. by K. Hanf and T. Toonen. Dordrecht: Martinus Nijhoff, pp. 33–70.

Glaser, Barney and Strauss, Anselm (1967). *The Discovery of Grounded Theory*. Chicago: Aldine.

Goggin, Malcolm L. (1984). 'Book review of Implementation and Public Policy, Daniel A. Mazmanian and Paul A. Sabatier, eds,' *Publius* 14 (Fall): 159–60.

Goggin, Malcolm L. (1986). 'The "too few cases/too many variables" problem in implementation research,' *Western Political Quarterly*, forthcoming.

Goodwin, Leonard and Moen, Phyllis (1981). 'The evolution and implementation of federal welfare policy,' in *Effective Policy Implementation*, ed. by D. Mazmanian and P. Sabatier. Lexington, MA: D.C. Heath, pp. 147–68.

Hanf, Kenneth (1982). 'The implementation of regulatory policy: enforcement as bargaining,' *European Journal of Political Research* 10 (June 1982): 159–72.

Hanf, Kenneth and Scharpf, Fritz, eds. (1978). *Interorganizational Policy Making: Limits to coordination and central control*. London: Sage.

Heclo, Hugh (1974). *Social Policy in Britain and Sweden*. New Haven: Yale University Press.

Heclo, Hugh (1978). 'Issue networks and the executive establishment,' in *The New American Political System*, ed. by Anthony King. Washington, D.C.: American Enterprise Institute.

Hinckley, Barbara (1981). *Coalitions and Politics*. New York: Harcourt, Brace, Jovanovich.

Hjern, Benny (1982). 'Implementation research – the link gone missing,' *Journal of Public Policy* 2(3): 301–8.

Hjern, Benny and Porter, David (1981). 'Implementation structures: a new unit of administrative analysis,' *Organization Studies* 2: 211–27.

Hjern, Benny and Hull, Chris (1982). 'Implementation research as empirical constitutionalism,' *European Journal of Political Research* 10 (June 1982): 105–16.

Hjern, Benny and Hull, Chris (1985). 'Helping small firms grow,' unpublished book-length manuscript, Management Institut, Science Center, Berlin.

Hjern, Benny, Hanf, Kenneth and Porter, David (1978). 'Local networks of manpower training in the Federal Republic of Germany and Sweden,' in *Interorganizational Policy Making: Limits to coordination and central control*, ed. by K. Hanf and F. Scharpf. London: Sage, pp. 303–44.

Hofferbert, Richard (1974). *The Study of Public Policy*. Indianapolis: Bobbs-Merrill.

Hogwood, Bryan and Peters, G. Guy (1983). *Policy Dynamics*. New York: St Martin's.

Hull, Chris and Hjern, Benny (1982). 'Helping small firms grow,' *European Journal of Political Research* 10 (June): 187–98.

Ingram, Helen (1977) 'Policy implementation through bargaining: federal grants in aid,' *Public Policy* 25 (Fall).

Jones, Charles (1975). *Clean Air*. Pittsburgh: University of Pittsburgh Press.

Jones, Susan (1984). 'Application of a framework for implementation analysis to evaluate groundwater management policy in two New York counties,' unpublished master's thesis, Department of City and Regional Planning, University of North Carolina, Chapel Hill.

Jordan, A. G. and Richardson, J. J. (1983). 'Policy communities: the British and European political style,' *Policy Studies Journal* 11 (June): 60–315.

Kirst, Michael and Jung, Richard (1982). 'The utility of a longitudinal approach in assessing implementation: Title I, ESEA,' in *Studying Implementation*, ed. by Walter Williams. Chatham, NJ: Chatham House, pp. 119–48.

Kiser, Larry and Ostrom, Elinor (1982). 'The three worlds of action,' in *Strategies of Political Inquiry*, ed. by E. Ostrom. Beverly Hills: Sage.

Knoepfel, Peter and Weidner, Helmut (1982). 'A conceptual framework for studying implementation,' in *The Implementation of Pollution Control Programs*, ed. by Paul Downing and Kenneth Hanf. Tallahassee: Policy Sciences Program.

Lazin, Frederick (1973). 'The failure of federal enforcement of civil rights regulations in public housing, 1963–71', *Policy Sciences* 4: 263–74.

Lester, James (1986). 'Intergovernmental relations and ocean policy: marine pollution, dumping, and incineration of hazardous wastes,' in *Ocean Resources and Intergovernmental Relations*, ed. by M. Silva. Boulder: Westview.

Levin, Martin (1980). 'Conditions contributing to effective implementation and their limits,' unpublished manuscript, Brandeis University.

Lipsky, Michael (1971). 'Street level bureaucracy and the analysis of urban reform,' *Urban Affairs Quarterly* 6: 391–409.

Lowry, Ken (1985). 'Assessing the implementation of federal coastal policy,' *Journal of the American Planning Association* 51 (Summer): 288–98.

MacIntyre, Angus (1985). 'The multiple sources of statutory ambiguity,' in *Administrative Discretion and the Implementation of Public Policy*, ed. by Hibbeln and Shumavon. New York: Praeger, pp. 66–88.

Majone, Giandomenico and Wildavsky, Aaron (1978). 'Implementation as evolution,' in *Policy Studies Review Annual – 1978*, ed. by Howard Freeman. Beverly Hills: Sage.

Mazmanian, Daniel and Sabatier, Paul (1983). *Implementation and Public Policy*. Chicago: Scott Foresman and Co.

Milward, H. Brinton and Wamsley, Gary (1984). 'Policy subsystems, networks, and the tools of public management,' in *Public Policy Formation and Implementation*, ed. by Robert Eyestone. Boston: JAI Press.

Murphy, Jerome (1973). 'The education bureaucracies implement novel policy: the politics of Title I of ESEA,' in *Policy and Politics in America*, ed. by Allan Sindler. Boston: Little, Brown.

Nakamura, Robert and Smallwood, Frank (1980). *The Politics of Policy Implementation*. New York: St Martin's.

Page, Ed (1985). 'Laws as an instrument in center–local relations,' *Journal of Public Policy* 5 (2): 241–65.

Pressman, Jeffrey and Wildavsky, Aaron (1973). *Implementation*. Berkeley: University of California Press.

Putnam, Robert (1976). *The Comparative Study of Political Elites*. Englewood Cliffs: Prentice Hall.

Rose, Richard (1984). 'From government at the center to nationwide government,' in *Centre–Periphery Relations in Western Europe*, ed. by Y. Meny and V. Wright. London: George Allen and Unwin.

Sabatier, Paul (1975). 'Social movements and regulatory agencies,' *Policy Sciences* 8: 301–42.

Sabatier, Paul (1984). 'Center–periphery relations in coastal zone regulation,' unpublished manuscript, University of California, Davis.

Sabatier, Paul (1986). 'Policy analysis, policy-oriented learning and policy change: an advocacy coalition framework,' Manuscript submitted to *Knowledge: Creation, Diffusion, Utilization*.

Sabatier, Paul and Klosterman, Barbara (1981). 'A comparative analysis of policy implementation under different statutory regimes,' in *Effective Policy Implementation*, ed. by D. Mazmanian and P. Sabatier. Lexington, MA: D.C. Heath, pp. 169–206.

Sabatier, Paul and Mazmanian, Daniel (1979). 'The conditions of effective implementation,' *Policy Analysis* 5 (Fall): 481–504.

Sabatier, Paul and Mazmanian, Daniel (1980). 'A framework of analysis,' *Policy Studies Journal* 8: 538–60.

Sabatier, Paul and Mazmanian, Daniel (1983a). 'Policy implementation,' in *Encyclopedia of Policy Studies*, ed. by Start Nagel. N.Y.: Marcel Dekker, pp. 143–69.

Sabatier, Paul and Mazmanian, Daniel (1983b). *Can Regulation Work? The implementation of the 1972 California Coastal Initiative*. N.Y.: Plenum.

Scharpf, Fritz (1978). 'Interorganizational policy studies,' in *Interorganizational Policy-Making*, ed. by K. Hanf and F. Scharpf. London: Sage, pp. 345–70.

Sharpe, L. J. (1985). 'Central coordination and the policy network,' *Political Studies* 33: 361-81.

Thrasher, Michael (1983). 'Exchange networks and implementation', *Policy and Politics* 11: 375–91.

Van Meter, Donald and Van Horn, Carl (1975). 'The policy implementation process: a conceptual framework', *Administration and Society* 6 (Feb.): 445–88.

Weatherly, Richard and Lipsky, Michael (1977). 'Street level bureaucrats and institutional innovation: implementing special-education reform,' *Harvard Educational Review* 47 (2): 171–97.

Weiss, Carol, ed. (1977). *Using Social Research in Public Policy Making*. Lexington, MA: D.C. Heath.

Wittrock, Bjorn *et al.* (1982). 'Implementation beyond hierarchy: Swedish energy research policy,' *European Journal of Political Research* 10 (June): 131–43.

Yin, Robert (1980). *Studying the Implementation of Public Programs*. Boulder: Solar Energy Research Institute.

Implementation, accountability and trust

Jan-Erik Lane

Abstract. According to standard dictionaries 'implementation' is ambiguous, as it means either the act of implementing or the state of having been implemented. This duality has characterized implementation theory, which models the process of implementation in different ways, each presumably conducive to successful implementation as an outcome. It is argued that one model of implementation as a process is most suitable for successful implementation meaning the fulfilment of policy objectives by programme technologies. However, there is no necessary relation between some model of implementation processes and implementation as an outcome. Public policies may be implemented in various ways and some policies do fail implementation or result only in political symbolism, but that does not warrant generalizations about the impossibility of successful implementation or create a case for some special model of implementation as hierarchical authority, or as evolution, learning or coalition. Basic to implementation is accountability, which restricts the amount of trust that gives autonomy to those responsible for the implementation of policies. The conceptualization of implementation as a combination of accountability and trust points in a new direction for the analysis of policy cycles.

Paul A. Sabatier, a pioneer in implementation analysis, raises some fundamental questions about the nature of implementation in a recent article which reviews the present state of implementation theory (Sabatier 1986). Although Sabatier's analysis of the two competing models of implementaton – top-down versus bottom-up implementation – as well as his attempt to launch a third model – a kind of coalition model – is perceptive and challenging, it may be argued that it misses a more basic problem concerning the nature of public policy implementation. As long as the concept of implementation remains unexplicated, any theory about the conditions for successful implementation will remain ambiguous. It must be recognized that modelling the process of executing public policies – the implementation process – is

ᐧ J.-E. Lane, 'Implementation, accountability and trust', *European Journal of Political* ᐧh, **15** (5), 1987, pp. 527–46.

different from evaluating the extent to which objectives have been accomplished – the implementation assessment. My argument is a theoretical one, but it may clarify some of the problems surrounding implementation analysis. It is based on the distinction between implementation as an outcome and implementation as a process.

Concept of implementation

The concept of implementation is characterized by a problematic structure. *Webster's Dictionary* (1971) states that 'implementation' means either the act of implementing or the state of having been implemented; it presents the following key words for 'implement':

> to carry out: accomplish, fulfill; to give practical effect to and ensure of actual fulfillment by concrete measures; to provide instruments or means of practical expression for . . .

'To carry out something' or 'to accomplish something' may sound intelligible and require little explication. A formal definition might be:

DEF. Implementation = F (Intention, Output, Outcome)   (1)

where implementation refers to the bringing about, by means of outputs, of outcomes that are congruent with the original intention(s).

It is readily seen that 'implementation' has a double meaning: 'to give practical effect to' or *execution* on the one hand, and 'fulfil' or *accomplishment* on the other. A policy that is executed need not result in the accomplishment of its objectives. Thus, we have a basic ambiguity in the notion of implementation: implementation as an end state or policy achievement, and implementation as a process or policy execution. *The Shorter Oxford English Dictionary* (1965) notes the same double meaning: 'to complete, perform; to fulfil'. The performance of activities need not lead to the fulfilment of objectives.

Implementation analysis could be considered a development of public administration whereby the execution of policies is expedited by the addition of evaluation research. Implementation analysis not only looks at what happens after political reforms have been enacted because implementation analysis goes beyond the focus on programme execution in public administration as it was traditionally conceived. The concept of implementation implies assessment; it is made by the actors involved in the implementation process, and one basic task of the implementation analyst is to evaluate the implementation. Given the ends and means of the policy, implementation analysis cannot be confined to a statement of what happens afterwards. The analyst may use the tools of evaluation research in order to arrive at an implementation judgement of the extent of successful implementation, the *first* major focus in implementation analysis. Success or failure are not the only relevant properties of the implementation of public policies. The process of enforcing a policy has its own logic, which is the *second* major focus of the implementation analyst. Aspects of the implementation process other than the accomplishment of the policy objectives that the analyst is interested in include: the strategies and tactics employed by various parties to the implementation game, the mechanism of delay as a decision parameter, the variety of motives among the participating actors, and the need for coalition building and fixing the game.

Implementation not only requires a state of affairs in which there is a policy objective and an outcome (or several objectives and outcomes) since, in addition, the concept of implementation implies that these two entities – objective and outcome – satisfy two different relationships: the causal function and the accomplishment function. Two ideas are fundamental to the concept of implementation: that the policy programme is the output that brings about the outcomes in such a way that the latter accomplish the objectives of the policy.

Implementation assessment focuses on the operation of a public policy and its consequences. It includes logically three separate activities: (a) clarification of the objectives involved (the goal function); (b) statement of the relationship between outputs and outcomes in terms of causal effectiveness (the causal function); and (c) clarification of the relation between objectives and outcomes in order to affirm the extent of goal achievement (the accomplishment function). Each of the three tasks presents its own peculiar problems. Together they imply that it may be difficult to judge the effectiveness of implementation.

The ends and means – the intentions – of policies are formulated and enacted by various kinds of actors in the political process. What is an end or a means is an intentional object to some actor, which means that any definition of implementation must specify the actors involved in the process. These actors may be divided into two sets, the formulators and the implementors. The idea is implicit in implementalist theory that the actors who decide on policy are different from the actors who are responsible for the implementation of policy. Though this is far from always the case, the implementation process is built up around an asymmetric relationship between the formulators of policy and the implementors of policy. The formulators may not be the initiators of policy; be that as it may, the theory of implementation assumes that public policy becomes a legitimate concern for implementors once it has been decided upon in formally defined ways.

By developing the original implementation formula we are now at a stage where a more powerful and complex concept of implementation may be introduced:

DEF. Implementation = F (Policy, Outcome, Formulator, Implementor,
Initiator, Time)   (2)

Suppose one asks about a policy whether it has been implemented. Then one needs information about the extent of *congruence* between policy objectives and outcomes, but that is not enough. In addition, there has to be a decision concerning the time span that may pass before an implementation judgement can be said to be neither premature nor belated. When is it appropriate to ask about a programme whether its objectives have been realized?

This is all about the concept of implementation. When we move to the theory of implementation processes, the conflicting views crop up. It is easier to introduce a formal concept of implementation than to model the evolving implementation process.

The implementation process

It does not follow that implementation exists just because it is possible to state what implementation would amount to if it came about. We could possess a clear and articulate concept of implementation but fail to identify cases of implementation. Actually, there are different arguments in the literature to the effect that implementation or successful implementation does not exist, because each and every process of impementation fails in its purpose. If implementation is impossible or difficult, it is not because we lack an adequate concept of implementation but because the relationship between policy and action is such that processes of implementation have a number of properties that are not conducive to the occurrence of successful implementation.

Let us focus upon the various models of implementation as a process. According to Sabatier these models may be classified as either top-down or bottom-up models of implementation. Although this distinction is essential in theories of implementation, it is certainly not the only or fundamental demarcation line between alternative approaches. Nor is it obvious that the top-down and bottom-up models of implementation were developed in the historical sequence that Sabatier describes, as the importance of the various versions of the Pressman and Wildavsky volume *Implementation* (1973; 1984) is underestimated.

Implementation as perfect administration

Hood (1976) ventures to suggest some hypotheses about what type of implementation process would 'produce perfect policy implementation' (1976: 6). Such a process would satisfy the conditions of 'perfect administration', listed as a unitary administrative system with a single line of authority, enforcement of uniform rules or objectives, a set of clear and authoritative objectives implementable on the basis of perfect obedience or perfect administrative control, perfect coordination and perfect information within and between administrative units, absence of time pressure, unlimited material resources for tackling the problem, and unambiguous overall objectives and perfect political acceptability of the policies pursued (1976: 6–8).

The model of perfect administration suggested by Hood is intended as an *ideal-type* construct instrumental in finding what went wrong in actually occurring processes of implementation failure (Hood 1976: 190–207). It is thus pointless to criticize the model for stating unrealistic assumptions. What is questionable is not the extent to which a concrete implementation process fulfils the model of perfect administration, but the hypotheses about the conditions conducive to successful implementation.

The model approaches implementation from the narrow focus of the concept of authority, as the characteristics of authority relations – hierarchy, obedience, control and perfect coordination – are viewed as the mechanism for the accomplishment of successful implementation. It is true that it has been argued that a basic explanation for failures in national government policy is to be found in the fact that the national government may have too little authority (Derthick 1972; Murphy 1971).

However, other empirical work on how implementation comes about has resulted in a different finding, viz. that mechanisms more symmetrical in nature – such as exchange, bargaining and negotiation – are more germane to the implementation process than authority and its characteristics (Barrett and Fudge 1981). These mechanisms for the implementation of policy are as important as structure of authority, if the work of Bardach (1977) is consulted. Both types of mechanisms for carrying out collective action are vulnerable to the complexity of joint action and the expression of resistance to change, resulting in delays (Pressman and Wildavsky 1973: 87–124).

It is questionable whether the model conditions listed really are conducive to perfect implementation. If no actual implementation processes satisfy the model, then maybe it is the model which is imperfect rather than the implementation that fails.

Implementation as policy management

It may be asked more generally what the *necessary* and *sufficient conditions* for successful implementation are. The answer to this problem will depend upon the state of implementation theory. A theory of an implementation process may imply the search for guidelines for successful implementation. Sabatier and Mazmanian (1979) offer a theory of the sufficient conditions for successful implementation. This task in implementation analysis goes beyond what social impact analysis (SIA) and evaluation research (ER) are up to, because it asks not only if policy objectives have been accomplished, but also what management changes are conducive to policy improvement or implementation. Sabatier and Mazmanian state:

> The program is based on a sound theory relating changes in target group behaviors to the achievement of the desired end-state (objectives). The statute (or other basic policy decision) contains unambiguous policy directives and structures the implementation process so as to maximize the likelihood that target groups will perform as desired. The leaders of the implementing agencies possess substantial managerial and political skill and are committed to statutory goals. The program is actively suported by organized constituency groups and by few key legislators (or the chief executive) throughout the implementation process, with the courts being neutral or supportive. The relative priority of statutory objectives is not significantly undermined over time by the emergence of conflicting public policies or by changes in relevant socioeconomic conditions that undermine the statute's 'technical' theory or poitical support. (Sabatier and Mazmanian 1979: 484–5)

The listing of these presumed sufficient conditions for successful implementation does identify crucial factors that affect policy accomplishment: technology, unambiguity of objectives, skill, support and consensus. However, it could be argued that it begs the question of what a 'sound' policy technology is. Moreover, what is 'substantial' policy skill and 'enough' policy support? And when is a policy 'significantly' undermined by conflict?

If the values of such crucial parameters in the policy implementation process are not specified, listing sufficient conditions may be mere empty tautology. The first Sabatier theory of the nature of the implementation process bypasses findings from the study of processes of implementation: if implementation means interaction between objectives and outcomes, if implementation is a process whereby objectives are redefined and outcomes are reinterpreted, and if implementation is a decision game requiring coalition formation, then it may very well be that the conditions put forward by Sabatier and Mazmanian are not to the point, because they model the policy process too rationally and top-down (May and Wildavsky 1979).

Implementation as evolution

The literature on implementation processes has cast doubt on the applicability of the naive concept of implementation: decide on the goals, find the means and bring about the outcomes. It is argued that the dynamic properties of implementation processes negate such a decision analysis.

Implementation is different from the simple execution of policies; implementation analysis combines the traditional public administration focus upon execution with the emerging interest in evaluation methodology (SIA and ER). If implementation is more than execution, then policy objectives must be determined in order to make evaluation possible. Thus, the concept of implementation implies that objectives be differentiated from outcomes. If the concept of a process of implementation implies the opposite, then we end up in a paradox: the concept of implementation cannot be applied because the concept of a process of implementation denies it.

Wildavsky has introduced the theory of a process of implementation as necessarily resulting not in implementation but in evolution:

> Implementation is evolution. Since it takes place in a world we never made, we are usually right in the middle of the process, with events having occurred before and (we hope) continuing afterward. At each point we must cope with new circumstances that allow us to actualize different potentials in whatever policy ideas we are implementing. (Majone and Wildavsky 1978: 114)

If implementation processes result in the redefinition of objectives and the reinterpretation of outcomes, then how could there be implementation? The evolutionary conception of implementation implies that implementation processes may not be neatly separated from stages of policy formulation mingling objectives and outcomes. It also implies that implementation is endless: 'Implementation will always be evolutionary; it will inevitably reformulate as well as carry out policy' (Majone and Wildavsky 1978: 116).

It devolves upon the implementation analyst to differentiate between policies: some policies may be more susceptible to implementation than others. A promising line to follow in implementation analysis may lie in attempting to identify such criteria: obviously, policies that do not have articulate objectives attached to them or whose objectives change rapidly would not be very interesting for the implementation analyst.

It is argued that there has to be a process of redefinition as policy failure is inevitable: 'Unless a policy matter is narrow and uninteresting (i.e. preprogrammed) the policy will never be able to contain its own consequences' (Majone and Wildavsky 1978: 116). This is an empirical argument that is open to refutation pending a major survey of programme accomplishments, to see whether it is possible to arrive at a consensus as to what is an interesting programme, and whether a particular programme really has attained its policy objectives. Is the Wildavsky generalization true of each and every implementation of innovations and new programmes?

Implementation as learning

If implementation is continuous and never-ending, then maybe there is some rationale behind this, other than the implications of complexity that objectives become transformed and technologies need revision. Perhaps there are some positive unintended functions in the fact that implementation is evolution?

Wildavsky has outlined yet another interesting interpretation of the nature of the implementation process (Browne and Wildavsky 1983). Implementation is modelled as an endless learning process where the implementors through continuous search processes come up with improved goal functions and more reliable programme technologies. There is no natural end to the process of policy implementation because each stage means an improvement in relation to earlier stages, so that over time the original objectives are bound to become transformed and the initial means replaced. There is the claim that:

> Implementation, rather than being a static subject, its ends safely tucked within the prescribed means, needs to become dynamic, with implementors learning how to overcome unforeseen obstacles. These obstacles (lack of knowledge, power, etc.) cannot be entirely assumed away. A prospective, anticipatory view of implementation concentrates on designing policies in advance so they are less likely to fail. Its opposite, a retrospective view, emphasizes the ability to cope after things break down. In our evolutionary (or learning) view of implementation – implementation as mutual adaptation – a little anticipation and a lot of resilience go a long way. (Browne and Wildavsky 1984: 230)

The theory that implementation is learning may be regarded as an optimistic explanation of the hypothesis that implementation is evolution. The kind of implementation process conceived of in the various versions of a top-down approach – naive implementation, perfect administration (Hood 1976), a hierarchical model (Vedung 1986), conditions for successful implementation (Sabatier 1986) – is suboptimal.

There is an objection that may be raised against the elaborate theory of implementation as evolution. Public policy implementation takes place under the norm of responsibility and accountability. The strong institutionalization of this norm in public administration implies that implementors may be held responsible for their implementation actions and their implementation outcomes. But how could there be accountability if implementation is evolutionary learning? Public policy failure and implementation errors would be both inevitable and self-correctable. Faced with unsuccessful implementation, each and every implementor could simply refer to the fact that things will shape up in the long run as a result of ongoing learning. Why blame people when they will learn tomorrow how successful implementation is to be done?

Implementation as implementation structures

If implementation appears to be troublesome from a top-down perspective, then what are the prospects of a bottom-up perspective? The events constituting a process of implementation are typically approached as pieces forming a whole. What is the nature of such wholes? First, there is a demarcation problem – how to separate what is part of an implementation process from what is not. Second, we have an identification problem – what are the basic pieces of a process of implementation. We need an answer to the identification problem to solve the demarcation problem. Hjern and Porter (1981) suggest solutions to these two problems. They state: 'An implementation structure is comprised of subsets of members within organizations which view a programme as their primary (or an instrumentally important) interest' (Hjern and Porter 1981: 216). This definition of an implementation structure has a fundamentally phenomenological tone, because what ties a set of actors together in an implementation structure is their attitude towards a programme.

The concept of an implementation structure raises some questions. Obviously, an implementation structure consists of sets of actors, but which sets of actors constitute one and only one implementation structure? Is it enough that these actors are members of organizations and have a 'primary interest' – whatever that is – in a programme? Is it not necessary for people who have a 'primary' interest in a policy also to wish or attempt to put it into effect? Could one not conceive of an implementation structure that includes actors with varying interests – even opposing ones – in relation to a programme, which they interpret differently?

The phenomenological approach to implementation structures follows from an emphasis on properties of processes of implementation other than those of the top-down perspective: organizational complexity, self-selection of participants, multiplicity of goals and motives, local discretion. Yet, if a process of implementation covers a longer time span, then it may be necessary to lay down objective criteria for demarcating who is and who is not part of an implementation structure.

Hjern and Porter also discuss the identification problem in the following way:

> Implementation structures are not organizations. They are composed of parts of many organizations; organizations are composed of parts of many programmes. As analytic constructs, implementation structures are conceptualized to identify the units of purposive action which implement programmes. They are 'phenomenological administrative units', partly defined by their participating members. (1981: 222)

The description of implementation structures as comprising units that implement programmes is, of course, of little help, as it is circular. The distinction between concrete and abstract units is more promising, as it breaks with the traditional idea of a single bureaucracy by itself implementing a policy. However, if the elements of an implementation structure are identified as parts of organizations that are not themselves an organization, then it is strange to read about failures 'to identify implementation structures as administrative entities distinct from organizations' (Hjern and Porter 1981: 216).

Either an implementation structure is a construct, simply a 'unit for administrative analysis', or 'implementation structures are administrative entities' (1981: 219); it cannot be both. The concept of an implementation structure is relevant for the analysis of implementation processes, but one has to be aware of the fallacy of reification or misplaced concreteness. Although it is not necessary to define 'implementation structure' phenomenologically, the set of initiators, formulators and implementors is best seen as a unit for administrative analysis, not as an administrative entity. If it is problematic to identify an implementation structure, then it is no wonder that implementation itself is typically described as difficult.

Implementation as outcomes

It may well be argued that perfect coordination, unitary administrative structure and perfect political acceptability do not ensure successful implementation. These model assumptions are connected more with a naive interpretation of the concept of implementation than with the evaluation of empirical evidence concerning processes of implementation. Fudge and Barrett state:

> Part of the literature we reviewed suggests that control over policy execution or the ability to ensure compliance with policy objectives is a key factor determining the success or failure of the policy . . . However, if implementation is seen as 'getting something done', then performance rather than conformance is the main objective and compromise a means of achieving it (Barrett and Fudge 1981: 258).

This assumes that a theory of the implementation process follows from a particular concept of implementation. If implementation is not 'putting policy into effect', Fudge and Barrett state, then: 'The emphasis . . . shifts away from a master/subordinate relationship to one where policy-makers and implementors are more equal and the interaction between them becomes the focus for study' (1981: 258). However, one may object that the concept of implementation and the concept of an implementation process should be kept separate analytically. Why could not organization complexity or autonomy, just like exchange and negotiation, be conducive to or compatible with implementation as 'putting a policy into effect', just as it could be the case that the perfect administration model may only achieve a state describable as 'getting something done'? Stating a definition of 'implementation' should be a neutral task in relation to the problem of finding what factors are conducive to successful implementation. It is one problem to analyze what must obtain in order to apply the concept of implementation, and quite another to state a model of how implementation – in particular successful implementation – comes about. Perhaps successful implementation depends on the right approach being adopted by the policy-makers and implementors?

Implementation as perspective

Williams (1980) argues strongly in favour of taking such a perspective. What does it amount to? Williams states succinctly:

> The basic need is for a decision making rationale and framework to shape choices that will orient social program organizations toward better field performance. The recommended decision framework for building action in social service delivery programs, I label the implementation perspective. (Williams 1980: 4–5)

Is the implementation perspective some kind of practical science of administration, a body of knowledge that policy-makers and implementors could draw upon as they approach the implementaton of policies? For Williams the implementation perspective is the perspective of the implementation practitioners, not that of the implementation theoretician:

> The implementation perspective will force a particular agency to ask hard questions about its *own* underlying commitment and capacity. At basic issue is whether the agency can alter its orientation and style of decision making to develop the resources and the organizational structure needed for *implementing* the implementation perspective. (1980: 101)

Williams' basic idea concerns the implementing of an implementation perspective and he argues that it is difficult for an organization to carry out (implement) an ambition to implement an implementation perspective – introducing an implementation perspective seems to result in an infinite process of implementing implementations.

However, it does not follow from the fact that actors are participating in something they label an 'implementation process' that implementation is really going on. As several implementation studies have testified, actors may execute policies believing that their actions will eventually bring about implementation, but they may be wrong. In order to state the extent to which an implementation perspective meets with successful implementation there must be a different implementation perspective, that of the theoretician.

Just as implementation is the putting into effect of a policy bringing about outcomes that are congruent with the objectives, implementation itself – i.e., successful implementation – may be regarded by policy-makers as an objective to be implemented. This is the implementation perspective of Williams (1976: 280–2). It is not infallible. Thus, the fact that an organization implementing programmes has an implementation perspective does not dispense with an examination of the extent to which the implementation perspective results in actual implementation or the extent to which the assessment made in an implementation perspective is correct.

Implementation as political symbolism

There is an interesting argument that highlights the use of an implementation process itself as a strategic target for political action. Fudge and Barrett state that an implementation perspective cannot be taken for granted:

> In this sense policy may become a substitute for action, to demonstrate that something is being done without actually tackling the real problem . . . governments or policy-makers wish to be seen to be responsive without necessarily really wanting to take responsibility for intervention. Equally, policy-makers wish to be seen as powerful. Symbolic policy also serves to avoid tackling the real issue of attempting to change the 'negotiated order' or upsetting powerful groups which might show up only too clearly the limits of the policy-makers' power. (1981: 276)

An insight gained from studies of implementation processes is not only that the implementors may resist change or approach both objectives and programme in terms of their own interpretation, but also that the policy-makers may find it necessary or advantageous to neglect policy execution.

The symbolic argument is often backed by statements to the effect that the policy process – the initiation, enactment and implementation of policies – is typically characterized by uncertainty, vagueness, complexity, conflict and pseudo-actions. Actually, the hypothesis that implementation is symbolism may be regarded as an application of the more general organizational theory of garbage can processes (March and Olsen 1976). Implementation processes are no doubt susceptible to the dangers of running into organized anarchy: confused goals, poor programme technologies, and fluid organizational participation. The strength of the garbage can model is to present a beautiful way of modelling what goes on when foolishness strikes organizations. However, how prevalent is organized anarchy in implementation processes?

Two reminders are not out of place here: The fact that a process of implementation exhibits political symbolism does not preclude the applicability of the concept of implementation; goals may be accomplished because they were intertwined with other goals, combined with pseudopolitical behaviour as well as executed on the basis of extensive uncertainty among the participants. The extent to which each and every implementation process has more or fewer symbolic elements, and what the consequences are for the possibility of goal accomplishment is an entirely empirical question. If all goals and all programmes are the result of pseudo-politics, then imple-mentation is indeed impossible, but this is hardly necessarily the case.

Implementation as coalition

Sabatier, once an adherent of some version of the top-down model of implementation, argues in an innovative way that the only way to develop implementation theory is to combine some aspects of the top-down model and the bottom-up model (Sabatier 1986). Implementation process consist of so-called advocacy coalitions: 'actors from various public and private organizations who share a set of beliefs and who seek to realize their common goals over time'. This new hybrid model is derived from two sources, the policy network framework (Richardson and Jordan 1979, Sharpe 1985) and the hypothesis that implementation is basically learning (Browne and Wildavsky 1983). Sabatier states:

> It assumes . . . that actors can be aggregated into a number of advocacy coalitions – each composed of politicians, agency officials, interest group leaders, and intellectuals who share a set of normative and causal beliefs on core policy issues. At any particular point in time, each coalition adopts a strategy(s) envisaging one or more changes in governmental institutions perceived to further its policy objectives . . . The end result is legislation or governmental decrees establishing or modifying one or more governmental action programs at the collective choice level. (1986: 25)

The new Sabatier theory very much seems to focus on earlier stages of the implementation process in contrast to his earlier top-down model. It may even be questioned if it is not more of a model of the general policy process, especially the policy enactment phase. However, Sabatier offers some clues to what the new theory of implementation means for the implementation process:

> These outputs at the operational level mediated by a number of other factors (most notably, the validity of the causal theory underlying the program), result in a variety of impacts on targeted problem parameters, as well as side effects. (Sabatier 1986: 26)

How can we be sure of this? Are we to interpret this as if any coalition of implementors – private and public – are bound to produce outputs that result in successful implementation? Maybe the effects on targets are dysfunctional?

The other component of the new theory of implementation is the emphasis on long-term learning in these advocacy coalitions. A distinction is made between the core and the secondary aspects of policy, where learning refers to the secondary aspects:

> While changes in the policy core are usually the result of external perturbations, changes in the secondary aspects of a governmental action program are often the result of policy-oriented learning by various coalitions or policy brokers. (Sabatier 1986: 27)

If implementation is to be understood as a long-term process where policy coalitions interact and learn about programme technologies and programme outcomes, then perhaps implementation is everything? Why is there this need for more learning? Obviously, because implementation does not work. But is this always a function of a lack of learning which benevolent coalitions may undo? The missing element in the new Sabatier theory seems to be implementation itself, what it is and how it comes about.

Simply having policy coalitions does not produce implementation, let alone successful implementation. Actually, some of the lessons from the implementation literature indicate that too many actors or too many coalitions may block the implementation process. And how can we ever make beneficial assumptions about the probability that so-called policy-brokers will make peace between and within so-called policy coalitions? Sabatier seems to say that if there is a policy coalition and its participants try hard to learn over a number of years, then there will be eufunctional outcomes. Perhaps but perhaps not.

Implementation as responsibility and trust

Obviously, an implementor gives practical effect to a policy by taking action in relation to the objectives of the policy. Hopefully, the implementor is sooner or later confronted with a set of outcomes that are positively relevant to the realization of the objectives. If these outcomes are congruent with the objectives, then there will be successful implementation. If the set of outcomes is related to the set of objectives in such a way that to each objective there is a corresponding outcome and vice versa – a one-to-one relationship – then we have policy accomplishment *par préférence*. But this is only theory. In actual practice objectives do not always find their outcomes, and there are outcomes that lack objectives. Outcomes have to be interpreted in terms of the objectives; one objective may be partly satisfied by several different outcomes, or it may be satisfied by one outcome but be in opposition to another. If a policy contains a number of goals – ends and means concerning various policy aspects – some of these goals may find their outcomes, whereas others may confront outcomes that are contrary to these objectives.

A judgement about implementation is not something that is mechanical. It depends on how the environment in which implementation takes place is interpreted. If a policy is only partly implementable from the very beginning, then maybe this fact has to be added to the evaluation. Implementation analysis could require evaluation criteria that are not strictly intersubjective. Whether a goal has been achieved or not depends on how the goal and the outcomes are perceived by the actors involved in the implementation process. Whether there is policy success or policy failure depends on how the actors perceive the environment and judge the implementability of the policy or the means to be employed. What is successful implementation to one group is failure to another because these groups perceive the ends, the means and the outcomes differently. There is no simple solution to these problems, and they all pertain to implementation as policy accomplishment or the extent to which objectives meet their outcomes independently of how the process of implementation is structured.

The first aspect of implementation is the relation between objectives and outcome – *the responsibility side*. The implementation of public policies takes place under an accountability norm which restricts the putting into effect of the public programmes. Political accountability and administrative as well as professional responsibility is impossible without the notion of implementation of public policy. If it is not possible to evaluate the extent to which objectives and outcomes match, then public accountability is meaningless. The fact that objectives sometimes do not find their outcomes or that outcomes sometimes cannot find their objectives does not imply that accountability is impossible. Implementation, according to this aspect, is simply the match between objectives and outcomes, perfect implementation being a perfect match as it were. In whatever way implementation takes place, it is always valid to inquire into the extent to which objectives have been accomplished and the degree to which outcomes have occurred that work against the objectives. This is the basis for judging the accountability of implementors and the responsibility of politicians and officials.

There are different arguments in the literature to the effect that implementation or successful implementation does not exist, because each and every process of implementation fails in its purpose. If implementation is impossible or difficult, it is not because we lack an adequate concept of implementation but because the relationship between policy and action is such that processes of implementation have a number of properties that are not conducive to the occurrence of successful implementation. If successful implementation is always impossible, then how about responsibility?

The second aspect of implementation refers to the process of putting policies into effect –*the trust side*. Implementation in a democratic system of government rests upon the public power entrusted to politicians and public officials, whether administrators or professionals. Politicians and officials are supposed to deliver on policies; this is the basic restriction on the degrees of freedom of decision-makers and implementors in relation to their principals, the citizens. How implementation is to be carried out is a task for the implementors, for which they are to be held accountable but where autonomy is vital. Without space for independent action the implementors cannot make use of their capacity to make judgements about what means are conducive to the ends, and adapt in relation to environmental exigencies securing flexibility. However, complete autonomy on the part of the implementors would mean a total absence of restrictions on the behaviour of the implementors so negating the fundamental accountability nature of the interaction between citizens and implementors. On the other hand, too many restrictions following a distrust in the implementors would jeopardize the possibility of successful implementation as it is impossible to outline once and for all a detailed plan as to how objectives are to be accomplished. Trust is basic to the implementation process, but this does not do away with the responsibility side of implementation.

Top-down models overemphasize the responsibility side, trying to nail down the inherent uncertainties of implementation processes in accordance with a firm plan or an outlined structure of control. Bottom-up models underline the trust side to much too high an extent in an attempt to safeguard as many degrees of freedom as possible to the implementor as a tool for handling the uncertainties by flexibility and learning. If responsibility is stressed unduly, then there will be too many restrictions on the implementors in the choice of alternative technologies for the accomplishment of objectives. On the other hand, if trust is the sole basis of the activities of the implementors, then there will be too few restrictions on the implementors, allowing even the replacement of the original objectives by new goals.

An implementation process is a combination of responsibility and trust both in the relation between citizens and the public sector in general and in the relation between politicians and officials. Without the notion of *implementation as policy accomplishment* there is no basis for evaluating policies and holding politicians, administrators and professionals accountable. On the other hand, *implementation as policy execution* rests upon trust or a certain amount of degrees of freedom for politicians and implementors to make choices about alternative means for the accomplishment of goals.

There is no single model of policy execution that will guarantee policy accomplishment. Implementation theory has thus far been the search for some pattern or way of structuring the process of implementation in such a manner that there will be a high probability of policy accomplishment. This has resulted in a controversy between those who believe in control, planning and hierarchy on the one hand, and on the other those who believe in spontaneity, learning and adaptation as problem-solving techniques. A reorientation of implementation theory would be to inquire into how accountability is to be upheld in the implementation of policies and how much trust is in agreement with the requirement of accountability.

The logic of the dynamics of implementation forces the analysis to take different types of implementation processes into account: continuous versus step-wise implementation, repeated versus unique implementation, innovation implementation versus maintenance implementation, and short-span versus long-term implementation. Processes of implementation may not fit a simple notion of the implementation process as the unique continuous implementation of a social innovation in a short span of time. The distinction between continuous and step-wise implementation processes alerts the implementation analyst to the possibility of suboptimization. A policy may comprise a number of subgoals which may only be implemented in a discrete fashion due to the interdependencies among the goals; once one subgoal has been implemented, another subgoal may be implemented, and so on. The time distinction draws attention to the fact that some programmes are commitments for long periods of time. The fact that such programmes require a substantial evolution over time does not necessarily imply that their objectives must change and that accountability is impossible; premature assessments about policy accomplishment are likely if the time dimension is neglected.

Programmes to be implemented are not all of one kind. Programmes may be approached differently depending on whether they are about to be initiated or in the process of consolidation and maintenance. Consider the differences between doing an implementation analysis of a standard programme for the surveillance of traffic rules and the unique programme to start a new university. The goals with regard to the former may be so apparent that they are trivial, while in the latter case they may be so complex that they contain goal conflicts and unrealistic goals. In the former case we have standard operating procedures which are oriented towards the maintenance of certain states whereas in the latter the programme offers innovation and social experiment. It may be the case that a programme that calls for repeated maintenance implementation has to be evaluated differently fom a programme that calls for major innovation, where the goals may be changed and the outputs revised. Also, it is pertinent to examine the point of time at which an innovative programme is redefined into a consolidating programme calling for an implementation analysis of how the accomplishments already made are being maintained.

The distinction between implementation as end state and as process is relevant when one is aware of the variety of implementation phenomena. The concept of implementation is suitable for the detection of goal changes, programme redefinition, discrepancies between innovation objectives and consolidation goals, short-term goals and long-term objectives – phenomena that the equation of implementation as evolution, learning, perspective or coalition interprets in a manner which makes accountability in implementation virtually impractical.

Conclusion

Sabatier has made the first attempt to integrate two of the major schools in implementation theory. It is interesting reading, highly relevant to coming to grips with the fundamental problems of implementation in order to escape the stalemate between the top-down approach and the bottom-up approach. The solution offered is to make implementation almost indistinguishable from the general policy cycle and identifying implementation with the learning over time that takes place in groups that have an interest in policy-making.

Implementation, all dictionaries tell us, is the accomplishment of objectives. There is no cause for controversy here. What is contested in theories about implementation is the nature of the implementation process. How are the public sector actors to go about successful implementation? Acording to one line of argument there can be no successful implementation because the whole notion of implementation rests upon the idea of the classical public administration model which is not suitable for implementation problems in the era of big government. Another line of argument suggests that implementation cannot take place because all policy processes constitute an unpredictable web of events as parts of an evolutionary process that refuses any specific goals or outcomes. The third mode of reasoning about implementation is to focus on actual programmes and outcomes at the street level. Implementation is what takes place at the bottom, i.e. implementation is the execution of policies, nothing more or less.

My argument is twofold. It is clarifying to distinguish between implementation or successful implementation as an outcome, and the implementation process or how implementation comes about. And there is no necessary link between implementation as an outcome and some special model of the implementation process – top-down, bottom-up or otherwise. Sometimes control and hierarchy may be conducive to successful implementation, sometimes exchange and interaction is crucial in implementation.

My second point is that whereas implementation as an outcome is rather unambiguous – to carry some policy into effect – the implementation process is a much more complex phenomenon. Implementation processes involve coalitions, learning, political symbolism and implementation perspectives, as well as control. But this is not enough for the general claims that implementation is advocacy coalitions, evolutionary learning or hierarchical control. Any kind of mechanism may be used in the implementation process, because of the loose connection between implementation as an outcome and implementation as a process.

References

Bardach, E. (1977) *The Implementation Game: What Happens After a Bill Becomes a Law*, Cambridge, MA: The MIT Press.

Barrett, S. and Fudge, C. (eds.) (1981) *Policy and Action. Essays on the Implementation of Public Policy*, London: Methuen.

Browne, A. and Wildavsky, A. (1983) 'Should Evaluation become Implementation?', in Pressman and Wildavsky (1984), pp. 206–31.

Derthiek, M. (1972) *New Towns in-Town*, Washington: The Urban Institute.

Dunsire, A. (1978) *Implementation in a Bureaucracy*, Oxford: Martin Robertson.

Elmore, R. F. (1978) 'Organizational Models of Social Program Implementation', *Public Policy* 26: pp. 185–228.

Elmore, R. F. (1982) 'Backward Mapping: Implementation Research and Policy Decision', in Williams (1982), pp. 18–35.

Fudge C. and Barrett, S. (1981) 'Reconstructing the Field of Analysis', in Barrett and Fudge (1981), pp. 249–78.

Hargrove, Erwin (1975) *The Missing Link: The Study of the Implementation of Social Policy*, Washington: The Urban Institute.

Hjern, B. and Hull, C. (1982) 'Implementation Research as Empirical Constitutionalism', *European Journal of Political Research* 10, pp. 105–15.

Hjern B. and Porter, D. O. (1981) 'Implementation Structures: A New Unit for Administrative Analysis', *Organizational Studies* 213, pp. 211–27.

Hood, C. C. (1976) *The Limits of Administration*, London: John Wiley & Sons.

Majone, G. and Wildavsky, A. (1978) 'Implementation as Evolution', in Pressman and Wildavsky (1983), pp. 163–80.

May, J. V. and Wildavsky, A. (eds.) (1979) *The Policy Cycle*, Beverly Hills: Sage.

Mazmanian, D. A. and Sabatier, P. A. (1983) *Implementation and Public Policy*, Palo Alto: Scott Foresman.

Pressman, J. and Wildavsky, A. (1973) *Implementation*, Berkeley: University of California Press.

Pressman, J. and Wildavsky, A. (1984) *Implementation*, Berkeley, University of California Press.

Richardson, I. F. and Jordan, A. G. (1979) *Governing under Pressure: The Policy Process in a Post-Parliamentary Democracy*, Oxford: Martin Robertson.

Sabatier, P. (1986) 'Top-Down and Bottom Up Approaches to Implementation Research: A Critical Analysis and Suggested Synthesis', *Journal of Public Policy* 6, pp. 21–48.

Sabatier, P. and Mazmanian, D. (1979) 'The Conditions of Effective Implementation: A Guide to Accomplishing Policy Objectives', *Policy Analysis* 5, pp. 481–504.

Sharpe, T. (1985) 'Central Coordination and the Policy Network', *Political Studies* 33, pp. 361–81.

Vedung, E. (1986) 'Policy Imperfection', Department of Political Science, University of Uppsala (mimeo).

Williams, W. (1971) *Social Policy Research and Analysis: The Experience in the Federal Social Agencies*, New York: Elsevier.

Williams, W. (1980) *The Implementation Perspective*, Berkeley: University of California Press.

Williams, W. (ed.) (1982) *Studying Implementation. Methodological and Administrative Issues*, Chatham, NJ: Chatham House Publishers.

Williams, W. and Elmore, R. F. (eds.) (1976) *Social Program Implementation*, New York: Academic Press.

Part V

Organizations, rules and bureaucrats

Introduction

In the companion textbook the exploration of further issues about policy implementation is organized into three closely integrated chapters on organizations, on the issues about the blend of rules and discretion in policy and on the issues about the behaviour of bureaucratic and professional staff within public policy delivery organizations. Because of the links between these topics, and because some of the key readings deal with more than one of them, this final part of the reader puts all three together.

The readings start with an extract from the work of the German sociologist Max Weber whose theory of bureaucracy has been the starting point for very many analyses of the characteristics of public organizations. The extract locates Weber's theory of bureaucracy in his wider theory of types of authority structures. Weber postulated that the characteristic authority system of the modern state was a 'rational-legal' one, providing thereby a framework of rules to regulate complex institutional life. Within specific organizations, and particularly within state organizations, Weber saw this order as manifested in his concept of bureaucracy. The characteristics of the ideal-typical bureaucracy are set out in the rest of the extract.

This is followed by an extract from a book by Pollitt, which shows how practical management thought evolved, during the twentieth century, from a perspective (Taylorism) which had many similarities to the Weberian ideal type of bureaucracy, in which subordinate participants were seen as pliant cogs in an organizational machine, to one in which the needs of individuals and the complexity of the 'culture' in which they operate were recognized. In his book Pollitt goes on to show that Taylorist principles continue to be asserted in the public sector. His argument on this is summarized at the end of the extract. Clearly, if public services are viewed in instrumental terms there is a justification for this, deriving, as has been suggested earlier in this book, from democratic models of the policy process.

The issues about models for organization are also explored by Elmore, in the extract that has been printed in Part IV.

The next chapter reminds us that in looking at organizations it is important to recognize that much important policy work occurs between rather than within organizations. Hudson's article explores some of the theory that needs to be taken into account where this is the case.

Much of this inter-organizational theory has been influenced by organization theory which stresses that many of the so-called boundaries between organizations are artificial constructs; human beings interact with each other in a complex milieu in which they have various organizational affiliations and in an overarching system of values and power. Various theoretical writings deal with these issues – in particular the work of Benson (1977, 1983) and Clegg (1989, 1990). One of the important concerns of this literature is to explore the scope for autonomous action by organization participants in a wider power structure. The article by Degeling and Colebatch reviews this issue in the public policy field with particular reference to theory about the relationship between structure and action, deriving from writers such as Giddens (1984). Degeling and Colebatch suggest ways in which two paradigms – a 'social action' and a 'structuralist' one – offer competing challenges to the 'instrumental' one (roughly their name for the principles embodied in Taylorism or for Elmore's 'systems management model'). In their chapter they show how these perspectives may be integrated. They end, since like so many of the contributors to this literature they aim to have something helpful to say to managers, by suggesting that where appeal to 'ascribed authority' may be little use managers nevertheless can 'be active participants in the shaping of the negotiated order of which they are a part'. This view puts a very different perspective upon the concept of 'policy-making' from that embedded in the top-down model.

The next extract seems to take us in a rather different direction, since it is written by a legal theorist and is about administrative discretion. Yet this is just another way of approaching issues about the influences upon policy outputs. Baldwin reviews the concerns of legal theorists like Davis (1969) about the importance of discretionary action in policy implementation and the scope for control over it by means of legally enforceable rules – that is, in the terms discussed earlier, 'top-down' or 'instrumental control'. Baldwin shows how there are wider sociological issues to be taken account about the nature of policy and the social and political context in which it is implemented. The extract ends not with a rejection of the legal approach, but with an exploration of the alternative kinds of policy issues (drawing upon the work of Mashaw 1983) and of the various 'legitimacy claims' which may be made by those who seek to exercise control over outcomes.

The contrast here between the legal approach to the issue of control and the social reality has been well highlighted in a clever analogy by Feldman:

> The difference between the formal limits and the social context limits to discretion can be likened to the difference between a wall and a rushing stream of water. The wall is firm, clearly delineated, and it hurts when you run into it. The rushing stream . . . moves; its speed varies; it is more powerful in the middle than on the edges. It does not always hurt to go into the stream; indeed it may at times be pleasurable. The wall, however, can be assaulted and broken down while the stream rushes on creating a path for itself against the mightiest resistance. (Feldman 1992, p. 183)

In other words the relationship between what is open to ready manipulation and what is structured in the policy process is a complex one. There is a set of issues about what policy makers try to control by rules and there is a different cross-cutting set of issues about what is influenced by culture and custom. These two sometimes coincide and sometimes do not.

The work of Michael Lipsky deals with these issues, but here the approach (adopted by a political scientist) is different again. In analysing his 'bureaucratic process model', in the article in Part IV, Elmore drew upon Michael Lipsky's theory of 'street level bureaucracy'. This has been of seminal importance for the examination of the impact of comparatively low level actors as the *de facto* creators of policy. The central thrust of Lipsky's argument is comparatively simple, it is then very carefully elaborated in his book. Here what has been chosen is a small extract from the beginning of Lipsky's book in which he sets out his essential ideas. This is followed by an article by Hudson in which he explores some key aspects of Lipsky's theory and draws upon a range of sources, including Lipsky's own pupils as well as some British writers, to illustrate the use of the theory.

Two key points about Lipsky's work should be emphasized. One is that he must not be taken to be saying simply that street-level bureaucrats subvert policy goals. Inasmuch as they do this, it is because of a lack of clarity in those goals or a lack of resources to achieve those goals. But often the goals are not clear, the painful problem for street-level bureaucrats is that they enter employment with ideals which they cannot realize in practice. They *do* make policy, but not in the way they would really like to. Coping strategies dominate their lives. In this sense Lipsky's work is more compatible with the bottom-up than with the top-down approach to implementation. In addressing the normative issue, which we have seen that debate raises, Lipsky does not regard the process by which actual policy is determined as an ideal one. In a section towards the end of his book he does suggest that greater accountability of street level bureaucrats to their clients may offer a way out of the 'dilemma', that is, of course, the characteristic bottom-up solution.

The second important point about Lipsky's work is that many of his street level bureaucrats are professional or semi-professional workers. Indeed the latter term has been particularly applied to professional workers in organizations who lack control over their working conditions (Etzioni 1969). Had space allowed it would have been desirable to explore the theme of professionalism in public service organizations more widely since:

(a) professionalism has tended to involve making claims to work autonomy, arguing that responsibility to clients overrides responsibility to political policy-makers;
(b) alternatively professionals have been seen as a group of bureaucratic employees particularly likely to engage in bureau-enlargement or bureau-shaping (see the extracts from Tullock and Dunleavy in Part II) and accordingly an alternative model is advanced for public control over professionals which aims to put them in a position in which they are forced to sell their services in competition with each other. (Friedson 1970)

The new public management movement (NPM) has already been mentioned as being influenced by the public choice concern about bureaucratic power. It has also been influenced by critiques of the Weberian ideal type of bureaucracy and of

Taylorism. Also embedded within it is a suspicion of professional autonomy and a desire to create public organizations in which discretion is curbed.

This is a complex mix, one might indeed say mish-mash, in which doctrines derived from suspicion of bureaucratic rigidity and those derived from distrust of official discretion sit incompatibly side by side. The final two chapters dissect the impact of this movement upon the public sector. The first by Hood explores the inconsistencies in NPM, the second by Hoggett suggests some of its consequences for public policy delivery.

All of the literature in this section deals in some sense or other with issues about control over implementation. The debate about that subject centres on questions about the desirability and/or feasibility of central control. Taylorism and much of the legal literature on discretion regards such control as desirable, and the Weberian theory on bureaucracy treats it as feasible too. Radical organization theory, much sociological writing on discretion and Lipsky's work raises doubts about the feasibility of control. Feasibility of control will vary according to the issue and the prospects, for the 'legitimacy claims' of those who seek to control will depend upon political or institutional context, or – to put it more generally – political and social culture. Obviously, if such control is not feasible it will be inappropriate to continue to be obsessed about desirability. The result is a quest for new models for the organization of policy activity – focusing on what happens at the 'street-level', acknowledging the importance of inter-organizational activities and accepting the phenomenon of discretion. Whether 'new public management' offers satisfactory new models is, as Hood and Hoggett suggest, open to doubt. It is certainly, however, an important manifestation of the contemporary search for solutions. That search is embedded in dilemmas arising from conflicts between different ideals of accountability and different expectations of fairness, responsiveness and predictability in policy processes.

For further explorations of these themes, the books from which the extracts by Pollitt, Lipsky and Baldwin are drawn are worth consultation. On organization theory the work by Benson and Clegg, cited above, is important, and a rather older monograph by Perrow (1972) remains valuable. On discretion the cited book by Mashaw and a collection edited by Hawkins (1992) are recommended. In Britain there is a great deal of work emerging on aspects of New Public Management. The Open University Press series of books on 'public policy and management' is particularly to be recommended. A key example from that source – ranging across most of the issues – is Tony Butcher's *Delivering Welfare* (1995).

References

Benson, J. K. (1977) 'Organizations: a Dialectical View',*Administrative Science Quarterly*, 22 (3), pp. 1–21.

Benson, J. K. (1983) 'Interorganizational Networks and Policy Sectors', in D. Rogers and D. Whetten (eds.), *Interorganizational Coordination*, Ames, IO: Iowa State University Press.

Butcher, T. (1995) *Delivering Welfare*, Buckingham: Open University Press.

Clegg, S. (1989) *Frameworks of Power*, London: Sage.

Clegg, S. (1990) *Modern Organizations*, London: Sage.

Davis, K. C. (1969) *Discretionary Justice*, Baton Rouge: Louisiana State University Press.

Etzioni, A. (1969) *The Semi-Professions and their Organization*, New York: Free Press.

Feldman, M. (1992) 'Social Limits to Discretion: An Organizational Perspective' in K. Hawkins (ed.) *The Uses of Discretion*, Oxford: Clarendon Press.

Friedson, E. (1970) *Professional Dominance*, New York: Atherton.

Giddens, A. (1984) *The Constitution of Society*, Cambridge: Polity Press.

Hawkins, K. (ed.) (1992) *The Uses of Discretion*, Oxford: Clarendon Press.

Mashaw, J. L. (1983) *Bureaucratic Justice*, New Haven, CT: Yale University Press.

Perrow, C. (1972) *Complex Organizations: A Critical Essay*, Glenview IL: Scott Foresman.

Rational-legal authority and bureaucracy

Max Weber

The three pure types of legitimate authority
There are three pure types of legitimate authority. The validity of their claims to legitimacy may be based on:

1. Rational grounds – resting on a belief in the 'legality' of patterns of normative rules and the right of those elevated to authority under such rules to issue commands (legal authority).
2. Traditional grounds – resting on an established belief in the sanctity of immemorial traditions and the legitimacy of the status of those exercising authority under them (traditional authority); or finally,
3. Charismatic grounds – resting on devotion to the specific and exceptional sanctity, heroism or exemplary character of an individual person, and of the normative patterns or order revealed or ordained by him (charismatic authority).

In the case of legal authority, obedience is owed to the legally established impersonal order. It extends to the persons exercising the authority of office under it only by virtue of the formal legality of their commands and only within the scope of authority of the office. In the case of traditional authority, obedience is owed to the *person* of the chief who occupies the traditionally sanctioned position of authority and who is (within its sphere) bound by tradition. But here the obligation of obedience is not based on the impersonal order, but is a matter of personal loyalty within the area of accustomed obligations. In the case of charismatic authority, it is the charismatically qualified leader as such who is obeyed by virtue of personal trust in him and his revelation, his heroism or his exemplary qualities so far as they fall within the scope of the individual's belief in his charisma. [. . .]

From M. Weber, *The Theory of Social and Economic Organization* (1947), edited and translated by T. Parsons, New York: The Free Press.

Legal authority with a bureaucratic administrative staff

Legal authority: the pure type with employment of a bureaucratic administrative staff
The effectiveness of legal authority rests on the acceptance of the validity of the
following mutually inter-dependent ideas.

1. That any given legal norm may be established by agreement or by imposition, on
grounds of expediency or rational values or both, with a claim to obedience at least on
the part of the members of the corporate group. This is, however, usually extended to
include all persons within the sphere of authority or of power in question – which in the
case of territorial bodies is the territorial area – who stand in certain social
relationships or carry out forms of social action which in the order governing the
corporate group have been declared to be relevant.

2. That every body of law consists essentially in a consistent system of abstract rules
which have normally been intentionally established. Furthermore, administration of
law is held to consist in the application of these rules to particular cases; the
administrative process in the rational pursuit of the interests which are specified in the
order governing the corporate group within the limits laid down by legal precepts and
following principles which are capable of generalized formulation and are approved in
the order governing the group, or at least not disapproved in it.

3. That thus the typical person in authority occupies an 'office.' In the action
associated with his status, including the commands he issues to others, he is subject to
an impersonal order to which his actions are oriented. This is true not only for persons
exercising legal authority who are in the usual sense 'officials,' but, for instance, for the
elected president of a state.

4. That the person who obeys authority does so, as it is usually stated, only in his
capacity as a 'member' of the corporate group and what he obeys is only 'the law.' He
may in this connexion be the member of an association, of a territorial commune, of a
church, or a citizen of a state.

5. In conformity with point 3, it is held that the members of the corporate group, in
so far as they obey a person in authority, do not owe this obedience to him as an
individual, but to the impersonal order. Hence, it follows that there is an obligation to
obedience only within the sphere of the rationally delimited authority which, in terms
of the order, has been conferred upon him.

The following may thus be said to be the fundamental categories of rational legal
authority:

(1) A continuous organization of official functions bound by rules.

(2) A specified sphere of competence. This involves (a) a sphere of obligations to
perform functions which has been marked off as part of a systematic division of labour.
(b) The provision of the incumbent with the necessary authority to carry out these
functions. (c) That the necessary means of compulsion are clearly defined and their use

is subject to definite conditions. A unit exercising authority which is organized in this way will be called an 'administrative organ.'

There are administrative organs in this sense in large-scale private organizations, in parties and armies, as well as in the state and the church. An elected president, a cabinet of ministers, or a body of elected representatives also in this sense constitute administrative organs. [. . .] Not every administrative organ is provided with compulsory powers. But this distinction is not important for present purposes.

(3) The organization of offices follows the principle of hierarchy; that is, each lower office is under the control and supervision of a higher one. There is a right of appeal and of statement of grievances from the lower to the higher. Hierarchies differ in respect to whether and in what cases complaints can lead to a ruling from an authority at various points higher in the scale, and as to whether changes are imposed from higher up or the responsibility for such changes is left to the lower office, the conduct of which was the subject of complaint.

(4) The rules which regulate the conduct of an office may be technical rules or norms. In both cases, if their application is to be fully rational, specialized training is necessary. It is thus normally true that only a person who has demonstrated an adequate technical training is qualified to be a member of the administrative staff of such an organized group, and hence only such persons are eligible for appointment to official positions. The administrative staff of a rational corporate group thus typically consists of 'officials,' whether the organization be devoted to political, religious, economic – in particular, capitalistic – or other ends.

(5) In the rational type it is a matter of principle that the members of the administrative staff should be completely separated from ownership of the means of production or administration. Officials, employees, and workers attached to the administrative staff do not themselves own the non-human means of production and administration. These are rather provided for their use in kind or in money, and the official is obligated to render an accounting of their use. There exists, furthermore, in principle complete separation of the property belonging to the organization, which is controlled within the sphere of office, and the personal property of the official, which is available for his own private uses. There is a corresponding separation of the place in which official functions are carried out, the 'office' in the sense of premises, from living quarters.

(6) In the rational-type case, there is also a complete absence of appropriation of his official position by the incumbent. Where 'rights' to an office exist, as in the case of judges, and recently of an increasing proportion of officials and even of workers, they do not normally serve the purpose of appropriation by the official, but of securing the purely objective and independent character of the conduct of the office so that it is oriented only to the relevant norms.

(7) Administrative acts, decisions, and rules are formulated and recorded in writing, even in cases where oral discussion is the rule or is even mandatory. This applies at least to preliminary discussions and proposals, to final decisions, and to all sorts of orders and rules. The combination of written documents and a continuous

organization of official functions constitutes the 'office' which is the central focus of all types of modern corporate action.

(8) Legal authority can be exercised in a wide variety of different forms [. . .]. The following analysis will be deliberately confined for the most part to the aspect of imperative co-ordination in the structure of the administrative staff. It will consist in an analysis in terms of ideal types of officialdom or 'bureaucracy.'

In the above outline no mention has been made of the kind of supreme head appropriate to a system of legal authority. This is a consequence of certain considerations which can only be made entirely understandable at a later stage in the analysis. There are very important types of rational imperative co-ordination which, with respect to the ultimate source of authority, belong to other categories. This is true of the hereditary charismatic type, as illustrated by hereditary monarchy and of the pure charismatic type of a president chosen by plebiscite. Other cases involve rational elements at important points, but are made up of a combination of bureaucratic and charismatic components, as is true of the cabinet form of government. Still others are subject to the authority of the chief of other corporate groups, whether their character be charismatic or bureaucratic; thus the formal head of a government department under a parliamentary regime may be a minister who occupies his position because of his authority in a party. The type of rational, legal administrative staff is capable of application in all kinds of situations and contexts. It is the most important mechanism for the administration of everyday profane affairs. For in that sphere, the exercise of authority and, more broadly, imperative co-ordination, consists precisely in administration.

Legal authority: the pure type with employment of a bureaucratic administrative staff – (continued)
The purest type of exercise of legal authority is that which employs a bureaucratic administrative staff. Only the supreme chief of the organization occupies his position of authority by virtue of appropriation, of election, or of having been designated for the succession. But even*his* authority consists in a sphere of legal 'competence.' The whole administrative staff under the supreme authority then consists, in the purest type, of individual officials who are appointed and function according to the following criteria:

(1) They are personally free and subject to authority only with respect to their impersonal official obligations.
(2) They are organized in a clearly defined hierarchy of offices.
(3) Each office has a clearly defined sphere of competence in the legal sense.
(4) The office is filled by a free contractual relationship. Thus, in principle, there is free selection.
(5) Candidates are selected on the basis of technical qualifications. In the most rational case, this is tested by examination or guaranteed by diplomas certifying technical training, or both. They are *appointed*, not elected.
(6) They are remunerated by fixed salaries in money, for the most part with a right to

pensions. Only under certain circumstances does the employing authority, especially in private organizations, have a right to terminate the appointment, but the official is always free to resign. The salary scale is primarily graded according to rank in the hierarchy; but in addition to this criterion, the responsibility of the position and the requirements of the incumbent's social status may be taken into account.

(7) The office is treated as the sole, or at least the primary, occupation of the incumbent.

(8) It constitutes a career. There is a system of 'promotion' according to seniority or to achievement, or both. Promotion is dependent on the judgement of superiors.

(9) The official works entirely separated from ownership of the means of administration and without appropriation of his position.

(10) He is subject to strict and systematic discipline and control in the conduct of the office.

The development of management thought

Chris Pollitt

In this [. . .] chapter, [. . .] the intention is to offer enough of a potted history to enable the reader to see how management thought has itself developed through several historical phases. [. . .] Those who wish for a fuller treatment of the history of management and administrative thought are advised to seek it through the more specialist references, particularly Child (1969), Dunsire (1973), Perrow (1979) and Thomas (1978).

Pushing simplification somewhere near to the point where its drawbacks begin to overtake its advantages, one may say that managerial thought grew up hastily in the final decades of the nineteenth century and has since moved through at least six broad phases. (Not too much should be made of these, since, in practice, they frequently ran side by side. The sequence here depicted is a logically neat summary of what was actually a fairly untidy process.)

In the first phase theorists struggled to come to terms with the process of industrialization, and the concomitant creation of large workforces concentrated at particular sites of production. How were these workforces to be selected, controlled, paid and prevented from endangering the increase in production and the accumulation of capital?

> Factory work involves specialization, sub division and fragmentation. Decisions about the general rules and procedures and detailed work specifications are vested in experts, managers or machinery. The speed and quality of work cannot remain with the individual workers . . . . These features required a new 'rational' work ethic on the part of the hands. (Salaman, 1981, p. 33)

Explicit theorizing on these questions was perhaps most noticeable in the US, which industrialized later and even faster than Germany or the UK. In the US in the 1870s and 1880s doctrines of Social Darwinism were widely expounded. Ideas of competition and natural selection suggested that entrepreneurs and owners need have little regard for the active welfare of their workers. Nature's 'laws' would in any case ensure the survival of the fittest, and the sensible employer should therefore go with the grain of

From C. Pollitt, *Managerialism and the Public Services* (1990), Oxford: Blackwell.

this 'legislation' by retaining the healthiest, strongest workers and not paying too much attention to the rest (Perrow, 1979, pp. 60–1).

By the beginning of the twentieth century, however, fresh theories were beginning to suggest that far more initiative lay in the hands of the owners and managers themselves. In the US the New Thought Movement emphasized not biology but the power of positive thinking. It spawned advisory texts with what now sound preposterously exhortatory titles such as *Your Forces and How to Use Them* or *Pushing to the Front* (Perrow, 1979, pp. 61–2). The emphasis was on willpower and mental energy – if individuals applied themselves keenly enough then wealth and success lay within reach (one can detect echoes of this in many popular expressions of contemporary 'new right' political and economic thought, for example Michael Heseltine's *Where There's A Will* (1987), or the Conservative Party's 1987 slogan 'The resolute approach').

Hard on the heels of the New Thought Movement came the considerably more detailed and practical body of thought most commonly associated with the name of Frederick Winslow Taylor. His *Principles of Scientific Management* (1911) became enormously influential, and its basic approach remains with us to this day. Though countless social scientists have subsequently criticized or scorned Taylor's techniques:

> A successful and durable business of management consulting and an endless series of successful books rest upon the basic principles of the classical management school. These principles have worked and are still working, for they addressed themselves to the very problems of management, problems more pressing than those advanced by social science. (Perrow, 1979, p. 59; see also Merkle, 1980)

Taylor's work was so seminal that it is worth quoting from it at some length:

> This paper has been written:
> FIRST. To point out through a series of simple illustrations, the great loss which the whole country is suffering through inefficiency in almost all of our daily acts.
> SECOND. To try to convince the reader that the remedy for this inefficiency lies in systematic management, rather than in searching for some unusual or extraordinary man.
> THIRD. To prove that the best management is a true science, resting upon clearly defined laws, rules and principles, as a foundation. And further to show that the fundamental principles of scientific management are applicable to all kinds of human activities, from our simplest individual acts to the work of our great corporations, which call for the most elaborate co-operation. (Taylor, 1911, pp. 5–7)

Taylor is perhaps best known as a pioneer of time and motion techniques, and for his studies of the detailed movements of workers dealing with particular, well-defined tasks. As the above manifesto clearly shows, however, his ambitions ran far beyond this [. . .]. Scientific management constituted: 'a clearly-marked complex that ties together patterns of technological innovation with techniques of organization and larger designs for social change, unifying its entire structure with an ideology of science as a form of puritanism' (Merkle, 1980, p. 11).

Two of his claims are of particular importance. First, there is the assertion that management can be a 'true science' (with all the connotations of discovering precise, impersonal laws). Second, a parallel claim is made for universality of application – *all* human activities are subject to the laws thus discovered. Both these claims, but perhaps especially the second one, can still be heard today – *anything* can, and should, be managed.

Taylor's ideas had considerable influence on both sides of the Atlantic, and in both private and public sectors. The notion that management could be divided off as a separate and scientific field of study combined very neatly with what was by the 1920s a popular view of public administration in the US. As long ago as 1887 Woodrow Wilson had written what later became an influential paper, 'The study of adminis-tration'. Here Wilson urged that 'administrative questions are not political questions' (Wilson, 1887). This had been widely interpreted as marking out a distinct sphere of 'administration' in which politics constituted an unwelcome and improper intrusion (Dunsire, 1973, pp. 87–94). Within this sphere, therefore, 'scientific' methods could be applied. Various attempts were made to do just this, especially among the 'progressive' reformers of municipal government (Schliesl, 1977, especially pp. 163–5).

In Britain the impact of Taylorism was less pervasive, but its spirit was nevertheless clearly present in some influential quarters. The Haldane Committee report on the machinery of government espoused the general idea of a set of functional principles by which the optimal pattern of government departments could be determined (Cd 9230, 1918). In 1922 the first issue of *Public Administration*, journal of the newly founded Institute of Public Administration (now RIPA), carried an article entitled 'Public administration: a science', and editorialized in favour of this stance. Then, as now, it was supposed that, if only management and administration could be established as a scientific discipline, then public officials would be better protected against the irrationalities of 'political interference'. [. . .]

From Taylorism flowed many attempts to identify and enumerate the correct prin-ciples for the design of organizations. This extensive literature, much of it published during the 1920s and 1930s, has become known as 'classical management theory'. Among its exponents was Luther Gulick, best known for the list of chief executive functions (POSDCORB) [. . .]. However, scientific management was not without its rivals. From the early 1930s a new perspective was developed, one which has been retrospectively dubbed the 'human relations school'. The key difference from Taylor-ism was the advancement of a considerably more sophisticated model of the individual worker. Whereas in early scientific management the worker was treated as an individual unit responding directly to some fairly simple incentives and punishments, the human relations school substituted a model of rather a complex being who respon-ded to a much wider variety of environmental factors, including behavioural norms created and sustained by informal groups of fellow workers. Whilst Taylor had been aware of work group solidarity he seems to have seen it as an obstacle to be overcome rather than as a phenomenon which needed to be understood and turned to manage-ment advantage. For human relations theorists, however, what was required for a smoothly functioning organization was no less than a rational assessment of the whole person, set in a context of the social relations of the workplace (Perrow, 1979, p. 49).

The human relations approach grew from roots in the work of industrial psychologists during the First World War, but the investigations which established it as a major force in management were the 'Hawthorne Studies', carried out between 1926 and 1932. The classic text, *The Human Problems of an Industrial Civilisation*, was published by the leading researcher, Elton Mayo, in 1933 (Mayo, 1933). The significance of this work for managerialist ideologies today is that it established the idea that *informal* relations within and without the organization are of considerable importance. It is not only the formal organization chart, distribution of functions and systems of work measurement which are important, but also the feelings, values, informal group norms and family and social backgrounds of workers which help determine organizational performance. 'Man is not merely – in fact is very seldom – motivated by factors pertaining strictly to facts or logic' (Roethlisberger and Dickson, 1969, pp. 54–5). Subsequently this general message has been developed in many and various detailed applications – modern techniques of job enrichment, participative management styles and 'self-actualisation' (Argyris, 1960) are part of the intellectual heritage of the human relations school.

It should be noticed, however, that the genuinely 'humanizing' tendencies of the human relations movement have their limits. Many critics of the approach: 'point to the excessive concern of the authors with consensus and co-operation . . . . Conflict is given little attention, such instances as are noted being attributed to worker irrationality' (Salaman, 1981, p. 149).

Furthermore:

whereas management like [a company] have a definite interest in recognizing more fully that production is social production – i.e. in recognizing that men are not simply commodities but thinking, social beings, with potentially valuable contributions to make, and with the potential to work together more productively – they also have an interest in limiting the development of these human potentials. And this is because, though it would suit workers to act as if there were really socialism inside work, managers themselves have to operate in a world in which market forces reign and impede the development of the very unstinted co-operation they wish to bring about. (Nichols, 1980, p. 298)

One might add that, in a contemporary public-sector context, one could substitute, without diminishing the accuracy of Nichols' generalization, the words 'cash limits, performance indicators and staffcuts' for 'market forces'.

The fifth main phase in the development of management thought is even harder to summarize than the first four. One problem here is that the sheer volume of material grew enormously during the three decades after 1945. This was in large part due to the rapid growth of management-related disciplines (social psychology, sociology, organization theory etc.) in universities and business schools. This growth was itself related to the emergence of new dominant organizational forms, especially the large multinational corporation in the private sector, and to the appearance in the UK of very large nationalized industries (mainly created by the 1945–51 Labour government) which greatly enlarged the public sector. In the face of this flood of ideas I have decided to term the period up to the mid 1970s the 'decisions and systems' phase. I do this because, alongside continuing work in the scientific management and human relations traditions, two major new foci emerged: first, a concern with the cognitive processes of individual and group decision making in organizational contexts and, second, attempts to understand the macro-features of organizational performance by characterizing them as 'open, socio-technical systems' (Sayles, 1958).

The decision-making focus is most closely associated with the name of Herbert Simon, although it has now diversified into dozens of sub-approaches (Simon, 1947). The 'systems approach' enjoys many well-known advocates, but none quite so pre-eminent. Both perspectives share a concentration on goal-directed activity (Bourn, 1974). They are centrally concerned with the processes of objective setting, the review of alternative courses of action, the weighing and selection of these alternatives, the implementation of choices once made and the feedback (or lack of it) the decision makers receive about the consequences of the strategies which have been implemented. The decision-making approach concentrates more on the detailed cognitive and emotional processes at the individual and small-group levels, whereas the systems approach typically operates at the level of the organization as a whole, its major inputs and outputs, and the nature of the wider environment in which it is set. Neither approach denies the importance of the formal structures and behavioural processes which interested the Taylorists, nor do they ignore the social processes which were highlighted by the human relations school. Rather they incorporate and modify these insights, claiming to provide a more dynamic (action-oriented) synthesis.

For our purposes the nature of these modifications is of particular significance. Instead of searching for a timeless 'one best way' of structuring any organization, the decisions and systems perspective attempts to relate structures to organizational objectives, to the nature of the organizational environment (stable, unstable, highly competitive, oligopolistic etc.) and to the particular productive technologies employed within the organization. Thus, instead of arriving at a set of fixed 'administrative proverbs', as the classical school/Taylorists tended to do, decisions and systems writers were likely to adopt a much more relativistic stance. They say, in effect, 'If your objectives are so-and-so, and the environment you face is like this, and the technology you use is of type *x*, *then* you should design your organization as follows'. Because of this, one sub-school of the systems approach (which became particularly prominent in academic circles during the 1970s) is known as 'contingency theory', reflecting the idea that the optimal internal structure for an organization will be determined by the 'setting' of key environmental contingencies (Clark, 1975; Pugh and Hickson, 1976).

Nevertheless, some broad features of the classical school are still discernible. The decisions and systems paradigm is usually assumed to be universal in its applicability. All organizations are systems, with inputs, outputs etc. All set goals and then need to shape decision processes to serve those goals. Figure 1, or something similar, has appeared in dozens, probably hundreds of publications, some aimed at corporate executives, some at chemical plant managers, some at local government managers, some at hospital administrators and so on.

The second common feature with the classical school is a seeming distaste for any analysis of politics and power struggles. Systems and decisions can, it is usually assumed, be discussed in a detached, rational, scientific manner. Values, of course, have their place, but they enter the analysis preformed, from 'outside'. Once there,

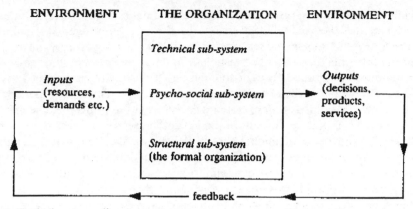

Figure 1 Typical systems diagram

they can be slotted into the decision calculus, but – with a few honourable exceptions, including Simon himself – most writers in this genre do not spend much time discussing the origins, formation or substance of the values which provide fuel for the whole decision process. Furthermore, 'systems theorists, whether functionalist or not, have . . . failed to provide a theoretically satisfactory framework for the satisfactory analysis of power relations' (Martin, 1977, p. 19). Clearly, therefore, if one regards the institutions of the welfare state as being imbued with a distinctive set of social and political values, values which are crucial to their modes of operation, then the decisions and systems corpus may be limited in its explanatory and diagnostic strengths.

Decisions and systems ideas, like scientific management, extensively penetrated government and the public sector, as well as the world of business and commerce. Like Taylorism, however, they influenced some parts of the public sector more than others. Their presence was probably most noticeable in the training of general administrators, especially in central government/federal departments, and in the general administrative, planning and policy formulation units of state, local and city government. The language of systems – 'feedback', 'inputs', 'environment', 'interface' etc. – was widely learned and used, even where the impact of these concepts went little beyond rhetoric. In some areas, however, the influence of 'decisions and systems' went considerably further. [An important example was] the introduction of planning, programming and budgeting systems (PPBS) in the federal government (from the early 1960s) and, later and on a smaller scale, in Whitehall (for brief summaries, see Patten and Pollitt, 1980; and Wildavsky, 1979, pp. 32–4). When British central government was restructured by Edward Heath's incoming government in 1970 the white paper *The Reorganization of Central Government* was redolent of this brand of thought. Its first aim was:

> To improve the quality of policy formulation and decision-taking in government by presenting ministers, collectively in cabinet and individually within their departments, with well-defined options, costed where possible, and relating the choice between options to the contribution they can make to meeting national needs. (Cmnd 4506; for a detailed discussion see Pollitt, 1984, pp. 82–106)

[. . .] Elaborate planning systems and data requirements were installed at the top of government but they made little change to the operating agencies and, it soon appeared, were not necessarily regarded as terribly interesting even by the ministers in whose departments they had been installed. In local government, too, new management systems were more likely to be found in the departments of the new (post-1972) chief executives than in social services or education. [. . .] The limited penetration of the operating arms of the welfare state by decisions and systems ideas seems to have been connected to both limitations in the ideas themselves and resistance (actual or anticipated) from the professional service deliverers. Doctors, teachers and social workers had their own practices, and their own professional cultures. The prospect of 'outsiders' refining *their* goals, streamlining *their* professional decision procedures and inspecting *their* 'feedback' was not an overwhelmingly attractive one.

If, however, specific borrowings could be made from this body of thought, and those borrowings could be kept under the control of the profession concerned, then that would be a different matter. Thus decision theory techniques have begun to be employed to assist doctors with problems in medical diagnosis. In other professions, too, the spread of computer-based 'expert systems' is widely predicted (for a survey of the techniques and their implications, see Dowie and Elstein, 1988).

From the beginning of the 1970s the decisions and systems perspective came under heavy attack. Criticisms centred on 'the incapacity of the dominant systems paradigm to deal with the inherent complexity of social action and the intellectual paralysis which this had produced within the field' (Reed, 1988, p. 36). An alternative 'social action' perspective was advanced which espoused a voluntaristic epistemology, emphasized the importance and legitimacy of differing perceptions of organizational 'realities' and rested 'on a moral philosophy which asserts the primacy of individual ethical choice over the normative imperatives entailed in institutions' (Reed, 1988, p. 37; for an influential early example see Silverman, 1970). Subsequently a more overtly 'political' critique directly attacked these normative imperatives by attempting to show that, far from being 'necessary' or unavoidable, they constituted a central element in a process of systematic domination by particular social groups (Burrell and Morgan, 1979). These methodological and ideological criticisms effectively dethroned the systems and decisions perspective (at least within the academic world) but they largely failed to provide a coherent new orthodoxy. Since the mid 1970s the field of organizational studies has been particularly kaleidoscopic – and therefore extremely hard to characterize in a brief summary such as this. Reed describes the situation as one in which there was a 'melee of competing theoretical perspectives that jockeyed for intellectual "poll position"' (1988, p. 40).

There has, however, been one special recent trend which merits particular mention. This – my sixth and final key development in management thought – emerged during the 1970s, and became very fashionable in the 1980s. I am going to call it 'culture management', because it borrowed the concept of 'culture' from anthropology and sociology and attempted to make it central to the study of organizations. Just as the human relations school had reacted against the mechanistic model of the individual deployed by the Taylorists, so the culture management advocates believed that most decision-theoretic and systems analyses neglected the importance of symbolism and ritual in organizational life (see, e.g., March and Olsen, 1984; Meyer and Rowan, 1977; Pettigrew, 1985; Westerlund and Sjostrand, 1979). They aired this view in both academic journals such as *Dragon*, and in more popular formats such as *In Search of Excellence* (Peters and Waterman, 1982). A comprehensive and widely read text which integrated cultural aspects with other salient issues in management thought was Charles Handy's *Understanding Organizations* (1976).

There are almost as many alternative definitions of 'culture' as of 'ideology' (indeed the two concepts are often used in overlapping ways). One useful and influential one was that offered by Donald Schon, who said that culture was the theoretical dimension of an organization which met the need for the 'inhabitants' of the organization to gain 'a view of itself, its role within some large system, the nature of its environment, its own operation and the norms which govern its behaviour' (Schon, 1971). Handy, similarly, refers to 'sets of values and norms and beliefs', and points out that, far from there being 'one best culture', cultures may legitimately vary both between and within organiza- tions (Handy, 1976, p. 176). Peters and Waterman tended to be more prescriptive. They argued that the successful companies they studied were 'value-driven' – that their staffs were motivated by carefully maintained cultures of excellence. The task of shaping the organizational culture was seen as one for senior management. 'Even management's job becomes more fun. Instead of brain games in the sterile ivory tower, it's shaping values and reinforcing through coaching and evangelism in the field – with the worker and in support of the cherished product' (Peters and Waterman, 1982, p. xxv).

Subsequently this cry was taken up in the public-sector context, and writers in the field of public management began to argue that one of the tasks of top public officials was to change the old culture of advice and regulation in favour of a much more responsive and proactive style. Thus Metcalfe and Richards claimed that: 'The values round which public management cultures should develop include learning, experi- mentation, adaptability and flexibility. The need for these values arises from the rate of change with which governments will have to cope in future' (Metcalfe and Richards, 1987, p. 85).

One problem with this approach is the generality of its key concepts. It is hard to derive very specific prescriptions for action from something as vague and elusive as 'culture'. Yet despite this vagueness the emphasis on culture also has its sinister side. For in crude or unscrupulous hands it is not hard to see how this line of thinking could be used to suppress dissent and harass staff who did not appear to have 'appropriate attitudes'. In the 'culture' movement one can see how Taylor's original attempt at direct, stick-and-carrot control of the workforce has long since given way to a much more subtle and indirect approach. Managers now work to create the right 'climate', to encourage identification with corporate goals, high motivation, internalization of 'constructive attitudes'. Those who can comply with these blandishments may be granted not simply higher pay but also discretion, status and other privileges (Salaman, 1981, pp. 172–4). Ultimately they may even cease to *see* contradictions or injustices within their employing organizations, to become what in political science terms might be termed the willing victims of the 'third dimension' of managerial power (Lukes, 1974).

Subtle managerial manipulations of organizational cultures may thus become a focus for growing concern. As yet, however, it is not clear that management possesses either the kinds of reliable theories or the kinds of inducements that would allow them to remould a given culture 'to order'. [. . .] Such attempts as have been recently mounted in British and American public services have been either crude or contradictory or largely ineffective or some combination of all three. Part of the difficulty lies in the oft-made assumptions that management somehow 'owns' an organization's culture, and that the culture can be spread homogeneously throughout the various vertical and horizontal sub-divisions of the department or agency in question (Lynn Meek, 1988). Such assumptions are contradicted by much empirical work which, by contrast, reveals that large organizations are usually honeycombed with different and contrasting cultures, many of which are deeply embedded in the belief systems of the staff concerned and are unlikely to be substantially altered by short-term management campaigns to promote a new 'image'. In sum, the cultural perspective can be of considerable value as a complement to more instrumental, goal- or decision-oriented approaches. It reminds managers (and academics) of the general importance of the symbolic dimension of organizational life, but it may never be able to furnish a practical 'toolkit' for producing new, 'management-designed' cultures on demand. Even if it could, there would remain a whole set of further questions concerning the nature of the links between belief systems and actual behaviours. Many studies have shown that staff are often involved in actions which do not appear to 'fit' their ostensible values and preferences. The links between culture and action are not straightforward.

Finally, I want to draw attention to a recently emerging analysis which sets distinct limits to the practical usefulness which managers may hope to derive from *any* general theory of management. Whitley notes that 'the goal of an integrated, coherent and practical "science of managing" seems, if anything, further away than it did in the 1950s' (1988, p. 48). This apparent failure he attributes to the fact that: 'managerial skills differ considerably from other sorts of expertise in their limited standardization across industries, their susceptibility to change, their specificity to situations rather than problems and their diffuse, varied knowledge base' (Whitley, 1989a).

[. . .] To the extent that we find the same, generic model of management being applied across a variety of non-standardized situations and tasks within the public services it will be appropriate to enquire how 'appropriate' or 'realistic' this appears to be to the 'locals' who actually run these services. Note that Whitley is *not* taking the extreme position that there are no common factors; rather he is arguing that these are of limited provenance, and that effective management will require a lot of local and particular knowledge besides:

> there are general and political skills which are common to all managerial jobs insofar as these involve working with people, and indeed are probably required for all those jobs where tasks are interdependent. However, where judgement and discretion are involved in complex tasks which are highly context-dependent, skills are much more specific to particular situations and

organizational fields. Here industry knowledge and personal networks are often crucial to effective management and skills are often not readily transferable. (Whitley, 1989b)

[...]

Summary

Even in such a compressed history as this it is plain that management thought has bequeathed to the modern manager a rich and varied armoury of theories, concepts and techniques. Various tensions are visible – for example between the desire for a hard-edged 'science' and the fascination with evidence of idiosyncratic leadership, the strength of informal processes or the existence of exotic organizational symbolism. Yet behind all these variations lies the broader, unifying set of [...] assumptions concerning the growing social importance of management and the special roles and responsibilities of managers. There may also be corresponding assumptions, often hidden, to the effect that other forms of social co-ordination and integration, such as political activity, voluntary co-operation or friendship, are less efficient and probably of relatively diminishing social significance.

Though most of the major developments in management thought had their origins in the private sector (Taylorism, the Hawthorne experiments, PPBS, culture management), many of them also left their mark in the public sphere. Yet this was not a uniform influence. It was more noticeable in those parts of public sector organizations dominated by general administrative or clerical work, and in 'industrial' type areas such as nationalized industries or local authority direct labour forces. The specialist, professionalized welfare services were among the least affected. But from the mid 1970s, in both the US and the UK, this began to change. By the mid 1980s these same services were at the focus of a major movement for management change. The driving force behind this movement was a generic model of management, that is to say one which minimized the difference between private-sector business management and the running of public services. What is more [...] the particular species of genericism which was dominant tended to be of a neo-Taylorian character.

References

Argyris, C. (1960) *Understanding Organizational Behaviour*, London: Tavistock.

Bourn, J. B. (1974) 'The administrative process as a decision-making and goal attaining system', Block 2, Part 2 of *D331 Public Administration*, Milton Keynes: Open University Press.

Burrell, G. and Morgan, G. (1979) *Sociological Paradigms and Organizational Analysis*, London: Heinemann.

Child, J. (1969) *British Management Thought*, London: Allen & Unwin.

Clark, P. A. (1975) 'Organizational design: a review of key problems', *Administration and Society*, 17 (2), August, 213–56.

Cd 9230 (1918) *Report of the Machinery of Government Committee* (the Haldane Committee), London: HMSO.

Cmnd 4506 (1970) *The Reorganization of Central Government*, London: HMSO.

Dowie, J. and Elstein, A. (1988)*Professional Judgement: A reader in clinical decision making*, New York: Cambridge University Press.

Dunsire, A. (1973) *Administration: The word and the science*, Oxford: Martin Robertson.

Handy, C. B. (1976) *Understanding Organizations*, Harmondsworth: Penguin Books.

Heseltine, M. (1987) *Where There's a Will*, London: Hutchinson.

Lukes, S. (1974) *Power: A radical view*, London: Macmillan.

Lynn Meek, V. (1988) 'Organizational culture: origins and weaknesses', *Organization Studies*, 9 (4), pp. 453–73.

March, J. G. and Olsen, J. P. (1984) 'The new institutionalism: organizational factors in political life', *American Political Science Review*, 78, pp. 734–49.

Martin, R. (1977) *The Sociology of Power*, London: Routledge & Kegan Paul.

Mayo, Elton (1933) *The Human Problems of an Industrial Civilization*, New York: Macmillan.

Merkle, J. (1980)*Management and Ideology: The legacy of the international scientific management movement*, Berkeley: University of California Press.

Metcalfe, L. and Richards, S. (1987) 'Evolving public management cultures', pp. 65–86 in J. Kooiman and K. A. Eliassen (eds.), *Managing Public Organizations: Lessons from contemporary European experience*, London: Sage.

Meyer, J. W. and Rowan, B. (1977) 'Institutionalized organizations: formal structure as myth and ceremony', *American Journal of Sociology*, 83, pp. 340–64.

Nichols, T. (1980) 'Management, ideology and practice', pp. 279–302 in G. Esland and G. Salaman (eds.), *The Politics of Work and Occupations*, Milton Keynes: Open University Press.

Patten, J. and Pollitt, C. (1980) 'Power and rationality: theories of policy formulation', Paper 8, Block 2, *D336 Policies, People and Administration*, Milton Keynes: Open University Press.

Perrow, C. (1979) *Complex Organizations: A critical essay*, 2nd edn., London: Scott, Foresman and Co.

Peters, J. and Waterman, R. H. (1982) *In Search of Excellence: Lessons from America's best-run companies*, New York: Harper & Row.

Pettigrew, A. (1985) *The Awakening Giant: Continuity and change in ICI*, Oxford: Blackwell.

Pollitt, C. (1984) *Manipulating the Machine: Changing the pattern of ministerial departments, 1960–83*, London: Allen & Unwin.

Pugh, D. S. and Hickson, D. J. (1976) *Organization Structure and its Context: The Aston programme*, Farnborough: Saxon House.

Reed, M. I. (1988) 'The problem of human agency in organizational analysis', *Organisation Studies*, 9 (1), pp. 33–46.

Roethlisberger, F. J. and Dickson, W. J. (1969) 'On organizational goals', pp. 51–62 in J. A. Litterer (ed.), *Organizations*, 2nd edn., Vol. 1, New York: Wiley.

Salaman, G. (1981) *Class and the Corporation*, Glasgow: Fontana.

Sayles, L. R. (1958) *Behaviour of Industrial Work Groups*. New York: Wiley.

Schliesl, M. (1977) *The Politics of Efficiency*, Berkeley: University of California Press.

Schon, D. A. (1971) *Beyond the Stable State*, New York: Norton.

Silverman, D. (1970) *The Theory of Organizations*, London: Heinemann.

Simon, H. A. (1947)*Administrative Behaviour: A study of decision-making processes in adminstrative organization*, New York: Macmillan.

Taylor, F. W. (1911) *The Principles of Scientific Management*, New York: Harper & Row.

Thomas, R. (1978) *The British Philosophy of Administration: A comparison of British and American ideas, 1900–1939*, London/New York: Longman.

Westerlund, G. and Sjostrand, S.-E. (1979) *Organizational Myths*, London: Harper & Row.

Whitley, R. (1988) 'The management sciences and managerial skills', *Organizational Studies*, 9 (1), pp. 47–68.

Whitley, R. (1989a) 'On the nature of managerial tasks: their distinguishing characteristics and organisation', *Journal of Management Studies*, May.

Whitley, R. (1989b) personal communication with the author, 22 March.

Wildavsky, A. (1979) *Speaking Truth to Power: The art and craft of policy analysis*, Boston: Little, Brown.

Wilson, W. (1887) 'The study of administration', *Political Science Quarterly*, 2, pp. 197–222.

Collaboration in social welfare
A framework for analysis

Bob Hudson

Collaboration is a paradoxical concept in the field of social welfare. There can be little doubt that the notion is in vogue. The desirability of some form of collaborative activity has become a *sine qua non* of effective practice within the welfare professions, both at practitioner and policy-making levels. However, we know remarkably little about how collaborative activity works, why it may initially be developed, how it may be measured or even how it may be defined.

Social science research on organisations has tended to be principally concerned with *intra*-organisational phenomena. Psychologists have studied the individual in an organisation; social psychologists have focused on the relations amongst members of a group in an organisation, and the impact of a group on the attitudes and behaviour of group members; sociologists have studied informal groups, formal sub-units and the structural attributes of an organisation. There has been relatively little attempt to focus on *inter*-organisational behaviour, particularly in the application to welfare policies in Britain. This paper attempts to outline a framework for the analysis of collaborative activity, which may then be applied to a variety of welfare settings.

The significance of inter-organisational behaviour

At a broad level, the significance of interlocking networks of organisations has been established at least since the publication of C. Wright Mills' *The Power Elite* in 1956, and it is now more widely accepted that it is interlocking organisations rather than individuals that are at the centre of power systems. Consumers or clients of welfare organisations are usually served, processed, changed or harassed not by a single organisation but by a number of related organisations.

From B. Hudson, 'Collaboration in social welfare: a framework for analysis', *Policy and Politics*, **15**, 1987, pp. 175–82.

One approach to this difficulty would be to encourage awareness on the part of the related organisations of the impact of their activities upon the individual client or consumer. This is premised upon certain assumptions about the motivation of principal decision-makers, most notably that a prevailing spirit of altruism will result in co-operation as soon as individual or community needs become known. However, it may be more realistic to assume not only that inter-organisational collaboration in social welfare has no qualities of spontaneous growth or self-perpetuation, but also that organisations strive to maintain their autonomy.

From an agency's viewpoint, collaborative activity raises two main difficulties. First, it loses some of its freedom to act independently, when it would prefer to maintain control over its domain and affairs. Second, it must invest scarce resources and energy in developing and maintaining relationships with other organisations, when the potential returns on this investment are often unclear or intangible. Hence it could be posited that an agency prefers *not* to become involved in inter-organisational relationships unless it is compelled to do so, and that simple appeals to client well-being may constitute an insufficient motivation.

A much more powerful motivation concerns the realisation of organisational goals. Welfare organisations do not normally possess or control the entire complement of resources needed for their goal accomplishment. Funds, facilities, personnel or other resources may be lacking in some measure, and organisations may therefore enter into exchanges with one another to acquire needed resources. Yuchtman and Seashore (1967) go so far as to define 'organisational effectiveness' as 'the ability of an organisation to exploit its environment in obtaining resources, while at the same time maintaining an autonomous bargaining position'.

In Britain, there is a small but growing empirical literature on collaborative welfare activity. Much of this stems from 'community care' policies and focuses in particular upon the relationship between health and personal social services authorities, but the collaborative theme has also been scrutinised in other diverse fields such as child abuse, the treatment of juvenile offenders and the housing/social services interface. What has been noticeably absent is a theoretical framework to bring some order to the findings. Transfers of resources among profit-making organisations are mediated by money and behaviour may be explained in terms of economic theory and market behaviour, but these concepts do not appear suitable for explaining interaction amongst welfare organisations. This chapter will attempt to provide a more appropriate framework.

Modes of organisational co-existence

Not all organisational relationships are conducive to collaboration. Litwak and Hylton (1962) identify three modes of organisational co-existence, each with different implications for the likely development of collaboration – independence, interdependence and conflict.

Two organisations may be said to be *independent* of one another if neither needs the other's resources to accomplish its goals, and neither is interfering in the other's goal achievement. When this occurs, there is little need for exchange between organisations, and since agencies do not generally co-operate unless they have to, one would predict a low level of collaboration. If the presence of collaboration is to be broadly accounted for, then perhaps the most general explanation for its occurrence may be found in the notion of organisational *interdependence*, where each organisation perceives that its own goals can be achieved most effectively with the assistance of the resources of the others.

Conflict arises when the goal achievement of one or more organisations occurs at the expense of the goal achievement of others. Although conflict *per se* may constrain or block inter-organisational exchange, its presence also indicates some potential for such exchange; therefore, inter-organisational conflicts may be considered a more favourable condition for collaboration than independence. Organisations may move from interdependence to conflict or vice versa, through relatively subtle shifts in goals or available resources. Molnar and Rogers (1979) further distinguish between structural and operational conflict. *Structural conflict* occurs over the basic identities and responsibilities that define a relationship, and reflects an inability to establish or maintain the basic rules or principles that govern the relationship. *Operating conflict* represents the disagreements over task expectations or role performance within an inter-organisational relationship, and can be viewed as a continual process of mutual adjustment between interacting organisations.

Given that some scope for collaborative activity seems feasible or actually exists, how can we explain any specific linkages that develop? A threefold focus is available: upon the environmental context; upon the comparative properties of an organisational network; and upon collaborative linkages themselves. These three approaches are not in conflict, but should be viewed as complementary approaches. A total analysis of inter-organisational relations would require a thorough understanding of the interplay between the variables operating on all levels, but such an analysis is dependent upon the delineation and operationalisation of these variables.

The environmental context

External factors in the environment may create the necessary preconditions for inter-organisational relations by affecting the ability of an organisation to function independently. In 'turbulent fields', individual organisations, however large, cannot expect to adapt successfully, simply through their own direct actions. Emery and Trist (1965) identify several indicators of 'turbulence' – a field containing a relatively large number of organisations; inability of agencies to satisfy the demand for services; an unstable social situation; a new programme or piece of legislation; a retrenching economy. Much of this could apply to Britain.

Although a turbulent environment establishes a context for collaborative decision-making and perhaps creates a necessity for action, the tendency of organisations to act as closed systems and resist such pressures to adapt is still powerful. In Emery and

Trist's research, it appeared that environmental pressures were great enough to induce agencies to talk together and enter a relatively loose confederative arrangement. It was not until much later, when the financial rewards for a closer relationship were tripled, that the agencies give up anything of value. Clearly the environment is important, but not of itself sufficient, to explain the existence and nature of inter-organisational relationships. More immediate factors require to be examined.

The comparative properties approach

The comparative dimension has been viewed as an initial determinant of the occurrence of collaborative activity and as a factor in its continued existence and success.

The comparative properties approach involves examining the similarities or differences of interacting groups or organisations on certain attributes or dimensions which constitute a set of conditions that continually shape the pattern of interaction. In effect, the comparative properties are seen as independent variables, and any subsequent collaborative mechanism as dependent variables. The literature identifies several comparative property prerequisites for the creation of collaborative activity.

Inter-organisational homogeneity

This variable is concerned with the degree to which the members of an interaction network exhibit functional and structural similarity. Reid (1969) takes the view that although similarity of goals is not necessary for collaboration to develop, it is likely to lead to additional cohesion, and more extensive and stable exchanges. Some of the literature on health/personal social services forums would certainly suggest that one obstacle to more fruitful collaboration is the difference in value-systems and goals amongst the participants. Whilst all may find virtue in a 'banner' goal of 'community care', the operationalisation of the goal may reveal conflicting underlying assumptions.

Hasenfeld (1972) makes a useful distinction between 'people-processing' and 'people-changing' organisations. Within the welfare field, the traditional focus has been upon the latter, whose explicit function has been to change client behaviour. Education and social work organisations are obvious examples.

'People-processing' organisations process people and confer public status upon them, and thereby shape people's lives by controlling their access to a range of settings. Examples would be Job Centres, Observation and Assessment Centres and Juvenile Courts.

'People-processing' organisations are much more likely to be involved in collaborative activity. Their *raison d'être* is the classification and disposition of clients, and the reactions to the status they confer occur mainly outside their boundaries. Staff activity will consist of transactions with clients at input, negotiations with them on a classification–disposition status at output, and exchanges with potential external recipients of the clients. 'People-changing' organisations are more likely to be insulated from the environment and from organisational boundary transactions. Hence it could be hypothesised that 'people-changing' organisations will be less attracted to collaborative activity than 'people-processing' organisations. This notion would help to explain why, for example, social work has a poor record of 'boundary transaction' activity with organisations concerned with social security and housing.

*

Domain consensus

There is some overlap between the notions of organisational homogeneity and domain consensus. Any discussion of inter-organisational analysis either explicitly or implicitly deals with the concepts of domain and domain consensus.

Thompson (1967) defines it as:

> a set of expectations, both for members of an organisation and for others with whom they interact, about what the other organisation will and will not do . . . it provides an image of the organisation's role in a larger system, which in turn serves as a guide for the ordering of action in certain directions and not in others.

Braito *et al.* (1972) operationalised it as an organisation's statement as to whether or not a particular organisation should be involved in an agency formed for a specific purpose.

The establishment of domain consensus requires the resolution of some potentially difficult issues. First it requires agreement on specific organisational goals. Second it assumes a compatibility of organisational goals, philosophies and reference orientations. Finally, it requires some agreement amongst kindred professionals upon their position in a hierarchy of professionals. Clearly these will not be attained easily. An organisation's history and association with a particular problem should increase the possibility of the problem being within its domain, but even this may be insufficient to maintain the domain consensus. The public, political or other organisations may become dissatisfied with the progress of a particular organisation, question its domain and withdraw legitimation. The manner in which in the 1940s local government lost its responsibility for both hospitals and poor law relief may be examined within this framework.

The establishment of a consensus over domain has two important implications. The most obvious is the securing of legitimated claims. Possession of a domain permits an organisation to operate in a certain sphere, claim support for its activities and define proper practices within its realm. Moreover, the authority to conduct activities is generally assumed to imply a claim upon money adequate to attain performance in a prescribed sphere.

The other implication is for collaborative activity itself, but the literature has conflicting views on this. When organisations have similar domains, they are likely to be aware of one another and to have the resources needed to help each other achieve their respective goals, but similar domains also increase the potential for territorial disputes and competition. Van de Ven (1976) proposes a concave-shaped relationship between domain similarity and collaborative activity, in which the polar ends of high and low domain similarity are unlikely conditions for collaboration, and the intermediate ranges the most likely.

Network awareness

It has already been suggested that interdependency is the most fertile ground for collaboration, but organisations must have *awareness* of their interdependence. Not only must they have knowledge of one another's existence, but they must also perceive a possible matching of goals and resources that would result in more effective goal achievement. Collaboration will also be affected by the extent of positive evaluation – the judgement by workers in the organisation of the value of the work of another organisation.

This may be affected by the length of time that organisations have been members of a network. A history of distinct administrative divisions, separate patterns of accountability and isolated patterns of training and professional socialisation all militate against positive network awareness. It is not uncommon in the literature to find not only a poor understanding of the roles of related professions and organisations, but also an unduly critical appraisal of any potential contribution. Most of the reports of inquiries into child abuse cases provide ample evidence of this.

Organisational exchange

The concept of 'exchange' can be traced back to the work of Marcel Mauss, who proposed an explanation for the seemingly one-way transfer of resources by suggesting that receipt of the gift created an obligation in the receipt. The concept, therefore, implies that no goods or services are ever transferred without reciprocity of some kind being involved. Theorists have utilised exchange notions to provide a loose conceptual framework for their analyses, but few attempts have been made to apply these to inter-organisational relationships in welfare.

In their seminal contribution, Levine and White (1961) defined 'exchange' as 'any voluntary activity between two organisations which has consequences, actual or anticipated, for the realisation of their respective goals and objectives'.

Cook (1977) points out that the problem with this definition is that it incorporates *any* form of voluntary activity, thereby rendering the term synonymous with *interaction*. She prefers to confine the concept to those situations where interactions are based upon reciprocal reinforcement – where exchange provides for *each* actor a reduction in organisational uncertainty.

An exchange analysis is fruitful because it focuses attention upon power processes, which are fundamental to an understanding of collaboration. In exchange relationships, power is linked to dependence. It is precisely because the needs of *both* participating parties need to be fulfilled by an exchange (i.e. it must be beneficial to both) that an integrated and rational system does not always evolve. There are many cases where a transfer of resources from one organisation to another may be desirable from the viewpoint of a co-ordinated system, but may be beneficial to only one party. The reluctance of the NHS to enter into unilateral resource transfers to local authorities in pursuit of a community-based scheme for some clients is an illustration of this. An exchange relation is balanced when the actors have equal power (or equal levels of dependency), but equality is not a precondition for exchange. What is necessary is that neither party is powerless in relation to others, otherwise exchange will amount to little more than the formalisation of the clear dominance of one party over another.

Alternative resource sources

An important element in organisational exchange is the availability of alternative sources. An organisation is less dependent upon exchange relations with other organisations in its network to the extent that it has accessibility to elements it needs from 'outside' sources. In terms of Hasenfeld's (1972) 'people-processing' organisations, the availability of such alternatives will increase the discretion of personnel responsible for processing and reduce the pressure to form links with any one outlet. Without such alternatives, the organisation would be under pressure to control either its intake or its output of clients, or both. It may, for example, only accept clients for whom disposition resources are available, or it may confer a 'holding' status, linking the person to an outlet but defining him or her as unready for disposition. Hasenfeld's study of employment placement agencies found that clients for whom job opportunities were not available were more likely to be classified as requiring counselling than similar clients for whom job opportunities were available. In Britain, this framework could help to explain the functioning of observation and assessment centres, the availability of assessments and statements under the 1981 Education Act, and the continued high use of custodial options by juvenile courts.

In the comparative properties approach, the basic unit of analysis is the network of organisations, consisting of a number of distinguishable organisations having a significant amount of interaction with each other.

Such interaction may at one extreme include extensive reciprocal exchanges, and at the other intense hostility or conflict. [The] variables [. . .] above may help us to explain such variations. Benson (1975) puts forward the notion of 'inter-organisational equilibrium'. An inter-organisational network is said to be equilibrated to the extent that participant organisations are engaged in highly co-ordinated, co-operative interactions based upon normative consensus and mutual respect. He hypothesises that there is a tendency towards equilibrium, and argues that increases in one equilibrium component (partly covering [the variables] above) will tend to be associated with increases in the others. Similarly, decreases in one will be associated with decreases in the others.

The focus on collaborative linkages

The third and final focus is upon the actual *dimensions* of interaction or exchange between organisations. Four key dimensions tend to be used for examining linkage mechanisms.

Degree of formalisation

Several analyses have noted variations in the extent to which the requirements and characteristics of collaborative situations are made explicit. There are two main ways in which we can attempt to assess the degree of formalisation of a relationship – the existence of administrative or legislative sanction, and the existence or otherwise of an intermediary co-ordinating body.

The extent to which an interdependency is given *official sanction* by the parties involved refers to the degree to which rules, policies and procedures govern inter-agency agreements and contracts. In social welfare settings, informal tacit arrangements occur quite frequently among organisations – cases may be referred from one agency to another and ideas can be exchanged – but formal agreements are less common. This may be in part attributable to the greater commitment required of a formal agreement, and the potential threat to organisational autonomy which it poses.

Formalisation increases as an agreement is verbalised, written down, contractual and, ultimately, mandatory. Mandated interactions involve laws or regulations specifying areas of domain, information and financial obligations, the most obvious form being one externally imposed by the legal or political system. Aldrich (1976) found that these tended to be more intense, unbalanced in favour of one of the organisations studied and associated with lower perceived co-operation.

Benson (1975) hypothesised that in voluntary, non-mandated situations, domain consensus and positive evaluation were preconditions for collaboration, and the organisations attempted to exert power as the exchange occurred. However, when collaboration is mandated by law, the roles of the interacting organisations have already been defined, and domain consensus should not be an issue.

In such situations, positive evaluation becomes a key issue for the interacting organisations. In the operation of joint finance, for example, a form of mandated relationship exists, but there may continue to be professional and organisational skirmishing over the respective abilities and perspectives of health and personal social services.

The second dimension of formalisation is the existence of an *intermediary co-ordinating body*, which offers a measure of *structural* as opposed to *agreement* formalisation. An agency may be considered 'co-ordinating' if one of its important functions is to bring about exchanges amongst other organisations. Reid (1969) distinguishes between two major strategies that may be used to achieve this – the facilitation and induction of interdependence.

The 'facilitation' of interdependence rests upon the assumption that the organisations to be co-ordinated are already close to interdependence or are ready to move in this direction. The degree of facilitation required will depend upon the degree of interdependence already present. At its simplest, this strategy could be executed by the development of inter-organisational awareness of potential interdependencies in relation to existing goals and resources.

A more common and problematic circumstance arises when a co-ordinating agency is confronted with either a high degree of independence or conflict among constituent organisations.

This may require interdependency to be 'induced' by effecting major changes in their goals and use of resources. This inducement may be generated by the use of resources which the co-ordinating agency possesses or controls and which other organisations desire. In this way, for example, the Housing Corporation may be said to have brought a degree of order to the voluntary sector of housing. Alternatively, inducement may be accomplished through the use of 'power' or 'influence', whereby organisational goals are modified by external influences. For example, in the 1970s the DHSS and Department of the Environment attempted, by the use of Circular (18/74) and then legislation (1977 Homeless Persons Act), to impose collaborative activity upon local authority housing and social services departments. Such an approach may be tenuous and subject to rupture.

Degree of intensity

The level of intensity indicates the amount of *investment* an organisation has in its relations with other organisations. Aldrich (1979) identified two measures of intensity. First, the *amount of resources* involved in a relationship. Among welfare agencies, the number of services, referrals and staff support provided to another organisation are common indicators of the intensity of a relation, but measurement is much easier in the profit-orientated sector. Second, the *frequency of interaction* between organisations, although cognisance needs to be taken of the nature of contacts and the authority level at which they take place.

Most social services contacts involve boundary-spanning personnel who arrange the referral of clients, but these contacts may not be critical to organisational survival.

Rogers (1974) has attempted to develop a scale of intensity in inter-organisational relationships, ranging through director acquaintance, director interaction, information exchange, resource exchange, overlapping membership and written agreements. *Ad hoc* case co-ordination draws only minimally upon the resources of an organisation, whereas some form of 'programme co-ordination' encompasses a much larger portion. Unless the success of a venture has been clearly established, organisations will be inclined to choose the less intense situation over that which is highly demanding.

Degree of reciprocity

The reciprocal dimension to a collaborative relationship is based upon the notion of 'exchange', discussed earlier. Interactions need not necessarily be symmetrical – some parties to an exchange may have greater influence in determining the bases and conditions of the activity than others.

There are several elements of reciprocation, of which the most common is *resource reciprocity* – the extent to which the resources in a transaction (or in the longer run, a relationship) flow to both parties equally or benefit one of them unilaterally. The units of value transacted between agencies may encompass money, physical facilities and materials, and client referrals.

Information flows are also important – messages or communications about the units of exchange or the nature of the relationship. Resource and information flows constitute the bases of a social action system, but measurement within welfare settings is problematic because such transactions cannot be assigned an unambiguous value.

This is even more true of an intangible such as prestige – the judgement by workers in one organisation of the value of the work of another organisation. Indeed, where such judgements are negative, self-validating ideologies may be internally generated which negate the assessment criteria used by external groups. Collaboration will be unlikely in such circumstances.

A related notion is *definitional reciprocity* – the extent to which the terms of a transaction are mutually agreed upon, with equal contributions from all participants. Interaction is not limited to situations in which both parties set the terms of the agreement. Many welfare agencies must follow regulatory or legislative guidelines in establishing collaborative relationships, therefore many of the terms are pre-set. However, an organisation may be predisposed to joint activity, but avoid a specific encounter because there is no give and take in problem definition.

Degree of standardisation

This represents another dimension taken from traditional models of bureaucratic structure. Just as internal standardisation of procedures smooths bureaucratic operations and promotes efficiency, so the standardisation of external relations is sought by cost-conscious administrators. Two aspects of standardisation can be distinguished.

First, *unit standardisation* – the extent of similarity between the individual units of the resources in a transaction. Litwak and Hylton (1962) hypothesise that the institution of formal collaborative mechanisms requires some reliable determination of the units of exchange and the repetition of the exchange. The argument implies that when the exchange elements are ill-defined and shifting, interaction is possible but formal interaction unlikely. Second, *procedural standardisation* – the degree of similarity over time in the procedures used for inter-organisational transactions. The intensity of interaction will have a positive effect on standardisation, because the larger the investment organisations have in each other, the more they are pushed into standardised modes of interaction for protecting their investments.

Standardisation does differ from formalisation. The latter refers to the extent to which there is an official agreement, but does not necessitate explicitness on details. An agreement that a relationship will be established may be found, but that agreement may leave open the nature and operation of the exchange.

Not all of the variables [above] are likely to be of equal significance. The resource indicator of intensity is particularly sensitive and likely to place constraints upon the others. In a situation involving large resources, one could anticipate formal agreements, standardisation of both units and procedures and reciprocal flow.

Marrett (1971) proposes two inter-organisational models. The first is characterised by a low degree of formalisation, standardisation and intensity and is represented by the kind of interaction that occurs among social welfare personnel over referrals. The second is highly formalised, standardised and intense, and is far less likely because it involves the kind of investments and commitments which organisations may not be inclined to make. Marrett argues that research is needed not so much on the first model as on the constraints to the realisation of the second.

Social change in inter-organisational networks

Given the preceding analysis, how might inter-organisational networks change in such a way as to promote collaboration? Benson (1975) identifies three sources of pressure.

Co-operative strategies
Change is sought through agreements and joint planning in which each affected social unit participates and exercises options, and any resultant network alterations are typically compromises agreed upon by the affected organisations. Such compromises will usually involve a process of negotiation and exchange through which each party voluntarily relinquishes some valued condition in exchange for similar concessions on the part of others. However, despite the frequency of co-operative strategies, the conditions for their success are restricted, since each party must hold something of value for the other party and be capable of resisting the other's demands. Agreements may cover a wide variety of products or behaviour – exchanges of funds, personnel, facilities and clients are among the most obvious, but agreements to cease disruptive and harassing activities may be of equal importance.

Incentives strategies
This constitutes the purposeful alteration of environmental constraints which may be inhibiting collaborative activity, but falls short of a directive. It may be seen as analogous to government regulation of the economy through manipulation of interest rates, tax rates and the money supply. Such a strategy may involve an alteration of the total volume of resources flowing into a network (as in the case of joint finance) or an alteration of resource channels as a means of changing priorities. Tactics such as these typically belong to an executive office or a legislative body.

Authoritative strategies
Organisations with common vertical ties may be *directed* to engage in joint activities that would not ordinarily occur on a voluntary basis. Relations between agencies may be precisely specified, covering the regulation of contacts, referrals, resource sharing and so forth. This is premised upon the possibility of an executive or legislative body utilising a dominant position in the flow of resources to *specify* the nature of programmes and linkages at subordinate levels, and not merely to encourage or reward such activities. This could cover the example of a local authority taking action to prevent 'departmentalism', as in the cases of corporate planning and the fusion of social services and housing departments in several of the London boroughs. It would also encompass attempts at national government level to rearrange boundaries in the pursuit of collaboration, such as the attempt to produce coterminous boundaries between health and social services authorities in the 1974 NHS reorganisation.
    Broadly, such a strategy could cover:

1. the introduction of new programmes of agencies;
2. the formalisation of linkages which had hitherto been informal or variable;
3. the rearrangement of an entire system of inter-agency boundaries and linkages.

Conclusion: a warning

This chapter has drawn upon American literature on management and the sociology of organisations to suggest an analytical framework for the analysis of collaborative activity in social welfare settings. The British approach to this important area has been unduly empirical. The usefulness of such a framework remains to be put to the test in a variety of settings. [. . .]

However, a provisional warning should be given against thinking that collaboration is likely to be a significant factor in resolving welfare dilemmas. Davidson (1976) has noted the paradox whereby:

> commentators on the effects of co-ordination are almost uniformly pessimistic, yet co-ordination continues to be promoted as a means of providing greater rationality in the delivery of services.

Warren *et al.* (1974) have also pointed to the frequent failure of structural arrangements for collaboration in attaining tangible results. They found that out of a total of 406 reports of structured co-ordination, only 125 instances of positive tangible results were obtained, and 29 of these were simply tautological references to improved communications.

The state of the art in assessing the feasibility of successful collaboration is not well enough developed to include precise operationalised measures for the variables involved, and further research is needed on operationalisation of the concepts and on testing the relationships between them. But at the end of the day, the fashioning of collaborative relationships of substance remains a job for talented practitioners.

References

Aldrich, H. (1976), 'Resource dependence and interorganisational relationships', *Administration and Society*, Volume 7.

Aldrich, H. (1979), *Organisations and Environments*, Prentice Hall.

Benson, J. K. (1975), 'The interorganisational network as a political economy', *Administrative Science Quarterly*, Volume 20, June.

Braito, R., Paulson, S. and Klongon, G. (1972), 'Domain consensus: a key variable in interorganisational analysis', in Brinkerhoff, M. and Kunz, P., *Complex Organisations and their Environments*, Wm. C. Brown.

Cook, K. (1977), 'Exchange and power in networks of interorganisational relations', *Sociological Quarterly*, Volume 18.

Davidson, S. M. (1976), 'Planning and co-ordination of social services in multi-organisational contexts', *Social Services Review*, March.

Emery, F. and Trist, E. (1965), 'The causal texture of organisational environments', *Human Relations*, 18.

Hasenfeld, Y. (1972), 'People processing organisations: an exchange approach', *American Sociological Review*, Volume 37.

Levine, S. and White, P. (1961), 'Exchange as a conceptual framework for the study of interorganisational relationships', *Administrative Science Quarterly*, Volume 5.

Litwak, E. and Hylton, L. (1962), 'Interorganisational analysis: a hypothesis on co-ordinating agencies', *Administrative Science Quarterly*, Volume 6, March.

Marrett, C. (1971), 'On the specification of interorganisational dimension', *Sociology and Social Research*, Volume 61.

Molnar, J. and Rogers, D. (1979), 'A comparative model of interorganisational conflict', *Administrative Science Quarterly*, Volume 24.

Reid, W. J. (1969), 'Interorganisational co-ordination in welfare: a theoretical approach to analysis and intervention' in Kramer, R. and Specht, H., *Readings in Community Organisation Practice*, Prentice Hall.

Rogers, D. (1974), 'Towards a scale of interorganisational relations among public agencies', *Sociology and Social Research*, Volume 59.

Thompson, J. D. (1967), *Organisations in Action*, McGraw-Hill.

Warren, R., Rose, S. and Bergunder, A. (1974), *The Structure of Urban Reform*, D.C. Heath.

Van de Ven, A. (1976), 'On the nature, formation and maintenance of relations among organisations', *Academy of Management Review*, Volume 1, Part 4.

Yuchtman, E. and Seashore, S. (1967), 'A system resource approach to organisational effectiveness', *American Sociological Review*, Volume 32, December.

Structure and action as constructs in the practice of public administration

Pieter Degeling and Hal Colebatch

The dominant paradigm and its critics

Until very recently the dominant paradigm in the study of organization and the teaching of administrative studies has been an instrumental one. That is, the organization is seen as an instrument for the attainment of given purposes, and both the nature of the organization and of the processes which take place in and around it are best understood in relation to its instrumental character.

Academic study of and teaching about organizations was seen as being about increasing their capacity to achieve these given purposes. Positivistic science was applied to the design of organizational processes, and to devising practices and techniques which would strengthen the scientific character of managerial decision-making, increase management's capacity to control, and hence enhance the strength of the organization as an instrument of rational purpose. The propagation of these ideas, practices and techniques then formed the content of management education.

This instrumental paradigm has, in the past two decades, been subject to question on a number of grounds. Within systems theory, research has pointed to the effects of factors outside an organization on organizational processes.[1] At the same time, the introduction into analysis of concepts such as power, dependence, coalition-formation and conflict has raised questions about the extent to which activity within organizations is and can be controlled and directed toward the rational pursuit of previously-defined goals.[2]

It has become clear, for instance, that while presentations of the organization as a coherent entity with a clear set of goals are important in the process of organizing, they are not accurate descriptions of the process.[3] Other studies have raised questions about the presumed primacy of managers and their capacity to impose their will over

From P. Degeling and H. K. Colebatch, 'Structure and action as constructs in the practice of public administration', *Australian Journal of Public Administration*, **53**, 1984, pp. 320–31.

organizational processes. Again it is clear that while the attribution of managerial primacy is a significant factor in the structuring of relations (that is, it is important in the exercise of managerial control), this is itself not an accurate and full description of how relations within organizations are structured and conducted.[4]

Recent studies have also questioned the presumption of managerial homogeneity implicit in the instrumentalist view of organization. Under examination, 'management' turns out not to be a single entity, and certainly not a single-minded one. Managers have been shown to be participants in continuing contests, characterized by contingent power and shifting coalitions.[5] The increasing focus on the processes in which managers are engaged has led some writers to question the assumption that positivistic science will produce 'efficient management'. Evered, for instance, points out that management:

- is centrally concerned with action-taking . . . yet nearly all published research (on management) ignores action.
- involves making projections which are not open to empirical research but require the creation of a new paradigm of inquiry which will overcome the crucial deficiencies of positivistic science.
- deals with diagnosis, judgement and interpretation of events and as such requires pattern recognition and a different kind of knowing that logic and rationality are conceived in positivistic science.
- is a political process, in which the exercise of power and influence is dependent on the social and historical context in which the actors are located. The approaches of positivistic science have proved inadequate for a satisfactory analysis of these processes.[6]

Evered concludes that managerial decisions and actions are both a product of and a reaction to the phenomena of organization as experienced and interpreted by participants. That is, outcomes are produced by the way that participants act in terms of their perceptions, their values and their experiences rather than the limited 'behavioural variables' which yield the universal categories (for example 'human needs') of the positivistic approach. Thus we need to develop non-positivistic theories that incorporate 'the unique experiential and phenomenal reality of the actors. We need theories in which the "field" is defined by the organizational participants rather than categorical scientists'.[7]

Social action theory and the practice of administration
Our understanding of organizations (and management processes) has been enhanced by the application of social action theory to their analysis.[8] Put simply, social action theory argues that the actions of organizational participants are only understandable in terms of the subjective meanings which actors attribute to the situations confronting them. This implies that analysis should focus on the meanings which actors attach to their own actions and attribute to the actions of others. Actors are depicted as intentional beings who, in casting their own actions and interpreting and evaluating the actions of others, make use of frameworks of meaning which are socially and historically based, are (in part) institutionalized and, in many instances, are perceived

by those involved as social facts. To the extent that particular frameworks of meaning are shared by numbers of actors and provide a basis for them to cohere, and people act in terms of these frameworks, their actions contribute to both the re-affirmation of these frameworks and the maintenance of social (and hence organizational) structure.

Social action theorists focus attention on the inter-subjective dimension of organizational life: that is, how it is constructed, sustained and changed by the actors in interaction with one another. When viewed from a social action perspective, the arrangement and practices used (relating to the definition and division of work, the exercise of control over personnel and clientele, and resource allocation and decision processes within organizations) cannot be taken as given. Nor can they be seen as products of past exercises in organizational design which, once promulgated, will automatically be binding on organizational participants.

Instead, social action theorists argue that the various dimensions of organization structure and process (and the arrangements and practices which give them form) can only be understood when they are examined from the perceptions that participants hold of them, and how they act accordingly. From this basis, it is then possible to demonstrate how particular arrangements and practices come to be accepted and taken for granted; how and why previously accepted and taken-for-granted constructions come to be challenged; and how what is regarded as accepted practice is subject to negotiation and can be changed over time.

The social action perspective demonstrates that organizations can no longer be viewed primarily as goal-directed instruments: that is, to explain and evaluate an organization in terms of its presumed functions or goals is an inadequate base both for understanding the organizational process and for locating oneself within it as an actor. Rather, organizations are seen as structures of order in which outcomes (goods and services, and also the patterning of relations) emerge from continuing processes of negotiation. Furthermore, managers can no longer be seen as framing and implementing unambiguous organizational goals; rather, their activities are seen to focus on the maintenance of negotiated order within and between organizations.

In the social action perspective, then, management requires a self-awareness on the part of practitioners. They need to be aware of how prevailing organizational arrangements and practices have differing meanings and significance for those who are subject to them as well as for those responsible for their operation. They need an understanding of how frameworks of meaning, and consequent modes of discourse, are developed and propagated, and how in their use, these modes of discourse shape the terms under which organizational relationships are conducted. In studying administration, both academics and practitioners will want to increase their awareness of the inter-subjective dimensions of social and organizational life and the implications that these hold both in the casting of our own actions and in interpreting and evaluating or judging the actions of others.[9] And they need to understand that different frameworks of meaning can be in use simultaneously, and that these can have different implications for the structuring of organizational relationships. For instance, if we were to look at public administration in relation to the Sydney milk supply, we might encounter a range of abstract concepts: 'market forces', or 'government policy', or 'orderly marketing'. Each of these emerges from a different set of assumptions about the way the world works, that is a different framework of meaning. They are not simply concepts, but are statements about the relationships between participants in a complex organizational situation, the Sydney milk supply, and they are mobilized to explain and legitimate particular sorts of relationships. In so doing they underwrite the claims of some participants, and discount those of others.

Social structure and the analysis of organizational life

This perspective on organizations as systems of negotiated order is contested by others who see them as media through which relations of domination are maintained in capitalist society. They see organizations as systems of order which reflect and recreate established relations of power and social and economic advantage within a society. These theorists, whom we shall call 'structuralists',[10] argue that organizational analysis should go beyond description of the behaviour of those who are involved in or affected by organizational processes, and should focus on the complexity of social and economic forces within a society which are given form and force by the actions of organizational participants. The structuralists argue that the social (and hence structural) make-up of these actions only becomes clear when analysis moves beyond the formalized arrangements and practices used in particular organizational contexts and takes account of the social/historical factors which affect and are reflected in the structuring of relations within a society. To structuralists this means that organizational analysis should focus on the interrelationship between the economic structure of society, its class relations, its ideologies, and how these are developed over time. From this basis it will then be possible to explain the structuring of relations within and between organizational contexts and how this constrains actions on the part of some and facilitates actions on the part of others.

Structuralists have brought into sharper focus the differences in power and advantage which are inherent in the conduct of relations in capitalist society, and in so doing they have brought into question the presumed neutral instrumentality of organizational processes inherent in functionalist analysis. However, the structuralists retain an instrumental orientation. This is demonstrated by their claims that their approach clarifies the way that organizations operate as media of control and how (in facilitating the control which some exercise over others) organizations contribute to the maintenance of existing modes of domination and reproduce prevailing differences of power and advantage within a society.

The instrumentalism inherent in the structuralists' accounts of organizations leads them to relate the way we think about management to those processes through which the existing structuring of relations within a society is reproduced.[11] To structuralists, the connections between thought, action and structure can be seen in the process of management education. The vocational nature of management education means that it is concerned first with equipping a particular group (existing and prospective managers) with the ideological forms which buttress the existing relations of power among capital workers, organizations and clients; and secondly, with providing this elite group with social technologies which can be used to maintain managerial primacy, and the continued operation of organizations as media of control. The structuralists argue that these outcomes can only be avoided by denying the legitimacy of the vocational orientations of the field of study and/or casting the educational process into a form which will offer a radical critique of capitalist society, capitalist modes of production and the location and practice of management within these.

Acceptance of these findings poses dilemmas for those of us – academics or practitioners – whose activities are oriented to the critical review of, and to having an impact on, administrative practice. When viewed from a structuralist perspective, we are either knowing collaborators in the perpetuation of structures of domination and inequality in our society; or as ineffective critics of these structures, we contribute to their stability: the system of repressive tolerance absorbs contradictions within our society, and the underlying legitimacy of the existing system of domination is not shaken.[12]

Framing an alternative paradigm

Social action theorists and structuralists provide covering fire for one another in their rejection of the instrumental paradigm, but diverge on the construction of an alternative – a divergence which emerges over such questions as power, consciousness, voluntarism and causality – in fact over the relationship between structure and action.

Social action theorists, stressing the importance of actors' perceptions in the creation of organization, question analyses which rely on some imputed force ('structure') which is independent of the actors themselves. They argue that to assume such a cause-and-effect relationship denies the capacity of actors: first, to ascribe meaning to the social and organizational world which both confronts them and is of their making; secondly, to make choices in the framing of their own actions and to act strategically; and thirdly, to make judgements about their own actions and actions of others.

Structuralists, by contrast, decry the voluntarism which they see as being inherent in the social action perspective. They argue that social action theorists, in their concern to take account of the way that the occurrences of social life are mediated and given meaning by actors, have given insufficient weight, first to the social and historical context in which action is taking place; secondly to the way that organizational actors are part of continuing structures of domination; and thirdly to the way that action within organizational contexts is shaped by and recreates relations of dependence and domination.

To overcome this impasse, we need to focus our attention on the relationship between structure and action. It is misleading to see these as distinct and opposed categories, since they are, in fact, parts of the same process. Cicourel,[13] for instance, argues for the abandonment of frameworks which depend on drawing distinctions (necessarily arbitrary) between so-called macro structures and the micro episodes of everyday life. Instead, analysis should be focused on the way that everyday encounters are both shaped by social forms, and in turn re-constitute[14] these social forms, whose existence and effect transcend the time and space of individual actions.

Habermas relates structure and action by focusing attention on the way that communicative modes (defined as ways of ordering and ascribing meaning to phenomena, and related approaches to reasoning and discourse) have emerged in particular social–historical contexts.[15] He argues that these communicative modes, by their use and by their consequent effect on action, constitute structure, both in interpersonal relations, and in an individual's relations with wider collectivities. Moreover, in industrial societies, the dominant communicative mode is one which places emphasis on rational choice, known goals, and instruments for their attainment, and which denies the significance of personal relationships (and hence 'inter-subjectivity') in both reasoning and social discourse. Habermas argues that the dominance of this communicative mode when combined with the stated values of a market economy, which emphasizes the necessity of continued economic growth, and the social and instrumental efficacy of calculable market relations, has led to the emergence of a system of order in which social relations are objectified and increasingly made subject to rational (calculative) and organizationally-based forms of control. With western industrial societies these outcomes are justified by the claim that rationalized forms of control ensure social and political order and expand a society's instrumental capabilities. The consequent devaluation of the significance of socially-negotiated (that is inter-subjective) meaning is seen as contributing to social and political integration and the continued growth of purposively instrumental organizations is seen as extending the society's ability to exercise control over the processes of social and economic production.

Habermas argues that the resulting rationalization of social life and the attendant denial of politics as an integral aspect of social life is self-sustaining, unless it is subjected to critique which focuses on the processes which, in western industrial societies, have led to the displacement of inter-subjective modes of discourse and which in present day society sustains the dominance of instrumentalism in social, political and economic life. The development of such a critique will first raise our awareness of both the nature of the existing structures of domination and the deleterious effects that these produce for both individuals and society; secondly, will raise our awareness of how these structures of domination are constituted and maintained by the actions of those who are subject to them; and thirdly, will demonstrate how through critique, and resulting forms of self-awareness and action, the existing structures of domination can be displaced by social forms which will allow for greater inter-subjectivity in social relations. This will lift the social (other-regarding) potential of individuals and social institutions to the mutual benefit of both individuals and society.

The importance which Habermas has attributed to instrumental modes of com-munication in present day society has provided a point of entry for researchers and teachers of public administration who approach their work from a perspective which has come to be called 'critical theory'.[16] The presumed instrumental rationality of institutional and organizational forms has been questioned. Attention has also been paid to the way that within these institutions, questions of choice involving contending values and interests are either not recognized, or translated into problems which are soluble by the application of impersonally derived rules and/or 'scientifically' derived techniques. It has also been shown that such procedural and technical approaches to choice and decision mask the exercise of power and legitimate existing structures of control. Denhardt has argued that the application of critical theory in research, teaching and administration will mean that questions about public policy and the operation of public organizations will be placed in 'larger normative and historical contexts in which they properly reside'. He argues that this use of critical theory will lead those involved in research, teaching and practice to lay 'the foundations for greater autonomy and responsibility within the bureaucracy and its interactions with others' and will raise our awareness of the '. . . essential connection between personal and social self-reflection, and personal and social development (including organizational development)'.[17]

How this restructuring is to be achieved is not clear. Habermas and Denhardt seem to assume that structural factors within a society can be altered, negated or removed simply by raising the awareness of those involved – a view of change akin to a debating society's belief in the ultimate power of reason. It collapses politics to reasoned debate (or in Habermas's terms, 'unfettered discourse') about preferred states of social being and does not address how and why those who are being advantaged (as well as those who are disadvantaged) by the existing structuring of relations will act to maintain or to change these. Furthermore, by locating the impetus for change in the consciousness of individual actors, this approach avoids or ignores significant aspects of the analysis (elsewhere in critical theory) of how these relations have come to be structured over time, and are restrained by continuing action in which the actors are involved.

We can see this in Denhardt's discussion of the potential for change. He argues that if they act from a critical perspective actors can change the values and frames of reference which underlie some of the existing arrangements and practices within an organization even though these changes 'might be at odds with the dominant values of the bureaucracy'. Denhardt recognizes that this possibility would be slighter 'if we assume that the dominant values of the bureaucracy are those of the society, but [s]ince bureaucracies take on a 'life' of their own and values of their own, we have reason to question the correspondence of organizational values and those of society at large'.[18]

But this position and its underlying assumptions seem open to question on a number of grounds. Denhardt, along with Habermas and others, has pointed to the pervasiveness of instrumental communicative modes in western industrial society, which is built upon bureaucratic organizations which are seen as rational, scientific instruments of control. The instrumental mode is not some private language for bureaucrats. If it were, the gulf between the values of officials and the values of the rest of society would in itself be a focus for change. And Denhardt's presentation of the problem does not address the question of interest and hence of content implicit in a challenge to the dominant instrumental paradigm.

At this stage, it is important to make two conceptual clarifications concerning the relationship first between structure and action, and secondly between organizational processes and interests. As we have said, structure and action are closely linked in that each is constituted by, and in turn constitutes, the other. In Giddens' terms, the social world enables, constrains and invokes action, and it is reproduced as skilled performance by actors, and in this way reconstituted.[19] Bourdieu argues that action should be seen as the merging of objectified history and embodied history.[20] By objectified history, he refers to the practices, beliefs and structured relations of power which are recognized as having been developed over time, and which govern relationships between the positions which actors occupy in social and organizational life. By embodied history, he means those aspects of historical experience which have been internalized by actors as part of their own selves, and which in this way shape their dispositions in continuing relations with others. In this way objectified history becomes 'historical action' (or enacted history), and the prevailing structuring of relations within a society and the position that this sets out for actors are re-formed. This means that social action cannot be seen as the product of some 'structural' force outside of the actors, nor can their actions be explained simply by reference to what is needful for the accomplishment of some objectified purpose external to the actors (for example 'the needs of capital' or 'the goals of the organization'). Rather the positions which the actors came to occupy and their interpretations of these, and the courses of action they see as being open to them, are themselves the outcomes of the actions of others, past and present, dominant and dominated, advantaged and disadvantaged. All individuals in the course of their involvement in struggles for power and advantage 'short of opting out of the game and falling into oblivion, have no choice but to struggle to keep up or improve their position in the field'.[21]

In the course of the struggles which take place, relationships are 'restructured', though not necessarily changed, and a society comes to be 'peopled' by institutional forms 'which no one designed and wanted' and which show little evidence of instrumental purpose or even of volition. The structuring of relations which results will be such that even those who are in positions of dominance, 'cannot say, even with the advantage of hindsight, how the formula was found, and are astonished that such institutions can exist as they do'.[22] Furthermore, in relation to the disposition of actors, Bourdieu notes 'that no one (actor or group of actors) can take advantage of the game, not even those who dominate it, without being taken up and taken in by it. Thus, there will be no game without a belief in the game and without the wills, intentions and aspirations which activate the agents'[23] as they seek to protect or enhance their positions. In this way the actors occupy positions, but are also appropriated by them. Through their actions in and reactions to the struggles which take place they contribute to the production and reproduction of social and historical processes (for example social structure) which shape both their positions in society and their dispositions in action.

To say that social practices, which include organizational forms, stem from objective and embodied history rather than from the instrumental purpose of one or some of the actors is not to imply that these arrangements, like other forms of social patterning, favour all of the actors equally. Practices used in the allocation of resources, the exercise of control, the attribution of legitimacy and standing, and the determination of access, eligibility and priority are obviously an important part of the structuring of inequality within society. In other words, the activity of organizing creates winners and losers – meaning not only that some people do better out of them than others, but also that the experience of this becomes part of the embodied history of the actors, and something which they are motivated to enhance, defend or challenge.

The analysis and practice of administration

Our analysis has led us away from the study of 'the organization' towards the contemplation of 'organizing'. There are many bases for organizing people; they emerge from historical experience rather than from some mechanical form of social engineering; and they are articulated by frameworks of interpretation of experience and modes of communication. In this way they generate order, and hence create the organization. But it is created by social action, not by the imposition of science; it is not self-sustaining, but is recreated by the experience of participants; and it is not morally neutral – it creates winners and losers.

This calls for a clearer view of both where managers stand in organizations, and the nature of the activities in which they engage. It becomes clear that managers are partisan players in the political processes which arise from and give shape to the structuring of relations. Their position and standing in these processes depends on their reputed and demonstrated ability to shape and maintain systems of order to which sufficient significant groupings within the organization and the wider society can subscribe. The activities in which they engage (that is mobilizing, co-opting, mediating, networking, brokering and enunciating or propagating generalized value/rule frameworks) are not neutral in content and intent. Rather, these activities are oriented toward shaping and/or sustaining the existing systems of order and sustaining their own positions both within and external to an organization.

So analysis and practice must recognize that organizational processes are shaped through structured contest. There are within social and organization (that is structured) contexts different bases for cohesion and for cleavage. These bases are given form through the activities of individuals who, in their efforts to fashion and maintain systems of order which are congruent with their definitions of meaning, their interests and their constructions of how relations ought to be conducted, bargain and negotiate with one another. Analysis which proceeds from a recognition of the structured (but nevertheless negotiated) nature of organizational life highlights the political nature of managerial involvement in the construction and maintenance of ordered relations within their organizations and with the society at large. The practice of managers who understand this will reflect their recognition that statements about 'managerial authority' have to be interpreted as part of a particular negotiated order rather than as descriptions of normal practice. These managers will see that an appeal to their ascribed authority is a frail basis for affecting outcomes; but that their impact on outcomes is a consequence of their activity in constructing and maintaining relationships, mobilizing frameworks of meaning, shaping discourse – in other words, being active participants in the shaping of the negotiated order of which they are a part.

Notes

1. Examples of so-called environmental factors recognized as having an influence on organizational processes include the incorporation of clients and possible opponents into organizational processes: P. Selznick, *TVA and the Grass Roots*, Berkeley, University of California Press, 1949; the penetration of wider social and economic factors into organizational contexts and their effects on the conduct of relations within primary work groups and between these groups and other segments of an organization; E. L. Trist *et al.*, *Organizational Choice*, London, Tavistock, 1963; the effect of market forces, technological change and other forms of uncertainty and relations of dependence on the practices and use in organizations; P. Katz and R. L. Kahn, *The Social Psychology of Organizations*, New York, Wiley, 1966; P. R. Lawrence and J. W. Lorsch, *Organization and Environment: Managing differentiation and integration*, Boston, Harvard University Press, 1967; J. D. Woodward, *Industrial Organization Theory and Practice*, London, Oxford University Press, 1965; J. D. Thompson, *Organizations in Action*, New York, McGraw-Hill, 1967.
2. A. W. Gouldner, 'Organizational analysis', in R. K. Merton *et al.* (eds.), *Sociology Today*, New York, Basic Books, 1959; C. Perrow, 'The analysis of goals in complex organizations', *American Sociological Review*, 26 1961, pp. 854–66; J. Stelling and R. Bucher, 'Autonomy and monitoring of hospital wards', *Sociological Quarterly*, 13, 1972, pp. 431–46.
3. For an overview of the notion of goals in organization theory and the sociology of organizations, see Richard Scholl, 'An analysis of macro models in organizations', *Administration and Society*, 13(3), 1981, pp. 271–98.
4. In essence the central concern of much of organization theory (to develop organization designs and methods of control whose use would enhance the position of management) bears witness to the contingent nature of managerial control. For an overview of the ideological nature of organization theory and its use in buttressing managerial primacy see J. Child, *British Management Thought*, London, Allen & Unwin, 1969. See also J. Pfeffer, *Power in Organizations*, Boston, Pitman, 1981, pp. 1–31.
5. See C. I. Barnard, *The Functions of the Executive*, Cambridge, Mass., Harvard University Press, 1938; M. Dalton, *Men Who Manage*, New York, Wiley, 1959; R. M. Cyert and J. G. March, *A Behavioural Theory of the Firm*, Englewood Cliffs, Prentice Hall, 1963; A. Jay, *Management and Machiavelli*, London, Hodder and Stoughton, 1967; C. Perrow, *Organizational Analysis: A sociological view*, London, Tavistock, 1970; Leonard R. Sayles, *Management Behavior*, New York, McGraw-Hill, 1964; A. Downs, *Inside Bureaucracy*, Boston, Little, Brown, 1967; A. M. Pettigrew, *The Politics of Organizational Decision Making*, London, Tavistock, 1973.
6. Roger Evered, 'Management education for the year 2000', in Gary L. Cooper (ed.), *Developing Managers for the 1980's*, London, Macmillan, 1981.
7. *Ibid.*, p. 75.
8. D. Silverman, *The Theory of Organisations*, London, Heinemann, 1970; D. Silverman, 'Some neglected questions about social reality', in P. Filmer *et al.* (eds.), *New Directions in Sociological Theory*, London, Collier-Macmillan, 1972; D. Silverman, 'Accounts of organisation: organisational "structures" and the accounting process', in J. B. McKinlay (ed.), *Cases in Organisational Behaviour*, London, Holt, Rinehart and Winston, 1975.
9. An extended discussion of these dimensions in administrative studies is provided in M. Harmon, *Action Theory for Public Administration*, London, Longman, 1981.
10. V. L. Allen, *Social Analysis: A Marxist critique and alternative*, London, Longman, 1975; Stewart Clegg and David Dunkerley, *Organizations, Class and Control*, London, Routledge

& Kegan Paul, 1980; J. K. Benson, 'Organisations: a dialectical view',*Administrative Science Quarterly*, 22, 1977, pp. 1–21. Some writers restrict the term 'structuralist' to Levi-Strauss and his close followers; we do not.

11. An account of this dilemma is provided in Rosemary Deem, 'The teaching of industrial sociology in higher education: an exploratory analysis', *Sociological Review*, 29(2), 1981, pp. 237–51.

12. H. Marcuse, *One-Dimensional Man*, London, Routledge & Kegan Paul, 1964.

13. A. V. Cicourel, 'Notes on the integration of micro and macro-levels of analysis', in K. Knorr-Cetina and A. V. Cicourel (eds.), *Advances in Social Theory and Methodology*, London, Routledge & Kegan Paul, 1981.

14. Literally 're-constitute'; that is, these social forms ('structure') only continue to have force to the extent that people act in this way, and in so doing, re-constitute the structure through their actions.

15. J. Habermas, *Toward a Rational Society*, London, Heinemann, 1971.

16. See Richard Bates, 'Educational administration, the technologization of reason and the management of knowledge: toward a critical theory', paper presented to the Annual Conference of the American Educational Research Association, Los Angeles, April 1981; Robert B. Denhardt, 'Toward a critical theory of public organisations', *Public Administration Review*, 41(6), 1981, pp. 628–35; Robert E. Denhardt and Kathryn G. Denhardt, 'Public administration and the critique of domination', *Administration and Society*, 11(1), 1979, pp. 107–20; Robert B. Denhardt, *In the Shadow of Organisation*, Lawrence, Kansas, The Regent Press, 1981.

17. Denhardt, *op. cit.*

18. *Ibid.*, p. 633.

19. Anthony Giddens, *Central Problems in Social Theory*, London, Macmillan, 1979, Ch. 2.

20. Pierre Bourdieu, 'Men and machines', in K. Knorr-Cetina and A. V. Cicourel,*op. cit.*, Ch. 11. For an earlier use of Bourdieu's work see Clare Burton, 'Labour market strategies in public sector and private sector organisations', paper presented to APROS Colloquium on the Public–Private Dichotomy in Organisational Analysis, Kuring-gai College of Advanced Education, Lindfield, NSW, August 1982.

21. Pierre Bourdieu, *op. cit.*, p. 307.

22. *Ibid.*, pp. 311–12.

23. *Ibid.*, p. 308.

Rules, discretion, and legitimacy

R. Baldwin

Rules have often been advocated as a means of controlling governmental discretions.[1] Indeed, when discussing how a governmental activity should be carried out there is a strong temptation (especially for lawyers) to ask: 'Should this activity be governed by rules or discretion?' Assessing governmental processes involves, however, far broader issues than arc encompassed in the 'rules versus discretion' debate. The operation of government gives rise to a host of questions concerning the exercise of power and the acceptability of various means to control or facilitate the exercise of that power.

Using governmental rules is one way of controlling or executing governmental functions but it is by no means the only one. Alternative controls include accountability to variously constituted bodies; scrutiny, complaints, and inspection systems; arrangements to ensure openness (such as requirements to publish performance indicators and statistics) and schemes for giving effect to consumer's views. Alternative executive devices include arbitrations, managerial decisions, inquiries, adjudications, contracts, and negotiations.[2] The notion of discretion is, moreover, unduly narrow if seen only in the context of rules. As Keith Hawkins has pointed out, lawyers may see discretion as constrained only by legal rules but social scientists are likely to see discretion as shaped also by political, economic, social, and organizational forces outside the legal structure.[3] The relationship between rules and discretion, may, of course, often be so close as to constitute a blending. Discretion suffuses the interpretation and application of rules (as in the processes of defining the meaning, relevance, and scope of rules). Similarly the nature and quality of rules will often bear on the kind of discretion encountered.[4] This is not to imply that rules, rather than other factors or processes, are the primary influences on discretion and to make this point is quite consistent with holding that discretion can be seen in the context of processes and constraints other than rules.

In asking whether, when, and how rules may best contribute to good government, it is necessary to bear in mind the potential of controlling or enabling devices other than rules, and to explore the array of values potentially served by different governmental processes. [. . .]

From R. Baldwin, *Rules and Government* (1995), Oxford: Oxford University Press, pp. 16–46.

The 'rules versus discretion' approach to process

The legal paradigm

The stereotypical 'lawyers' view' of the world is one built on a particular set of approaches and values. It generally favours the regulation of human activity by means of clear, previously announced rules.[5] As Nicola Lacey has argued:

> Problems are typically seen as arising from ambiguities or 'gaps' in the rules, calling for clearer interpretation or further legislative or quasi-legislative action. Disputes are seen as calling for resolution on the basis of the given rules and according to standards of due process. This approach is closely associated with the ideal of the 'rule of law' and hence with liberalism as a doctrine of political morality.[6]

The paradigm, of course, gives rise to difficulties in areas where governance by rules is inappropriate or cannot be arrived at, but a slowness to recognize the existence of such areas is an inescapable aspect of the paradigm. Owing much to Dicey's concept of the rule of law, the approach is eager to build processes around the courts and to protect individuals' procedural rights. The concept of collective rights, of public policy issues is alien.[7] A model of justice built on fairness to individuals looms sufficiently large to obscure such values as efficiency in the public interest, since it focuses on procedures and, instead of a concern for substantive results, there is, as Lacey notes: 'faith in the idea that openness, rationality, generality and predictability (values centrally located in the rule of law ideal) will conduce to fairness'.[8] It has been argued, notably by Jeffrey Jowell,[9] that in spite of its well-known deficiencies, the rule of law nevertheless provides 'a principle which requires feasible limits on official power'.[10] This argument is not, however, without dangers. If the notion of the rule of law is treated as useful in pointing to certain values that are relevant in assessing governmental processes, this is relatively unproblematic. Much remains to be said, however, about the other values to be served by such processes and how 'rule of law' values relate to these – hence Jowell comments: 'The scope of the Rule of Law is large, but not, however, large enough to serve as a principle upholding a number of other requirements of a democracy.'[11]

If, however, centrality is given to the notion of the rule of law so that it becomes a focal point or a principal bench-mark for assessing processes then it may well be countered that the 'rule of law' vision constitutes a view of the world through legalistic eyes and a distorting perspective.

To see the world as essentially governable by rules leads naturally to the 'rules versus discretion' approach; it moreover encourages an understating of the drawbacks of rules and an exaggeration of their virtues. Such a vision tends to evaluate administrative procedures according to standards designed to ensure a fair trial and it leads to a neglect of non-lawyerly ways of seeing and evaluating governmental processes.[12] As a result, lawyerly critiques of governmental modes of operation tend to produce calls for more rules, more trial-type processes – in short, more of the trimmings of formal justice. The failings of a particular governmental process may be fundamental and may require substantial rethinking of such matters as broad governmental strategy, schemes of accountability, scrutiny procedures, organizational frameworks, and goals. To respond according to the prescriptions implicit in the legal paradigm may not prove merely obfuscatory, but, as shall be seen below, counter-productive.

These points can be understood in relation to rules by examining the 'legalistic' case for rule-making as put forward by Kenneth Culp Davis.

The legalistic case for rules

In his highly influential book *Discretionary Justice*[13] Davis argued that the greatest need and hope for improving justice for individuals in the government and legal system lay in the area where decisions depended more upon discretion than upon rules and principles, and where formal hearings and judicial review were mostly irrelevant.[14] The goal, he said, should be to eliminate unnecessary discretionary power in government, not to eliminate all discretionary power.'[15] To this end, he argued that three techniques might profitably be employed: confining discretion by fixing its boundaries with statutory or administrative standards; structuring discretion by using rules and policy statements to control the manner of its exercise; and checking its use by having one official monitor another 'as a protection against arbitrariness'.[16] The way forward was not to improve the use of statutory standards but lay in 'earlier and more elaborate administrative rule-making and in better structuring and checking of discretionary power'.[17]

Davis freely conceded the need for discretion in a governmental of laws and men. Indeed, he criticized the 'extravagant version of the rule of law'[18] that had no place for discretion: 'The answer is in broad terms that we should eliminate much unnecessary discretionary power . . . The goal is not the maximum degree of confining, structuring and checking; the goal is to find the optimum degree for each power in each set of circumstances.'[19]

In cases of doubt, however, Davis was not disposed in favour of discretion. He argued that 90 per cent of injustice in administration flowed from discretionary activity and that: 'In a government of men and laws, the portion that is a government of men, like a malignant cancer, often tends to stifle the portion that is a government of laws.'[20]

In spite of Davis's assertions about the indispensability of discretion for the individuation of justice, the use of such language portrayed discretion as a corrupting force, a nasty growth that eroded the basis of 'justice'.[21] Thus Davis commented: 'Our governmental and legal systems are saturated with excessive discretionary power which needs to be confined, structured and checked.' His central concern was to do what could be done 'to minimise discretionary power'. As Judge Henry Friendly put it: 'Discretionary justice thus begins to look suspiciously like non-discretionary justice.'[22]

Davis directed attention to the less rule-governed areas of government and he did much to encourage the growth of governmental rule-making. His prescriptions for the use of rules were, however, legalistic and it is necessary to bear in mind the limitations of Davis's thesis when analysing governmental rule use. Five main difficulties can be identified.

DAVIS'S CONCEPT OF JUSTICE

Davis's yardstick for evaluating governmental procedures – that of 'justice' – is highly legalistic. We might ask why this should provide the basis for assessing the acceptability of governmental activities and processes. Davis, after all, focuses not on social justice or policy-making but states his concern to be: 'that portion of discretionary power which pertains to justice, and with that portion of justice which pertains to individual parties'.[23]

It is this concern with individualistic justice that slants his account and restricts its wider applicability. His focus is on decisions that are made by individuals rather than by organizations or groups and on discretion that affects private citizens and not, say, sectors of the population. Attention is directed to the exercise of discretion in the handling and disposal of cases rather than to the ways in which choices are made about policy. There emerges a concept of administrative justice that plays down policy considerations and makes it easy both to focus attention on those demands typically made of administrators by subscribers to the legal paradigrn (fairness, openness, predictability, etc.) and to minimize the importance in public decision-making of such factors as efficiency, adaptability, and the furtherance of public rather than private interests.

Such narrowness overlooks the substantial policy-making discretions that legislatures often give to administrative officials in order to deal with the subtleties and uncertainties of individual regulatory problems. Thus commentators have questioned an approach to administrative law that is preoccupied with individuals rather than policies addressing collective issues.[24]

It would thus be a mistake to think that any governmental procedure can be improved by adding ever more legalistic trimmings and accessories (the 'Escort XR3i' approach to processes). Davis's thesis, however, almost boils down to a simple plea for greater openness in government. Thus, in one article,[25] Davis reduced his whole position to the twelve-word slogan: 'As far as feasible – open standards, open findings, open reasons, open precedents.' This might be an attractive proposition on its face value but it is too simple as indeed is the notion that justice is an agreed, unproblematic, apolitical bench-mark. Within the same bureaucracy a number of different notions of justice may exist and there may be found within any group of parties affected by a decision-maker some very different conceptions of 'justice'. Thus, for example, when considering the decision of a body that distributes air transport licences, a large airline may consider that a 'just' system is one that is judicialized, rational, based on published rules, mindful of the *status quo*, and amenable to low-risk planning (one, incidentally, that constitutes a formidable barrier to new entrants to the industry). A newer, smaller, more aggressive operator who benefits from some disturbance of the *status quo* may consider a just regime to be one that is fast-reacting, not necessarily based on slowly developing rules, open to innovation, and rewarding of enterprise.

RULES AND THE PURSUIT OF JUSTICE

A legalistic approach to rules does not merely operate with narrow bench-marks for evaluating processes, it tends also to exaggerate the potential of rules. A second major difficulty with the Davis thesis on rules is the view that to subject discretion to open rules, policy statements, and so on will generally push matters in the direction of 'justice'.[26] In fact, rules will often simply fail to work. As Albert J. Reiss Jr has pointed out[27] rules may frequently be used by bureaucracies to circumvent the interests of individuals. Nor is it clear that 'unjust' or 'arbitrary' action necessarily occurs when discretion is unstructured by rules. Attempts to regulate with rules may in some circumstances lead to more, rather than less, of the mischief to be avoided. An example is provided by Susan Long's analysis of US tax laws (a body of legislation whose detailed drafting Davis admired). Long found that the very complexity of such detailed provisions did not decrease but increase the agency's effective discretion: 'Varying fact patterns present in individual tax situations make determining the "correct" tax a matter of judgment on which opinions differ even among experts . . . Complexity itself adds to the potential for tax violations. Today . . . it is difficult to speak of a correct return.'[28]

It is thus not clear whether structuring with rules *will* reduce discretion at all. Administrators who can choose *which* rule to apply or who can make a new rule on the spot can hardly be taken to be strictly constrained by existing rules. For Davis the only course is to advocate 'the right mix of rule and discretion'[29] in relation to each individual action. He gives little help, however, in describing how the 'optimum' level of control over discretion may be recognized or arrived at. He repeats that the general objective should be to go 'as far as is feasible in making rules to confine and guide discretion in individual cases'[30] but states in a footnote: 'Unfortunately, how far is feasible, is a question that must be determined for each discretionary power in each particular context.'[31]

For rule-users, however, the issue of feasibility is central. How to decide what is and what is not feasible is the crucial question but on this point Davis's reader may feel stranded.

It may even be rash to assume that an activity involves such a degree of recurrence of factual considerations as to make it governable by rules at all. Daniel Gifford[32] has argued that what is wrong with the Davis thesis in the regulatory context is the idea that the needed narrowing of discretion will come from rules, standards, and precedents which gradually emerge as an agency acquires information through repetition of the decisional process itself.

Gifford contends that such an approach assumes that factual considerations recur. In real life, he suggests, many issues bear little in common with previous events. Thus, Davis's notion of agency decision-making differs from that of, say Sharfman,[33] historian of the Interstate Commerce Commission, who emphasizes not standards or rules in decisions but the non-repetitious caseload of the agency and its *ad hoc* or 'managerial' mode of decision-making. Gifford seems to be on firm ground in concluding that both the ability to develop standards or rules and their worth in controlling regulatory activity will be a function of: *inter alia*, the degree of recurrence of issues and the value of precedents in resolving cases under decision.

THE NATURE OF DECISION-MAKING

A legalistic conception of decision-making underplays the complexity of decisions and tends to see the 'decision' as existing at a particular point in the administrative process, as an isolated event logically separable from its surroundings.[34] This conception in turn produces a particular rule-centred view about the control of discretionary powers. Decisions, in short, are seen as simple, discrete, and unproblematic as opposed to complex, subtle, and woven into a broader process.

An examination of parole decision-making demonstrates the point. The 'decision' of a parole board is typically treated within the legalistic paradigm as a choice by an individual or panel based on 'factors' or 'criteria'.[35] This mechanistic analysis, however, little reflects decision-making as a continuing process, as a subtle and shifting affair that is the result of substantial human interpretative work. Such an approach pays too little attention to the problematic nature of the information upon which the decision is based, to the judgements involved in defining issues as relevant and to the ways in which cases or policies proceed through the organizational handling system. 'Facts of the case' are thus treated as some taken-for-granted reality rather than as the results of complex processes in which reality is socially constructed and reconstructed. In contrast with such a mechanical approach, 'decisions' can be seen as involving interpretations of reality, as reflecting the moral or ideological stances of various participants in a process, and as the products of a whole series of frameworks within which the decision-makers work: symbolic, socio-political, economic and organizational.

A product of the mechanical view of decisions is the idea that much discretionary behaviour tends to be 'arbitrary' or 'capricious' – it is then easy to assume that if a decision is not rule-governed it must be free from all constraints and explanations. It is necessary, however, to question how 'disparity' is assessed. Close investigation often reveals that a patterned, rational process is at work even in those kinds of decision (like parole or sentencing judgments) that are readily characterized by lawyers as exercises of 'unfettered' discretions. Some commentators have for this reason gone so far as to argue that aggregate patterns of 'discretionary' behaviour are usually so clear that discretion, in the sense of an individualized decision on the merits, is in fact a 'myth'.[36] What can at least be argued with conviction is that it is the narrow legalistic conception of 'decision' upon which many accusations of capriciousness are founded and that it is this narrow conception that implies that the answer lies in structuring with rules.

A further consequence of the 'discrete' notion of decisions is the belief that, since discretionary power exists at a particular point in the legal or administrative process, it can be controlled effectively by attention at that one point. In fact, discretion often so permeates a process that such simple controls are rarely feasible.[37] To structure or confine discretion at one point without attention to the shaping of that discretion often leads to the phenomenon of displacement. Squeeze in one place and, like a tube of toothpaste, discretion will bulge at another. Thus sentencing and parole practice in California was revised in the mid-1970s following concern at the use of discretion by the Adult Authority (the State's administrative sentencing and parole board). The response was to remove all post-conviction discretion to fix or change prison terms.

In addition, the legislature rejected a discretionary sentencing model in favour of determinate sentences fixed by statute. The result of such changes was not, however, to eliminate discretion but to displace it. Since convictions for particular offences were tied to defined sentences, and since pre-trial plea and conviction bargaining continued unabated, this meant that real authority to fix sentences of imprisonment was effectively transferred to prosecutors – unaccountable officials doing their work by (highly discretionary) bargaining in private. Thus, even in a case where confining or structuring is 'feasible', it may (within Davis's own terms) have adverse consequences.

RULES, RIGHTS, AND PROTECTIONS

A further difficulty inherent in the legalistic approach lies in its assumption that making rules to foster openness and give rights to individuals will actually improve the position of those individuals. In practice, the introduction of lawyers and rights may not only fail to eradicate discretion but it may prejudice the very people that it is supposed to benefit. Thus it has been argued that to legalize welfare decision-making may not benefit recipients if they have to go through the process of hiring and instructing lawyers and have to endure the vastly increased decision-making times that are likely to result.[38] On this point Davis himself argues that the way to improve welfare administration is not to increase emphasis on adjudicative rights but to improve informal procedures. The real point, however, is that administrative formalization of procedure can no more be assumed to improve the recipient's position than can resort to 'lawyers" law in the courts. If the key defect of legal rules in this field is, as Titmuss argued,[39] their slowness to respond to rapidly changing human needs and circumstances, it cannot be taken for granted that administrative rules will prove more responsive.

Procedural justice, moreover, cannot be taken as ensuring substantive justice. Procedures can be made more open to the point of inefficiency – thus two farmers may dispute shares in a fruit crop by an open, fair, and lengthy procedure while the fruit rots. Not only that, but procedural concessions may be used to disguise poor substantive rights.[40] Without proper regulation, rule-making procedures may lead to as much 'injustice' as adjudication – for example, by allowing poorly trained staff to administer a complex scheme for the purposes of bureaucratic convenience,[41] or by excluding small or poorly organized groups from rule-making in favour of larger and more powerful groups.[42] Thus Jeffrey Jowell has pointed out that administrators under certain conditions use rules as 'shields' to allow decisions to be routinized, reasons for any findings to be produced with ease, and decision-makers to be both insulated from political pressures and lent authority for any particular exercise of power.[43]

Even within the legal paradigm there are circumstances in which it may be 'better' for an administrative body to resist the temptation to make rules and, instead, to rely on adjudicative processes. Thus, where decisions are taken in conditions of rapid (perhaps economic) change, then to purport to decide on the basis of rules that are outdated may help no one. Policy-making by trial-type adjudication has a number of advantages over rule-making,[44] notably its flexibility and its ability to focus on those closely affected by the policy. Again, it cannot be assumed that a discretion limited by rules or standards is necessarily 'better' or more helpful to individuals than one that is less confined but more often reconsidered.

THE FEASIBILITY OF STRUCTURING

Davis is happy dealing with rule-following bureaucrats (here the mechanistic model is at home) but he is less concerned with the problems of technocratic or expert decision-makers. As Reiss has commented: 'Bureaucracies are built on rules and on the notion that decisions must be made according to those rules and with relatively little choice is applying them. Professional decision-making is based on quite the opposite model – the necessity to exercise judgment when confronted with the individual case.'[45]

Davis's approach is thus attuned to the 'transmission-belt' model of administration in which statutory objectives are applied to particular facts in an unproblematic fashion, but this model is of diminishing relevance to systems of government that delegate ever-broader powers to agencies.[46] Thus Unger argues[47] that in the movement from the liberal to the welfare state, government assumes managerial responsibilities in areas where the complexity and variability of factors are too great to allow recourse to general rules. There is a rapid rise in the use of open-ended standards in legislation, administration, and adjudication. This is accompanied by a movement from *formalistic* styles of reasoning (in which all legal choices can be deduced sufficiently from rules) to *purposive* reasoning, in which decisions on how to apply rules depend on judgements on how the purposes ascribed to rules may most effectively be achieved. A formal notion of justice, Unger points out, is persuasive in the realm of exchanges between individuals but is less so when dealing with issues of government and distribution.

Put in other terms, certain areas of activity may be ill suited to governance according to rules, because the issues are 'polycentric'[48] in nature. In polycentric (as opposed to yes/no, or binary) issues, many factors interact and shift the grounds of decision beneath the decision-maker's feet. In deciding these issues rational justifications offer less solid foundations than do balanced judgements. To attempt to control such decision-makers by use of rules may thus be to use the wrong tools for the job. The danger here may not be an under-structuring of discretion but an over-use of rules. Davis gives the impression that in general it is useful to increase structuring via administrative rules, but his approach contrasts with that of other commentators. Thus Eugene Bardach and Robert Kagan focus their attention on the tendency of US officials to regulate excessively by filling in the 'holes' in regulatory schemes with over-indulgent rule-making.[49]

Governments, moreover, may adopt modes of operation that are not highly conducive to the control of discretions by means of rules. Thus the last decade and a half has seen the rise of the 'new public management' in British government.[50] The emergence of this approach reflected concerns in successive Conservative govern-ments that administrative bureaucracies were expensive, inefficient, and unrespon-sive. The answer was seen to lie in a new philosophy phacing emphasis on reducing the size of government; shifting away from public towards the private provision of services and pursuing effectiveness, as seen in terms of satisfying consumer demands. A series of measures was introduced. Against the background of a continuing privatization process, the Next Steps programme transferred a mass[51] of 'executive' functions from central departments to independent agencies which were to operate under framework documents but which were to enjoy the 'freedom to manage'.[52] Public services were to be provided by establishing internal markets (as in the National Health Service) so that purchasers of public services were separated from providers. Arrangements for compulsory competitive tendering were introduced (as in local authority construction work)[53] so as to increase the contracting-out of tasks to private enterprises. Competition was extended by providing for the market testing[54] of every function of government, central and local, NHS and nationalized industry, unless it was part of the 'core' business of the organization. The Citizens' Charter was launched so as to emphasize the rights of individuals to choice and quality in services.[55]

The new public management is based on the notion of separating policy-making from service delivery. The nature of the service is treated as free from policy implications but a new emphasis is put on the effective delivery of the service by professional managers. The latter are accordingly accountable for producing results. A variety of contractual devices serves to distance the citizen from the policy-maker and the public are seen, not so much as participants in the policy-making process as consumers of services.[56] Accountability operates not at the level of policy-making (or service definition) but at the point of delivery – on market-derived principles. Thus Hood has noted the debt owed by the new public management: first, to 'reform doctrines built on ideas of contestability, user choice, transparency and close concentration on incentive structures . . . doctrines very different from traditional military–bureaucratic ideas of "good administration"'; second, to 'ideas of professional management expertise as portable, paramount over technical expertise, requiring high discretionary power to achieve results (free to manage)'.[57]

Whatever the merits or demerits of the new public management,[58] it should be noted that the potential part to be played by rules may be quite different under such a system than in arrangements relying more heavily on public bureaucracies. Clearly, rules will be required in order to establish, for example, the frameworks under which the Next Steps agencies are to operate,[59] but in any system built on 'expert', 'managerial' discretions which are exercised quite freely under 'contractual' frameworks and which are evaluated according to results (rather than questioned as to policies pursued) special attention has to be paid to control devices other than rules, and which are attuned to a quasi-contractual context rather than the exercise of statutory discretions by a public bureaucracy. Thus, emphasis might be placed on audit mechanisms; systems of inspection and evaluation; performance targets and indicators; competition as a yardstick for effectiveness; quality controls; managerial incentives; complaints and redress mechanisms; and the capital markets as sources of scrutiny and discipline.[60] To view the administrative process in legalistic terms is not helpful in assessing the place of either 'alternative' controls or of rules in such a context.

A final problem with the legalistic argument for rules stems from its tendency to overlook those practical and political realities that demand flexibility rather than a rule-bound consistency. Thus it might be argued that, for the sake of fairness and justice, all polluters should be treated equally. If, however, fixed standards are set and enforced on polluters in a mechanical way and without discretionary intervention, larger enterprises might be in a position to comply, but a number of smaller operators might well go out of business. The regulatory agency would then face a public outcry against oppressive regulation, lose esteem in the public eye, and be likely to pay the political price. In short, the mechanical approach would not be politically feasible. Other considerations, such as limitations on resources and time, also rule out non-discretionary enforcement. In practice, street-level enforcers of all kinds have to operate by negotiation and bluff.[61] Automatic resort to law would be extravagant in terms of resources, it would risk exposing the low penalties that accompany many regulatory offences, provoke damaging attacks by opponents where penalties were substantial, and possibly make enforcement enormously difficult for individual inspectors. A system based on a large measure of discretion might thus be preferable on a number of counts.

To summarize, the above analysis of Davis is not offered in order to deny the value of rules within government but to show, first, that in assessing the role of rules it is necessary to recognize values other than those implicit in the legal paradigm and, second, that a narrowly legalistic approach can produce unrealistic expectations as to the practical potential of rules. Davis is open to criticism on a number of counts. His notion of justice is bound up with lawyers' values and so is question-begging. In many areas of government the application of rules is not feasible and it cannot be assumed that rules will protect individuals' interests. The Davis approach builds on a narrow view of governmental decision-making and offers prescriptions whose appropriateness to modern governmental processes may increasingly be questioned.

Above all, Davis offers no convincing means of justifying any particular method of carrying out government business in any particular context. This challenge was avoided by stating that what was 'feasible' had to be considered in each individual context and by operating with an unexplained bench-mark of 'justice'. The latter notion served only to invoke, in an imprecise manner, certain values implicit in the legal paradigm.

Earlier it was argued that the real test of a governmental process should be whether it furthers recognized and acceptable values. What, then, are those values if they are not (or at least are not exclusively) those encountered within the legal paradigm? In both making a case for certain values and suggesting a method of evaluating govern-mental processes it is useful to consider how approaches to evaluating procedures have developed in a number of key respects since Davis wrote *Discretionary Justice*.

Evaluating governmental processes

The search for process values
Six years after *Discretionary Justice* was first published, Richard Stewart, in a celebrated article,[62] attacked the 'traditional' view of administrative law and examined the case for seeing such law as a system for ensuring the representation of affected interests. His analysis deals with a series of different bases for judging the appropriateness of governmental procedures.

Stewart contrasted the 'interest-representation' model of administrative law, marked by its emphasis on ensuring the adequate representation of affected interests in decision-making, with the 'traditional' model and its focus on whether governmental intrusions into private liberty and property interests were authorized by the legislature.

The traditional view, according to Stewart, required of government a number of essentials, notably that coercive controls on individuals be authorized by the legislature; that the legislature must promulgate rules, or principles, to guide the exercise of delegated powers; that officials should apply legislative directives rationally; and that judicial review be available to ensure the above. In short, the traditional view saw the governmental official or agency as a mere 'transmission belt' for implementing legislative directives.

The debt such a view owes to the Diceyan notion of the rule of law is clear and it encounters similar problems in dealing with discretion. Vague, general, or ambiguous statutes create discretion and threaten the legitimacy of actions under the transmission-belt theory since the relevant statute does not dictate the decision or policy and, instead, the priorities of officials, who are unaccountable to the electorate, hold sway. Such statutes have proliferated on both sides of the Atlantic. The idea of objective goals for administrators had by the mid-1970s been discredited and Stewart wrote: 'Today the exercise of agency discretion is inevitably seen as the essentially legislative process of adjusting the competing claims of various private interests affected by agency policy.'[63]

It was, he argued, no longer possible to legitimate agency action by the transmission-belt theory. Nor was another model of legitimation still convincing. This was the 'expertise' model put forward in the 1930s by defenders of the New Deal and the practice whereby Congress delegated sweeping powers to a host of new agencies. Championed by James M. Landis,[64] proponents of the expertise model offered no apologies for the broad discretions operated by agencies and officials. They maintained that these discretions were necessary for successful planning and management. 'Expertise' was thus held out as a solution to the 'problem' of discretion since the application of specialized knowledge, skills, and experience was the means with which to effect agency goals. Administrators, according to this view, were not political but professional, and public administration was treated as objective in nature.

Faith in the expertise model waned, pointed out Stewart, as experience eroded the general belief in an objective public interest, in the disinterestedness of agencies and in their ability to achieve goals. The unravelling of the objective notion of the public interest made way for the pluralist interest-representation model. This model looked to the affirmative side of government, which has to do with the representation of interests during the development of policies, in contrast with the negative approach of the traditional model and its focus on the checking of governmental power. What was not possible, argued Stewart, was any revived application of the traditional model by means of closer legislative specification of policies (the 'non-delegation doctrine'). This was 'neither feasible nor desirable'[65] and could not realistically be demanded by the judges. Nor could administrative rules remove 'inevitable' discretions.[66] Stewart lodged a further objection to Davis's notion that judges should locate the optimum degree of structuring in each respect for each discretionary power, calling it 'unrealistic and unwise' given limitations on judicial experience and specialized knowledge.[67]

Did this mean that the notion of interest representation was left as the appropriate yardstick for assessing governmental procedures? In the end this was also said to fail as a general structure for legitimating agency action. The case for valuing the representation of interests in governmental decisions was based on a number of points: such representation would improve agency decisions; make then more responsive to the needs of various interests; give citizens a sense of involvement in government; and increase confidence in the fairness of government decisions. A number of objections, however, pointed to the limitations of the notion: unlimited provision for interest representation would lead to chaos and the stultification of government; the courts, if chosen as the arbiters of participatory rights, would be given too much control over access to decision-making and ultimately a power to control policy choices; whether judicial protections for participating rights were better than political or administrative measures was contentious; to formalize participatory rights would not only prove intolerably burdensome but would increase the expense of participation and thus would discriminate against participation by certain groups; limiting participatory rights in the interests of effective decision-making was a process that itself involved highly discretionary decisions, and whether participation would *influence* governmental decisions was also problematic.[68]

For Stewart, the unavoidable conclusion was that, although interest representation might have a useful role, it provided no comprehensive yardstick for assessing governmental procedures. Failing the prospect of interest representation maturing into a more convincing model, the real issue could be stated as how best to use different measures to control power. In response, the 'nominalist thesis' suggested that governmental tasks, functions and contexts be classified and then:

> Such a classification . . . might be parallelled by a similar classification of the various techniques for directing and controlling administrative power, including judicial review, procedural requirements, political controls, and partial obligation of agency functions. The two systems of classification might then be meshed to determine the most harmonious fit between the purposes and characteristics of particular agencies and various control techniques.[69]

Such an approach offers at first sight a number of useful rules of thumb for the designers of governmental processes but, again, it fails to provide any coherent basis for evaluating such processes. It does not, for example, tell us how to decide what indeed is 'the most harmonious fit' between powers and controls.[70]

In order to progress from this point it is necessary to come to grips with the problem of identifying the broad array of values that is to be served in the governmental process. This challenge has notably been taken up by Denis Galligan.

In his book, *Discretionary Powers*, Galligan looks at the role of ideas of legality in restraining and directing the exercise of discretion and argues that legal accountability is not 'self-contained and independent of political morality'.[71] He emphasizes that the law serves a number of purposes: 'It is not clear why we should expect there to be one central idea of what law is, or of the tasks it is meant to perform or of the values it is supposed to serve.'[72]

How, then, can one evaluate the acceptability of governmental processes involving the exercise of discretionary power? Galligan's view is that: 'there is no fundamental and irreducible ideal or principle, but rather . . . law and legal institutions are part of the political and social composition of a society and that they can be made instrumental in upholding values several and diverse. What those values are depends on the political theory and practice of a society.'[73] Thus, he argues that to separate law from political considerations gives an unduly narrow approach. The task is to identify the set of political values that is to serve as the basis for developing legal principles relevant to the control of discretion. At this point in his argument Galligan appears reluctant to argue for a particular set of values or an underlying theory of democracy. He says choice of values 'must depend on a certain degree of personal preference both as to the values selected and the importance of each'.[74] In a quest for further content, however, he adopts an eclectic approach:

> reflection on the political theories that underlie modern, democratic, liberal societies would tend to suggest that the following have a position of importance and that each provides scope for the development of more specific legal principles. The four basic values suggested are: stability in legal relations, rationality in decision-making, fair procedures and, finally, a rather loose residual category of moral and political principles.[75]

Each item is explained. *Stability in legal relationships* is a value traditionally associated with the rule of law; *rationality in decision-making* is said to be a 'fundamental' value; and *fair procedures* to be central to the legal enterprise but to have a place within a wider political framework where 'the concept of participation is of undoubted importance'. It is, however, the residual category of *moral and political principles* that proves the most problematic. This set of principles is said to generate constraints on discretion and examples are of non-discrimination and 'general ideas of justice and equity'. There is, however, no unifying basis for such values (for example a rationale founded on respect for persons) and this is a conscious aspect of Galligan's eclecticism. All four of these values are nevertheless problematic since it is not clear whence they derive. Why, one might ask, are these values rather than any others important in any system of good government? Why should these be the bench-marks? A further issue is whether different *systems* of government are based on the same set of values and whether there is a particular or 'core' model of liberal democracy being offered. (If so what is it like?)

These difficulties make the identification of good governmental processes a complex task. Galligan notes that a combination of procedure and substance is involved: 'Good government means more than good results in terms of one or other set of political goals, it depends partly on consideration of and compliance with a range of values and ideals in arriving at those results.'[76] He summarizes:

> I have suggested that there are certain values which are important in any system of good government, and that these may be the basis for creating a framework of legal principles, or principles of process, which constitute constraints on the exercise of discretionary authority.

Such principles complement rather than compete with more direct methods of political accountability by contributing to the over-all justifiability and legitimacy of discretionary decisions.[77]

The strength of Galligan's approach is that it recognizes that many issues arising in modern government are best resolved by institutions other than courts and according to strategies other than rules and adjudications; that the balance of political and legal accountability is itself an aspect 'of a wider sense of political accountability'. More problematically, though, a principle for selecting certain values is difficult to discern in Galligan's account and, as a result, there fails to emerge a convincing explanation of how justifications for particular governmental processes can be made and evaluated.

The seeds of an explanation do lie, however, in Galligan's notion that values play a role in justifying and legitimating particular governmental procedures. The legitimacy of an administrative process can thus be seen in terms of the persuasive power of the arguments made in its favour. Such an approach is consistent with the focus adopted by Christopher Hood and Michael Jackson in their book *Administrative Argument*[78] in which they concentrate not so much on the performance of processes as on the 'link between argument and acceptance'.[79] As they put it: 'administrative argument is typically not a process of validation and disproof using hard data, but rather a process of persuasion'.[80]

The American administrative lawyer Jerry Mashaw adopted elements of such a strategy in *Bureaucratic Justice* in 1983. He contended: 'The justice of an administration system . . . means simply this: those qualities of a decision process that provide arguments for the acceptability of its decisions . . . These justificatory structures, once identified, should appear to be ubiquitous in the legal structure of public institutions and in ordinary experience.'[81] Mashaw suggests that there are three types of justice argument.[82] The *bureaucratic rationality* model of justice demands that decisions be accurate and efficient concrete realizations of the legislative will. The *professional treatment* model calls for the application of appropriate special skills and recognizes the incompleteness of facts, the singularity of contexts, and the intuitive nature of judgements. The *moral judgement* model requires fairness and independence in decision-making and promises a 'full and equal opportunity to obtain one's entitlements'.

How, though, do the models interact? Mashaw argues that they are 'distinct conceptual models' which are each coherent and attractive but, while not mutually exclusive, they are 'highly competitive'.[83] It follows that: 'the internal logic of any one of them tends to drive the characteristics of the others from the field as it works out in concrete situations'.[84]

A problem for Mashaw (and, indeed, for Hood and Jackson) is, however, the notion of acceptability. One might ask not only: 'What constitutes acceptable?' but also: 'Acceptable to whom?' On the latter point, it can be questioned whether the judges of a bureaucratic process are to be the consumers of services, the general public, the management of the agency, the front-line officials, the government, the media, or some other grouping. Without further theoretical underpinning it seems that Mashaw is exposed to many of the objections faced by the participatory model.

Mashaw concedes that his technique for developing the models is 'in part empirical and in part intuitive and analytic'.[85] It is the eclectic nature of this technique that is the root of many of the problems encountered in using his models. Thus a particular difficulty is the relationship between different models of justice. Mashaw argues that these are competitive but not that they are mutually exclusive. They are theoretically inconsistent, they contain internal tensions that reflect alternative justice perspectives, and they compete to achieve dominance as the accepted model. The notion is of three models or 'visions'[86] of justice each of which may serve to legitimate a particular process but which all exist in a stressed relationship. There is by no means 'a happy blending of justice models'.[87] Without clarification on the matter of 'acceptability' it is accordingly difficult to justify either the 'triumph'[88] of one model or the appropriateness of a particular mixing of models. One might protest that the offer of the different bench-marks for administration is of limited utility if one is not told which bench-marks are appropriate and when.

Five rationales for legitimacy claims

An explanation can be offered, however, which explores the nature of legitimacy claims or attributions and employs the notion of a *discourse* of justification within which certain values operate. Such a notion holds that evaluations of procedures are, as a matter of practice, argued out with reference to certain recognized values. Language users, on this view, distinguish between claims that bureaucratic processes are justifiable or appropriate (let us call these 'legitimacy claims'[89]) and claims that processes are constitutionally correct, legal, or morally praiseworthy. When legitimacy claims are made, those involved can recognize both relevant and irrelevant arguments and can see that relevant arguments invoke certain understood values and only these. Thus different persons may employ different models of the optimal democracy but each is able to recognize the basis of the arguments as to legitimacy being made by the other. They may each place different emphasis on the furtherance of certain values but they share a common recognition that certain values are relevant.

When there is talk of this or that process being legitimate or illegitimate, in the sense that certain values are argued to be satisfied or left unsatisfied, reference is made to a limited set of values or justificatory arguments. Thus Gerald Frug argues that in justifying bureaucracy: 'we have adopted only a limited number of ways to reassure ourselves about these institutions'.[90]

These justifications are all problematic in some respects but, as will be argued, it is their cumulative force that justifies.[91] The types of claim can be outlined as follows:[92]

THE LEGISLATIVE MANDATE CLAIM

This claim attributes value to achieving objectives that are set out in legislative form (it echoes Mashaw's 'bureaucratic rationality' model). Thus in Britain a support claim would point to the existence of an authorizing mandate from parliament. The proponent of the claim is in effect stating: 'Support what is being done because that is what parliament, the fountain of democratic authority, has ordered.'[93]

There are, of course, problems with this rationale as were pointed out by Stewart in his attack on the traditional model of administrative law.[94] The claim is weakened in so far as the legislature has provided administrators with broad discretions ('What *did* parliament order?'). Implementation of the mandate demands interpretation and, accordingly, legitimacy claims become problematic. Nor is it usually feasible for the legislature to overcome such problems by setting down precise standards and objectives. Parliament has neither the time nor the expertise to solve all problems in advance and, indeed, it may deliberately decline to do so and give, say, a regulatory agency, a set of discretionary powers so as to allow it to make judgements on policies and implementing strategies.

THE ACCOUNTABILITY OR CONTROL CLAIM

Like the legislative mandate claim this model seeks justification in the assent of the people but, instead of relying on the people's voice as expressed in parliament, it looks to more narrowly defined groupings as conduits for the democratic voice.[95] Thus, where a particular interpretation of the mandate is put into effect, the imple-menter(s) may claim that they are accountable for that interpretation to a represen-tative body and that this oversight renders the chosen mode of implementation acceptable. Rights of participation and consultation are valued, as is openness.[96]

This claim is not unproblematic. Deciding to whom the bureaucrat is to be made accountable is controversial. In so far as a system of accountability or control is not exercised by parliament or elected persons, it may be open to criticism as unrepresentative. Where control is exercised by means of certain institutions (e.g. courts) then the competence of those institutions in a specialist area may be called into question.

THE DUE PROCESS CLAIM

This claim values the use of certain procedures which imply a respect for individuals and fairness or even-handedness in government. Support claims are based on the level of consideration that has been shown, not to the broad public will, but to the interests of those persons affected by the process, decision, policy, or action.[97]

As a complete claim this is again limited. There is no guarantee that maximizing the recognition of individuals' rights will deal with collective or social issues or will produce an efficient decision (it may lead to stagnation and indecision). The dictates of such a claim may not correspond with the legislative mandate and to pay heed to process rights beyond a certain point may not be consistent with the development and exercise of necessary expertise and judgement.

THE EXPERTISE CLAIM

Many governmental, and particularly regulatory, functions require that expert judgements be made and applied. In such cases the issues are often polycentric[98] and the decision- or policy-maker has to consider a number of competing options and values so as to form a balanced judgement on incomplete and shifting information. Where this is so, it is inappropriate to demand either that rules or guidelines be set out in advance so as to govern the matter or that, beyond a certain point, reasons and justifications can be given. The expertise claim urges that the expert will take the most appropriate action when given an area of freedom in which to operate and that his/her performance will improve over time.[99] As Mashaw put it in relation to his 'professional treatment' model:

> The basis for the legitimacy of professional treatment is that the professional is master of an arcane body of knowledge and supports his judgement by appealing to expertise. But whereas the bureaucrat displays his or her knowledge through instrumentally rational routines designed to render transparent the connection between concrete decisions and legislatively validated policy, the professional's art remains opaque to the lay man.[100]

This comment points to the problems of making claims to expertise. Lay observers find it difficult to understand the bases for expert judgements and often impossible to assess the success with which the expertise has been applied. The patient who is not a surgeon tends not to know if the operation was as successful as it might have been. The observer may not know what would have happened if alternative strategies had been adopted. It is, moreover, difficult for the expert to explain why *this* issue demands expert judgement. Attacks on the competence and independence of experts serve further to undermine claims. Such attacks are fostered by an instinctive distrust of those who claim to 'know best', who fail to give full reasons, or who pursue a specialist or arcane mode of analysis.[101] Where expert opinions conflict within a field or between disciplines, this again undermines legitimacy claims.

THE EFFICIENCY CLAIM

Two kinds of claim can potentially be made on the basis of efficiency. First, that stated objectives are being achieved in an effective manner, and second, that economically efficient actions are being taken.[102] The first kind of claim can be considered a version of the legislative mandate claim and, accordingly, problems arise in so far as it is difficult to define the content of the given objectives. Even if objectives are clear, the absence of comparators usually makes it difficult to demonstrate that the most effective approach is being taken at any one time – what might have happened had another approach been adopted is often impossible to judge.

The second form of claim – that efficient results are produced – is highly contentious, indeed it is the most dubious form of claim discussed here. It is difficult to see efficiency as a value independent of distributional considerations and, unless there is legislative authority for taking 'efficient' action there is liable to be a degree of conflict between the dictates of efficiency and the distributional implications of a statute. All efficiency claim may have a role, however, in so far as support may be claimed according to a particular efficiency-based interpretation of a legislative mandate.

Notes

1. Notably by K. C. Davis in *Discretionary Justice* (1971).
2. Primary legislation is a further option not to be overlooked. On the variety of governmental modes of control and execution see generally C. Hood, *The Tools of Government* (1983).

3. K. Hawkins, 'The Use of Legal Discretion: Perspectives from Law and Social Science', in K. Hawkins (ed.) *The Uses of Discretion* (1992).

4. On different approaches to discretion see Hawkins, 'The Use of Legal Discretion', and Galligan, *Discretionary Powers*, chs. 1 and 2.

5. On discretion generally see Galligan, *Discretionary Powers*; Hawkins (ed.), *The Uses of Discretion*; Davis, *Discretionary Justice*; M. Shapiro, 'Administrative Discretion: The Next Stage' (1983) 92 Yale LJ 1487; G. Bryner, *Bureaucratic Discretion* (1987); R. Dworkin, *Taking Rights Seriously* (1977); M. Adler and S. Asquith (eds.), *Discretion and Welfare* (1981).

6. N. Lacey, 'The Jurisprudence of Discretion: Escaping the Legal Paradigm' in K. Hawkins (ed.), *The Uses of Discretion*, 362.

7. See J. W. P. B. McAuslan, 'Administrative Law, Collective Consumption and Judicial Policy' (1983) 46 MLR 1. On the 'traditional' view of public law and Dicey see P. Craig, 'Dicey: Unitary, Self-correcting Democracy and Public Law' (1990) 106 LQR 105.

8. Lacey, 'The Jurisprudence of Discretion', 369.

9. J. Jowell, 'The Rule of Law Today', in J. L. Jowell and D. Oliver (eds.) *The Changing Constitution*, 3rd edn (1994).

10. *Ibid.* 78.

11. *Ibid.* 76.

12. Lacey, 'The Jurisprudence of Discretion', 372. On why aiming to control discretion is 'unacceptable' as a route to 'sound government' see Edley, *Administrative Law*, 217– 21.

13. (1971) Illinois. See the critiques by Lacey, 'The Jurisprudence of Discretion', and Baldwin and Hawkins, 'Discretionary Justice: Davis Reconsidered', 570. I am grateful to Keith Hawkins for allowing me to deploy here a number of points that owe their origins to him.

14. Davis, *Discretionary Justice*, 216.

15. *Ibid.* 217.

16. *Ibid.* 142.

17. *Ibid.* 219.

18. *Ibid.* 28–44.

19. *Ibid.* 3–4.

20. *Ibid.* 25.

21. *Ibid.* 27.

22. H. J. Friendly, 'Judicial Control of Administrative Action' (1970) 23 JLE 63, 65.

23. Davis, *Discretionary Justice*, 5–6; see A. W. Bradley, 'Research and Reform in Administrative Law' (1974) 13 JSPTL 35.

24. Patrick McAuslan has said: '[Administrative Law] has, even where collective agencies of grievance-handling have been created, concentrated overwhelmingly on refining, elaborating, extending and discussing remedies for individuals against the administration. The [administrative processes of collective consumption] have developed a multitude of agencies, processes and systems for deciding upon policies and allocating resources between the different programmes of collective consumption where the law is facilitative rather than regulatory . . .' see McAuslan, 'Administrative Law, Collective Consumption and Judicial Policy', 1.

25. K. C. Davis, 'An Approach to Legal Control of the Police' (1974) 52 Tex. LR 703.

26. Davis, *Discretionary Justice*, 226–7.

27. Book Review of *Discretionary Justice* (1990) 68 Mich. LR 794.

28. S. B. Long, 'Social Control: The Civil Law: The Case of Income Tax Enforcement', in H. L. Ross (ed.), *Law and Deviance* (1984), 206–7.

29. Davis, 'An Approach to Legal Control of the Police', 703, 706.
30. Davis, *Discretionary Justice*, 221.
31. *Ibid.* 221 n. 15.
32. D. J. Gifford, 'Decisions, Decisional Referents and Administrative Justice' (1972) 37 LCP 3.
33. I. L. Sharfman, *The Interstate Commerce Commission* (1931).
34. On discretion in making legal decisions see (1986) 43/4, *Washington and Lee Law Review* and articles by K. Hawkins, D. R. Novack, E. Kimbrough, J. M. Thomas, and P. K. Manning; see also Hawkins and Thomas (eds.), *Making Regulatory Policy*.
35. See K. Hawkins, 'On Legal Decisionmaking' (1989) 4 *Washington and Lee Law Review* (1989) 1161.
36. See M. P. Baumgartner, 'The Myth of Discretion', in Hawkins (ed.), *The Uses of Discretion*.
37. On the selective enforcement of even clear-cut rules see Jowell, 'The Rule of Law Today'.
38. See R. M. Titmuss, 'Welfare "Rights" Law and Discretion' (1971) 42 Pol.Q. 113; J. L. Jowell, *Law and Bureaucracy* (1975); cf. C. Reich, 'Individual Rights and Social Welfare: The Emerging Legal Issues' (1965) 74 Yale LJ 1245.
39. Titmuss, 'Welfare "Rights"', 124.
40. See Adler and Asquith, *Discretion and Welfare*, 16–18 and 169–70.
41. See T. Prosser 'The Politics of Discretion', in Alder and Asquith, *ibid.*
42. See B. A. Hepple, book review of *Discretionary Justice* [1969] CLJ 313.
43. Jowell, *Law and Bureaucracy*, 20–1.
44. See D. L. Shapiro, 'The Choice of Rule Making or Adjudication in the Development of Agency Policy' (1965) 78 Harv. LR 921.
45. A. Reiss Jr, review of *Discretionary Justice* (1970) 69 Mich. LR 792.
46. See R. B. Stewart, 'The Reformation of American Administrative Law' (1975) 88 Harv. LR 1667.
47. R. M. Unger, *Law in Modern Society* (1976); T. Lowi, *The End of Liberalism* (1969), 133–41. See also C. Diver 'Policymaking Paradigms in Administrative Law' (1981) 95 Harv. LR, 393.
48. M. Polyani, *The Logic of Liberty* (1951); P. Weiler, 'Two Models of Judicial Decision-making' (1968) 46 Can. BR 406; L. Fuller, *The Morality of Law* (1964), 83; Jowell, *Law and Bureaucracy*, 151–5, 213–14.
49. See E. Bardach and R. Kagan, *Going by The Book: The Problem of Regulatory Unreasonableness* (1982).
50. See e.g. C. Hood, 'A Public Management for All Seasons' (1991) 69 Pub. Admin. 3; I. Harden, *The Contracting State* (1992); N. Lewis, 'The Citizen's Charter and Next Steps: A New Way of Governing' (1993) Pol. Q 316; G. Drewry, 'Mr Major's Charter: Empowering the Consumer' [1993] PL 248; M. Henkel, 'The New Evaluative State' (1991) 69 Pub. Admin. 121; A. Barron and C. Scott, 'The Citizens' Charter Programme' (1992) 55 MLR 526; J. McEldowney, 'Contract Compliance and Public Audit as Regulatory Strategies in the Public Sector', paper to Citizens' Charter Conference, Univerity of Warwick, 23 Sept. 1992; C. Scott, 'Rule Versus Discretion in the New Public Sector', paper to Citizens' Charter Conference, University of Warwick, 23 Sept. 1992; N. Lacey, 'Government as Manager, Citizen as Consumer: The Case of the Criminal Justice Act 1991' (1994) 57 MLR 534.
51. In five years the transfers involved some 90 agencies and 350,000 staff – see J. Mayne, 'Public Power Outside Government' (1993) 64 Pol. Q. 327.
52. See Prime Minister's Efficiency Unit, *Improving Management in Government: The Next Steps* (London 1988); and *Making the Most of Next Steps* (London 1991).
53. See Local Government Planning and Land Act 1980; Local Government Act 1988; Harden, *The Contracting State*, 18.

54. I.e. testing in-house public service bids against those from the private sector.
55. See *The Citizens Charter: Raising the Standard* (Cm 1599, 1991).
56. On citizen as consumer see Barron and Scott, 'The Citizens' Charter Programme', 543–5 and Lacey, 'Government as Manager, Citizen as Consumer', 534–5, 553.
57. See Hood, 'A Public Management for All Seasons' (1991) 69 Pub. Admin. 3, 5–6.
58. A style of government that can be evaluated by the bench-marks offered in this chapter.
59. As noted, the status of such rules may be problematic, see Harden, *The Contracting State*, ch. 5.
60. See Scott, 'Rule versus Discretion in the New Public Sector'.
61. See K. Hawkins, *Environment and Enforcement* (1984) and K. Hawkins and J. Thomas (eds.), *Enforcing Regulation* (1984); Richardson *et al.*, *Policing Pollution*, chs 5 and 6; B. Hutter, *The Reasonable Arm of the Law?* (1988), chs. 5 and 6. For an economic justification of compliance-seeking by negotiation see P. Fenn and C. G. Veljanovski, 'A Positive Economic Theory of Regulatory Enforcement' (1988) EJ 1055; C. G. Veljanovski, 'The Economics of Regulatory Enforcement', in Hawkins and Thomas (eds.), *Enforcing Regulation*. See also S. Shavell, 'The Optimal Structure of Law Enforcement' (1993) *Journal of Law and Economics* 255.
62. Stewart, 'The Reformation of American Administrative Law', 1667.
63. *Ibid.* 1683. For a defence of bureaucratic rationality and an important neo-Weberian endorsement of bureaucracy as 'the best hope for justice and rationality' see J. Mashaw, *Bureaucratic Justice* (1983); quotation from book review of Mashaw by L. Liebman and R. B. Stewart, 'Bureaucratic Vision' (1983) 96 Harv. LR 1952.
64. See J. M. Landis, *The Administrative Process* (1938).
65. Stewart, 'The Reformation of American Administrative Law', 1695. A number of commentators have argued that the US Supreme Court should ensure that Congress does not unnecessarily delegate social policy discretion to administrators: e.g. J. Ely, *Democracy and Distrust* (1980), 131–4; J. Freedman, *Crisis and Legitimacy* (1978), 78–94; T. Lowi, *The End of Liberalism* (1969), 129–46, 297–9. On US courts and delegation see S. Breyer and R. Stewart, *Administrative Law and Regulatory Policy* 3rd edn (1992), 66–91; E. L. Rubin, 'Law and Legislation in the Administrative State' (1989) 89 Col. LR 369, and P. L. Strauss 'Some Comments on Rubin' (1989) 89 Col. LR, 427.
66. Stewart, 'The Reformation of American Administrative Law', 1712.
67. *Ibid.* 1701.
68. *Ibid.* 1803–5. See also P. P. Craig, *Public Law and Democracy in the United Kingdom and the United States of America* (1990), 128–36. On the practicalities of participation see Mashaw, *Bureaucratic Justice*.
69. Stewart, 'The Reformation of American Administrative Law', 1810.
70. Stewart does offer three 'bases' for administrative intervention in a later article. These are: securing rights; promoting efficiency; and protecting 'non-commodity values'. See R. Stewart, 'Regulation in a Liberal State: The Role of Non-Commodity Values' (1983) 92 Yale LJ 1357. For criticisms of Stewart's concept of 'non-commodity values' and of his claims to neutrality, see P. H. Schuck, 'Regulation, Non-Market Values and the Administrative State: A Comment on Professor Stewart' (1983) 92 Yale LJ 1602; G. E. Frug, 'Why Neutrality?' (1983) 92 Yale LJ 1591.
71. Galligan, *Discretionary Powers*, 4.
72. *Ibid.* 89. On 'discovering fundamental values' see Ely, *Democracy and Distrust*, ch. 3.
73. Galligan, *Discretionary Powers*, 89–90.
74. *Ibid.* 90.

75. *Ibid.*
76. *Ibid.* 98.
77. *Ibid.* 99.
78. C. Hood and M. Jackson, *Administrative Argument* (1991).
79. *Ibid.* 200.
80. *Ibid.* 26.
81. Mashaw, *Bureaucratic Justice*, 25–5.
82. *Ibid.*, ch. 2, and also James O. Freedman, *Crisis and Legitimacy* (1978), 11. Freedman argues that the legitimacy of the administrative process may be supported by public recognition that administrative agencies are indispensable in the constitutional scheme of government; that they are accountable; that they are effective in meeting their statutory responsibilities; and that their decision-making is fair.
83. Mashaw, *Bureaucratic Justice*, 23.
84. *Ibid.*
85. *Ibid.* 17. For an attempt to derive some process values from the American liberal democratic tradition see J. Mashaw, 'Administrative Due Process: The Quest for a Dignitary Theory' (1981) 61 BULR 885.
86. *Ibid.* 7.
87. *Ibid.* 40.
88. *Ibid.* 46.
89. On legitimacy see D. Beetham, *The Legitimation of Power* (1991); R. Barker, *Political Legitimacy and the State* (1990); and 'Legitimacy, Obedience and the State', in C. Harlow (ed.), *Public Law and Politics* (1986); W. Connolly (ed.), *Legitimacy and the State* (1984); Freedman, *Crisis and Legitimacy*; P. McAuslan and J. McEldowney (eds.), *Law, Legitimacy and the Constitution* (1985); J. Habermas, *Legitimation Crisis*, trans. T. McCarthy (1976).
90. See G. E. Frug, 'The Ideology of Bureaucracy in American Law' (1984) 97 Harv. LR, 1277.
91. On the 'deception' involved in combining rationales see Frug, 'The Ideology of Bureaucracy', 1378–9. For an argument that rationales should be used in an integrated fashion so that they cannot be teased apart see C. Edley, *Administrative Law: Rethinking Judicial Control of Bureaucracy* (1990), ch. 7.
92. See R. Baldwin and C. McCrudden, *Regulation and Public Law* (1987). In 'The Ideology of Bureaucracy' Frug offers four models of bureaucratic legitimacy: formalist; expertise; judicial review; and market/pluralist. The formalist, expertise and market/pluralist models correspond to what are termed here the legislative mandate, expertise, and accountability rationales. Frug's judicial review model can be seen as a sub-category of the accountability rationale (judicial control being a particular species of accountability). The efficiency rationale discussed here may be subsumed to some extent under Frug's formalist heading, and the due process rationale, though not stressed by Frug, is reflected in his comments on judicial review and its role in controlling processes. Edley, *Administrative Law*, argues that three paradigms underpin prescriptions about administrative procedure: the adjudicatory fairness; the scientific (or expertise); and the political (interest-balancing/participatory) paradigms. See also J. Freedman's analysis of justificatory rationales in *Crisis and Legitimacy*.
93. Disputes may, of course, arise as to the need for any kind of public mandate – as for example when it is asserted that an action is purely of private concern. Where functions of an arguably public nature are contracted out to private bodies such disputes are likely to arise – see Harden, *The Contracting State*, ch. 8. On legal and bureaucratic authority see H. Gerth and C. W. Mills (eds.), *From Max Weber: Essays in Sociology* (1958); see Frug, 'The Ideology of Bureaucracy', 1207–300 (on the 'formalist' model).

94. Stewart, 'The Reformation of American Administrative Law', 1671–87.
95. See Freedman, *Crisis and Legitimacy*, ch. 5. See also Frug, 'The Ideology of Bureaucracy' on accountability through the political and market processes as well as by judicial scrutiny (pp. 1355–61 and 1334–9).
96. On participation see Stewart, 'The Reformation of American Administrative Law'; Freedman, *Crisis and Legitimacy*, ch. 10; C. Pateman, *Participation and Democratic Theory* (1970); and *The Problem of Political Obligation* (1985); N. Poulantzas, *State, Power, Socialism* (1980); C. B. Macpherson, *The Life and Times of Liberal Democracy* (1977); D. Held, *Models of Democracy* (1987), 254–64. But cf. the New Right theorists and their hostility to democratic as opposed to market-based processes within the minimalist state, and e.g. F. A. Hayek, *The Constitution of Liberty* (1960); R. Nozick, *Anarchy, State and Utopia* (1974), and the discussion in P. Dunleavy and B. O'Leary, *Theories of the State: The Politics of Liberal Democracy* (1987), ch. 3.
97. On protecting individual interests as a first priority of administration and administrative law see e.g. J. Dickinson, *Administrative Justice and the Supremacy of Law in the United States* (1927). On rationales for due process see Craig, *Public Law and Democracy*, 137–9.
98. See references at n. 48 *supra*.
99. For a defence of expertise see J. M. Landis, *The Administrative Process* (1938). See also Mashaw's 'professional treatment' model, Mashaw, *Bureaucratic Justice*, 26–9; Frug, 'The Ideology of Bureaucracy', 1318–22, 1331–4; Freedman, *Crisis and Legitimacy*, 44–57. A recent example of the rationale in operation occurred when Mr Neil Hamilton defended the regulation of accountants by their own professional bodies. The then Corporate Affairs Minister said: 'There is a possibility of conflict. But the great merit of self-regulation is that it uses experts', *Financial Times*, 26 Nov. 1992.
100. Mashaw, *Bureaucratic Justice*, 28. The 'new public management' places a good deal of faith in the manager as expert. It is expertise that is held to justify the 'freedom to manage'; see Hood, 'A Public Management for All Seasons', 6; Harden, *The Contracting State*, 70.
101. Harold Macmillan expressed such distrust: 'We have not overthrown the divine right of kings to fall down before the divine right of experts.' See N. Beloff, *The General Says No* (1963), 59, quoted in P. Hennessey, *Whitehall* (1989), 159.
102. On the role of economic appraisals in rule-making, see Ch. 7 *infra*. For a citique of efficiency as the measure of governmental success see Lacey, 'Government as Manager, Citizen as Consumer'.

References

Adler, M., and Asquith, S. (eds.), *Discretion and Welfare* (London, 1981).
Baldwin, R. and Hawkins, K., 'Discretionary Justice: Davis Reconsidered' [1984] PL 570.
Baldwin R. and McCrudden, C., *Regulation and Public Law* (London, 1987).
Bardach, E. and Kagan, R., *Going by the Book: The Problem of Regulatory Unreasonableness* (Philadelphia, PA, 1982).
Barker, R., 'Legitimacy, Obedience and the State', in C. Harlow (ed.), *Public Law and Politics* (London, 1986).
Barker, R., *Political Legitimacy and the State* (Oxford, 1990).
Barrett, S. and Fudge, C. (eds.), *Policy and Action* (London, 1981).

Barron, A. and Scott, C., 'The Citizens' Charter Programme' (1992) 55 MLR 526.

Baumgartner, M. P., 'The Myth of Discretion' in K. Hawkins (ed.), *The Uses of Discretion* (Oxford, 1992).

Beetham, D., *The Legitimation of Power* (London, 1991).

Beloff, N., *The General Says No* (London, 1963).

Bradley, A. W., 'Research and Reform in Administrative Law' (1974) 13 JSPTL 35.

Breyer, S. and Stewart, R. B. *Administrative Law and Regulatory Policy*, 3rd edn (Boston, MA, 1992).

Bryner, G., *Bureaucratic Discretion* (New York, 1987).

Connolly, W. (ed.), *Legitimacy and the State* (Oxford, 1984).

Craig, P. P., *Public Law and Democracy in the United Kingdom and the United States of America* (Oxford, 1990).

Craig, P. P., 'Dicey: Unitary, Self-correcting Democracy and the Public Law' (1990) 106 LQR 105.

Davis, K. C., *Discretionary Justice* (Chicago, IL, 1971).

Davis, K. C., 'An Approach to legal Control of the Police' (1974) 52 Tex. LR 703.

Dickinson, J., *Administrative Justice and the Supremacy of Law in the United States* (1927).

Diver, C. S., 'Policymaking Paradigms in Administrative Law' (1981) 95 Harv. LR 393.

Drewry, G., 'Mr Major's Charter: Empowering the Consumer' [1993] PL 248.

Dunleavy, P., and O'Leary, B., *Theories of the State: The Politics of Liberal Democracy* (London, 1987).

Dworkin, R., *Taking Rights Seriously* (Cambridge, MA, 1977).

Edley, C., *Administrative Law: Rethinking Judicial Control of Bureaucracy* (New Haven, CT, 1990).

Ely, J., *Democracy and Distrust* (Cambridge, MA, 1980).

Fenn, P., and Veljanovski, C. G., 'A Positive Economic Theory of Regulatory Enforcement' (1988) 98 *Economic Journal* 1055.

Freedman, J., *Crisis and Legitimacy* (Cambridge, 1978).

Friendly, H. J., 'Judicial Control of Administrative Action' (1970) 23 JLE 63.

Frug, G. E., 'Why Neutrality?' (1983) 92 Yale LJ 1591.

Frug, G. E., 'The Ideology of Bureaucracy in American Law' (1984) 97 Harv. LR 1277.

Fuller, L., *The Morality of Law* (New Haven, CT, 1964).

Galligan, D. J., *Discretionary Powers* (Oxford, 1986).

Gerth, H., and Mills, C. W. (eds.), *From Max Weber: Essays in Sociology* (London, 1958).

Gifford, D. J., 'Decisions, Decisional Referents and Administrative Justice' (1972) 37 LCP 3.

Habermas, J., *Legitimation Crisis*, trans. T. McCarthy (London, 1976).

Harden, I., *The Contracting State* (Buckingham, 1992).

Hawkins, K., *Environment and Enforcement: Regulation and the Social Definition of Pollution* (Oxford, 1984).

Hawkins, K., 'On Legal Decisionmaking' (1989) 4 *Washington and Lee Law Review* 1161.

Hawkins, K., 'The Use of Legal Discretion: Perspectives from Law and Social Science', in K. Hawkins (ed.), *The Uses of Discretion* (Oxford, 1992).

Hawkins, K., and J. M. Thomas (eds.), *Enforcing Regulation* (Boston, MA, 1984).

Hawkins, K., and J. M. Thomas (eds.), *Making Regulatory Policy* (Pittsburgh, PA, 1989).

Hayek, F. A., *The Constitution of Liberty* (London, 1960).

Held, D., *Models of Democracy* (Oxford, 1987).

Henkel, M., 'The New Evaluative State' (1991) 69 Pub. Admin. 121.

Hennessey, P., *Whitehall* (London, 1989).

Hepple, B. A., Review of *Discretionary Justice* [1969] CLJ 313.

Hood, C., *The Tools of Government* (London, 1983).

Hood, C., 'A Public Management for All Seasons' (1991) 69 Pub. Admin. 3.

Hood, C., and Jackson, M., *Administrative Argument* (Aldershot, 1991).

Hutter, B. M., *The Reasonable Arm of the Law?* (Oxford, 1988).

Jowell, J. L., *Law and Bureaucracy* (Port Washington, New York, 1975).

Jowell, J. L., 'The Rule of Law Today', in J. L. Jowell and D. Oliver (eds.), *The Changing Constitution*, 3rd edn (Oxford, 1994).

Jowell, J. L. and Oliver, D. (eds.), *The Changing Constitution*, 3rd edn (Oxford, 1994).

Lacey, N., 'The Jurisprudence of Discretion: Escaping the Legal Paradigm', in K. Hawkins (ed.), *The Uses of Discretion* (Oxford, 1992).

Lacey, N., 'Government as Manager, Citizen as Consumer: The Case of the Criminal Justice Act 1991' (1994) 57 MLR 534.

Landis, J. M., *The Administrative Process* (New Haven, CT, 1938).

Lewis, N., 'The Citizen's Charter and Next Steps: A New Way of Governing' (1993) Pol. Q. 316.

Liebman, L., and Stewart, R., 'Bureaucratic Vision' (1983) 96 Harv. LR 1952.

Long, S. B., 'Social Control: The Civil Law: The Case of Income Tax Enforcement', in H. L. Ross (ed.), *Law and Deviance* (1981).

Lowi, T., *The End of Liberalism* (New York, 1969).

McAuslan, P., 'Administrative Law, Collective Consumption and Judicial Policy' (1983) 46 MLR 1.

McAuslan, P., and McEldowney, J. (eds.), *Law, Legitimacy and the Constitution* (London, 1985).

McEldowney, J., 'Contract Compliance and Public Audit as Regulatory Strategies in the Public Sector', paper to Citizen's Charter Conference, University of Warwick, 23 Sept. 1993.

Macpherson, C. B., *The Life and Times of Liberal Democracy* (Oxford, 1977).

Mashaw, J., 'Administrative Due Process: The Quest for a Dignitary Theory' (1981) 61 BULR 885.

Mashaw, J., *Bureaucratic Justice* (New Haven, CT, 1983).

Mayne,J., 'Public Power Outside Government' (1993) 64 Pol. Q. 327.

Nozick, R., *Anarchy, State and Utopia* (Oxford, 1974).

Pateman, C., *Participation and Democratic Theory* (Cambridge, 1970).

Pateman, C., *The Problem of Political Obligation* (Cambridge, 1985).

Polanyi, M., *The Logic of Liberty* (London, 1951).

Poulantzas, N., *State, Power, Socialism* (London, 1980).

Prosser, T., 'The Politics of Discretion' in M. Adler and S. Asquith (eds.), *Discretion and Welfare* (London, 1981).

Reich, C., 'Individual Rights and Social Welfare: The Emerging Legal Issues' (1965) 74 Yale LJ 1245.

Reiner, R., *The Politics of the Police*, 2nd edn (Brighton, 1992).

Reiss, A., Jr., review of *Discretionary Justice* (1970) 69 Mich. LR 792.

Richardson, G., Ogus, A., and Burrows, P., *Policing Pollution* (Oxford, 1983).

Rubin, E. L., 'Law and Legislation in the Administrative State' (1989) Col. LR 369.

Schuck, P. H., 'Regulation, Non-Market Values and the Administrative State: A Comment on Professor Stewart' (1983) 92 Yale LJ 1602.

Scott, C., 'Rules versus Discretion in the New Public Sector', paper to Citizen's Charter Conference, University of Warwick, 23 Sept. 1993.

Shapiro, D. L., 'The Choice of Rulemaking or Adjudication in the Development of Agency Policy' (1965) 78 Harv. LR 921.

Shapiro, M. 'Administrative Discretion: The Next Stage' (1983) 92 Yale LJ 1487.

Sharfman, I. L., *The Interstate Commerce Commission* (New York, 1931).

Shavell, S., 'The Optimal Structure of Law Enforcement' (1993) Journal of Law and Economics 255.

Stewart, R., 'Regulation in a Liberal State: The Role of Non-Commodity Values' (1983) 92 Yale LJ 1357.

Stewart, R. B., 'The Reformation of American Administrative Law' (1975) 88 Harv. LR 1667.

Strauss, P. L., 'Some Comments on Rubin' (1989) 89 Col. LR 427.

Titmuss, R. M., 'Welfare "Rights" Law and Discretion' (1971) 42 Pol. Q. 113.

Unger, R., *Law in Modern Society* (New York, 1976).

Veljanovski, C. G., 'The Economics of Regulatory Enforcement', in K. Hawkins and J. Thomas (eds.), *Enforcing Regulation* (Boston, MA, 1984).

Weiler, P., 'Two Models of Judicial Decision-making' (1968) 46 Can. Br 406.

Street-level bureaucracy

An introduction

Michael Lipsky

Dilemmas of the individual in public services

This book is in part a search for the place of the individual in those public services I call street-level bureaucracies. These are the schools, police and welfare departments, lower courts, legal services offices, and other agencies whose workers interact with and have wide discretion over the dispensation of benefits or the allocation of public sanctions.

I have tried to show how people experience public policies in these important realms. Too often social analysts offer generalizations about organizational and governmental actions without concretely explaining how individual citizens and workers are affected by the actions, how the behavior of individuals, when aggregated, gives rise to the actions, or how and why the actions in question are consistently reproduced by the behavior of individuals. For example, it is suggested, persuasively, that the administration of public welfare has the effect of minimizing the extent to which people seek welfare assistance. But since welfare workers do not as a rule explicitly discourage welfare recipients from applying (although some of this does go on), we need to know what welfare workers do that results in a systemic bias affecting welfare participation. Similarly, we know that service bureaucracies consistently favor some clients at the expense of others, despite official regulations to the contrary. To understand how and why these organizations often perform contrary to their own rules and goals, we need to know how the rules are experienced by workers in the organization and to what other pressures they are subject.

This study is grounded in observations of the collective behavior of public service organizations and advances a theory of the work of street-level bureaucracies as individual workers experience it. I argue that the decisions of street-level bureaucrats, the routines they establish, and the devices they invent to cope with uncertainties and work pressures, effectively *become* the public policies they carry out. I argue that

From M. Lipsky, *Street-level Bureaucracy: Dilemmas of the individual in public services* (1980), pp. xi–xv, New York: Russell Sage Foundation. Used with permission of the Russell Sage Foundation.

public policy is not best understood as made in legislatures or top-floor suites of high-ranking administrators, because in important ways it is actually made in the crowded offices and daily encounters of street-level workers. I point out that policy conflict is not only expressed as the contention of interest groups but is also located in the struggles between individual workers and citizens who challenge or submit to client-processing.

One aspect of the way workers, clients, and citizens-at-large experience street-level bureaucracies is the conflicts that they encounter in wanting their organizational life to be more consistent with their own preferences and commitments. For example, people often enter public employment, particularly street-level bureaucracies, with at least some commitment to service. Teachers, social workers, public interest lawyers, and police officers in part seek out these occupations because of their potential as socially useful roles. Yet the very nature of this work prevents them from coming even close to the ideal conception of their jobs. Large classes or huge caseloads and inadequate resources combine with the uncertainties of method and the unpredictability of clients to defeat their aspirations as service workers.

Ideally, and by training, street-level bureaucrats respond to the individual needs or characteristics of the people they serve or confront. In practice, they must deal with clients on a mass basis, since work requirements prohibit individualized service. Teachers should respond to the needs of the individual child; in practice, they must develop techniques to respond to children as a class. Police officers should respond to the implications of the presenting case; in reality, they must develop techniques to recognize and respond to types of confrontations, and to process categories of cases accordingly. At best, street-level bureaucrats invent benign modes of mass processing that more or less permit them to deal with the public fairly, appropriately, and successfully. At worst, they give in to favoritism, stereotyping, and routinizing – all of which serve private or agency purposes.

Some street-level bureaucrats drop out or burn out relatively early in their careers. Those who stay on, to be sure, often grow in the jobs and perfect techniques, but not without adjusting their work habits and attitudes to reflect lower expectations for themselves, their clients, and the potential of public policy. Ultimately, these adjustments permit acceptance of the view that clients receive the best that can be provided under prevailing circumstances.

Compromises in work habits and attitudes are rationalized as reflecting workers' greater maturity, their appreciation of practical and political realities, or their more realistic assessment of the nature of the problem. But these rationalizations only summarize the prevailing structural constraints on human service bureaucracies. They are not 'true' in an absolute sense. The teacher who psychologically abandons his or her aspirations to help children to read may succumb to a private assessment of the status quo in education. But this compromise says nothing about the potential of individual children to learn, or the capacity of the teacher to instruct. This potential remains intact. It is the *system* of schooling, the organization of the schooling bureaucracy, that teaches that children are dull or unmotivated, and that teachers must abandon their public commitments to educate.

In the same way, the judicial system 'teaches' that police officers must be impersonal and highly reactive to hints of disobedience among youth, and that judges are unable to make informed determinations or consign defendants to institutions that will help the offender or deter future offenses. Although the potential for thoughtful and useful determinations and interventions is not contradicted in any individual instance, the system teaches the intractability of the juvenile crime problem.

Street-level bureaucrats often spend their work lives in a corrupted world of service. They believe themselves to be doing the best they can under adverse circumstances and they develop techniques to salvage service and decision-making values within the limits imposed upon them by the structure of the work. They develop conceptions of their work and of their clients that narrow the gap between their personal and work limitations and the service ideal. These work practices and orientations are maintained even while they contribute to the perversion of the service ideal or put the worker in the position of manipulating citizens on behalf of the agencies from which citizens seek help.

Should teachers, police officers, or welfare workers look for other work rather than perpetuate unfair, ineffective, or destructive public practices? This would leave clients to others who have even less concern and interest in service ideals. It would mean giving up the narrow areas in which workers have tried to make a difference or in which some progress is foreseen.

Should they stay on, contributing to discredited and sometimes brutalizing public agencies? If current patterns repeat themselves this would mean fighting the losing battle against cynicism and the realities of the work situation, and watching as service ideals are transformed into struggles for personal benefits.

Should they struggle from within to change the conditions under which citizens are processed by their agencies? This path seems the hardest to maintain and is subject to the danger that illusions of difference will be taken for the reality of significant reform.

The structure of street-level bureaucracy confronts clients with dilemmas bearing on action. Consumers of public services, once they have decided on or been consigned to a place of residence, with rare exceptions cannot choose the public services to which they will be subject. They must accept the schools, courts, and police forces of their communities. If they are poor they must also accept the community's arrangements for health care, welfare, public housing, and other benefit programs. In approaching these institutions they must strike a balance between asserting their rights as citizens and accepting the obligations public agencies seek to place upon them as clients. As citizens they should seek their full entitlement; as bureaucratic subjects they feel themselves obliged to temper their demands in recognition of perceived resource limitations and the agencies' organizational needs. Although it is apparent that exceptions are often made and additional resources often found, clients also recognize the potential costs of unsuccessfully asserting their rights.

On matters of the greatest urgency and moment, such as health care, education, justice, housing, and income, clients passively seek the benign intervention of public agencies when evidence and experience suggest that their hopes will go unrewarded.

The dilemmas of action are particularly acute if clients are poor, and racially, ethnically, or linguistically different from most of the public employees. Should I wait my turn and submit to the procedures of the agency, despite reservations? I risk being unable to gain attention to my particular needs and concerns. Should I speak out forcefully and demand my rights? I risk the antagonism of the workers by disrupting office procedures.

Clients experience similar uncertainties in attempting to obtain proper services through collective action. The parent who organizes others to protest school actions, or the welfare recipient who challenges welfare policy, even if he or she perceives the possibilities of collective responses, risks receiving a reputation as an unreliable troublemaker toward whom favorable treatment should not be extended.

A final set of dilemmas confronts citizens who are continuously, if implicitly, asked to evaluate public services. This occurs in as focused a forum as a referendum on a school budget, and as diffuse an arena as Proposition 13 and other expressions of dissatisfaction with the nature and quality of public services. Indeed, recent legislative initiatives to limit state and local spending have largely been understood as attacks on governmental performance and the ineffectiveness of social services.

What are the policy alternatives? When all the 'fat' has been trimmed from agency budget and all the 'waste' eliminated, the basic choices remain: to further automate, systematize, and regulate the interactions between government employees and citizens seeking help; to drift with the current turmoil that favors reduced services and more standardization in the name of cost effectiveness and budgetary controls; or to secure or restore the importance of human interactions in services that require discretionary intervention or involvement.

But how much can human intervention be eliminated from teaching, nursing, policing, and judging? The fact is that we *must* have people making decisions and treating other citizens in the public services. We are not prepared as a society to abandon decisions about people and discretionary interventions to machines and programmed formats. Yet how can one advocate greater attention to the intervening and discretionary roles of street-level bureaucrats in the face of the enormous and often well-deserved popular discontent with the effectiveness and quality of their work?

I try to address these questions in this book. I do not exonerate street-level bureaucracies, excuse their deficiencies, or urge their support as currently structured. Rather, I locate the problem of street-level bureaucrats in the structure of their work, and attempt to identify conditions that would better support a reconstituted public sector dedicated to appropriate service and respect for clients, one that would be more likely to produce effective service-providers. In developing the street-level bureaucracy framework, I identify the common elements of occupations as apparently disparate as, say, police officer and social worker. The analysis of street-level bureaucracy helps us identify which features of people-processing are common, and which are unique, to the different occupational milieux in which they arise.

Michael Lipsky and street level bureaucracy

A neglected perspective

Bob Hudson

Over the past decade in Britain, there has been renewed political and academic interest in the problem of 'policy implementation'. The concern of a right-wing government to reduce the scale and role of public service bureaucracies has left the air rife with talk of 'value for money', efficiency, effectiveness, performance review and so forth. Policy-makers find themselves under intense pressure to ensure that policy impact reflects the intended direction of change. The broad problem confronting policy-makers is that policy is rarely applied directly to the external world, but is mediated though other institutions and actors. Policy impact is therefore at risk of distortion by these mediators.

In health and welfare agencies, the traditional focus upon the individual has tended to inhibit scrutiny of the collective context within which such activity takes place (Roberts, 1982). Those research studies which have led to theoretical speculation have stemmed mainly from work within industrial organisations, and have tended to see 'implementation deficit' as a problem for top-level policy-makers (Hill and Bramley, 1986). Concerns about over-elaborate structures have been a major preoccupation of administration textbooks for both the public and private sectors and issues about hierarchical control have been the traditional concern of 'management science'. The primary technique for studying behaviour has been the case study.

This is clearly a very limited way of examining social policy implementation. A fresh avenue of inquiry has concentrated upon the behaviour of 'street level' personnel – those actors who do the 'actual' work of the agency – and the ways in which their activities affect the way the public bureaucracy fulfils its public responsibility. In particular, Michael Lipsky (1980) has attempted to synthesise much of the research done in America on the activities of such personnel, and to elaborate a new body of theory on the roles of 'street level bureaucrats'.

From B. Hudson, 'Michael Lipsky and steel level bureaucracy: a neglected perspective', in L. Barton (ed.), *Disability and Dependency* (1989), London: Falmer Press.

Lipsky's analysis has enormous potential for helping us to make sense of the relationship between service providers and service consumers, yet it has had a curiously muted impact. This may be because as Professor of Political Science at Massachusetts Institute of Technology, Lipsky is in the 'wrong' discipline for influencing those studying social welfare. Equally his Goffmanian eclecticism may not appeal to all, for somehow he does manage to address almost every question that occurs to the reader. This chapter will suggest that Lipsky's under-utilised theory has as much significance for understanding welfare service bureaucracies as Goffman's work has had for the understanding of closed institutions.

Lipsky uses the term 'street level bureaucrat' to describe those public service workers who 'interact directly with citizens in the course of their jobs and who have substantial discretion in the execution of their work'. Typical street level workers are teachers, social workers, police officers, doctors, health visitors, certain social security officers, certain housing officers and so forth. It is therefore a notion which encompasses a wide range of welfare services as well as embracing both professionals and non-professionals. By focussing upon this tier of organisational life, Lipsky gets us away from traditional analyses of legislative activity and high ranking policy-makers. By attempting to transcend the limitations of case study, he seeks to develop a body of theory on street level activity. He directs our attention to a very large class of people at the sharp end of welfare activity, who routinely behave in ways that remain essentially unexplained.

The essence of Lipsky's case is that street level bureaucrats have enormous power which is scarcely acknowledged in the literature on public administration; that this power extends not only to control over service consumers but also to a considerable autonomy from their employing agency; and that this power is accompanied by the dilemma of working at the sharp end of resource allocation in a situation where demand far exceeds supply. Street level bureaucrats therefore end up making policy in circumstances which are not of their own choosing and which impel them to devise strategies to protect their working environment. In this way, Lipsky is addressing the process whereby zeal is eclipsed and idealism corrupted. It is significant that Lipsky's title refers not to the *power* but to the *dilemma* of the street level bureaucrat.

What is the source of this power? The crucial source is the inescapable exercise of *discretion*. Inescapable, because street level bureaucracies *require* people to make decisions about other people. Indeed, in defence of their activities, organisations will frequently point to the expertise of their members rather than to the success of their endeavours. But once an agency admits that its members have special skills, it also admits to a limitation of the right to define appropriate street level behaviour.

Unlike lower level workers in most organisations, street level bureaucrats have a considerable amount of discretion in determining the nature, amount and quality of benefits and sanctions provided by their agencies. Policemen decide who to arrest and whose behaviour to overlook; teachers make subtle decisions on who is teachable; social workers on who is socially salvageable; health care workers on who has a life worth preserving; housing lettings officers on who gets accommodation; social security officers on who gets a community care grant and so on. The discretion is therefore largely brought to bear in the rationing of resources in a situation where demand for them exceeds supply.

Lipsky writes at great length, drawing widely upon evidence, to indicate the techniques used by street level bureaucrats in allocating resources between competing clients. To understand what is taking place, he emphasises the need to take a phenomenological view of street level behaviour – we need to understand the subjective states of mind of the actors. His analysis of the routines developed starts with the proposition that they contribute to control over a difficult and ambiguous work environment. He identifies three broad responses: modification of client demand; modification of job conception; and modification of client conception.

I shall look very briefly at each of these, but this does not do justice to the richness of Lipsky's analysis of modification of client demand. Although street level bureaucrats can rarely charge for their services, most other forms of demand control are open to them, such as perpetuating delay, withholding information, and stigmatising the process of service delivery. Social policy has yet to address this field effectively at an empirical level.

If necessary, street level bureaucrats can simply *control* clients, or at least obtain their cooperation with client processing procedures. Several aspects of practice contribute to the routine control of clients. First, street level bureaucrats interact with clients in settings that symbolise and limit their relationship – this may encompass such matters as uniforms, location, and the content, timing and pace of interaction. Second, clients are isolated from one another, and are therefore more likely to see themselves as responsible for their situations – indeed street level bureaucrats will tend to resist client organisation when it arises. Third, the procedures and services of street level bureaucrats are presented as benign and always in the best interests of clients.

But street level bureaucrats do not simply deal with occupational hazards by limiting client demand. They also modify their *own* activities and perceptions of their jobs and clients. Modification of job conception basically means that street level bureaucrats modify their objectives to match better their ability to perform. Lipsky gives several examples. One is 'psychological withdrawal', resulting in a workforce relatively unbothered by the discrepancy between what they are *supposed* to do and what they *actually* do. By accepting limitations as fixed rather than problematic, innovation is discouraged and mediocrity encouraged. It is a situation not unfrequently chronicled in research into the functioning of long-stay psychiatric and subnormality hospitals.

Modification of client conception is even more subtle. Lipsky argues that street level bureaucrats who are unable to provide all clients with their best efforts develop conceptual mechanisms to divide up the client population and rationalise the division, even though the consequence of this may be at variance with the formal goals of the organisation. This may involve 'creaming off' those clients who seem most likely to succeed in terms of bureaucratic success criteria; or it may simply involve differentiating between those clients deemed to be deserving and undeserving.

Even with this brief review, I hope to have conveyed something of the power exercised by the street level bureaucrat. But to what extent can the street level bureaucrat act autonomously of the employing agency? Lipsky himself argues that accountability to the organisation is virtually impossible to achieve where street level bureaucrats exercise a high degree of discretion. I shall return to the issue of accountability shortly, but for now it is worth re-emphasising that street level bureaucrats do carry out much of the difficult rationing at client level, and it is therefore often convenient for organisations to permit this discretion to continue relatively unabated. The exercise of street level bureaucrat discretion can be functional to the organisation.

Lipsky's analysis is useful for helping us to understand a wide range of public welfare activities, including services for people with a disability. Disappointingly little attempt has been made, in any field of activity, to put Lipsky's ideas to the test. I shall look briefly at some areas of provision for people with a disability which could benefit from Lipsky's work and which do at least have some data on the activities of street level bureaucrats.

First, Special Educational Needs. In the USA an attempt has been made by one of Lipsky's associates, Richard Weatherley (Weatherley and Lipsky, 1977), to apply the street level perspective to the study of the implementation of special education reform in Massachusetts, where the Comprehensive Special Education Law introduced provisions very similar to those in Britain's 1981 Education Act. Schools were required to operate much more sophisticated procedures for assessing needs and for developing individualised programmes for children, and, as in Britain, were expected to do this without significantly more resources. Weatherley shows how the realities at street level constrained and distorted the reforms hoped for by state legislators – assessments were not conducted; limits were placed on the number of assessments held; assessment schedules were biased in favour of children likely to be inexpensive; parental deference to professional authority was sought, and so forth. In short, street level bureaucrats sought to secure their work environment.

In Britain, no attempt to apply Lipsky's theory explicitly has been made, but in her study of 'statementing' under the 1981 Education Act, Nicki Cornwell (1987) does reveal some telling detail about the *modus operandi* of street level bureaucrats, which can help us to explain the wide variation in the percentage of school populations with statements. I shall take only two of her many illustrations, the first in relation to modifying demand by reducing service levels. In the London borough she studied, she found that although administrators had to follow the advice of psychologists about placement, somehow demand and supply had to match. She writes that: 'Some negotiation might be needed with psychologists about this, and a gentleman's agreement reached about not putting the borough in an embarrassing situation.' Again, on modification of job conception, she argues that statementing amounts to little more than a continuously loaded conveyor belt in which decisions on outcomes are made as soon as the child is referred for assessment, but it is important in order to keep up the appearance of open and rational decision making. This is not only for the purpose of legality, but also for the psychological well-being of the street level bureaucrats involved. She writes: 'The appearance of negotiation can help to obscure the reality of the situation from the professionals involved, who can remain convinced that they are taking part in a rational assessment.'

In the field of social work Carol Satyamurti (1981) has written tellingly of the adoption of stereotyped responses to clients. She argues:

> In the social work literature, the client is often spoken of as though he were a fully consenting adult participant in the social work relationship. In practice, however, it often seemed that a parent–child relationship was a more powerful model, as far as the social worker was concerned, for her dealings with clients. This was true both at the level of face-to-face encounters, and at the level of decision-making affecting the client.

As illustrations of this, Satyamurti cites the way in which social workers encouraged dependent behaviour in their clients, the way in which social workers treated appointments and called without warning on clients, the terms in which social workers discussed clients and the assumptions they made about client 'irresponsibility'.

A third area which could usefully draw upon Lipsky's work is that of income maintenance policies, which affords a useful example of street level bureaucrats who do not hold professional status. Folk-lore is rich with tales of encounters between social security officers and claimants, but research is at a premium. An important exception is Cooper's (1985) detailed consideration of the former supplementary benefit scheme at a range of offices.

Much of Lipsky's theory is reflected in Cooper's findings. The impact of unmanageable demand is evident. He writes: 'In most offices, most of the time, the emphasis was on getting the work done at all, rather than on doing it well. . . . Many of the difficulties found in relationships between staff and claimants could be interpreted in part as devices used by staff for controlling the amount of work with which they were required to cope.' In the pursuit of coping practices, relatively junior staff were left pretty much to their own devices, but it is clear that much of this is delegated autonomy which it is functional for the organisation to permit. He notes: 'In keeping with the emphasis on "getting the work done", it was apparent on several occasions that the calibre of junior staff was judged by their ability to dispose of cases rapidly and without follow-up work, with scant reference to the outcome for claimants.'

One of the prime coping mechanisms described by Cooper is illustrative of Lipsky's notion of modification of client conception. Treatment of claimants was found to vary according to a judgement made about them by officers on the basis of very little information and a brief acquaintance. People with a disability tend to emerge from these encounters better than most, but sympathy is hardly the stuff of citizenship. Cooper's vignettes are illuminating. I shall take two contrasting examples, both dealt with by the same officer.

> . . . a married man in his 50's who had been out of work for a number of years owing to a chronic chest condition. He had called to drop in his latest medical certificate and to put a general enquiry about extra help with fuel costs over the winter. Mike (the officer) treated him very decently, asking after his and his wife's welfare, and thanking him pleasantly for the certificate. He then gave an outline of help available for fuel costs and passed over the relevant leaflet, saying, 'This will tell you how to apply. The form is on the back, see? If you have any doubts or queries come back in and we'll sort it out, OK?'

The next caller was less fortunate:

... there followed Mr. Z., a young Pakistani who had recently been made redundant, bringing in his rent book and last three wage slips. He appeared shy and confused in the office environment. Mike's approach was abrupt. He wanted to know why Mr. Z. had come in. Mr. Z. said he had been told to bring the documents. 'You must have heard wrong,' said Mike. 'We tell people to post them in. Why don't you leave it with the man on reception?' Mike took the papers and dismissed Mr. Z., with the words 'Right enough, we'll keep these and you'll get them back sometime in the post. There was nothing else was there?' As Mr. Z. retires, evidently disconcerted, Mike remarked 'What do you make of that one? Bloody odd. The best thing you can do is get them in and get them out when they're like him. We get quite a few Pakis like that, wandering in like lost sheep.'

It is worth emphasising that Cooper is describing the implementation of the 1980 Social Security Act which ostensibly afforded claimants legal entitlement to benefits. The 1986 Social Security Act has largely replaced entitlement with discretion and will make the street level bureaucrat–claimant relationship even more one-sided. The first set of figures on the community care grant, for example, reveals that six of the London DHSS offices spent none of their budget, and elsewhere the variation is huge.

If Lipsky's analysis has validity, then concern about the accountability of street level bureaucrats is bound to be high, for accountability is the link between bureaucracy and democracy. Lipsky himself argues that such accountability is virtually impossible to achieve where workers exercise a high degree of discretion, and since he also takes the view that discretion itself is inescapable, the likelihood of securing accountability seems slim.

This pessimistic appraisal has not diminished the zeal with which various forms of accountability are pursued. Four main types can be distinguished: accountability to the organisation; accountability to consumers; accountability to the law; and accountability to professional norms. Each is problematic.

Accountability to the organisation

Attempts to increase accountability to the organisation through administrative controls (both sanctions and incentives) is the most common effort to increase congruence between worker behaviour and agency policy. But for the street level bureaucrat, the formal rewards of agencies are likely to play only a minor role in directing behaviour.

Prottas (1978) points out that in many public service bureaucracies, the turnover of street level bureaucrats is very high, therefore the relevance of promotions, salary increases and retirement benefits is correspondingly low. The same is true when the street level bureaucrats are established professionals, as in law and medicine, and have other career alternatives.

It is, in any case, difficult for the agency to decide when it is appropriate to deploy such controls as it has available. Street level bureaucrat performance is notoriously difficult to define and measure, and much of the performance occurs in places inaccessible to supervisors. Greater demands can be made for written records to serve as an independent check, but when matters are ambiguous, they are less than useful; they either support the decision of the street level bureaucrat or do not mention it. Indeed, Prottas (1978) suggests that: 'The most striking characteristic of client files in many public bureaucracies is their sparseness'.

Organisational measures to *increase* scrutiny of street level activity are strewn with difficulty. Conceivably, someone could replicate the street level bureaucrat's interaction with clients, but this is a desperate measure, of use in inhibiting flagrant abuses, but not a practical means of assuring routine compliance. Similarly, close supervision will be resisted. Alvin Gouldner (1964) showed clearly that all workers have an idea of what constitutes normal supervision, and any attempt to exceed that norm will be identified as 'close supervision'.

Downs (1966) called it a 'law' of organisational behaviour, that 'the greater the efforts made to control subordinated officials, the greater the efforts by those subordinates to evade or counteract such control'. This is borne out by the discussion by Fox (1974) on the relationship between rule-imposition and low-trust relationships. Coming from a concern with industrial relations, he shows how a 'top-down' concern with detailed prescription creates and reinforces low-trust relationships. Subordinates therefore feel little commitment, which results in an even further tightening of control, and a further diminution of commitment. Hill and Bramley (1986) note: 'Low motivation in a rule-bound context produces restriction of output, working to rule, industrial sabotage and strikes. In public administration, there is often another person or member of the public, rather than a machine, to feel the effects of low official morale.'

Accountability to consumers

Proposals for greater client autonomy tend to suffer from the fact that clients generally remain relatively powerless, but there nevertheless remains a *potential* for contributing to changing street level relationships. There are two main variants.

One approach is to attempt to *eliminate street level workers as buffers* between government and citizens. A class of proposals utilising such an approach is represented by the voucher system, which promises to import consumer sovereignty into the production of welfare services. In Britain, two major reports have come out in favour of vouchers – the Griffiths Report on community care (1988) and the Wagner Report on residential care (1988).

The debate is a complex one, but it will be very difficult to establish the conditions under which consumers of services are fully informed about the wide variety of options, and it is therefore difficult to create the rudiments of competition upon which the theory depends. Given Lipsky's argument that *agencies* find it difficult to assess the appropriateness of street level behaviour, it would clearly be difficult for *clients* to assess the appropriateness of a service.

An alternative route to consumer sovereignty is to *eliminate public workers from service contexts*, which, with proper support, might be handled by citizens with little assistance. Advocacy, and particularly self-advocacy, would fit into this route, and this represents one of the more exciting developments relating to people with disabilities. But at this stage, it would not be wise to make anything other than provisional claims for the success of such experiments. It has to be remembered that while clients seek services and benefits, street level bureaucrats seek control over the process of providing them, and they will not easily relinquish their grip.

A further possibility, and an increasingly fashionable one, is to democratise through forms of participation close to service delivery level – decentralisation. In social work in Britain, such notions have become increasingly popular since the Barclay Report (1982), but again, claims can be little more than provisional. In terms of Lipsky's analysis, if decentralisation intensifies pressure upon street level bureaucrats by making them more accessible, then they will develop new strategies for protecting themselves.

Accountability to the law

Judicial processes might be used to secure 'rights' to public benefits and services. Legal philosophers such as Dicey (1905), saw the growth of the 'collective state' as a threat to liberty, and the intervention of the judiciary as a brake upon the state. However, not only are procedures inaccessible to underprivileged citizens, but the legal system is not well equipped to deal with the problems associated with the exercise of discretion by street level bureaucrats.

Rather closer to organisational level, clients can bring information to the attention of other members of the bureaucracy. The ubiquity of appeals procedures in many welfare bureaucracies testifies to the hope that the availability of this channel will increase the compliance of street level bureaucrats. However, we still know relatively little about the actual uses to which appeals procedures are put, and about their effects upon street level behaviour.

Lipsky, with characteristic scepticism, argues that from the street level perspective, appeals procedures should exhibit three qualities. First, it must look as though the channels are open. Second, the channels must be costly to use, rarely successful and (if successful) not well publicised. Third, a single client should not be able to gain redress for a class of clients. This does seem to encompass much tribunal and appeal activity in Britain.

Accountability to professional norms

Lipsky concludes that most street level work is not open to meaningful revision by limiting discretion, removing public employees from interaction with clients, or modestly altering the bureaucratic structure. He stresses the idealism and commitment of many practitioners, but sees this idealism undermined by work situations and organisation structures.

In his concluding chapter, he seems to opt for the enhancement of professionalism as a way of coping with the problems of street level bureaucracy. The argument, he says, '... comes down simply to the realisation that control of occupational groups must come from within group members'. This is perhaps a rather insipid up-shot, particularly since he also recognises that: 'The problem with the "professional fix" lies in the gap between the service orientations of professionals in theory and in practice'.

Hill and Bramley (1986) take the view that '... it is far from certain that professional monopolies are not greater evils than the forms of discretion and "street level" behaviour they profess to bring under control'. This is broadly in line with Wilding's (1982) review of professional power, which concluded: 'Professional self-regulation is unsatisfactory. No profession has shown anything but the most luke-warm interest in monitoring and maintaining the standard of work of its members ... There is little or no acceptance of a consumer's right to comment on, or complain about, the substance of the service offered'.

The intractability of the street-level bureaucrat

There would therefore seem to be clear limits on the extent to which the freedom of action of front-line staff can be circumscribed. Lipsky argues that a bureaucratic accountability *policy* should possess four pre-requisites. First, agencies must know what they want workers to do; where objectives are multiple and conflicting, agencies must be able to rank their preferences. Second, agencies must know how to measure workers' performances. Third, agencies must be able to compare workers with one another, to establish a standard for judgment. And finally, agencies must have incentives and sanctions capable of disciplining workers.

These preconditions tend *not* to apply to street level bureaucrats, because street level bureaucracies *require* people to make decisions about other people. To say that human interaction is required in service delivery is to suggest that the situation requires judgments to be made about potentially ambiguous situations; the requisite human judgment simply cannot be programmed.

Hill (1982) reminds us that many examples of deviation from the apparent intentions of policy can be seen as situations in which the centre has no real concern that its policy should become manifest. There is a degree of 'sanctioned unaccount-ability'. As Hill puts it: 'Delegation may owe more to a desire to obscure political responsibility, than to an acceptance of the need to come to terms with street level bureaucracy'. It would seem that the best that can be managed is a little reining in here and a little wing clipping there.

Changing street level behaviour: the wider context

Ultimately, the contradictory tendencies in street level bureaucracies cannot be understood without examining their role in society, and the way in which society impinges upon the character of bureaucratic relations. The main danger of Lipsky's phenomenological approach is that it can be construed as a form of ideological relativism, largely ignoring the question of *why* one 'weltanschauung' is considered more legitimate than another. Such studies usually operate at a level of analysis which is divorced from any notion of power in social relations.

Although Lipsky does not systematically attempt to link his analysis to a broader perspective, he does point us in that direction. The influence of the wider context is raised at two levels. First, that the character of client treatment at the hands of street level bureaucrats reflects and reinforces class and ethnic divisions. The extent to which the clients are prepared for the impersonalism, hierarchy and institutionalisation of bureaucracy is also a reflection of such divisions.

But he also goes beyond this, in raising an even more fundamental question – in what ways do street level bureaucracies reflect and perpetuate the values of the larger society? An adequate analysis of the actual exercise of discretion at 'face-to-face' level must be informed by an understanding of the structural position of welfare institutions and their relationship to the broader social, political and economic framework of society. Novak (1988) makes some attempt to do this in his Marxist interpretation of relief of poverty by the state, but overall there has been little attempt to connect and reconcile micro- and macro-sociological concerns.

The poorer people are, the greater the power that street level bureaucracies have over them. In the 1960s and 1970s, a typical government response to social problems was to commission a corps of street level bureaucrats to attend to them, for as Lipsky notes, '. . . it is easier to develop employment for street level bureaucrats, than to reduce income inequalities'. It is through street level bureaucracies that society organises the control, restriction and maintenance of relatively powerless groups.

Despite his focus upon intra-organisational processes, Lipsky nevertheless concludes: '. . . the reconstruction of street level bureaucracies is unlikely to take place in the absence of a broad movement for social and economic justice. . . . Isolated reform efforts cannot plausibly be expected to bear the full weight of social change'. This is not a message in mood [*sic*] with the political spirit of the 1980s, in Britain or the USA. It may help to explain the relative neglect of Lipsky's analysis.

What, then, is the message to come out of Lipsky? It is not that street level bureaucrats are simply malicious and cunning functionaries interested only in their own comfort. Rather, it is that in looking at the dilemmas in their working day, we can see just how problematic a role they are asked to play in the policy making system. Academically, the pressing need is to find out more about how street level bureaucrats are actually behaving. Getting at the truth would be problematic, but must be confronted. If we wish to understand policy implementation, we must understand the street level bureaucrat.

References

Barclay Report (1982) *Social Workers: Their role and tasks*, Bedford Square Press.

Cooper, S. (1985) *Observation in Supplementary Benefit Offices*, Supplementary Benefit Working Paper C, Policy Studies Institute.

Cornwell, N. (1987) *Statementing and the 1981 Education Act*, Cranfield Press.

Dicey, A. V. (1905) *Lectures on the Relation Between Law and Public Opinion in England*, Macmillan.

Downs, A. (1966) *Inside Bureaucracy*, Little, Brown.

Fox, A. (1974) *Beyond Contract: Work, power and trust relations*, Faber.

Gouldner, A. (1964) *Patterns of Industrial Bureaucracy*, Free Press.

Griffiths Report (1988) *Community Care: An agenda for action*, HMSO.

Hill, M. (1982) 'Street level bureaucracy in social work and social services departments', *Research Highlights*, 4, University of Aberdeen.

Hill, M. and Bramley, G. (1986) *Analysing Social Policy*, Blackwell.

Lipsky, M. (1980) *Street-Level Bureaucracy: Dilemmas of the individual in public services*, Russell Sage Foundation.

Novak, T. (1988) *Poverty and the State*, Open University Press.

Prottas, J. D. (1978) 'The power of the street level bureaucrat in public service bureaucracies', *Urban Affairs Quarterly*, 13, 3.

Roberts, E. (1982) 'A presentation of perspectives of organisational theory relevant to social work', *Research Highlights*, 4, University of Aberdeen.

Satyamurti, C. (1981) *Occupational Survival*, Blackwell.

Wagner Report (1988) *Residential Care: A positive choice*, HMSO.

Weatherley, R. and Lipsky, M. (1977) 'Street-level bureaucrats and institutional innovation: implementing special education reform', *Harvard Education Review*, 47, pp. 171–97.

Wilding, P. (1982) *Professional Power and Social Welfare*, Routledge & Kegan Paul.

Contemporary public management: a new global paradigm?

Christopher Hood

Abstract. This paper takes another look at the much-canvassed idea of a 'new global paradigm' emerging in contemporary public management. It argues that, linguistic usage apart, the 'globality' and monoparadigmatic character of contemporary public management change seems to be exaggerated. Three interrelated objections are advanced against the claim of an emerging new global paradigm. First, it is argued that contemporary reform ideas, particularly those advanced by Osborne and Gaebler, are culturally plural rather than homogeneous. Second, it is argued that there are substantial biases towards exaggerating international similarity in public management reforms, but that the similarity weakens when we go beyond semantic packaging to examine the specific content of reform initiatives. Third, it is claimed that there are also built-in biases for overstressing the continuity of contemporary public management reforms, but that in fact there are major obstacles to the emergence of a stable new paradigm in public management. One is the underlying mutual repulsions of the multiple reform paradigms today, and the other is the frequency of self-disequilibrating processes in public management reform associated with the production of unintended side-effects and reverse effects.

The claim of a new global paradigm in public management

It has become commonplace to assert that an unstoppable new 'global' model is developing in contemporary public management. The claim is made explicitly by David Osborne and Ted Gaebler, in their 1992 best-seller *Reinventing Government*. They say that the world-wide ascendancy of a new 'global paradigm' in public administration is historically as inevitable as the rise of 'progressive' public management ideas in the USA in the late nineteenth and early twentieth century (Osborne and Gaebler 1992: 325 and 328). Those progressive era ideas embraced a faith in institutionalized

From Christopher Hood 'Contemporary public management: a new global paradigm', *Public Policy and Administration*, **10**(2), 1995, pp. 104–17.

science and public service professionalism, allied with general process rules to limit malfeasance and insulate public management from political control of case decisions over entitlements, contracts and the like (cf. Hood 1994).

Osborne and Gaebler are the most famous exponents of this view. But they are not the only ones. Peter Aucoin (1990: 134) strikes the same note, arguing that there is an 'internationalization' of public management: 'What has been taking place in almost every government in developed political systems . . . is a new emphasis on the organizational designs for public management . . . This internationalization of public management parallels the internationalization of public and private sector economies.' And in similar vein, Michael Barzelay (1992: 116ff.) writes of a 'postbureaucratic paradigm' replacing an earlier 'bureaucratic paradigm' that was appropriate for most of the twentieth century but is now outdated (*ibid.*: 133).

Some observers and commentators link a general shift in public management style to developments in technology, particularly in 'informatization' (that is, the linking of computers and telecommunications to produce new information networks). Christine Bellamy and John Taylor (1994: 26) see 'New Public Management' changes as just a part of a broader 'attempt to deliver the transformational properties of informatization'. The 1993 US National Performance Review (Gore 1993: 6) makes similar claims: 'Throughout the developed world, the needs of information-age societies were colliding with the limits of industrial-era government. Regardless of party, regardless of ideology, . . . governments were responding.' And Patrick Dunleavy (1994) even argues that the production of many public services may be set to be globalized through giant corporations who have specialized in making a particular product part of their 'core competencies', along the lines of McDonald's or Coca-Cola, interacting with 'decentralized nets of implementing agencies' (*ibid.*: 56). This development, too, seems to imply a steady move towards a uniform rather than a diverse model.

It is easy to be carried away by grand claims of historical inevitability and global convergence on some new epoch-making paradigm, especially when they come from such eminent writers. But the argument here is that such claims should be treated with some scepticism. Certainly, there does seem to have been a movement away from the doctrines of progressive era public administration in several OECD states. And undoubtedly, the same managerial catch-words have such a wide currency that one can speak of a new global vocabulary. The question of 'when is a paradigm not a paradigm' is potentially one of those angels-on-the-head-of-a-pin issues. But if that term means anything more than common linguistic usage, it is less certain that the move is truly universal, and the idea of a new 'global paradigm' seems to exaggerate the underlying uniformity and coherence of current developments, for three reasons.

First, establishing the partial retreat of traditional approaches to public administration does not necessarily demonstrate that any single new style of public administration will 'inevitably' be adopted worldwide to replace the progressive-era style, or even that the old style will everywhere disappear. Instead of the claim by Osborne and Gaebler and others to have identified a 'new paradigm' in public administration with some underlying coherence, it can be argued that the many contemporary reformers and would-be reformers of public management share few fundamental premises, and where they do, they seem to be united more by what they are against than by what they are for. There is no single alternative to the progressive-era public administration model.

Second, the idea of a new global paradigm ignores the very different and typically 'path dependent' local political agendas to which contemporary public management changes are responding. Where the same thing is happening, it is often for quite different reasons, reflecting different underlying political agendas. And when we go below the superficial level of common global management 'seminarspeak', very different concrete things seem to have been happening in public service changes. It is tempting to suggest that whatever is global is not a 'paradigm' in a meaningful sense, and that what is a paradigm is not 'global'.

Third, the notion that a stable new structure is emerging worldwide seems to overplay the elements of continuity in contemporary public management change and to downplay the typically self-disequilibrating capacity of public management doctrines as a result of the unintended effects they produce – that is, their tendency to turn into 'fatal remedies', leading to the introduction of quite different doctrines as a corrective. It seems most unlikely that contemporary public management ideas can be exempt from this normal fate.

Coherent new paradigm – or Babel of Tongues?

Speaking of a global shift from one paradigm to another implies both that there is a single old paradigm and a single exit route from it. Both of these implied premises are contestable, though, as noted earlier, much depends on what is counted as a 'paradigm'. If that elusive word is taken to mean a coherent ABC of public service organization or a collection of management doctrines that fit together without contradiction, the idea of a clear-cut move from one paradigm to another seems of doubtful plausibility.

I have argued elsewhere (Hood 1995) that traditional public administration systems vary in ways that are likely to make substantial differences to the motive and opportunity to adopt 'new public management' measures. Countries with a 'big government' profile in spending and staffing are likely to provide more *motive* for politicians to attempt money-saving administrative reform measures than small government states, while countries where the public administration system is capable of being changed from a single point are likely to produce more *opportunity* to adopt such measures. Accordingly, it is the big-government states with an 'Archimedean lever' for regulation of their public services which are likely to display the most dramatic shifts towards 'new public management' profiles, because the necessary conjunction of motive and opportunity will be strongest there. Indeed, any 'old global paradigm' that embraces the juridified German public service style with its tradition of semi-independent public authorities and a Parliament dominated by public servants, the British 'Whitehall village' portrayed by Heclo and Wildavsky (1974) and the American 'government of strangers' must be a very broad affair (cf. Silberman 1993).

Even if there really is a global 'old paradigm' corresponding to the American progressive-era recipe, there is still room for doubt as to whether that structure is giving way to a single 'new paradigm', because conventional public administration attracts a range of very different critiques and contradictory recipes for improvement. Indeed, Osborne and Gaebler's own set of alternatives to progressive public administration is a collection of remedies which are more notable for their diversity, and even their internal contradictions, than for any single coherent underlying theme. In fact, much of the broad appeal of Osborne and Gaebler's collection may lie precisely in the way that they combine a set of elements that are fundamentally incompatible rather than readily combinable threads of a coherent 'paradigm' (cf. Goodsell 1993: 86). The ability to convey different messages to different audiences simultaneously has often been said to be a key to persuasive power.

With Patrick Dunleavy (Dunleavy and Hood 1994), I have argued that critiques of 'New Public Management' (NPM) can be arrayed in ways that correspond with each of the four polar types defined by the coordinates of the grid-group cultural theory (cf. Douglas 1982; Thompson, Ellis and Wildavsky 1990), and in that sense culturally different variants of NPM can be identified. Osborne and Gaebler's collection of reinventions seems to link to most of those polar types, suggesting that there may be three or more different paradigms rather than a single one.

Osborne and Gaebler's much-quoted emphasis on 'steering', a public service ethos and strong leadership from the top is a reflection of an 'hierarchist' worldview applied to public management. Hierarchism in the cultural theory frame means a set of attitudes and beliefs in a ladder of authority, orderly structures and the primacy of organized expertise. The progressive-era faith in scientists and expert professionals is one expression of that worldview. Its contemporary variant is a managerial view of the world which stresses the difference that visionary leadership can make, the need to modernize public services through state-of-the-art informatization, and an emphasis on broad strategic vision to counter what are otherwise seen as the besetting sins of the policy process, such as inconsistency, 'tunnel vision' and 'random agenda selection' (terms used by Breyer 1993).

Elsewhere, however, Osborne and Gaebler's approved recipe for 'reinvention' relates to the conventional individualist cultural worldview, in which the main recipe for improving public management is competition and market-type consumerism. Such remedies link with the doctrines of 'government by the market' (Self 1993) in order to make producers responsive to their consumers. And in yet other places, Osborne and Gaebler tap into egalitarian cultural themes. Egalitarians in cultural theory share with individualists an antipathy to 'leaderism' and ordered authority. But they differ from individualists in preferring collective organization to markets and rivalry. In that sense, Osborne and Gaebler's ideas of 'empowering' local collectivities reflect the egalitarian recipe for improving public management (see Goodsell 1993: 86).

Indeed, the modish word 'empowerment', much used by Osborne and Gaebler, illustrates the potential plurality of paradigms with which they are engaged. Like every rhetorical word, it means different things in different cultural contexts. For individualists, empowerment means marketizing reforms designed to enhance consumer sovereignty in public services at the expense of entrenched producers. But, to egalitarians, empowerment means the very opposite: putting political power – to override markets – in the hands of local collectivities. Since not everyone can be 'empowered' at the same time, who is to be empowered against whom is a key test of cultural bias.

In fact, Osborne and Gaebler's 'new paradigm' looks like another case in public administration where doctrinal 'tendency and counter-tendency are present simultaneously' (Spann 1981: 14). As has happened before in the history of public administration ideas (for example in pre-unification China and nineteenth-century Germany) 'managerial' recipes for better government clash with 'legalist' ones (stressing due-process rather than free-to-manage solutions), and corporate-producer solutions (such as business-style privatization) clash with communitarian ones (coproduction, community self-organization). Many of the critics of contemporary public administration are hostile to conventional bureaucracies, but beyond that what seems to unite them is what they are *against*, not what they are *for*. A 'global paradigm' to be worthy of the name should amount to more than that.

Superficial similarity, underlying differences?

It is easy to see how a bias towards overstressing similarity in contemporary public management changes can arise. Powerful international organizations such as the OECD and the World Bank are by their *raison d'être* committed to a view of international convergence on some single 'best practice' model which it is their institutional role to foster, in helping the 'laggards' to catch up with the vanguard. And within the domestic context, managers, politicians and bureaucrats facing criticism often try to build up bipartisan support for reshaping organizations in their preferred direction by arguing that what they are doing reflects 'international best practice', as has been the case in the UK since the early 1990s and applied to the US 1993 National Performance Review, with its conveniently vague references to changes sweeping through public administration from Sweden to New Zealand. Public management gurus will likewise aim to convey the impression that their favoured path to salvation is spreading everywhere. (Countervailing tendencies to exaggerate distinctiveness by spurious badge-engineering exist too, sometimes alongside the exaggeration of similarity.)

Given such built-in biases towards exaggeration of similarity in public management changes, it is important to weigh such claims carefully. Even though the general direction of change in many countries seems to be away from the model of progressive-era public administration, it does not follow that the old model will disappear everywhere, or that there will be a single route taken away from that model. And contrary to Osborne and Gaebler's claim that there is an 'inevitable' and 'global' movement to a coherent 'new paradigm', it seems more plausible to expect multiple future states rather than a single one, for three reasons.

First, in spite of Osborne and Gaebler's claim that the paradigm change is 'global', it would appear that the movement away from 'progressive public administration' in the 1980s and early 1990s was in fact far from universal (cf. Hood 1995). For example, the EU bureaucracy showed no discernible movement away from progressive-era principles of lifelong career service and highly legalistic operating procedures over that period (cf. Hay 1989) and indeed the OECD bureaucracy showed no signs of itself adopting the 'New Public Management' principles that it has so earnestly canvassed as the wave of the future to its member states. In the key case of China, some of the important public administration developments of the 1980s – such as the return to a traditional-style grading system and the resumption of examination rather than political patronage for public service recruitment – look more like a partial return to progressivism than a move away from it.

Second, even where apparently similar changes have been made, it does not necessarily follow that they were undertaken for the same reasons or will automatically have the same results. After all, progressive-era tenets themselves may have been adopted for different reasons to suit particular domestic political agendas, in which 'efficiency' in a narrow sense was not always paramount. Hans Mueller (1984) has argued that eighteenth-century Prussia and nineteenth-century Britain adopted the same 'old paradigm' measure (meritocratic examination systems for the recruitment of public servants) for diametrically opposed political reasons – to push the landed gentry out of public service in the first case and to retain its grip on the bureaucracy in the second. In the same way, contemporary managerialization of contemporary public services can be undertaken as a tactic of 'conservative change' (to stave off demands for deeper change in the state's role, as, say, in Sweden under the Social Democrats) or for the very opposite reason, as a first step to what is intended to be a radical rollback of the state (as, say, in the UK under Margaret Thatcher). That does not mean that the results will necessarily be what the reformers intend, an issue to be discussed in the next section.

Third, even if there is a tide flowing against progressive-era doctrines in several OECD countries, it is far from clear that the reform measures adopted by different countries amount to the same 'new paradigm'. It is true that the same management buzzwords tend to be very widely diffused, but that on its own is a trivial level of convergence: the key question is whether what is happening underneath is also uniform, and that seems doubtful. For example, while states like New Zealand and the UK have concentrated on 'managerializing' their core public services, Germany has hitherto left the style of its public service largely intact at federal level, at least, and concentrated instead on by-passing it for key functions (like regional economic development) by the creation of private-law companies. The Australian Commonwealth government resisted 'agencification' of its structure, on the grounds that it was dangerous to separate policy from execution, while New Zealand and the UK took exactly the opposite course. France and Spain concentrated on regional devolution as the centrepiece of their public sector reform programmes in the 1980s, while the UK if anything went in the opposite direction. In Japan more rather than less stress seems to have been put into 'legalistic' styles of administration by written documents (for example in business regulation). The US emphasis on deregulation *within* government, as stressed by the 1993 National Performance Review, has not been strongly followed elsewhere, no doubt because the US separation of powers structure produces a pattern of Congressional micromanagement of the bureaucracy that is not reproduced in other OECD states. To see these very different ways of reforming traditional public administration systems as reflecting a single new 'global paradigm' would seem to require creative interpretation of a high order.

A new stable paradigm or a succession of self-disequilibrating solutions?

The third question mark over the notion of a coherent new paradigm in public management is the issue of whether the agenda for public management reform has been stable enough over the last decade or two to be counted as a single set of ideas and practices. It is often argued that those developments have defied what observers in the past have often seen as the peculiar vulnerability of public management to fad and fashion (cf. Spann 1981) – Japanese management styles yesterday, New Ageist methods of releasing inner energy today (Huczynski 1993), some new, equally superficial and short-lived, panacea tomorrow.

But just as there may be an institutional bias towards exaggerating international convergence in public management, so is there frequently a propensity to overstress continuity over time, particularly in circumstances like those of the UK where the same party has been in office for over a decade. Over the long imperial period, Chinese officials tended to exaggerate the continuity of their public management institutions and practices, and in the same way there may be some built-in biases towards playing up the stability of the contemporary 'New Public Management' agenda.

In the UK case, it is notable how many of the underlying public management themes and agendas have kept changing over the past twenty years. Christopher Pollitt (1993) has pointed to the shift from the 'neo-Taylorist' late-1970s emphasis on cutting public service numbers at any cost to the opposite stress on public service 'quality' emerging from the later 1980s. A related change is the move from the emphasis on 'results' or 'outputs' that were the catchwords of public management reformers in the early 1980s to the stress on 'governance' (apparently a euphemism for 'process') as the hot topic of the mid-1990s, with concerns about sleaze and the 'proper conduct of public business'. Nor are those the only shifts that have taken place. Others include the shift from stress on manager power' ('free to manage') of the late 1970s to the late-1980s stress on consumer power ('free to choose' or at least 'free to know') allied with ministerial attacks on the proliferation of managerial 'suits' in the NHS; and the shift from the early-1980s effort to equip ministers to manage through devices such as MINIS to the late-1980s effort to take management away from ministers by creation of executive agencies. It is hard to see what basic public management paradigm these very different successive approaches reflect.

Indeed, there would seem to be at least two serious obstacles to the emergence of a stable new paradigm in public management. One is the difficulty that mutual repulsion among different recipes for good public management poses for arriving at a convergent solution. The other is the propensity of polar approaches to public management to turn into 'fatal remedies' producing the opposite of the intended effect.

Problems of arriving at a convergent solution
In principle, the idea of producing a hybrid mixed-salad approach to public management drawing on the strengths of different approaches is an attractive one (even if there might be a problem about seeing a mixed-salad approach as a single paradigm). But achieving any sort of stable 'balance' among approaches which reflect different basic worldviews is likely to be problematic because each approach of that type involves an underlying logic which, if taken to its limits, will tend to destroy all the others. In such circumstances, the appropriate metaphor may be not so much a mixed salad as a set of dogs and cats – a collection of mutually repulsive elements.

That is, if all the emphasis is placed on the individualists' preferred remedy of competition, regulation and system guidance will be hard to operate because no one will be above the fray, peer-group processes will be undermined by free-riding and elements of deliberate unpredictability in the design of organization may be hard to sustain against pressures to create internally cohesive competing units. If, on the other hand, all the emphasis is placed on the egalitarians' favourite remedy of group interaction, regulation and system guidance will be rejected as inappropriate 'top-down' interference, competition will be incompatible with 'groupiness' and the group bonds will likewise work against maintaining unpredictability as a mechanism of control. Again, if the hierarchists' preferred recipe of regulation and system guidance is pursued single-mindedly, competition will be no more than lobbying of the regulators, group interaction will be trumped by authority and control by deliberate unpredictability will be hard to maintain in the face of generalized rules and concentrated authority. Equally, if all the emphasis goes on to the approach which seems closest to the fatalist position, namely controlling public management by making its operation unpredictable (to limit opportunities for bribery and extortion), the elements of cooperation required to organize for competition, group mutuality or regulation are likely to be damped down.

Given the force of mutual repulsion which each of these recipes for good public management exerts against each of the others, it seems inherently difficult for public management controls to settle down into a stable hybrid form, at least for very long. Rather, such systems seem more likely to keep 'hunting around' among the various types, as surprise and disappointment over the capacity of one approach to deliver satisfactory results leads to increasing support for one of the other options. In such circumstances, self-exciting paradigmatic instability seems a more likely outcome than a settled approach.

Fatal remedies
If each cultural worldview involves an approach to public management that has built-in strengths and weaknesses, it follows that those weaknesses (as well as the strengths) will tend to become more glaring the more weight is put on any one approach. Hence

side-effects and even reverse effects from public management changes will be wide-spread, and those unintended outcomes will tend to produce shifting emphases from one public management approach to another.

Side-effects and reverse effects – unintended effects of policy and management measures – are a recurring theme in social science (cf. Hood 1976; Sieber 1981). Much of the debate about 'new public management' has been over the alleged side-effects of measures like contractorization and outsourcing. An example is market-testing obligations on public bodies, which are ostensibly designed to reduce costs, but may turn out to cut across other policy goals, such as the desire to involve prisoners in the running and maintenance of prisons as part of vocational training programmes (cf. *Annual Report of HM Chief Inspectorate of Prisons for Scotland 1993–4*, Cm 2649 1993–4, London, HMSO: iii).

There are other ways too that public management changes may unintendedly produce results that are very different from those claimed or intended by their champions. In earlier work (Dunleavy and Hood 1994; Hood 1995), I have called attention to two ways in which ambitions to move from a 'public bureaucracy state' to a 'minimal purchasing state' may unintendedly produce outcomes that fit neither of the conventional dichotomies of the state-versus-market debate.

One possible unintended outcome is a 'Headless Chicken State', in which a public sector remalns distinct from the private sector in staffing and organization, but there is no orderly structure of rules or conventions within which the component organizations work. The Headless Chicken State is a structure of 'no-one-in-charge management' (Bryson and Crosby 1992) in which everything is up for grabs at every stage and there are no clear rules of the road or demarcation of responsibilities.

A second possible unintended outcome is a 'Gridlocked Contract State' in which there is no distinct public sector presence or style. Public service provision is a matter for private corporations or organizations operating in a business look-alike style. But the structure of service provision is nevertheless 'juridified' into an 'iron rule book' which has a life of its own and is impervious to management or common sense (Teubner 1987). Juridification can come from general rules imposed by insurance companies, rule by law courts through litigation, regulatory pressures from domestic or international authorities, or some mixture of the three.

No public management reformer sets out with the intention of creating such effects. And these two outcomes are less commonly discussed than the conventional alternatives of hierarchical bureaucracy and marketized individual provision. But they are far from remote or exotic possibilities. The Headless Chicken State is common-place in US public administration and the fragmentation of local public services in the UK in the 1980s/90s, away from the nineteenth-century style of uniform and inclusive elected local authorities towards a set of quangos under appointed leadership, is producing a similar style. The US healthcare system of the 1980s (and large parts of its public utility provision) is an obvious case of the Gridlocked Contract State, and some have seen juridification rather than freedom to manage as the shape of things to come in UK public service provision (cf. Jacob 1991).

Indeed, the possibility that contemporary public sector management changes may produce not just side-effects but *reverse effects* (achieving the opposite of the desired effect) deserves more discussion than it has hitherto received. Perhaps that discussion has been inhibited by question-begging labelling for the new style (such as 'economic rationalism', as used by Pusey 1991), or by the well-known difficulties of obtaining clear evidence of reverse effects, for example by interview-based studies. But many of the contemporary changes in public management are potentially vulnerable to all the seven 'conversion mechanisms' identified by Sieber (1981) as ways in which social interventions can turn into 'fatal remedies', achieving the very opposite of the effect desired.

Table 1 presents Sieber's conversion mechanisms in summary form, together with an indication of possible ways in which 'New Public Management' measures can succumb to those conversion processes. The argument is *not* that 'New Public Management' is uniquely vulnerable to reverse-effect problems. It is that any system of control over public management drawn from one of the polar worldviews identified by cultural theory is likely to produce such outcomes, for two reasons.

First, the more reliance is placed on any one polar approach to control the more serious its blind spots are likely to become, producing reverse effects through 'functional disruption' and 'placation'. For example, over-extending the egalitarian recipe of communitarian peer-group interaction where there is no inherent cultural homogeneity may tend to weaken control, not strengthen it (as with the well-known story of 'maximum feasible participation' in the US Great Society programme of the 1960s (Moynihan 1969)). Moreover, if the public management application of each of the polar cultural types comes to be presented as a general answer to improving public services, it will tend to create the conditions for reverse effects through overcommit-ment, as it moves from its natural heartlands into more problematic territory.

Second, each polar approach will tend to antagonize those who prefer alternative approaches to public management, creating the conditions for reverse effects through 'exploitation', 'provocation' and 'classification'. For example, hierarchist measures of review and oversight, designed to tighten up control, may in fact weaken it if the result is either to provoke open challenge or covert avoidance. A case in point is Jabbari's (1994: 194) discussion of the application of natural justice requirements to prison boards of visitors' and governors' disciplinary hearings, having the possible effect of driving prison discipline underground, 'such that formal disciplinary procedures become less important than informal and less open methods of control'.

Figure 1 summarizes the argument sketched here. Two of of Sieber's reverse-effect mechanisms, namely functional disruption and placation resulting from comfortable blind spot assumptions going unchallenged, seem more likely to be linked with heavy emphasis on any one polar approach to improving public management, fitting with what is known about the effects of 'groupthink' and the sources of military incompe-tence (cf. Dixon 1976). Three of the other reverse-effect mechanisms in Sieber's set, on the other hand, seem more likely to come into play when the emphasis is placed on a single cultural paradigm of public management but the social context is culturally heterogeneous (exploitation, provocation and classification resulting from processes which cross boundaries of trust and shared beliefs and thereby invite 'bending-back' responses).

Table 1 Sieber's 7 'Conversion Mechanisms' and Public Management Reforms

Mechanism	Causal process	Example
FUNCTIONAL DISRUPTION	The unintentional frustration of a 'system need' in public service organization has the effect of worsening the condition which the reform is intended to improve	Power's (1994) argument that the 'audit explosion' weakens effective regulation by turning responsible (self-regulating) professionals into cheating regulatees
EXPLOITATION	Public management reforms can create opportunities for opponents or opportunists to use in ways that achieve the opposite of the desired effect	Dunleavy's (1991) argument that contracting out and hiving off leads to welfare-reducing over-outsourcing by high public servants for private benefit
GOAL DISPLACEMENT	An instrumental value becomes a terminal value in a way that defeats the basic objective	Nethercote's (1989a: 17 and 1989b) argument that NPM tends to be defeated by middle-level bureaucratization turning reporting requirements from a means to an end
PROVOCATION	Measures intended to increase compliance with authority have the opposite effect because of the antagonism they stir up, producing loss of cooperation	The argument that strict rule enforcement produces principled dissidence and reduces high-trust compliance (Bardach and Kagan 1982; Heclo and Wildavsky 1974)
CLASSIFICATION	Labelling or categorization has reverse effects as intended stigmas are treated as badges of glory or intended prizes are treated as stigmas	Martin's (1993) claim that stress on management produces negative motivation in work groups; standard critiques of performance pay as demotivating
OVER-COMMITMENT	Intervention is self-defeating because it exhausts resources in pursuit of objectives that cannot be achieved	Sieber's (1981: 162) argument that administrative reforms defeat themselves by initial hype that produces later disillusion
PLACATION	Intervention causes situations to deteriorate by compromises that come unstuck or illusions of success which produce complacency	Argument by Dunleavy and Hood (1994) that NPM schemes can worsen policy-making quality by deflecting attention from large-scale substantive problems to endless reorganization

Figure 1 How control systems destroy themselves (*Source*: Sieber 1981)

Conclusion

Today's prophets of a new 'global paradigm' in public management are not the first to proclaim that history is on their side. Today it seems ironic that Max Weber could have believed that turn-of-the-century Prussia provided a universal model of modern organization on which other societies could be expected to converge as they developed (Douglas 1987: 95–6). Doctrines and ideas which have been confidently consigned to the 'dustbin of history' (in Lenin's famous and equally ironic phrase) have a habit of appearing in a recycled form (Hood and Jackson 1991). This chapter suggests that we should be cautious about claims of an inexorable one-way march of history and critical of 'habits of *Gleichshaltung*, the deeply-ingrained worship of tidy-looking dichotomies' (Austin 1962: 3).

Though progressive-era doctrines of public administration are currently in retreat in a number of countries, both the past and the future of public management may be more plural and contradictory than the sweeping prognostications of Osborne, Gaebler and Aucoin might lead us to think. A cultural theory analysis suggests that it is far from certain that public administration in the nineties is heading towards a new 'global paradigm', unless 'paradigm' is defined so broadly as to be drained of meaning.

If the arguments advanced earlier are correct, 'New Public Management' seems likely to face either or both of two possible fates. One is to embrace incompatible doctrines simultaneously (as Osborne and Gaebler do) rather than a single clear-cut paradigm, papering over the cracks with a rhetoric of 'empowerment' which will mean different things to people with different worldviews or local agendas. The other is to embrace the alternative doctrines sequentially, with the emphasis shifting among different approaches, as awareness develops of unintended side-effects and reverse effects. Indeed, it was suggested earlier that there are signs of both processes occurring in the brief history of NPM.

References

Aucoin, P. (1990), 'Administrative Reform in Public Management', *Governance*, 3, pp. 115–37.

Austin, J. L. (1962), *Sense and Sensibilia*, London: Oxford University Press.

Bardach, E. and Kagan, R. A. (1982), *Going by the Book: The Problem of Regulatory Unreasonableness*, Philadelphia: Temple University Press.

Barzelay, M. (1992), *Breaking Through Bureaucracy: A New Vision for Managing in Government*, Berkeley: University of California Press.

Breyer, S. G. (1993), *Breaking the Vicious Cycle: Toward Effective Risk Regulation*, Cambridge, MA: Harvard University Press.

Bryson, J. and Crosby, B. (1992), *Leadership for the Common Good: Tackling Public Problems in a Shared-Power World*, San Francisco: Jossey-Bass.

Dixon, N. (1976), *The Anatomy of Military Incompetence*, London: Pimlico.

Douglas, M. (1987), *How Institutions Think*, Routledge: London.

Dunleavy, P. J. (1991), *Democracy, Bureaucracy and Public Choice*, Hemel Hempstead: Harvester Wheatsheaf.

Dunleavy, P. J. (1994), 'The Globalization of Public Services Production: Can Government be "Best in World"?' *Public Policy and Administration*, 9 (2).

Dunleavy, P. J. and Hood, C. (1994), 'From Old Public Administration to New Public Management', *Public Money and Management*, 14 (3), pp. 9–16.

Goodsell, C. T. (1993), 'Reinvent Government or Rediscover It?' (review of Osborne and Gaebler's *Reinventing Government*), *Public Administration Review*, 53 (1), pp. 85–7.

Gore, A. (1993), *Creating a Government that Works Better and Costs Less: Report of the National Performance Review*, Washington: US Government Printing Office.

Hay, R. (1989), *The European Commission and the Administration of the Community*, Luxembourg: Office for Official Publications of the European Community.

Heclo, H. and Wildavsky, A. (1974), *The Private Government of Public Money*, London: Macmillan.

Hood, C. (1994), *Explaining Economic Policy Reversals*, Buckingham: Open University Press.

Hood, C. (1995), 'The "New Public Management" in the 1980s: Variations on a Theme?' *Organizations, Accounting and Society*.

Hood, C. (1995), 'Beyond Progressivism' *International Journal of Public Administration*.

Hood, C. and Jackson, M. W. (1991), *Administrative Argument*, Dartmouth: Aldershot.

Huczynski, A. (1993), *Management Gurus*, London: Routledge.

Jabbari, D. (1994), 'Critical Theory in Administrative Law', *Oxford Journal of Legal Studies*, 14 (2), pp. 189–215.

Jacob, J. (1991), 'Lawyers Go To Hospital', *Public Law*, Summer 1991, pp. 255–81.

Martin, S. (1993), *Managing Without Managers*, Beverly Hills: Sage.

Mueller, H. E. (1984), *Bureaucracy, Education and Monopoly*, Berkeley: California University Press.

Nethercote, J. R. (1989a), 'Public Service Reform: Commonwealth Experience' paper presented to the Academy of Social Sciences of Australia 25 February 1989, Canberra: Australian National University.

Nethercote, J. R. (1989b), 'Revitalising Public Service Personnel Management' *Canberra Times*, 11 June.

Painter, M. (1990), 'Values in the History of Public Administration', ch. 4 in J. Power (ed.) *Public Administration in Australia: A Watershed*, Sydney: RAIPA/Hale and Iremonger, pp. 75–93.

Pollitt, C. (1993), *Managerialism and the Public Services*, 2nd edn, Oxford: Blackwell.

Power, M. (1994), *The Audit Explosion*, London, DEMOS.

Pusey, M. (1991), *Economic Rationalism in Canberra*, Cambridge: Cambridge University Press.

Self, P. (1993), *Government by the Market*, London: Macmillan.

Sieber, S. (1981), *Fatal Remedies: The Ironies of Social Intervention*, New York: Plenum.

Silberman, B. S. (1993), *Cages of Reason*, Chicago: Chicago University Press.

Spann, R. N. (1981), 'Fashions and Fantasies in Public Administration', *Australian Journal of Public Administration*, 40, pp. 12–25.

Teubner, G. (ed.) (1987), *Juridification of Social Spheres*, Berlin: de Gruyter, ch. I 'Juridification: Concepts, Aspects, Limits, Solutions', pp. 3–48.

New modes of control in the public service

Paul Hoggett

Controversy exists regarding whether recent changes in the organization of the public services in the UK and elsewhere constitute a paradigm shift towards a post-bureaucratic form. This chapter argues that in Britain three fundamental but interlocking strategies of control have been implemented over the last decade. First, there has been a pronounced shift towards the creation of operationally decentralized units with a simultaneous attempt to increase centralized control over strategy and policy. Second, the principle of competition (often attached to the development of market relations but sometimes not) has become the dominant method of coordinating the activities of decentralized units. Third, during the most recent period there has been a substantial development of processes of performance management and monitoring (including audits, inspections, quality assessments, and reviews), again a phenomenon largely directed towards operationally decentralized units.

Taken together, these three strategies do not describe a simple movement from a bureaucratic to a post-bureaucratic form, rather they combine strong elements of innovation with the reassertion of a number of fundamentally bureaucratic mechanisms. This may be a peculiarly British phenomenon, certainly the excessive elements of centralization and formalization appear to depart from the ideal-type of the post-bureaucratic organization. It is argued that this 'British trajectory' can best be understood in terms of the continued relative decline of the British economy and the Conservative response to it, i.e. the drive to create a 'high output, low commitment' workforce.

Getting more for less

One of the earliest and most consistent signs of the slow death of the Keynesian welfare state was manifest in the tendency towards fiscal crisis and the continued questioning of spending levels on collective consumption (Pickvance and Preteceille

From P. Hoggett, 'New modes of control in the public service', *Public Administration*, **74**, 1996, pp. 9–32.

1991). The desire to get 'more for less' (Hood 1991) has therefore emerged as a persistent theme within public management in the UK and elsewhere. It will be my thesis in this chapter that the restructuring of the public sector in the UK has nevertheless assumed a particular trajectory, one to a considerable extent determined by the unique circumstance of an economy in persistent relative decline (Crafts 1991; Hutton 1995; Nairn 1993). Given this circumstance the need to find ways of intensifying the public sector labour process has taken on added urgency.

My argument is that in Britain the 'success' of successive Conservative governments since 1979 has been to create a high output/low commitment public sector workforce. This combination is clearly counter-intuitive. It has been an assumption of management thought since the work of MacGregor (1960) that, in the absence of coercive mechanisms, high output is best achieved via a motivated workforce. As Lowe and Oliver (1991) note, much of the modern Human Resource Management movement is based on the assumption that productivity is best achieved by eliciting high levels of worker commitment rather than through compliance or passive accommodation, i.e. by moving towards 'self-control' and away from 'external control' (Guest 1987). Yet in Britain most of the evidence suggests that levels of job satisfaction, stress and morale within much of the public sector is at an all-time low (Bogg and Cooper 1995; British Medical Association 1992; Caplan 1994; Cooper and Kelly 1993; Labour Research Department 1994; Institute of Employment Studies 1994; Rees and Cooper 1992; Royal College of Nursing 1994; Travers and Cooper 1993; Sutherland and Cooper 1992) whilst levels of productivity if measured in terms of throughput (in hospitals, schools and universities, etc.) has greatly increased.

The key to unlocking this paradox lies with the issue of control. The attempt to develop new and more sophisticated forms of organizational control have been an essential underlying theme of the restructuring of the public sector in the UK. I will argue that changes in the organization of the British public sector combine strong elements of self-control with new and old forms of external control (i.e., elements of both post-bureaucratic and bureaucratic management). The introduction of a variety of market mechanisms has undoubtedly been central to this task but to understand the role they play it is necessary to see them as a complement to two other control strategies – the development of centralized decentralization and extended forms of performance management – which have emerged during this period.

Beyond bureaucracy?

Recent analyses of developments in both public and private sectors have pointed to the emergence of 'post-bureaucratic' (Heydebrand 1989) or 'post-modern' (Clegg 1991) organizational forms. In an earlier article (Hoggett 1991) I indicated some of the difficulties in defining 'bureaucracy' precisely. Weber's (Albrow 1970) ideal-type has four guiding principles – functional specialization within a firmly ordered hierarchy; a comprehensive, impersonal body of rules and procedures, the precise definition of powers and responsibilities invested in each organizational role; formal equality of treatment regarding recruitment and promotion. We would expect to find that the majority of these principles would either no longer apply to post-bureaucratic organizations or would apply in a radically different form. Clearly the emergence of radical forms of organizational decentralization appear to contradict Weber's first principle and the development of forms of flexibility appears to contradict the third.

Clegg (1990) specifies a further dimension along which the post-modern departs from the modern. Specifically Clegg draws upon Lash's (1988) notion of de-differentiation, the process by which under conditions of post-modernity boundaries become blurred and distinctions undermined. Crucially the boundary between the organization and its environment, and hence the subjective distinction between being on the inside or the outside of the organization, began to collapse as the traditional industrial and public bureacracies made increasing use of profit centres (Eccles and White 1986), internal markets, transfer pricing (Eccles and White 1988) and other combinations of decentralist and market mechanisms. In the context of the public sphere the resort to such processes has also led to a considerable blurring of the distinction between the public and the private. We now speak of 'quasi-markets' (Le Grand and Bartlett 1993) in education and the health services and refer to organizations such as housing associations and even hospital trusts as 'not-for-profit' organizations which inhabit a 'murkier third terrain that is both public and private' (Rein 1990).

Many of the recent changes in the organizations of the British public sector appear to be quite novel. However, if we consider the image of the ideal-type of post-bureaucratic organization that writers such as Heydebrand (1989) provide then clearly we can see that some elements are reflected in a rather distorted fashion in the British public sector today. For Heydebrand, the post-bureaucratic form 'would tend to be small or located in small sub-units of larger organizations; its object is typically service or information, if not automated production; its technology computerized; the division of labour is informal and flexible; and its managerial structure is functionally decentralized, eclectic and participative' (p. 327). At first sight this description would seem to fit neatly an NHS trust or decentralized district within the Benefits Agency. But a closer look would reveal elements not in Heydebrand's picture. Far from being more participative in many parts of the NHS there has been a resort to far more coercive and simple (Edwards 1979) forms of control. We also find much higher degrees of job insecurity consequent upon flexibilization and, in many areas, an increasing resort to proceduralism and extensive forms of performance monitoring. So there is a danger that by giving emphasis to what's new our attention is drawn away from the study of what is not new – rather than thinking of organizational changes simply in terms of 'advance' or 'progress' it may be possible that in some situations organizations adopt many trappings of the post-modern form whilst also resorting to a number of old techniques with renewed vigour. The impact of new forms of organizational control may well be felt in different sectors at different intervals. Moreover, even within a sector, such as the UK public sector, there may be differential impacts in different service areas.

I wish to argue that in Britain public sector restructuring, far from describing a smooth movement from bureaucratic to post-bureaucratic forms of control, in fact combines strong elements of innovation with the reassertion of a number of fundamentally bureaucratic mechanisms. Following Jessop (1994) we could think of the organization of the British public sector in the 1990s as a form of 'flawed' post-bureaucratic regime. The use of the term 'flawed' suggests 'failed' and indeed I do intend to argue that the emerging hybrid of bureaucratic and post-bureaucratic elements has in several ways proved to be both politically and organizationally dysfunctional.

Rather than a single movement towards some presumed post-bureaucratic end-state, I will argue that three distinct but interlocking strategies of control can be discerned within the UK public sector:

- the introduction of competition (market and non-market based) as a means of co-ordinating the activities of decentralized units;
- the attempt to decentralize operations whilst centralizing strategic command;
- the extended development of performance management techniques.

A fourth trend emerges but more ambiguously and this concerns the nature of work itself and the extent to which it is subject to processes of standardization and deskilling.

I will now look at each of these developments in more detail.

Markets and competition

When speaking of competition and markets it is necessary to differentiate between a number of quite distinct phenomena which are sometimes confused or lumped together. Three different strategies can be perceived in the UK:

1. the introduction of competition within producer markets where units compete to supply goods and services to government which remains the main or sole direct purchaser;
2. the introduction of competition within consumer markets where units compete to supply services to individual purchasers or their proxies;
3. the promotion of competition without markets where units are engaged in competing for government's resources but where government does not adopt the role of purchaser.

The introduction of CCT and market testing should be distinguished from the implementation of internal markets. Competitive tendering corresponds to the development of competition within producer markets where supplier organizations compete to provide goods and services for purchaser organizations. In contrast, internal markets in education resemble a form of managed consumer market where the purchasers are individual service users, or rather their proxies (for example, parents). This market is therefore primarily concerned with the relationship between producers and end-users. The so-called internal market for health care is in fact a strange hybrid of both a producer market where government through the agency of the district health authority remains the key purchaser and a consumer market where GPs act as proxy purchasers for individual users. Glennerster and Matsaganis (1993) refer to these strategies in terms of 'top-down' and 'bottom-up' approaches to decentralization.

Public sector markets in the UK have a number of distinctive characteristics. One of the main effects of the development of producer markets, such as CCT, has been to enhance labour flexibility (particularly time and pay flexibilities) and reduce labour costs. This is true even where, as in the majority of cases, contracts are won in-house. Trade unions are well aware that successful in-house tendering can only be achieved as a consequence of rationalization and the consequent intensification of labour (Cousins 1988; Foster 1992). This does not necessarily mean that the effect of CCT has been cost-saving for, as Walsh (1991) indicates, for some services such as street cleaning the impact of reduced labour costs have been offset by increased standards of service.

A number of observers would regard the increased resort to sub-contracting as a sign of the development of the post-bureaucratic organizational form. Clearly one should recognize that such a claim continues to be contested, some writers being inclined to suggest that such extended forms of sub-contracting have existed all along, academics only just having discovered it (Pollert 1988). My inclination is to believe that there has been a significant shift (at least within a number of key industrial sectors in Western-type economies) away from vertically integrated forms of production. What is distinctive about the UK is that within the public sector this strategy has been primarily politically driven and focuses on the objective of promoting competition around cost rather than quality. The introduction of compulsory forms of competition within a sector where norms of accountability and probity still remain strong has also led to the development of forms of highly proceduralized, 'arms-length' contracting quite unlike the more 'relational' forms of contracting which are more the norm within the private sector (Taylor and Hoggett 1994).

It is clear that the neo-Liberal fetish of 'the free market' serves to mask a desire to diminish the power of government in order to give corporate power a free reign. But such is the power of their rhetoric that when speaking of markets there is now a great danger that we all become prone to reifying the very object we seek to understand. For example, 'the market' is often counterposed to 'regulation' or emphasis is given to the 'quasi' character of an internal market as a way of distinguishing it from the real thing. To avoid such dangers we need to understand that all markets are social constructions. As such they constitute sites or arenas in which different players with different positional power compete for resources according to fluctuating rules (Ball, Bowe, and Gewirtz 1992; Glatter and Woods 1994). The distinctive characteristic of producer markets within the public sector is that the state typically remains in the position of being the monopsony purchaser and therefore has the power to dictate many of the rules of the game, often according to a fluctuating political agenda concerned to buy legitimacy for the reforms which have been put in motion. Within the education market the hand of government is no less powerful for not being directly in control of the purchasing function (Ball, Bowe, and Gewirtz 1994). Here the rules of the market, the positional power of the players (including the 'price' that different kinds of children carry on their heads), the stakes that are played for and even the process of refereeing are all initially determined by government.

The final characteristic of public sector markets in the UK which needs noting is the way in which the cash limited nature of public service funding forces the players to engage in a zero-sum game in which 'the market of one is only expandable at the expense of another' (Harrison et al. 1994). Indeed, in the context of producer markets not only do we have a zero-sum but one in which the number of players increases as organizations from the private sector are drawn into competition.

So far we have discussed the extension of producer and end-user markets within the public services but over the past decade we have also witnessed the increasing promotion of competition without markets. Among several examples we can cite the use of competition via the City Challenge Initiative as a means of distributing urban regeneration resources, the use of Estate Action money in social housing for estate improvements, and the operation of the Research Assessment Exercise in Higher Education. In each instance we see the increased use of narrow concepts of performativity rather than equity and social justice as the criterion for resource allocation (De Groot 1992; Malpass 1994) – performance criteria being set either directly by government or by its arms-length agencies.

What, then, are some of the effects of the introduction of markets and competition, within the public sector? First, by combining radical forms of operational decentralization with the introduction of markets and competition the devolved service units so created increasingly take on the form of Small and Medium Public Enterprises (SMPEs). These enterprises can assume a variety of forms depending upon the way in which they are constituted, their executive structure, the extent of oper-ational devolution they enjoy, and the nature of the market environment in which they operate. In some instances, such as TECs, the new units are actually constituted as private companies but, as we shall see, ones which operate within a highly restricted market. In other instances, such as the NHS trusts, some analysts (Bartlett 1995) have suggested the model of the non-profit firm is the most appropriate but, in this case, one which is a composite of a management firm and a medical firm. One casualty of this development in some parts of the public sector has been any semblance of open government. Many of the new bodies have resorted to hiding behind the shroud of 'business secrecy' as a means of avoiding scrutiny by either the public or their own employees (*British Medical Journal* 1994). In this light it is noteworthy that the initial progress report of Public Concern at Work (1994), a charity recently established to support whistle-blowers in the workplace, indicated that the largest single group of requests for support came from employees within the NHS.

A second impact has been the fragmentation (Alexander 1991) of the public service and the undermining of lateral solidarities linking service user to service user, worker to worker and professional to professional. Speaking of the education sector Ball (1993) notes, 'for both parents, acting in the best interests of their children, and senior teachers, acting in the best interests of their school the market leaves little alternative but to engage in individualistic, competitive activity' (p. 109). Whilst we should not underestimate the strength of professional and departmental boundaries in the old public service, such phenomena were nevertheless construed as forms of bureaucratic dysfunction which tugged against the grain of a corporate ethos. But the loyalty that always existed to our school, our hospital, or our department now takes on a new character. The 'us' is no longer contained within a wider imagined community (the National Health Service, the civil service) but becomes reconstituted as an isolated unit, at times almost a gang, pitched into a partly real and partly phantasized life and death struggle against other units who are equally fearful. In management-speak this gang becomes 'the enterprise' or business unit, the managers of which are trained in business planning with all the paraphernalia of SWOT analyses, strategic market reviews, etc.

To some extent the discourse of enterprise is cathected in different ways by different actors according to their positions. For some managers this cathexis appears to relate to the pre-pubescent boy's phantasy of being 'big', one's potency being judged according to the size of one's budget. For workers and staff the cathexis is based much more upon feelings of fear and vulnerability and the sense of one's own survival has become linked inextricably to the strength of the unit one works for rather than the strength of one's trade union or professional association. In either case, the main casualty would appear to be some kind of ethic (sometimes referred to as 'the public service ethic') which is able to transcend the particularism of one's own situation.

Third, there can be no doubting the powerful effect that markets are having on the behaviour of the vast majority of public sector employees. The distinction between the concepts of discourse and organizational culture can further our understanding of the 'grip' of the market here. In a later section I will argue that the attempt to shift public sector organizations' cultures by persuasion, example, training, etc. appears to have failed. However, the introduction of markets and competition to vast areas of the public sector since 1987 does appear to be bringing about a major change in the way in which workers and managers behave. The crucial difference seems to be this – for a culture to be operative within an organization actors must, to some extent, adopt the values and beliefs of that culture; for a discourse to be operative however actors simply need to participate in the practices that comprise it. The concept of discourse therefore offers to take us further than the related concepts of organizational culture and ideology, for, as Du Gay and Salamon (1992) note, 'the dominance of a discourse is not so much inscribed in people's consciousness as in the practices and technologies to which they are subjected'. Competition can be thought of as an extremely powerful form of practice which shapes the behaviour even of those whose value systems embrace traditional notions of public service rather than the new values of public enterprise. Drawing on the distinction between 'values in use' and 'espoused values' made by Argyris and Schon (1974) we can see how the discourse of competition forces a wedge between the consciousness and practice of workers in the public sector. The point is that such a split can only be sustained for so long, after which, following the logic of dissonance reduction, the new practices are abandoned or consciousness will align itself to the new forms of practice. It is interesting to note that early proponents of the 'new wave' in management such as Peters and Waterman (1982) and Schein (1985) deliberately drew attention to the implications of cognitive dissonance theory when insisting that attitudes tend to follow behaviour and not the other way around.

The final effect of markets to be examined concerns the way in which they have served to strengthen the hand of centralized government. Clegg's use of the concept of de-differentiation has considerable value in drawing attention to the blurring of the boundary between the organization and its environment, as Heydebrand (1989: 333) puts it, 'organizations tend to disappear as distinct and bounded units'. In place of the NHS we find a plethora of trusts and purchasers, the territory of the local education authority fades away before our eyes to be replaced by a mass of small education enterprises. Specifically we can liken the pre-1979 public setor to one built upon vertically integrated forms of organization in which the vast majority of functions necessary to support the task of service delivery were performed in-house. Current reforms have not only sought to out-place these support functions but have also sought to distance government from the process of service provision itself through the development of the purchaser – provider split. As a consequence, what we now observe is the emergence of quite radical forms of horizontally integrated production but within which central controls are stronger rather than weaker than before. In other words, rather than witnessing the replacement of hierarchy by market, what we observe is the development of a 'plural mode of governance' (Bradach and Eccles 1989) in which elements of market are combined with elements of hierarchy. Heydebrand (1989: 330) takes this line of analysis further by suggesting that 'hierarchicalness' and 'marketness' can be considered as two discrete and orthogonal dimensions along which any organization can be located.

This has important implications. The creation of managed markets introduces an entirely new mode of control, one where the locus of control is to be found in the structured sites or fields in which public business units are forced to compete. In other words, rather than simply focusing upon the exercise of control within the organiz-ation, the new context forces us also to examine the operation of control within a field, partly structured by central government, in which the organization operates. DiMaggio and Powell's (1983) concept of 'organizational fields' therefore has considerable potential value in explaining patterns of control in de-differentiated organizational settings. According to these authors, 'by organizational field, we mean those organiza-tions that, in the aggregate, constitute a recognized area of institutional life: key suppliers, resource and product consumers, regulatory agencies, and other organiza-tions that produce similar products and services' (p. 148). They add that organizations in a structured field 'respond to an environment that consists of other organizations responding to their environment' (p. 149). Because the field is structured by the organizations within it as well as by the government that establishes it a certain indeterminacy inevitably arises which means that outcomes may not be strictly as government intended.

DiMaggio and Powell (1983) adopt the concept of 'isomorphism' to describe the constraining process that forces one unit in a field to resemble other units that face the same set of environmental conditions. Arguably this kind of process may account for the way in which voluntary organizations in the community care sector which have been drawn into the contract culture appear to be losing many of the distinctively voluntarist characteristics which made them so attractive to government in the first place (Taylor *et al.* 1995). Whilst DiMaggio and Powell focused primarily upon the institutionalized environments of the public sphere prior to the current period of restructuring, Hannan and Freeman (1977) were concerned to examine the process of competitive isomorphism which occurred within market environments. These authors suggested that we think of markets as populations of organizations within which processes analogous to 'natural selection' take place. If we consider (in a manner which Hannan and Freeman themselves reject) the population ecology perspective as a potentially useful metaphor then it may be possible to side-step the probably unresolvable and in any case misleading question whether quasi-markets are 'real' markets or not, for the key question is whether those operating within such environments act 'as if' they are involved in a market which can have real effects.

Simultaneous centralization and decentralization

The previous discussion has already indicated the paradox of a public sector which has apparently been subject both to more centralization and decentralization. Within virtually all parts of the public sector there has been a pronounced movement towards the creation of more devolved forms of management (Hoggett 1991). The Education Reform Act of 1988 gave headteachers and school governing bodies responsibility for the administration of school budgets and the power to seek grant maintained status. The NHS and Community Care Act of 1990 promoted the development of 'self-managed' units within health districts, based upon hospitals or clusters of similar services. The same act encouraged the development of care management within the social services sector through which care budgets would be devolved to care managers who would act as decentralized purchasers of care acting on behalf of social service clients. Within other parts of local government, agencies such as the Audit Commission have been advocating devolved forms of financial management for several years now (Audit Commission 1989) and the extension of competition legislation to professional services has further stimulated processes of bureaucratic disaggregation via the creation of internal business units. Within the civil service the Next Steps initiative launched in 1988 has led to the creation of devolved agencies operating on an arms-length basis in relation to government departments. Some of these, such as the Benefits Agency, are themselves radically devolved internally.

I have argued that the introduction of market mechanisms in the public sector has been accompanied by the creation of a range of small and medium-sized public enterprises such as schools, direct service organizations and hospital trusts which nevertheless operate within a field or arena in which the hand of central government still remains strong. Ball (1993) notes that one of the paradoxes of contemporary management is that it both liberates and enslaves. Whilst operational managers may be given real control over the resources necessary to do the job right the centre (of the firm or the government) retains control over key strategic questions such as the allocation of resources to operational units and the framework of financial and personnel rules and performance targets within which devolution over operational matters is allowed to occur (Hoggett 1991). Countless examples of this process of maintaining 'tight' central control over essentials can be given. Within the civil service central controls are enshrined in the Framework Documents which govern the relationship between government department and executive agency (Fry *et al.* 1988). Within the educational sector the 1988 Education Reform Act which, even at the time of its introduction, was seen by commentators as both centralist and decentralizing in intent (Maclure 1988), introduced local management of schools but also introduced both national testing and the national curriculum and imposed a restrictive formula upon LEAs with which to allocate resources to schools (Thomas and Levacic 1991).

For many observers of public sector change this phenomenon of simultaneous centralization and decentralization at first seemed contradictory and a sign of the lack of coherence of government strategy (Pollitt 1990). But the concept of centralized decentralization has become an established part of the new organizational literature (Aldrich 1978; Heydebrand 1979; Murray 1983; Hoggett 1987) and should be regarded as a distinctive element of post-bureaucratic control (Heydebrand 1989). What is distinctive about Britain is the way in which the new organizational technologies became harnessed to a political project which was designed to destroy virtually all alternative power bases within society which might challenge Conservative hegemony. There can be no denying the reality of the freedoms which many service managers now enjoy compared to the past – freedoms to transfer moneys between different budget headings, to hire, fire and promote staff, to develop local personnel and manpower planning strategies, etc. But what has been striking about developments in the UK public sector over the last decade is the way in which the shift towards forms of operational decentralization has been promoted by successive Conservative administrations which even by 1988 had already created one of the most centralized forms of government Britain has experienced this century (Burns *et al.* 1994).

Operational decentralization has proceeded against the background of governmental centralization and has, if anything, served to reinforce centralization processes. Thus the legitimate concern for the spread of non-elected bodies at the local level such as TECs, hospital trusts, and city technology colleges can serve to deflect attention away from the fact that current research indicates that many of these bodies have little real autonomy (Ferlie *et al.* 1995; Kearns 1991; Peck 1993; Power *et al.* 1994; Weir and Hall 1994). Whilst operations have been devolved to business units such as schools, trusts, or agencies, control over policy and the allocation of resources has become increasingly concentrated within Whitehall, centralized but arms-length agencies such as the Funding Authority for Schools and the Further Education Funding Council or the new regional arms of central government (Stewart 1994). Whilst the development of performance management systems will be examined in the next section we should note here the link which has developed between performance-based funding and centralized control. Increasingly, the centre does not simply prescribe performance targets for operational managers but offers incentives and sanctions for meeting targets. Such forms of outcome funding have proved particularly powerful in shaping operational behaviour within the training sector where units have become increasingly tied to delivering short-term programmes for the unemployed (Peck 1993) or producing qualified students within the NCVQ framework (Elliot and Hall 1994).

There is a danger that naturalistic assumptions may guide policy-makers and organizational analysts which obscure how the boundaries of the 'operational' and 'the strategic' are in fact always socially constructed. Indeed perhaps one of the main ways in which the 'mobilization of bias' is achieved through government is precisely by relegating to 'the operational' matters, such as distributive questions, which might otherwise be thought of as strategic. In the absence of any more direct or bottom-up forms of political accountability the danger is that the attempt to formalize an operational sphere leads to the depoliticization of public life. For example, in some sectors, processes of operational decentralization have been accompanied by an explicit emancipatory rhetoric which encouraged managers to perceive devolution in terms of deliverance from the dead hand of bureaucratic control. But this sometimes obscured the fact that the escape from local bureaucracy was swiftly followed by capture by Whitehall and its arms-length agencies (Halpin et al. 1993) and moreover that the perceived locus of local bureaucratic control (for instance the local education authority) was also the locus of immediate democratic control. At times, the effect of this process has been to render the real locus of decision-making increasingly invisible, particularly where public services are transferred to local non-elected bodies such as TECs or UDCs. Commenting on the directors, governors, and management committee members of the new bodies, Davis and Stewart (1994: 8) note, 'public accountability, if it exists at all, is through a long and uncertain line . . . to the Minister who appointed them, or who appointed the people who appointed them'.

There is a further difference between government and the firm which means that the effects of centralized decentralization have quite different consequences. Whilst the firm is primarily oriented towards production and capital accumulation, public institutions, particularly those engaged in welfare service provision, are primarily exercised by the problem of resource rationalization. In other words, there is a quite different understanding of resources in the two sectors. In the private sector a resource is essentially capital to be deployed in order to generate further capital; in the public sector resources consist of revenues obtained through taxation to assist the reproduction of labour (through provision of health, education, and other services). It follows that the function of strategic control in the two sectors differs substantially. Whilst the firm may face capital shortages its decentralized units are essentially profit centres and what counts in the last analysis is not how much has been spent but by how much income exceeds expenditure. Within the governmental sector decentralized units are essentially cost centres, they may operate within internal markets but ones where the overall volume of demand is fixed by government cash limits (Harrison et al. 1994). For governments undergoing a prolonged period of fiscal crisis and budgetary constraint, extended operational decentralization combined with tight centralized expenditure control therefore constitutes a subtle attempt to pass difficult rationing decisions down the line not only to service managers but to various publics themselves. There is now some evidence to indicate the way in which representatives of users of different kinds of services have been drawn in to the process of constraining public expenditure (Martin 1994). This clearly poses a dilemma for advocates of user participation and control. In this light the recent revolt of school governors against what they see as the government's attempt to make schools pay for the salary improvements of their own staff is a fascinating example of the struggle of local citizens to avoid collusion with government strategy.

The new formalization: extended forms of performance management

In virtually all sectors operational decentralization has been accompanied by the extended development of performance management systems. Such systems seem designed to both monitor and shape organizational behaviour and encompass a range of techniques including performance review, staff appraisal systems, performance-related pay, scrutinies, so-called 'quality audits', customer feedback mechanisms, comparative tables of performance indicators including 'league tables', chartermarks, customer charters, quality standards, and total quality management (TQM).

I wish to argue that although some current forms of performance management are, in this sense, post-bureaucratic the dominant impact of the development of this strategy in the UK contradicts the idea of a movement towards more 'hands off' forms of organizational control. On the contrary, it appears to be leading to the development of new kinds of formalization, ones Pollitt (1990) argued were akin to 'neo-Taylorism'. This should cause us to pause before claims that I, among others, have made that what is emerging is a distinctively post-bureaucratic form of organization.

The classic studies of centralization and formalization conducted by Aiken and Hage (Hage and Aiken 1967; Aiken and Hage 1968) may help elucidate the trends at work here. Aiken and Hage outlined three dimensions of formalization:

1. job codification: 'the degree to which jobs are specified';
2. rule observation: 'the degree to which the job occupants are supervised in conforming to standards established in job codification';
3. job specificity: 'the degree to which procedures defining jobs are spelled out'.

As I noted in my introduction, one of the essential characteristics of bureaucracy lay in the precise and detailed specification of jobs and responsibilities of personnel within ordered hierarchies of command. How therefore does the development of performance management relate to this principle of formalization?

The first thing to note is that in contrast to the traditional model contemporary forms of performance management shift the emphasis away from input controls to output controls. Kikert (1995) likens this to a paradigm shift in control strategies, i.e. a movement from *ex-post* (input) to *ex-ante* (output) control. I suggest that this development, particularly where the achievement of targets is linked to sanctions and incentives, is a distinctively new and potentially powerful behaviour shaping tech-nology. Second, within the traditional bureaucracy the work of officials was also subject to close but impersonal supervision, i.e. 'rule observation'. In a response to the work of Aiken and Hage, Dewar and his colleagues suggested that the rule observation dimension could more accurately be described as 'surveillance' (Dewar *et al.* 1980). In the post-bureaucratic organization I would suggest that while the dimension of surveillance remains strong its locus shifts away from close and visible forms of supervision to an increasingly remote and sometimes invisible centre. The use of information technology to provide the centre with the means of monitoring behaviour from a distance can, in this sense, be likened to a form of remote or arms-length surveillance. The concept of 'job specificity' refers to the third and more procedural aspect of formalization. Most commentators on the New Public Management (Aucoin 1990; Hood 1991) suggest that process controls would largely disappear within the post-bureaucratic organization. The picture that therefore emerges is one of an operationally decentralized organization with a strong but distant centre engaging in performance monitoring and shaping activity by concentrating on a few key indicators which give emphasis to results rather than inputs or processes (Aucoin 1990; Handy 1989). As I put it in an earlier paper, performance indicators constitute part of the boundaries within which operational freedoms are realized (Hoggett 1991). Within these boundaries the self-regulation of sub-units is based largely on forms of cultural control, specifically a commitment at all organizational levels to core organizational values.

I would suggest that within the British public sector the way in which performance management systems have been developed largely contradicts this picture of the post-bureaucratic organization. First, although there has been a shift from *ex-post* to *ex-ante* forms of control, in many instances there has been such a proliferation of performance indicators that what appears to be taking place is not so much a process of organizational de-differentiation (Clegg 1991) but rather one of re-differentiation. Job codification remains strong but the locus has shifted from the job specification to the performance specification.

Second, far from being remote and largely invisible the majority of public sector organizations in the UK today appear to be overwhelmed by forms of performance monitoring. Scrutinites, audits, performance review systems, inspections, client or pupil progress reports, peer assessments, appraisals, routine statistical returns, etc. now appear to consume an enormous amount of time in all of the educational sectors and many parts of the health service and local government.

Third, there has been a decline in traditional forms of proceduralism such as were found in the vast numbers of personal, financial and other rules which surrounded managers and staff in formal bureaucracies (these rules, it should be added, often served to secure the robustness and probity of the organization concerned (Hood 1991)). In recent years we have seen the emergence of new forms of proceduralism which, paradoxically, have been facilitated by the coming of markets and quality to the public sector.

The contract specification and monitoring process incurs considerable transaction costs when conducted in an inter-organizational environment characterized by declining trust, on the basis of arms-length and legalistic rather than relational models of contracting (Taylor and Hoggett 1994), and within environments where purchasers operate in situations of high information uncertainty. These days, jokes abound about contract specification documents which come thicker than telephone directories and facility managers who have more regular contact with contract compliance officers than their own operational bosses.

Regarding service quality, proceduralist models of quality control have tended to dominate over more developmental models of quality assurance in the UK public service. These two contrasting strategies for implementing quality parallel what Barley and Kunda (1992) refer to as rational systems and normative models of control. Drawing largely from an analysis of the private sector management discourse in the USA, Barley and Kunda suggest that the present period, characterized by the various excellence cults, is one which gives primacy to aspects of an organization's culture. Indeed, much of the literature on the post-modern organization emphasizes the role of trust, shared values, clan-like forms of organizational solidarity, and so on. But whilst attempts by senior management to shape the culture of public organizations in local government and the NHS were characteristic of the late 1980s and have gathered strength within some of the executive agencies in the 1990s, I suggest that normative control strategies in the public sector have largely failed, existing largely as symbolic and rhetorical artifacts towards which the majority of staff are highly cynical (Harrison *et al.* 1994; Colville *et al.* 1993). Normative strategies are based upon consensualist assumptions. But for many staff the talk of a shared organizational mission, commitment to quality and customer responsiveness flies in the face of their experience of increased class sizes, inadequate nursing cover, disappearing job security, voluntary and compulsory redundancies, etc.

Normative approaches to quality in the UK public services find clearest expression in the total quality management approach and rely upon participative methods of employee involvement in processes of continuous product or service improvement. As Florida (1991) notes, it is concerned as the Japanese say to 'harness the gold in the worker's brain'. The rational systems model, however, is less concerned to harness human resources than it is to design new forms of process controls. Exemplified by the British Standards approach, it is deeply mechanistic. Rather than seeking to build quality into the work culture it tries to build quality into inputs, systems, and procedures. It is this model which is implicit in the Citizen's Charter initiative and the associated 'Chartermark' awards. Again however, we should beware of overgeneralization. Whilst the trend appears to be towards greater proceduralism (typified by the coming of quality audits to higher education) counter examples (such as the introduction of TQM within the Employment Service) can always be cited.

To summarize, detailed performance specification, routine monitoring, and proceduralization can all be thought of as elements of a rational-systems model of control. Together they spin a myriad of little threads around the SMPEs. Contrary, therefore, to what is sometimes thought to be the current trend there is no obvious sign of a reduction in the formalization of organization within the UK public service; if anything quite the reverse appears to be true. How can we explain this? I offer three arguments which may go some way towards providing an answer.

First, the development of very detailed forms of performance monitoring in sectors such as schools, education, and housing management appears to be directly linked to the attempt to extend central government control over operational matters in some electorally sensitive areas. Second, in the absence of strong normative controls, formalization becomes a 'solution' to the absence of trust. Given the intensification of public sector labour, the collapse of morale and the prevalence of cynicism within many occupational groups, the development of overextended forms of performance management can be seen as a return to hands-on control over the newly created SMPEs. Third, many forms of routine monitoring may be the consequence of bureau-shaping activities (Dunleavy 1991) but of a largely non-rational form. In other words, rather than being an expression of bureaucratic control they are the means by which senior officials maintain an illusion or simulation of control within a decentralization system; thus the experience that many staff have that nothing ever happens after the inspection, review or audit has occurred. In fact perhaps, in these cases nothing is meant to occur for this may be a form of symbolic policy-making largely designed to reassure anxious senior bureaucrats unused to operating on a hands-off basis.

Performance management systems, even of a symbolic kind, clearly shape behaviour but whether they shape behaviour in the direction policy-makers intend is another, and little researched, question. Clearly, many individuals and groups have become highly adept at impression management whilst others have become equally skilled in the art of performing to target, even though this may run counter to the need to do the right job. Furthermore, the resort to hands-on control exacerbates the problem it seeks to address. It further undermines trust than builds trust (Fox 1974), both in terms of the contractual relation between employer and employee and in terms of inter-organizational relations (witness the rampant proceduralism involved in much of the contract specification which occurs in competitive tendering). Finally, the shift from input towards output controls sharpens and deepens the principle of performativity against which both organizations and individuals are judged. For many professionals this leads to the invalidation of work which is non-visible and non-measurable – crucially this means that the care and attention given to service users or fellow members of staff suffers as it fails to contribute directly to the immediate output measures upon which the organization's success stands or falls.

Control at a distance

In the previous sections I have outlined the elements of three distinctive strategies of control – managed competition, centralized decentralization, and performance management. In some parts of the public services, such as the education sector, all three control strategies have been implemented simultaneously; in other areas, such as the civil service, the diffusion of competition has been confined to producer rather than consumer markets. Finally, there are some areas, such as social services for than consumer markets. Finally, there are some areas, such as social services for children and families, where competition has made virtually no inroads but where the use of other methods (i.e. process and performance controls) has been intense (Packman and Jordan 1991).

Attempts to comprehend the change processes presently underway need to go beyond traditional binary oppositions such as that between freedom and constraint. For example, Eustace's (1994) article reflecting upon change within the university sector is severely hampered by his reluctance to envisage any state in between direct 'hands on' control, on the one hand, and 'autonomy' on other. But the point about the introduction of markets and decentralization to the public sector is that they combine elements of both regulation and autonomy. Indeed my guess is that if we are to properly understand post-modern organizational forms then we have to get used to thinking in terms of paradox and contradiction rather than the either–or binary logic of the past.

Interestingly enough, post-modern theory itself is not entirely free from the old forms of thinking. Here recent debates about change within the public sector overlap with wider discussions concerning the nature of power and the way in which it is exercised. For example, one finds a number of writers such as Clegg (1989), Kikert (1993) and Mulgan (1988) anticipating the arrival of a new era in which power has become dispersed into a myriad of micro-circuits which no single super-ordinate body has the capacity to command. This line of analysis sometimes explicitly draws upon Foucault's notion of the demise of sovereign power (Jessop 1990: 336). The danger with this approach is that by concentrating upon the dispersal of power it draws our attention away from the new forms of power, concentrating within more remote and less visible centres of corporate and state governance.

In place of what he calls 'the hierarchical notion of a controller', Kikert (1993) puts forward the idea of a 'self-governance autonomy of social institutions'. But this concept of self-regulating actors operating within dispersed networks constantly runs up against his own experience of the reform of higher education in Holland. Kikert notes that one of the chief motives prompting reforms was economic, 'the responsibility to decide how savings were to be made was delegated to the institutions themselves. They were in effect granted the power to perform painful cutback operations on themselves – not the most desirable autonomy one could imagine' (1995: 144). As a consequence one tends to find two quite separate lines of analysis within Kikert's writing, the one emphasizing self-governance and autonomy 'where coordination and integration are practically impossible' (1995: 149), the other giving emphasis to what he calls 'steering from a distance'.

The ambiguity within Kikert's analysis is clearly illustrated in the following:

> Assuming that in a network of nearly autonomous actors no coercive steering can be exercised by any actor, steering has to be non-coercive and has to take place by stimulating the various actors to display the collectively desired behaviour of their own free will. Central top-down control has to be replaced by a varied system of incentives which influence the actors and push them directly into a particular desired direction. This is steering by 'incentives' or behavioural stimuli of a non-coercive nature.

But then he adds, 'Steering by means of incentives is almost a form of non-steering' (1995: 149–50).

His difficulty in seeing steering as a powerful means of hands-off control shows up once more in an adjacent passage where, having asserted that coordination within a multirational network which lacks a common overall goal cannot work, Kikert adds a footnote which states 'in such a situation the only form of "co-ordination" which can take place is at the meta-level of the rules of the game' (1995: 156). But the British experience indicates that steering by use of incentives and sanctions and the setting of meta-level rules (what DiMaggio and Powell (1983) call 'the power to set premises') can be an extremely effective form of 'hands-off' control, indeed probably much more powerful than 'hands-on' regulation and direction. My feeling is that the obituaries currently being read for the collapse of sovereign power are premature; certainly successive Conservative governments in Britain seem unaware of them.

In an earlier publication, I tried to picture this combination of regulation and autonomy in terms of 'freedom within boundaries' (Hoggett 1991). I was aware that a key element of the boundary within which devolution occurred was constituted by the burgeoning systems of performance management, and in this chapter I have tried to give more emphasis to this in terms of the shift from input to output-based forms of control. But the idea of 'freedom within boundaries' now seems too static and organizationally focused. Hence, given the systematic introduction of market and non-market-based forms of competition to the public services, my interest in shifting the focus of analysis from the organization to the field in which it operates. I am aware that many have criticized the Population Ecology perspective for its determinism. Reed (1992), for example, notes how this perspective 'emphasizes the operation of a systems logic which works its way through behind the backs of social actors' (pp. 144–5). But, despite such structures, it is precisely this idea of a covert or implicit logic into which social actors are dragged that I feel does helpfully illuminate some of the many processes through which collusion with the market presently occurs. As successive Conservative governments in Britain have never tired of telling us, 'you cannot buck the markets'. As forms of market and non-market-based competition have been progressively introduced into the British public sector an initial moment of opposition has been followed by a reluctant but inevitable entrapment in the logic of structured competition. In saying this I do not wish to deny that the markets have not been shaped, even subverted, in some instances by these actors. As we noted before, markets resemble fields consisting of other organizations responding to the same field. But for public sector markets in particular we must remember that such fields are also pre-structured by government, a government which moreover remains a key player so long as its monopsony purchasing role remains intact.

Both rowing and steering

In this final section, I wish to return to the hypothesis I outlined at the beginning of this chapter, that the restructuring of governance in Britain has been strongly influenced by the country's relative decline. I have tried to describe a new model of organizational governance built around the principle of regulated autonomy. Clearly such a mode of governance could be used for a variety of different strategic purposes – as in Britain, to reduce public expenditure and heighten inequalities, or, as is equally possible, to provide a framework for regional development and the renewal of local democracy. Nor does regulation necessarily have to be top-down; more genuinely egalitarian and organic forms of the self-regulation of production do appear to be emerging in certain regions and sectors of the global economy (Nohria and Eccles 1992; Camagni 1991). But I hope that I have also made clear that there are a number of important respects in which the restructuring of governance in Britain departs from the trajectory of regulated autonomy or hands-off control. Specifically, I have in mind the degree of centralization and formalization the public sphere has been subject to.

Given the deep-seated weaknesses of the British economy, fiscal crisis hit earlier and harder compared to the majority of its competitors. The social costs of economic restructuring combined with the demands of an ageing population has made the quest 'to get more for less' from the public sector in Britain an urgent and persistent problem. There can be no doubt that successive Conservative governments have risen to this challenge – elements of British approaches to privatization, competitive tendering, performance management, operational decentralization and internal markets have been adopted widely by countries as diverse as Singapore and Sweden. But if the British government has acted as a global innovator in this respect some aspects of its approach have not been subject to emulation elsewhere. The restructuring of the public sector in Britain demonstrates several elements of hands-off control systems (e.g. the development of structured markets, the linking of resource allocation to performativity, the new forms of operational decentralization), but these have to some extent been dwarfed by visible elements of centralization (e.g. the destruction of the autonomy of local government, the development of the quango state) and the extended use of hands-on systems of performance management creating a form of 'evaluative state' (Henkel 1991).

Thus whilst strategic centralization and 'tight-loose' performance management systems have a part to play in sustaining hands-off control within the Briish public sector we have experienced far more centralization and formalization than is required by the model. This has had a number of dysfunctional consequences. Excessive centralization has proved to be politically dysfunctional. Despite its attempts to pass responsibility down the line, the hand of central government has at times become so visible that it is now widely held by the British public to be responsible for the perceived failings of the public service in areas as diverse as the prison service, community care, and education. Reed (1992) notes that the 'capacity to "control at a distance" is never total and is always contested in some form or another by those who constitute its primary targets'. Given the flawed character of this approach in the UK, it is not surprising that at times the hand of government has been far from hidden and processes of public service reform continue to be contested within virtually every sector. Moreover, the separation between strategy or policy on the one hand, and operations on the other, is not always easy to maintain, particularly in the context of government rather than the firm. This the Major government has discovered to its cost as repeated crises within the Child Support Agency, the Student Loans Company and HM Prison Service dogged the Conservatives in late 1994 and early 1995. Within schools education, parents and teachers have repeatedly contested the government's right to dictate educational strategy as evidenced by the struggle over aspects of the national curriculum and pupil testing in 1994 and the revolt of school governors against cuts in education spending in 1995. Finally, as I hope I have demonstrated, excessive formalization has proved to be organizationally dysfunctional, creating new layers of bureaucracy engaged in contract specification and monitoring, quality control, inspection, audit and review and diverting the energies of professional staff away from service and programme delivery into a regime of form-filling, report writing and procedure-following which is arguably even more extensive than that which existed during the former bureaucratic era.

The paradox of Britain in the 1990s therefore is the co-existence of an unregulated economy with an excessively regulated public sphere. If Britain has an economic strategy then it appears to be one which relies on attracting inwards investment into an unregulated, low-wage economy in contrast to the dominant European model which looks towards more endogenous forms of growth around emerging regions and sectors. Thus, unlike the Utopia of a high trust, high skill, participatory firm commitment to quality drawn by some variants of the flexible-specialization thesis, what we seem to be heading towards in both private and public sectors in the UK is the development of a high output, low commitment work culture in which trust has become a value of the past and where quality counts for far less than quantity. In other words what we seem to have is a form of 'flexible mass production' (Piore 1991) in which workers and managers are subject to the progressive intensification of labour in the context of a Britain undergoing continued relative economic decline. As I hope I have demonstrated, the public sector in Britain in particular exemplifies this uneasy combination of the new and the old, the hands-off and the hands-on, the sophisticated and the crude, freedom and surveillance, quality and quantity.

Conclusion

In providing these general reflections I am aware that there are some developments that I have not dealt with adequately. For example, the spread of individually based employment contracts, performance-related pay and decentralized pay bargaining clearly parallel the three dominant strategies described in this chapter. Nor have I dwelt upon the interface between managerialism and professionalism, a phenomenon which also seems to be seeking different forms of resolution in different sectors. In education, increased centralized control of the curriculum (which has been a highly contested process) has served to undermine teacher discretion and has had a direct impact upon the labour process of the professionals concerned undermining considerable areas of work autonomy (Shaw 1990). Within the social security service the impact has been more ambiguous. This was already an area of low discretion but the impact of IT combined with the introduction of the 'whole person concept' has certainly led to the introduction of multiskilling in a number of front-line jobs (Hoggett 1994b). The emergence of the professional-manager which I anticipated in a couple of articles a few years ago (Hoggett 1990; 1991) has developed more unevenly – for example, the process of converting senior professionals into managers seems to have gone much further in the education and primary health care sectors than in others. On the other hand, the diffusion of performance management systems has clearly had the effect of reducing professional autonomy across a wide number of different sectors. Clearly, anyone seeking to provide an overview of developments in the entire public service will fall short in a number of areas of detail which are necessary to provide a flavour for the specific changes occurring in each policy sector. The usefulness of an overview however lies in the possibility of being able to provide a sense of perspective, i.e. to see the wood for the trees.

What I am offering here is one perspective, clearly there are several others which are possible. Like any other perspective the one here draws upon my own values and experiences. As I see it, writing in mid-1995, Britain's political future flow seems very much in the balance. On the one hand, a further Conservative victory might well imply that the crucial question becomes not whether Britain will be dragged reluctantly towards Europe but whether Europe will be dragged reluctantly towards unregulated, low-wage Britain. On the other hand [. . .] the Conservatives might not win. Would a Blair led government arrive with a mandate to restore the commitment and reduce the exploitation of the public sector workforce and dismantle the massive centralization of state power which has accumulated in the last decade and a half? This, as they say, may be the $64,000 question.

References

Aiken, M. and J. Hage (1968) 'Organizational interdependence and intra-organizational structure', *American Sociological Review* 33, 912–30.

Albrow, M (1970) *Bureaucracy*, London: Macmillan.

Aldrich, H (1978) 'Centralization vs. decentralization in the design of human service delivery systems: a response to Gouldner's lament' in R. Sarri and Y. Hasenfield (eds.), *The management of human services*, New York: Columbia University Press.

Alexander, A (1991) 'Managing fragmentation – democracy, accountability and the future of local government', *Local Government Studies* 17, 6, 63–76.

Argyris, C. and D. Schon (1974) *Organizational learning*, Reading, MA: Addison-Wesley.

Aucoin, P. (1990) 'Paradigms, principles, paradoxes and pendulums', *Governance* 3, 2, 115–37.

Audit Commission (1989) *Better financial management*, Management Paper 3, London: HMSO.

Ball, S (1993) 'Education policy, power relations and teacher's work', *British Journal of Educational Studies* 41, 2, 106–21.

Ball, S., R. Bowe and S. Gewirtz (1992) *Circuits of schooling: a sociological exploration of parental choice in social class context*. Working Paper, London: Kings College.

Ball, S., R. Bowe and S. Gewirtz (1994) 'Schools in the market place: an analysis of local market relations' in W. Bartlett, C. Propper, D. Wilson and J. Le Grand, *Quasi-markets in the welfare state*, SAUS: University of Bristol.

Barley S., and G. Kunda (1992) 'Design and devotion: surges in rational and normative ideologies of control in managerial discourse', *Administrative Science Quarterly* 37, 363–99.

Bartlett, W (1995) 'Privatisation, non-profit trusts and contracts', *Studies in decentralisation and quasi-markets* 20, SAUS: University of Bristol.

Bogg, J. and C. Cooper (1995) 'Job satisfaction, mental health, and occupational stress among senior civil servants', *Human Relations* 48, 3, 327–41.

Bradach, J. and R. Eccles (1989) 'Price, authority and trust: from ideal types to plural forms', *Annual Review of Sociology* 15, 97–118.

British Medical Association (1992) *Stress and the medical profession*, London: BMA.

British Medical Journal (1994) 'The rise of Stalinism in the NHS', 309, 1640–5.

Burns, D., R. Hambleton and P. Hoggett (1994) *The politics of decentralisation: revitalising government*, Basingstoke: Macmillan.

Camagni, R. (ed.) (1991) *Innovation networks: spatial perspectives*, London: Belhaven Press.

Caplan, R. (1994) 'Stress, anxiety, and depression in hospital consultants, general practitioners, and senior health service managers', *British Medical Journal* 309, 1261–3.

Clegg, S. (1989) *Frameworks of power*, London: Sage.

Clegg, S. (1990) *Modern organisations: organisation studies in the post-modern world*, London: Sage.

Colville, I, K. Dalton and C. Tomkins (1993) 'Developing and understanding cultural change in HM Customs and Excise: there is more to dancing than knowing the Next Steps', *Public Administration* 71, 4, 549–66.

Cooper, C. and M. Kelly (1993) 'Occupational stress in head teachers: a national UK study', *British Journal of Educational Psychology* 63, 130–43.

Cousins, C. (1988) 'The restructuring of welfare work: the introduction of general management and contracting out of ancillary services in the NHS', *Work, Employment and Society* 2, 210–28.

Crafts, N. (1991) 'Reversing relative economic decline? The 1980s in historical perspective', *Oxford Review of Economics* 7, 3, 81–98.

Davis, H. and J. Stewart (1994. *The growth of government by appointment: the implications for local democracy*, Luton: Local Government Management Board.

De Groot, L. (1992) 'City challenge: competing in the urban regeneration game', *Local Economy* 7, 3.

Dewar, R., D. Whetten and D. Boje (1980) 'An examination of the reliability and validity of the Aiken and Hage Scales of centralisation, formalisation and task routineness', *Administrative Science Quarterly* 25, 1, 120–8.

DiMaggio, P. and W. Powell (1983) 'The iron cage revisited: institutional isomorphism and collective rationality in organizational fields', *American Sociological Review* 48, 147–60.

Du Gay, P. and G. Salaman (1992) 'The (cult)ure of the customer', *Journal of Management Studies* 25, 5, 615–33.

Dunleavy, P. (1991) *Democracy, bureaucracy and public choice*, Brighton: Harvester Wheatsheaf.

Eccles, R. and H. White (1986) 'Firms and market interfaces of profit centre control' in S. Lindenberg *et al.* (eds.), *Approaches to social theory*, New York: Sage.

Eccles, R. and H. White (1988) 'Price and authority in inter-profit centre transactions', *American Journal of Sociology* 94 (supplement): S17–51.

Edwards, R. (1979) *Contested terrain*, New York: Basic Books.

Elliot, G. and V. Hall (1994) 'Further education incorporated: the business orientation in FE and the introduction of human resource management', *School Organisation* 14, 1, 3–10.

Eustace, R (1994) 'University autonomy: the 80s and after', *Higher Education Quarterly* 48, 2, 86–117.

Ferlie, E., L. Ashburner and L. Fitzgerald (1995) 'Corporate governance and the public sector: some issues and evidence from the NHS', *Public Administration* 73, 3, 375–92.

Florida, R. (1991) 'The new industrial revolution', *Futures* (July/Aug.), 559–76.

Foster, D. (1993) 'Industrial relations in local governnient – the impact of privatisation', *The Political Quarterly* 64, 1, 49–59.

Fox, A. (1974) *Beyond contract: work, power and trust relations*, London: Faber.

Fry, G., A. Flynn, A. Gray, W. Jenkins and B. Rutherford (1988) 'Symposium on improving management in government', *Public Administration* 66, 4, 429–45.

Glatter, R. and P. Woods (1994) 'The impact of competition and choice on parents and schools' in W. Bartlett, C. Propper, D. Wilson and J. Le Grand, *Quasi-markets in the welfare state*, SAUS: University of Bristol.

Glennerster, H. and M. Matsaganis (1993) 'The UK health reforms: the fundholding experiment', *Health Policy* 23, 179–91.

Guest, D. (1987) 'Human resource management and industrial relations', *Journal of Management Studies* 24, 5, 505–21.

Hage, J. and M. Aiken (1967) 'The relation of centralisation to other structural properties', *Administrative Science Quarterly* 12, 72–92.

Halpin, D., S. Powers and J. Fitz (1993) 'Opting into state control? Headteachers and the paradoxes of grant-maintained status', *International Studies in Sociology of Education* 3, 1, 3–23.

Handy, C. (1989) *The age of unreason*, London: Hutchinson.

Hannan, M. and J. Freeman (1977) 'The population ecology of organizations', *American Journal of Sociology* 82, 929–64.

Harrison, S., N. Small and M. Baker (1994) 'The wrong kind of chaos? The early days of an NHS trust', *Public Money and Management* 14, 1 (Jan.–Mar.), 39–46.

Henkel, M. (1991) 'The new "evaluative state"', *Public Administration* 69, 1, 121–36.

Heydebrand, W. (1979) 'The technocratic administration of justice', *Research in Law and Sociology* 2, 29–64.

Heydebrand, W. (1989) 'New organisational forms', *Work and Occupations* 16, 3, 323–57.

Hoggett, P. (1987) 'A farewell to mass production? Decentralisation as an emergent private and public sector paradigm' in P. Hoggett and R. Hambleton. (eds), *Decentralisation and Democracy*, SAUS Occasional Paper 26, School for Advanced Urban Studies: University of Bristol.

Hoggett, P. (1990) 'Modernisation, political strategy and the welfare state: an organisational perspective', *Studies in decentralisation and quasi-markets* 2, School for Advanced Urban Studies: University of Bristol.

Hoggett, P. (1991) 'A new management in the public sector', *Policy and Politics* 19, 4, 143–56.

Hoggett, P. (1994a) 'The politics of the modernisation of the UK welfare state' in R. Burrows and B. Loader (eds.), *Towards a Post-Fordist welfare state?* London: Routledge.

Hoggett, P. (1994b). 'A case study of quality initiatives within the Severnside benefits agency'. Unpublished Report to The European Foundation for the Improvement of Living and Working Conditions 'Consumer-oriented Action in the European Public Services' Programme, Dublin.

Hoggett, P. and G. Bramley (1989) 'Devolution of local budgets', *Public Money and Management* (Winter), 9–13.

Hood, C. (1991) 'A public management for all seasons?' *Public Administration* 69, 1 (Spring), 3–19.

Hutton, W. (1995) *The state we're in*, London: Jonathan Cape.

Institute of Employment Studies (1994) *Opening the door: employment prospects and morale of newly qualified nurses*, Brighton: Institute of Employment Studies.

Jessop, B. (1990) *State theory*, Cambridge: Polity Press.

Jessop, B. (1994) 'The transition to post-Fordism and the Schumpeterian workfare state' in R. Burrows and B. Loader, *Towards a Post-Fordist welfare state?* London: Routledge.

Kearns, A. (1991) *Active citizenship and accountability: the case of the British housing association movement*, University of Glasgow: Housing Associations Research Unit Discussion Paper 2.

Kikert, W. (1993) 'Autopoiesis and the science of (public) administration: essence, sense and nonsense', *Organisational Studies* 14, 2, 261–78.

Kikert, W. (1995) 'Steering at a distance: a new paradigm of public governance in Dutch higher education', *Governance* 8, 1, 135–57.

Labour Research Department (1994) *Stress at work: a trade union response*. London: Labour Research Department.

Lash, S. (1988) 'Postmodernism as a regime of signification', *Theory, Culture and Society* 5, 2–3, 311–36.

Le Grand, J. and W. Bartlett (eds.) (1993) *Quasi-markets and social policy*, London: Macmillan.

Lowe, J. and N. Oliver (1991) 'The high commitment workplace: two cases from a high-tec industry', *Work, Employment and Society* 5, 3, 437–50.

MacGregor, D. (1960) *The human side of enterprise*, New York: McGraw-Hill.

Maclure, S. (1988) *Education re-formed*, London: Hodder and Stoughton.

Malpass, P. (1994) 'Policy making and local governance: how Bristol failed to secure city challenge funding (twice)', *Policy and Politics* 22, 4, 301–12.

Martin, L. (1994) 'A case study of user-involvement and advocacy in community care in Wiltshire'. Unpublished Report to the European Foundation for the Improvement of Living and Working Conditions 'Consumer-oriented action in the European Public Services' Programme, Dublin.

Mulgan, G. (1988) 'The power of the weak', *Marxism Today* (Dec.).

Murray, F. (1983) 'The decentralisation of production: the decline of the mass collective worker', *Capital and Class* 19.

Nairn, T. (1993) 'The Sole Survivor', *New Left Review* 200, 41–8.

Nohria, N. and B. Eccles. (eds.) (1992) *Networks and organizations*, Boston, MA: Harvard Business School Press.

Packman, J. and B. Jordan (1991) 'The Children Act: looking forward, looking back', *British Journal of Social Work* 21, 4, 315–27.

Peck, J. (1993) 'The trouble with TECs . . . a critique of the Training and Enterprise Council initiative', *Policy and Politics* 21, 4, 289–306.

Peters, T. and R. Waterman (1982) *In search of excellence*, New York: Harper and Row.

Pickvance, C. and E. Preteceille (1991) *State restructuring and local power*, London: Pinter.

Piore, M. (1991) 'Corporate reform in American manufacturing and the challenge to economic theory' in M. Piore, *Collected essays on management for the 1990s*, Oxford: Oxford University Press.

Pollert, A. (1988) 'Dismantling flexibility?' *Capital and Class* 34, 42–75.

Pollitt, C. (1990) *Managerialism and the public services: the anglo-American experience*, Oxford: Basil Blackwell.

Power, S., K. Halpin and J. Fitz (1994) 'Underpinning choice and diversity? The grant maintained schools policy in context' in S. Tomlinson (ed.), *Alternative Education Policies*, IPPR, London: Rivers Oram Press.

Public Concern at Work (1994) *The advice service: second report*, London: Public Concern at Work.

Reed, M. (1992) *The sociology of organisations*, Brighton: Harvester Wheatsheaf.

Rees, D. and Cooper, C. (1992) 'Occupational stress in health service workers in the UK', *Stress Medicine* 8, 79–90.

Rein, M. (1990) 'The social structure of institutions: neither public nor private' in S. Kamerman and A. Kahn. (eds.), *Privatisation and the welfare state*, Princeton: Princeton University Press.

Royal College of Nursing (1994) *The morale of nurses working in the community: a study of three NHS trusts*, London: Daphne Heald Research Unit, Royal College of Nursing.

Schein, E. (1985) *Organizational culture and leadership*, San Francisco: Jossey-Bass.

Shaw, K. (1990) 'Ideology, control and the teaching profession', *Policy and Politics* 18, 4, 269–78.

Stewart, M. (1994) 'Between Whitehall and town hall: the realignment of urban regeneration policy in England', *Policy and Politics* 22, 2, 133–46.

Sutherland, V. and C. Cooper (1992) 'Job stress, satisfaction and mental health among general practitioners before and after introduction of new contract', *British Medical Journal* 304, 1545–8.

Taylor, M. and P. Hoggett (1994) 'Quasi-markets and the transformation of the independent sector' in W. Bartlett, C. Propper, D. Wilson and J. Le Grand (eds.), *Quasi-markets in the welfare state*, Bristol: SAUS, University of Bristol.

Taylor, M., J. Langan and P. Hoggett (1995) *Encouraging diversity: voluntary and private organisations in community care*, Aldershot: Arena.

Thomas, G. and R. Levacic (1991) 'Centralizing in order to decentralise? DES scrutiny and approval of LMS schemes', *Journal of Educational Policy* 6, 4, 401–16.

Travers, C. and C. Cooper (1993) 'Mental health, job satisfaction and occupational stress among UK teachers', *Work and Stress* 7, 3, 203–19.

Walsh, K. (1991) *Competitive tendering for local authority services: initial experiences*, London: HMSO.

Weir, S. and W. Hall (1994) *Ego trip: extra-governmental organisations in the UK and their accountability*, Colchester: University of Essex and Charter 88 Trust.